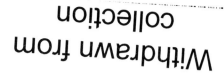

MAN, MYTH & MAGIC

VOLUME 11

Time – Zurv

Library of Congress Cataloging in Publication Data

Main entry under title:

Man, myth, and magic

   Bibliography: p.
   1. Occult sciences. 2. Psychical research.
I. Cavendish, Richard. II. Deutch, Yvonne.
BF1411.M25 1983   133   82-13041
ISBN 0-86307-041-8 (set)
ISBN 0-86307-052-3 (v.11)

British Library Cataloguing in Publication Data

Man, myth and magic.
   1. Mythology - Dictionaries
   2. Religion - Dictionaries
I. Cavendish, Richard
291.1'3'0321   BL303

   ISBN 0-86307-041-8 (set)
   ISBN 0-86307-052-3 (v.11)

Reference Edition Published 1983

© Marshall Cavendish Limited MCMLXXXIII
© B.P.C. Publishing Limited MCMLXX

Printed and Bound in Italy by L.E.G.O. S.p.a. Vicenza.

Published by Marshall Cavendish Corporation,
147 West Merrick Road,
Freeport, Long Island
N.Y. 11520

Distributed in India by Standard Literature.

MAN, MYTH & MAGIC

The Illustrated Encyclopedia of Mythology, Religion and the Unknown

Editor-in-Chief
Richard Cavendish

Editorial Board
C. A. Burland; Professor Glyn Daniel;
Professor E. R. Dodds; Professor Mircea Eliade;
William Sargant; John Symonds;
Professor R. J. Zwi Werblowsky;
Professor R. C. Zaehner.

New Edition edited and compiled by
Yvonne Deutch, B.A. University of Exeter;
M.A. University of Kansas, Lawrence, Kansas.

MARSHALL CAVENDISH
NEW YORK, LONDON, TORONTO

CONTENTS Volume 11

TIME

Awareness of time has made man conscious that he is inexorably subject to decay, old age and death, and his reactions to this grim fact have been expressed in his religions: the myth of the Golden Age states the general human conviction that history is a process of decline, that things are worse than they used to be

THE MYSTERIOUS NATURE of time, as it is presented to human experience, has been described in a celebrated passage by St Augustine of Hippo (354–430). He writes in his *Confessions*: 'What then is Time? If no one asks me, I know; but if I wish to explain it to one that asketh, I know not. Yet I say boldly, that I know that if nothing passed away, Time past were not; and if

nothing were coming (into existence), a Time to come were not; and if nothing existed, Time present were not. These two Times, then, past and to come, how are they, seeing the past now is not, and that to come is not yet? But the present, if it were always the present, and never passed into Time past, would surely not be Time, but Eternity.'

The enigma of time is of fundamental importance, for time is one of the two dimensions of our consciousness, the other being space. We are aware of time through the change of phenomena presented to our senses; for, as Augustine saw, if the present pattern of our experience did not change, we should have no sense of time, but be in a state of timelessness or eternity. In other

'To the last syllable of recorded time': clock shop in Camden Passage, London. Man's consciousness of time is one factor distinguishing him from other species and has profoundly affected his view of life, death and the gods

words, normal human consciousness consists of awareness of the three temporal categories: past, present and future.

On analysis, it is impossible for us at any given moment to define exactly what is the present. The 'here-now' of the present is an ever-moving point separating our past and future. Indeed, psychologically our 'present' includes our immediate past experience and anticipates the continuance of our experience into the immediate future. However, when we reflect on our experience over a longer

For whereas the animals suffer the experience of dying without the long anticipatory knowledge of mortality, man contemplates his end from the moment of his first discovery that all life dies

period, we can distinguish more clearly what is 'past' and what is 'future', although the existential reality of what is past and future constitutes problems of great metaphysical subtlety and complexity.

Enigmatical though time is and replete with problems beyond the comprehension of most persons, it constitutes a factor that has profoundly affected the evolution of the human race. For man, in contra-distinction to all other species, is endowed with an acute time-consciousness which he has exploited with amazing results. Because man is so acutely aware of time, he is by nature a 'planner': he is for ever drawing upon past experience in the present to provide for future needs. This trait finds expression in the earliest evidence we have of mankind. For the Paleolithic peoples were tool-makers, and the making of a tool, for example, a stone axe, involves the anticipation of the future need of such an axe and busying oneself in the present to make it. Through his ability to anticipate and so provide for his future needs, man has succeeded, since Paleolithic times, in dominating the world and eliminating or enslaving all his animal competitors. The complex scientific and technological civilization which we now enjoy is a sophisticated product of our time-sense. And its range is enormous: from the planning of a nuclear power station to the taking out of an insurance policy, past experience is being utilized in the present to meet future contingencies. In short, the time-consciousness of man has been, and is, a primary cause of his success in the struggle for existence.

But this endowment has a kind of debit side. Man's time-consciousness has not only enabled him to plan ahead to ensure his physical well-being; it has also made him acutely aware that he is subject to the flux of time that brings change, decay, aging and finally death to every form of life. Accordingly, every human being learns early in childhood to anticipate his own death. In this sense, it has been truly said that man has invented death. For whereas the animals suffer the experience of dying without the long anticipatory knowledge of mortality, man contemplates his end from the moment of his first discovery that all life dies.

This awareness of his mortality, which stems from his ability to project himself mentally into the future, produces in man a fundamental sense of insecurity. It

prevents him from immersing himself wholly in the enjoyment of present well-being. He ever fears that changing time will bring misfortune; and he knows that it is surely bearing him towards that dread moment of personal extinction to which he has seen so many of his fellow-beings come.

This ambivalent endowment of acute time-consciousness has found expression in human history in a twofold quest for security. As we have seen, the whole complex structure of civilization is designed, on its final analysis, to ensure constant and adequate provision for the material needs of man. But beyond the satisfaction of these needs, the prospect of death has remained as the ultimate menace. Mankind's reaction to this grim fact has found expression in religion.

In Search of Security

It can be reasonably shown that all religions are basically concerned with the problem of security after death. The logic of experience has precluded any serious attempt to provide immunity from physical death in this life (the quest of some Taoist magicians in China to find an elixir of immortality is notable only for its persistence against all evidence of failure). But though forced to accept the inevitability of death, mankind has generally believed that some part of the personality survives physical disintegration and needs to be secured against post-mortem perils. In conceiving of such security, man's fear of the destructive process of time is reflected in a variety of imagery expressive of his instinct to transcend time. Behind this imagery certain distinctive forms of belief and action can be discerned by the comparative study of religion.

What is undoubtedly the most primitive attempt, so far as thought and action are concerned, to gain everlasting post-mortem security from the destructive process of time occurred in ancient Egypt. There the elaborate mortuary ritual, including mummification, was designed to effect two things. By embalming the corpse, it was hoped that physical decomposition would be stopped and the body preserved intact for ever. Through the magical efficacy of the ritual 'Opening of the Mouth' it was believed that the ability to see, breathe and take nourishment was restored to the mummified remains, so that the deceased might live, together with his *ka*, a kind of double or

second self, and revisited by his *ba*, an entity separated from the human body at death, in his 'house of eternity', the tomb, for ever. Arrangements were also made for the perpetual offering of food at the tomb, and it was hoped that the dead, revivified and immune from decay, and 'perfectly equipped' with magical spells, would be eternally secure, 'coming forth' each day to the portal of the tomb, to see the sun and feed on the mortuary offerings. The other purpose of the mortuary ritual was to assimilate the dead person to the god Osiris, and among the various virtues that would accrue from such assimilation was transcendence of time. This was achieved, as a text in the Book of the Dead shows, by magically incorporating time into one's own being. The dead person, who had become one with Osiris, exclaims: 'I am Yesterday, Today and Tomorrow' (see BOOK OF THE DEAD; EGYPT; MUMMIFICATION; OSIRIS).

The idea of gaining immunity from the destructive flux of time by union with a supernatural being regarded as eternal, which lies behind this passage in the Book of the Dead, finds various forms of expression in many religions. It appears in a non-Osirian context in Egypt as far back as the Pyramid Texts. The dead pharaoh is imagined as flying up to heaven to join the sun god Re in his solar boat, in which he daily crossed the sky; on this unceasing journey he would be beyond temporal change. In Christianity, the 'beatific vision', which constitutes the final reward of the redeemed, is an eternal communion of the individual soul with God. In the Apocalypse of St John, an attempt is made, in an esoteric imagery, to represent the transcendence of time in the eternity of worship. The four living creatures about the throne of God 'never cease to sing, "Holy, holy, holy, is the Lord God Almighty, who was and is and is to come!"' (chapter 4). Indian thought similarly conceives of the effect of the individual's ultimate realization of Brahma: 'Verily, for him who knows thus, this mystic doctrine of Brahma, the sun neither rises nor sets. For him it is day for ever' — in other words, he is beyond time, whose passage is marked by the succession of day and night. Nirvana, in Buddhist imagery, is likewise a state beyond time's changing phenomena (see NIRVANA). The Buddha is represented as teaching: 'There, monks,

I say there is neither coming nor going nor staying nor passing away nor arising. Without support or going on or basis is it. This indeed is the end of pain.'

'Know I Am Time'

Concern about time has not only expressed itself in religion by imagining states of beatitude beyond its range. Since man is so disturbingly aware of his subjection to time in this world, his religions reflect his preoccupation with its nature and the significance of its operation throughout the universe. This preoccupation has led to the deification of time among some peoples. The rich imagery of Hinduism provides examples that are both impressive in their dramatic portrayal and significant in their theological implication. In the famous *Bhagavad Gita*, which is one of the foundational documents of Hinduism, the god Vishnu, in his form of Vasudeva, is equated with time (see BHAGAVAD GITA; VISHNU). This aspect of Vishnu is revealed in the culminating vision given to the prince Arjuna. At first Vishnu had revealed himself as the Creator and sustainer of the world. This was a revelation of the beneficent providence of the deity. Arjuna was impressed; but feeling that he had not seen all, he asks that a full revelation be made. His request is granted, but he is appalled by what he then beholds. Vishnu appears as a monstrous being, into whose awesome mouths, beset by hideous fangs, all forms of life are seen passing swiftly to destruction. And Vishnu announces: 'Know I am Time,

Man can never escape from death, and from early childhood he learns to anticipate his own end: 'he knows that Time is bearing him towards that dread moment of personal extinction which he has seen come to so many of his fellow beings' *Above left* 'Inexorable Fate' *Above right* 'Time changes, and we change with it', both engravings from the 16th century book *Fiacci Emblamata*

that makes the worlds to perish, when ripe, and come to bring on them destruction.'

This account is significant both for the ambivalence of its concept of deity and its identification of the supreme deity with time. It reflects the Indian conviction that creation in the empirical world inevitably entails destruction, that life involves death, and that time governs this alternating rhythm that never ends. This Vaishnavite theology is paralleled by a similar conception in Shivaism. The god Shiva (see SHIVA), on one side of his being, personifies the dynamic persistence of life, in all its teeming abundance and complexity of form, which is symbolized by the *lingam*, the mighty generative organ of the god. In his other aspect, he is Bhairava, 'the terrible destroyer', and Maha-Kala (great Time), and Kala-Rudra (all-devouring Time). An even more remarkable conception is that of Kali, the goddess who personifies *kala* (time). She derives from the concept of Shiva's *shakti*, or activating energy. Her iconography is horrific, being thus designed to portray the baleful nature of time. She is depicted as black in hue, and wearing a chaplet of

severed heads; her many hands hold symbols of her destructive power – the exterminating sword, scissors that cut short the thread of life. Yet, like Shiva, her lord, from whom she emanates, Kali is of ambivalent character; for she also holds the lotus of eternal generation and her body is expressive of vigorous fecundity (see KALI).

This deification of time is related to the Indian view that the empirical world is not ultimately real. It is a view designed to account for human destiny, and it involves a belief that time moves in cycles, which will be considered later.

The Infinite and the Finite

The ancient peoples of Iran had a god of time called Zurvan. How old this deification of time may be is unknown; there is some evidence that such a god was worshipped as far back as the 12th century BC. The earliest reliable information, however, comes from a Greek scholar, Eudemos of Rhodes, who explained in the 4th century BC that the well-known gods of Persian dualism, Ohrmazd and Ahriman, were derived by the Persians from time and space. Although the native Iranian writings which witness to this deification of time are comparatively late, they are very definite about the primordial nature of time and its religious significance. Thus in the *Rivayat* it is stated: 'it is obvious that, with the exception of Time, all other things have been created. For Time no limit is apparent, and no height can be seen nor deep perceived, and (Time) has always existed and will always exist . . .

Picturepoint, London

The Timeless Gods

All we wax old and wither like a leaf.
We are outcast, strayed between bright sun and
　　moon;
　Our light and darkness are as leaves of flowers,
　Black flowers and white, that perish; and the noon
　　As midnight, and the night as daylight hours.
　A little fruit a little while is ours.
　　　　And the worm finds it soon.

But up in heaven the high gods one by one
　Lay hands upon the draught that quickeneth,
Fulfilled with all tears shed and all things done,
　And stir with soft imperishable breath

The bubbling bitterness of life and death,
And hold it to our lips and laugh; but they
Preserve their lips from tasting night or day,
　Lest they too change and sleep, the fates that
　　spun,
The lips that made us and the hands that slay;
　Lest all these change, and heaven bow down
　　to none,
Change and be subject to the secular sway
　And terrene revolution of the sun.
Therefore they thrust it from them, putting time
　away.

　　　　Swinburne *Atalanta in Calydon*

Time is both Creator and the Lord of the creation which it created.'

The Iranians, however, distinguished between two forms of Zurvan. Zurvan *akarana* was Infinite Time; Zurvan *daregho-chvadhata* was 'Time of the long Dominion' or Finite Time. This latter form of Zurvan represented the time that rules in this world, and which brings age, decay and death to all men. Although its dominion was believed to be long, extending to 12,000 years, it was finite. During the Sassanian period (226–637 AD), it appears that a cult of Zurvan developed which explained mythically the relation of Zurvan to Ohrmazd and Ahriman, who personified the opposing forces of good and evil in Zoroastrian dualism. According to this myth, Zurvan, as the primal being, desired to have a son who would create the universe. To this end he offered sacrifice for 1000 years. But before the millennium had been completed, Zurvan doubted for one brief moment the efficacy of the sacrifices. This momentary doubt had a fatal consequence; for it caused a second son to be conceived, who was to be Ahriman. And so, when the time was fulfilled, two sons were born to Zurvan: Ohrmazd, radiant with light; Ahriman, dark and foul. And when Ohrmazd created that which was good and beautiful, Ahriman countered by creating the evil and the ugly (see AHRIMAN; OHRMAZD; ZURVAN).

This Iranian deification of time appears to have been incorporated into Mithraism, which originated in Iran and gradually spread westwards into the Roman Empire (see MITHRAS). The form in which it found expression was strange but significant. Images were set up, in the cave sanctuaries of Mithras, of a nude man with a lion's head, the mouth being open in a menacing grimace. About the body a huge snake was entwined, and on the body the signs of the zodiac were carved. The monster was winged, and usually held a staff and keys. These images undoubtedly represented Zurvan *daregho-chvadhata*, with whom Ahriman appears to have been identified. Of the significance of such images in the cult of Mithras no certain evidence survives. But there is reason for thinking that they signified the sovereignty of 'Time of the long Dominion' over mankind in this world. It is possible that the devotees of Mithras thus recognized the cosmic dominion of time,

but looked to Mithras for salvation from its baleful tyranny.

The influence of this form of Zurvan can be traced also in the figure of Phanes in the Greek Mystery religion known as Orphism (see ORPHEUS). The Persian concept of Infinite Time was also carried into the Graeco-Roman world, where it was identified with the supreme deity under the names of Cronus (see CRONUS) and Aion. In Egypt, the cult of Cronus was closely associated with that of Serapis (see SERAPIS) and, according to the Latin poet Macrobius, the cult image of Serapis in Alexandria symbolized this connection with time in a curious way. Serapis was portrayed accompanied by a three-headed monster: the middle head, that of a lion, represented time present; the wolf's head to the left signified time past, and that of a 'fawning dog' to the right depicted future time.

Janus, the ancient Roman god associated with beginnings (see JANUS), has sometimes, erroneously, been regarded as a time god, his two faces being interpreted as looking to the past and the future. So far as the Romans did deify time, it was in the form of Aeternitas, which derived from the Alexandrian concept of Aion. The most notable depiction of Aeternitas is in a bas-relief adorning the base of the column of the Emperor Antoninus Pius in Rome. Aeternitas is represented as a heroic male figure, nude, with eagle's wings, and holding a serpent-encircled globe in his left hand: he bears the dead emperor and his wife Faustina to heaven.

The Sorrowful Weary Wheel

In contrast to these personifications of time, in other religions time has been regarded as an impersonal cyclic process, to which all life in this world is subject and obliged to conform. This view of time is linked with the idea of metempsychosis, or the transmigration of souls. It forms a basic concept of Hinduism and Buddhism, of Orphism and some forms of Gnosticism.

The impression that time is cyclic in its movement, and unceasingly reproduces the same pattern of events, is an obvious deduction to make from natural phenomena. The succession of day and night, the rotation of the seasons, and the movements of the heavenly bodies, all suggest that time moves in cycles. This view has sometimes led to a

Clocks express a variety of ideas about time: the movement of the hands round the face suggests inexorability and the 'weary wheel' of time as a cycle in which man is imprisoned; a clock stopping suggests escape from the cycle, death, timeless eternity *Above left* **The cuckoo is linked with time and with clocks because its call heralds the changing of the seasons with the coming of spring** *Right* **Photo montage of a grandfather clock and alarm clocks, by Erich Lessing**

cynical evaluation of life such as finds expression in the well-known verses of the book of Ecclesiastes (1.9–10): 'What has been is what will be, and what has been done is what will be done; and there is nothing new under the sun. Is there a thing of which it is said: "See this is new"? It has been already, in the ages before us.'

But it has been in connection with the idea of the transmigration of souls that the cyclic pattern of time has been most impressively utilized. The Indian sages taught that the individual self or *atman*, by mistaking the phenomenal world for reality and becoming attached to it, is involved in the stream of time. By the process of *samsara* or rebirth, the atman is continually reincarnated in this world in a form determined by its previous actions or *karma* (see KARMA). Hence it becomes subjected to an unceasing process of births and deaths, with all their attendant pain. To emphasize the unending misery of such existence and impel the self to seek salvation, Indian thinkers invented an elaborate chronology based on the cyclic nature of time. A *maha-yuga* was conceived, which was a period of 12,000 years; but these were reckoned as years of the gods, each being equal to 360 human years. One thousand of such maha-yugas made up one *kalpa*, which represented one day of Brahma, and that one day spanned the whole period from the creation of a world to its destruction. On the dawning of the next day, Brahma creates the world anew, and the dreary wheel of existence begins to turn for another kalpa, through which the unenlightened soul is doomed to a further succession of births and deaths. Both Hinduism and Buddhism claim to provide a way of salvation from this 'sorrowful weary wheel' of time.

The expression 'sorrowful weary wheel' actually comes from an Orphic text; for a

National Gallery

According to Hesiod, a Golden Race, the earth's first human population lived like gods, free from pain, toil and old age. In Rome the Golden Race turned into the Golden Age, an idyllic period far in the past, when man lived happily, simply and naturally: *The Golden Age*, after Giorgione

similar view of the fate of the uninitiated soul was held in ancient Greece by the members of the Pythagorean and Orphic Mystery cults. Plato also conceived of the errant soul as having to endure a series of incarnations for 10,000 years before it could return to its former happy state. And the mysterious philosopher and poet Empedocles tells of having for 'thrice ten thousand seasons' wandered 'far from the blessed, being born throughout that time in the forms of all manner of mortal things and changing one baleful path of life for another'. For those who thought thus, salvation was to break out from time's inexorable process, or, as it is eloquently phrased on an Orphic grave tablet by one who thought that he had achieved deliverance: 'I have flown out of the sorrowful weary wheel; I have passed with eager feet to the Circle desired.'

To believe that the course of time is cyclical has been the more common view; but the idea that time's movement is linear has been a basic concept of four great religions – Zoroastrianism, Judaism, Christianity and Islam.

Both Judaism and Christianity (and the Islamic view has essentially followed the same pattern) equate the process of time with the unfolding of the purpose of God. This view finds expression in the Old Testament in what is virtually a philosophy of history (see HISTORY). The main theme is the gradual revelation of Yahweh's providence for Israel, which starts with the call of Abraham (Genesis, chapter 22). Christianity

took over this interpretation of the temporal process, but adapted it to its own recognition of Jesus of Nazareth as the promised Messiah and of the Church as becoming the true Israel, consequent on the rejection of Jesus by historic Israel. From these basic notions there was gradually evolved the great synthesis of medieval Christianity, in which both the destiny of mankind and of its individual members were related in a time scheme that commenced with the Creation and would end with the Second Coming of Christ. The theme of this cosmic drama was the redemption of mankind after the Fall of its original parents, by the vicarious sacrifice on the cross of the incarnate Son of God.

This view of time has found significant expression in the division of its process into two parts, labelled respectively the era 'Before Christ' and the era *Anni Domini*, the 'years of the Lord'. In medieval iconography, the end of time was symbolized by the catastrophic destruction of the world, and its replacement by a new and eternal order (see END OF THE WORLD). But the most impressive statement, as it is also the most concise, of the Christian view that God incorporates and transcends time is surely given in Revelation (chapter 22) when the Glorified Christ is represented as saying: 'I am the Alpha and the Omega, the first and the last, the beginning and the end.'

It is interesting, in conclusion, to notice briefly the evolution of the idea of Father Time. The Christian view of God precluded any deification of time, but it did not prevent its personification. In the Middle Ages there were two lines of tradition concerning human destiny which finally coalesced, during the Renaissance period, in the figure of Father Time. One tradition was astrological, through which the image of the pagan god Saturn survived as a grim old man, armed with a sickle and hour-glass, symbols of the termination of human life. In the other tradition, Death was personified as a skeleton, armed with a scythe or dart with which he gave the death-blow. These two figures were eventually fused into the figure of Father Time, complete with hour-glass and scythe. In the iconography of Western mythology his figure still symbolizes, perhaps a little vapidly, man's ancient association of time with death.

S. G. F. BRANDON

Living Backwards

Alice was just beginning to say 'There's a mistake somewhere − ,' when the Queen began screaming, so loud that she had to leave the sentence unfinished. 'Oh, oh, oh!' shouted the Queen, shaking her hand about as if she wanted to shake it off. 'My finger's bleeding! Oh, oh, oh, oh!'

Her screams were so exactly like the whistle of a steam-engine, that Alice had to hold both her hands over her ears.

'What *is* the matter?' she said, as soon as there was a chance of making herself heard. 'Have you pricked your finger?'

'I haven't pricked it *yet*,' the Queen said, 'but I soon shall − oh, oh, oh!'

'When do you expect to do it?' Alice asked, feeling very much inclined to laugh.

'When I fasten my shawl again,' the poor Queen groaned out: 'the brooch will come undone directly. Oh, oh!' As she said the words the brooch flew open, and the Queen clutched wildly at it, and tried to clasp it again.

'Take care!' cried Alice. 'You're holding it all crooked!' And she caught at the brooch; but it was too late: the pin had slipped, and the Queen had pricked her finger.

'That accounts for the bleeding, you see,' she said to Alice with a smile. 'Now you understand the way things happen here.'

'But why don't you scream *now*?' Alice asked, holding her hands ready to put over her ears again.

'Why, I've done all the screaming already,' said the Queen. 'What would be the good of having it all over again?'

Lewis Carroll *Through the Looking Glass*

The Golden Age

Strictly speaking, the Greek myth was not of a 'Golden Age' but of a Golden Race which was the earth's first human population. Hesiod (c 700 BC) tells the story in his *Works and Days*. They lived when Cronus was king of the gods, and they lived like gods themselves, free from pain and toil and old age. The earth bore them its fruits untilled, and death came to them gentle as sleep. Now they have become invisible spirits that watch over men and bring them prosperity. They were succeeded by a Silver Race, foolish, violent, and irreligious: their childhood lasted 100 years, but then they aged rapidly. They have become spirits of a lower order, the Mortal Blessed. The gods next made a Bronze Race, out of ash trees, more stern and brutal still, who destroyed themselves and left no trace. They were the first to kill animals for food. Then the succession of metals and the moral decline was interrupted: the fourth race was that of the noble heroes who fought at Troy and elsewhere, and who now live in the Isles of the Blessed and are revered as demigods. But now we have an Iron Race, doomed to toil, suffering, and eventually destruction, as their wickedness increases and children begin to be already grey-haired at birth.

The metal names do not have a single consistent significance. Of the Bronze Race, Hesiod says that their armour, tools and houses were of bronze, for there was no iron then. This evidently represents a memory of the 'Bronze Age' of our archeologists, which in Greece gave way to the Iron Age about 1100 BC. At the same time, the Iron Race's name is appropriate to its inhumanity; while gold and silver join up with bronze to form a scale of absolute value. (Iron, however, ranked as a precious, not a base metal.) Thus the myth represents a compromise between abstract theory and a genuine memory of the past. The conflict shows itself again in the way the Heroic Age is accommodated between the Bronze and Iron Races. It has often been assumed that Hesiod was adapting a mythical scheme in which there were four races instead of five: Gold, Silver, Bronze, Iron, each worse than its predecessor. It may have been of oriental origin. Medieval Persian texts, which certainly contain some ancient material, tell how Zoroaster saw in a vision a tree with four branches, of gold, silver, copper and iron, and Ahura Mazdah explained to him that these were the four kingdoms of Iran that were to succeed one another, each worse than the last. We recall, too, Nebuchadnezzar's dream in the book of Daniel (chapter 2) in which four successive kingdoms are represented by the gold, silver, brass, and iron and clay parts of an effigy in human form. The metal symbolism has been thought to point to Babylon, where alchemy was practised early, and metals were assigned to each of the planets. In India, there developed a theory of four world ages, of advancing badness and decreasing length, associated with different colours of Vishnu, though not with metals. Here too the last age is characterized by encroachment of old age upon youth.

Hesiod's poem has a double theme, honesty and industry. The myth serves to show how human morality has declined from a perfect state, and also how it has become necessary to work for a living as the earth has withdrawn her bounty. In the time of the Golden Race, righteousness went together with leisure. The general conviction of mankind that the times are growing worse, that today's men are inferior to yesterday's, here finds systematic expression. The details of the idyll follow from a negation of all that is most bothersome at the present day: toil, pain, war, want, worry, old age. Even the residual guilt over animal sacrifice is purged away in the recollection of the time of innocence when men lived in amity with each other and their fellow creatures. The statement that Cronus was king may be connected with the fact that he presided over a summer festival at which conditions approached those enjoyed by the ideal race.

The Philosophers

Later Greek and Roman accounts all derive ultimately from Hesiod, but show a perspective that gradually changes with the times. Philosophers and moralists constructed their own accounts of the development of human society. Reflection, and observation of more backward peoples, brought a new awareness of the fact of technical progress. In 5th century BC accounts, the blessed vegetarians of the earliest age have been replaced by shivering cave-dwellers subsisting on acorns and whatever else they can find. So far from declining, on this view, man's state has constantly improved. This has little in common with Hesiod's picture, and at first there was no attempt to reconcile the two. Plato more than once makes use of Hesiod's metal races, adapting them freely in myths of his own. In his *Republic*, he proposes justifying his strict class structure to the citizenry by persuading them that God has fashioned them with different metals in their constitutions, gold, silver, bronze or iron. Here the metals keep their qualitative significance, but there is no idea of temporal succession. Elsewhere, too, while he allows the idea of world cycles, Plato is disinclined to link virtue and happiness to them too firmly.

Later in the 4th century BC, the philosopher Dicaearchus gave a rationalistic interpretation of Hesiod's description of the life of the Golden Race. Naturally their food grew of its own accord, because they had no agriculture, and that was why they were free from toil and care. They did not fall sick, because their diet was sparse and simple. There was no warfare, because there was nothing worth taking. So the myth is brought into harmony with more recent speculation about how early man's life must have been. As yet there is no exaggerated insistence on the virtue and nobility of the primitive, no connection is seen between technical progress and moral regress. The influential Stoic writer Posidonius (135−50 BC), praising the benefits that philosophy had conferred on mankind, claimed that in the Golden Age the rulers were philosophers, who taught their subjects wisdom, restraint and justice, besides providing for their wants. It was the passing of power to tyrants that brought about the decline, and the need for laws. But the philosophers remained active as makers of these laws, and in developing the arts and crafts.

It is when we pass to Rome that we find the Golden Race turned into a Golden Age, as a result of the ambivalence of the Latin word *saeculum*. Other new developments can also be explained from Roman conditions. The myth is given political applications. In his famous fourth Eclogue (40 BC), Virgil announces that the wheel has come full circle, and that a return of the Golden Age is imminent. Within 20 years or so, he says, the earth will become generous again, fruit and crops will grow of their own accord, honey will run from the

Allegory with Time, by the Venetian painter Tiepolo: the figure of Father Time goes back partly to the astrological image of Saturn as a grim old man, armed with a sickle and hourglass as symbols of the ending of human life, and partly to the image of Death as a skeleton, reaping men's lives with a scythe; the two images fused in Father Time

National Gallery

oaks, the snake will bite no more, warfare and commerce will disappear, the sheep will even grow coloured wool to save us dyeing it artificially. Obviously Virgil did not believe all this literally, and it is hard to say what he meant by it. But later, in the *Aeneid*, it becomes the reign of Augustus that he celebrates as the new Golden Age. His enthusiasm was sincere, but he was setting a bad precedent. To speak of 'this golden age' became a commonplace in the art of emperor-flattery.

Freedom of the Primitive

Virgil has a new concept of the connection between the end of the Golden Age and the growth of civilization. In the *Georgics*, he explains that Jupiter put a stop to the life of ease in order to stimulate mankind to resource and discovery, and 'so that his kingdom should not bask in torpor'. Deprived of automatic sustenance, they were forced to find out how to grow crops, strike fire from the flint, navigate, hunt, saw wood; harsh necessity was the mother of invention. This favourable view of human progress was soon to be challenged. The complexity of life in the big city, and the diversity of luxury and ostentation that flourished there, increasingly provoked the censure of moralizers and satirists. Hence the advances of material civilization finally came to be identified as the symptoms and concomitants of moral degeneration. Seneca (60 AD) voiced the opinion that it was better to live in caves and hollow trees than in towering tenements that threaten to collapse, with locking doors that only encourage avarice; the primitive's freedom was more valuable than our pastrycooks and ornamental ceilings. Man's essential needs can be very easily satisfied in simple ways.

Thus mankind is made fully responsible for its own fall. It was not the gods' will or the exhaustion of Nature that put an end to the Golden Age, but man's folly.

M. L. WEST

FURTHER READING: S. G. F. Brandon, *History, Time and Deity* (Manchester Univ. Press, 1965); J. Fraser ed., *Voices of Time* (Allen Lane, 1968). See E. Rohde, *Psyche* (Harper Torchbooks, N.Y., 1966 reprint) for a discussion of Hesiod's myth from the point of view of religious history.

The tinkers who still travel the roads of Scotland and Ireland are probably the descendants of an ancient caste of itinerant metal-workers, whose skill once endowed them with great prestige

TINKERS

IN SCOTLAND and Ireland, as well as in parts of Scandinavia, there are still to be found nomadic or quasi-nomadic groups whose way of life resembles that of the gypsies, although they have little or no gypsy blood in them. It is impossible to speak with certainty of their origin, but it seems likely that they are the descendants of a very ancient caste of itinerant metal-workers whose status in tribal society was probably high. One of the trades associated with them from early times was that of tinsmith, and it is clear that to primitive man the ability to use metals seemed very close to magic; consequently, both 'black' and 'white' smiths for long enjoyed immense prestige, not only as craftsmen but as wielders of secret powers (see SMITH).

When the gypsies arrived in Western and Northern Europe in the 15th and 16th centuries (see GYPSIES), there was no doubt a certain amount of biological and socio-cultural mixing between them and the aboriginal itinerants whom they encountered (and in some areas appeared to have displaced). In certain regions a measure of fusion took place between the two groups, and a mixed 'tinkler-gypsy' race came into being, but at the present day the gypsies and tinkers view each other as quite distinct groupings; and there is not much love lost between them.

The ranks of the Scots tinkers were augmented at various periods as a result of events in the country's troubled history. Writing in the 1690s, Fletcher of Saltoun stated that as a result of repeated famine and breakdown in trade there were at least 200,000 people wandering homeless in Scotland, and reduced to begging for their bread. Many of these must have become absorbed in the tinker clans. Dynastic and religious wars, and the ultimate disaster of Culloden (1746) sent sizeable new contingents to join the fraternity, and some of the victims of the Highland clearances (mass evictions) no doubt added their quota. Tinkerdom, therefore, constitutes not so much an ethnic as a socio-cultural group; it has been described by F. Rehfisch, in an unpublished thesis, as 'cultural inasmuch as many of the cultural norms of the fraternity are different from those of the Flattie (the non-tinker), and social because most members interact with fellow tinkers and generally not with outsiders, if it can be avoided.'

The tinkers' fear of persecution finds expression in their belief in 'burkers', body-snatchers supposed to lie in wait to murder them; especially suspect were medical students who seized bodies to sell to the anatomy departments of hospitals
Top right A tinker's camp, north of Perth
Centre Tinkers round a camp-fire *Right* A tinker family near Kintyre in Argyllshire

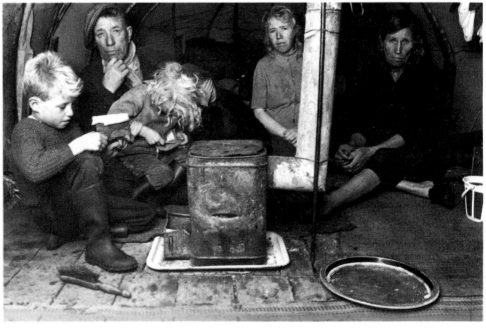

Hamish Henderson

Travellers From the Past

Some of the tinker groupings, both in Scotland and in Ireland, make up a kind of 'underground' clan system of their own, and individuals are intensely conscious of kinship and family ties. They want nothing to do with tramps and other solitaries, feeling themselves as distinct from this type of itinerant as they are from the Romany gypsies. A very intelligent tinker youth once put the distinction in a nutshell when, referring to an Irish tramp who used to wander around Scotland, he declared: 'That sort of lad just lives from day to day, but we (tinkers) live entirely in the past.' (It should be stressed at this point that the term 'tinker' itself is disliked by the fraternity because of its frequent use in a derogatory context; tinkers call themselves 'travellers'.)

There were, of course, many tinkers in the south as well as in the countries of the 'Celtic fringe', but in England the gypsies seem to have taken over their role in society and to a large extent put them out of business. It may safely be conjectured that the organized tinker groupings survived longer in Scotland and Ireland than in the south because a semi-tribal state of society lingered until a much later date in these countries.

Unlike the true gypsies, whose language is (or used to be) Romany, the tinkers use a cover-language known as 'cant'. The cant of the tinkler-gypsies of Galloway and southeast Scotland has quite a strong admixture of Romany in it, but north of the Forth-Clyde line the amount of recognizable Romany in the cover-tongue is hardly more than 15%. The tinkers of the North and West and of the Hebrides, whose native language is Gaelic (or was, until very recently) have a cover-tongue of their own which resembles one of the secret languages of Ireland. Their name for it is 'Beurlacheard', or 'lingo of the cairds' (the tinkers). That this is a very ancient cover-tongue is shown by the fact that some of the vocabulary which it reflects and deforms is archaic Gaelic.

The Black Coach

Although the 'flattie' (non-tinker) population for long feared that the tinkers were child-stealers (witness the lullaby 'Hush ye! Hush ye! Dinna fret ye! The black Tinkler winna get ye'), the folklore of the tinkers shows clearly and even poignantly that they lived in much greater fear of the ordinary population than the 'flatties' did of them. This persecution complex found, and still finds, expression in gruesome folklore about 'burkers' (body-snatchers) who were supposed to be continually on the wait to waylay and murder travelling folk, and sell their bodies to the anatomy schools. An Aberdeenshire tinker, quite well known as a country dance-band musician, told me in 1954: 'I mind, once upon a time, when ye couldna

In the north and west of Scotland the tinkers use a language that resembles one of the ancient and secret tongues of Ireland, which the tinkers call 'Beurlacheard' or 'lingo of the cairds': tapestry of Irish tinkers

William MacQuitty

pass the Marischal College or the King's College, for the students would fairly tak a haud o' ye with a cleik (a hooked piece of iron) by the leg . . . they took ye right inside — they wanted fresh bodies.'

Writing four years later Rehfisch stated: 'To my surprise, I discovered that there is still a real belief in 'burkers', the villains of many of the most hair-raising tinker stories. We were told that the neighbourhood of the University of Aberdeen was a dangerous place to visit at night, and is so even today. One of our Blairgowrie informants claimed to have been chased by two or three red-robed students not more than five years ago. She said she knew their aim was to kill her and sell her body to the Anatomy Department . . . Another informant noticed a sign posted in the neighbourhood of that same university stating that it was dangerous for persons alone to frequent the area after dusk. Still another one said that the missing persons column in the Sunday newspaper *The News of the World* was concrete evidence that the body-snatchers were still active . . . She explained that in all probability those whose names appeared in that column were for the most part victims of these villainous burkers.'

Paraded by an accomplished storyteller at the camp-fire, the ghoulish trappings of the burker stories conjure up a phantasmagoric *grand guignol* world reminiscent of Dylan Thomas's 'The Doctor and the Devils'. Lum-hatted black-frockcoated noddies (medical students) drive the 'burker's coach' into the countryside to try and find isolated tinker encampments; the coach is long and black-draped, looking like a hearse; bloodhounds lope silently beside it; the horse's harness is swathed in cloth to prevent it chinking; the horse's hooves have rubber pads on them. In some of the stories the tinker victim gets his throat cut, and his relatives discover too late that he is missing; in others, there are hair's-breadth escapes from the villainous doctors and noddies. Looking at the faces round the camp-fire, I could well believe statements made to me that Perthshire tinkers would (until quite recently) leave their encampments and rush in panic to the hill on the appearance of a suspicious vehicle.

Although we can well believe that defenceless ragged nomads were occasionally the victims of murderous body-snatchers, we must probably look further back in history in order to understand the deeper-lying reasons for this persecution complex. In the 17th century it was a capital crime in Scotland merely to *be* an 'Egyptian' – Egyptian, for the courts, meaning not merely a gypsy, but any sort of wanderer, vagabond minstrel or travelling tinsmith of no fixed abode. If it could be proved that a travelling man of uncertain occupation was 'halden and repute to be an Egyptian', he was as good as dead. Among the victims of this law was the famous fiddler James MacPherson, who was hanged at Banff in 1700.

Like the gypsies, tinkers sometimes make money by telling fortunes. Quite a number are believed (by themselves and others) to possess the gift of 'second sight', but this gift is not at the beck and call of its possessor and is never exploited commercially. The tinkers believe, as do many ordinary Scots country folk, that the seventh child of a seventh child is likely to possess this strange psychic gift.

The Uncanny MacPhees

Belief in the existence of fairies is still very widespread among the tinkers. In *A Dictionary of British Folk-Tales,* Dr. K. M. Briggs prints several allegedly true stories about fairies recorded by the School of Scottish Studies from tinker informants. These include stories about brownies, elves, changelings, water-kelpies, fairy funerals, fairy music heard by mortals, and — last but not least — 'a wee green man' seen in the Sma' Glen. Rehfisch reports (in 1958): 'Some of our informants had seen one or more fairies, with never any harm to themselves. One had found a fairy's coffin with a little corpse inside! They kept it for some time until one day it mysteriously disappeared. Ghosts are feared, though there are but few tales of them harming living persons. The number of our informants who claim to have actually seen one or more of them is legion.' Belief in witches and the black art is also common.

Finally, one rather curious item of tinker folklore deserves mention. A sort of mystical aura surrounds the name of the MacPhees, one of the Scots tinker clans. The MacPhees are regarded by some as the 'original' tinkers, the 'first on the road', but even so an undoubted 'hoodoo' seems to lie over their very name: it is bad luck to hear or speak the name MacPhee, and a substitute name such as MacFud, MacaFud or Maca-Tuttie, is supposed to be used in place of it. If the first person one sees when leaving for work in the morning is a MacPhee, it is advisable to turn back; no good will come of the day's endeavours. Some tinkers believe that to say the words 'cold iron' constitutes an effective counter-spell.

HAMISH HENDERSON

FURTHER READING: Scottish Dev. Dept., *Scotland's Travelling People* (H.M.S.O., 1971).

The grotesque physical appearance of the toad does nothing to endear it to humans: indeed in England a toad might be a witch's familiar and in Europe it could be the witch herself

TOAD

THE IMPORTANCE of the toad in world folklore seems to derive more from its basic characteristics than from any diffusion of notions about it from one area to another. Being associated with water, toads and frogs are involved in rain-making and other fertility rites. Moreover, the fact that toads resemble grotesque, miniature human beings arouses the ambivalent feelings so often inspired by mysterious and possibly sinister creatures. Not only are the faces of toads reminiscent of a very wide-mouthed human face but their attitudes while swimming and copulating bear some resemblance to human postures and human movements.

The toad is rightly regarded as venomous. If irritated, toads exude a substance, from glands on the skin, which carries two separate poisons sufficiently violent to cause dogs to foam at the mouth and become feverish. During the Middle Ages, bandits sometimes forced a toad into the mouth of one of their victims. Thus there are adequate grounds for regarding toads with repugnance.

In England, particularly in East Anglia, the toad had an evil reputation. A toad might be a witch's familiar and she was said to make a magic lotion of toad spittle and the sap of the sow-thistle. With this concoction, she outlined a crooked cross on her body, and so could make herself invisible. In parts of central Europe, toads were believed to be witches and in many areas their evil repute was such that they were killed, but in Rumania a toad killer was believed capable of murdering his mother and therefore they remained unmolested.

Toads have an evil reputation in many parts of Europe, and were often believed to be in league with the Devil or to be witches' familiars *Above* **Toads dancing at a sabbath and** *(below)* **a toad flying to a sabbath, from De Plancy's** *Dictionnaire Infernal*

In Cambridgeshire certain men, called toadmen, were believed to have special power over horses, and to be able to make them stand still despite all efforts to get them to move. They could also render horses uncontrollable. Such a person might be regarded as in league with the Devil and viewed with some anxiety. A man wishing to acquire this power had to skin a toad, or peg it to an ant-hill until its bones were picked clean. He then carried the bones in his pocket until they were dry, and at midnight, when there was a full moon, he floated the bones on a stream. They would screech and one bone would set off upstream. If he secured this bone, he gained the powers of a toadman. Such men were said to be found in Cambridgeshire up to 1938. It is difficult to decide the extent to which this ritual was actually carried out or taken seriously.

Also in Cambridgeshire, toads were regarded as predicting storms. It was believed that they could hear distant thunder, inaudible to human ears, and could then be seen making their way to water. The origin of this belief may be that toads move from their winter quarters to their breeding place with remarkable unanimity within a period of a few days, and thunderstorms may occur around this time.

Toads, or parts of them, were considered efficacious as charms. A Herefordshire man declared that he could steal as much as he liked, and would never be found out, because he wore a toad's heart around his neck. In Devonshire, toads were burnt because they were believed to be in league with the Devil. Perhaps on the principle 'Set a thief to catch a thief', the toad was reputed to be able to drive away noxious things. In a book on gardening which appeared in 1593, Thomas Hyll recommended that before sowing seeds a toad should be drawn around the garden, then placed in an earthenware pot and buried in the centre of a flower bed. He advised that after the seeds had been sown the toad should be dug up, otherwise the vegetables growing round about would acquire a bitter taste. Having taken these precautions, the gardener could feel confident that no creeping thing would injure his crops. This appears to be a version of an ancient belief: the Greek writer Apuleius and the Roman writer Pliny advocated placing a toad in an earthenware pot in a field to avert storms, and two years after Hyll's book appeared another writer repeated this timeworn recipe for protecting the fields.

There was said to be enmity between toads and spiders. Toads do indeed eat spiders, and possibly by an extension of this observed fact the creatures were credited with being able to repel evil.

Jewelled Head

A toadstone (in practice, any stone that resembled the toad or frog in shape or colour) was believed to have the power of curing bites and stings, when applied to the affected part. You could always tell whether such a stone was genuine by holding it in front of a toad; if the toad jumped forward to snatch it from you the stone was no counterfeit.

During the Middle Ages and later, it was believed that the toad concealed a precious jewel in its head. In Shakespeare's *As You Like It*, the Duke remarks:

Sweet are the uses of adversity;
Which like the toad, ugly and venomous,
Wears yet a precious jewel in his head.

Earlier writers also refer to this belief. One, in 1569, commented: 'There is to be found in the heads of old and great toads a stone they call borax or stelon, which being used in a ring gives a forewarning against venom.' The fear of assassination by poison was very real among the upper classes in some countries during the medieval period and the Renaissance. Lyly, the Elizabethan playwright, wrote in *Euphues*: 'The fayrer the stone is in the toades head the more pestilent the poyson is in hir bowelles.' Thus association proceeded from the fact that the toad produces a poisonous secretion to the supposition that it carries within itself an antidote.

The belief in the toadstone's efficacy against poison dates from at least as far back as the 12th century. But the poisonous characteristics of the toad were recognized much earlier. Pliny said that the creature was full of poison and Aelian (3rd century AD) added his own touch of exaggeration, remarking that people had been killed instantly by drinking wine to which the blood of a toad had been added. Milton, influenced by his classical learning, relates in *Paradise Lost* that Satan transformed himself into a toad in order to squat by

Eve's ear and inject poison into her blood.

Probably because the toad and the fabulous basilisk were both reputed to be venomous, they were brought into association during the Middle Ages. The basilisk was said to kill shrubs by touching them and smash stones by breathing on them. Writers of the 12th and 13th centuries stated that it was born from an egg laid by a cock in old age and hatched by a serpent or toad.

In general, and especially in ecclesiastical circles, the toad was regarded during the medieval period as a revolting, Satanic creature. A story was told of a monk who, during Lent, caught a cock in order to cook and eat it. When he put in his hand to extract the entrails he pulled out a toad. Another tale relates that as an extremely avaricious money-lender lay dying he begged his wife to place a purse full of money in his tomb. This she did, as stealthily as possible, but the secret leaked out. Searching for the money, some people went to the grave and opened it. They saw there two toads, one in the opening of the purse and the other on the man's breast. 'One with its mouth was extracting coins from the purse, the other taking those that had been extracted and putting them into his heart. It was as if they said: "We will satisfy that insatiable heart with money."' Those who concocted such stories were not interested in natural history but in edification, so they associated a revolting creature with self-indulgence and greed. A sculpture at Strasbourg entitled *The Seducer of Unfaithful Virgins* depicts snakes and toads climbing up a handsome youth's back while he holds forth an apple.

The fact that one of the Zoroastrian sacred books states that toads are evil creatures and should be killed, shows that the dislike of toads is not confined to Christendom and confirms that their appearance and characteristics awaken a deep-seated and widespread repugnance.

Such feelings may account for the toad being among the animals which in various parts of the world are treated as scapegoats. In Togoland the Hos enacted an elaborate ceremony annually to expel noxious things and influences from their midst. After they had besought evil spirits and witches to enter into bundles of creepers, which they carried out of town, they swept their houses and yards, and washed their faces with magical medicine. At night, a toad, tied to a palm leaf, was drawn through the streets. Among the shamanistic Gilyaks of Northern Asia the toad also figured as a scapegoat. After bears had been ritually sacrificed, the figure of a toad, made of birch bark, was placed peering in through a window while inside the house a dummy bear, dressed in Gilyak costume, occupied a bench of honour. The guilt of slaying the bear was laid upon the toad.

E. A. ARMSTRONG

TOBACCO

WHEN white explorers reached the New World, tobacco was grown abundantly in the West Indies, Latin America and much of what is now the United States. It was cultivated by many agricultural Indian tribes and also by some who were not agriculturalists. Most western and south-eastern Indians gathered wild tobacco, if they did not grow their own. Other tribes, who could neither grow it nor find it, acquired it by trade or theft. Certainly they almost all smoked it. They stuffed the dried and crumbled leaves into hollow reeds, like primitive cigarettes, or rolled the leaves themselves into cylinders like cigars, or packed their tobacco in superbly crafted, decorated and far from primitive pipes.

Smoke of all kinds – from burnt offerings or incense, for example – has always been used as a carrier of man's prayers and praises upwards to the gods, and American Indians used tobacco smoke for this purpose. At the beginning of any holy or otherwise important enterprise, honour would be paid to the gods and their blessings sought by four (or six) puffs of smoke from a ceremonial pipe, passed among the chiefs and warriors: four puffs to each of the sacred four directions (and often two more to the other two directions, upwards and downwards). The Incas and other South American peoples used this ritual; it is thought that the early Mound Builders, prehistoric inhabitants of the eastern woodlands of North America, did too, for they had numerous and sophisticated pipes.

When the Plains Indians performed this tobacco ritual, using their glorious calumet (reed-stemmed) pipes, the paramount chief smoked first, facing east, and the pipe passed to the right, sunwise. But there were variations: a smoker might dance briefly with the pipe, or the pipe stem itself might be presented to the four corners (giving the spirits a puff) instead of the smoke. The Pawnee used enormous calumet pipes, with stems four feet long, and bowls that rested on the ground, too large to pass from hand to hand.

But if outward forms differed, the ceremonial purpose remained the same. The act of smoking together bound the smokers in a pact or covenant, and called down the sanction of the spirits on their intentions. Western films have provided a typically over-simplified idea of 'the peace-pipe', but certainly such ritual smoking together did take place when warring tribes drew up treaties.

Smoke Offering to the Gods

Smoking to the four directions was by no means the only occasion at which tobacco was used in Indian ceremonial. Most south-eastern tribes offered tobacco smoke to gods and spirits whenever the occasion demanded – even smoking to the spirits of trees before cutting them down. They also put tobacco in the graves, along with other gifts, to ensure the dead person's well-being in the next world.

The Iroquois and other north-eastern tribes made their smoke offerings by placing tobacco directly onto a fire during dances and ceremonies. The hunters of the Labrador region of Canada might blow smoke onto some talismanic object that bore their personal good luck; similarly, a Plains warrior might offer pipe smoke to the magical objects within his medicine bundle.

Tobacco smoke is sometimes part of a purifying ritual that precedes most Pueblo ceremonies. Under the supervision of a special Tobacco clan, smoke from reed cigarettes or special clay pipes will be blown over altars, magical objects and prayer-sticks. And the meeting of the Pueblo men to discuss and plan a major

> ## Sovereign Remedy
>
> King James I's *Counterblaste to Tobacco*:
> Tobacco was widely thought to possess rare medicinal power and to be a cure for all and sundry disorders; and the bulk of the *Counterblaste* is a scathing attack upon these claims. The King's notions of medicine and anatomy are, of course, absurd . . . Yet he is on solid ground in challenging the therapeutic powers claimed for tobacco. Smoke flies up into the head, he scoffs, yet is supposed to cure gout in the lower limbs. It is a remedy for diseases directly opposed to each other. It makes a drunken man sober and a sober man drunk, it induces sleep yet quickens and awakens the brain.
> D. H. Willson *King James VI and I*

ceremony becomes itself a ritual occasion on which tobacco is formally and communally smoked.

Tobacco can function as more than an offering to the spirits. The Crow Indians consider it to be an object of religious veneration in its own right. Their myths say that a high spirit called a Star Being came to earth in the form of tobacco, but was recognized by a culture hero who declared the plant and its cultivation to be sacred. (Many other tribes have comparable legends of tobacco as a gift from the gods.) The Crow developed a Tobacco Society that devoted itself to the ceremonial planting, harvesting and curing of tobacco as a major part of the year's religious observances. The Omaha Indians had a different cult, centred on sacred pipes. Two special pipes served as the tribe's main totem objects, brought out and smoked by the great chiefs before any major event.

Healing Powers

In general the tobacco used by Indians of North America was a rough variety, strong enough to make men dizzy and mildly 'high', and some used it to induce visions. The Indians also used tobacco in healing. They believed that the smoke was good for asthma and lung complaints, but they especially found the leaves useful in poultices for sores and wounds.

Folk medicine (mainly American) also uses tobacco in more overtly magical cures, often linked with the traditional healing powers of human breath and spittle. Blowing smoke into the ear cures ear-ache; blowing smoke onto a baby's stomach cures its colic; spitting tobacco juice onto warts causes them to disappear. Chewing tobacco is also believed to forestall pain while treating snakebite, and anglers can spit tobacco juice onto their bait, for extra luck. The raw tobacco leaf serves in a cure for indigestion, by crossing two leaves on the sufferer's stomach; and to keep the household from disease all winter, hang a tobacco leaf in the chimney all summer.

Today with all the medical warnings surrounding the habit, smokers know that smoking is itself unlucky. On a slightly happier note, it is said that if your cigarette keeps going out, it is a sure sign that you are in love.

Tongs

American term for Chinese secret societies, frequently combining religious and political aims with racketeering; in the 1850s the Tongs fought gang wars in the United States, wearing warpaint and armed with hatchets: these societies originated in China, among rebels against the established government and the state religion.
See CHINA.

Torah

Hebrew for 'teaching', applied in the first instance to the Pentateuch, the first five books of the Bible, traditionally believed to have been dictated to Moses by God, and by extension to the other books of the Old Testament; there is also the oral Torah, the teachings held to have been conveyed by God to Moses by word of mouth, together with the commentaries of the rabbis during the first five centuries AD.
See JUDAISM.

Keystone Press

'For those who live within a totemic culture, it is the very basis of their understanding of the world'; a totem is a hereditary badge or emblem of a tribe or other group, usually representing an animal after which the group is named; the word is also applied to the animal itself

TOTEM

THE WORD TOTEM comes from the North American Indians, who did not so much believe in descent from animals as that their early ancestors were partially divine and could change their shape from time to time to suit their convenience. Echoes of this belief remain in some of the Greek myths, quite as much as among Indian tribes, such as the Haida of Queen Charlotte's Islands, British Columbia, who have left remarkably beautiful carvings illustrating their mythology. The development of totemic animal myths into romantic epics, symbolized in the carved house poles and decorated costumes of the tribal leaders, is not unlike the system in the early Middle Ages when mythology first developed into the rich artistic heritage of heraldry. A Haida chief who belonged to the bear clan and wore symbols of Bear Mother on his clothing was not so very different from the ancient Earls of Warwick who, from a family tradition, adopted a bear with a ragged staff as their badge.

On the great plains of North America, the tribes of the prairie were also interested in animals which symbolized the spirit world. Young men would hope for revelation of an individual totem creature. On reaching puberty they would go through a short period of instruction from the elders and magicians of the tribe, and were then sent out on a difficult journey to find their protective spirit. The young man would walk away from the village into the open prairie: he would carry neither clothes nor blanket, but he was allowed a bow and arrows. He was expected to abstain from all food for the four days of his journey and as he went through the days and nights he asked the Power Above and Earth Mother to grant him protection and to give him a spirit helper who would stand beside him through life, warn him of danger and lead him into paths which would be honourable and profitable. In a state of semi-starvation, combined with near ecstasy in his prayerful relation with the spirit world, he would naturally experience many visions, like waking dreams. At some point he would see an animal which might possibly talk to him, but in any case he would become aware that this was the creature which was meant to be his totem. He was expected to shoot it, kill it and skin it. Then he would keep some special portion: claws, or skull, or some of

Australian aborigines held totemic dances in which the men dressed to resemble their totemic ancestors and believed that they entered the Dreamtime and became their ancestors: carvings of a totemic dingo and whale

the bones which would go inside the dried skin. This was what Europeans would call his 'medicine bag'. He would carry it with him tucked in his belt: it would be his protector in battle and his guide in times of peace. This was the traditional totem.

The Continuity of Life
There are examples of this type of attitude throughout humanity. One may think of the young squire kneeling in prayer all night, asking for the blessings of heaven and for the care of a patron saint in the days to come when he would be a knight and become a leader in peace and in war. Among the peoples of ancient America, symbolic animals and birds were regarded as sent from the spirit world. Among the Inca, the respect paid to the condor and the puma was characteristic of this belief, and even in ancient Britain, the blackbird was a messenger of the dead and the magpie a kind of fairy bird. However, the basic feeling for totemism rarely reaches the development that it had among the North American Indians, and also among the far more primitive Australian aborigines.

The aboriginal tribespeople of Australia lived a reasonably comfortable life with early Stone Age equipment. The primary skills of hunting animals, finding edible roots and supplies of water allowed them to live well in regions of the Australian desert which are quite uninhabitable to Europeans. The philosophical elders among the aborigines considered that in the long ago, in the Dreamtime (see AUSTRALIA), the world was not so well organized as

today. Land and water were not properly separated, there were trees and grasses that were living beings which could move about, man and animals were somehow all one, so that the beings which finally developed as men had quite probably inhabited animal forms previously. Within any given tribe there were several divisions; each was named after an animal or other creature from the Dreamtime, who had developed his human side and so become a direct ancestor of that part of the tribe. It was very important for people to know about their totem ancestor. They not only held ceremonies in his honour, but also it was well known that people of one totem might only marry people of a specified other totem; it was a way of making sure that intermarriage was not too close between related groups.

The aborigines did not believe that death was the end. The body was often thrown away to decay, except perhaps for a few bones that were removed for magical use, for the body was but a temporary house for the reality of the living being. Aborigines believed that after the body died, the personality escaped, sometimes into sacred trees, sometimes to hide in caves. Among the aborigines of central Australia, the spirits went back into sacred slabs of stone or wood which had been carved with patterns representing the emergence of the totem ancestor in the ancient Dreamtime. The soul would rest in one of these *churinga*, as they were called, and wait until a likely mother passed by.

This magic was known to the elders of each tribe and was not shared by women. All the women were allowed to know was that somewhere in a sacred area which they were not allowed to visit there were the souls of ancestors waiting to enter their bodies and be born as new babies. Since in the wandering, hunting life of the aboriginals it was difficult to look after many children, women were usually careful to keep away from these magical places. It appears that they knew that babies could not be born without the help of man, and also that intercourse would not necessarily result in the birth of a child; pregnancy would occur only when the spirit had entered them and so given life which could properly develop into a baby. When a child was born, the elders of the tribe consulted together and decided whose spirit was in the child. They then removed the appropriate sacred churinga from its store, and it was kept in another place for the whole lifetime of the newly born person. At death the soul was thought to have re-entered the churinga and it was then placed with the remainder, where souls were waiting rebirth into the pleasant world.

The belief that people belonged to certain selected groups of totem ancestors, related to the non-human world, led to many interesting ceremonies. These were conducted by the men, mostly in places which women would not visit. Women took part only in the social *corroboree*, an occasion for singing and dancing, in which very often the men might wear the secret painted decoration of the totem ancestors. The women, of course,

Jeffrey Craig

did not know the meaning of the designs. They had dances of their own, and when the men were putting on their little theatrical ballet about the ancestors, the women could join in the rhythm and beat out the time on pieces of wood or bundles of kangaroo skin on their laps.

But at the really important occasions where the history of the totem ancestor was mimed, no women were allowed. The men painted themselves with red and yellow ochre and white pipe-clay. They decorated themselves with white tufts of down from the feathers of the larger birds which they stuck to themselves by making little cuts in their skin so that the blood would act as glue. From their hair, they often built up elaborate head-dresses of sticks and grass, all painted with ochre which made them in some way resemble their own ancestral totem, such as the emu or the kangaroo. Then, to the accompaniment of explanatory chants by their elders, they would dance around sacred objects which represented the places where the ancestors had emerged from the earth and they would pretend to be once again in the Dreamtime where man and animal were indistinguishable.

In imitating the animal, one could see through the disguise to the shape of a man who was going to develop into the totemic ancestor. Among the Australian aborigines this was not just a representation, it was so important a ritual that the people taking part really believed that they had entered another time and were at one with their ancestors. In fact, it was perfectly clear to

Above Australian aborigines believed that spirits waited for rebirth in churingas, sacred slabs of stone or wood, carved with patterns representing the emergence of the totem ancestor in the ancient Dreamtime *Right* Totemic figures from British Columbia: an American Indian totem might be a man's individual guardian spirit or the spiritual protector of an entire group; it would usually show itself in the form of an animal or bird

them that since their spirits had come from sacred churinga they had formerly inhabited a human body. Before that, the soul had been in the churinga; and so on through time, from man to storage stone and back, and back into the Dreamtime itself. They believed that they were the same people who had been the ancestors, though they were now living in a modern body in a modern time. So to the Australian aborigines, the totem belief was a belief in the continuity of human life from the very beginning of things when man and animal were all one.

In a way, this is reminiscent of the scientific teaching about the evolution of man through the humanoids from a physical animal ancestry, but of course the aborigine was not interested in studying the origin of species. He just believed that the chants and the words handed down to him from the elders in the past were the sacred truth about the nature of humanity and the relationships between man and the totem.

The totemic idea is very widespread, but in many cases it amounts to little more than

Picturepoint, London

relationship with mankind. One called, or asked the wise man to call, in a specially receptive state of mind, and the answer would come. The 'medicine bag' would be handled or even displayed on such occasions, because it represented the first firm contact with the world in which one's personal totem was at home. Rapport with the hidden powers was important since they were man's supporters in the quest of life.

Although the American Indian was no longer as totally dependent upon the gifts of uncultivated Nature as the aborigine, he relied on many more spirit powers for help. There were the animal spirits who would affect his success in hunting by their willingness or unwillingness to yield their bodies to feed humans. There were the spirits of maize, tobacco, beans and pumpkins, who must be asked to give their fruit abundantly, as well as to produce living seed for future sustenance. All these were influenced by this gentle mystery of the totem who was the protector of the individual and his community. Maybe this was a projection of the 'unconscious', but to the Indian this was no matter for introspection. The powers were felt to be external, and the totem spirit was an external protector.

The transition from the diffuse feeling of a spirit being, as expressed in North American totemism, to organized religious systems with hierarchies of defined divinities is a natural one. It can be seen in the ceremonies of such highly cultured societies as those of the Pueblo Indians, whose *kachina* spirits partake of both the generalized vagueness of the totem and the clear-cut line of action expressed in a formalized mythology characteristic of incipient gods (see PUEBLO INDIANS). Though one must remember that to all known American Indian societies there was an awareness of a being which Europeans have called the Great Spirit, but which may best be described in the Iroquois term *Wa'nkonda*, the 'Power Above'.

The Watchful Ancestors

A kind of totemism has existed in almost every branch of the human race. In the late Paleolithic in Europe, the engravings and paintings suggest that there was some magical connection between the painting on the wall of a deep cave and the bringing of animals to be hunted in the outer world (see CAVE ART). Numerous implements, such as spear throwers, have engravings of animals on them: one is led to imagine that they represent either good-luck charms or are the owner's marks, symbolic of the owner's name. However, we have no real factual information about the mental processes of our remote ancestors, only the knowledge that they must have had much experience in common with other peoples at the same stage of cultural development. Is the reindeer carved on a bone staff the totem of a hunter, or a sign to help the staff throw a dart at a reindeer? We do not know.

The idea of the relation of man to Nature was important in Polynesia, but it can hardly be said to be expressed in any recognizably totemic form. In the background of Polynesian religion was the idea

poetic simile. People of certain occupations were supposed to be like the animals which were symbolic of their activities, so that they were distinguished by the names of animals and birds, more or less as one might give someone an appropriate nickname. In Aztec Mexico there were two groups of military orders, one of which was named for the wild cat, the ocelot. These were the people who were sent out as scouts to hide among the rocks and find out about the disposition of the enemy and, when possible, to leap upon one and seize him, making him prisoner for sacrifice, just as the wild cat among the rocks of the mountains might leap upon an unsuspecting traveller. The other warriors, who led frontal attacks on the enemy, were dedicated to the eagle; they were thought of as the people who descended from above upon the foe and seized him in their talons, and so wrapped him up to be taken as an offering to the gods. These were poetic images as well as the badges of the particular clans of warriors.

Sometimes, however, certain creatures have been regarded as sacred. In many tribes where an animal totem was respected, this totem was never eaten by members of its related social group, for this was considered insulting to a relative.

This idea of relationship between man and animal occurs occasionally in everyday life, when we compare each other to some creature which exhibits the characteristic we are talking about. To say that a person is a cat is something of an insult, but it does imply a quality of personality. To say that a

person is hawk-eyed implies that he possesses the keen vision of the bird. Such habits of speech help us to understand totemism as something perfectly natural. The idea has so many different origins that it is quite wrong to think that it is the same thing in every part of the world. The relationship is in a certain community of ideas and not of direct meaning. It is best to use the word to relate to those groups of people who believe in their descent from an animal ancestor; and this is much more true of the Australian aborigines than of the North American Indians.

As has already been noted, the word totem had a North American Indian origin, derived from a Chippewa dialect of the Algonquian group of languages. The word was originally *ototeman*, which refers to a close relation like a brother or sister. A boy obtained a personal spirit protector through his visions during the lonely vigil of his days of initiation, but he also had a group totem, a symbolic being who protected all members of his social group. This group totem was usually in the form of an animal or bird, though representing a kind of hidden power. It was symbolic of the *orenda* or inner power which inspired the community.

Although the American Indian totem was not directly ancestral, as among the Australian aboriginals, it was also an expression of the human relationship with the powers of Nature. The spiritual quality of orenda was something which men shared with all other creatures and objects in Nature. To the American Indian all Nature was instinct with life and capable of being brought into

Detail of a totemic carving of 'double-headed snake', executed in 1958 by Chief Mungo Master of the Kwakiutl Indians of British Columbia: the word totem itself comes from the North American Indians but the idea of a close relationship between the human and the animal is known all over the world

that the Creator had brought forth the first ancestor of all classes of being; that the oceans, islands, birds, plants and fishes were as much the children of the Creator as the tribes of men. The relationship was expressed in sexual life. Everywhere the descent of man from the gods was a family matter, and was expressed by reduplicating the race generation after generation. Similarly, the other creatures descended as great families, all eventually linked in a common ancestry to the Supreme Being.

Melanesian societies often have a more clearly distinguishable totemic belief. For instance, for the village agriculturists of New Ireland their ancestors have become watchful spirits who look after the welfare of their descendants and protect them from evil forces. Wood sculpture, brightly painted, represents the more important citizens at their funeral ceremonies. The protective departed is usually shown as a bird holding a fish, and clutching a serpent in its talons.

In Africa there are remnants of totemism in the spirits worshipped in animal form, like the Old Man Mantis who was an important divine being to one group of Bushmen. Similar fragmentary survivals of the totemic idea can be found among many peoples, but the usual type of belief which looks like totemism is more of a comparative nature. People are named after animals, both factually and jokingly, but they are not seriously thought of as being descended from animals. Mpande, a Zulu king, was saluted as the Great Black Elephant, not because he was a member of an elephant clan, but as a description of his great power and his rich darkness. It was an honorific nickname, like that accorded to the English king Richard the Lion-Heart. In many African regions, the old initiation ceremonies represented human-animals but these were symbolic of the animal side of raw human nature before it had been reformed by the initiation rituals. True, some tribes have stories, which may find expression in masked dances, in which distant ancestors are supposed to have had animal forms, but this rather undefined totemic idea is widely scattered and not totally African.

In the religions of the East there is little of the ancient animal magic and totemism of some of the Siberian tribes. There are ideas of reincarnation and transmigration from animal to man, and vice versa, in Hinduism and Buddhism, but in no sense can the animal be considered the ancestor of the man. These religions derive from a rich philosophical background, and not from the simple animal ancestor cults which are most properly described as totemistic.

In both Norse and Celtic mythology there is a close relationship between gods, heroes and magical animals. Some clans were described in a vague way as being descended from animal ancestors, of which the bear and the wolf seem to have been most popular. But in all their rich poetry, and poetic history, there is little which can truly be said to go back to the world in which totemic beliefs were the accepted explanation of man's place in Nature. One can hardly regard the shape-changing propensities of demigods or witches or werewolves as totemic activities.

The most one can say is that the folklore of Europe is full of animal stories and that this may well imply that in ancient times totemic ideas were common; but mostly they seem to rely simply on the comparison of various human characters with traits of animal behaviour.

Totemism as an idea must be treated as a diffuse subject of much obscurity and confusion. Whatever definition of the totemic cults one may take, there remain confused areas where the totemic merges into other systems of primitive belief. Perhaps it is best to consider it as a useful research tool which had a widespread vogue when introduced by 19th century anthropologists, and which must now be more closely defined and limited to more exact categories of belief before it can become of much practical scientific value. But for those who live within a totemic culture, it is the very basis of their understanding of the world.
(See also GREAT PLAINS INDIANS; NORTH AMERICAN INDIANS; PACIFIC NORTH-WEST INDIANS.)

C. A. BURLAND

Though the Touareg are Moslems, it has been suggested that they were once Christians, for they use the cross as an amulet

TOUAREG

THESE are the most mysterious and, at the same time, the most easily recognizable race of people in Africa. The men wear a 'veil' which allows only their eyes to be seen through a slit, and this alone gives these tall, robed men a vaguely sinister appearance, especially in the desert when mounted on their racing camels. A genuine Touareg wears the veil inside as well as outside his tent, and only raises it to eat.

The Touareg live in scattered groups throughout the Sahara, especially in those regions which are farthest away from civilization. Born and bred to a nomadic existence, they despise cities and the urban way of life. Yet they are by no means a primitive people, and their aloofness is a matter of choice.

The Touareg belong to the white race. Taller than the general run of Europeans, their average height is six feet; they are small-boned, graceful, and even rather languid in their movements. Yet their history shows them to have been the most dreaded warriors of the Sahara, with a reputation until quite recently for brigandage and rebellion. Today, they are still the great caravanners of the desert.

Though they are nominally Moslems, they are considered by strict Mohammedans to be extremely lax, for they flout the basic religious code in allowing their women to go unveiled, and in fact the degree of liberty permitted their women is unique among Moslems. For not only is a woman entitled to take part in public life, but she can own her own property and even choose her own husband. Before marriage the Touareg girl is permitted to have as many lovers as she likes, though she is expected to be loyal and faithful to the man she eventually marries.

Like all desert-dwellers, the Touareg are very religious in the sense of being conscious and to some extent fearful of forces outside their control. Consequently they rely to a great extent on charms and amulets to ward off misfortune; and one of the objects most used by them is the cross. This has led some ethnologists to suggest that the Touareg were once Christians, for it is difficult to explain otherwise their predilection for this Christian symbol, specifically proscribed by Moslems. The cross appears on a great many items of their equipment – the pommels of camel saddles, the bosses of shields, the handles of swords and even on their spoons.

Like Knights of Old
The theory that the Touareg were actually Christians during the Roman occupation of North Africa may help to explain the unique status of women in Touareg society, for nowhere else in Africa do women have equality with men, let alone so much freedom. The Touareg seem to idolize women, somewhat in the manner that medieval knights in Europe idealized their ladies. As their contribution to this tradition of chivalry, well-born Touareg women devoted themselves to the arts of music and poetry, as the men devoted themselves to war and hunting.

In the sand seas of the central Sahara and the mountain ranges of the Hoggar and Air, where they are still found in their traditional communities, the Touareg retain many of their old customs. Their medicine, for instance, is still based on the efficacy of charms which they combine with barbarous practices picked up from the Arabs. 'Firing', or burning wounds and infections with red-hot irons, is still used for liver complaints, tuberculosis, hernia, and even blindness. Great use is also made of urine and dried dung: the urine of the male camel – but never of the female – is considered excellent for diseases of the skin, while a paste made of dried donkey dung mixed with wood ash is applied to abscesses.

But though Touareg medicine, by Western standards, is a combination of ignorance and superstition, the people themselves have nothing resembling the witch-doctors of pagan Africans. The reason is that they have kept themselves aloof from both black Africa and white Europe, although it is becoming obvious that they cannot resist what we call progress much longer. Camels are their principal source of wealth, and conducting caravans across the sand seas is their principal activity, but both camels and caravans are becoming things of the past. More modern forms of transport are replacing them, and it is increasingly difficult for the Touareg to survive.

The abolition of the slave trade has also affected the situation. During the 19th century, the slave caravans moved continuously across the Sahara to the North African ports. This trade was organized by Arabs, but the running of it was in the hands of the Touareg whose knowledge of the desert and the location of the wells made them the link between Central Africa and the Mediterranean.

Many of the Touareg today are being slowly absorbed into the modern world of factories and machines. The discovery of oil in the Sahara has been, perhaps, the major factor in this change, for oil exploitation has brought American standards as well as methods to the desert. Touaregs can now be found driving Land Rovers, working on oil rigs and laying pipelines, where in the old days any sort of manual labour was considered beneath their dignity. Jobs and wages have led many of the younger men to abandon the traditional way of life and to think in terms of Western values. The veil is discarded; their language (called *Temajegh* when it is spoken and *T'ifinagh* when written) is tending to disappear; and some sort of a house, even if made of mud, is preferred to the traditional tent.

But there are still vast areas of the Sahara where the Touareg live as their ancestors did, notably in the Hoggar Mountains of southern Algeria and the Aïr Mountains of the Republic of Niger. These tribesmen continue to measure their wealth in terms of their camel herds and the number of serfs or retainers who serve them. They still wear the veil and the long cotton gown, usually black, which has always been the distinguishing garb of the genuine member of their nation. They still live the free, simple and rigorous life of their forefathers. Their food, for instance, is coarse and unvaried — an endless diet of goat's milk and cheese, bread made from millet flour, dates, and only very occasionally, meat. Most of these true nomads are still uneducated in the Western sense, for the children are sent out with the camels and goats instead of attending school.

Lords of the Desert

Yet the last of these genuine Touareg retain the classic virtues of their race — independence, pride, courtesy, respect for women, and a simple belief in God. At the same time, it would be unrealistic to regard them as the 'noble savages' of romantic literature. They are manifestly harassed by poverty, malnutrition and disease. It may be hard for the Western observer to understand why they do not try to improve their way of life, except that if you are born in a country of sand and eroded mountains it is very difficult to do so. But the fact is that the old-fashioned Touareg has no desire to change, for he is still convinced that his way of life is preferable to that of the city-dweller.

What is happening to the Touareg is that progress is changing the life and philosophy of many of the younger men, while tradition is driving the older generation deeper into the wastelands of the Sahara. But it is extremely unlikely that even the most obstinate of the old guard can continue to keep alive the traditions of the 'Lords of the Desert', as was once their boast. The veiled warrior mounted on his white camel, armed with a spear and shield, will never be seen again, except at folklore festivals put on for the benefit of tourists. Gone, too, are the famous 'courts of love' at which Touareg girls entertained with music and poetry the young warriors who had ridden a hundred miles or more to find perhaps a lover for a few nights, perhaps a wife for a lifetime.

JAMES WELLARD

FURTHER READING: Francis Rennell Rodd, *People of the Veil* (Humanities, 1966); James Wellard, *Lost Worlds of Africa* (Dutton, 1967).

Below The Touareg are nominally Moslem but they flout orthodoxy by allowing their women to go unveiled; some experts believe they were once Christians, for the cross features as a symbol on many items of their equipment: Touareg men at a tea-drinking ceremony *Right* The men wear a veil which covers the face, except for a slit for the eyes, and gives them a sinister appearance in keeping with their old reputation as dreaded warriors

George Rodger/Magnum

TOWER OF BABEL

THAT the original language of mankind was Hebrew was assumed in the Judaeo-Christian tradition down into modern times and, as Sir James Frazer remarked, 'when the science of philology was in its infancy, strenuous but necessarily abortive efforts were made to deduce all forms of speech from Hebrew as their original'. The story of the tower of Babel in Genesis (chapter 11) was an attempt to explain how the various nations of men, all descended from the sons of Noah, who with their wives had survived the Flood, came to speak in a 'confusion of tongues'.

When 'the whole earth had one language and few words', the descendants of Noah migrated from the east to the land of Shinar (Babylonia), where they decided to build a city, called Babel (Babylon), and a tower 'with its top in the heavens'. God came down to look at the city and the tower, and said: 'Behold, they are one people, and they have all one language; and this is only the beginning of what they will do; and nothing that they propose to do will now be impossible for them.' And God confused their language and scattered them over the face of the earth.

This brief story, which so strongly conveys that inability to communicate is

Left **The Tower of Babel, from the Bedford Book of Hours, 15th century**

one of the great obstacles to man's overweening and potentially godlike power, is based on the *ziggurats* or temple towers of Mesopotamian cities, and perhaps on the confusing medley of tongues spoken by citizens and traders in their streets. A ziggurat was a tall tower which might well look as if its top was in the heavens, often constructed in seven stages which were probably connected with the planets, and evidently regarded as a means of communication between gods and men. The ziggurat of Marduk in Babylon, which some have identified as the original of the tower of Babel, was said to have a shrine at the top to which the god descended each night (see RELIGION).

According to later Jewish traditions, the tower was built in deliberate rebellion against God. Some said it was constructed by Nimrod, 'the first on earth to be a mighty man' and 'a mighty hunter before the Lord' (Genesis, chapter 10, where he is King of Babel), who was a great-grandson of Noah. Nimrod's father bequeathed to him the garments of skins which God had made for Adam and Eve (Genesis, chapter 3), and when Nimrod put them on he became immensely strong and a bold and skilful hunter. He was the chosen king of the descendants of Noah's son Ham, and in his monstrous pride he built the tower so that he could invade heaven and take revenge on God for drowning his ancestors in the Flood.

The tower eventually rose 70 miles high, according to some accounts, and had seven

stairways on the eastern side up which the bricklayers climbed, and seven on the western side down which they descended (following the course of the sun). Others said that the tower was so high that it took a year for a hod-carrier to reach the top. If he fell off and was killed, the people did not weep for him but mourned over the brick because it would take so long to get it to the top again. From the top the builders fired arrows into heaven, which fell back to them stained with blood. They assumed they were doing fierce execution among God's court, and continued building with enthusiasm.

In the end God lost patience and with the 70 angels who surround his throne he descended and confused the language of the builders, which caused quarrels and violence. A man would ask his helper for mortar and be given a brick, and after a while would become so angry that he hurled the brick at his helper's head and brained him. The work was abandoned. One third of the tower sank into the earth, one third was destroyed by fire and only one third was left standing. Nimrod was eventually killed by Esau, who robbed him of the sacred garments of skins, which were in turn stolen from him by his brother Jacob.

According to both Jewish and local traditions, the original tower of Babel was a temple of Nabu, or Nebo, master of writing and wisdom, and the god of Borsippa (modern Birs Nimrud), a city close to Babylon.

However a trance is induced, whether by drugs or by mystical or magical techniques, the result is that part of consciousness is split off from the whole. The symptoms of trance are readily apparent, but its true nature is still not understood

TRANCE

QUITE ORDINARY words are often used by occultists and magicians in a sense different from their everyday meaning. In the case of the word trance, however, there is no such semantic divergence and a majority of occultists would have no quarrel with the dictionary definition: 'state suggesting that the soul has passed out of the body; ecstasy, rapture, extreme exaltation'.

Such a state can sometimes be induced by physical causes, a brain tumour or, more typically, a blow on the head. I remember a player in a rugby game suffering a trance of this type; he continued to play the game, although perhaps rather more erratically than usual, and it was not until the final whistle had blown and it was seen that he continued to play against a totally non-existent opposing team that his peculiar condition became apparent. It was this aspect of trance – the combination of a grossly abnormal state of mind with the continuation of conventional behaviour patterns and even comprehensible speech – that probably originated the idea that the soul had temporarily left the body. Once this theory had been accepted, it was an easy

step to the concept that the soulless body could be used by non-human entities, that the entranced person could become, quite literally, a mouthpiece of the gods.

In many societies the use of such a divine mouthpiece became an established part of the prevailing religious culture; in ancient Greece the Delphic Oracle was consulted not only by citizens of the Greek city-states but by representatives of colonies as far away as Spain, and wherever Hellenic culture was dominant the Delphic Oracle was held in veneration. In pre-Communist Tibet, not only did every major monastery have an individual oracle who, while in trance, answered questions and gave spiritual and mundane advice, but the Dalai Lama and his government had their own state oracle.

Such official oracles did not, of course, have their trance states induced by anything so crude as a blow on the head; in Tibet the oracles almost all appear to have been epileptics, looked upon as people in whom trance could be particularly easily induced, but rhythmic drumming, dancing and (possibly but not certainly) psychedelic drugs were used to achieve the desired disassociation of consciousness. At Delphi, the oracle inhaled the smoke of burning laurel leaves. This would have contained both a small amount of hydrocyanic acid and a certain amount of complex alkaloids, and it is probable that inhaled in sufficient quantity it produced a state of cerebral intoxication highly conducive to trance and other abnormal mental states. In any case,

however, it seems likely that as in Tibet, oracles were chosen for their inherent ability to achieve a voluntary disassociation of consciousness.

There is no doubt that trance is most easily attained by the use of such drugs as LSD and *anhalonium* (mescaline), but while the states of consciousness attained in this way seem fundamentally identical with the trances of the mystic and the magician, their effects do not seem to be either as permanent or as profound as those produced by more physically and emotionally demanding techniques, such as those of the *Spiritual Exercises* of St Ignatius Loyola or the frenzied dancing of Haitian Voodoo. In the trance experienced by participants in Voodoo rites the entranced worshipper is not just the mouthpiece of the god but actually becomes the god.

The White Darkness

Voodoo is a synthetic religion, a blend of elements derived from West African religious cults, popular Catholicism and the debased ceremonial magic of the printed grimoires (textbooks of ritual magic) of 18th century France. Its central religious rite is the invocation of the *loa* (gods) by drums, dance and sacrifice, and these invocations normally end in the entrancement and possession ('mounting') of one or more of the participants in the ceremony by the particular loa invoked – each loa has its own particular dance pattern and drum rhythm. Sometimes, however, an unwanted loa makes a spontaneous appearance but in this case it is made clear to it that it is not welcome and the possessed worshipper comes out of his trance fairly quickly.

In the last analysis, all trance, whether mediumistic, drug-induced or the result of mystical, magical or Voodoo techniques, is identical; that is to say, a part of consciousness is split off or disassociated from the whole. Nevertheless, most of those who have experienced trance have been unable to communicate to others even a faint idea of the nature of the subjective experience they have undergone. Fortunately, the late Maya Deren, who was herself frequently possessed by the goddess Erzulie (the Haitian Venus), has left us a clear description of the processes of Voodoo trance; and when due allowance has been made for the cultural variations between Haiti and, say, Tibet, her account throws a great deal of light on the nature of trance in general.

Maya Deren, a maker of avant-garde films with a particular interest in choreography, first visited Haiti in 1947 with the object of filming Haitian dance forms. She began to attend Voodoo rituals, soon realized that the dance could not be separated from the mythology, the rapture from the religion, joined the dance, and was entranced and 'mounted' by the loa Erzulie. She described her experience of entrancement as being 'the white darkness' – a contradiction in terms that is reminiscent of the paradoxes used by mystics of all ages in an attempt to communicate the incommunicable. She wrote: 'Resting . . . I felt a strange numbness . . . I say numbness, but that is inaccurate . . . To be precise I must call it a white darkness, its whiteness a glory and its darkness terror. It is the terror which has the greater force . . . The white darkness starts to shoot up . . . My skull is a drum . . . This sound will drown me . . . The white darkness moves up the veins of my leg like a swift tide rising, rising; is a great force which I cannot sustain or contain, which, surely, will burst my skin. It is too much, too bright, too white for me; this is its darkness. "Mercy!" I scream within me. I hear it echoed by the voices, shrill and unearthly: "Erzulie". The bright darkness floods up through my body, reaches my head, engulfs me. I am sucked down and exploded upward at once. That is all.'

Maya Deren had no memory of her actions while entranced, but as the *hougan* (Voodoo priest) assured her that she showed all the signs of genuine 'mounting' by Erzulie we can be sure that her behaviour pattern followed the conventional lines of possession by this loa. Her first act would have been to perform an elaborate toilet with the consecrated comb, perfume, face-powder and mirror always kept ready in the temple for Erzulie's use. She would have followed this by donning bangles, ear-rings, necklaces and three wedding rings (Erzulie is married to more than one of the male loa).

Her toilet completed, she would have chosen several handsome men to accompany her on a tour of the congregation, shaking hands with the men but extending only her little finger to the women. Following this she would have perhaps asked for songs, dances or delicate food, or she may simply have sat in a chair, flirtatiously basking in the admiration of her worshippers. The whole period of entrancement and divine possession probably extended over two or three hours.

The Magical Method

Western magicians have a number of ways of inducing trance, and all of them show some similarity with the techniques of Voodoo, although they do not usually involve the complete cessation of normal consciousness: in some little corner of his mind the magician retains his individuality and can observe the actions performed by the disassociated aspects of his own consciousness.

One of these methods involves the performance of a mystery play (Aleister Crowley particularly recommended the *Bacchae* of Euripides for this purpose) with the actors so strongly identifying themselves with the characters they play that they become those characters. At the Abbey of Thelema in Sicily, Crowley and his disciples performed such a magical version of Oscar Wilde's *Salome*, seemingly with considerable success. Years earlier, Crowley had stage-managed the public

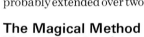

In trance, 'a part of the consciousness is split off and disassociated from the whole': the condition has long been valued because it puts man in touch with planes of experience beyond his normal grasp. Techniques of trance include rhythmic drumming and chanting, as in the Jamaican Pocomania cult *(above left)*, or the dangerous and unsatisfactory use of drugs *(left)*

René Burri/Magnum

Magnum

performance of a series of dramatic rituals incorporating music and dance, the *Rites of Eleusis*, during which the poet Victor Neuburg became entranced and, according to Crowley, literally inspired (see also CROWLEY).

Curiously enough, the technique of achieving partial trance by the conscious and deliberate identification of oneself with an imagined being or situation has been known and used by non-occultists. The great physiologist Galton once spent a day in London strongly imagining himself as the most hated and evil man in the world; so strongly did his abnormal state, a light trance, change his bearing and appearance that it affected other people. Respectable looking men jostled him off the pavement; women crossed the street to avoid him; shopkeepers falsely stated that the goods he required were out of stock; finally he was violently kicked by an aged and usually docile cab-horse. Similarly, in his novel *The Thirty-Nine Steps*, John Buchan gave a fictional description of how a wanted man succeeded in being mistaken for a road-mender by persistently imagining himself as one and thinking of nothing but stones, hammers and roads.

Other Western methods of achieving trance and possession are the processes of invocation and evocation (see MAGIC). Here the idea is to achieve 'one-pointedness' by surrounding the practitioners with the symbols of the force invoked, and to achieve the frenzied psychic escape — a form of trance — by 'enflaming oneself with prayer'

Left The Diolas of Senegal celebrate major festivals with several days of dancing which culminates in a state of collective trance **Right** The solitary trance of a yogi; the attainment of *samadhi* demands extraordinary discipline to achieve total control over all mental and physical faculties

and chanting the barbarous words of evocation. Once this suspension of everyday consciousness has been achieved, the god invoked is enabled to manifest himself in one or more of the practitioners. In a variant version of this system, sex, sometimes deviant sex, is used to induce trance; in *The Great Beast*, John Symonds gives a fascinating description of how a ceremony of this type, part of the so-called 'Paris Working', resulted in the entranced Victor Neuburg being obsessed by a 'demon' who demanded human sacrifice.

The word trance is also used in a secondary sense by Western occultists; in this sense it is approximately equivalent to the word 'rapture', and reference is made to the 'Trance of Wonder', the 'Trance of Indifference' and even the 'Trance of Sorrow'. During such a trance, ordinary consciousness is not in any way interrupted; the occultist is able to carry on a conversation or go about his ordinary business, while at the same time undergoing the extraordinary subjective experiences associated with, for example, the Trance of Wonder. In this meaning of the word, every authentic occult operation partakes of the character of trance. Aleister Crowley wrote that: 'The essence of the idea

of Trance is indeed contained in that of Magick, which is pre-eminently the transcendental Science and Art. Its method is, in one chief sense, Love, the very key of Trance; and, in another, the passing beyond normal conditions . . . Nor need any man fear to state boldly that every Magical Operation soever is only complete when it is characterised (in one sense or another) by the occurence of Trance. It was ill done to restrict the use of the word to the supersession of dualistic human consciousness by the impersonal and monistic state of Samadhi . . . it is the first necessity as it is the last attainment of Trance to abolish every form and every order of dividuality.'

Interesting, and perhaps important, as such magical trances are, there is no doubt that the types of trance which are most familiar to the layman are those of the Spiritualist medium on the one hand, and of the yogi on the other. Mediums can be divided into three broad groups; the deliberately fraudulent, who are a small minority; the self-deceived, of whom there are a surprisingly large number; and the genuine — genuine not, of course, in the sense that they are necessarily in authentic contact with the dead but in the sense that they enter a trance state. While the phrase 'trance medium' is usually confined to those who lose normal consciousness during a sitting, it seems probable that all genuine mediumship, even the mildest clairvoyance, is characterized by disassociation of some sort or another.

When in deep trance and the mouthpiece

of a 'guide' or other supposedly discarnate communicator, the mental state of the medium seems remarkably similar to that of a Voodoo devotee who has been mounted by one of the loa. He, or she, appears to be the vehicle of a distinct personality in its own right, and Professor H. H. Price has commented that, 'If all this is just subconscious dramatization on the medium's part it is comparable to Ruth Draper at her very best.'

One of the main differences between Spiritualistic and Voodoo possession is that the latter almost always follows a highly conventional pattern, the loa using the entranced worshipper's body in the way that it is expected to use it. This difference, however, originates in contrasting cultural patterns, not in any profound variation between one sort of trance and another.

The same is true of the trances experienced by devotees of Yoga. While it may seem that there is an enormous gulf between the silent entrancement of a yogi experiencing Samadhi and the behaviour of the medium possessed by her spirit guide, there is considerable evidence to show that on a physiological and psychological level they are undergoing the same experience. This is not, of course, to say that the two are spiritually of equal value.

Finally, we come back to our dictionary definition of trance – and we find it not so much a definition as a description. For today we are only a very little nearer to comprehending the real nature of trance (and its first cousin, hypnotic trance) than were our ancestors. It is true that there are a multitude of psychological explanations – Freudian, Jungian, Behaviourist – of the phenomenon, but the very fact that so many conflicting hypotheses can be defended so vigorously by men of real intellectual integrity is an indication that we are still far from understanding what trance really is. (See also DRUGS; ECSTASY; MEDITATION; MEDIUMS; MESMER; ORACLES; POSSESSION; SEX; SHAMAN; VOODOO; YOGA.)

FRANCIS KING

FURTHER READING: M. Deren, *Divine Horsemen* (Thames & Hudson, 2nd edn, 1969); Stewart Wavell, *Trance* (Allen & Unwin, 1966).

Transmigration

Or metempsychosis, the passage of the soul into another body after death; the idea is basic to Hinduism and most schools of Buddhism, and is also found in various forms in many other religious traditions: the soul is sometimes believed to be reborn in higher or lower forms of life, according to its past behaviour and its spiritual needs.
See REINCARNATION.

Transubstantiation

In the Eucharist, the changing of the 'substance' (the underlying reality) of the bread and wine into the body and blood of Christ, though the outward appearance (the 'species' or 'accidents') of the elements remains unaltered; the doctrine is central to the Roman Catholic Mass; many Protestants have denied it, interpreting the 'real presence' of Christ in the sacrament in a spiritual or symbolic sense.
See MASS.

Keystone Press

The tradition still persists that buried treasure is accursed; perhaps a relic from the days when treasure-seekers had to protect themselves against demons and spirits who would resist man's attempts to plunder the earth

TREASURE MAGIC

THE LURE of buried treasure has fascinated man for centuries. Burial mounds, prehistoric monuments, Iron Age hill forts, and sometimes natural outcrops of rock have all been regarded as likely sites of buried hoards, providing an irresistible temptation to grave robbers and other vandals, despite the fact that comparatively little gold has been discovered interred with the dead. The majority of deposits of gold and silver that have come to light have consisted simply of wealth hidden in times of danger, when the safest place to conceal it was below the earth's surface.

It is true, of course, that some treasure has been found in burial sites, as for example, the gold cape discovered at Mold, Flintshire, on a site haunted by a knight in golden armour. The famous find of treasure at Sutton Hoo in Suffolk and coins in Roman graves are further instances; but there is good reason to believe that some of the treasure recovered from burial mounds had been placed there at a later date for safekeeping, in the belief that no treasure seeker would risk angering the ghost of the deceased by invading his grave.

Traditionally, the domain of the Earth Mother was peopled by hideous spirits, dwarfs, Germanic gnomes, Cornish knockers (spirits of the tin mines), and other treasure-guarding elementals (see CORNWALL; DWARFS; FAIRIES), to whom supplication and sometimes sacrifices had to be made before the earth could be disturbed. Even then, the most elaborate magical ceremonies were undertaken before disturbing the soil. It is said that when Irish grave robbers discovered only calcined bones and ashes in a grave, they assumed that the fairies had transformed the gold into this form in order to outwit them.

Terrifying treasure guardians were supposed to lie in wait, deep within the bowels of the earth, ready to curse the sacrilegious sorcerer's apprentice unprotected by magic. Dragons were among the most frequently encountered monsters (see DRAGON), as were phantom dogs, usually jet black, extremely fierce and hideous. On the other hand, in some legends, there are references to dogs which actually led the treasure-seeker to the hidden hoard. In later anecdotes, the treasure guardian was often Satan or one of the minor fiends of hell.

The Vibrating Ring

Elaborate magical rites were considered necessary for the discovery of the treasure and for its successful recovery. Divining for metals or hidden veins of ore by means of a forked hazel twig, a device borrowed from the miners of Germany, was the method usually employed, but to be really effective the twig had to be cut from the tree on St John's Eve. Dactylomancy, or divination by means of a magic ring, was also popular among the treasure conjurers, the ring being suspended on a fine thread over a round table marked with the letters of the alphabet. The ring, as it travelled or vibrated over the table, stopped at the various letters, supplying answers to the questions asked. In 1577 Robert Mantell, an Essex alchemist, was in trouble with the authorities for having in his possession 'a familiar in a ring', who guided him in his treasure-hunting exploits.

Another method in common use was scrying or crystal gazing, in which the conjurer was accompanied by a pure young boy, that is one who had not yet attained puberty. Catoptromancy or mirror magic was also used, the glass being suspended over a holy well, where it reflected the secrets hidden in the water. In hydromancy, a thin film of oil was spread upon the surface of a bowl of water upon which would then be seen, usually in symbolic form, the site where the treasure lay hidden.

Once the treasure had been located, the conjurer and his assistant had to protect themselves from the anticipated anger of the ghost, phantom dog, dragon, or demon, by a complicated system of rituals. Often, a magic circle some 30 feet in circumference would be drawn, at the centre of which the magician stood, wand in hand, invoking the demon of the treasure by name. The position of the planets was also considered; and it was the generally accepted view that

Sunday was the most favourable time for the start of operations. Treasure-guarding demons expected to be paid for their information with a human sacrifice, a demand usually modified to a dog, cat, or black cock following a blasphemous baptism. A human offering was by no means excluded, however, and as late as 1841 there occurred a case in which a boy was murdered by some Italian treasure-seekers.

A Snorting Devil

During the 16th and 17th centuries it was taken for granted that any disturbance of a burial mound containing treasure would be followed at once by a furious outburst of thunder. It is recorded that at the very time that the famous wizard, Dr Dee (see DEE), brought to light a hoard of gold in Brecknockshire, 'a mighty storm and tempest was raised'. Sometimes the barrow would collapse, crushing the pillagers to death beneath a mountain of fallen earth and stone. There were even occasions when a fiend actually materialized, chasing the audacious tomb robber from the scene. In 1549 William Wycherley, a treasure-hunter from London, fled for his life when a devil, snorting furiously, lunged wildly towards him. He later discovered that his attacker had been a blind horse.

During the height of the treasure-seeking mania, the conjurers seem to have concentrated their attention on the counties of Norfolk, Hertfordshire, Worcestershire and Gloucestershire. This says little for their psychic faculties, since most of the recorded discoveries of treasure have been made elsewhere.

The authorities seem to have regarded treasure-hunting with suspicion, but even when the law was invoked against the conjurers the penalties were relatively light for an age when witchcraft was sometimes punished by death. If found guilty, a treasure-magician might be sentenced to stand in the pillory with a whetstone suspended from his neck, or compelled to parade barefoot through the streets of the town, and ordered to limit himself each Friday for 12 months to a strict diet of bread and water. His books, wands and other magical paraphernalia would be burned.

Beneath the Crosses

During the first half of the 16th century there is evidence to suggest that a number of superstitious individuals began to bury their surplus gold beneath the stone crosses which usually stood at the crossroads outside the villages; presumably they imagined that their property would be inviolate on such sacred sites. The result was perhaps predictable. The treasure conjurers immediately transferred their attentions from burial mounds to this novel and extremely profitable field of exploitation; they destroyed the village crosses without the slightest compunction. Indeed the Witchcraft Act of 1542 makes special provision for this offence in a clause beginning: 'Whereas divers and sundry persons unlawfully have devised and practised invocations and conjurations of spirits, pretending by such means to understand

Mansell Collection

Among the elemental spirits of the earth which jealously guarded buried treasure and might have to be appeased or outwitted by treasure-seekers were dwarfs and gnomes, who were sometimes said to cheat grave-robbers by turning buried gold into bones and ashes
Above The Elf-king asleep, by Richard Doyle
Right The modern counterparts of the old elementals are the aptly-named 'Gnomes of Zürich' *Below* The Blackgang gnomes counting their treasure

Picturepoint, London

" *Of course it would be fatal to international finance if the least suspicion leaked out that the Gnomes don't understand it either. . .* "

Hans Tasiemka

Treasure Magic

Those who seek gold, the elixir of power, must sometimes pay too great a price to fulfill their desires; legend says that treasure-guarding spirits often demanded a life in return for gold. There is a story that King Midas, who asked the gods to turn to gold all that he touched, turned his daughter to gold: illustration by Arthur Rackham

and get knowledge for their own lucre in what place treasure of gold and silver should or might be found or had in the earth or other secret places . . . ' , and which goes on to condemn as felons those who 'have digged up and pulled down an infinite number of crosses within this realm'.

The Magic Black Box

The methods used by the treasure-seekers could be applied equally well to divining for lost and stolen property, a practice that was also made illegal by the same act. William Lilly, the famous 17th century English astrologer, is said to have charged his clients half a crown for seances of this character.

Treasure-hunting reinforced by magic never seems to have completely died out, for it was practised as late as the 19th century by Cunning Murrell, the famous Essex witch-doctor (see MURRELL). Very similar techniques were used by gold and oil diviners in the United States of America. Here the conjurer, armed with hazel stick and 'doodle bug', as his magic black box was known, could usually be found prowling in some abandoned graveyard which he believed to be a treasure site.

Many treasure-seekers also turned their attention to the buried treasures of the 17th century Scottish sailor Captain Kidd and other pirates which, like the gold of European burial mounds, were supposed to be protected from the searchers by some foul fiend or a dead man's curse.

Even today the tradition persists that all buried treasure is accursed; and even money which has been picked up in the street is considered so unlucky that superstitious people will spit upon it, for safety's sake. No doubt this attitude is a relic of the terror once inspired by the treasure-guarding spirit who had to be propitiated with the gift of a life as the price of that elixir of power, gold.

ERIC MAPLE

Chris Barker

Tree of Life

The concept of the universe as a tree is best known in its Scandinavian form, where the ash, Yggdrasil, is the world tree, but also appears in other traditions, in some of which the cosmic tree bears fruits which the gods eat to ensure their immortality; the garden of Eden contained the tree of life (Genesis, chapter 2); in the Cabala, the Tree of Life is a diagram of God, man and the universe.

See ASH; CABALA; EVIL; FIRST MAN; PATHS; TAROT; TREES.

TREES

2873

A great tree with its roots drawing strength from the earth and its head commandingly in the sky, with a lifespan far longer than that of man, with sap flowing like blood in its veins and its leaves rustling in the wind as if it had speech, has frequently been seen as an image of the world and all Nature, as the tree of life. The network of branches springing from the trunk suggests relatedness and a complex pattern unifying all things: *The Co-Existence Tree*, a modern variation on this theme, by E. Box *(previous page)*
Right The tree of Jesse, showing the descent of David's line in the form of a tree: from Cyprus, 15th century *(above)* Tree of life, from the church of St Dominic in Oaxaca, Mexico *(below) Facing page* Genealogical tree of the Mackay family

At Phlius in the Peloponnese a sacred grove of cypresses provided a refuge for fugitives from justice, and the trees were entwined with prisoners' discarded chains: sacred trees and the gods or spirits associated with them have played a great variety of roles in religion and magic

WITH THE EARLIEST glimmerings of man's intelligence came, one surmises, the need for an explanation — where had he come from, who was responsible, what did it mean? In that far distant epoch all that early man could do, presumably, was to look around him. His environment was land and water, animals and plants. Everywhere around him were plants and, at a time when a very large proportion of the land was covered with forests, trees were dominant. To short-lived man, any tree must have seemed immortal, especially the evergreens which remained changeless whatever the time of year.

Man's instinct was, perhaps to venerate the trees, and once his need for more or less identifiable deities had crystallized, it was a short step to identify tree with god, or make tree embody deity. It seems clear that trees in general, and some trees in particular, were very widely venerated among early peoples.

We can see how deep-rooted tree worship must have been by examining the earliest records available to us. Representations of sacred trees are to be found on Chaldean and Assyrian engraved cylinders and, from slightly later periods, on temples. The tree seems to have been an essential symbol of Chaldean religion; it is sometimes shown stylized or, later on, more clearly represented as a palm, pomegranate or cypress.

In ancient Egypt, the numerous deities were frequently supposed to inhabit trees, chiefly the sacred sycomores (*Ficus sycomorus*, not to be confused with our sycamore). These sycomores were thought to exist on the borders of the great desert that lay between this world and the next, and the souls of the departed, on reaching these trees, would receive from the deities supplies of food and water. Paintings in the Book of the Dead, and in tombs, depict such meetings on the soul's travels.

In the Old Testament there are many references to sacred groves and to the setting up of altars in these groves and under trees, notably oaks; the history of

Sonia Halliday

ZFA, Düsseldorf

To short-lived man, any tree must have seemed immortal, especially the evergreens which remained changeless whatever the time of year

Old Testament religion is of a struggle between the worship of a unique, omnipresent deity and that of a great many lesser ones, such as the Canaanites held in regard. Similarly, the earliest Christian missionaries often had to contend, as in ancient Germany, with sacred groves, trying to destroy them or to build their churches within them.

Even when lesser deities had been overthrown, the need to placate the tree, or to use its magic power, was such that temples carried representations of them, as in the temple of Ezekiel's vision where, echoing Assyrian and Babylonian motifs, the decoration included 'cherubim and palm trees, a palm tree between cherub and cherub. Every cherub had two faces; the face of a man toward the palm tree on the one side, and the face of a young lion toward the palm tree on the other side' (Ezekiel, chapter 41).

The concept of the tree as a god's dwelling place appears in Persian mythology: the cypress was considered especially sacred, symbol of Ahura Mazda or Ohrmazd, chief of the pantheon. Tree worship was widespread in India; Gautama Buddha was reputedly incarnated as a tree spirit some 43 times, and he received spiritual illumination while meditating under the bo-tree. Many ancient Indian sculptures show a stylized sacred tree, surrounded by devotees and often hung with garlands. On the Stupa of Barhut there is one showing elephants paying homage to a banyan. There were not dissimilar decorations in Mexico.

The God-Boxes

The original object of veneration was doubtless the tree itself, as continued to be the case until very recently, with primitive peoples in Africa, Malaya, Sumatra and elsewhere. Later an erect tree-trunk might suffice, and an altar might be placed before the tree or trunk for offerings. The next logical step is to transform the trunk into a pillar which, like a cut trunk, can be erected in a suitable place. Standing stones in Britain and menhirs in Brittany are examples. The upright stones which represented gods in ancient Phoenicia may well derive from such pillars. In his book *From an Antique Land*, in which he christens such stone pillars 'god-boxes', Sir Julian

Radio Times Hulton Picture Library

Huxley brought this possibility into his description of the Obelisk Temple at Byblos in the Lebanon as a 'savage forest of primitive stone pillars' (see also STONES).

Later comes the combination of pillar and sacred animal foreshadowed by Ezekiel: the ancient world was full of representations of a pair of animals facing each other on either side of a stone pillar, such as the lionesses over the famous gate at Mycene, or the antique slabs within St Mark's, Venice, which show a stylized tree between pairs of monsters. A further stage in the stylization of the worshipped tree is the placing on it of a mask or cloak to represent the god, and finally the carving of the trunk into a statue.

The statue treatment is, of course, very familiar to us in the religions of ancient Greece and Rome, where personified deities abounded. In both countries gods were worshipped in connection with individual trees or groves. The symbolized tree is frequently seen on Greek paintings, vases and tablets. Many of the deities had particular trees: Artemis was in different places goddess of the cedar, hazel, laurel, myrtle and willow. Pausanias (2nd century AD) records the cult of the 'hanging Artemis' in Arcadia, presumably in reference to a mask hung on a sacred tree. The laurel, sacred to Apollo, became very important both in religious and lay ceremony, as did the olive, Athene's tree. Could the impressive pillars of Greek temples — as indeed of Egyptian ones before them — have derived from tree trunks; like the Byblos obelisks,

That trees are divine, or are the abodes of gods or spirits is widely believed *Above* Grove of sacred banyan trees in India, from an 18th century French print *Below* Hindu women, praying for long life for their husbands, wind cotton thread round and round a banyan, and offer it flowers and milk

B. Bhansali

a formal statement of the sacred grove? They were certainly decorated with vegetation motifs, while in many places they were combined with a sacred grove planted outside the temple.

In his form of Jupiter Feretrius, the chief god of Rome appears to have been a sacred tree, and Rome was reputedly founded where the floating cradle of Romulus and Remus became entangled in the roots of a fig tree, the *ficus Ruminalis*. The 'King of the Wood', the priest of the sacred grove of Diana at Nemi, was the king of the trees, 'the incarnation of the spirit of all vegetation' (see KING). Maximus of Tyre, writing during the 2nd century AD, refers to the continuing worship of individual trees, notably at the festival of Dionysus, when anyone with a tree in his garden dressed it up to represent the god.

Fruit of Goodly Trees

Throughout Eastern countries there was the practice (and still is, here and there) of hanging gifts on any particularly sacred tree, or attaching pieces of clothing to it so that luck and good health would attend the wearer. In Greece and Rome, sacred trees received the trophies of the chase and the arms of conquerors.

Sacred texts from Chaldean times describe the use of tree branches at ceremonies, while the Israelites, at the Feast of Tabernacles, were told to 'take the fruit of goodly trees, branches of palm trees, and boughs of leafy trees, and willows of the brook, and you shall rejoice before the Lord'

Right The Naga Kalika and his wife comfort Buddha as he takes his seat under the bo-tree: it was while meditating under this tree that the Buddha received spiritual illumination
Below Adam and Eve with the serpent and the tree of knowledge, which bears the forbidden fruit: from a late 13th century manuscript. The other sacred tree in Eden was the tree of life

C. M. Dixon

(Leviticus 23.40). In Greece wreaths of the tree of the deity being honoured were both placed upon it and worn by worshippers. In the nine-yearly ceremony of the Daphnephoria in honour of Apollo, a branch of laurel was carried to the temple by the laurel-bearer, a specially chosen young man. Another important Greek festival was Eiresione, a harvest festival and fertility rite combined, in which a branch of laurel or olive, decorated with fruits, cereals and ribbons, was carried and finally fixed over the farm door, its predecessor being ceremonially burnt.

A holy tree might also afford the right of asylum. There are many classical allusions to tree-sanctuaries, such as the holy tree at Ephesus where the Amazons found refuge. Orestes fleeing from the Furies found safety under Apollo's laurel, while at Phlius in the Peloponnese a sacred cypress grove gave fugitives refuge from the normal course of justice, and the trees were entwined with prisoners' discarded chains. Such sanctuaries were pre-Homeric in origin, and often sacred to heroes rather than gods; and beside them the Greek games were often held.

Early rituals were frequently designed to ensure fertility, and in the cradle of civilization the tree mainly involved was the date palm. The representations associated with the date often show kings or priests approaching the tree, holding an object resembling a pine cone, which represents the male flowers of the palm, since it was necessary to fertilize palms artifically to ensure good crops. Long after the connections of trees with specific gods had disappeared, the feeling of the tree as a beneficent fertility symbol remained. From it undoubtedly derives the carrying of various kinds of tree sprig, including myrtle, pine, hawthorn, hazel, oak and ivy, by brides at their weddings, as well as the whole complicated ceremony of the Green Man or Jack-in-the-Green (see GREEN) and the May Day observances (see HAWTHORN; MAY DAY). These included the choice of a King or Queen of the May, almost always finally symbolically sacrificed, who was typically clothed in oak leaves. A Puritan commentator, Stubbs, described the maypole as a 'stinckyng idoll'; after the populace had set it up, he goes on, 'then fall they to banquet and feast, to leape and daunce

British Museum

2877

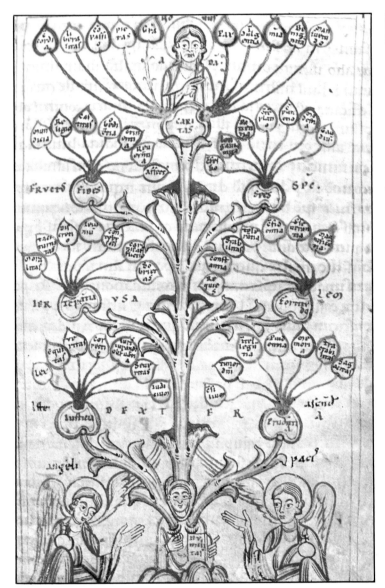

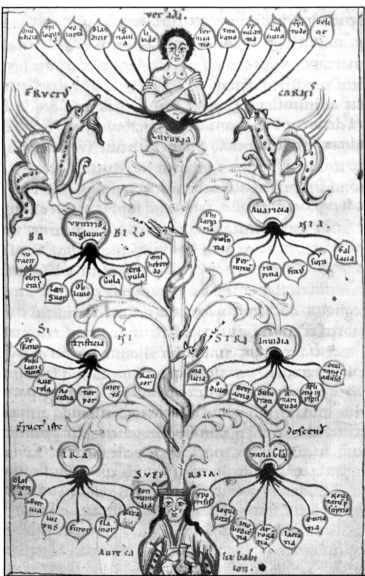

British Museum

'But of the tree of the knowledge of good and evil you shall not eat': virtues *(left)* and vices *(right)* depicted as fruits growing on trees in two German manuscript illustrations of the 12th century, reflecting the tradition of the tree of knowledge in Eden

around it, as the Heathen people did at the dedication of their idolles, whereof this is a perfect patterne, or rather the thyng itself.'

The Long Parliament of 1644 forbade the maypole, and though it came back after the Restoration the leaping and dancing was never quite the same. The importance of the May Day ceremonies, lasting certainly into the 17th century, all over Europe as well as in Britain, testify to the importance and spread of tree worship. In the north European countryside the harvest-May ceremony was exactly parallel to the antique Greek Eiresione. In many ways the Christmas tree and greenery are very similar observances, while the burning of the Yule log, usually of oak, is another symbolic sacrifice for future fruitfulness (see CHRISTMAS; FIR; HOLLY AND IVY).

Trees as Oracles

Among the sacred groves of the ancient world one of the most notable was that of the oaks of Zeus at Dodona, which apparently flourished for at least 2000 years. The laurel at Delphi has perhaps achieved more notoriety. The tree oracle was thought to be connected by its roots with the underworld and hence to the wisdom and foreknowledge of the dead. In Mesopotamia the cedar was both deity and oracle; it was

sacred to the god Ea, whose name was supposedly engraved on its innermost core.

Many oracular trees are mentioned in the Old Testament, such as the 'tree of the diviners' at Shechem, mentioned in the book of Judges (9.37); 'the tree of the revealer' in Genesis (12.6); and the mulberry trees which gave David the signal to attack the Philistines (2 Samuel, chapter 5). Tree oracles are recorded from Armenia, Arabia and Persia, while in Rome there was a prophetic ilex grove on the Aventine hill. Tree omens remained important to the Romans, among many other types of augury; major examples are the withering of laurels which foretold Nero's death, and the fall of a cypress which did the same for Domitian.

The Scythians practised divination with the aid of willow rods, and the Druids used 'omen sticks', perhaps of fruit branches in similar manner. Such wands and rods lead on to sceptres, heralds' wands, generals' staffs and perhaps even the policeman's truncheon – all symbols of power and

inviolability, partly deriving from the original sacredness of the tree. In a rather different field there is the divining rod, for the finding of water, treasure or metal. Such rods were cut from all manner of trees, notably hazel but including fruit trees, willow, blackthorn and mistletoe, with special ceremony at specific times (see DOWSING; WAND).

In many societies, people have believed in lesser spirits who inhabit trees. They were responsible for the well-being of their trees, and sometimes of other plants and animals, and if not propitiated might be hostile to humans. Those most similar to man were likely to be least hostile.

The jinn of ancient Arabia, for example, inhabited trees and thickets among other places, and were monstrous creatures capable of assuming different forms (see JINN). Unfriendly Egyptian monsters of similar type inhabited trees or posts and were likely to waylay the spirits of the dead on their difficult journey. Similar monsters appear in the Bible, translated as 'satyrs' or 'devils', but in the original they are 'hairy monsters', and similar to jinn.

Greek and Roman mythology has a wide range of wood-inhabiting creatures, including the centaur and cyclops, haunters of forests, and the man-goat combinations

The Greenwood

Enforced to seek some covert nigh at hand,
A shady grove not far away they spied,
That promised aid the tempest to withstand:
Whose lofty trees yclad with summer's pride,
Did spread so broad, that heaven's light did hide,
Not pierceable with power of any star:
And all within were paths and alleys wide,
With footing worn, and leading inward far:
Fair harbour that them seems: so in they
    entered are.

And forth they pass, with pleasure forward led,
Joying to hear the birds' sweet harmony,
Which therein shrouded from the tempest dread,
Seemed in their song to scorn the cruel sky.
Much can they praise the trees so straight and
    high,
The sailing Pine, the Cedar proud and tall,
The vine-prop Elm, the Poplar never dry,
The builder Oak, sole king of forests all,
The Aspen good for staves, the Cypress funeral.

The Laurel, mede of mighty Conquerors
And Poets sage, the Fir that weepeth still,
The Willow worn of forlorn Paramours,
The Yew obedient to the bender's will,
The Birch for shafts, the Sallow for the mill,
The Myrrh sweet bleeding in the bitter wound,
The Warlike Beech, the Ash for nothing ill,
The fruitful Olive, and the Platane round,
The carver Holm, the Maple seldom inward
    sound.

Spenser *The Faerie Queene*

of pans and dryads. Pans had many human attributes; protectors of herds, they were generally friendly to man, but by no means beyond playing unkind tricks on him. Satyrs and sileni, and their Roman counterparts, fauns and silvani, were more bestial; Hesiod described these wood spirits as 'a useless and crafty tribe'. Within the last century Greek peasants believed in malicious demons which were half human and half goat. Many of these creatures later became specific: Pan, Silenus and Silvanus became particular spirits, representations of their class (see PAN: SATYRS).

The spirits most closely connected with trees were the female hamadryads. Consorts of the sileni, it was into their care that Aphrodite put the infant Aeneas. When they died, the trees did too. There was also a whole family of nymphs linked with trees — Rhoea with the pomegranate, Daphne with laurel, Helike with willow, Philyra with lime. Tales such as that of Daphne turned into a laurel to escape from Apollo (see APOLLO) are probably inversions of older associations. Lucian's parody *Verae Historiae* describes vines, part of which were in the form of girls; if you tried to pick the grapes growing from their fingers they cried in agony. It was frequently held that trees bled if cut. The reverse is shown by legends surrounding elder — a basically evil tree in which witches were supposed to reside. If you cut an elder branch, some old woman living nearby would be sure to appear with her arm in a sling. There was always a strong feeling that it was bad luck to cut down a tree, particularly those especially associated with fairies or tree spirits like hawthorn, oak, birch and rowan. In Dalmatia, within the last century, it was customary to sacrifice a chicken before cutting down a tree.

East and West alike have tales of spirits, elves, pixies and similar creatures inhabiting trees, especially in central and northern Europe. Such were the Scandinavian 'wild people' covered in moss, the German moss-women, the Tyrolean wild women, the Russian wood demon, often one-eyed, all of whom lived in woods. The Japanese had wood-spirits with a man's body, hawk's head and claws, and a proboscis, which emerged from eggs; the primitive South Americans a wood-ghost who lured men to death (see WILDWOOD).

The Tree of Life

The concept of the tree as the universe is best known in its Scandinavian form, where the ash, Yggdrasil, was the world tree (see ASH); in India it was the fig, Asvattha. But the idea is found in many other parts of the globe. With this tree the world of man rises in a mountain, where the gods live; the tree's trunk springs from this mountain, its outspread branches forming or supporting the sky, and the stars and planets, while its roots reach into the abyss or underworld, forerunner of hell. The fact that the branches held the stars may account for the frequent Eastern jeweller's conception of golden trees hung with jewels. An infinity of symbolic detail accompanies the different parts of the world-tree. Metal world-trees were conceived in China and Russia. Charlemagne destroyed the Saxon 'Irmensul' or World-pillar, which was

A tree of immortality, like other conifers, the yew was planted in graveyards, and so it came to be believed that to sleep in its shade meant death: 15th century illustration

Radio Times Hulton Picture Library

a tree-trunk representation of this belief.

The cosmic tree often bore fruits which the gods ate to ensure their immortality: and so it became a tree of life. The Persian *haoma* and Indian *soma* are examples of such life-giving trees; and so of course are the mystical trees of the paradise from which Adam and Eve were expelled — the tree of life and the tree of knowledge (see FIRST MAN). Man was created within this paradise and, if he spent a righteous life, would return to another, such as that described by Esdras in which were 'twelve trees laden with divers fruits' as well as a tree of life. The Talmud (the code of Jewish law) specifies two paradises, connected by a pillar, up which the souls of the righteous ascend on the sabbath to enjoy the light of the Divine Majesty. In the Cabala, the structure of the universe is conceived in terms of the 'tree of life' (see CABALA). Indian, Chinese and South American legends mention the souls of the dead climbing into heaven up the trunk of a tree.

In India the tree of life and knowledge was, yet again, the fig. In the Koran, paradise — the 'seventh heaven' — contains the enormous Tooba tree, covered with many kinds of fruit, and from which rivers spring, flowing with water, milk, honey and wine.

In Greek myth the garden of the Hesperides is supported on Mount Atlas, which Herodotus describes as the Pillar of Heaven; Hercules overcame the multi-headed dragon that guarded the sacred tree and snatched its golden apples, the fruits of knowledge.

Family Trees

These stories show how deeply the sense of sacred trees was fixed in man's mind. He came to regard the tree as embodying earth, heaven and hell, as the paradise of the departed and even as the origin of the human species, as well as a symbol of immortality. Many widely separated mythologies describe the origin of the human race from trees. In the Norse *Edda*, Odin and his brothers change two trees on the seashore into male and female humans who become the parents of mankind. One Greek story was that men had germinated from tree seeds: Hesiod specified ash, but in the *Odyssey* it was the oak.

These stories link up with such myths as the story of the birth of Adonis, who appeared when the tree into which his

C. Barker

mother Myrrha had been transformed was struck by a sword. Attis originated in an almond, and was later imprisoned by Cybele in a pine tree, from which every spring he was reborn. Parallel with Attis is Osiris, whose image was annually imprisoned in a hollowed pine log, which was burned a year later. From these legends came the pine cone as a symbol of resurrection. Many Greek and Roman gods were supposed to have been born under a tree.

This notion is inverted in the widespread custom of planting trees to celebrate the births of children, whose progress could be forecast by the trees' behaviour — a practice of the Romans, reported equally among less civilized peoples from, for example, western Africa and New Guinea.

Philemon the Oak and Baucis the Linden Tree, **by Arthur Rackham: Philemon and Baucis were a devoted husband and wife who after death were turned into trees by Jupiter, their branches intertwining at the top**

Such trees, if they survived, became 'family trees', and it seems likely that surnames based on tree names are a result of such associations.

It goes almost without saying that the trees which became particularly revered for various reasons, notably the ash, birch, hawthorn, hazel, holly, oak and rowan in north temperate countries, were protective against evil and its manifestations — witches, fairies and the like. Pieces of these trees, especially birch and rowan,

would safeguard the individual if carried, and his house or his cattle if fixed to porch or byre. Some trees protected against lightning, such as bay laurel, elm, holly, oak and olive; some indeed were reputed to have sprung from lightning. A birch, fir, or other tree is still placed on houses being built, and on bridges, dams and other large constructions, to avert any disaster.

(See also ANIMISM; BUILDERS' RITES; CRETE: CROSS; DRUIDS; ORACLES; VEGETATION SPIRITS; and articles on individual trees.)

A. J. HUXLEY

FURTHER READING: J. G. Frazer, *The Golden Bough* (St. Martin's Press, 1980).

TRICKSTER

'Trickster is comic relief; he is psychic catharsis on a deep and vital level; he is a hero whose own evolution perhaps mirrors that of mankind . . .'

THE MYTHOLOGICAL character generically called Trickster has many dimensions and roles. Often he is called Trickster-Transformer, to emphasize the fact that he is not single-natured, but a culture hero who transforms aspects of the world for man's benefit, as well as a player of pranks. The ethnologist Paul Radin, author of a pioneering study of this figure, defines the totality of Trickster as 'at one and the same time creator and destroyer, giver and negator, he who dupes others and who is always duped himself'. Radin found Trickster prominently in the myths of the Winnebago Indians, a tribe from the Nebraska area. But he found him also in various forms in the mythology of nearly every North American Indian tribe.

Generally, Trickster is the hero of a group of myths or tales, usually only loosely interrelated, which is called a cycle. He is pictured as a primordial being, who existed from the beginning of things or at least from soon afterwards. The Blackfoot and Crow Indians give their trickster-transformer the name of 'Old Man', but they do not see him as a doddering ancient. He is Old Man because he is ageless, as old as time.

Most other tribes give their trickster an animal name: Rabbit or Hare in the east and south-east of America, Bluejay or Mink in the north-west, Raven on the Pacific coast of Canada, Spider among some Siouan peoples and, among tribes of the Plains, the Great Basin, the south-west and California the incomparable Coyote. The Crow Indians' 'Old Man' is sometimes also known as 'Old Man Coyote'.

Most of these animals have reputations, in reality, for being clever or mischievous. But the animal form of Trickster is more metaphoric than literal. He is not a little furry creature with cunning ways. He possesses and embodies the essence of the animal — or of animalism, in general — and it is unrewarding to try to pin down his form, precisely and consistently.

Within the same story there may be mention of Coyote's tail, and of his hands. Raven is sometimes described in a decidedly human way, but then he pulls on his 'Raven mask' and costume, and flies off. We must take Trickster as he comes — seeming man-shaped here, seeming an animal there, seeming a giant or a monster or merely shapeless elsewhere. As a supernatural being he can change shape if he wishes; and quite often, he can set parts of his body free in an independent existence.

Though he may bear the name of a reputedly wily creature, Trickster is not always clever. In some of the most crudely enjoyable tales he is the fool, whose stupidity leads him into trouble or causes him to be tricked by other creatures. One recurring plot shows him setting a part of his body, usually his anus, a task. It fails and he foolishly punishes it, thereby causing himself great pain. The Winnebago Trickster finds that his right arm quarrels and fights with his left, wounding it severely and painfully. These comic blunderings have been explained as a mythic expression of life on an animal level — instinctual, lacking in self-awareness, with an undeveloped consciousness.

Trickster is usually highly curious, unable to leave well alone, unable to avoid interfering in the doings of others, usually with disastrous results all round. Several tales show Coyote getting his head stuck in a buffalo skull because he had to peer inside to watch a ceremony being performed by mice, or flies. Comparable tales reflect his stubbornness: he is obsessively, mindlessly persistent when he wants something, and his wants are on a primeval level. He is a creature of his appetites, and these are usually a voracious hunger and an equally voracious and gross sexuality. Raven is the hungriest North American trickster, constantly led into trouble by his lust for food — as when he dives to the sea-bed to steal a fisherman's bait, is caught by the hook and loses his beak. The Siouan

The Scandinavian god Loki has been interpreted as a trickster figure, mischievous, amoral or sometimes evil, a shape-changer who plays comic or revolting pranks but is also a culture hero who brings benefits to men: 19th century illustration of Loki in chains

lose his sight. Of course he does, the threat is realized, and he has to use trickery to cheat some other animal of its eyes in order to regain his vision.

But the myths also picture Trickster as a positive being, a transformer, if not a fully-fledged creator, who brings benefit to the world. Sometimes, these positive achievements happen by accident, as a side effect of some blunder or some trick. Many of the myths that purport to explain the growth of certain customs, or the invention of certain artefacts, have this element of Trickster's random and unintentional creation.

The world and man also receive benefit from one of the most universal acts of the trickster-transformer: the stealing of fire. Usually the trickster wheedles his way into the confidence of the powerful Fire People (or whatever the fire's supernatural guardians are called) and seizes the moment to take up a bit of fire and run. The guardians pursue, and often the fire is passed along a relay of other creatures until finally it is lodged in Wood or Tree. The Fire People cannot get it out, but the trickster teaches man how to get fire from wood (by rubbing two sticks together).

In most examples of the fire myth, and in other comparable tales, the Trickster has become a straightforward hero, whose good deeds are not the result of trickery or accident, but of his heroic devotion to the good and the right.

There are also tales in which Trickster is identified with the original creator-god, the Prime Mover and First Cause, who made the world and everything in it, like the Old Man of some Plains tribes, who sends the diver bird or some other creature to the bed of the primal sea for a bit of soil from which to mould the earth. The Blackfoot Old Man, seen at one point losing his sight in the eye-juggling idiocy mentioned before, is in the same cycle of tales seen sculpting the shapes of men and beasts and infusing life into them. So Trickster-Transformer is identified by the Indians as encompassing simultaneously a blockhead, an amoral practical joker, a hero who aids mankind and changes the world, and a god who creates mankind and the world.

Brer Rabbit and the Tar Baby
The North American Indians have no monopoly on the trickster figure. He is found in myths and folktales throughout the world, for example in the jackal and hare of Indian folktales. In most of Africa Hare is the trickster, though Tortoise is prominent in some places. But West Africa has its own trickster, the spider Anansi. Anansi is a high-powered trickster who rarely appears as a dolt or fool; and he is seldom seen as a creator god, but he does perform his share of heroic and 'transforming' acts. He was taken to the Americas by the West African slaves, and now has a starring role in Caribbean traditional folk-tales, under a variety of names, including 'Aunt Nancy'.

Legba, a trickster figure of Dahomey, made his way also to the Caribbean and is now an important *loa* of Voodoo religion (see VOODOO). He acts as an intermediary,

Trickster is shown finding a land of women without men and teaching them about sex by practical example. Many Indian tales echo the Winnebago stories of Trickster's enormous penis: once he stupidly mistakes it for a flagpole, and another time he sends it off to rape a chief's daughter by, as it were, remote control.

In all such tales we are seeing man's 'animal nature' in action. Other aspects of this nature are less comic, reflecting the vicious amorality of a being who knows nothing of ethical or moral values. Trickster lies and cheats and steals and kills, without guilt or hint of conscience. He talks Deer or Buffalo to the edge of a precipice, and then pushes him over for supper; Coyote cons Porcupine into a jumping contest with some

meat as the prize, making Porcupine forget that he cannot jump. Here is Trickster less doltish, more crafty, but also cruel and treacherous. He does not always escape the consequences of his actions: it is often Trickster who is credited with introducing death and pain into the world; but in a Maidu tale it is Coyote's own son who is the first creature to suffer death.

The Theft of Fire
Lacking values and any sense of propriety, Trickster naturally comes into conflict with customs, rules, laws and taboos. In the widely told tale of Coyote learning to juggle with his own eyes, he is told by his instructor never to take his eyes out more than three times a day, or he will

appearing first at a ceremony to open the way for people to be later possessed by other loa. The Hare trickster of southern Africa is thought to have made his way to the New World, to be reincarnated in southern Negro folktales as 'Brer Rabbit', though the Indian tribes of the south-eastern United States also have a notable Hare trickster who resembles Brer Rabbit.

Brer Rabbit appears in the folktales retold in a stage-Negro dialect by 'Uncle Remus', the journalist and folklorist Joel Chandler Harris. Like Anansi, the Rabbit is rarely seen to be a fool, though now and again he slips up. Every American child knows the story of the Tar Baby — a sticky figurine made by Brer Fox, which holds Brer Rabbit fast when he assaults it. Not every American child or adult knows that the motif of the 'stick-fast' trap recurs in Trickster cycles round the world. But not all of them get away from the trap so neatly as Brer Rabbit, who tricks the fox into flinging him into the briar patch, where he will be safe.

Trickster figures also exist in more sophisticated mythologies of the past, Monkey in China, for example, a supernatural being who defeats by magic and trickery various monsters and demons, and then forces the high gods to recognize and respect his power. Yet he remains a monkey, constantly getting into trivial and comic scrapes. Eventually his defiance of the gods is crushed by Buddha and he is imprisoned, but is later released (no less bumptious than before) to aid a noble traveller on a heroic quest.

Trickster and Devil

Upon his release, the Monkey story shades from the trickster theme into that of the 'clever animal' who aids the hero in his hour of need. Even in his trickster aspects Monkey is a long way from the more primitive Coyote or Anansi. Even farther are the Greek god Hermes (see HERMES), who has been classed as a trickster because of the mischief he plays as a child, and the hero Prometheus, classified as a trickster because of the fire-stealing myth (see PROMETHEUS). But many primitive tricksters have something in common with Hermes. Most North American tricksters have myths in which they are killed and yet revive themselves effortlessly (often by tricking the powers of death into freeing them). Hermes, too, as psychopomp — guide of souls to the realm of death — moves freely into that realm and out again. And, oddly, the Dahomean Legba is an intermediary between gods and men just as is Hermes (the messenger of Zeus).

The mythology of the Teutonic and Norse peoples provides another parallel in the figure of Loki. One of the Aesir (as Hermes was one of the Olympians), Loki appears in many tales as a mischievous but not

Facing page Brer Rabbit has again outwitted his enemy Brer Fox in this illustration to the 'Uncle Remus' stories: the African trickster Hare is thought to have influenced the figure of Brer Rabbit, though Indian peoples of the eastern United States also have a notable Hare trickster *Right* The fairy tale hero Jack is another trickster figure

demonic trickster. But in other myths he is an embodiment of amorality and evil, the killer (by a trick) of Balder, the father of the Fenris wolf and the Midgard serpent, the ultimate author of world-ending Ragnarok (see LOKI; SCANDINAVIA).

Here the trickster figure overlaps with the figure of the Devil or comparable personification of evil. Another example is the apparent mingling in early Christian times of the classical god Pan, lord of all that is instinctual and animal (see PAN), and the horned, split-hooved Satan. Pan has much in common with the animalistic, amoral tricksters, who are identified by many primitives with powerful demons. And it is often the trickster who introduces pain and death into an Eden-like, paradisal world.

The Navaho explicitly ally their Coyote with forces of outright evil, and also say that the sight of a real coyote at the start of some enterprise is a frightful omen.

Other tales of Trickster refer to him as someone who has been a high god, but who has fallen or been cast down from those heights. A comparable theme is the trickster's background as the prodigal and reprehensible son or brother of a high god, as Raven is in many north Pacific tales, as Loki is sometimes said to be the brother of Odin, as Legba is the youngest son of the Dahomey creator. The myth is not being strained when we link it with the fall of Lucifer and other aspects of the Christian Devil. Indeed, as Joseph Campbell points out, many primitive tribes after being

Victoria and Albert Museum

Christianized adopted the figure of Satan as a trickster, and imposed onto him many of the usual themes from trickster cycles, including in some instances giving him a hand in creating the earth.

There is another interesting parallel in the ancient but still extant tradition of the fool, harlequin, Lord of Misrule or the like, who cavorts and plays rude pranks during the great pre-Lent carnivals. Here is Trickster in his flouting of authority,

Punch, abbreviated from Punchinello, a character in 17th century Italian comedy, is a bully and clown with hooked nose and humped back who kills his wife and baby, and outwits the law: from the Raymond Mander and Joe Mitchenson Theatre Collection

taboo-shattering mode; and many of these European fools appear, interestingly, in animal guise (see FOOL; SPRING).

The Middle Ages also spawned trickster characters outside the conventions of Carnival, like Till Eulenspiegel, hero of comic German tales on the theme of a crafty peasant outwitting pompous city folk who underestimate him. Still older were the fables that came together in the French *roman* of Reynard the Fox, a classical trickster.

Farther afield, some writers have seen traces of Trickster in what Ali Baba does to the thieves, but there is more to be found in the ancient, hilarious but meaningful Sufi tales of Mulla Nasredin, recently reintroduced to the West by Idries Shah.

The Mulla is in the Eulenspiegel tradition of the 'cunning fool'; foolery masks his ability to puncture self-importance, show up prejudice and undermine narrow minds. He is Trickster ignoring the rules, the proprieties, the rigid and sterile dogmas of minds that have stopped expanding.

In this century, folklorists see echoes of the blockhead trickster in widespread joke cycles about the 'Little Moron' and his ilk, and other echoes in similar jokes about cunning fools like the 'clever Yankee'. But perhaps the fullest recent flowering of the trickster figure was in the multi-faceted comedy of men like Charles Chaplin, in films like *The Pawnbroker* — where the hero is capable of great stupidity at times, but able always to rise to the occasion (if, sometimes, by accident) to thwart a bully, aid the distressed and leave a much benefited and 'transformed' world behind him.

Angel and Ape

How can one mythological character contain at the same time a benighted idiot, an amoral villain with a certain low cunning, and a culture hero or god to whom man owes most or all of his humanity? Most authorities see in these apparently irreconcilable elements a fusion (or confusion) of two age-old strands in primitive myth-making. Paul Radin's interpretation of the Winnebago myth structure seems to support this view, because the Winnebago have not made (or have unmade) the fusion. Their trickster is the animalistic blockhead with occasional flashes of animal cunning — and nothing more. He is not a culture hero. That role is filled by Hare, in a separate myth cycle, and by other even more heroic figures in their myth cycles: and where Hare retains some of the craftiness of a true trickster, these other heroes have evolved past that stage.

So the Winnebago appear to show us the two strands for what they are. Radin, looking at the animalistic trickster in the light of Jungian psychology, sees him as representing the early, dim stumblings of humanity from a state of 'undifferentiated' animalism towards a humanized state of self-awareness, with a firm grasp on identity and social values. He suggested that the archetypal hero myth passes through four stages, representing the human consciousness on its way to a full flowering. Trickster is stage one — full of blundering, of a single-minded urge to satisfy primal desires.

Trickster myths are usually of extreme antiquity and Radin calls Trickster 'the oldest of all figures in American Indian mythology, probably in all mythologies'. The true culture-hero activities and the less animalistic aspects of Trickster cycles can be seen as later additions to the original figure. It may be that increasingly sophisticated shamans and priests gradually altered the old tales over the generations, so that the original doltish, obscene Trickster changed and improved, and gained heroic, or even divine, stature.

No doubt this fusion of dullard and deity did not disturb the primitive sense of religious propriety, as it would disturb ours. American Indians themselves in our day have expressed puzzlement and

QUADRILLE BY

Mander & Mitchenson

distress at the contradictions in their trickster tales. But their ancestors — and ours, in pagan Europe — knew better. Their gods were humanized, and Trickster is the most human of all, a clear expression of man's true nature, angel and ape in one.

C. G. Jung believed that the human ego, the bright nucleus of the conscious mind, has in the unconscious an exact counterpart or reverse image, which he called the 'shadow'. It appears in dreams as a 'compensatory' figure, pointing up a lack of balance or harmony in the psyche. And the animalistic Trickster, Jung felt, is a mythological shadow figure, the reverse image of the saint or angel; he is the ape or imp or dark opposite, without which a balance, a psychic wholeness, could not be achieved.

The tales are a primary source of entertainment, whether we laugh at the doltish trickster blundering into trouble or the wily trickster outwitting others. They were also used as a means of moral instruction for the young. The Coyote stories of treachery, stupidity, cowardice and taboo-smashing were effective ways of communicating to Indian children the need to obey tribal laws and aspire to the high virtues of warriors. But besides instruction and entertainment, the stories have a primary purpose which recalls Jung's theory of the 'shadow'. The myths are cathartic. They provide an outlet for the tensions that inevitably build up in societies bound by ritual, taboo, hierarchical order and the requirements of a highly

Trickster survives in Europe and the Americas in the fool, harlequin or Lord of Misrule of the carnival season before Lent who cavorts about playing rude pranks, flouting established authority and convention: Harlequin, from the Mander and Mitchenson Theatre Collection

Mander & Mitchenson

organized and demanding religion which permeates every fibre of the social structure.

Most tribal societies are so permeated, and have their tricksters. Prominent in the ceremonies of the Pueblo Indians, for example, are the holy fools, the *koyemshi*, daubed in mud and excrement, screeching obscenities, mocking the chants and songs, embodying and purging every individual's yearning to break free of his society's cumbersome demands. Other tribes had their variants of the koyemshi, and their trickster tales. Medieval Europeans found their cathartic release in the wild revelry of Carnival, led by a trickster figure. Perhaps we find ours in the films, watching the modern successors to Chaplin and Keaton.

So it seems that the many roles of Trickster blend and fuse. Trickster is comic relief; he is psychic catharsis on a deep and vital level; he is a hero whose own evolution perhaps mirrors that of mankind towards a higher consciousness and social maturity. And, embodying all these essentials, he is deathless — no ethnological museum piece but alive and flourishing today as in the primeval past.

(See also GREAT PLAINS INDIANS; PACIFIC NORTH-WEST INDIANS; PUEBLO INDIANS.)

DOUGLAS HILL

FURTHER READING: Paul Radin, *The Trickster* (Schocken, 1972); Joseph Campbell, *The Masks of God: Primitive Mythology* (Penguin, 1976).

Trinity

A set of three forming a unity or closely connected: in Christianity, God is One and also Three (Father, Son and Holy Ghost): in Hinduism, Brahman is One and also Three: deities grouped in sets of three occur in pagan religions, especially among the Celts: numerologically, the number 3 is held to reveal a pair of opposites and the Unity which reconciles and transcends them.
See BRAHMAN; CELTS; CHRISTIANITY; THREE.

TRISTAN

THE STORY of Tristan and Ysolt is one of the great love stories of all time. It is a tale of illicit passion, for Tristan is the nephew and favourite champion, and Ysolt the beloved wife, of Mark, the kindly but irresolute king of Cornwall, whom both regard with feelings of deep respect and affection. Like all the greatest love stories, it is about a pair in equal bondage to their passion rather than about a great lover wooing and winning the object of his desire. Tristan and Ysolt have gained the immortality of Romeo and Juliet, not that of Paris and Helen of Troy.

The Tristan legend is of great antiquity

and during its long history from early Celtic tales through medieval Arthurian literature to Wagner, Tennyson and Thomas Mann the style of its presentation and interpretation has varied greatly. But the two finest of all the versions of the legend, though separated by over 600 years, share to a marked degree the same subtle psychological framework in which the story is set, though many details of the narrative are different. These are the *Tristan* of Gottfried von Strassburg, one of the masterpieces of early 13th century German poetry, and Wagner's opera *Tristan und Isolde*. Both works profoundly analyse the mainsprings of the most powerful of human emotions and their tragic outcome in this particular version of the eternal triangle.

In both works, the first element of the passion of Tristan and Ysolt that gives it its archetypal quality is the equality of the lovers. It is moreover, a 'passion' in both senses of the word: no pair was ever more rapturously in love and because of that rapture, much suffering came to them and to others who were dear to them. It is this sorrow, willingly accepted on their own behalf but bitterly regretted when caused to others, that is the second of the main archetypal themes. Love, in one of its aspects, is inevitably a destroyer and lovers may despairingly watch their own actions, which they are powerless to control, damage or ruin the well-being of good people with whom they have enjoyed relations of trust and affection. At the same

The legend of Tristan and Ysolt has a long history from its beginning in Celtic tales through Arthurian romances to treatments by Wagner, Tennyson and Thomas Mann *Right* A tournament scene from *Roman de Tristan*, French, 15th century *Left* Tristan arrives at a castle below the sea: from a Flemish MS, c 1500

time, at least in the eyes of the world, the lovers are destroying themselves and their position in it. The good hurt the good; the innocents, almost, are massacred without the need of a butcher. Yet the lovers, caught in a web of deceit and circumstance, trying, in their more lucid moments, to balance an impossible account of lust, worldly honour and human decency, may themselves sometimes be brought to attempt vile deeds. They will later suffer remorse or be shamed by the generous forgiveness or loyalty of their intended victim.

The third archetypal strand also relates to the helplessness of the lovers. Tristan and Ysolt fall in love, at least in the simple terms of narrative, not as they might in a modern novel but because they unwittingly drink a love potion. How far the swallowing of this fatal draught absolves them of their moral responsibilities, of which they remain painfully aware, is uncertain. But it does symbolize love as an exterior force, an elemental power that strikes at mortal men and women and drives them 'mad'. The more powerfully are such mortals struck, the more total does their love become as the intensity of their spiritual union matches the pitch of their physical passion and, thereby, the further removed they become from choice, guilt or blame. Indeed, in extreme cases, like that of Tristan and Ysolt, an 'illegitimate' love acquires a sanctity that is recognized and revered even, and indeed especially, by those whom it has harmed. Such are the main themes against which both Gottfried and Wagner set their versions of the story of Tristan and Ysolt. The summary of the legend which follows is close to that of Gottfried's narrative.

The Splinter in the Bone

Tristan was the son of Blancheflor, sister of Mark, king of Cornwall, and Rivalin, the lord of a part of Brittany. Rivalin was killed in battle before Tristan's birth and Blancheflor died in childbed. Brought up by his father's loyal marshal, Tristan grew to be strong and handsome, skilled in hunting, literature and music. Stranded by misadventure in Cornwall, he made a favourable impression at Mark's court, and was recognized as the king's nephew and knighted.

At that time one of the great sorrows of Cornwall was the tribute exacted by the Irish. Every year Morold, champion of the king of Ireland, would appear and demand the handing over of a party of noble youths for service in Ireland. So fearsome was he, no Cornish knight dared oppose him, but Tristan challenged him to combat. After a long and savage duel, Tristan slew Morold by cleaving his skull, a splinter of his sword remaining in the bone when the body was taken back to Ireland. But Morold had wounded Tristan with a poisoned spear: the wound would not heal and his life was feared for. It was known that the only person skilled enough to cure him was, of all people, Morold's sister Ysolt, the queen of Ireland. Tristan therefore made a typically bold plan. He sailed to Ireland and, off Dublin, his friends set him adrift alone in a small boat disguised as a minstrel named

Tantris. The locals pitied him and took him to court, where the queen did indeed cure his wound. Tantris became a great favourite and was engaged as tutor in literature and music to the young princess, also called Ysolt.

When he finally returned to Cornwall, some of the courtiers began to be jealous of this young paragon who was the king's heir. They persuaded Mark that he should marry and have sons; and who better for bride than the young Ysolt, whom Tristan had praised so vividly for her beauty and intelligence and whose hand would bring peace between the two nations? Mark agreed and Tristan was sent to put the proposal.

Tristan landed in Ireland and found the country ravaged by a dragon so terrible that the king had promised his daughter in marriage to any knight who slew it. Tristan killed it and cut off a large piece of its tongue which he kept under his shirt. Now the king's steward (a cowardly man who was the princess's unwelcome suitor) happened to be riding past and could not believe his luck when he saw the reptile dead and nobody about — for Tristan, sorely wounded and overcome by the foul fumes exhaled by the monster, had fainted in a nearby wood. The steward lopped off the dragon's head and hurried to court to claim Ysolt's hand, to the dismay of the princess. But her wily mother knew the steward was incapable of this heroic deed. She and her daughter, accompanied by her niece Brangane, searched in the neighbourhood and found a stricken man whom to their astonishment they recognized as 'Tantris'. Under the queen's care, Tristan speedily recovered. But the young Ysolt noticed to her horror that a nick in the blade of his magnificent sword exactly matched the splinter she had taken from the skull of her beloved uncle Morold, whom she had sworn to avenge.

In a scene of high comedy, as Tristan sits helpless in his bath, Ysolt rails at him and tries to kill him with his own sword. Her mother, to whom Tristan confesses all and discloses the object of his present mission, calms her down and declares that bygones should be bygones — and that if the truth is not brought out before the king, Ysolt will have to marry the hateful steward. The princess agrees but remains implacable in her hostility to Tristan. When, at court, the steward is humiliated by Tristan producing the dragon's tongue, the king agrees to the alliance. Tristan sets sail for Cornwall with Ysolt, Brangane and all the youths who had been taken in tribute.

Now begins the passion. During the voyage, Tristan and Ysolt, still barely on speaking terms, call for a drink. By a fatal error, a lady-in-waiting gives them the flask containing a love potion brewed by the queen for Ysolt to give to Mark. It has an immediate and catastrophic effect, and by the

time they make port Tristan and Ysolt have consummated their love. Terrified, Ysolt persuades her virgin cousin Brangane to lie in the dark with her husband the king at the beginning of the wedding night. The stratagem is successful: Ysolt comes to bed before wine and lights are brought. Later, she orders Brangane to be secretly murdered, lest the truth come out. But her assassins have not the heart to kill the girl who protests her innocence so eloquently. Ysolt and Brangane are reconciled.

Tristan and Ysolt then begin a long period of hidden tortured love. Rumours begin to go about of an attachment between them, and Mark is tormented by doubt and indecision, above all by the horrible possibility that the gossip might be true. Various traps are laid for the lovers but although there is a mass of circumstantial evidence there is no proof. Finally it is agreed that Ysolt should submit to the ordeal: if she swears her innocence as she grasps a red-hot iron she will not be burned. In this passage, one of the most remarkable episodes, Tristan disguises himself as a ragged pilgrim in the watching crowd. Ysolt arrives in a boat at the appointed place and Tristan carries her ashore. He slips 'so that his fall brought him to rest lying in the Queen's lap and arms'. Thus Ysolt can swear that no man has lain with her save Mark and the pilgrim – and the iron did not burn her.

Mark's doubts are laid to rest; but only for a little while. The talk goes on and, indeed, it is now obvious, even to Mark, that Tristan and Ysolt love each other.

In the Cave of Lovers

Some people are smitten with curiosity and astonishment, and plague themselves with the question how these two companions, Tristan and Isolde, nourished themselves in this wasteland? I will tell them and assuage their curiosity. They looked at one another and nourished themselves with that! Their sustenance was the eye's increase. They fed in their grotto on nothing but love and desire. The two lovers who formed its court had small concern for their provender. Hidden away in their hearts they carried the best nutriment to be had anywhere in the world, which offered itself unasked ever fresh and new. I mean pure devotion, love made sweet as balm that consoles body and sense so tenderly, and sustains the heart and spirit – this was their best nourishment. Truly, they never considered any food but that from which the heart drew desire, the eyes delight, and which the body, too, found agreeable. With this they had enough. Love drove her ancient plough for them, keeping pace all the time, and gave them an abundant store of all those things that go to make heaven on earth.

Gottfried von Strassburg *Tristan*
(trans A. T. Hatto)

King Mark and Tristan, and Ysolt nursing Tristan, by Aubrey Beardsley: an essential element in the love-story of Tristan and Ysolt is the suffering which their passion inflicts on those who are dear to them, especially King Mark, who is Ysolt's husband

At last the desolate king admits this to himself. He summons the pair before the court and in a speech of great nobility and generosity he tells them that he loves them both too much to harm them. They must leave and go their own way. Then follows the most extraordinary part of Gottfried's poem. Tristan and Ysolt, accompanied only by Tristan's faithful retainer Curvenal and his hunting dog Hiudan, repair to the wilds to live in the 'Cave of Lovers'. Here they dwell in a gentle rapture in which the desires of body and spirit fuse in a mystical union. The lovers' condition, and the cave and its furnishings, are described in language which overtly uses the vocabulary of the Christian mysticism of the period.

Meanwhile, Mark is mourning their absence. Out hunting one day, he happens on the cave and through a window sees the pair asleep on the bed but between them Tristan's great sword – a symbol of chastity. The wretched king summons them back to court but is still suspicious, and one day actually finds them asleep in a garden, close and naked in each other's arms. As he rushes off to fetch witnesses (as the law required), Tristan awakes and sees him. Tristan rouses Ysolt. It is the end: they will both be killed if the witnesses see them and now they can never be happy together. 'Keep me in your heart; for whatever happens to mine, you shall never leave it.' Ysolt gives him a ring as a token of their love and to use to confirm any message he might ever have to send. She passionately bids him an agonized farewell.

Tristan tries to forget his sorrows in warfare, in Spain, in Germany, back in his homeland. He allies himself with a lord named Kaedin who has a sister, also called Ysolt – Ysolt of the White Hands. Tristan finds himself attracted to her, but he cannot understand his own feelings: is he trying to forget his true Ysolt by allowing (or even urging) himself to fall in love with another; is he drawn to Ysolt of the White Hands because she seems, by her very name, like a dream of Ysolt of Ireland? (Around this point Gottfried's poem breaks off and the story is continued in a fragment of the *Tristran* of Thomas 'of Britain', whom Gottfried admired and had used as one of his chief sources.) Finally Tristan commits the culpable folly of marrying this other Ysolt – and finds himself incapable of consummating the marriage.

Eventually, in a battle, as so many years before, Tristan is wounded by a poisoned spear and the wound will not heal. He suffers atrociously and knows that only Ysolt who learned her mother's skills can cure him. He sends Kaedin with the ring, to beg Ysolt to come. Overheard by Ysolt of the White Hands, Tristan asks that the ship, when it returns, should carry a white sail if Ysolt is on board and a black if she is not. Kaedin sets out, finds Ysolt and has little trouble in persuading her to come.

At last the ship comes into view and Tristan, rousing himself on his bed, asks his wife the colour of its sail. 'Black,' she replies. 'At this,' in the words of Thomas, 'Tristan feels such pain that he has never had greater nor ever will, and he turns his face to the wall and says: "God save Ysolt and me! Since you will not come to me I must die for your love. I can hold on to life no longer. I die for you, Ysolt, dear love!" Ysolt lands, and hearing of Tristan's death cries that she will die for him in return. She lies beside him, kisses him and dies. There, in Thomas, the story ends, in the love-death, the same *Liebestod* that brings Wagner's opera to its tragic end.

C. DE HOGHTON

FURTHER READING: Gottfried von Strassburg's *Tristan* and Beroul's *Romance of Tristan* are available in the Penguin Classics series.

TROLL

THIS elemental spirit of northern European mythology belongs to that supernatural fairy community which was once assumed to exercise dominion over Nature, a class of spirit regarded with considerable apprehension since all elementals were known to be capricious, treacherous and frequently hostile. Elementals were in the main associated with particular sites, in the case of trolls mountain caverns from which they emerged after nightfall. Broadly speaking, there were two classes of trolls: the giant and the dwarf, both of which were reported to steal women, exchange human children for their own hideous offspring and indulge in a good deal of petty theft. It has been generally assumed that all trolls were originally of giant stature but that, especially in areas like Denmark and Finland, they became gradually reduced in size. Giant trolls, however, abounded in mountainous countries like Norway and Sweden, where they were the spirits of the mountains, and were in the main dull-witted, hairy cannibals with huge noses for smelling out the blood of their human prey. An allied species, the trow, haunted the Orkneys and Shetlands, frequenting both land and sea.

The dwarf trolls in their own particular way were quite as hideous as their giant counterparts and were recognizable by their humped backs and red caps. They were good mechanics and clever dancers, and they possessed beautiful wives but, unlike the giants, they seem to have been extremely sharp-witted although their cunning was of a low order. One species at least must have been extremely small, hence the words of an old Danish ballad: 'Out then spoke the tiny troll, no bigger than an emmet'.

Scandinavian folklore contains a great deal of interesting information about the habits and idiosyncrasies of the troll population. All trolls hated noise, an aversion they acquired in the days of old when the Teutonic god Thor dedicated much of his time to hurling his hammer in their direction. Their instinctive hostility to the Christian faith led to an intense loathing of church bells, the sound of which could reduce the most powerful troll to a heap of pebbles. As creatures of darkness, trolls were terrified of sunlight, which could petrify them.

Giant trolls were frequently credited with building mighty structures like castles, bridges and churches, and legends abound describing how they were cheated of their wages (usually human souls) by their sharper-witted clients. At the root of this tradition lay the belief that some kind of payment was due to the owner of the soil when land was set aside for building or cultivation, the landlord, in this case, being an earth elemental demanding his rent in blood or souls.

Anyone who managed to learn a troll's name had the power to destroy him by repeating it. There is a famous Norse

Figure of a troll, from Sweden: the lore of these nightmare creatures of past belief has been revived in the interests of the tourist trade, though trolls are no longer credited with eating human flesh

legend about a troll named Wind and Weather, who contracted to build a church in return for which he was to receive as wages the sun and moon. Alas, his client, the saintly King Olaf, discovered his name by accident, and cried out: 'Hold, O Wind and Weather, you've set the spire askew', and the troll crashed to the ground, being reduced to a large heap of flints.

Despite the useful work performed by church-building trolls a pronounced antipathy existed between mankind and trolls in general, due largely to the trolls' deplorable habit of stealing babies and seducing wives. Trolls could be kept at bay, however, by attaching sprigs of mistletoe to crib and byre and bedroom ceiling, and by lighting huge bonfires known as Baldur's Bale Fires at crossroads on St John's Eve, using nine varieties of wood, and at the same time hurling toadstools into the flames. In Sweden fires were lit at Eastertide, the peasants firing warning shots in all directions.

A rapid degradation in the status of the troll followed the advance of Christianity into northern Europe which had the effect of transforming all Teutonic elementals into what can only be described as Christianized devils. Among the 17th-century evil spirits referred to by Burton in his *Anatomy of Melancholy* were 'Robin Goodfellows, trolls etc., which as they are most conversant with men do them the most harm'. Many of the basic characteristics of the troll are clearly discernible in the attributes of devils, the troll wife-stealer becoming in time the demon lover, the incubus seducing women in their sleep (see INCUBUS).

With the departure of devils from the modern mythological scene troll-lore has undergone an encouraging revival, largely in the interests of the Scandinavian tourist industry. Toy trolls, huge, long-nosed and hairy, often brandishing flint axes, are now available in Norwegian shops and the traveller is carefully reminded that trolls wearing their traditional red caps can occasionally be seen at night in the proximity of hills and mounds. Fortunately, modern trolls have developed more sophisticated appetites than their ancestors for, according to the last vagary of folklore, they no longer demand tribute in the form of souls but request heaped platefuls of bananas and cream.

ERIC MAPLE

TROUT

IN CELTIC regions of the British Isles the trout was long regarded as a 'fish of wisdom' and was credited with supernatural powers of a high order. Sacred trout were quite often found in holy wells, sometimes in the company of eels which were frequently assumed to have similar powers. In Wales, at the well of Ffynnon Beris in Caernarvonshire, there were two trout whose movements showed what fate held in store for those who consulted them by throwing bread into the water. If no fish put in an appearance, the omen was bad, but if they could clearly be seen swimming in the water, the auspices were favourable. The local people jealously guarded the fish, and a similar brace of trout in the well at Ffynnon Gwyfan, near Disserth Church, were also protected.

In Ireland, the trout of the well at Kilmorne were regarded as guardian spirits and were said never to vary in size over the centuries. There were two beautiful trout at Tober Kieran, one of which showed its supernatural qualities in a most startling manner. An irreverent soldier, wanting a fish for dinner, caught it with rod and line, but discovered to his astonishment that he had hooked a beautiful woman instead. Overwhelmed, he let her fall back into the water, where she again became a trout. The well at Tullaghan in County Sligo was tenanted by two miraculous trout, which were invisible to those without second sight.

In the Crammag River in the Isle of Man there is a pool which has a reputation for bringing misfortune to those who fish there. It is said that long ago an angler tried to catch trout there, but fainted on seeing a host of tiny fairy creatures clothed in red, which rose from the pool and then vanished.

Trout fishermen, like other anglers, have their own lore and superstitions. The saying, 'You must lose a fly to catch a trout', has a hint of a sacrifice required in return for the acquisition of so uncanny a fish. Some fishermen spit on the bait before casting the line, and some will never change rods after catching their first catch. The first of the catch is sometimes returned to the water 'for luck'. The cry of the cuckoo, first thing in the morning means no luck in fishing that day.

According to Homer, the Greek princess Helen, the loveliest of mortal women, was seduced and abducted to Troy by Paris, the son of King Priam: to recover her, the Greeks besieged Troy for ten years and took it in the tenth. Though formerly dismissed as fiction, it is now clear that the story of the siege was based on fact

TROY

THE PRINCIPAL sources of our knowledge about Troy are twofold and complementary; the Homeric epics, and archeological investigation in modern times. It is as a result of archeological investigation that there is now general acceptance of the view that there is a historical reality behind Homer; and that the tale of a ten-year siege of the city by an expedition under the command of the Achaean overlord Agamemnon from mainland Greece had a real basis. In addition, as the result of recent researches into the techniques of orally transmitted poetry, there is also wide acceptance of the theory that, no matter what the precise date may have been when the *Iliad* and the *Odyssey* were first written down in their present form, the sagas about the Trojan War and its aftermath could have been commemorated by bards soon after the actual events. These early sagas would then have formed the basis of the epic tradition, which was refined and enlarged by succeeding generations of poets depending upon memory and improvisation. It seems likely that the Trojans and Achaeans not only had the same kind of material culture but were perhaps of similar 'Indo-European' extraction.

The name of Homer is primarily associated with the two great epic poems, the *Iliad* and the *Odyssey*. Each of them is independent but their common background is the Trojan War. The central feature of the *Iliad* is the 'Wrath of Achilles', or the quarrel between Achilles and his overlord, Agamemnon (see ACHILLES). As a result of this quarrel, Achilles refused to continue fighting and the Greeks are pressed back. Then Achilles takes up arms again and kills Hector, the Trojan prince. The *Iliad* ends with Hector's funeral.

The *Odyssey* contains much about the Trojan War too, but it starts at a point in the tenth year after the war ended. There is a council of the Olympian gods, at which it is decided that Odysseus, who has been wandering about as a result of the anger directed against him by the sea god Poseidon, should be brought home to his kingdom of Ithaca. The nucleus is a cunning man's voyage overseas among miracles and monsters, his revenge on his enemies who took advantage of his absence, the faithful wife at home, the young son growing to maturity in the absence of his father. Though the adventures extend over ten years, all but the last are concentrated in a single section. As in the *Iliad*, a large subject is embraced in one view by focusing on a single portion.

The Towers of Ilion

Epic poetry is simply recitation; and Greek epic is written in hexameters, a single verse constantly repeated, saved from monotony by the device of a shifting caesura or 'pause' in the line. One of the features of epic diction is the use of stock phrases, many of them very old. They frequently consist of a half-verse preceding or following the caesura. The formality of these set verses, used repeatedly and without variation whenever the subject requires them, stamps them as archaic. The roots of the *Iliad* and *Odyssey* lie far back in the Mycenean Age, though the poems as a whole appear to have taken shape in Asia Minor during the 10th and 9th centuries BC; and they were still expanding in the 7th.

Homeric archeology is a comparative study. Its object is to interpret the poems in the light of the excavated remains, and the remains in the light of the poems. There are elements in the poems — descriptions of material objects and social usages — which have accordingly been dated to definite periods, early or late, from the 15th to the 7th centuries BC.

From a reading of Homer we gather that Troy was an extensive city, defended by mighty walls and towers and it is called either Troy (*Troie*) or Ilios (later to be Ilion), both conventionally described as 'well-walled', but each having more distinctive epithets. Troy is a 'broad city', 'a great city', 'the city of the Trojans', with 'deep rich soil'; it is the 'city of Priam', having 'lofty gates' and 'fine towers'; and Ilios is 'well-built', 'very windy' but 'a comfortable place to live'; it is also 'steep', 'sheer' and 'frowning', as well as 'holy' and 'sacred'; since it was the city of the Trojans ('those tamers of horses') it not surprisingly has 'fine foals'. It has been conjectured that the city of which Homer gives us these revealing glimpses could have sheltered as many as 50,000 people. A great city indeed must have been required for the indigenous people and the many allies of the Trojans with their horses and war-gear.

There was an open *agora* (place of assembly) in the upper part of the citadel outside the palace of King Priam. This magnificent place 'was fronted with marble colonnades, and in the main building behind there were 50 apartments of polished stone, adjoining each other, where Priam's sons slept with their wives. His daughters had separate quarters, on the other side of the courtyard, where 12 adjoining bedrooms had been built for them, of polished stone and well roofed in. Priam's sons-in-law slept with their loving wives in these.' Nearby were other palatial residences, including those of Hector and Paris, the latter built by Paris himself with the aid of the best workmen to be found in the land of Troy.

There were temples of Apollo and of Athene. The latter seems to have had a seated image of the goddess, for Hector (*Iliad*, book 6) bids his mother Hecuba to take a robe, the loveliest and biggest she can find, the one she most prizes herself, and lay it on the knees of the goddess. She is to promise to sacrifice a dozen yearling heifers, if only Athene will take pity on the town, on the wives and children of the Trojans. Homer then describes how Hecuba went into the palace and ordered her attendant ladies to gather the old women together from all parts of the city. Then she entered her bedchamber, where she stored her embroidered robes, woven by the women of Sidon whom Paris had brought back with him on the voyage on which he had fetched Helen. One of these robes, the largest and most richly adorned, lying at the bottom of the pile like a cluster of brilliant stars, she picked out as the gift for Athene. The old women thronged after her to the shrine in the citadel, and the door was opened to them by Theano, daughter of Kisseus and wife of Antenor, whom the Trojans had

J. R. Freeman

chosen to be priestess. They lifted their hands to Athene, and Theano took the robe and laid it upon the lap of the goddess.

Was this magnificent city, doomed to destruction at the hands of the besieging Greek forces, conjured out of poetic imagination? Did the Trojan War really take place? The search for the site, the work of excavation, the correlation of material objects with Homeric description — all this has led to impressive archeological discoveries in the past hundred years, making impossible that kind of scholarly scepticism which once dismissed the age of the Greek heroes as entirely fictitious. We have now been able to discern a basis of hard fact in many cases, though inconsistency, exaggeration and imaginative adornment must always be taken into account as possibly operative factors.

There is general agreement that no other city in the Troad (the north-west promontory of Asia Minor) except Hissarlik has any good claim to be the site of Troy. It also seems clear that the settlement known as Troy VI was severely damaged by an earthquake at the beginning of the 13th century BC, and was succeeded by the settlement known as Troy VII(a), which had real continuity with Troy VI. Troy VII(a) was destroyed by fire about half a century later, apparently through human agency. It is therefore Troy VII(a) which has strong claims to be regarded as the Homeric Troy.

From the fourth century BC onwards, Greek historians reckoned years in Olympiads, from 776 BC (see GAMES;

Above The Greeks finally entered Troy by what has become the far-famed stratagem of concealing warriors inside a wooden horse: *The Building of the Trojan Horse*, by Tiepolo *Following page* Flemish tapestry of the siege: the tale of Troy was immensely popular in the Middle Ages

Ulysses Remembers Troy

Much have I seen and known; cities of men
And manners, climates, councils, governments,
Myself not least, but honour'd of them all;
And drunk delight of battle with my peers,
Far on the ringing plains of windy Troy . . .

The lights begin to twinkle from the rocks:
The long day wanes: the slow moon climbs: the deep
Moans round with many voices. Come, my friends,
'Tis not too late to seek a newer world.
Push off, and sitting well in order smite
The sounding furrows; for my purpose holds
To sail beyond the sunset, and the baths
Of all the western stars, until I die.
It may be that the gulfs will wash us down:
It may be we shall touch the Happy Isles,
And see the great Achilles, whom we knew.
Tho' much is taken, much abides; and tho'
We are not now that strength which in old days
Moved earth and heaven; that which we are, we are;
One equal temper of heroic hearts,
Made weak by time and fate, but strong in will
To strive, to seek, to find, and not to yield.

Tennyson *Ulysses*

ZEUS), though local events continued to be dated by the names of annual magistrates and calculations for earlier times were based on the traditional genealogies. It is the Parian Marble, a long inscription of the 3rd century BC, which embodies the first attempt to work out a comprehensive chronology. Some time afterwards another effort was made by the Alexandrine scholar Eratosthenes, whose *Chronographicae* in nine books (known to us in fragments) started with the capture of Troy, dated to 1184 BC, as compared with 1209 BC. Other historians and chronographers gave different dates and their conjectures ranged over a period of two centuries. A destruction date for Homeric Troy around the middle of the 13th century BC, would roughly agree with that given by the historian Herodotus.

'The archaeological Troy,' wrote Carl Blegen, 'the Troy that was built by masons, carpenters and labourers, of rough stones or squared building blocks, and crude bricks made with straw, of wooden timbers and beams, of clay and probably thatch for the roofing — that Troy, in its ruined state today, differs greatly, so far as its appearance is concerned, from the glamorous citadel pictured in the epic poems. But — if one is blessed with a little imagination — when one stands on the ancient hill top in the extreme north-western corner of Asia Minor and looks out over the Trojan plain and thinks of some of the many exciting scenes it has witnessed, one cannot escape feeling that this Troy, too, has a powerful touch of enchantment.'

The ruins, called Hissarlik, he continues, occupy the western tip of a low ridge coming from the east and ending somewhat abruptly in steep slopes on the north and west and a more gradual descent toward the south. Some four miles distant to the westward, across the flat plain of the tree-bordered Scamander, and beyond a line of low hills, is the Aegean Sea. On it, to the southwest, floats the island of Tenedos – which was sacked by Achilles – and much farther northward is Imbros, where, the sorrowing Hecuba says, some of her sons who had been captured by Achilles were sold into slavery. Behind Imbros, on a clear day, one sees the twin-peaked height of Samothrace, and often when the weather is at its clearest, one can even make out the summit of Mount Athos. Looking on all this, one remembers the old story told by Aeschylus of the fire-signals that flashed from peak to peak across the sea and land to Mycenae, announcing to Clytemnestra that Troy had been captured.

The Mound of Hissarlik

Heinrich Schliemann, a German business-man turned archeologist, started to excavate the hill of Hissarlik in 1870 and he conducted seven major campaigns before he died in 1890. His work was then continued by his architect and assistant, Wilhelm Dörpfeld, in two large-scale campaigns in 1893 and 1894. His discoveries were published in his *Troja und Ilion* (1902). Then, between 1932 and 1938, seven campaigns of three to four months were arranged by the University of Cincinnati, with the aim of

investigating anew the stratification and other problems. The results of this work under Carl Blegen have now been published in the series called *Troy*.

The evidence of inscriptions found at Hissarlik caused it to be identified more than a century and a half ago as the site of Hellenistic and Roman Ilion. However, some of those who believed in a historical reality behind the Homeric poems considered that the site could be identified in the stronghold known as Bali Dagh, above the gorge through which the Scamander flows from the hills into the lower plain. In 1822 Charles Maclaren collected, in his *Dissertation on the Topography of the Plain of Troy*, all the relevant data from the *Iliad* and compared it with the best modern maps. As a result he revived the idea, prevalent from classical to Roman times, that Hellenistic and later Ilion lay upon the same site as the Homeric Troy. Frank Calvert, some 50 years later, arrived at a similar conclusion and, in 1865, put his theory to the test of actual excavation on a small scale. This produced Roman, Hellenistic and prehistoric pottery and other objects. When Schliemann visited the Troad in 1868, Calvert showed him the site. He agreed that Hissarlik was a more likely possibility for

Scenes from Lydgate's *Siege of Troy*, early 15th century *Left* Agamemnon, the Greek leader, in his tent *Right* King Priam, the ruler of Troy, mourns for Hector, the most redoubtable of the Trojan champions, who was killed by the Greek Achilles

the site of Troy than Bali Dagh, and determined to begin his excavations there.

The Hissarlik mound had a length of about 200 metres maximum and was under 150 metres wide. It went up to about 31 metres above the level of the plain at its northern extremity. As Blegen says: 'For an administrative centre and a capital the situation was admirably suited, both for security and for economic reasons. It lay near enough to the sea to have landing places and perhaps a small port or two within easy reach, and yet far enough away to be reasonably safe from sudden hostile attacks or piratical raids. It also controlled a land route that apparently came up along the western coastal region of Asia Minor to the shortest crossing of the straits from Asia to Europe. From its vantage grounds it could no doubt likewise dominate traffic up and down the straits, and perhaps tolls of some kind were exacted from those who passed.'

In *Troy and the Trojans* Blegen gives the following chronological table:

Troy		
I	3000–2500 BC
II	2500–2200
III	2200–2050
IV	2050–1900
V	1900–1800
VI	1800–1300
VII(a)	1300–1260
VII(b)1	1260–1190
VII(b)2	1190–1100
VIII	700–

He is, however, careful to point out that the

dates given, making no claim to represent more than a general approximation, with a wide margin of error in each direction, essentially follow the conclusions of the Cincinnati Expedition. Though these have been accepted by some scholars, they have been rejected in varying degrees by others. Also, a general chronology, as he says, cannot safely be worked out from the evidence of any one site alone. This must be based on the results obtained at many sites, with due allowance for local accidents and vicissitudes. The large establishments often afford a less trustworthy record than more modest settlements, which sometimes escaped the disturbance caused by grading, changing of levels, and deep digging for the foundations of palaces and great structures. Whole underlying layers could easily be eliminated by ambitious works in later times, as is well illustrated in the central part of the citadel at Troy itself.

Break with the Past

The archeology of Troy, then, dates back for about 5000 years. The first five settlements belong to the Early Bronze Age and are marked by a stratified deposit of some 12 metres in thickness. From the beginning the settlement was a kind of fortified stronghold and the debris of Troy I alone consisted of no less than ten phases of building. The fortification wall in this first phase of the occupation of the site is its most peculiarly impressive feature, some of it found standing to a height of about ten feet 5000 years after its construction. Well-built houses were sometimes coated with plaster and there were woven mats on the floors.

Troy VI of the Middle Bronze Age shows marked and novel differences from what had gone before. Blegen is not alone in thinking that these differences indicate a clear break with the past, and the arrival and establishment of a new people endowed with a heritage of its own. This new people could well have been culturally, perhaps ethnically, closely related to the Mycenaean Greeks.

R. F. WILLETTS

FURTHER READING: M. Forrest ed., *Troy and the Early Greeks* (Cambridge U. Press, 1973); C. W. Blegen and others, *Troy* (Princeton Univ. Press, 1950–58, 4 vols).

TRUMPET

'BEHOLD, I show you a mystery; we shall not all sleep, but we shall all be changed, in a moment, in the twinkling of an eye, at the last trump: for the trumpet shall sound, and the dead shall be raised incorruptible, and we shall be changed' (1 Corinthians, chapter 15). This tremendous passage in St Paul was familiar to generations of Christians through its use in the funeral service, and the picture of the great archangel sounding the last trump and the dead rising from their graves in response was part of the traditional Christian picture of what would happen at the Last Judgement.

In 1 Thessalonians (chapter 4) St Paul again refers to Christ descending from heaven, 'with the archangel's call, and with the sound of the trumpet of God', to judge the living and the dead. And in Matthew (chapter 24) Jesus is quoted as describing what will happen at 'the close of the age': the sun and moon will be darkened, the stars will fall from heaven, and all the people of the earth will see 'the Son of man coming on the clouds of heaven, with power and great glory; and he will send out his angels with a loud trumpet call, and they will gather his elect from the four winds, from one end of heaven to the other.'

This Christian association of the trumpet with the judgement at the end of the world goes back directly to a verse in Isaiah (27.13) which says that in the days to come a great trumpet will be blown and all the scattered people of God will reunite to worship him in Jerusalem. More generally, it goes back to the use of trumpets in Jewish ritual and the Old Testament association of the trumpet with the voice, power and judgement of God.

In many parts of the world the harsh, strident, carrying call of a horn or trumpet has been regarded, on occasion, as the voice of a supernatural being, and the same sound has also been used to attract the attention of supernatural beings. When God descended

The trumpet or horn has a heart-stirring sound, connected with its use in hunting and war, and in salutes to kings and heroes. War horns and trumpets were originally blown to convey signals and to frighten the enemy

John Moss

Giraudon

Left Sacred trumpets, made from ram's horns, and blown by priests, were used at Jericho to create a blast of sound which knocked down the walls: *The Fall of Jericho,* by Jean Fouquet, c 1475 *Right* An angel with a trumpet, from a window in Oxford Cathedral

on Mount Sinai to deliver the Ten Commandments, 'there were thunders and lightnings, and a thick cloud upon the mountain, and a very loud trumpet blast', which made all the people afraid (Exodus, chapters 19, 20). The author of Revelation heard behind him 'a loud voice like a trumpet', and turned to see that the speaker was Christ in majesty (chapter 1). It was the Jewish custom to blow trumpets at all religious feasts, on the first day of each month, and at the daily sacrifice, when the sound of the trumpet was the voice of the people calling to God. The deity himself had instructed Moses to have silver trumpets made, which were to be sounded to remind him of the people's presence and needs (Numbers, chapter 10).

The Feast of Trumpets was held in the autumn, on the first day of the seventh month, which was later termed the New Year but was originally the opening of the yearly period of repentance that reached its peak on the Day of Atonement (see JUDAISM). The day of the Feast of Trumpets was said to be the day on which God judged mankind and allotted rewards and punishments, and some said that the trumpets were sounded to confuse Satan, the prosecutor in the heavenly court. This reinforced the connection between the trumpet and God as Judge, already suggested by the trumpet blast on Sinai.

The rabbis also connected the trumpets of Exodus and Isaiah, and the Feast of Trumpets, with the story of how Abraham obeyed God's orders to sacrifice Isaac, his son (Genesis, chapter 22). He bound Isaac and laid him on the altar but at the last moment his instructions were changed, and instead of Isaac he sacrificed a ram which he found nearby, caught by its horns in a thicket. This ram, it was said, had been specially created by God. It was the ram's left horn which God sounded on Sinai, and it was the right horn which would be blown in the time of the Messiah to summon the strayed sheep of Israel back to Jerusalem. The sacrifice of the ram had occurred on the first

day of the seventh month, and the sounding of ram's horn trumpets on that day had been commanded by God, to remind him of Abraham's obedient binding of Isaac and as a sign that the congregation regarded themselves as bound offerings to God.

The Horn of Heimdall

The use of an animal's horn as a musical instrument, like the Jewish *shofar* of ram's horn, would naturally tend to carry the associations of power, virility and aggression linked with horns (see HORNS). In many societies trumpets have been used to herald the accession of a king, for sounding alarms and for signalling in battle, because the sound carries well and in the hope of frightening the enemy. The fall of Jericho was accomplished by the blast of the ram's horn trumpets, combined with the magic of the number seven (see SEVEN), creating so formidable a battering ram of sound that the walls of the city fell down flat. The trumpets were blown by the priests who escorted the sacred ark of God, and when the ark was brought to Jerusalem by King David seven priests blew trumpets before it (Joshua, chapter 6; 1 Chronicles 15.24).

These priests reappear in the book of Revelation (chapter 8) in the form of the seven angels who stand before God, who are given seven trumpets. They blow them in turn and appalling plagues and horrors strike the world. When the seventh trumpet sounds (chapter 11), voices are heard in heaven proclaiming that the kingdom of the world has become the Kingdom of God.

The association of the trumpet or horn with the end of the world appears again in Norse mythology. Heimdall, the watchman of the gods who never sleeps, lives beside Bifrost, the rainbow bridge, at the point where it reaches the sky. At the first signs of the approaching end, he will blow his great horn Gjallarhorn (ringing horn), whose note is heard through all the worlds (see SCANDINAVIA). There is a rough parallel here with the Christian belief that an archangel, Gabriel or Michael, will wake the dead at the end of time with the blast of the last trump.

In Bali spirits were summoned by blasts on horns or trumpets, which were blown again to drive them away. In some societies a medicine-man talks through a trumpet when he is speaking with the voice of a god or spirit, and the spirits of the dead played trumpets at shows staged by some 19th century mediums. In the Alps the wooden trumpet called the Alphorn, used for calling cattle and signalling over long distances, was believed to protect men and beasts from evil when sounded at dusk. Some ceremonial trumpets are of enormous size, the lengthening of the tube deepening the note. Metal trumpets carried in funeral processions in China are so long that they can only be played when rested on the ground during a pause in the procession, and the Tibetans and Mongols used copper trumpets 16 feet long.

Triton, the Greek merman, who played only a very minor role in mythology, was a favourite subject in art and was frequently shown blowing a conch shell. Virgil's *Aeneid* (book 6) tells the story of how Misenus, the Trojan trumpeter, who excelled all others in his skill at 'stirring hearts with his trumpet of bronze and kindling the blaze of battle with his music', rashly challenged the gods to outdo him. The jealous Triton trapped him among rocks at the sea's edge and drowned him.

The horn or trumpet has indeed a heart-stirring sound, connected with its use in hunting and war, and in salutes to kings and heroes. In Bunyan's *Pilgrim's Progress* the pilgrims come to the river of death, the last barrier that separates them from the Celestial City, and Mr Valiant-for-truth is summoned to cross: 'So he passed over, and all the trumpets sounded for him on the other side.'

TURIN SHROUD

THE TURIN SHROUD is a piece of linen, 13½ feet (4 m) long by 3½ feet (1 m) wide, supposed by many people to be the actual shroud used to wrap the body of Christ. It bears a faint, brownish image of the front and back of a bearded, male human figure, 'hinged' at the head, and superimposed are darker stains, said to be blood, found on the left hand side, wrists, feet and head.

Despite a battery of the most sophisticated tests, and the combined resources of modern technological methods, the shroud has stubbornly refused to yield up its mys-

teries. The exact nature of the image – paint? dye? sweat and embalming fluids? – remains inexplicable except to those who regard it as the result of supernatural radiation or burning produced at the moment of resurrection; and all the efforts of sceptics have failed to show that the shroud is a fake. Furthermore, the shroud has a habit of surprising investigators with still deeper mysteries: for instance, it was not until 1898, when the first photographs were taken of it, that the image was discovered to be a perfect photographic negative. The negative of a photograph of the shroud image shows up the features and body far more clearly – the original marks being rather blurred and hard to interpret. As yet no one has sug-

gested how a mediaeval forger could have achieved this effect, though some bizarre attempts at reconstruction have been made.

The details of the 'bloodstains' on the shroud correspond exactly with the details of Christ's crucifixion as we now know them. They indicate that the body was scourged, crowned or capped with thorns, crucified, by nails through the wrists and feet, and pierced in the side. The apparent scourge marks, covering the entire body in parallel pairs, correspond to what we know of Roman scourges or *flagrae*, two-thonged whips tipped with pieces of lead or bone. The wrist wounds are in the correct position for crucifixion, since a body could not be supported by nails through the hands, as the flesh would tear; this recent discovery is of course contrary to the popular artistic image of the crucified Christ, with the nails through the hands – another point making the forgery theory unlikely. Even the way the blood has run is correct. Blood from the wrist wounds has run up the arms towards the elbows, as it would if the arms were in a crucified position; and it has run at two slightly different angles, consistent with modern knowledge of how crucifixion tortured the victim – he alternately raised himself on his pierced feet and hung from the wrist nails. Many other correspondences have been found by medical experts.

. The earliest certain historical reference is in 1389, when we hear of the shroud being exhibited for money in France by a knight named Geoffrey de Charny. There are possible references to it earlier than this, and Ian Wilson in his *The Turin Shroud* has reconstructed a very plausible history right back to its possible creation, suggesting that a famous image of Christ's face known as the Mandylion was in fact the face section of the shroud. He supports this with a wealth of historical and art-historical evidence, but it remains unproven. We do know that in 1453 the shroud was given or sold by the de Charnys to Louis, Duke of Savoy, and it has remained in that family ever since. The present Duke of Savoy, ex-King Umberto of Italy, owns the shroud, which is kept at Turin Cathedral. In 1532 the shroud was damaged by fire; holes were burnt in it by melted silver from its case, and patched by

nuns two years later.

In 1973 pollen grains from the shroud were analyzed, and found to contain some examples from plants found in Palestine. Middle-Eastern cotton plants had been used to make the linen. In 1974 pictures of the shroud were scanned with a VP-8 image analyzer by two American scientists, and the three-dimensional model they produced led to the launching of the Shroud of Turin Research Project in 1977. In 1978 36 scientists from various disciplines met to examine the shroud with the most sophisticated equipment at their disposal.

The results of this arsenal of tests have not yet been published fully, but the major questions still remain unanswered. Evidence on the 'bloodstains' showed that they could be, and probably were, blood. The image seems not to be pigment of any kind, except that a small amount of iron oxide was found. One expert, Dr Walter McCrone, concluded from this that the image must be an artist's forgery, probably of the 14th century; but most of the investigators agreed that the image is not painted on or the result of a chemical reaction. One expert found that it 'may have been caused by a violent burst of radiant heat'. But what natural process could have produced this result?

The 1978 tests did not include dating by the carbon-14 method, as this would have meant destroying part of the shroud. New methods would use only small samples and could be accurate within 150 years, but this test has not yet been authorised. Even if the

Above The Turin Shroud

shroud was shown to be of the right date, this would not prove that it was Christ's shroud; and if it was shown to be of a later date, science still has to explain what formed the image. This paradoxical object, with its ability to reveal new puzzles as fast as new tests are devised, remains a baffling challenge to sceptics.

TWELVE

IN THE CLOSING chapters of the book of Revelation, the holy city, new Jerusalem, is seen coming down out of heaven from God, 'its radiance like a most rare jewel, like a jasper, clear as crystal.' One of the striking things about this vision of perfection and loveliness is the repeated use of the number 12. The city's wall has 12 gates, at which 12 angels stand and on which are inscribed the names of the 12 tribes of Israel. The wall has 12 foundation-stones, on which are written the names of the 12 apostles and which are adorned with 12 jewels. Within the city stands the tree of life with its 12 kinds of fruit, yielding its fruit each month. The city's dimensions are stated in terms of 12. It is a cube, 12,000 stadia long, broad and high, and its wall stands 144 cubits high. But the stadia and cubits are not earthly measurements; the cube means perfection, and 12 is used all through this passage as a number of completeness.

The year is made of 12 months, at the end of which the sun and the life of Nature return to their starting point, as it were, to run their course through the seasons again, and so 12 is the number of an entire cycle or a whole set. It is related to 7, another number of completeness, because both are made of 3 and 4, multiplied or added, and both are regarded by the numerologically minded as linked with the

essential underlying structure of the universe. There are the 7 planets of antiquity, 7 days of the week, 7 colours, 7 notes of the musical scale, and the 12 months, 12 zodiac signs, 12 hours of the day. Some Christian writers said that Jesus chose 12 disciples to make known the Trinity to the four corners of the world, and to show that he is the spiritual day or the perfect year, with the apostles as the hours or months (see also SEVEN; THREE).

The earliest code of Roman laws was written on 12 tablets.

In Exodus (chapter 28) there are instructions for making the vestments of the high priest, including the mysterious 'breastpiece of judgement' on which were to be set four rows of precious stones, three in each row: sardius (or cornelian), topaz, carbuncle; emerald, sapphire, diamond; jacinth, agate, amethyst; beryl, onyx, jasper. The 12 stones were to be engraved with the names of the 12 tribes. 'So Aaron shall bear the names of the sons of Israel in the breastpiece of judgement upon his heart, when he goes into the holy place, to bring them to continual remembrance before the Lord.' Much later, in the 1st century AD, the philosopher Philo Judaeus thought that the 12 jewels stood for the signs of the zodiac, and the historian Josephus said that the high priest's robes symbolized the entire universe, with the jewels representing either the months or the zodiac signs.

In Numbers (chapter 2) there are instructions for the order of march and the pitching of camp when the Israelites are travelling

Twelve is the number of a complete cycle or set of things, as in the 12 months of the year, the 12 signs of the zodiac; another example is the 12 days of Christmas ending on Twelfth Night, which inspired carols and songs in which the 12 days are connected with ideas or creatures or objects. The illustrations to 'The Twelve Days of Christmas' on the following pages are by 'Herry', published by Basil Blackwell, Oxford, 1926

through the wilderness towards the Promised Land. The camp is to be laid out in a square, like the holy city of Revelation later, with three tribes on each side and the Levites in the middle. When Elijah was engaged in his contest against the priests of Baal, he built his altar of 12 stones, to stand for the 12 tribes (1 Kings, chapter 18).

The gospels do not explain why Jesus chose 12 apostles, rather than some other number, but he is quoted as telling them that 'in the new world' they would sit on 12 thrones to judge the 12 tribes of Israel (Matthew 19.28). They are listed in St Luke (chapter 6) as Simon Peter, Andrew, James and John, Philip, Bartholomew, Matthew, Thomas, another James, Simon the Zealot, Judas the son of James, and Judas Iscariot.

In the book of Revelation (chapter 7) an angel appears and 'seals' the servants of God, making God's mark on the foreheads of 12,000 from each of the 12 tribes, 144,000 in all, who are later (chapter 14) seen standing on Mount Zion with the Lamb and singing a new song before the throne of God. Here the 12 tribes presumably stand

Three French Hens

Four Calling Birds

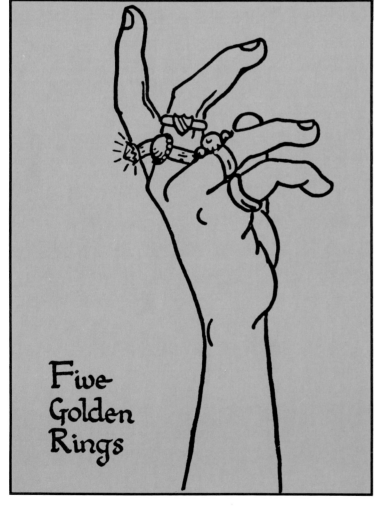

Five Golden Rings

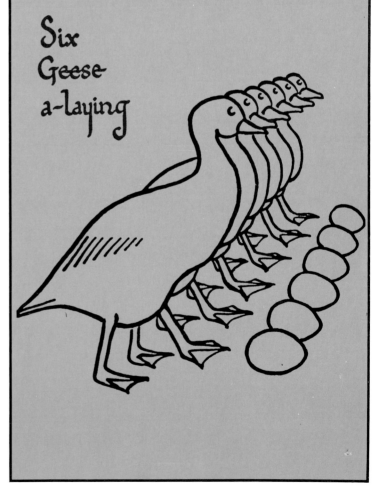

Six Geese a-laying

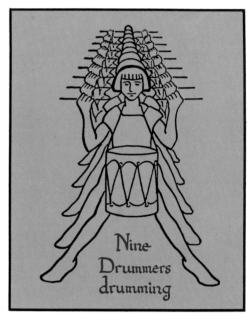

for the whole body of God's people and the 144,000 for the Christian martyrs slaughtered in the persecutions, with the counting in terms of 12 again a mark of completeness. The list of tribes in chapter 7 omits the tribe of Dan, apparently because the author of Revelation, following up Jewish traditions, expected the Antichrist to emerge from their ranks.

A New Dial

The 12 stars in the crown of 'the woman clothed with the sun' (chapter 12) are generally agreed to be the signs of the zodiac, but whether there is any astrological significance in the repeated use of 12 in the vision of the holy city is doubtful. The description of the city draws on the account of the Israelite camp in the wilderness and on the city of Ezekiel's vision, which also had 12 gates for the 12 tribes (Ezekiel, chapter 48). The 12 jewels which adorn the foundation stones are evidently related to the stones on the high priest's breastpiece, but they are given in a different order and they are now connected with the 12 apostles instead of the 12 tribes, presumably as a sign that the 'new Israel' of Christianity has

replaced the old. The order of the jewels is a puzzle and, if they are related to the zodiac signs at all, they seem to be listed in the reverse order.

A still surviving example of a cycle of 12 is the 12 days of Christmas, ending on Twelfth Night (the evening of 5 January) which used to be an occasion of feasting and revel (see BEAN; CHRISTMAS). A parallel was seen between the 12 days of Christmas and the 12 months of the ensuing year, hence the old belief that it is unlucky to take down the Christmas decorations before Twelfth Night, because to shorten the festive season is to curtail the prosperity of the months ahead and possibly the life of a member of the family, who may die before the year is out. This has in turn created the comparatively new superstition that it is unlucky to leave the Christmas decorations in place after Twelfth Night, which is to go beyond the proper limits, and so is dangerous.

The Christmas season also inspired carols and songs in which the 12 days are connected with ideas or creatures or objects, as in 'The Twelve Days of Christmas', in which the days are linked with a partridge in a pear tree, two turtle-doves, three French

hens, four calling birds, five gold rings, six geese a-laying, seven swans a-swimming, eight maids a-milking, nine ladies dancing, ten lords a-leaping, 11 pipers piping and 12 drummers drumming. The 12 hours on the clockface could similarly inspire a counting song of this sort, such as 'A New Dial', which begins (in the version in *The Oxford Book of Carols*): 'What are they that are but one? One God, one Baptism, and one Faith, one Truth there is, the scripture saith.' It continues with two Testaments (the Old and the New), the three persons of the Trinity, four evangelists, the five senses, the six working days of the week, the seven liberal arts, the eight beatitudes (of the Sermon on the Mount), the nine Muses, the ten Commandments, the 11,000 Virgins of Cologne (legendary martyrs massacred by the Huns), and finishes triumphantly with the 12 apostles and 12 articles of the Apostles' Creed. Here again, in crude form, is the attempt to picture the structure of the universe as arranged in terms of 12.

FURTHER READING: G. B. Caird, *The Revelation of St John The Divine* (Black, 1966).

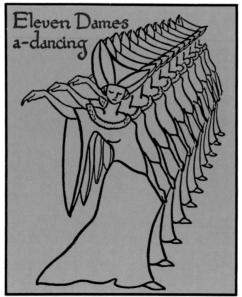

'If telepathic communication is to be found anywhere, it is much more likely to exist between identical twins than between ordinary persons': that there is something uncanny about twins has long been recognized, and in many societies the birth of twins has been greeted with fear — fear of both the children and their mother

TWINS

THE PHENOMENON of twins appears always to have exercised a remarkable fascination. Statistically it is not uncommon, and yet it is sufficiently unusual to call for comment and to arouse interest. As we follow the phenomenon back into the labyrinths of religion, mythology and folklore, however, we find other aspects besides the innocent curiosity of the envious bystander. There is also the aspect of fear — fear of both the children and their mother — which demanded special precautions, or worse, on birth, and continued respect and reverence afterwards. In addition, many peoples have worshipped at least one pair of twin gods, either brothers or brother and sister, reflecting some of the concerns and taboos which have surrounded human twins. Twins have been useful material for many novelists and scientific investigators, not least because of the extraordinary affinity which has been seen to exist between them. In short, twinship shows a type of human relationship consisting not only in similarity of appearance

The reason for the psychic affinity that sometimes exists between twins still eludes investigators. This is reflected in Tweedledum and Tweedledee, the best-known twins in literature; when Alice meets them, only the words 'dum' and 'dee' are visible; 'Tweedle', the mysterious element they have in common, is hidden from her. Illustration to *Through the Looking-Glass*, by Sir John Tenniel

but in something more mysterious and intangible; it is this intangible quality which has left such fascinating traces in all the frontier sciences.

It is common knowledge today that twins are of two kinds: identical twins, of the same sex, having developed from one fertilized egg (monozygotic twins); and fraternal twins, who may or may not be of the same sex, but who have developed from two independently-fertilized eggs (dizygotic twins). In pre-literate societies, however, this important distinction is as a rule not known, or at least known only by its effect; and in comparison with the primary belief that normal human births take place strictly one at a time, the birth of two children more or less simultaneously from the same mother is inevitably regarded as a special manifestation of supernatural power. (This of course applies even more strongly to triplets and other 'supertwins'.)

In the so-called primitive and archaic cultures, which have been dominated by a thoroughgoing belief in the reality and influence of a supernatural order alongside and within the natural, the act of giving birth has always been hedged about with taboos, since there the supernaturals are active (see BIRTH; FERTILITY). But since humans normally have only one child at a time, the birth of twins seems always to have been regarded as a temporary disturbance of the balance between Nature and the supernatural, and therefore 'uncanny'. Man's reactions to such manifestations have varied more or less as his reactions to any holy or sacred manifestation have varied – between horror, fear, fascination and devotion. As a rule, though, definite measures have had to be taken in order to restore the balance. Sometimes the offending infants have been put to death, together with their mother; sometimes one child has been destroyed, one saved; sometimes all three have been reverenced as repositories of divine power. Always rituals were resorted to in order to appease the unusually active spirits.

'Betrothed' in the Womb

Since sacredness was the peculiar property of the spirit world, it could provoke one of two reactions in primitive societies. One was to destroy whatever was so affected and thus return it to the spirits, on the principle of its being too dangerous to tolerate. The other was to accord the manifestation special honours, since it was too dangerous not to tolerate. It is recorded that in the Niger delta area at the turn of the century a woman who had given birth to twins was simply too dangerous to touch; she was allowed neither to touch anything belonging to ordinary people nor even to drink from the same spring. As a result both she and her twins might die from hunger and exposure, not because of callousness, but from fear. It is also reported that to say to a woman, 'May you become the mother of twins!' was tantamount to a curse. It seems to have been commonly held that since a man could normally father only one child at a time, the second twin was the result either of the infidelity of the mother, or of the direct intervention of the spirits.

In Togoland, if the twins were of different sexes, the boy was kept, the girl disposed of; if both were of the same sex, only the stronger was kept. In such cases, the surviving child might be given a carved piece of wood, said to represent the deceased twin; this may have been to prevent the survivor from pining for the deceased, but may also have served the

Mansell Collection

Castor and Polydeuces, the Dioscuri or 'heavenly twins', returning to their parents' home; scene from a Greek amphora, c540 BC. Best known for their protection of travellers, the Dioscuri are representative of the many twin deities, particularly pairs of brothers, who occur in Indo-European culture and who are regarded as helpers of mankind in a special sense. A body of mythological material concerning the classical 'heavenly twins' was assimilated to Christian themes and resulted in the legend that the Apostle Thomas, called Didymus, 'the twin', in the New Testament, was the twin of Jesus Christ; although they were outwardly alike, Jesus was divine and Thomas was human

practical purpose of giving the ghost of the child who had died somewhere to return to, other than to the living body of the survivor. One Borneo tribe gave the need to preserve the life of one twin as a motive for killing the other. In a dangerous world, twins, by reason of the bond of sympathy between them, were subject to a double share of danger and misfortune, since each was liable to all the ills which might befall the other.

To some extent, this attitude survives today. According to Professor E. E. Evans-Pritchard, twins are still regarded as one single social personality (although not as one individual) among the Nuer. In practice this means that on certain important ritual occasions they must act together. When the senior twin marries, for instance, the junior has an important role to play in the marriage ceremonies; female twins should be married on the same day. When one twin dies, no mortuary ceremonies take place, since it is not possible for the one symbolically to enter into the future life without the other. Among the Lele, according to Mary Douglas, the parents of twins are believed to have been especially honoured by the spirits (the 'positive pole' of sacredness); they are treated as diviners, and are exempted from the normal rituals which are carried out by those who wish to obtain magical powers. A woman who has borne twins does not suffer from the ritual disabilities which normally affect women; she is allowed to attend conferences on 'twin magic' on the same footing as men. As a rule, though, the parents of twins have to be secluded in a special hut for almost a month, until the proper customs have been carried out.

In parts of Nigeria, women who had given birth to twins were sent to live in 'twin towns', where they were maintained by their husbands, but were in effect living in a state of divorce. A variant was in some cases provided by the 'twin-market', where women who had already had twins offered goods for sale, and where something was bought on behalf of the new-born (four-month-old) infants. This again is a means of restoring the disturbed balance of Nature, and of receiving mother and children back into the normal fellowship of the tribe. A woman who died in childbirth was always regarded as dangerous, and it goes without saying that one who died in the course of giving birth to twins was thought to be doubly so.

It is interesting that there seems to have been a close analogy between the second of a pair of twins and the placenta of an ordinary child, which was sometimes called 'the twin'. In either case, the fate of the one (whether child or afterbirth) was closely bound up with that of the other. In parts of India, the connection of boy and girl in the womb seems to have been taken almost as a form of pre-natal incest, while it is on record that in Bali, twins of different sexes were called 'betrothed'.

The Twin Brother of Jesus

There are two kinds of mythological twins: brother and sister, and two brothers. Many myths in which sun and moon are brother and sister, condemned by some primeval transgression, possibly incest, to pursue each other across the heavens, fall into the first category. However, the twin motif is less marked in these stories than in the ancient Indian myth of the first human pair, Yama and Yami. In a hymn of the *Rig-Veda* the first man, Yama, is wooed by his sister, Yami, and in later tradition the two become rulers of the underworld (though in practice Yami fades away almost entirely). The similarity of the names is significant; in many pairs of mythological twins, the closeness of the bonds that bind them together is marked by the practically identical names that they bear.

Far more mythological material has gathered around pairs of brothers than around twins who are brother and sister. In some cases it may well be that the stories have a basis in historical fact. For example there are the two pairs of Old Testament twins, Esau and Jacob (Genesis, chapter 25), and Perez and Zerah (Genesis, chapter 38), the twin sons of Tamar. In the latter case, the mother is said to have conceived twins as a result of harlotry, a belief that has primitive roots. The practice of binding a thread on the first of the infants to emerge from the womb, presumably in order to avoid later complications when it came to determining questions of precedence, is mentioned in the second story.

A curious example, also from the Judaeo-Christian tradition, concerns the Apostle Thomas, who is called Didymus, 'the twin', in the New Testament, and who is traditionally regarded as the first missionary to India. According to a late legend, Thomas was the twin of Jesus Christ, born to Mary shortly after Jesus. The three Magi, when they brought their gifts to the infant Jesus, asked for his swaddling-band as a memento, but were given that of Thomas instead. Jesus and Thomas grew up together, making ploughs and yokes in their father's carpentry shop; the two were outwardly alike, but in reality Jesus was divine, Thomas human. What has happened here is that mythological material concerning the classical 'heavenly twins', the Dioscuri (see below), has become assimilated to Christian themes.

Another interesting example from the borders of the Christian tradition concerns Mani, the founder of Manicheism, who probably lived in the 3rd century AD. Mani claimed to have a 'twin self' in the heavens, who came down and united with him, bringing revelations from the deity. This 'twin' was in fact none other than the Holy Spirit (see GNOSTICISM; MANICHEANS).

However, the best known examples of twin deities come from the wide area of Indo-European culture, from India in the east to Scandinavia in the north. Although the details vary considerably, the outlines are constant: the worship of two brothers who are in a very special sense the helpers of mankind. They are connected in a general way with fertility, and with human birth (not surprisingly, in view of the primitive view of twin births); but in addition they have special links with horses and chariots and harnesses, they make yokes for oxen, and they are believed to be connected with the craft of stonemasonry and the building of cities. They also protect travellers, particularly those who travel by water. These details are not easily reconcilable with one another, and it is impossible even to speculate on the origins of such a wide variety of belief concerning one mode of deity; nevertheless all these points recur frequently.

In Indian tradition, the twin deities are called the Asvins, who are charioteers, rainmakers, and givers of fertility to humans and to the earth. They are also called

Mythological twin brothers are often associated with horses, chariots and harnesses, and with stonemasonry and the building of cities; Romulus and Remus, the legendary founders of Rome, traced the boundaries of the future city with a bull and heifer, symbols of fertility, yoked together: statue of the twins being suckled by a wolf
Mansell Collection

natasya, 'healers', but the fertility aspect is the most prominent; they are invoked in the Hindu marriage ritual, and in the *Rig-Veda* it is said of them: 'You place the child in a woman's womb, you place the seed in all beings, that it may grow.'

In the Greek tradition, the heavenly twins were called the Dioskouroi, 'sons of Zeus'. Together with their sister Helen they were born of Zeus and Leda – though in some versions there is an echo of the idea of divided paternity in the tradition that only one, Polydeuces, was fathered by Zeus; the other, Castor, was the son of Tyndareus, King of Sparta. Their worship early passed to Rome, where they received the better-known names of Castor and Pollux. They still retained a wide range of functions, being connected with the sky, thunder and storms, as well as guarding hospitality and oaths. It was, however, for their role in the protection of travellers that they were best known. A minor illustration of this is found in the Acts of the Apostles (28.11) where Luke and Paul 'set sail in a ship which had wintered in the island (Malta), a ship of Alexandria, with the Twin Brothers as figurehead'. This ship was clearly believed to be under the special protection of the patrons of navigation.

Incidentally, for seamen to catch sight of the constellation of Gemini (the heavenly prototype of Castor and Pollux, and probably of all other Indo-European twin gods as well) in a bad storm, was a sign of the greatest good fortune. The following lines by Macaulay refer to a ball of fire which is sometimes seen

playing round ships' masts in a storm, and which was once identified with the visible presence of Castor and Pollux:

Safe comes the ship to harbour
Through billows and through gales,
If once the Great Twin Brethren
Sit shining on her sails.

Another name for this electrical phenomenon is 'St Elmo's Fire'.

A similar combination of mythological motifs is found in the story of Romulus and Remus (see FOUNDING OF ROME). They were builders; one, Romulus, was divine; and the bounds of the future city were traced out by a bull and a heifer, both symbols of fertility, yoked together. Another building myth ascribes the founding of Thebes to

Amphion and Zethus. Amphion was immortal, Zethus mortal, and both were tamers and riders of horses.

Mention has been made of the link between the Dioscuri and the constellation Gemini. There is no evidence that human twins were believed to be under the special influences of this sign of the zodiac, but twins

In societies that regarded normal twins as uncanny, a temporary disturbance of the balance between Nature and the supernatural, the birth of twins who were joined together physically must have been a fearsome event; in more sophisticated societies, Siamese twins were often exhibited as freaks. 'Anna Belle Grey', from *Dear Dead Days: A Family Album*, edited by Charles Addams

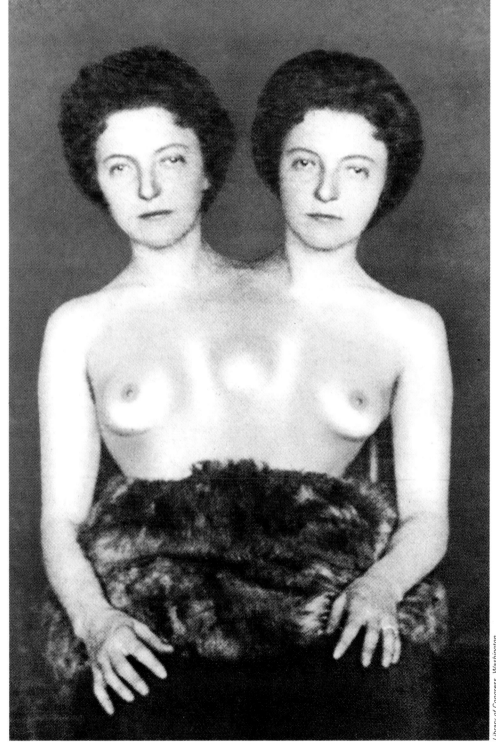

Library of Congress, Washington

would clearly have identical, or virtually identical, astrological horoscopes. The convinced believer in astrology finds no difficulty in explaining certain aspects of the psychical affinities that have been observed in twins in terms of identical planetary influences at every stage. In fact, twins, even when they are identical, are not always identical in behaviour or temperament; but some startling facts have been reported.

In 1962, for instance, two 32-year-old identical twin sisters died in different wards of an American hospital within moments of each other, having been admitted with identical schizophrenic symptoms, and having deteriorated in precisely the same way. There are, of course, many reports of twins who have known when their 'other half' was ill, in danger or in trouble. Like the twins Esteban and Manuel in Thornton Wilder's novel *The Bridge of San Luis Rey*: '. . . there existed a need of one another so terrible that it produced miracles as naturally as the charged air of a sultry day produces lightning. The brothers were scarcely conscious of it themselves, but telepathy was a common occurrence in their lives, and when one returned home the other was always aware of it when his brother was still several streets away.' Twins in school have been known to submit examination papers so nearly identical as to suggest to the authorities that there had been collusion, and there have been many other coincidences of thought and action.

Recent research has attempted to demonstrate and chart twin telepathy; J. B. Rhine, one of the foremost authorities in this field, has tested many pairs of twins for evidence of telepathic communication, and although he has not achieved spectacular results, he has recorded that 'cases have been reported to us from time to time of what would appear to be exceptional telepathic rapport between identical twins'. Patterns of the rhythmic electrical changes in the brains of identical twins are often remarkably similar, and although some scientists are disposed to explain away similarities of thought and behaviour as resulting from identical environmental influence, this explanation is forced. The Danish scientist Dr N. Jule-Nielsen has studied identical twins brought up for the most part in different environments, and has shown how similar their aptitudes and personalities are. Since 1953 a Roman scientist, Professor Luigi Gedda of the Gregor Mendel Institute has studied well over 15,000 pairs of twins. He put forward a 'clock-of-life' theory to explain the amazing coincidences in twins' lives. He describes these in his book *Chroagenetics* (1978), citing many cases of telepathy.

There are therefore solid reasons why twins should have exercised a perennial fascination, and why so many aspects of the phenomenon should have been recorded and commented upon. Perhaps the genetics of twinship are more thoroughly known now than at any time in the past; but the psychology of twinship is still very largely a closed, or at all events an unread book.

We may perhaps end with an allegory. The best-known twins in literature are

Ibedji from western Nigeria: because they believe that the affinity that exists between twins while they are alive continues after the death of one twin, the Yoruba make an effigy of the child who has died. The survivor is taught to tend and care for the statue

Lewis Carroll's Tweedledum and Tweedledee (whom no one now remembers to have been originally the 18th century musicians Handel and Bononcini, whose music the critics professed not to be able to tell apart). In *Through the Looking-Glass* they are introduced thus: 'They were standing under a tree, each with an arm round the other's neck, and Alice knew which was which in a moment, because one of them had 'DUM' embroidered on his collar, and the other 'DEE'. "I suppose they've each got 'TWEEDLE' round at the back of the collar," she said to herself.' If Alice is the eternal investigator, although she may be able to tell a certain amount about the twins in front of her, the writing on the back of their collars — the element which they genuinely have in common — still eludes her. Some day, though, she may find her way round to the back.

ERIC J. SHARPE

FURTHER READING: J. Rendel Harris, *The Cult of the Heavenly Twins* (Cambridge Univ. Press, 1906); Luigi Gedda, *Twins in History and Science* (C. C. Thomas, 1961); Peter Watson, *Twins* (Viking Press, 1982).

John Moss

TWO

TRADITIONALLY, 2 is the number of evil and the number of woman, long regarded in male-dominated societies as an essentially evil creature (see WOMAN). From the Pythagoreans onwards, 2 has carried a connotation of evil, but modern numerologists are reluctant to classify any number as inherently vicious and in their picture of 2's characteristics this old link is largely submerged. But the link with woman has remained, and in modern numerology 2 is regarded as the number of femininity and as the opposite of 1 (see ONE). Two is passive where 1 is active, negative where 1 is positive, weak where 1 is strong and, as a result of the sexual roles of male and female, receptive where 1 is thrusting.

Someone whose name adds to 2 (see ALPHABET) will be described as a quiet, unassuming, gentle person. He is tactful and diplomatic, a follower rather than a leader, and if he gets his own way at all, it is by persuasion and co-operation instead of by the forceful methods of 1. Unambitious and disliking the limelight, he is content to stay in the background, and since he is obedient, neat, modest, helpful and good at keeping a secret, he makes an admirable subordinate. Good-natured, sympathetic and understanding, he gets on well with people but is likely to be rather shy and timid. He likes detail and settled routine and is worried by new departures, bold initiatives, sudden changes of plan. He probably undervalues himself and because he loves peace and quiet, and fears argument and quarrels, he is always in danger of being trampled on by other people. He is likely to be deeply uncertain of himself, insecure and restless, and he will find it hard to make his mind up and almost impossible not to change it again.

People whose number is 2 have considerable charm and, being of a romantic disposition, they fall in love easily and are readily moved to tears. Though frequently worried and upset themselves, they are good at comforting and soothing other people and binding up their physical or psychological wounds (an obvious reference to woman's role as nurse). They are probably fussy and nervous, and inclined to take up fads, in religion or politics or food. They are intuitive rather than intellectual, and their inclination is always for reconciliation and compromise. Patient and frugal, they dislike risks and are uneasy with responsibility, and they often seem to lack any clear purpose in life. Easy-going, soft, indulgent, they are generally not as physically strong as those whose numbers are 1 or 3, and they are not such strong characters. Deep in their personalities is a strain of malice, cruelty and deceit, and at their worst they can be liars and mischief-makers, spineless and sulky, pessimistic and cowardly.

Two By Two

All this is a picture of woman, not as housewife and mother and partner of man, which is more the preserve of 6 (see SIX), but as the opposite and subordinate of man. The characteristics apply equally to a day or year which adds to 2, which numerologists expect to be a time of peace and quiet, of gentle progress by way of harmonious co-operation with others, of negotiation and reconciliation. As one numerologist puts it, the seed sown in a 1-year is quietly growing in the 2-year. Another says that in a 2-year you should pull in your oars, sit on the sidelines, reap what you sowed in the year before. And for businessmen, since 2 is the number of receptivity, a 2-day ought to be a good time to collect accounts receivable.

The Twin Pillars

Hiram of Tyre makes the bronze pillars for the Temple at Jerusalem:

He cast two pillars of bronze . . . He also made two capitals of molten bronze to set upon the tops of the pillars . . . Then he made two nets of chequer work with wreaths of chain work for the capitals upon the tops of the pillars; a net for the one capital, and a net for the other capital. Likewise he made pomegranates; in two rows round about the network, to cover the capital that was upon the top of the pillar; and he did the same with the other capital . . . He set up the pillars at the vestibule of the temple; he set up the pillar on the south and called its name Jachin; and he set up the pillar on the north and called its name Boaz. And upon the tops of the pillars was lily-work. Thus the work of the pillars was finished.

1 Kings, chapter 7

Two is the number of woman and wickedness because it is the first of the even numbers, which are evil and female (see NUMEROLOGY). It is evil because it is the first number to break away from the wholeness of 1. It sets up a pair of opposites, so creating antagonism and division, and it represents the second and unfavourable term in all the pairs of opposites seen in the structure of things – good and evil, one and many, male and female, light and darkness, active and passive, right and left, infinite and finite, and the rest. It is connected with lifeless, passive matter, because in it the One begins the process of making itself manifest in the world by splitting itself into two segments, the spiritual and the material.

The 'not-One' is fundamentally unstable. It may be an old lovers' saying that two's company and three's none, but in numerological theory a pair of opposites alone is readily divided and the number 3 has to be brought in to link them together in harmony and stability (see THREE). This accounts for 2's lack of clear purpose, lack of physical and psychological strength, uncertainty, restlessness and tendency to be easily upset.

Christian numerologists found confirmatory evidence of 2's evil and unstable nature in the Bible. The first chapter of Genesis does not say that 'God saw that it was good' after the work of the second day of creation, though it does say it about the creations of the other days. And in the story of the Flood, God told Noah to take with him in the ark seven pairs of all the clean animals but only one pair of the unclean ones (Genesis, chapter 7). Commenting on this, St Augustine said that the clean animals went into the ark in sevens and the unclean in twos 'as good and bad take part in the sacraments of the Church', and that the bad were in twos 'as being easily divided, from their tendency to schism'. In the 12th century Hugh of St Victor said that because 2 is the first number to recede from unity, it represents sin, which deviates from original good, and is the mark of things which are transitory and corruptible.

The Cloven Hoof
As the evil number which sets up an opposite to 1, 2 naturally belongs to the Devil, the principle of evil and the arch-opponent of God. The reversed pentagram, with two points upwards, is a symbol of evil and the Devil (see PENTAGRAM). The cloven hoof is a mark of the Devil and so is the forked tongue of the serpent. The Devil's fondness for horns may have something to do with his link with 2, and he was said to have two faces, one in the conventional position and one at his backside. Pierre de Lancre, a notorious French witch-hunter of the 17th century, said that the Devil appeared in the form of a goat with the face of a black man under his tail, and it was this face

The first of the even numbers, which are evil and female, two is traditionally the number of woman and the Devil, and the Devil's fondness for horns may have something to do with his link with the number: horned demon tempting a woman, from Chartres Cathedral

C. M. Dixon

which his worshippers kissed in homage. The fact that the Roman god Janus was represented with two faces (see JANUS) has given him a certain sinister air which he did not originally possess.

This link with the Devil accounts for the streak of malice and cruelty which numerologists attribute to 2, and the characteristics of telling lies and making mischief come from the Prince of Darkness. The sense of 2 as evil and deceitful survives in several common expressions. To double-cross an ally is to cheat or betray him, to be two-faced is to be insincere, to be in two minds is to be indecisive, to speak with forked tongue is to deceive, double dealing is trickery. Your 'double' is a shadowy counterpart of yourself, a second self, which usually has sinister associations, and twins have been widely regarded as uncanny and sometimes as evil (see DOUBLE; TWINS).

Of course, not all connotations of two and double are evil by any means. The members of the three highest Hindu castes are called 'twice-born', approvingly, because their initiation involves a second and spiritual birth (see CASTE). Janus had two faces because he was the god of entrances and passages, which run in two directions. Entrances consist, at a minimum, of two uprights and a space between them, and may mark the point of transition from one spiritual condition to another (see THRESHOLD). Solomon erected two massive pillars of bronze, named Jachin and Boaz, in front of the Temple at Jerusalem (1 Kings, chapter 7). They stood 27 feet high and were 18 feet round, with elaborate capitals on top. Beyond them was the vestibule of the Temple, beyond that the main hall, and beyond that again the Holy of Holies itself.

The names of the pillars are used as passwords in Masonic initiation ceremonies. Occultists tend to interpret them as showing the opposites in balance, with the space between them as the entrance to the divine, to eternity, to ultimate truth, to the One. The connection with woman reappears again, since the two pillars and the entrance can be taken as a female sexual symbol. In some Tarot packs the trump numbered 2, the Female Pope or High Priestess, shows a woman enthroned between two pillars, one black and one white for the opposites. Between the pillars is a veil, and the card is a symbol of the gateway to heaven.

Tyr
Scandinavian sky god, worshipped as Tiw in Anglo-Saxon England; his early Germanic name was probably Tiwaz, related to Greek Zeus and Roman Jupiter; he had only one hand, the other having been bitten off by the Fenris wolf; he gave his name to Tuesday, but had declined in importance by the Viking Age.
See GERMANIC MYTHOLOGY.

Umbilical Cord
Part of a newly born child, and so believed to be intimately linked with its life and fate; sometimes thought to be the seat of the 'free soul', which wanders in dreams and finally departs from the body in death; it was important to prevent it from falling into the hands of people who might use it to work magic against the child; also used as a cure for barrenness. See BIRTH.

Umbrella
In the East a symbol of majesty, carried over the heads of dignitaries on ceremonial occasions; though only introduced into the West comparatively recently, several superstitions have become linked with it; it is unlucky to open an umbrella indoors or to give one as a present, and to open one in fine weather brings rain. See SKY.

Unction
Anointing with oil, as a religio-magical rite through which a person or object is endowed with supernatural power or grace, or set apart as sacred; frequently a crucial part of coronation ceremonies; extreme unction is a Christian sacrament administered to those near death, 'for the health of soul and body'. See OIL.

This bearded female saint is one of the oldest figures thrown up by the medieval cult of saints: created by a misunderstanding of the significance of depictions of Christ crucified in a long robe, she was offered oats in London by wives who wanted to be 'uncumbered' of their husbands

ST UNCUMBER

THE MEDIEVAL CULT of saints was as prolific as Greek mythology in creating fantastic figures out of ancient objects and customs no longer understood. For example, the priest whom St Alban, the first British martyr, sheltered during the Diocletianic persecution (c 305), was venerated as St Amphibalus, owing to his being confused with the *amphibalus* or priest's cloak in which St Alban was disguised when arrested. St Barlaam and St Joasaph, two popular medieval saints, owed their origin to a confused account of the Buddha that found its way into Eastern Christendom. And St Ursula and the 11,000 virgins martyred with her at Cologne, whose adventures were so graphically depicted by Flemish artists, probably originated from the fanciful interpretation of an ancient inscription found there.

The 'Manly Virgin'
But no medieval saint was stranger in nature and origin than St Uncumber. Known also as Santa Liberata, Sanct Oncommer, Sainte Wilgeforte, and the Maid Uncumber in various parts of Europe, she was depicted as crucified, wearing a long robe and crown, and bearded.

According to the odd legend associated with her, she had been a daughter of a pagan king of Portugal, whose hand was sought in marriage by a king of Sicily. To preserve her virginity, she prayed fervently to God to disfigure her so that she might escape the abhorrent marriage. Her prayer was answered; God gave her an abundant beard *(prolixam barbam)*. Rejected in disgust by her princely suitor and publicly professing her devotion to Christianity, she was taken out and crucified by her enraged father.

How this strange legend originated can be reasonably explained. Although the portrayal of the crucified Christ unclothed goes back to the 5th century (as the Crucifixion scene carved on the doors of Santa Sabina in Rome shows) Syrian Christians from about the same period preferred 'to represent him as wearing a long tunic, a *colobium*, on the cross.

Well before the 12th century an image of the crucified Christ in this Syrian tradition, at Lucca in northern Italy, became famous as the 'Volto Santo', known in English as •the Holy Face of Lucca. Its popularity among pilgrims led to its reproduction elsewhere in Europe for a time; but the more realistic presentation of the unclothed Christ eventually prevailed. When the significance of the enrobed crucifixes had become forgotten, a new explanation was sought. The long robe was taken as indicating that the crucified figure was that of a female saint; and the beard was explained, in France, in terms of the legend of Sainte Wilgeforte, the name probably being a popular corruption of the Latin *virgo fortis*, which means 'manly virgin'.

Offering Oats to the Saint
The English name 'Uncumber' for the saint seems to have given rise to another curious explanation. According to Michael Nodde, writing in 1554, 'If a wife were weary of a husband she offered oats at Poules (St Paul's) in London to St Uncumber'. Speculation about this custom is recorded by Sir Thomas More in his *Dialogue*. It was suggested that the oats were offered to the saint, 'because she should provide a horse for an evil husband to ride to the devil upon, for that is the thing that she is so sought for as they say. In so much that women hath therefore change her name, and instead of saint Wilgeforte call her saint Uncumber, because they reckon that for a peck of oates she will not fail to uncumber them of their husbands'.

The cult of this strange saint flourished in France, Belgium, England, Spain, Germany and Bohemia. Her bearded image was still being venerated at Saalfeld, near Weimar in Germany, until comparatively modern times.

S. G. F. BRANDON

FURTHER READING: G. G. Coulton, *Five Centuries of Religion* (Octagon Books, 1979), Vol. 1.

Giraudon

Born of misunderstood travellers' tales, nurtured by the error of biblical translators and adopted by the alchemists, the legend of the unicorn who combines male and female in one beast is rich in the symbolism of opposites

UNICORN

A FABULOUS BEAST born of man's imagination, the unicorn plays a leading role in some of his most ancient myths and legends. Its form and function are as variable as the minds and religions of men; but whatever its shape — and it has been described as an ox, ram, goat, bull, antelope, wild ass, horse, rhinoceros, serpent or fish, and as a monster

in which the characteristics of several of these animals are combined — a one-horned beast was always a symbol of supreme power, connected with gods and kings. It concentrates into a single horn the vigour and virility associated with the two horns of real animals (see HORNS).

An early distinction was made between the caprine unicorn, a gigantic one-horned goat, and the equine unicorn, in the form of a horse. The latter, the unicorn *par excellence*, was gracefully adapted by the College of Heralds as a symbol of 'the very parfit gentil knight'.

The first to mention the unicorn in the West was Ctesias of Cnidos, a Greek historian and doctor who was court physician to the kings of Persia for some 17 years. A

16th century French tapestry illustrating the belief that only a virgin holding a mirror can tame a unicorn; the sexual symbolism, which includes the flagstaff, the crescent motif on the flag, rabbits, holly berries and oak leaves, suggests that the tapestry depicts the traditions of courtly love

fragment of his book on India, written about 398 BC, is the most important Western document concerning the unicorn: 'There are in India,' wrote Ctesias, 'certain wild asses, which are as large as horses, and larger. Their bodies are white, their heads dark red, and their eyes dark blue. They have a horn on the forehead which is about a foot and a half in length. The dust filed from this horn is administered in a potion as a protection against deadly drugs. The base of this horn is pure white, the upper part is sharp and of a vivid crimson; and the remainder or middle portion is black. Those who drink out of these horns made into drinking vessels are not subject, they say, to convulsions or the holy disease. Indeed they are immune even to poisons if, either before or after swallowing such, they drink wine, water, or anything else from these beakers . . .'

The Ctesian unicorn is a compound of three animals: rhinoceros, wild ass and a rare, fierce Himalayan antelope which, in profile, appears to have one horn. This confusion of the attributes of different animals, and the inability to distinguish between the artificial and the natural, is a perpetual stumbling-block in the complex history of the unicorn; but it was inevitable in a time when travellers' tales were the only sources of information. Ctesias had never seen a rhinoceros, but it is assumed that he saw a cup made from rhinoceros horn, which had been brought from India where these were commonly used as drinking vessels by potentates and princes, and often decorated with bands of colour – white, black and red. These are of course the colours on the horn of the Ctesian unicorn.

The Great Re'em

Aristotle (384–322 BC) mentions two kinds of unicorn, the Indian ass and the oryx, a kind of antelope that is single-horned in profile; and the Roman writers Pliny (23–79 AD) and Aelian (170–235 AD) between them muster seven different kinds, the most important being the rhinoceros, though, like Ctesias, neither realized they were describing that beast. Pliny emphasized the fact that unicorns could not be captured by men, and Aelian their love of solitude and their indomitability.

The most momentous thing that happened to the Western unicorn was a mistake. The Greek translators of the Old Testament rendered the word *Re'em* as *monoceros*, 'single-horned' or unicorn. This magnificent error conferred on the unicorn a lifespan far exceeding that of the rest of the mythical menagerie and lasting well into the 18th century. Through this mistranslation the unicorn became part of the Bible and to doubt its existence was to question the inspired word of God. The battle over the true identity of the Re'em was long and complex, but it was eventually identified as *bos primigenius*, the giant aurochs, a species of wild buffalo that was extinct in Mesopotamia by about 500 BC (see BULL).

Sir Austen Layard identified the aurochs with the superbly sculptured 'bulls of Nineveh', dating from the time of Nebuchadnezzar (6th century BC) which were seen by the Jews at the time of their captivity. The beasts are shown in conventional profile and therefore look single-horned. However, as Odell Shepard points out in *The Lore of the Unicorn*, there is little in the Hebrew text of the Bible to suggest that the Jews themselves thought of the Re'em as anything but two-horned, since the word for 'horn' is almost invariably in the plural.

Later Jewish commentators exaggerated

the Re'em out of all proportion. A young unicorn becomes as large as Mount Tabor and as high as the sky. Because it could not fit into Noah's ark, the unicorn had to be towed by a rope attached to its horn; and another tradition states that it perished in the waters. Talmudic texts link the unicorn firmly with the lion: 'And in our land there is also the unicorn, which has a great horn on its forehead. And there are also many lions. And when the lion sees a unicorn it draws him against a tree, and the horn pierces so deep into the tree it cannot pull it out again, and then the lion comes and kills the unicorn – but sometimes the matter is reversed . . .'

Bestiaries, collections of moral tales about real or fabulous animals, were very popular all through the Middle Ages. Texts varied according to local and religious influences, but all recounted the most famous of all legends about the unicorn – its capture by a virgin. According to this tale, the unicorn, a small kid-like beast armed with a sharp pointed horn, is too fleet and fierce to be taken by hunters. Only a virgin seated alone under a tree in a forest can capture it; because it is irresistibly attracted by the odours of virtue, the unicorn approaches

A symbol of supreme power, a one-horned beast concentrates into its single horn the strength associated with animals that have two horns: the demon Amduscias, who commanded 29 legions, is depicted with a man's body and the head of a unicorn: illustration from Collin de Plancy's *Dictionnaire Infernal* (1863)

the virgin, lays its head in her lap and permits itself to be caressed into sleep. She breaks its horn, the dogs leap, the huntsman pounces, and the unicorn is taken to the palace of the king.

Details vary, vividly, from text to text; in some the unicorn indulges in familiarities remarkably unsuited to virginal virtue, and in others the virgin is a boy in disguise. Although this legend, of unknown provenance, is transparently erotic, it was tortured into ill-fitting Christian significance. The treacherous virgin was identified with the Mother of God, and the unicorn with Christ and also, despite its dubious familiarities, with purity. The single horn was said to symbolize the unity of Father and Son, and also the 'horn' of the cross, the upright beam projecting above the transverse. The huntsman became the Holy Spirit acting through the angel Gabriel, and the king's palace was heaven. The dogs represented truth, justice, mercy and peace, despite the fact that their function was to tear the unicorn to pieces; they were said to couple at the beast's death, signifying that, though seemingly irreconcilable, truth, justice, mercy and peace were now one.

Another famous legend concerns the virtues of the alicorn, the beast's horn, as an antidote to poison. The animals gather at sunset to quench their thirst, and find the 'great water' poisoned with venom discharged by a serpent. Unable to drink, they await the unicorn. The beast approaches, makes the sign of the cross over the water with its horn and instantly the water is cleansed. The

horn symbolizes the cross, the serpent the Devil, and the poisoned water stands for the sins of the world.

As a result of this legend, drinking cups made from horn were commonly found on the banqueting tables of the Middle Ages and the Renaissance, as a defence against death by poisoning, a common hazard besetting those in high places. The horn was said to sweat in the presence of poison. Alicorns, bought and sold at formidable prices, were rated among the most precious items of princely and papal treasure. For the rich there were cups made from alicorn or pieces of it; while for the poor there were scrapings of horn or *l'eau a la licorne*, water into which the horn had been dipped. Apothecaries kept an alicorn chained to their counters, for it was considered to be the most effective panacea for a variety of evils; finally, it was claimed to raise the dead.

A veritable library of learning has been built up in search of the beast providing the 'true alicorn', and it is sad to reduce that quarry of forgotten lore to a brief citation of the main providers: rhinoceros, antelope, mammoth tusk, and the tusk of narwhal, a marine mammal. Practically all the pictures in ancient books show a horn based on the last of these. By 1600 Europe boasted at least 19 famous alicorns.

Unicorns held a high place in the religion and sacred writing of Persia: '. . . the three-legged ass . . . stands amid the wide-formed ocean . . . its feet are three, eyes six, mouths nine, ears two, and horn one. Body white, food spiritual and it is righteous . . . The horn is as it were of pure gold and hollow . . . With that horn it will vanquish and dissipate all the vile corruption due to the efforts of noxious creatures . . .' However, the one-horned ass is frequently thought to have been imported from an older culture; it is thought that the one-horned beast that haunts the high snows of the Himalayas has the most ancient tradition, and many authorities cite Tibet as the most likely source of unicorn legends, though there was a time when the Mountains of the Moon, heaving high over Ethiopia, held pride of place. The tradition was long and strong, and four brazen unicorns dominated the court of the Ethiopian kings.

In Tibet, antelope horns were used for magical and ritual purposes for centuries, particularly the horn of a fierce fleet antelope known as *Anthlops Hodgsoni*, named for a 19th century British resident of Nepal who identified its horn. In profile, the beast looks single-horned. The unicorn is frequently depicted in the paintings and sculptures of Buddhist temples; the circle containing the body of a dead lama was drawn with the horn of the sacred antelope. From Tibet the unicorn is assumed to have spread into China.

The Chinese unicorn does not have the fierceness of its counterpart further west; it is so gentle that it will not tread on so

The lion and the unicorn, which have long been associated together in legend and heraldry, are the supporters of the shield in the English royal coat of arms

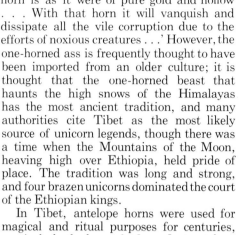

much as a blade of grass, and its backward sweeping horn is fleshy-tipped, indicating that it was not used for attack. Called the *ki-lin*, the Chinese unicorn was believed to appear at the start of a beneficent reign or the birth of a man equal to an emperor in stature; traditionally it announced the birth and death of Confucius. But there is more to the unicorn than that. The 'key' to the beast lies hidden in its Chinese name, *ki*, 'male', *lin*, 'female'.

The unicorn's most vital function has been as a symbol, whether of power or virility, or purity, or the combination of opposites, of the male horn and the female body. Many modern interpreters regard this last role as the crucial one and relate it to the symbolism of the soul as the spark of divine light in the darkness of matter and evil, the body, and to the concept of the hermaphrodite as the perfect union of opposites (see OPPOSITES).

This explains the unicorn's place in the symbolism of alchemy. The 'great work' of alchemy was an attempt to liberate the divine spirit of light from its prison of darkness by transforming base metal into gold by means of the Philosophers' Stone, and by transforming the alchemist himself into the psychic equivalent of gold, a being who was spiritually purified, who had liberated the god within himself. Mercury, the 'male-female', the androgyne, was an essential element in the work, and the personification of Mercury as the precursor of triumph, proclaiming victory over darkness was the unicorn. (See also ALCHEMY; MERCURY; PHILOSOPHERS' STONE.)

The moment for which every alchemist laboured is illustrated in *The Book of Lamb-sprinck* (1625) by a picture which shows a deer and a unicorn meeting in a forest, with the text: 'In the forest (body) there is a soul (deer) and spirit (unicorn) . . . He that knows how to tame and master them by art, and couple them together, may justly be called a master, for we judge rightly that he has obtained the golden flesh.' Another of the many symbols of Mercury as androgynous god and precursor to triumph was the green lion wounded in the lap of the virgin. Because both were figures for Mercury, green lion and unicorn were often considered one, and certainly the image echoes with familiar resonances for those acquainted with the legend of the 'virgin capture'.

The French scientist, Baron Cuvier (1769–1832) dealt the final blow to man's belief in unicorns as an actual species when he declared that beasts with cloven hooves had cloven skulls, and that no horn could grow in the cleft. Although Dr Dove, an American biologist, proved Cuvier wrong in 1933 when he transplanted the horn buds of an Ayrshire calf into its skull cleft, and produced a synthetic unicorn, this did nothing to resurrect belief in the beast.

JUNE GRIMBLE

FURTHER READING: Willie Ley, *The Lung fish, the Dodo and the Unicorn* (Viking Press, 1948); Odell Shepard, *The Lore of the Unicorn* (Harper and Row, 1979 reprint). See also C. G. Jung, *Psychology and Alchemy* (Princeton Univ. Press, 1968).

UNITED STATES
OF
AMERICA

American folklore is still developing; contemporary superstitions and tales of the supernatural are absorbed into the mainstream tradition with its frontier and pioneer lore, and the 'yeasty oral tradition' of the Negro

NOT SO LONG AGO the idea that there might be a fully distinguishable body of American folklore was generally dismissed as just so much . . . folklore. The United States might be swollen with folk traditions, it was said, but these were in fact European, where they were not Asian or African. While some authorities might have admitted that these transplanted traditions seemed to be flourishing, others insisted that the foreign folk materials existed in America like pressed flowers between the pages of a book.

The basic idea of the transplant is indisputable. Folklore came to the New World with its people, on the *Mayflower* and its successors. The early colonists in New England held the beliefs and followed the customs of their fathers, the usual folk superstitions, the ghost stories, the seafarer's tales of monsters and phantom ships, the herbal remedies, the old songs and ballads. Because many of the colonial folktales grew out of Puritan preoccupations, there were examples of the Devil's work among men, and of visitations of the wrath of God upon the sinful.

But not all the lore was explicitly of the Old World. The settlers of Massachusetts may have brought the witch tales of Britain to the innocent soil of Salem (see SALEM WITCHES), but more general beliefs and

tales concerning pagan magic were imputed to the Indians, and these formed a relatively new strain. At the same time some of the white Americans' race myths about the craftiness, cruelty and superstitious ignorance of the Indians took root; and other myths about New World marvels were promulgated, including wildly unlikely natural history. Many of these exaggerated the fertility of the land, where every seed grew 100 stalks and edible wild creatures were impossibly fat and almost begging to be caught. But other wild creatures were terrible in their danger to men and tales were told of fearsome snakes, monstrous bears, alligators and the like. In these tales another new note is struck; the awe of the new American confronted by all that space, most of which was then howling wilderness. Even in the earliest days of American history, certain apparently indigenous strands were being woven into the lore of the folk. However, those who scoff at the idea of an American folk tradition choose to consider these indigenous elements as mere reworkings of older European themes.

Much of the refusal to believe in an American folklore, a refusal that has been less in evidence in the years since the Second World War, stems from the fact that America likes to think that she has no 'folk', in the sense of *Volk*, the peasant classes that hold on to, and perpetuate, old oral traditions. Democratic, egalitarian, freedom-loving America, it is said, has no classes of any kind, and certainly no peasant class. How then can she have folklore?

In fact, America has a superabundance of small, close-knit rural and agricultural communities. More or less isolated before 20th century transport and communication bridged all gaps, these settlements supplied the requirements for the perpetuation of oral folk traditions. Regional variations naturally occurred: the themes of favourite folktales in rural New England differed from those of the cornfields of Iowa, for instance.

Although cars and aircraft, radio and television, put much of the old lore to death, a few communities nevertheless resisted integration. These were generally pockets of people who were isolated by geography and topography, and content to remain that way; predominant among them were the so-called 'hill-billies', who lived in mountains and foothills like those of the Ozarks on the Missouri-Arkansas border (see OZARKS), or the region called 'Egypt' in Illinois.

The hill-billies were the most prominent producers of a sort of music that was in fact the property of the whole of rural America, and which is known as 'Country and Western'. The songs of the country folk, played on banjo and fiddle and primitive instruments like the jews' harp, tended to be fairly recognizable versions of Old World songs, which had undergone many permutations on their journey through New England to the backwoods. Many such songs continued to journey westward, with the migrating 'folk'; and country dancing recalled the quadrilles and 'contre' dances of Europe transmuted into a genuine American folk tradition (see DANCE; SONG).

The early colonists held the beliefs and followed the customs of their fathers, but tales of pagan magic were imputed to the Indians, forming a relatively new strain

Out of these pockets of mainstream folklore also come abundant superstitions and legends. The Ozarks, for instance, were rich in ancient folk medicines and herb doctoring, and rich too in legends of fabulous animals very similar to those spawned by colonists in the 17th century. To a large extent the same kind of folk material is prominent in the lore of the 'Egyptians' of Illinois. Tall tales and unlikely legends are innumerable, including many that provide contradictory explanations of how the region got its name. One version suggests that the corn crop in neighbouring regions failed, and people went to 'Egypt' for corn as Joseph went to the real Egypt in the Old Testament. Egypt has an Ozarkian plenitude of witch tales and folk medicines, but seems to

specialize above all in ghost stories. The number and variety of apparitions is astonishing, and many seem to reflect ghost motifs similar to those in English tradition.

None of this hill-billy material, or the traditions of backwoods communities generally, is unusual in the overall picture of American folklore. Indeed, Richard Dorson finds in Egyptian lore a reflection of 'general American patterns' and others have said the same about Ozarkian or Appalachian elements. It seems that such backwoods communities, which are mainly dominated by white Anglo-Saxon Protestants, and which hark back to colonial and old British traditions, provide the basis of America's folk culture.

But there are also other cultures whose

folklore is embodied in other languages. These belong to the 'ethnic' minorities, some of whom immigrated to the United States shortly after the first British colonists, some of whom are more recent arrivals.

In most cases these 'foreign' communities managed to retain a good deal of their old traditions, though in time certain adaptations and alterations naturally crept in. The Germanic folklore of the Pennsylvania 'Dutch' settlements is a case in point: their tales still relate the trickster adventures of Till Eulenspiegel, but according to Dorson this traditional character has become less of a cruel jokester, and even his name has undergone certain changes. The penchant for proverbs, for sound Germanic folk remedies, for homely folk beliefs and

Previous page Covered wagons: 'America is a land of heroes, perhaps because in pioneer days individual strength and courage were at a premium, or perhaps because of a rose-coloured nostalgia for those days.' The Wild West with its larger-than-life heroes and villains, cowboys and Indians, the U.S. Cavalry, marshals and gunmen, has become part of the hero mythology of the world
Facing page 'Buffalo Bill' Cody, frontiersman, gold prospector, cavalry scout, buffalo hunter, marksman and showman, who killed and scalped Chief Yellowbrand of the Sioux in 1876: books about his exploits made him a household name *Right* 'Custer's Last Fight': General George A. Custer *(above)* and a force of cavalry were defeated and massacred by the Sioux at the Little Big Horn in 1876

The modern myth of the Wild West has been created largely by the cinema and television, and the true folklore of the cowboy has been overwhelmed by the 'fakelore' of the gunfight and the chase: John Wayne *(far left)* epitomizes the tough lawman to filmgoers all over the world; Butch Cassidy (seated right in the top group in this montage) is one of many outlaws who have been romanticized as devil-may-care rebels, while Wyatt Earp (third from the right in the bottom group) is one of the few lawmen who have been immortalized. The Apache Indian *(left)* is a stock figure in Western films. *Top* Poster offering a reward for the capture of Jesse James; a murderer and robber, he and Billy the Kid *(above)* were both transmuted into 'good criminals', popular figures in modern American folklore

Pen on Tour

Culver Pictures

superstitions is much the same as it would have been in Europe. But the equally traditional fear of witchcraft has become to some extent Americanized. There is a famous story about a 'Dutch' couple who bought a new car and found it bewitched by a neighbour, but who were aided by a witch-finder, a *braucher*, who provided a counter-spell. The basic tale is very old; the car is an American addition.

French folklore has also found its way into America. Among the 'Cajuns' of Louisiana, for instance, who still speak a special patois, remnants of traditional French children's games and dances are strongly apparent, while their Shrove Tuesday celebrations are the equivalent of the Mardi Gras of New Orleans, a festival that was introduced to what is now the state of Louisiana by French settlers (see SPRING).

The Mexican-Americans of the southwest have struggled to retain their ethnic homogeneity against many social pressures; and also to retain their religious beliefs, their customs and their self-respect in the face of discrimination. Their folklore, which reaches back to Spanish colonial days and to Spain itself, is a major aid in this struggle. Some aspects, such as their traditional ballads, superstitions and folk beliefs are plainly European. But they have also added local colour to their store of folk materials, such as the additions to their folksong traditions. The *canciones* may reflect older matters, but the *corridos* grew very much out of the American experience of this people and, because of the nature of that

experience, many of them are in some way protest songs.

Some of the corridos attack the Americans by lauding the deeds of Mexican border heroes such as Jacinto Trevino, the scourge of the Texas Rangers. There is something of the same reflection of the Mexican-American experience in the newer additions to the hoard of folktales, or *cuentos*. These are often comic stories with an edge to them, in which a pompous Anglo-Saxon American is made to look a fool by his ignorance of Spanish and his lack of Latin social graces. Needless to say, the outwitting or humiliating of the outsider, who is usually some far from silent representative of the majority, is a common theme in the lore of most ethnic minorities in America.

The German, French and Spanish-speaking cultures have been part of America since colonial times, but more recently, during this century, the American melting-pot has received ingredients from nations not previously represented in the New World. Each of these groups naturally brought its own folklore, and to some extent these traditions flourished, especially in rural areas where the group could form a tight little community cut off from many of the conformist Americanizing pressures. Out of such communities come gobbets of European and Asian folk material: gloomy Scandinavian tales, southern Italian witch fears, Greek songs and dances, Japanese ghosts and shape-shifters. The folklorist Americo Paredes has called these ethnic incursions 'tributaries to the mainstream', a phrase

Above Poster advertising Buffalo Bill's 'Wild West and Pioneer Exhibition'; a brilliantly successful showman, he brought the legendary Wild West of cowboys and Indians, the Union Pacific Railroad, Wells Fargo and the train hold-up, to life: Annie Oakley *(right)* one of the stars of the show, has been immortalized in the musical *Annie Get Your Gun*

that sets up some interesting reverberations. It asserts, primarily, that these cultures are making a visible and positive contribution to the folklore of the majority.

Perhaps one of the first, most noticeable effects that America has on this transplanted lore is reflected in the satiric stories or bitter protest songs that spring up when a recently arrived minority feels victimized and oppressed. One of the last effects occurs when the second or third generation can no longer remember the old songs and stories, can no longer even speak the old tongue.

But how does the transplanted folklore affect the American mainstream? One of the most obvious effects is also one of the least attractive: it is the appearance of cruel new joke-cycles and anecdotes about the 'stupid immigrant', stupidity being defined as inability to speak English, and inexperience of American ways.

Equally unpleasant are jokes that revolve around some supposedly innate characteristic of an immigrant group; jokes about Jewish craftiness, Irish drunkenness, Swedish or Slavic thick-headedness. If this is all that American mainstream folklore can derive from the wealth of ethnic cultures in

its midst, one might say that it does not deserve that wealth.

But of course that is not all. The minorities give much to the majority, as Americo Paredes states: 'There is a trend in the United States away from the uncompromising 100 per cent Americanism of earlier times when the country was younger and less sure of itself. There is a tendency to admire the values of minorities and to recognize their role in the enrichment of the majority culture . . .' Because this trend is still fairly new, detailed folklore investigation still needs to be done in order to value that enrichment correctly. Part of the difficulty, perhaps, lies in the fact that the minority contributions are made on a regional scale. The outsider may notice the

place names, the use of dialect terms in ordinary speech, the majority awareness of the folksongs, and perhaps even some of the stories from the minority traditions. For instance, there is the effect that Mexican-American songs have had on the development of the Western or 'cowboy' song: and there is the pervading presence of Yiddish dialect terms, and Jewish jokes – or the whole Jewish approach to joke-telling and humour generally – in the urban 'folk culture' of New York. Because New York is a communications centre these Jewish materials have diffused outwards to pervade much more of America than just that region. Other aspects of minority folk traditions have similarly diffused on a broader scale.

Strangely enough, the wealth of American Indian culture has had little or no effect on the mainstream. It has retreated into a kind of limbo, accessible for ethnological or anthropological study, but no longer an entirely living tradition open to folk borrowings and diffusions. But the other non-white folk culture of the United States is the broadest, most effective and most pervasive tributary of them all.

The black man arrived in the United States as a slave, not as a colonist or immigrant. This was not an ideal situation for the retention of traditional culture; families were broken up by the slave-owners and their dealings, quite apart from the effect that the trade had on village or tribal groupings. In a very short time the Negroes had lost their

White America took the blues and New Orleans jazz and other forms of Negro music and made it not black or white, not southern or northern, not urban or rural, but all-embracingly American

Africanness and, in order to survive, had begun to acquire the white man's language, religion and to some extent his customs.

But during the time of slavery and afterwards the Negro had been making what Dorson calls a 'yeasty oral tradition' all his own from the white folk materials accessible to him. Eventually the whites took an interest, and from that point the Negroes began to enrich American folklore by feeding back into it the wholly altered material that they had adopted long before.

But the whites did not easily recognize their own traditions. They saw a host of supernatural beliefs and superstitions in Negro lore, and believed these to be the products of an inferior mind or remnants of African primitive belief, or a combination of both. Yet most of the ghost and witch stories, the sorceries and taboos and omens that have been collected among Negroes of the old South can be traced directly to Europe and Britain.

It seems clear that any direct connection with African tradition stops at the West Indies, for several geographical and sociological reasons. As many folklorists have discovered with surprise, the West African spider-trickster Anansi (see TRICKSTER) occurs in folktales throughout the Caribbean, but never among black North Americans. However, the latter have produced another notable trickster, and in so doing have made a sizeable contribution to American folktales. This is Brer Rabbit, hero of the Uncle Remus stories gathered and retold by Joel Chandler Harris.

Negro contributions deserve the dominant place in a survey of American folk music. Indeed, most musicians would agree that indigenous American music owes most of its special and separate character to the Negroes. No one needs to be reminded of all those intertwined musical roots, going back to the condition of slavery and oppression: the spirituals, work songs, gospel songs, party songs; the advent of the blues, the birth of jazz with all its later forms and variations, and the even more recent protest songs, and all combinations of these. Experts may argue about whether a specific work song or 'holler', for instance, has any roots in African chant or singing. What is more important is that white America took the blues and New Orleans jazz and the other forms of Negro music and made it not black or

white, not southern or northern, not urban or rural, but all-embracingly American. In the process it was also torn up from its folk roots and made highly commercial, but that seems to be an inescapable aspect of the American way of folk diffusion. Jazz went on to influence serious 'highbrow' music, and became in itself an international highbrow concern. And the blues and work songs and ballads permeated and influenced every sort of basic folk song in America: their presence can be felt in even the purest hill-billy music, in cowboy ballads, and in the 'rhythm and blues' that gave birth to most of modern pop music.

Lore of the Frontier

The Negro contribution is undeniably the greatest single ethnic tributary to the folklore mainstream. But there is also another category that adds further dimensions to the American traditions, because of the nature of the nation's history. This includes the more heroic and romantic of the traditional occupations associated with that epic history.

Farming itself was once such an occupation, in the days of pioneering when a farmer was also hunter, woodsman and fighter of Indians. Eventually these occupations became separated; but they left behind the remarkable lore of the frontiersman. This was mainly a collection of heroic legends telling of Daniel Boone and Davy Crockett on the old frontier, Kit Carson and the mountain men in the far West. But there were also plenty of tall tales about adventures experienced and marvels seen. There is the tale of the 'wonderful hunt', for instance, in which a crack shot manages to kill a huge array of game with only one bullet, thanks to some fortuitous ricochets and other unlikely bits of luck. Variations on this theme crop up in nearly every region, ascribed to different hunters.

Other equally dramatic occupations became prominent. American seamen off the New England coast developed their own lore to add to the British seafaring traditions they had inherited. Inland, on the great commercial freeway of the Mississippi, the river men evolved their special songs, customs, taboos and superstitions, and of course their own heroes. The lumbering industry developed its set of folkways and beliefs, often with traces of Scandinavian lore from the many Swedish and Norwegian

lumberjacks. The tales are especially rich, and tell of haunted trees, magical trees and trees that are impossibly high.

Railroading later brought new tales, legends and songs into the mainstream. Songs like 'Casey Jones', for instance, or 'John Henry' which tells of a Negro culture hero who died in competition with a track-laying machine. Coal miners in the East added their own variations to old British and European superstitions about mines, and these were themselves increased, as were mining ghost tales, by gold seekers in mid-19th century California. More recently, the steel industry cast up a quasi-folk hero in Joe Magarac, a Hungarian-American man of steel, who paddled unconcernedly in the molten metal.

Prominent among the special characteristics of mainstream folklore is the American love of story-telling, with the emphasis on particular types of comic stories. One of the favourite kinds is the short 'anecdote' which tells of some brief humorous events or action, and often features an eccentric person, a trickster or a dullard. The way in which minority groups use trickster anecdotes to underline their solidarity at the expense of the outsider, and how the majority has utilized the 'stupid' immigrant as a favourite dullard stereotype has been noted previously. Other dullard stories avoid ethnic generalization and use some local character, for instance, whose stupidity becomes a legend.

The people of the frontiers, and of the backwoods in general, had a parochial dislike for the stranger, and out of this came the cycle of 'clever Yankee' stories, in which the shrewd rural New Englander may appear to be a yokel but always thwarts the city slicker. There are similar Western anecdotes in which an old-timer, or even an Indian, is the trickster. Sometimes no real trick is involved, but merely a crushing retort — another favourite form of American humour. There is the story of how a tourist was trying to get directions from a Yankee farmer. The farmer knows nothing about the highways or towns that the tourist is seeking, and the visitor calls him a know-nothing yokel. The farmer squelches him with, 'Mebbe so, but I ain't lost'.

A slightly longer story is often called a 'yarn', and may be a straightforward account of an experience of the narrator,

or someone known to him. Old-timers who had had long and eventful lives were supposed to be great tellers of yarns, whether they had been sailors, buffalo hunters or gold miners. But a well-told yarn may often acquire a little extra dramatic effect and audience interest by exaggeration and elaboration; if it does it may become a 'windy' or 'tall tale', an American speciality.

The story of the 'wonderful hunt' is such a tale. Others, which are usually devoted to natural marvels, are said to have arisen out of lying contests, good-natured rivalry among people from different localities. So, 'down our way', horse-flies grow so big they don't bite horses, they carry them off. Down our way the ground is so fertile that corn grows visibly; one time a farmer got caught on a stalk and whisked skyward so fast he would have starved to death if people hadn't shot food up to him from guns.

There are also miraculous animals, including the evergreen tale of a dog that was split in two by a buzzsaw, or as a result of some similar accident. Its owner stuck the two halves together in such a hurry that two feet were upwards and two were downwards. The dog is now twice as good a hunter as it was, for it runs on one pair of legs until they are tired, then runs on the other pair.

Land of Heroes
Of course there are stories of miraculous human beings. And at this point the tall tale becomes that other American folklore favourite, the hero legend. America is a land of heroes, perhaps because in pioneer days individual strength and courage and other heroic attributes were at a premium, or perhaps because of a rose-coloured nostalgia for those days. Certainly there is an emphasis on brute strength and aggression, brawn before brain, in the American folk hero; men like Paul Bunyan and Mike Fink, for instance, are not merely skilled in their occupations but are physical giants, a characteristic that is the sole basis for many of their legendary exploits.

Folklore tends to resist categories, and American folk heroes resist them especially. Davy Crockett is a good example. A real person, many tales told about him are mainly biographical: Davy as the shrewd yokel showing up affected city folk, Davy the honest man of the people thwarting clever or crooked politicians, Davy the skilled hunter

and woodsman fighting grizzly bears, Davy the patriot dying gloriously at the Alamo. But in other stories he becomes a fictional demigod, a mythical being; his terrible grin kills bears and cougars, he rides on the moon after a tiring hunt, he saves the world by greasing its axis to restore its spin.

Many American heroes combine this sort of honest biography with myth. The New England giant named Barney Beal, a real person whose feats of strength are recorded by Dorson, acquired a legendary reputation after his death: so did such other 'real-life' characters as 'Buffalo Bill' Cody, Kit Carson, Daniel Webster, and even Abraham Lincoln. Sometimes there is something more than physical prowess in these men, as there is in the legend of Johnny Appleseed, who is depicted as a gentle and primitive mystic scattering seeds through the wilderness, unharmed by wild beast or Indian. In fact the prototype, John Chapman, was a fairly rugged frontiersman who set up orchards on a businesslike basis.

America also specializes in the good criminal, the Robin Hood, the anti-villain, as it were. One aspect of the basic pattern of the hero myth is the character's individualism, his indifference to staid authority and restrictive rules. American lore takes this notion of the devil-may-care rebel who defeats the stodgy and the conventional, a step or two further. Robin Hood was an outlaw only in the eyes of a corrupted and evil law; but Billy the Kid was a vicious killer and thief in terms of any kind of law. Yet it is Billy, not Pat Garrett, the

indomitable lawman who tracks him down, who gallops heroically through American folklore, along with Jesse James, Pretty Boy Floyd and countless similar villains. All of them have had their villainy whitewashed and any number of heroic and legendary deeds are ascribed to them. The few lawmen, such as Wyatt Earp, who have been similarly immortalized are outnumbered and overshadowed by criminal heroes.

The abundance of 'supermen', the overall American penchant for heroes, hints at what is perhaps the most important single characteristic of United States folklore. Other nations have only recently grown self-conscious about their traditions, as collections and analyses grew and overlapped. But, because her folklore developed and merged in an age of print, and later of more sophisticated media, America has always been self-conscious about her lore. The bright lights of America's skills at self-examination, publicity and salesmanship were turned on its oral traditions almost from their inception.

The fact of this observation affected that which was being observed. To over-simplify a complicated system of inter-relationships, it seems that the publicizers picked up various aspects of the oral tradition, put them together in different garb, smoothing the language, for instance, or clarifying the regional references, and published them in forms ranging from stiff novels to cheap thrillers and semi-comic insertions in farmers' almanacs. Eventually this material filtered back to the 'folk', sometimes even

Victoria & Albert Museum

Culver Pictures

replacing the oral original, as with the whitewashing of Western outlaws.

The professional folklorist has difficulties enough trying to unravel the processes by which folk materials diffuse from one region or community or culture to another. But in America the influence of the media complicates the problem of diffusion even further. Looked at from one angle, American lore can be divided into categories such as regionalism, ethnic grouping, sectarianism, and occupational grouping. From another viewpoint, however, the media have spread much of that lore throughout the nation, so that it is not only thoroughly diffused, it has also become standardized.

At the same time, and as a result of the same process, the original folk materials were often expanded or entirely transmuted by the media into 'fakelore', to borrow Dorson's splendid term. The process can be seen in action by a look at the body of material that deals with the Wild West.

More than a century of Western history has been mined for every scrap of excitement, colour and heroic drama, which has then been put through the media mill. The cowboy has become a myth, and the traditional folklore of his occupation has been buried under mountains of gunfights, saloon brawls, chases and other fakelore.

Unavoidably, the media have created much of what is now American folklore. They created Davy Crockett, not in the Crockett fad of the 1950s, but in the 'almanacs' and spurious adventure tales of the 1830s and afterwards. Similarly,

Thanksgiving Day, first celebrated by the Pilgrim Fathers in 1621, was originally an American version of the European harvest festival; a national holiday, it has gradually taken on more secular and patriotic associations: *The First Thanksgiving*

commercial writers created most of the Western heroes and villains. In this century, books, films and cartoons have often made 'folk' heroes — out of virtually nothing. Paul Bunyan's legend rests on a few sparse fragments of true lumberjack lore, and a great deal of commercial imagination. Pecos Bill, the Texas demigod hero who pulled rivers straight and lassoed clouds to overcome drought, was mostly invented by a magazine writer. These are manufactured heroes; they are no more outgrowths of an oral tradition than are the 'folk songs' written last week for a pop group's latest album, yet they seem to answer much of the same need, for the mass of the 'folk', as did the pure original material. As the folklorist John Greenway has put it, 'the folk nowhere make the niggling distinctions between "genuine" and "factitious" that folklorists do, so long as the article feels right in their culture'. If people get what 'feels right' from mass-media fakelore, it may simply be a recognition that those media are with us now, and that no living oral tradition is going to remain untouched by them.

American folklore is still developing. As fast as pop culture absorbs folk elements, more is churned out. Some of it is naturally adapted from old motifs; superstitions that

were once ascribed to horses and carriages, for instance, now recur in terms of cars, and there are even tales of phantom automobiles. A ghost story involving a real car is told, with innumerable variations, all across the United States. The story is of a young man who picks up a pretty girl hitchhiker. She directs him to her home, but on the way there she disappears from the car. The driver visits the house, describes the girl, and is told that she was the householder's daughter who died years before. This plot occurs in folktales all over the world, and the modern American versions owe nothing to mass culture.

Equally authentic is the mass of folklore found among modern servicemen. This includes hero tales told among the Marines, and stories of phantom ships like the one detected off the West Coast by naval radar. All the old taboos and omens arise again in modern dress. These examples are as much tributaries to the American mainstream as are any of the strands discussed earlier. They show that the mainstream is still flowing; that, in Richard Dorson's words, the 'idea that folklore is dying out is itself a kind of folklore'.

(See also NEGROES.)

DOUGLAS HILL

FURTHER READING: Richard M. Dorson, *American Folklore* and *Buying the Wind* (both published by Univ. of Chicago Press, 1971 and 1964 respectively); Tristram Potter Coffin ed., *Our Living Traditions* (Basic Books, 1968).

URANUS

The rain that fertilizes the earth is sometimes represented as the seed of the Greek god Uranus, whose name means sky or heaven; in astrology the planet called after him is a harbinger of violence, revolution and upheaval

URANUS is the Greek name for sky or heaven, whether as a common noun or personified as a god. In the earliest Greek literature the sky is imagined as a solid roof to the world, made of bronze or iron and garlanded with stars. (For the ancients there was nothing humdrum about metal; it comes from the womb of earth, and there is an air of magic about the working of it.) Nothing is said about its shape. The sun 'goes up into' it and 'comes down from' it. It is supported by Atlas, or by pillars. It is the seat of the gods, for the peaks of Mt Olympus, where they have their houses, reach up to it.

Considered as a god himself, Uranus is the consort of Ge, Earth. The rain that fertilizes the earth and makes things grow is sometimes (from the 5th century BC on) represented as his seed, though this may be a rationalistic interpretation of the mythical marriage rather than its basic meaning. The mythical offspring were not, for example, vegetation spirits, but Titans, Cyclopes, and ogres with 100 hands, none of whom has any place in our present world. At their birth Uranus kept them pressed down inside Earth. In her discomfort she consulted with them, and Cronus (see CRONUS) was emboldened to take an adamantine sickle and castrate his father when he came at night to resume intercourse with Ge. Various divine or semi-divine beings sprang up from where the drops of blood fell on the earth. Cronus threw the severed genitals in the sea, and in the foam that formed round them Aphrodite was born. (Her name suggested 'foam'.) Cronus now became king of the gods, and Uranus played no further part in the divine history.

The episode represents a combination of two myths. One is about the separation of heaven and earth. Many peoples tell how the sky originally lay on the earth and later rose or was pushed to its present position. Sometimes a physical link such as a tree or navel-cord has to be severed; in Polynesian myth, heaven and earth were an embracing couple, Rangi and Papa, and Rangi's arms were cut through. Secondly, we have an Asiatic myth: in the Hittite version, Heaven is king of the gods for nine years and is then castrated; gods are born from his severed members. In the Babylonian version he is less prominent. The motif of children hated by their father and confined within their mother is there, and it is a son of Heaven who overthrows the father, but the primeval parents here are Apsu and Tiamat, the subterranean waters and those of the sea (see MESOPOTAMIA).

The personified Uranus owes his existence to these oriental models. He has no other significance in myth or cult. Indian evidence proves that Zeus was the original Father Sky and consort of Mother Earth; and he remained the real Greek sky god.

M. L. WEST

Uranus in Astrology

In 1781 Sir William Herschel identified a new planet, which was named first for King George III, then for Herschel himself and finally for the Greek sky god Uranus. The discovery of Uranus, and later of

Neptune and Pluto, wrecked the traditional astrological picture of the order of the universe, in which the seven planets of antiquity corresponded to numerous other groups of seven, and round which so many religious, mystical and magical ideas had gathered (see CORRESPONDENCES; SEVEN). In the circumstances, it is not surprising that 'change' is the key notion which astrologers have come to associate with Uranus, especially change of a sudden, disruptive and revolutionary sort.

Astrologers say that it is only when a new planet is recognized that human beings seem to respond to its influence, even though the planet has been in existence, unrecognized, all along. They see the influence of Uranus behind all the violent and revolutionary upheavals of the modern world, from the French Revolution onwards, behind the accelerated pace of change, new inventions and discoveries, and progress in science and technology, especially in the fields of electricity and magnetism. Someone strongly influenced by Uranus is likely to be highly original and inventive, free-thinking and rebellious, independent, wilful, unconventional, wild and unorthodox, impatient of old systems and accepted ideas.

Some see the planet casting its shadow before it, as it were, in the American Revolution of 1776, and Uranus is believed to have played an important role in American history. It was in the ascendant sign, Gemini, when the Declaration of Independence was signed. It returned to Gemini, in an ominous conjunction with the two baleful planets Saturn and Mars, in 1860, the year before the outbreak of the Civil War. It was again in Gemini, and again in conjunction with Mars, in 1942, when the United States was again at war.

FURTHER READING: For a discussion of the Greek myth, see F. M. Cornford, *Principium Sapientiae* (Peter Smith); P. Walcot, *Hesiod and the Near East* (Verry, Lawrence, 1966).

As a god Uranus is the consort of Ge, Earth; their mythical offspring were Titans, Cyclopes and ogres with 100 hands. He was castrated by his son Cronus, who became king of the gods, and divine or semi-divine beings sprang up where his blood fell on the earth: statuette from Tanagra in Greece

Mansell Collection

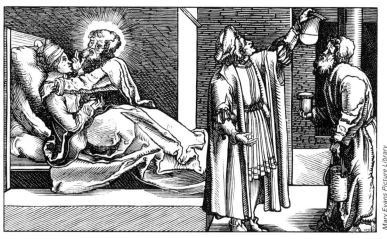

Mary Evans Picture Library

Urine

With other bodily secretions and excretions, valued in magic and alchemy because it was thought to retain some of the vital energy of the body from which it came and to provide a magical link with that body: a witch bottle was a device for turning a witch's spell or poison against her by boiling some of the victim's urine in a bottle; a person's urine was also bottled because its condition would reveal whether he was well or ill, safe or in danger, while away from home.

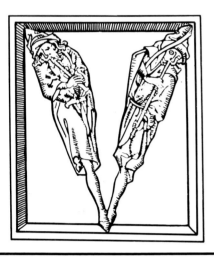

Valhalla

The hall of the slain, the paradise ruled by Odin in Norse mythology, to which heroes and distinguished warriors went after death, conducted there by the Valkyries, Odin's battle-maidens; there they fought all day and those who fell were restored again in the evening, to feast on pork and mead.
See ODIN.

The vampire in this 19th century engraving of a 'vampire kiss' has bat's wings, a comparatively modern addition to the legend, dating from the discovery of the 'vampire bat' of South America. The Victorians generally played down the strong sexual element in the vampire tradition, preferring to regard vampire legends as good gory horror stories, grown out of primitive beliefs about the dead

VAMPIRE

TOGETHER with the golem in his guise as Frankenstein's monster, the vampire has become the world's best-known supernatural monster, the result of decades of horror films capitalizing on the imagination and researches of an Irish author named Bram Stoker. Before Stoker, the vampire legend had attracted attention, and had even become something of a fad in Europe, but it was jumbled, tangled, overgrown. Stoker pruned it, performed some judicious grafting, dressed it up in a richly purple prose, and added *Dracula* to the list of classic horror stories.

The name of his vampire was borrowed from the name of a 15th century Balkan nobleman whose sadistic cruelties justified his name; *dracul* means 'devil' in Rumanian. It was not difficult for Stoker to project the vampire evil onto the ugly actuality of the true story. And he did it so successfully that folklorists are sometimes surprised to find how often he has affected the more modern concepts of vampires.

Rumanian Vampire Beliefs

In the district of Teleorman, on the third day after a death, when people go to the house of mourning in order to burn incense they carry with them nine spindles, and these they thrust deep into the grave. Should the vampire rise he would be pierced by their sharp points. Another method is to take tow, to scatter it upon the grave, and to set fire to it there, for it is believed that the occupant will scarce venture through the flames. Sometimes the anathema of a priest will confine the vampire in his tomb.

In the Romanati district the vampire is stripped and the naked carrion thrust into a stout bag. The clothes and cerements are sprinkled with holy water, replaced in the coffin which is secured and again buried in the grave. The body is taken away to the forest. The heart is first cut out, and then it is hacked piecemeal limb from limb and each gobbet burned in a great fire. Last of all the heart is flung into the flames and those who have assisted come near so that they shall be fumigated with the smoke. But all must be consumed, every shred of flesh, every bone. The veriest scrap if left would be enough to enable the vampire again to materialize. Occasionally the ashes of the heart are collected, mingled with water and given to sick people as a powerful potion.

At Zarnesti after a female vampire had been exhumed great iron forks were driven through the heart, eyes, and breast after which the body was buried at a considerable depth, face downwards . . .

It is held to be imperative that the vampire should be traced to his lair and destroyed at the very first opportunity. If he is sufficiently cunning to avoid detection so long at the end of seven years he will become a man again, and then he will be able to pass into another country, or at any rate to a new district, where another language is spoken. He will marry and have children, and these after they die will all go to swell the vampire host.

Montague Summers *The Vampire in Europe*

It is also surprising, considering the wide fame of the vampire motif, to realize that the legend is comparatively young and that it was for a long time highly localized. Corollaries and ancestors of the vampire, several times removed, are fairly plentiful. Evil bloodsucking demons or witches and blood-hungry ghosts abound in primitive belief. And the ancient world also offers antecedents in the blood-consuming ghosts in the *Odyssey*, in Ovid and elsewhere. There is also the demonic Lilith of ancient Hebrew legend, who had many vampire traits, and the Romans conceived of the lamia, a near relation of the vampire, who enticed men sexually and then feasted on their blood (see INCUBUS; LILITH). The Arabs believed in blood-eating spirits, and the ancient Irish told of a comparable demon. But none of these creatures was a vampire, as it is now defined, although such legends probably blended and crystallized to give rise to the concept. Almost exclusively a creature of the Slavic regions and Balkan states of eastern Europe, the vampire first made its appearance in its present form in the 16th century.

The word 'vampire' comes from various eastern European terms, including the Magyar *vampir*. By the 17th century, the word was on a great many lips; vampire activity seems to have burgeoned rapidly in the Balkans, and to have occurred as far afield as Greece, where fearsome tales of the *vrykolakas* spread from town to town. Balkan clergy reported the spread of such tales, and their superiors spoke of a new offensive by the Enemy. Then in the 17th century a Greek writer named Leone Allacci separated the concept of the vampire from standard Christian demonology.

Travellers began to pick up hints of the new horror, and patched them together in their writings for the rest of Europe. The first stage of the legend's spread was completed in 1746 when a French monk named Dom Augustin Calmet published a learned treatise on vampires.

Late 18th century romanticism had fallen in love with the Gothic, and vampires suited the fashion nicely. Goethe wrote some vampire verses and in the following years so did Byron and Southey, Gautier and Baudelaire.

The vampire soon reached the theatre; a successful play in Paris in the 1820s spawned imitators, and as the years passed hardly a stage in Europe lacked its vampire. A singing vampire entertained German opera audiences in 1828; Alexander Dumas wrote a successful stage play on this theme in the 1850s; the London stage also presented vampires, and was in fact still doing so in 1925 with a dramatization of *Dracula*. In 1931 the cinema took over, and assured the immortality of Bela Lugosi who played Count Dracula (see FILMS). But long before that the fashion for vampires had reached a new height in prose fiction, with the publication in 1847 of a story called *Varney the Vampire*, some 800 pages of horrification, gory action and nauseous over-writing. It was an instant bestseller; but it was eclipsed at the end of the century when Bram Stoker published his classic blend of folklore and fantasy.

From then on, the vampire's world-wide notoriety was assured. And although other great vampire stories exist, the creature as he is now known is almost indistinguishable from his incarnation as Count Dracula. In studying the folklore vampire it is never possible to get very far away from the evil Transylvanian aristocrat.

It must be remembered that the vampire is a resuscitated corpse, not an immaterial

The vampire theme was well suited to the late 18th century with its love of the Gothic, and Goethe and Byron were among the poets who wrote verses on the subject. In the 19th century the vampire fashion reached new heights in prose fiction with the publication of *Varney the Vampire* (1847)

spirit. Primitive people often fail to draw our distinction between the body of someone who has died and the spirit; they may feed the corpse in order to placate the ghost. And it is rarely clear whether tribesmen think of the dead as returning in bodily form or as insubstantial apparitions. This confusion is found to some degree in vampire lore. But basically the vampire is a walking corpse with some of the powers and functions of a non-corporeal spirit.

As a cadaver, the vampire looks cadaverous: lean, pale with the pallor of death, icy cold to the touch. Some tales describe him as skeletal and withered, like an Egyptian mummy, and he may be clothed in a shroud. But more usually he is said to be merely gaunt to an extreme, and to wear

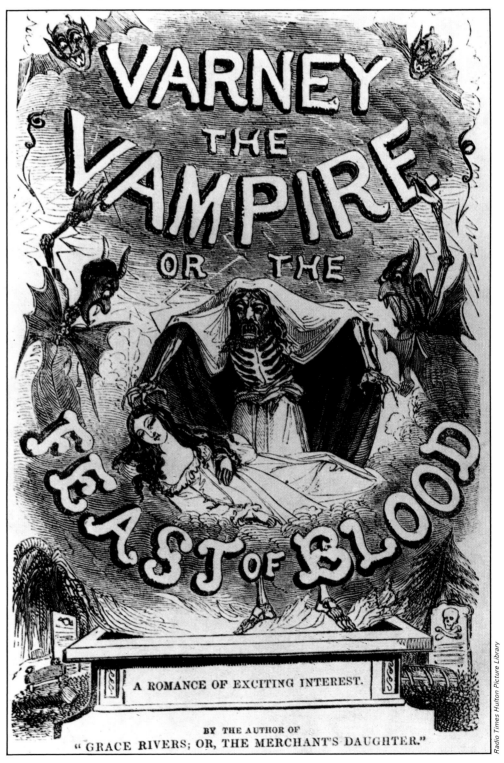

A ROMANCE OF EXCITING INTEREST.

BY THE AUTHOR OF
" GRACE RIVERS; OR, THE MERCHANT'S DAUGHTER."

normal clothing with perhaps a touch of the theatrical, like Dracula's entirely black costume. His thinness may vanish, in some cases, when he is well fed; when, like a leech, he is horribly swollen with engorged blood. At these times he may be decidedly hot to the touch. But more usually the only sign of life about his face will be the thick ruddiness of his lips, which are frequently drawn back to display long, pointed canine teeth.

The vampire's eyes gleam, and sometimes flash redly, and his ears may be pointed, as were Dracula's. These features seem to be borrowings from the older tradition of the werewolf (see WEREWOLF); similarly, the vampire will have sharp curved finger nails, eyebrows that meet above the nose, and he will be extremely hairy, with hair on the palms of his hands. His limited diet gives him foul breath but also makes him preternaturally strong despite his thinness.

A few isolated groups of tales add some special features, for extra horror effects. There is the Bulgarian suggestion that a vampire has only one nostril, or the old Polish idea that his tongue has a sharp point or barb. Vampire tales from Greece described the creature as having blue eyes; but this was merely a way of saying that blue-eyed people, rare creatures in Greece, were probably vampires. Anyone who is 'different' in some way has always been a convenient victim when the conforming majority is looking for enemies of the *status quo*. People with hare-lips, or red hair, or odd birthmarks, and children born with teeth, have all been persecuted for alleged vampirism.

These victims may well have wished that they *were* vampires, for folklore endows the creature with some impressive supernatural powers. The old eastern European legends underline its character as one of the 'walking dead' by stating that it can get in and out of its grave through six feet of soil. According to some Balkan stories, the grave of a vampire is punctuated by numerous small holes, which are channels down to the coffin through which the creature filters up to the surface. This is one of the main examples of the lack of distinction between corpse and ghost: the vampire is a material body with some of the abilities of an immaterial spirit. Hungarian tales overcome the problem by giving vampires the magical ability of changing into clouds of mist, a trick that Bram Stoker borrowed for Dracula; the Count could slip into locked and sealed rooms through the space under a door, or the keyhole, to reach a victim.

The shape-changing powers of the vampire also enable it to turn into various animals, usually noxious or nocturnal creatures with long-standing supernatural associations. And the vampire will sometimes have such animals at its beck and call, as aides in its evil-doing. Dracula had a pack of wolves under his control to terrify travellers; and the old tales similarly include wolves, or werewolves, among the vampire's animal companions, along with cats, owls, rats, and sometimes even flies. The vampire sometimes changed itself into animals such as these, most often a wolf or a cat. Dracula for

instance was able to change into wolf form. And of course he also turned himself into a bat, a metamorphosis that has been emphasized in films. Stoker, however, used the bat sparingly. The old vampire tales of eastern Europe almost never depict the creature assuming this last form.

When the 19th century globe-trotting urge sent Europeans as far afield as South America, their travellers' tales sometimes told of the curious fauna of the continent, including a strange bat which fed solely and exclusively on the blood of animals or people. The world reached into folklore to give it its popular name – the vampire bat; and folklore and fiction incorporated it in the supernatural vampire tradition.

One further special power attributed to the vampire, apart from filtering out of a grave or tomb, and shape-changing, is its ability to hypnotize its victims, preventing them from struggling while it feasts, and also from remembering their fearful visitor the next morning. The vampire can therefore return again and again to the same victim, who will complain merely of having had shadowy nightmares and feeling anaemic.

A Stake Through the Heart

According to tradition, if people become aware of the presence of a vampire there is a battery of defences and reprisals that can be brought into action against it. The creature is bound up in a more extensive array of 'rules', within which it must operate, than any other folklore horror; and these rules contain defences against the vampire. It must of course be active only at night; but because it is a walking corpse, it must not only rest by day but must rest in its own grave or tomb. A few Balkan tales describe vampires moving freely around during the day, but this is generally thought to be cheating. On the other hand, the old tales do not say that sunlight is actively harmful to the vampire; this idea is a contribution of horror fiction, and films.

In fact many things can hurt, or at least ward off, a vampire. It shuns silver, as evil creatures have done since antiquity, and also hates garlic, and the plant's pungent flowers are useful to have at the window, or around the neck, if vampires are about. Since Christian times, the creature has actively feared the crucifix in any form, an idea that is partly the result of belief that all evil is in some way derived from Satan, the Enemy, and that the symbol of Christ will therefore oppose it. But older tales, from a Devil-oriented age, are sometimes more explicit: theories by European churchmen of the 17th century suggested that the corpse

Left John Haigh as a choirboy; accused of murdering nine people, whose blood he was said to have drunk, he has been called the 'vampire of London'. Isolated cases of people who suffer from a mania for consuming blood may have provided a factual basis for some legends of vampirism *Right* A fairground 'vampire' in Sydney, Australia; the embodiment of repressed sexual wishes, and guilts that come 'from the unconscious world of infantile sexuality', the vampire is one of the most popular of supernatural monsters

which became a vampire was in fact activated, or powered, by a demon from hell, and not by its original soul. Therefore it would especially fear the cross.

Silver, garlic and the cross are forms of protective magic; but vampire lore also specifies preventive magic which is widely used in lands riddled with the vampire fear. In these regions it seems that every deceased person would be ringed round with charms to bind him into his grave. These often resemble primitive methods for keeping the dead from rising. The Chiriguono tribe of South America, for instance, fastened a corpse into its grave with pegs, which also kept the ghost down, and some old Slavonic tales suggest thrusting iron skewers through the earth over a grave, so that the corpse would be magically pinned down. The iron works the magic: evil things shun cold iron almost as much as silver. Many European people simply placed a lump of iron in a dead man's coffin, to keep him in his grave. Other methods of ensuring this included putting a branch of hawthorn or some similar sacred tree, or a wreath of garlic flowers, on the coffin.

There are also all the practices by which, in European lore, any ghost is kept down when there is cause to believe that he may walk — this applies to suicides, executed criminals and so on. They are buried under running water, or at crossroads, or the corpse has a stake driven through its heart. In lands where belief in vampires took precedence even over ghosts, these techniques became charms against vampires.

However, if neither preventive nor protective magic is effective, there are still ways in which the monster can be destroyed. First, though, the vampire must be captured. Few vampires are as gregarious as Dracula, who invited people to stay at his castle, where the truth about him was revealed in several ways: his appearance, his absence by day, or the fact that he had no reflection in a mirror.

If vampire activity broke out in a particular region the locals would repair to the cemetery and examine the graves. Hopefully, they might find one with the small tell-tale perforations through which the monster filtered up from its coffin. Or they might borrow an old Hungarian test for vampirism. In this a white stallion that has never stumbled and never been to stud is taken to the cemetery; the horse will refuse to walk on a vampire's grave.

If there were no indications above the ground of vampire activity, the hunters would have to open the graves, and look for a corpse that had not decomposed. These trials could take place with perfect safety during the day while the vampire was dormant, but the searchers had to give themselves time to get back indoors before sunset. The uncorrupted corpse would bear additional signs of vampirism: the typical facial appearance, and traces of blood on mouth and face.

Once a vampire has been caught, it can be easily destroyed. For that matter, the monster could be shot with a silver bullet at night, while it was active, provided the

hunter could avoid the creature's hypnotic eyes for long enough. Ideally the bullet should be made from a melted-down crucifix, or at least blessed by a priest. A safer method is to find the vampire in its coffin and to employ some homely magic to keep it there. The main technique is to drive a short, sharp stake into its heart.

The tales recommend using sacred wood for the stake, perhaps the thorn, or aspen. According to some traditions only one blow must be used to drive it home, or the 'pinning' magic will not work. Albanian tales suggest using a consecrated dagger, in the shape of the cross, instead of a stake. Other legends recommend that the monster be decapitated as well as staked; and specify that the beheading must be done with the sexton's spade. Sometimes the beheaded and staked vampire is then conclusively destroyed by the purification of fire.

These powerful defensive and offensive rituals and charms seem to give the living an advantage over the vampire, who at night can be balked by garlic or the cross, and who is wholly at the hunter's mercy during the day. But the vampire has one magical power not mentioned so far. He can recruit his victims into the ranks of vampirism. According to some tales, anyone who dies from loss of blood as the result of a vampire's continued attacks will instantly rise again as a new vampire. Other traditions suggest that even one or two non-fatal attacks by a vampire will cause the victim eventually to rise again after his or her natural death. For every vampire staked and destroyed,

British Film Institute

Dracula, the most famous of all vampires, was created at the end of the 19th century by Bram Stoker, so effectively that the character has passed into modern folklore: scenes from the 1931 film with Bela Lugosi as Count Dracula *(left)* and from the 1958 film in which the part of the vampire count was played by Christopher Lee *(right)*

several new ones will have been created.

Nor is this recruitment the only way in which vampires can come into existence. The lands most rife with vampire lore associated many supernatural traditions that are elsewhere ascribed to ghosts with these creatures. In the Balkans, anyone dying in a state of sin, without the Church's blessing, would rise again as a vampire; this category would especially include suicides and ex-communicants. Perjurers and people cursed by their parents, in fact any exceedingly wicked person, might also walk as vampires after their deaths, as would anyone who dabbled in black magic.

According to western European folklore, such evil-doers must come back after death as insubstantial haunts, punished with eternal restlessness for their evil ways, and bound to this earth in a dreadful shadowy immortality. Western European tales also insist that the victims of evil return as haunts; and similarly, in eastern Europe, such victims return, through no fault of their own, as vampires. A murdered man whose death goes unavenged becomes a vampire (especially in Greek tales); so does a child who dies unbaptized, or a man whose

corpse does not receive a Christian burial.

In addition to these borrowings from the older ghost traditions, vampire lore has produced some original ideas about the creation of the monsters. In Rumania, for instance, men who are werewolves reappear after death as vampires. Greek legends assert that anyone born on Christmas Day runs the risk of becoming a vampire; and other tales suggest that a seventh son, or a child born with a 'caul', might rise as a vampire after death. According to Rumanian tradition, if a vampire stares at a pregnant woman she will give birth to a potential vampire, unless a priest's blessing can cancel out the evil.

Hungry for Blood

The weird assortment of ways in which vampires are bred do not reflect the purpose for which the creature arises. Unlike ghosts, witches and demons, the vampire is not impelled by any of the familiar evil urges or intentions such as revenge, terrorizing or tempting souls from the righteous path. The vampire is merely obsessively hungry. He seeks blood to give him the pseudo-life he needs to seek more blood.

Folklore contains many instances of the animation of the dead by blood. In the *Odyssey* shadowy phantoms regain substance and the power of speech after drinking blood; witches fed their familiars on their own blood. And there is the story of a 19th century French doctor who pumped blood into the severed head of a guillotined prisoner, and was convinced that the head

came briefly to life and took on a 'puzzled' expression.

The fascination of the vampire legend may be explained, to some extent, by the few nuggets of reality that lurk within the folklore. Some writers, for instance, make much of the parallel between vampires rising from the grave and the prevalence in past centuries of premature burial. Inadequate medical knowledge meant that people were sometimes buried before they were dead; and folklorists find some possible explanation for the 'uncorrupted corpse' aspect of the legend in this fact.

In the 16th and 17th centuries it was not uncommon for a number of people in a village to die, apparently inexplicably, from what were then unknown diseases. If a number of graves were later opened, and it was found that one of the recently buried corpses had not yet started to decompose, seemed to have changed position, and had a frightful expression on its face and blood on its hands, vampirism seemed to be the obvious explanation. In fact, the corpse would have been that of a person buried prematurely who had awoken in the grave and died horribly, trying to claw his way out.

There are also numerous cases of long-dead corpses remaining intact; examples may be found especially in accounts of Christian saints. There is also a supposedly true story from Italy which tells how the body of a woman buried in 1820 was exhumed 30 years later and found to be wholly uncorrupted. One of the exhumers accidentally cut the corpse's leg with a

2927

DOAMNE

APARA-MA DE DRACULA

A cross bearing the inscription in Rumanian, 'My God, save me from Dracula': *dracul* means 'devil' in Rumanian and Bram Stoker gave his vampire the name of a 15th century nobleman, noted for his sadistic cruelties. Vampires are said to fear the cross of Christ, which can be used as a weapon against them

spade, and blood gushed from the wound, as blood is supposed to flow from a vampire when it is staked, after which decomposition set in rapidly. In a superstitious age incidents such as these might well have given rise to a number of 'vampire' tales.

Finally, we must look behind a curtain drawn over the vampire theme by the moralizers of the 19th century. In Victorian times explicit accounts of brutality and violence were perfectly proper for widespread dissemination, but anything containing more than a hint of sexuality required censorship. This attitude produced the view that vampire legends are just good gory horror stories, grown out of primitive superstitions about the dead. In fact, vampirism is a blatantly sexual motif, riddled with oral eroticism and sadomasochism.

The old Balkan tales rarely omitted the sexual side of vampirism: married vampires arose from the grave to bestow their terrible attentions on their marriage partners, while those who were unmarried visited attractive young persons of the opposite sex. And it was not solely blood lust that impelled them. But in later tales, and in fiction, the sexual angle was more oblique.

The vampire bites his victims; and anyone with the slightest knowledge of Freud knows that a bite is a sado-erotic kiss; in *Dracula* the female vampires around Jonathan Harker's bed comment that his health and strength mean 'kisses for us all'. Even the creature's appearance, his thick red lips and unusual hairiness, corresponds to widely-held folk beliefs about excessively sex-oriented people.

Blood is profoundly involved with sexuality in man's psyche, a belief that is reflected in the widespread taboos placed on menstruating women. And modern psychology has shown the predominance of blood and blood-letting in the erotic fantasies of many psychiatric patients.

The British author Maurice Richardson has described the vampire legend as 'a kind of incestuous, necrophilous, oral-anal-sadistic all-in wrestling match'. The vampire embodies repressed sexual wishes and guilts which come 'from the unconscious world of infantile sexuality'. This view may unsettle some people who have enjoyed reading fictions like *Dracula*, or Sheridan Le Fanu's story *Carmilla* (1872), which has an unmistakable theme of lesbianism. But it is these undercurrents which are the main reason for the vampire's staying power, in the forefront of our favourite supernatural horrors.

DOUGLAS HILL

FURTHER READING: David Bischoff, *Vampires of the Night World* (Ballantine, 1981); Montague Summers, *Vampire in Europe* (Universal Books, 1961).

VEDANTA

Robert Skelton

Vedanta begins with the proposition that there is an eternal all-pervading Reality which remains unchanged amidst changing appearances

Vedanta is not a cult, but a philosophy which can be used to describe and interpret any of the great religions of the world *Previous page* A London group receive instruction in Vedanta; they are affiliated to the Ramakrishna Mission (*inset*), named after the modern Hindu saint who taught that all religions are true
The various methods of achieving union with the Atman are suited to different temperaments: bhakti yoga works through worship, prayer and concentration on a divine personality, while jnana yoga offers to its disciples salvation through intellectual effort
Above A rajah, holding a rosary as he makes *japam*, worships the god Rama, his wife and brother *Above right* Rama and his brother visit four hermits, who have withdrawn to the forest to devote themselves to meditation

According to Vedanta, the meaning and purpose of life for every person on earth is to know Brahman-Atman, the all-pervading Reality: four main paths lead to this ultimate union — the way of devotion, the way of knowledge, the way of action and the way of meditation

VEDANTA is a Sanskrit word which means 'the end of the *Vedas*', the scriptures which form the basis of the Hindu religion. There are four of them; the *Rig*, the *Sama*, the *Yajur* and the *Atharva*. The traditional Hindu belief is that they were composed by seers at the very beginning of human history. In any case their origin is obscure and exceedingly ancient.

The Hindus regard the *Vedas* as being

divine truth — truth known by men through experience of union with the divine in man — but their attitude toward them is not the same as that of the devotees of other religions toward their own sacred books. The Hindus do not demand that the *Vedas* shall be approached in a spirit of uncritical faith. On the contrary, they insist that each individual must verify the truths taught by the *Vedas* through his own effort and practice, in his own life.

The content of the *Vedas* is varied, and scholars have divided it into two categories which they call the Work Portion and the Knowledge Portion respectively. Each of the four *Vedas* contains both a Work and a Knowledge portion. The Work Portion includes prayers, hymns, rules of conduct,

instructions for the performance of sacrificial rites and religious duties. The Knowledge Portion consists of the *Upanishads*.

The word *Upanishad* means 'sitting near one's spiritual teacher (guru) in a mood of devotion'. Its further meaning is 'the secret teaching', in other words, the teaching which may be imparted only to those disciples who are fit to receive it. Of the 108 *Upanishads* included in the *Vedas*, ten are regarded as being of major importance. Some of them are direct expositions of spiritual truth; others are set forth as dialogues between a teacher and one or more disciples. Their teaching may be conveyed in the form of a story; for example, the story of the boy Nachiketa's visit to the house of the King of Death, in the *Katha*

Robert Skelton

Upanishad. Or it may be contained in a poetic image, as when, in the *Brihadaranyaka Upanishad*, the noise of the thunder, *Da*, is interpreted by three different classes of pupils to mean three different things: *damayata* 'be self-controlled', *datta* 'be charitable', *dayadhwam* 'be compassionate'.

Vedanta means 'the end of the *Vedas*' in two senses. First, the Knowledge Portion does in fact come after the Work Portion in each *Veda*. Second, the word *anta*, like 'end' in English, also means goal or purpose. Vedanta is therefore the purpose of the *Vedas*, the reason for their existence; that is, their teaching. And since the teaching of the *Vedas* has been restated and explained by many commentators in many books, the word Vedanta may also be used to describe this vast literature, which is still being added to today.

Unchanging Brahman

Vedanta is sometimes used as a synonym for the Hindu religion, but this is inaccurate. In one sense, the Hindu religion is something more than Vedanta, since it includes the cults of numerous aspects of God and of divine incarnations – Rama, Krishna, Durga, Kali, Vishnu, Shiva, Ramakrishna, to name only a few. In another sense, Vedanta is something more than the Hindu religion, since it is not a cult but a philosophy and as such can be used to describe and interpret any of the great religions of the world. One could, for example, be simultaneously a Christian and a Vedantist – always provided that one was

ready to agree that Jesus was not the only divine incarnation. Vedanta, by the terms of its own philosophy, must be universal.

Vedanta begins with the proposition that there is an eternal all-pervading Reality, without characteristics or attributes, which remains unchanged amidst the changing appearances of our universe. When spoken of as external, or transcendent, this Reality is called Brahman; when spoken of as internal, or immanent, it is called the Atman (see BRAHMAN). But, since the Reality is both external and internal, these names imply absolutely no difference in essence, only in one's subjective viewpoint. The Brahman around us *is* the Atman within us.

Brahman-Atman is described as being *Sat-chit-ananda*, absolute existence, absolute consciousness, absolute bliss, but these are not to be thought of as attributes. Brahman *is* existence, *is* consciousness, *is* bliss. It is the existence through which all else exists, the consciousness which contains all knowledge, the bliss which is beyond all desire and fear and is therefore absolute peace.

There are those who mistakenly describe Vedanta as pantheistic. (Pantheism, as defined by *Webster's Dictionary*, is the doctrine that the universe, taken as a whole, is God.) But Vedanta makes a clear distinction between Brahman and the universe, although it sees them as intimately related. The universe is called an effect of Brahman, inseparable from Brahman in the same sense that heat is an effect of fire and inseparable from fire. Nevertheless, heat is not identical with fire and Brahman is not

identical with the universe. The universe changes; Brahman does not change.

In the *Upanishads* one finds nothing which can be described as pantheism. But there are two interpretations of the Brahman-universe relationship which at first sight seem contradictory. In certain passages it is stated that nothing but Brahman exists; in others, that Brahman and universe co-exist eternally. This seeming contradiction arises because two different levels of mystic perception are being described. The seer who has experienced the reality of Brahman and who then returns to normal consciousness may declare that the universe he sees around him has no substance and that there is in truth nothing but Brahman. But this same seer, if he is on the level of mystic perception which is between the normal and the supernormal, may declare that he sees both Brahman and the universe, both inner and outer, simultaneously.

Vedanta's second proposition is that Brahman-Atman, being the true nature of man, as of all creatures and objects, can be known by man. To know yourself, according to Vedanta, is to know the Atman within you, not the ego-personality, labelled Mr Smith or Mrs Brown, with which you ordinarily identify yourself. Indeed, this ego-personality can never be fully known, since it is subject to continual change and since it is like an onion: when you have removed all of its skins there is nothing left. The process of knowing the Atman is therefore a process of ceasing to identify yourself with the ego-personality. The ego's fundamental claim is

Robert Skelton

that it is separate from and other than its neighbours and surroundings. But the seer who knows the Atman within him knows in the same instant that he is essentially one with his neighbours and surroundings, since their true nature is also Brahman-Atman.

Vedanta's third proposition is that the meaning and purpose of life for every individual on earth is to know Brahman-Atman, and that all his activity should be directed toward that goal. If you accept Vedanta's first two propositions it would seem that you are forced to accept this one, at least in theory. Surely, if Brahman is *Sat-chit-ananda*, everyone must wish to be united with it and find safety? Surely, if Brahman is the true Fact of Life, then to refuse to accept it is to turn one's back on sanity and prefer to inhabit a world of madness? This is what mystics of all ages and races and faiths have held to be self-evident, and this is why they have devoted their lives to the search for union with the Eternal within themselves. Why do the overwhelming majority of the inhabitants of the earth fail to follow their example?

No Absolute Good and Evil

Even though you have accepted Vedanta's first two propositions, you may still not put the third one into practice, because you are bewildered by *Maya*. Maya is the basis of mind and matter and therefore the stuff of the universe, the effect of which Brahman is the cause. As individuals we exist and perceive and think and act within Maya. Within Maya we are Mr Smith or Mrs Brown. As long as we believe in the absolute reality of our perceptions within Maya, we cannot know the Atman. Maya is multiplicity, Brahman-Atman is one.

If Maya makes us ignorant of our true nature, and if Maya is an effect of Brahman, then is not Brahman evil? Vedanta says that such a statement cannot be made, because evil and good are merely relative concepts, existing within Maya. The question 'Why does God permit evil?' is as meaningless in an absolute sense as 'Why does God permit good?', since it is we who are defining what is good and what is evil. This universe is a place of mixed and changing values, of interaction and evolution. The greatest mystics, such as Ramakrishna (see RAMAKRISHNA), have likened it to a game and laughed at it, not because they were callous toward mankind's suffering or indifferent to its well-being but because they saw the Reality behind the shadow-show. When we ask, 'Why does this ignorance exist, why have we lost awareness of our true nature?', that question cannot be answered either, since it is asked from a standpoint within Maya and the answer lies outside Maya. The mystics who transcended Maya assure us that all is ultimately well; each individual, sooner or later, will free himself from Maya and know his identity with the Atman, and in doing so will realize that his ignorant flounderings in illusion were a necessary part of the game.

How is Brahman-Atman to be known? This has been the main theme of the literature of Vedanta. The principles set forth in the *Vedas* themselves have been elaborated by hundreds of later writers. Among the major classics of Vedanta are the *Bhagavad Gita* (see BHAGAVAD GITA), Patanjali's *Yoga Aphorisms*, Shankara's *Crest-Jewel of Discrimination* and the *Gospel of Sri Ramakrishna*. What follows is a digest based upon these four books and several others.

There are four distinct methods or disciplines by which union with the Atman may be achieved. They are called yogas. Yoga is the Sanskrit ancestor of the English word 'yoke', and it means both the act and the method of uniting. A man who practises yoga is called a yogi or a yogin; a woman who does so is called a yogini. The four principal yogas are bhakti yoga, jnana yoga, karma yoga and raja yoga.

Four Ways to Unity

Bhakti yoga is the method of union with the Atman through devotion. It is followed by means of ritual worship, prayer and *japam*. To make japam is to keep repeating one of the names of God — usually one's own mantra (see MANTRA), the name of one's chosen ideal. A rosary is often used in combination with making japam, in order to count out a prescribed number of repetitions. The object of devotional worship is, generally speaking, one of the many aspects of God with attributes, a divine personality or a divine incarnation (avatar). This kind of spiritual exercise is said to be easier than any other, since it only demands that the worshipper shall sublimate his natural urge to love and fix it upon the divine. The vast majority of believers in any religion are fundamentally bhakti yogis.

Bhakti yoga leads to ultimate union with the Atman but it does so indirectly, so to speak, achieving non-dualism by a dualistic approach. The devotee may theoretically accept the idea that he is essentially the Atman and yet find it impossible to believe this at first. Looking inward, he can see no farther than his own ego-personality and its defects. Bhakti yoga teaches him, therefore, to look outward and choose some other personality which is more evidently god-like than his own. (The importance of making a definite choice and keeping to it is stressed

Surely, if Brahman is the true Fact of Life, to refuse to accept it is to turn one's back on sanity and prefer to inhabit a world of madness

because the emotions need an unchanging focus. To worship at every shrine is to disperse the emotional powers.) As the worshipper's devotion increases, he begins to understand that the object of his worship is the Atman within himself and one with Brahman; so in the perfected state of yoga, worshipper and worshipped become one.

The bhakti yogi (also called a bhakta) may choose not only the object of his worship but also the particular relationship which he wishes to establish between it and himself. For example, he may take the attitude of servant toward Master, of child toward Father or Mother, of parent toward Child, of friend toward Friend, or of lover toward Beloved. Exponents of all these relationships may also be found among the mystics of the Christian tradition.

Jnana yoga is the method of union through intellectual discrimination, often called the Path of Knowledge. The jnani is non-dualistic: he seeks to reach Brahman-Atman by constant and rigorous analysis of the nature of all phenomena. Instead of using the approach of dualism within Maya in order to transcend Maya, he denies the essential reality of Maya from the outset. His watchwords are 'not this, not this', as he continually reminds himself that the apparent universe is other than Brahman-Atman. The jnani hopes to discover the Reality by a process of elimination. He makes use of the intellect just as the bhakti makes use of the emotions. This explains why bahkti yoga is for the many and jnana yoga for the few. The pursuit of jnana yoga calls for tremendous willpower and mental clarity. The jnani, by dispensing with devotion and the aid of a chosen ideal, makes his path much harder for himself. Yet there are those who are temperamentally suited to jnana and who might otherwise not embrace religion in any form. The path of jnana

Above left Worshippers at a shrine sacred to Krishna; in the foreground musicians are singing devotional songs. Bhakti yoga is said to be the easiest kind of spiritual exercise, 'since it only demands that the worshipper shall sublimate his natural urge to love and fix it upon the divine' *Right* Yoga, particularly raja yoga, includes physical as well as mental disciplines: an ascetic performs his devotions by the banks of a river, seated in the lotus position – a technique of yoga

Robert Skelton

What is Joy?

What is joy?
Think of a young man, well read, ambitious, firm, strong, noble; give him all the wealth of the world, call him one unit of human joy.

Multiply that joy a hundred times, and call it one unit of the joy of those brought to the celestial choir by their good deeds. A man full of revelation, but without desire, has equal joy.

Multiply that joy a hundred times, and call it one unit of the joy of choir-born spirits. A man full of revelation, but without desire, has equal joy.

Multiply that joy a hundred times, and call it one unit of the joy of the fathers, living in their eternal paradise. A man full of revelation, but without desire, has equal joy.

Multiply that joy a hundred times, and call it one unit of the joy of heaven-born gods. A man full of revelation, but without desire, has equal joy.

Multiply that joy a hundred times, and call it one unit of the joy of gods brought to godhead by their good deeds. A man full of revelation, but without desire, has equal joy.

Multiply that joy a hundred times, and call it one unit of the joy of ruling gods. A man full of revelation, but without desire, has equal joy.

Multiply that joy a hundred times, and call it one unit of the joy of Indra, god of Power. A man full of revelation, but without desire, has equal joy . . .

He who lives in man, He who lives in the sun, are one.

He who knows this, cries goodbye to the world; goes beyond elemental Self, living Self, thinking Self, knowing Self, joyous Self. Here is my authority:

'He who knows the spiritual joy mind cannot grasp nor tongue speak, fears nothing.'

The Ten Principal Upanishads
trans. Shree Purohit Swami and W. B. Yeats

---

yoga appeals to the intellectual agnostic.

Karma yoga is the method of union through selfless work. Karma means a mental or a physical act, and also the consequences of that act (see KARMA). In a long-term sense, it means the sum of the consequences of all the acts performed by an individual in this and in previous lives. An individual's karma is made up of his *samskaras*, the tendencies or potentialities which are created in his mind by his actions and thoughts. Thus one karma motivates another, bringing with it happiness or unhappiness or a mixture of both. The samskaras make up what, at any given moment, we call the 'character' of an individual, but no one is helplessly in their power. An individual can always begin to modify them by performing acts and thinking thoughts which are contrary to their tendency. Thus a man's karma can be changed, for better or for worse.

According to Vedanta, it is karma which drives the individual soul, after death, to seek rebirth in a new body. The theory of reincarnation is therefore inseparable from the theory of karma. But the individual can free himself from this cycle of birth-death-rebirth through realization of his oneness with the Atman. When the Atman is known, the law of karma ceases to operate.

Work for Work's Sake
To work selflessly is to work sacramentally, offering every action and its results to God. This means in practice that every action must be performed to the very best of one's ability, since it is an offering to God; and that the doer must have no desire for any resulting fame or other material advantage and no fear of unpleasant consequences. He works, as the *Gita* says, 'for the work's sake only and not for the fruits of work', without fear and without desire.

Properly speaking, the karma yogi must perform every action according to this principle, even when the act is performed in solitude and without reference to other people. For the karma yogi must regard himself as the witness of his actions and not as the doer. He identifies himself with the Atman, and not with the physical and psychological drives which cause the action. But in general, the path of karma yoga is followed by rendering service to mankind through education, medical care or some other type of social work. The karma yogi is

reminded, however, that he is not really benefiting mankind by his service: to believe that he is doing so is to lapse into delusion and vanity. All action is really symbolic, for how can Brahman-Atman help, heal or harm Brahman-Atman? The yogi who seemingly helps others is actually helping himself, for his efforts are bringing him nearer to union with the Atman. Therefore he is told to bow down in gratitude to those who accept his service.

To speak of an action creating 'good' or 'bad' karma is to raise the question: in what manner does the law of karma relate to ethics? One may say that the Christian concept of sin is generally dualistic. The Christian thinks of himself in relation to a personal Father-God. A sin is an act of disobedience and ingratitude toward this Father. If the Father punishes it, that is only right and proper. Meanwhile the sinner begs his forgiveness and tries to feel sincere contrition. The Vedantist, being a non-dualist, is taught to regard sins as obstacles which he himself has placed in the way of his own enlightenment. He has not offended a divine Father; he has done himself an injury. He is not expected to feel contrition and beg for forgiveness; he is expected to resolve not to make the same mistake again. The danger of the Christian approach is that it may lead to exaggerated self-loathing and hence to weakness and despair. The danger of the Vedantist approach is that it may lead to a self-indulgent permissiveness.

Each one of us, considered as an individual within Maya, has different virtues and weaknesses; each has varying duties according to the way of life he has chosen. This natural duty is called *dharma*. The *Gita* warns us never to undertake the dharma of another person but to prefer to die doing our own duty. The dharma of the individual determines what is 'right' or 'wrong' for him at that particular stage in his growth. What is right for him at one period in his life may be wrong for him at another. Acts of desire and fear must be harmful because they put a man into greater bondage. But problems of conduct are seldom easy. No act in itself can be regarded as absolutely right or wrong, under all circumstances, for all individuals. The act can only be evaluated in relation to the search for union with the Atman.

Royal Yoga
Raja yoga, meaning literally royal yoga, is the method of union through the practice of meditation. It is followed by a systematic training and controlling of the mind, concentrating it one-pointedly on the Atman until complete absorption is achieved.

Raja yoga is also concerned with the study of the human body as a vehicle of spiritual energy. According to Patanjali, whose *Aphorisms* is the classic textbook on the yogas, there is an immense reserve of this energy situated at the base of the spine. It is called the *kundalini*, meaning 'that which is coiled up' (see KUNDALINI); hence it is sometimes referred to as 'the serpent power'. In normally unspiritual people, the kundalini is seldom and only partially aroused. The aim of raja yoga is to arouse it fully. In the *Gospel of Sri Ramakrishna*, which is a record of his teachings, Ramakrishna explains that the mind dwells only in the lower centres of consciousness as long as it remains attached to the objects of worldly desire. When, through the practice of yoga, the kundalini is aroused and has moved up the spine to the centre of the heart, man experiences his first spiritual awakening. If the kundalini can be made to ascend farther, to the centres of the throat, the forehead and the top of the head, man becomes enlightened.

It may be admitted that raja yoga is primarily for those who are prepared to lead predominantly contemplative lives; its techniques are too exact and thorough to be practised amidst the distractions of a busy life in the world. But its description of human physiology has great significance for us all. It teaches that there is no sharp division between mind and matter: the two are interrelated within a process which may be thought of as a series of superimposed coverings, the outermost increasingly material, the innermost increasingly mental or subtle. Furthermore — and this is a most important lesson for the puritan — there is no sharp division between pure and impure, between spirit and flesh. The same energy, the power of the kundalini, is expressed in physical appetite, sexual desire, artistic creation, compassion for others, the longing for God and finally the highest spiritual experience.

The disciplines, usually known as the 'eight limbs', of raja yoga are: *yama*, the

Robert Skelton

practice of truthfulness, continence, abstention from greed and the exploitation of others for one's own gain; *niyama*, mental and physical purity, contented acceptance of one's lot in life, performance of ritual worship, practice of japam, devotion to God, study of the scriptures; *asana*, choice of a suitable place and a correct posture for meditation; *pranayama*, control of the vital energy through the practice of breathing exercises; *pratyahara*, withdrawal of the mind from sense-objects; *dharana*, holding the mind within a centre of spiritual consciousness inside the body or fixing it upon a divine form; *dhyana*, an unbroken flow of thought toward the object of concentration (this is often compared to pouring oil from one vessel to another in an unbroken stream);

'The process of knowing the Atman is . . . a process of ceasing to identify yourself with the ego-personality'; to this end the sannyasin, meditating by the river in the holy city of Benares, has renounced all material possessions

samadhi, the superconscious state in which man experiences his identity with the Atman.

Samadhi is the goal of the Vedantist and of many other practising mystics; Buddhists call it Nirvana and Christians the Mystic Union (see MYSTICISM). There are degrees of samadhi – in the lower samadhi, some sense of duality still remains – but samadhi is always a state of superconsciousness in which, to quote Patanjali, 'the true nature of the object shines forth, not distorted by the mind of the perceiver'.

For convenience, the yogas have to be described one by one, but of course they are not to be thought of as mutually exclusive. Indeed nobody can practise any one yoga to the absolute exclusion of the others. To call oneself a bhakti, a jnani, a karma or a raja yogi is merely to define one's general approach to yoga. But discrimination without devotion is ultimately sterile, devotion without discrimination must degenerate into shallow emotionalism, some meditation is necessary even for the most active, and no human being can avoid action altogether. A classical simile likens man's character to a bird in flight: love and knowledge are its two wings, meditation is its tail.

(See also BREATH; HINDUISM; YOGA.)

CHRISTOPHER ISHERWOOD

Vedas

Hindu sacred texts, consisting primarily of the *Rig-Veda, Yajur-Veda, Sama-Veda* and *Atharva-Veda*; incorporating three main strata, in order of date, the *Samhitas* (hymns), the *Brahmanas* (manuals of ritual and prayer) and the *Upanishads* (philosophical treatises); the language of the Vedas is Vedic, a form of Sanskrit; the word *veda* means 'wisdom' or 'knowledge'.
See HINDUISM; INDIA; VEDANTA.

VEDDAS

THE VEDDAS, a primitive forest tribe of Ceylon, and the numerous ethnic groups of similar physical appearance represent one of the most archaic surviving racial types of Asia. They are of slight build and small stature, with dark brown skin colour and wavy or curly black hair. The forehead is low, the eyes are deep set under heavy ridges, the nose is short and broad and often depressed at the root, the lips are full and the chin tends to be receding. Some of the jungle tribes of Southern India closely resemble the Veddas, and it can be safely assumed that all these populations are remnants of an ethnic stratum which during the late Stone Age extended over large parts of Asia.

When at the end of the 19th century the Veddas were first studied by Western scholars, they were found to live solely by hunting and collecting, dwelling in caves surrounded by jungle. Excavations proved that these caves had been inhabited by people of the late Stone Age, and much points to the assumption that the Veddas are the direct descendants of the Stone Age cave-dwellers whose roughly flaked stone implements lie only a few inches below the surface. The cultural evidence from these cave deposits coincides largely with what is known about the style of life of the modern Veddas, and this too suggests that in the wooded highlands of Ceylon there was an unbroken cultural sequence from the Stone Age to the present time.

The traditional style of Vedda life persisted until the first quarter of the 20th century, when the British anthropologist C. G. Seligman undertook a study of this ancient people. The majority of Veddas had already been partly assimilated to the Sinhalese peasantry, but there were still groups of Veddas who led a semi-nomadic life in the forest and used rock shelters as habitations. The average Vedda community consisted then of about five families, who shared the rights of hunting over a tract of land within which they gathered honey, edible roots and tubers, fished in streams and used natural rock shelters. But the whole of the community did not commonly move about its territory as one band.

Each group exercised property rights over a clearly defined territory, and there was a tradition that in the old times an intruder entering the land of another group without the owners' permission would have faced death. Membership of a group descended through the female line, and it was customary for a man to join his wife's group on marriage and live in their territory. As the membership and size of a group changed from generation to generation territorial boundaries also changed, and the whole system of land holding was extremely elastic.

As the inroads of peasant cultivators restricted the hunting grounds of the Veddas, many of them had to seek new means of subsistence. Most took to a simple form of shifting cultivation, clearing small patches in the forest and planting millet, maize and various vegetable crops. They also acquired some cattle, and gradually adapted themselves to the way of life of small-scale cultivators. Today there are no true forest Veddas left, and the Ceylonese government has provided facilities to aid the process of transition from semi-nomadic hunting and food-gathering to settled agriculture. But although there is no longer an essential difference between the economies of the Veddas and other backward rural communities, the Veddas remain culturally outside the society of the Buddhist Sinhalese.

Corpses Left in Caves

When they were first studied, more than half a century ago, the religious practices and beliefs of the various groups of Veddas proved to be of great complexity. It was impossible to isolate any body of beliefs which could be regarded as the original Vedda religion: while the material aspects of Vedda life seemed to reflect a fairly accurate picture of conditions among South Asian food-gatherers of the Stone Age, the same could hardly be claimed of the religious phenomena met among the Veddas. Some customs, however, are certainly of considerable antiquity. For instance, the funeral practices of the forest Veddas present a striking contrast to Sinhalese practice. When a man or woman died from natural causes the body was left in the cave or rock shelter where the death occurred, and was covered with leaves and branches. The cave was then abandoned for some time but could be reoccupied later, when the remaining bones were thrown out unceremoniously. An alternative method of disposal of corpses was burial in a simple grave dug by the brothers or other close kinsmen of the deceased. While most graves were not marked and no objects of any kind were buried with the departed, the spirits of the dead were treated with great respect and were given offerings of food.

There is a belief, still current among Veddas, that for a short time the spirit of a dead man remains near the site where he died, but later on joins the company of the ancestor spirits. These spirits are known as *yakku*, the same term which the Sinhalese employ for demons. The Veddas believe that life in the realm of the yakku remains the same for all time: that is, they are not reborn in a different shape. Although there are male and female spirits they are 'like the wind' and do not have sexual relations. Some Veddas say that all yakku lead a more or less similar life, but others believe that even among the yakku 'good people' occupy a higher and 'bad people' a lower position. The good yakku are helpful towards the living, while bad yakku are liable to harm their surviving kinsmen. Acts of violence, even the harsh treatment of a dog, annoy the ancestor spirits and endanger those who have aroused their wrath.

Distinct from the ancestor spirits are spiritual beings also described as yakku but named according to localities. These yakku have the character of local deities and are associated with certain features of the landscape. Some of them are believed to control wild animals; when Veddas were still mainly hunters, they used to cut off the head of whatever game they had killed and leave it in the forest as an offering to the gods of the chase.

In most Vedda communities there is one man who has the power and the knowledge to establish contact with the ancestor spirits and the nature deities. At ceremonies when the spirits of the dead are given offerings of food, one of them may possess this priest and, speaking through his mouth in hoarse guttural accents, declare that he approves the offerings and that he will assist his kinsmen in hunting, often stating the direction in which a hunting party should go. Each priest trains his

The Veddas are one of the oldest surviving racial types of Asia, preserving elements of the culture of their cave-dwelling ancestors

Illustrations from C. G. Seligman's *The Veddas* (1911) *Left* To determine the cause of an illness, a Vedda recites an invocation: when the spirit causing the sickness is named the bow should swing to and fro *Below left* Group of Veddas: semi-nomadic hunters, they would offer a portion of each kill to the spirits

successor, and the pupil learns to repeat the invocations of spirits recited at ceremonies.

The method of invoking spirits is essentially the same in all Vedda ceremonies: an invocation is sung by the priest and often by the onlookers, while the priest dances round the offering prepared for the spirits. Special veneration is accorded to two spirits, known by individual names, who are believed to exercise control over other spirits and who must sanction any assistance which those under their authority give to men. These two spirits were specially invoked in order to obtain game, and when hunters had been successful, pieces of flesh from the neck and chest of the animal were roasted in the ashes of a fire and offered to them before being consumed by the Veddas. It was believed that if part of the meat was not presented to the spirits, the hunters would experience bad luck in future and might even be attacked by wild animals.

Contacts between Veddas and Sinhalese must occasionally have occurred ever since the latter, emigrants from Northern India, settled in Southern Ceylon in the 6th century BC. As free hunters the Veddas were accorded a high status by a society which greatly valued martial qualities, and traditions tell of various unions between members of the Sinhalese nobility and Vedda girls. The memory of such associations is reflected also in Sinhalese mythology. Kataragama, one of the most renowned Sinhalese deities, who presides over an important temple and centre of pilgrimage, is said to have fallen in love with Valliamma, the daughter of a Vedda chief; to this day Valliamma is worshipped as Kataragama's mistress and has a shrine of her own in the temple grounds, which is not inferior to the shrine of Kataragama's legitimate divine consort. Thus the Veddas, though gradually losing their tribal identity and merging with the Sinhalese peasantry, continue to figure in folk beliefs and mythology as the oldest indigenous inhabitants of the island.

C. VON FÜRER-HAIMENDORF

Seligman: The Veddas, 1911

Within the darkness of the pharaohs' tombs, 'mummies' filled with Nile mud and planted with corn sprouted with new life: the decay and resurrection of the seed-corn, personified in a vegetation god, was invested by ancient man with a deep religious significance

VEGETATION SPIRITS

THE EARLIEST human beings known to us, those of the Paleolithic or Old Stone Age (c 30,000 to 10,000 BC), are generally designated 'food gatherers' by anthropologists; for they either found their food in the form of nuts, berries and roots, or they hunted animals for it. During the succeeding Neolithic or New Stone Age a great transformation of economic activity occurred, which has aptly been called the 'Neolithic Revolution'. Man gradually changed from being a 'food gatherer' to being a 'food producer'. The two basic factors in this change were the invention of agriculture and the domestication of animals. The origins of agriculture have been much debated by scholars; but no generally agreed conclusions have yet been established about how and where this momentous change in human economy was first achieved. We can only speculate about the likely places (for example, the ancient Near East), where wild corn-bearing grasses might first have been purposely planted and tended by man.

This revolution in his economy had a profound effect upon man's life and thought. It led to the establishment of settled communities, from which emerged the first towns and cities; it prompted the formation of the first calendars, since seed-time and harvest had to be predicted; and it promoted the invention of writing and a scribal class, as agrarian transactions grew more complicated and required the keeping of accounts and records. The beginnings of all these institutions have been discerned in the ancient Near East.

But the change to an agrarian way of life also deeply affected man's religious ideas. As an agriculturist, he became intimately involved with the annual cycle of Nature's life. He realized that his existence and well-being depended upon the yearly miracle of the germination of the seed-corn, upon its steady growth and the increase of its fruits until harvest. The process of the seasons took on a new significance for him. He saw it as an annual drama of life and death. For in the Near Eastern lands the cycle of Nature's year has the aspect of a dramatic contest between the forces of life and death. Spring comes quickly, clothing the landscape in verdant green, bedecked by flowers. Under the increasing power of the sun the corn quickly ripens to harvest. But as summer advances and no rain falls, vegetation withers and dies, and the ground seems cursed with sterility and death. Yet from this seeming death, vegetation awakens again next spring to a new life, and the miracle of Nature's resurrection provides mankind once more with food.

Son and Lover
But the early peoples of this area saw in the annual rebirth of vegetation a significance deeper than that of the assurance of their food. For them the truth it intimated was twofold, and inevitably they interpreted it in mythic imagery. The idea of a 'Great Goddess', who was the source of all living things, seems already to have found expression in the Paleolithic era in the many carvings of the female form, showing the maternal attributes grossly exaggerated while the facial features were undelineated (see EARTH; FACELESS GODDESSES; MOTHER GODDESS). This primitive conception of the 'Great Goddess' was naturally associated with the earth, from which all forms of vegetation grew and within which the dead were laid. The vegetation was thus the offspring of the Earth Mother, and it was easily personified as a divine spirit that manifested itself in the trees and grass, and in the corn.

Hence developed the idea of a divine couple who embodied the fecundity of the earth and the crops which it bore, and upon which man's life depended. But the imagery of mother and son did not completely portray the whole complex of Nature's annual cycle. To give birth to vegetation, the Earth Mother had to be impregnated. A variety of imagery suggested itself: the plunging blade of the plough or the fall of rain. Some lines from the *Danaids* of the Athenian dramatist Aeschylus (c 499–458 BC) significantly portray the anthropomorphic images in which the ancient Greeks envisaged the process: 'Love moves the pure Heaven to wed the Earth; and Love (*Eros*) takes hold on Earth to join in marriage. And the rain, dropping from the husband Heaven, impregnates Earth, and she brings forth for men pasture for flocks and corn, the life of men.'

From such sexual imagery emerged the concept of a virile god who impregnated the Earth Mother with his seed. The form of this deity could vary between the animal and the human. The bull provided an obvious type-figure, and at Catal Hüyük, the oldest known sanctuary (c 6000 BC) of the Great Goddess, frescoes of bulls and bulls' horns signified the incorporation into her

cult of the principle of male virility. In Greek mythology Zeus, in the form of a bull, carried off Europa, and the Minotaur (half-man and half-bull) was the offspring of the Queen of Crete, Pasiphae, and a divine bull. In these 'faded myths' were probably preserved folk-memories of the associated cults of 'Great Goddesses' and sacred bulls. (See BULL.)

Mythic thought is characteristically imprecise, and it easily embraces ambivalent or contradictory ideas. So it is not surprising to find, in many myths of the ancient Near East, a male deity who is both the son and the lover of a fertility goddess. An example of such complex imagery is succinctly expressed in a title of the Egyptian god Amun-Re, descriptive of his relation to the goddess Nut. 'Bull of his Mother, the first on his field', he impregnated the goddess who gave him birth.

In his role of vegetation god, the offspring of the Earth Mother, this ambivalent male deity was also a 'dying and rising god' (see DYING GOD). For he personified the annual death of vegetation in the fierce summer heat and drought of the Near Eastern lands, and its resurrection in the spring. As such he became the subject of a complex of myth and ritual. Lamentations commemorated his death as the vegetation withered and died; ceremonies were performed to ensure his return from death; and joyous festivals acclaimed his resurrection as the new green of reviving vegetation appeared in the spring. From this basic drama of death and resurrection, manifest in Nature each year, there stemmed a rich tradition of idea and fantasy which embodied some of the deepest of human emotions – the instinct for life and the fear of death, sexual love and motherhood, the pathos of early death, aversion from the withering touch of time, aspiration for the assurance of immortality.

Life in the Tomb
The ancient Egyptian god Osiris (see OSIRIS) has been regarded by some scholars, most notably by Sir J. G. Frazer, as the classic example of the dying and rising god of vegetation. Subsequent research has not endorsed the view that this was the original character of Osiris; but the deity certainly became closely associated with fertility and the death and resurrection of the corn. This association was graphically portrayed in Egyptian art and ritual. The dead Osiris was frequently depicted lying supine, with phallus erect and plants sprouting from his body. A similar idea inspired other scenes representing the goddess Isis, in the form of a falcon, impregnating herself on the phallus of the dead Osiris. The meaning of such depictions seems clear: Osiris, as the deification of Nature's life-cycle, retained his fertility even in death, from which he triumphantly rose again.

A more spiritually significant idea motivated the making of 'corn-mummies', which were placed in tombs. The specimen found in the tomb of Tutankhamen consisted of an image of Osiris, constructed of wood and linen, which had been filled with mud from the Nile and planted with corn. It was bandaged like a mummy and placed in a wooden

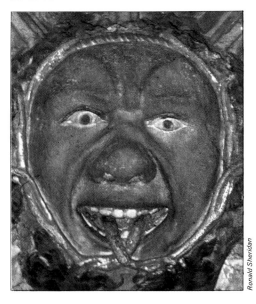

The 'foliate heads' in many medieval churches, depicting a human head covered with foliage, or with leaves and tendrils sprouting from the mouth and ears, are evidence of our ancestors' concern for the spirit of vegetation. 'No inscriptions explain their meaning; doubtless they needed none for people whose lives were so closely bound up with the fields and woods': painted roof bosses from Canterbury Cathedral

box. Enclosed in bandages and coffin, the seeds in this particular example could not have germinated as they did in less elaborate versions, which sprouted with corn in the warm darkness of the tomb, symbolizing the renewal of life after death. But it is probable that they were intended also to assist, by means of imitative magic, in achieving the resurrection of the dead person, buried in the tomb, to a new life.

The significance which the death and rebirth of the seed-corn, personified in a vegetation god, had for man's hope for immortality, invested the annual drama of the alternation of life and death in Nature with a deep emotive significance. The hope which the corn-mummies signified to the ancient Egyptians was presented anew for Christians in the well-known words of St Paul: 'But some one will ask, "How are the dead raised? with what kind of body do they come?" You foolish man! What you sow does not come to life unless it dies. And what you sow is not the body which is to be, but a bare kernel, perhaps of wheat or of some other grain . . . So it is with the resurrection of the dead. What is sown is perishable, what is raised is imperishable . . . It is sown a physical body, it is raised a spiritual body' (1 Corinthians, chapter 15).

Baal Avenged

The mystique of the annual death and resurrection of vegetation is seen in its clearest and most dramatic form in the cult of Osiris. But the mythologies of other ancient Near Eastern dying and rising gods better illustrate the connection between the god of vegetation and the fertility goddess: those of Adonis (see APHRODITE), Tammuz (see TAMMUZ), Baal and Attis.

'Baal' was a title meaning, in Hebrew, 'possessor' or 'lord' of the land (see BAAL). It was used to designate the Amorite god Hadad ('the thunderer'), who personified the winter rains and their accompanying storms. Since the rain was recognized by the Canaanites as an essential factor in the fertility of the fields and the growth of vegetation, Baal was identified with vegetation in its annual cycle of life and death. The mythology of Baal has become known through the discovery of texts, inscribed on clay tablets, at the site of the ancient city of Ugarit, on the Syrian coast north of Beirut. In these texts, which date from the latter half of the second millennium BC, a triad of deities is concerned in the drama of Nature's year. Baal's sister and lover is the fertility goddess Anat, who is generally depicted nude, with the sexual attributes emphasized. The enemy of Baal is Mot, who is the

The worship of the god of vegetation was associated in many agricultural communities with that of the goddess of fertility or Earth Mother; the god might be thought of as both her son and lover, issuing from her womb, to die and rise again in due season *Left* Aztec Earth Goddess, Coatlicue *Right* Head of an Aztec maize god, the 'flayed god' Xipe Totec, a form of Tezcatlipoca, who died by being skinned alive so that men might receive the maize; his priests wore the flayed skins of their victims to symbolize the rebirth of the crops

personification of drought and sterility, and hence of death.

Owing to the fragmentary state of the tablets, it is difficult to reconstruct with certainty the myth which described the relations of these deities. It would seem that Baal, for some obscure reason, had to descend into the realm of Mot. Before departing, he had intercourse with a heifer, from which a bull-calf was born: this bestial act may perhaps relate to the association of a bull cult with Baal, which was a feature of the fertility rites of the Great Goddess, already noted.

The disappearance of Baal caused sterility: 'the furrows in the fields are cracked with drought'. Anat took vengeance on Mot for the death of her lover. Seizing Mot, she 'ripped him open with a sword, winnowed him in a sieve, burnt him in the fire, ground him with two mill-stones, sowed him in a field'. This punishment inflicted on Mot has a curious significance; for it parallels the fate of the corn – some being ground into flour for bread; some being sown as seed. What the action signified in the myth is uncertain; but consequent on it, Baal returns to life. It is possible that since Mot had apparently devoured Baal, the sowing of fragments of Mot, intermixed with Baal, caused the resurrection of the dead god of vegetation. The revival of Baal is symbolized in the myth by poetic imagery: 'the heavens rained oil, the ravines ran with honey'. These myths probably served as a kind of libretto to fertility rites, performed each year to assist the germination of the seed-corn and ensure a good harvest. The licentious nature of such Canaanite rites, involving as they did sacred prostitution, was vehemently denounced by the Hebrew prophets.

Youthful Lover

Attis was the youthful lover of Cybele, the great mother goddess of ancient Phrygia (see CYBELE). The spring festival of the goddess was mainly a ritual commemoration of the death and resurrection of Attis. There are variant versions of the myth accounting for his death, which seems to have resulted from self-castration. It is difficult to make out a coherent myth and ritual complex from these versions and the rites associated with the cult of Cybele and Attis. The fact that the pine was sacred to the young god might indicate that originally he was a tree spirit; it is interesting in this connection to note that an episode in the legend of Osiris concerns a marvellous tree that quickly grew and enshrined his body. Cybele was served by eunuch priests called *galli*, who were reported to have buried their severed parts in the earth, perhaps to promote the fertility of the Earth Mother. Similarly suggestive are the repulsive rites of the *criobolium* and the *taurobolium*, in which a ram and bull, symbols of male virility, were sacrificed, their blood providing a regenerating baptism for initiates into the mysteries of the goddess (see BAPTISM).

Some scholars have claimed to find in many religions of the ancient Near East a definite 'myth and ritual' pattern connected with the life-and-death cycle of vegetation.

According to them, the king represented the vegetation god at the New Year festival, in which the death and resurrection of the deity was ritually enacted in a series of related episodes. These comprised, besides a dramatic representation of the death and resurrection of the god of vegetation, the recitation or symbolic representation of the myth of creation; a ritual combat, in which the triumph of the god over his enemies was portrayed; a sacred marriage; and a triumphant procession, with the king playing the part of the god, followed by a train of lesser gods.

This 'myth-and-ritual' complex, so it is explained, originated from a primitive custom of killing the king when his physical vigour began to diminish; for, since the fertility of the land was magically connected with his virility, it would be disastrous to have an aged impotent monarch. His youthful successor ensured the continuance of the fecundity of the soil by his marriage with the queen or high priestess. These barbaric rites, it is argued, had been gradually transformed into a ritual death and resurrection of the king, which was celebrated each year. In the subsequent sacred marriage, the queen or priestess represented the fertility goddess. The case for the existence of this 'myth and ritual' pattern has not been generally accepted by scholars as proven. But much evidence concerning the reaction of the ancient peoples of the Near East to the death and rebirth of vegetation does suggest that their kings were deeply involved in the annual fertility rites.

Return of the Corn Maiden

In ancient Greece, the famous Mystery cult of Eleusis witnesses to the mystic significance that men there found in the annual drama of the seed-corn (see DEMETER; ELEUSIS). The two deities connected with this cult differed notably, however, from those of the Near Eastern cults. Instead of a naturally interdependent pair of fertility goddess and vegetation god, the Eleusinian divinities were related as mother and daughter. Demeter, the corn goddess, was the mother of Persephone, the corn maiden. The myth of the abduction of Persephone by Plouton, the lord of the underworld, provided the rationale or explanation of the secret rites performed at Eleusis (see PERSEPHONE; PLUTO). Distracted by the loss of her daughter, Demeter forgot her task as the corn goddess. So the ground grew sterile and famine afflicted the race of men, until the supreme god Zeus was obliged to intervene and bid Plouton restore the corn maiden to her mother. But the restoration could not be complete, because Persephone had tasted a morsel of food in the underworld. Zeus ruled, in consequence, that Persephone should spend two parts of the year above ground with Demeter and one part in Hades with Plouton. The return of Persephone brought fruitfulness again to the fields, which soon waved 'with long ears of corn, and its rich furrows were loaded with grain'. There has been much speculation as to the exact significance of this division of the year between Persephone's stay with her mother and with Plouton,

but it is generally agreed that the division relates to the life cycle of the seed-corn — perhaps to the time the seed lies buried in the ground until its emergence in the fresh vigorous upsurge of life in the following spring.

In the Eleusinian Mysteries the death and resurrection of the seed-corn was undoubtedly interpreted as presaging a rebirth to a new and immortal life for those who were initiated. Very little is known of the rites which were performed in the great Telesterion or Hall of the Mysteries at Eleusis; but there is evidence that the culminating revelation made to the initiate, who had been subjected to experiences simulating death, was that of 'a reaped corn-stalk'. The meaning of the symbol must surely have then been apparent to him, and perhaps that meaning implied an insight similar to that ascribed to Christ in St John's gospel (12.24): 'unless a grain of wheat falls into the earth and dies, it remains alone; but if it dies, it bears much fruit'. However that may be, the Homeric Hymn to Demeter, which records the Eleusinian myth, ends with the assurance: 'Happy is he among men upon earth who has seen these mysteries; but he who is uninitiate and who has no part in them, never has lot of like good things once he is dead, down in the darkness and gloom.'

It was Sir James George Frazer who first showed, in *The Golden Bough*, the enormous influence that agriculture has had upon religion. The titles of some of the volumes that make up the work significantly indicate aspects of the theme: *The Dying God; Adonis, Attis, Osiris; Spirits of the Corn and of the Wild*. In the first volume of the series, *The Magic Art*, Frazer evokes, in a masterly passage, the memory of the mysterious priest-king who served the goddess Diana in her sacred grove at Nemi (see KING). This sinister being bore the title *Rex Nemorensis*, the 'King of the Wood'. Whoever was bold or desperate enough to challenge the 'ghastly priest', proclaimed his challenge by breaking off a bough of the sacred tree — the 'golden bough', according to certain ancient writers.

The Green One

Frazer set himself the task of explaining this strange institution. After a long and involved investigation of ancient literature and folklore, he conclude that 'at Nemi the King of the Wood personated the oak-god Jupiter and mated with the oak-goddess Diana in the sacred grove'. Originally this priest-king was named Virbius, which Frazer translated as 'the Green One'. The sacred union of Virbius and Diana, or the priestess who impersonated the goddess, was intended 'to make the earth gay with the blossoms of spring and the fruits of autumn, and to gladden the hearts of men

The growth of vegetation was often interpreted in human terms, as the result of a cosmic sexual act: human fertility continues to be associated with the fertility of Nature, in a modern Chinese poster showing the prosperity to be expected under Communism

and women with healthful offspring'. Frazer identified the mystic Golden Bough with the mistletoe which, growing on the oak, was believed by ancient peoples to be the life or soul of the tree (see MISTLETOE).

In his quest for the origins of the priest-king of Nemi, Frazer was led to investigate a widespread cult of tree spirits which has been practised in northern lands to make the corn grow. The custom of the Harvest May, observed by various peasant peoples of Europe, is particularly notable. A large branch of may or hawthorn was brought home with the last load of harvest, and decorated with ears of corn. Sometimes it was fastened to the roof of the farmhouse, remaining there for a year, or planted in the cornfield, with the last sheaf tied to it. To those who made it, the Harvest May evidently embodied or represented the spirit of vegetation, upon whose fructifying influence next year's harvest depended.

It was from this primitive belief in vegetation spirits that the custom of the maypole took its origins. The maypole, which the Puritan writer Phillip Stubbes perceptively, if humourlessly, condemned as a 'stinking idol', was the symbol of the vegetation god. The institution of the May Queen, so essentially associated with the maypole, preserves an ancient folk-memory of the sacred marriage to promote the fertility of the herds and fields. In the May Day customs the spirit of vegetation was also represented by the Green Man or Jack in the Green. At Knutsford in Cheshire, the Green Man still leads the annual procession of the May Queen —

Pearl Binder

a strange and somewhat eerie figure, completely enveloped in greenery (see GREEN; MAY DAY).

Frazer collected a mass of evidence from the folklore of many lands expressive of a sense of tragedy at the time of harvest. Sometimes the last sheaf of corn has been ritually threshed and treated as a sacrificial victim, recalling perhaps a human sacrifice that was once made on the harvest field to the god of vegetation. The fate of the corn in its transformation to bread has also been seen as the passion of the Corn Spirit. A Danish folktale describes the sufferings of the rye: 'In the autumn you will be sown, deeply buried in earth; in the spring you will rise; in the summer you will be parched in the sun, drenched in the rain,

then cut and dried, carted to the barn and threshed; then, carted to the mill and ground.'

Today in many medieval churches the so-called 'foliate heads' still witness to our ancestors' concern for the spirit of vegetation. These strange emblems, carved in wood or stone, depict a human head with leaves and tendrils sprouting from the mouth and ears.

There are no inscriptions to explain their meaning; doubtless they needed none for people whose lives were so closely bound up with the fields and woods. A faint memory of these old beliefs lingers on in the 'corn dollies' made for harvest festivals (see HARVEST). They are the last relics of a tradition that reaches far back to the

dying and rising gods of the ancient Near East.
(See also FERTILITY; TREES.)

S. G. F. BRANDON

FURTHER READING: J. G. Frazer, *The Golden Bough* (St. Martin's Press, 1980 reprint); E. O. James, *The Cult of the Mother Goddess: Seasonal Feasts and Festivals* (Barnes and Noble, 1959 and 1963 respectively); E. O. James, *The Tree of Life* (Brill, Leiden, 1966); S. H. Hooke ed., *Myth Ritual and Kingship* (Oxford Univ. Press, 1958); John C. Gibson, *Canaanite Myths and Legends* (Attic Press, 1978); G. E. Mylonas, *Eleusis and the Eleusinian Mysteries* (Princeton Univ. Press, 1961).

VENUS

The Italian Venus was identified with the Greek goddess of love, Aphrodite, who was the mother of Aeneas and so an ancestress of the Roman people: the 'Venus of Rhodes', Greek sculpture of the 1st century BC

THE WORD *Venus* is related to English 'wish' and, more remotely, 'win'. The Latin common noun means 'charm', 'attraction', 'delight'. Its derivative verb *venerari*, which in antiquity also meant 'venerate', primitively signified the sacral act of alluring or enticing something from beyond mankind's power. Thus a famous literary echo of an old prayer reports the formal enticement of willingness from the god Quirinus (*veneror horam Quirini*). The goddess who sprang from the abstract *venus* forever kept the skill of wheedling.

Rome's foremost expert in religious history, Varro, was struck by the absence of Venus's name in the oldest records. Indeed Venus could not boast an old priesthood or festival or shrine at Rome. Further, Venus was unique in Italy. Etruscans spoke of Turan, 'Lady'. In the Oscan dialect the

comparable goddess was Herentas, very similar in concept because the name is related to the aforementioned Latin 'willingness' and to English 'yearn'. There is reason to believe that Venus had not even been universal to the Latins of central Italy. She seems especially Roman and thus contrasts with Jupiter whom all the Indo-European speakers knew, or with Mars who, though native to Italy, was shared by all peninsular inhabitants (see JUPITER; MARS).

Most of Venus's cult remains unknown to us. Some Romans insisted that the month of April was named after Aphrodite, her Greek equivalent. However, this folk etymology was based on the cult of Venus on behalf of vegetable gardens. As early as the late 3rd century her name signified the garden produce itself. The Romans consecrated gardens to Venus on 19 August, and vegetable gardeners kept the day holy.

There is no certain answer as to why Venus was related to the Vinalia, two wine ceremonies in the civil calendar on 23 April and 19 August. These festivals belonged to the sky god Jupiter. Aside from the coincidence of their worship on days of the Roman Vinalia, there is some Campanian evidence of a state cult of Venus Jovia. This worship can be construed in one of two ways. Either Venus is already identified as Aphrodite whom Zeus (Jupiter) fathered according to one Greek myth (see APHRODITE), or the goddess originated as the sky god's *venus* or, to use the local term, *herentas*. Of course, vineyards do not greatly differ from gardens. Also, in a sense, all plants need to be coaxed or wheedled to put forth their fruits. Such coaxing may be enacted by sexual representation. Be that as it may, no clear and direct evidence of such religious practice emerges from the ancient evidence on Venus.

Produce and Prostitution

At least as early as 290 BC, Venus was somehow associated with the August Vinalia because her first temple was dedicated on that day by a patrician, Fabius, who had built it with fines exacted for ladies' debauchery. Although it stood at least 600 years, this temple's activities are rarely mentioned. Venus's epithet Obsequens, 'compliant', and the source of the building funds point to an already existing identification of the goddess with the Greek Aphrodite and the

Etruscan Turan, who were definitely goddesses of female sexuality. Despite the sexual aspects of both the cult title and the ladies' misbehaviour, Fabius had a personal reason for the choice of his piety. He claimed that Venus had submitted to the wishes (*obsequi*) of his father and himself. The two Fabii had fought together in several campaigns against the Samnites and after the last Samnite war Venus Obsequens received her temple. Unfortunately, we do not know whether the Samnite Venus was worth conciliating in war.

Venus perhaps exercised some political sway among the Latins, for there existed two large precincts a few miles south-west of Rome where Aphrodite or Frutis, sometimes called Venus, were annually worshipped by all the Latins. One or both shrines, purportedly of great age, may have actually been related in cult to the widely renowned goddess of Mt Eryx on the western tip of Sicily. The Erycine sexual goddess was variously identified with Aphrodite and the Phoenician Ishtar (see ISHTAR). The Latin Frutis was said to have received her cult statue from Erycina.

One tradition explicitly equated Venus Erycina to the Aphrodite who bore Aeneas. Accordingly, the Trojan hero gratefully transported her cult to Cyprus, to Sicily and to Latium. Aphrodite occasionally had the epithet *Aineia*, which was interpreted to commemorate her maternity. The maritime route of Aeneas's legendary wanderings can be traced from one to another of Aphrodite's shrines. Some place-names of the western Italian coast preserved indications of Aphrodite in her role as protector of seafarers. Venus inherited these places as Roman rule spread.

After successive humiliations from Carthage's great general Hannibal, a direct descendant of the two Fabii observed what seems a family tradition and dedicated a temple to the true Venus Erycina in 215 BC. By this gift Fabius and the Romans placated a deity who had protected Carthage during the earlier Punic war and who was also an ancestress of the Roman people, through Aeneas who came to Latium and founded Romulus's line (see FOUNDING OF ROME). Venus Obsequens had received her temple at roughly the same time as the Romans first reared a statue group of

Ronald Sheridan

Left Gold votive figure of a Mycenean love goddess, with birds; doves were sacred to Venus *Right* A goddess of gardens and pot-vegetables, Venus became the embodiment of female allure and sexuality: *Venus* by Titian

Left Gold votive figure of a Mycenean love goddess, with birds; doves were sacred to Venus *Right* A goddess of gardens and pot-vegetables, Venus became the embodiment of female allure and sexuality: *Venus* by Titian

Romulus and Remus being suckled by the she-wolf. Venus Erycina had been integrated into the Roman tradition of their non-Italian ancestry. Consequently Rome's Capitoline Hill, reserved for truly Roman gods, allowed a site for Venus of Eryx.

Venus is certainly connected with the month of April by the dedication in 181 BC of a third temple on the earlier Vinalia of 23 April. This Venus, another Erycina, had been promised a temple during a war with the Ligurians of northern Italy, whom the Romans reckoned distant relatives of the Sicilians. Situated just outside the city, the new shrine reproduced the very temple on Mt Eryx where temple prostitution still thrived. Rome's Erycine precinct attracted the city's less savoury residents. On 23 and 25 April prostitutes and the offspring of prostitution and pimping kept their holy days here. Late April and early May had become holidays given over to sexual promiscuity and stage plays. Since the 3rd century such rites, introduced under the influence of the Greek Sibylline Books, had been consecrated to Flora, spirit of blossoming. They had their likely model in the cult of Aphrodite Antheia (Flora in Latin). For centuries the Floral Games provided notorious spectacles of sexual licence. Venus herself was not directly worshipped with Flora; nevertheless as divinity of produce and prostitution Venus belongs to the same kind of religious mentality.

The Sibylline Books reinforced the association in 114 BC, when the Romans were prompted to dedicate a temple to Venus Verticordia, 'Turner of Hearts'. Her name was intended to commemorate the acquittal of two Vestal Virgins charged with breaking their vows. Whatever the intent of the title, which is supposed to suggest the conversion from lust to chastity, Venus clearly retained her latent power of coaxing.

Political Promotion

Through Cornelius Sulla, who briefly engrossed the Republican government by his dictatorship of 82–79 BC, Venus entered the realm of personal politics. Sulla, also her devotee in other ways, adopted the style *Epaphroditos*, 'Aphrodite's darling', which he rendered *Felix* in Latin. The latter style, which he may also have applied to a Roman Venus, comprised all notions of fertility, prosperity, success and good luck. At Pompeii a coastal colony of Sulla's veterans accorded Venus unusual prominence. The Pompeian cult perhaps combined Sulla's patroness with the town's continuing adoration to Venus Physica, Venus of Nature (*physis*), which preserved the Greek idea of growth.

In 55 BC Pompey the Great dedicated a temple to Venus Victrix 'the Winner', atop his theatre, which was the first permanent theatre in Rome. Opposition to its construction was probably blunted by the consecration to Venus. At about the same time, Rome's great poet Lucretius published his philosophical poem on Nature, in which he invoked for poetic inspiration Venus, ancestress of the Aenead race, and which he dedicated to Memmius whose clan corporately worshipped Venus.

The patrician clan of Julii asserted even stronger proprietary rights of ancestral cult for Venus since they claimed direct descent from Iulus, the Trojan son of Aeneas. Julius Caesar surprised no one by emphasizing his clan's rise to power in his own person by vowing a temple to Venus Genetrix during the battle of Pharsalus, at which Pompey was defeated. Caesar raised the temple (perhaps the first built entirely of marble at Rome) in his new forum and dedicated it in 46 BC, although his adopted son Augustus completed the work. Beside the statue of his ancestress Caesar set a golden statue of Cleopatra.

In the Greek East subject provincials joined Aphrodite with deified Rome in a religious demonstration of loyalty to the Empire and to the imperial house which Caesar had generated. Ultimate expression of the catholic loyalty of the Empire is met during the reign of Hadrian (117–128 AD). This emperor of Spanish birth devoted himself to the adornment of Rome, Italy and the Empire, whose ideal he generously cultivated with lovely and magnificent buildings. Hadrian did much to accord the provincials a sense of merit for their role in the Empire's government. To amplify his notion of imperial unity Hadrian built Rome's largest and handsomest temple to Venus and Roma, which he situated beside the Colosseum. Adoration of Roma, a provincial concept, remained unique to this temple. Each goddess had her own precinct, placed back to back. By universal usage this double temple was referred to as the City's Shrine. Hadrian chose to dedicate the temple on 21 April, the feast of Parilia, in order to honour Venus in her month and Roma on her birthday in the city's 888th year.

At Rome Venus was worshipped under other cult names. Most of these are easily understandable; Placida, 'pleasing'; Alma, 'nurturing'; Pudica, 'demure'. A few are most obscure, for instance Calva, 'bald'. The goddess's popularity extended throughout Italy and the Latin-speaking western Empire. She invited identification with lesser local divinities and found herself acquainted with universal notions. Thus she provides other examples of the Roman capacity to enlarge the concept and identity of their gods.

The Dead and the Sewers

Near the great cemetery on the Esquiline Hill once stood a holy grove called Libitina where corpses were prepared for burial. The profession of undertaker was also *libitina*. Cult for and in groves was quite common but a grove cult for the dead was extraordinary. By the Imperial age the Grove of Libitina was no more than an address, and very probably just the name of a street. From the name of the grove, or from that of its tutelary deity, the Romans thought up a goddess Libitina. At some later point they could not intellectually tolerate the

Colorific

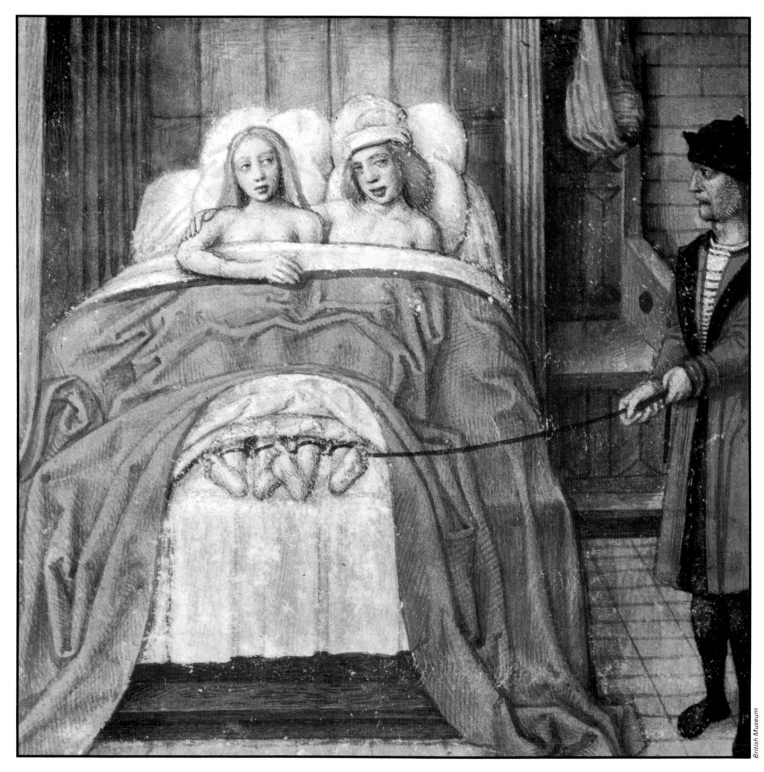

British Museum

The myths associated with Venus were taken from the Greek myths of Aphrodite: Venus is caught in bed with Mars by her husband Vulcan, in a 15th century Flemish illustration from *The Romance of the Rose*

plethora of insignificant divinities. Perhaps the very distaste for the subject of funerals had prepared the Romans to believe Libitina governed sexual desire (*libido*); thence the easy next step carried them to apply Libitina to Venus and to rear a temple to this goddess of lust. The word Libitina seems to have entered Latin from Etruscan, where it meant 'dead'. Libitina was not necessarily an Etruscan goddess, but a euphemism for death and its sequel.

Another example of a latterday Venus can be derived from a known locality. In early times the Romans knew the Little Aventine Hill as Mt Murcus. The valley between the Aventine and Palatine Hills was named the Murcia and was ultimately given over to the construction of the enormous Circus

Maximus; this embraced a number of old religious sites, among which was an altar to Murcia. Murcia shared her name with the turning posts at that end of the racecourse. Being overwhelmed physically by the affairs and structures of the Circus and her link with the locality having been forgotten, Murcia became the subject of learned speculation. Her name was derived from the Greek *myrtea*, 'myrtle'. Since this shrub was sacred to Aphrodite, Murcia came to be another name for Venus. With the discovery of her new

identity Murcia's cult seems to have perished.

Next and more perplexing is the case of Venus Cloacina. *Cloaca* is the Latin word for sewer. In uniformity with the need for a deity to oversee every place and structure, a shrine to Cloacina was put up in the Forum over the Cloaca Maxima, the town's main sewer. The Romans fancied that cloaca was derived from a verb of cleansing. Further, they supposed that the goddess of cleansing must be Venus, because the local plant used for sacral cleansing was the same as the myrtle. Finally, both Cloacina's shrine and Murcia's altar were situated over running water. This Venus was humanly represented and her statue held a flower of some kind. By involutions peculiar to the ancient mind Venus became mistress of funerals, racecourse turning posts and sewers.

A last instance of Venus's acquisition of alien functions illustrates another Roman religious peculiarity. When the Romans entered Carthaginian Africa, they readily acknowledged the native goddess Venus Caelestis, 'heavenly' Venus. The existence of an obscure Greek deity, Aphrodite Ourania, perhaps promoted the Romans' acceptance of Caelestis. At any rate the ground was soon prepared for the introduction of the planetary week and the convictions of astrology. In the wake of these innovations Venus lent her name to the sixth day of the new week which still keeps alive Mesopotamian astrology in Italy, France and Spain, where Ishtar's planet is commemorated in Venus's day. Our own Friday is just a further step in the equation. 'Friday's child is loving and giving!'

The Roman Venus exhibits different modes of divinity. From first to last her state cult contributed to the grandeur of the Empire and the glory of certain élite clans. Venus goddess of pot-vegetables gave way to the Venus of female sexuality, whose myth and cult are based upon Greek and oriental precedents that became peculiarly Roman only insofar as they included accounts of Aphrodite as the mother of Aeneas. Whatever else the cult of the abstract *venus* had once contained, the aspect of charm and allure was transferred to a female goddess of procreation.

R. E. A. PALMER

Venus the Planet

The Babylonians connected the morning and evening star with the goddess of love, and so did the Greeks and Romans, possibly because its appearances mark the limits of night, the time of love-making. Venus is the only planet named for a female deity and its astrological symbol is widely used outside astrology as a symbol of the female, the corresponding male symbol being that of Mars, the god who was the lover of Venus in classical mythology.

In astrology Venus is traditionally the ruler of love and desire, beauty and relationships — not confined to sexual partnerships but extending to relationships with friends and in business. It is also considered essentially beneficent, a force making for harmony, reconciliation, peace, affection, love of beautiful things, physical attractiveness. The position of Venus in your birth chart is thought to affect all these matters, but especially your ability to enter into relationships with other people and your attitudes to beauty, the arts, and the pleasures of life. If Venus is fortunately placed, it should tend to produce a warm, gentle, sympathetic, graceful and artistic person, contented, tactful and probably rather sentimental. The planet is particularly associated with music and is said to produce composers and musicians.

If not so fortunately placed, the influence of Venus may be less harmonious. The old belief was that Venus in conjunction with Saturn and Mercury in a horoscope threatened death by the treachery of a woman or by poison, traditionally the woman's weapon, but this has been reinterpreted by at least one modern authority to mean the threat of being dominated by a woman, or women, in life. It is often said that a man born when Venus is close to the Sun in the zodiac is likely to be effeminate, his character (Sun) being unduly influenced by the feminine planet. Saturn square to Venus, as in Hitler's horoscope, is supposed to indicate selfishness and egotism.

The influence of Venus on love-life varies with its placing in the zodiac. According to Margaret Hone's *Modern Text Book of Astrology,* a person who has Venus in Taurus will be 'steadfast in love, but possessive' and 'slow to make partnership but reliable when once settled'. Venus in Gemini, however, means that 'affection is changeable and often for more than one at a time', and if Venus is in Scorpio 'love tends to be more intense, more sexual, more secretive and passionate'. Venus in the eighth house, incidentally, is a good sign, traditionally foretelling an easy death.

In magic the force of Venus is connected primarily with love and sex, and with fertility and the teeming life of Nature. Copper, as the metal of Venus, is useful in love charms, and operations of love, lust, pleasure and friendship should be timed in the hour and day of Venus (see CORRESPONDENCES; DAYS; FORCES).

FURTHER READING: For the Roman goddess, see G. K. Galinsky, *Aeneas, Sicily and Rome* (Princeton Univ. Press, 1969).

In 1901, visiting the Petit Trianon – a building in which the ill-fated Marie Antoinette, Queen of France, had lived before the French Revolution – Miss Moberly and Miss Jourdain apparently stepped back in time to the year 1770

VERSAILLES ADVENTURE

THE STORY published under the title *An Adventure* in 1911 has been described by one of its critics as 'the arch ghost story of all time'. It is the account of the experiences of two English women, Miss C. A. E. Moberly and Miss E. M. Jourdain, who were both of academic standing and unimpeachable integrity.

The story began in 1901. While they were staying together in Paris for a short visit, they went on 10 August to see, for the first time, the Petit Trianon at Versailles. They knew very little about the place, beyond the fact that Marie Antoinette had lived there for some years before 1789. They came away that afternoon having seen in the garden persons and features, seemingly real at the time, but afterwards found to have been inappropriate to the circumstances of 1901.

They did not discuss the matter until a week had elapsed, when they came to the conclusion that the place was haunted. Three months later they discovered, on talking over the events of the August visit, that their recollections did not in all respects agree with one another. They accordingly decided to write independent accounts and these, with minor alterations and additions, constitute the main narratives of *An Adventure*. Both accounts are commendably brief, occupying only some five pages and four and a half pages respectively.

About the same time, November 1901, Miss Jourdain heard from a French friend that Marie Antoinette was regularly seen on a certain day in August sitting outside the garden front of the Petit Trianon. The conclusion was quickly reached that the haunting had to do with Marie Antoinette, and all later researches and visits were directed to the task of reconciling their recollections of the 1901 visit with what was known of the background of Marie Antoinette's time.

There have been five editions of *An Adventure,* and each one has elicited from reviewers and others fresh solutions of the mystery. For instance, it has been suggested that the two visitors on 10 August 1901 failed to take in their surroundings at all accurately, because they were too much engrossed in conversation, or overcome by unaccustomed French food and wine. They may have seen men in long coats of old-fashioned appearance, who were really Robert de Montesquiou and his friends, who were alive in 1901, holding a costume party in the garden of the Petit Trianon, and have mistaken them for 18th century gardeners.

One critic expressed surprise that people still paid any attention to the story, considering that Miss Moberly had confessed on her death-bed that it was a hoax. But this allegation was never substantiated and Dr Joan Evans, who knew both the ladies well, denied that any such confession had been made.

Time Out of Joint

Whatever influences may have been at work to bemuse or mislead the two visitors on 10 August 1901, the fact remains that their descriptions of what they saw on that afternoon cannot, without making extravagant assumptions, be reconciled with the surroundings as they were either in 1901, or in the time of Marie Antoinette. Their descriptions may, of course, have been pure fantasy. But it is a curious fact that the visitors, apparently without realizing the significance of what they saw, described some garden features characteristic of the period of the 'Anglo-Chinese garden', a fashion which was at its height in the early 1770s. A first attempt by the present writer to date the visions from internal evidence put the year at 1774, but later research by A. O. and M. E. Gibbons pointed to an earlier date for them, 1770.

Briefly, the visitors, in the course of a walk of a few hundred yards, saw and described eight features which were manifestly 'wrong' for 1901, and can be shown by pictures and plans to have been 'wrong'

What They Saw

From Miss Jourdain's description:

'We walked for some distance down a wooded alley, and then came upon the buildings of the Grand Trianon, before which we did not delay. We went on in the direction of the Petit Trianon, but just before reaching what we knew afterwards to be the main entrance I saw a gate leading to a path cut deep below the level of the ground above, and as the way was open and had the look of an entrance that was used, I said, "Shall we try this path? it must lead to the house," and we followed it . . .

'. . . there was a feeling of depression and loneliness about the place. I began to feel as if I were walking in my sleep; the heavy dreaminess was oppressive. At last we came upon a path crossing ours, and saw in front of us a building consisting of some columns roofed in, and set back in the trees. Seated on the steps was a man with a heavy black cloak round his shoulders, and wearing a slouch hat. At that moment the eerie feeling which had begun in the garden culminated in a definite impression of something uncanny and fear inspiring. The man slowly turned his face, which was marked by smallpox, his complexion was very dark. The expression was very evil and though I did not feel he was looking particularly at us, I felt a repugnance to going past him.'

Earlier, Miss Moberly and Miss Jourdain had asked the way from two men in greenish clothes and three-cornered hats. They saw a cottage with stone steps, a woman and a little girl. They saw the man in the dark cloak, his face marked with smallpox. Then a man with long dark hair directed them to another path and they crossed a stream by a rustic bridge. When they reached the Petit Trianon, Miss Moberly saw a woman in a large shady white hat with sketching paper.

---

for 1789. All eight features, as shown by garden plans and documents, make sense in relation to the surroundings of the year 1770.

The idea that the two visitors may have had a 'glimpse of the historic past' does not rest solely upon the *Adventure* story. There are a few stories of a similar kind which have so far defied attempts to explain them away. Each story, taken separately, can be criticized on grounds of deferred reporting, poor documentation and lapses of memory. But if, as here, the person who has had the experience has thereby acquired knowledge about the past which could only have been acquired normally by research, it is unreasonable to assume that research had been previously carried out but had been forgotten.

The alternative hypothesis, that the correspondences between vision and fact were due entirely to chance, seems implausible in a case where there were so many 'hits' on the target and no manifest 'misses'.

It is disappointing that so little is known about the day-to-day life at the Petit Trianon in the years 1770–74, and there is no certain clue to the identity of any of the persons who were seen on that August afternoon. But to the lover of beautiful buildings there is some compensation in the thought that the two visitors may have seen the Petit Trianon in its perfection, as it came from the hand of the architect, before its surroundings had been marred by the demands and whims of a later generation. The reader's verdict, however, should be founded not on sentiment but on the evidence of the visions themselves, examined against the recorded history of the house and garden.

G. W. LAMBERT

FURTHER READING: The 5th edition of *An Adventure* was published by Faber & Faber in 1955, with a useful preface by Dr Joan Evans. For the 'dating', see A. O. Gibbons ed, *The Trianon Adventure* (Museum Press, 1958). See also Lucille Iremonger, *The Ghosts of Versailles* (Faber & Faber, 1957); Andrew Mackenzie, *The Unexplained* (Arthur Barker, 1966).

R. G. Foord

VERVAIN

WHAT WE CALL vervain today is *Verbena officinalis*, an insignificant plant. But vervain is also identified with a plant, now unknown, which was important in classical times. Pliny called it *sacra herba*, the sacred herb, and other classical names applied to 'verbena' included Cerealis, Demetria, Persephonion, Mercury's Blood, Tears of Juno or of Isis, all of which suggest a close link with fertility ceremonies. Besides using it in religious rites, the Romans kept evil spirits from their homes with it, and made it into charms to ward off bodily harm. Ambassadors and heralds parleyed with enemies wearing a 'verbena' crown. Roman witches employed it too, as the poet Virgil notes.

In ancient Persia 'vervain' branches were carried in rites associated with sun worship, while its juice was used by magicians: smeared on the body, it enabled one to gain the affection even of an enemy. Cutting of vervain was done when neither sun nor moon were visible, and honey was poured on the ground as an offering in exchange. Similar observances are recorded of the Druids, who made special use of the plant in prophecy. During the 18th century revival of interest in Druids, the finding of vervain anywhere near a stone circle convinced antiquarians of the monument's druidical past.

In medieval times, when *Verbena officinalis* took over from the unknown classical plant, its religious importance diminished in relation to its use by herbalists and sorcerers. Charms of all kinds, including love potions, were made with vervain. It was something of a cure-all, used as an amulet, especially against snake-bite and accident, and recommended for dozens of different ailments from cancer to plague, the 'bloody flux' to piles. Tumours could be dealt with by cutting a vervain root in two, hanging one round the sufferer's neck and smoking the other over a fire. As this shrivelled the tumour was supposed to do likewise. If the smoke-shrivelled part was retained by an ill-disposed person and placed in water, the tumour would return as the root swelled up.

Vervain kept away witches and their works, as many authors testify, and was frequently used in conjunction with dill, and also rue. This did not stop witches from themselves making use of vervain, so much so that it was called the Enchanter's Plant. It was one of the plants supposed to open locks magically: a thief would embed a fragment of the leaf in a cut made in his hand, and would then only have to touch a locked or bolted door or chest to open it.

Vervain was associated with St John's Eve, 23 June (see ST JOHN'S WORT), when bonfires were lit while, to quote a contemporary poem,

> . . . young men round about with maids
>   do dance in every street,
> With garlands wrought of Mother-wort,
>   or else with Vervain sweet.

Frazer relates how in Germany, in the 16th century, the chaplets of mother-wort (mugwort) and vervain were finally thrown onto the St John's Eve bonfires. On this night also, protective garlands of vervain, often mixed with flax, were hung in houses.

The use of vervain as a love philtre and securer of affection has been recorded within the last century, together with its use against illness. In Germany a wreath or hat of vervain was placed on a bride's head, harking back to classical times when the plant was sacred to Venus and the bridal wreath was picked by the bride herself. In the Victorian language of flowers, vervain stands appropriately enough for enchantment.

Vesta

Roman goddess of the hearth, equivalent of the Greek Hestia: worshipped at home as the deity of the family hearth, her public cult was conducted in a circular shrine, the 'hearth' of the community, where a perpetual fire burned, tended by the Vestal Virgins; her favourite animal was the ass.
See HEARTH.

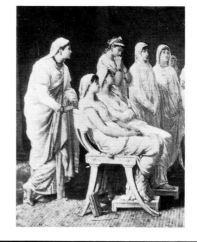

Vestal Virgins

Priestesses of the sacred fire of Vesta in Rome; probably the successors of the King's daughters who originally tended the fire on the royal hearth; if they let the fire go out, they were beaten; chosen as small girls, they served for 30 years, during which time they had to remain chaste.
See FOUNDING OF ROME; HEARTH.

That our lives are influenced by mysterious universal vibrations has become a common notion, largely based on the taking over into occultism and astrology of theories drawn from 19th century science

VIBRATION

IN THE PAST a few rationalists have gone so far as to allege that all those who claimed to have experienced 'occult phenomena' were, quite literally, mad. Today, few would openly admit to such an extreme point of view, but it is true that occultists and schizophrenics have always shared a tendency to attempt to explain the interior experiences they have undergone in terms of the generally accepted beliefs of the societies in which they lived. Thus in the 17th and 18th centuries a schizophrenic would usually attribute his peculiar mental state either to the activities of spirits and witches or to the punishment of a jealous Calvinistic deity.

With the decline of popular belief in witchcraft such rationalizations were replaced by others of a more 'scientific' type, and the schizophrenic tended to blame his condition on the activities of evilly disposed individuals broadcasting 'death rays' or mysterious 'telepathic radiations'. The recent occult revival has brought signs of a reversion to earlier modes of explanation and a surprisingly large number of seriously disturbed patients in mental hospitals claim to be the victims of either black magic or 'astral attacks'.

Like the schizophrenic, the occultist of the last century attempted to explain his beliefs and experiences in the light of the science of his own day; the astral light of Eliphas Levi, for example, showed much more resemblance to the luminiferous ether of 19th century physics than to the astral light of Paracelsus. Similarly, the prominence which the concept of vibration assumed in the occult theorizing of the last quarter of the 19th century owed much to the importance of vibrational frequency in the wave theory of light. Spiritualists took over the idea and explained the invisibility of the spirit world (supposed to interpenetrate the ordinary world of matter) to ordinary individuals as being the result of varying 'rates of vibration'. Mediums, so it was claimed,

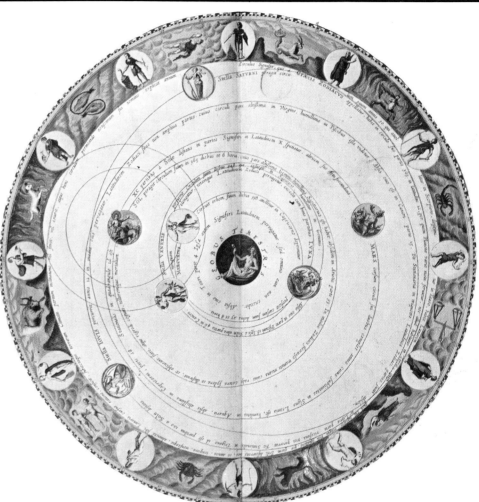

'The universe visible to man can be likened to a web of tiny interlacing octaves of vibrations': one source of this analogy is the old Pythagorean theory of the 'music of the spheres', that the motions of the heavenly bodies create a harmony of musical sounds; 17th century diagram of the planetary spheres

were those who were able partially to adjust their vibrational rates to those of the spirit world.

Madame Blavatsky and her theosophical following were particularly prone to use vibration as an explanation of supernormal events; indeed they seem to have seen it as the bridge which would eventually link up the dogmas of the physicists with their own syncretistic brand of oriental occultism

(see BLAVATSKY; THEOSOPHY). They held that there existed a mysterious 'inter-etheric force' which could be controlled by the use of the vibrations of sound and would ultimately provide mankind with a free source of energy, enabling a complete control over its physical environment.

The theosophists seem to have derived this idea from a charlatan named John Worrell Keely, 'inventor' of the notorious Keely motor, of which its creator wrote: 'In the conception of any machine heretofore constructed, the medium for inducing a neutral centre has never been found. If it had, the difficulties of perpetual-motion seekers would have ended, and this problem would have become an established and operating fact. It would only require an introductory

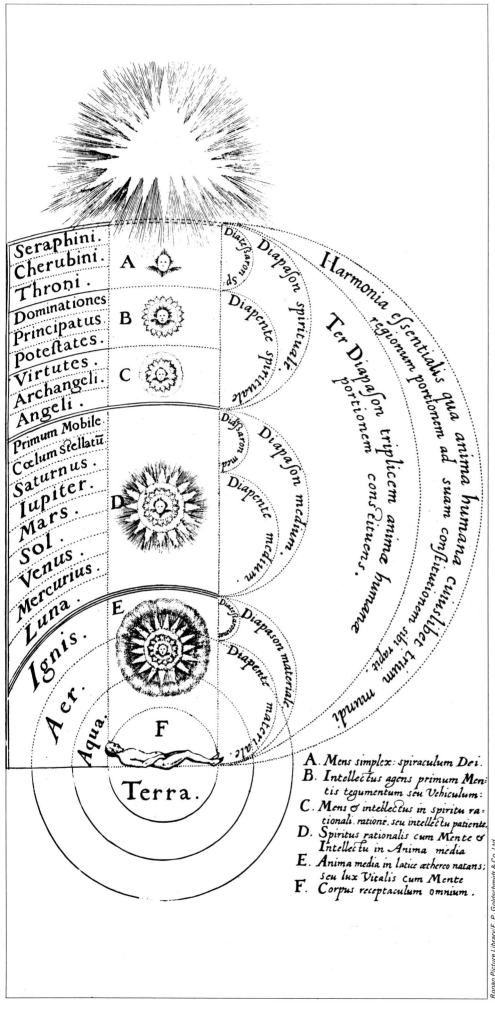

Seraphini.
Cherubini.
Throni.
Dominationes
Principatus
Poteftates.
Virtutes.
Archangeli.
Angeli.
Primum Mobile.
Cœlum ftellatū
Saturnus.
Iupiter.
Mars.
Sol.
Venus.
Mercurius.
Luna.
Ignis.
Aer.
Aqua.
Terra.

A. *Mens simplex: spiraculum Dei.*
B. *Intellectus agens primum Mentis tegumentum seu Vehiculum:*
C. *Mens & intellectus in spiritu rationali. ratione, seu intellectu patiente.*
D. *Spiritus rationalis cum Mente & Intellectu in Anima media*
E. *Anima media in latice æthereo natans; seu lux Vitalis cum Mente*
F. *Corpus receptaculum omnium.*

impulse of a few pounds, on such a device, to cause it to run for centuries. In the conception of my vibratory engine, I did not seek to attain perpetual motion but a circuit is formed that actually has a neutral centre, which is in a condition to be vivified by my vibratory ether, and, while under operation by said substance, is really a machine that is virtually independent of the mass (or globe), and it is the wonderful velocity of the vibratory circuit which makes it so. Still, with all its perfection, it requires to be fed with the vibratory ether to make it an independent motor . . .'

Madame Blavatsky appears to have been much impressed by Keely. In the *Secret Doctrine* she referred to him as 'a natural-born magician' and quoted with approval a description of him as being 'great . . . in soul, wise . . . in mind, and sublime . . . in courage . . . the greatest discoverer and inventor in the world . . .' He was, in reality, a fraud who managed for many years to enjoy a comfortable existence on the money he had extracted from those gullible enough to invest in his 'Vibrational Self-Motor'. After his death it was discovered that the working model of his motor which, seemingly set in motion by the vibration of a violin string, had so impressed visitors to his laboratory was in reality powered by a secret supply of compressed air. In spite of this fiasco theosophists and other occultists continued to attach great importance to 'vibrational energy', and to the Keely motor; even today there are those who defend Keely as a great occultist and physicist.

Music of the Universe

In the present century vibration has ceased to occupy an important place in the theoretical framework of most occult systems and its place has been taken by other, more fashionable, scientific (or pseudo-scientific) concepts. Thus some 19th century astrologers attempted to provide a rationale for their art by arguing that each planet had its own vibrational frequency which, transmitted by radiation through the ether, blended with the vibrations of the other planets to influence the child at birth; today such theories have been largely abandoned by astrologers in favour of Jungian 'synchronicity' — the belief that everything done at a certain moment of time has the qualities of that moment of time.

Nevertheless, vibrational theories have survived, and indeed have been developed much further in attempts to provide a semi-physical explanation for the phenomena of dowsing and radiesthesia (see DOWSING; RADIESTHESIA). Such explanations often involve a belief that the vibrational frequencies of the ordinary musical scale have an occult significance of cosmic importance. Dr H. Tomlinson, an Australian radiesthetic and homoeopathic practitioner, has claimed that: '. . . the notes of the tonic sol-fa system are a universal constant . . . The universe visible to man can be likened to a web of tiny interlacing octaves of vibrations. These octaves are of two sorts, ascending and descending. A descending octave is progress from matter of higher vibrating rate to matter of lower vibratory rate . . . An ascending octave is progress from denser matter to more spiritual matter . . . The diviner . . . is operating in a web of interlacing celestial octaves . . . Every substance, when tested by radiesthetic methods, can be found to react to one of the notes of the octave . . .'

On the whole, those who follow what has sometimes been called the Western Esoteric Tradition – largely MacGregor Mathers's personal synthesis of the Christian Cabala, occidental ritual magic and certain elements derived from Madame Blavatsky's theosophy – are not particularly concerned with such semi-physical, semi-spiritual theories of vibration, for in the Cabalistic doctrines regarding emanation they have available to them a much more sophisticated conceptual framework (see CABALA; GOLDEN DAWN). Western occultists have, however, been concerned with vibration as a mode of pronunciation, used as a means of inducing religious ecstasy. In an unpublished Golden Dawn document written by Wynn Westcott *c* 1893 four modes of spiritual development are described; one of these is 'the procuring of the influence of Divine Powers through the peculiar modes taught in our Order of Vibrating the Divine Names'.

This method of vibration was described in detail in the second part of another Golden Dawn document, *Flying Roll XII*:

In vibrating the Divine Names the Operator should first of all rise as high as possible towards the idea of the Divine White Brilliance, keeping the mind raised to the plane of the loftiest spiritual aspiration. Unless this is done, it is dangerous to vibrate only with the astral forces, because the vibration attracts a certain force to the operator, and the nature of the force attracted rests largely on the condition of mind in which the operator is.

The ordinary mode of vibrating is as follows: Take a deep and full inspiration and concentrate your consciousness in your heart, which answers to Tiphareth. (Having first, as already said, ascended to your Kether, you should endeavour to bring down the white Brilliance into you heart, prior to centering your consciousness there).

Then formulate the letters of the Name required in your heart, in white, and feel them written there. Be sure to formulate the letters in brilliant white light, not merely in dull

whiteness as the colour of the Apas Tattwa. Then, emitting the breath, slowly pronounce the Letters so that the sound vibrates within you, and imagine that the breath, while quitting the body, swells you so as to fill up space. Pronounce the Name as if you were vibrating it through the whole Universe, and as if it did not stop until it reached the further limits.

All practical work which is of any use, tires the operator or withdraws some magnetism, and therefore, if you wish to do anything that is at all important, you must be in perfect magnetic and nervous condition, or else you will do evil instead of good.

When you are using a Name and drawing a Sigil from the Rose, you must remember that the Sephira to which the Rose and the Cross

DE ARITHMETICA   MVSICA .

Regula

Two diagrams from *Utriusque Cosmi Historia* by Robert Fludd, concerned with the universe as a harmony of musical vibrations
Left The relationship of the harmonies and notes of a monochord *Above* The different spheres which make up the macrocosm are shown to produce a universal harmony

Ronan Picture Library/E. P. Goldschmidt & Co. Ltd

are referred, is Tiphareth, whose position answers to the position of the heart, as if the Rose were therein. It is not always necessary to formulate before you in space the telesmatic angelic figure of the Name. As a general rule, pronounce the Names as many times as there are letters in it.

From this brief instruction it is not clear whether the magicians of the early Golden Dawn regarded the vibrations they created as physical, mental or spiritual. Probably they were supposed to partake of all three. In any case it seems likely that each practitioner had his or her own private interpretation of the vibratory process.

Trembling With Energy

Certainly at the present day, those occultists who are devotees of either the original Golden Dawn magical system or of one or other of its many derivatives – mostly greatly inferior to the original – give widely varying descriptions of both what is actually done and what is subjectively experienced when a Divine Name is vibrated. The best descriptions – which ultimately seem to derive from Aleister Crowley (see CROWLEY) – take it for granted that the experiences undergone are subjective in nature but that, nevertheless, a *psychologically* real vibration is felt. One occultist has described himself as having his consciousness so filled with the spiritual essence of the Divine Name he is vibrating that not only his body but 'the universe itself seems to be shaking, trembling and vibrating with the energy of the God-name invoked'.

In the sense that the word vibration is interpreted by contemporary Western magicians its use is likely to continue. It seems at least possible, however, that the semi-physical theories of vibration associated with radiesthesia will slowly die out and that practitioners of radionics will turn towards a more traditional terminology and philosophy in future attempts to explain their science.

(See also NAMES.)

FRANCIS KING

FURTHER READING: H. P. Blavatsky, *The Secret Doctrine* (Theosophical Publishing House, 1980); S. L. MacGregor Mathers, *Astral Projection, Ritual Magic and Alchemy* (Spearman, London, 1971).

Tate Gallery

Vigil
A watch by night: in early Christianity, a service celebrated during the night before a festival, surviving in the midnight Mass on Christmas Eve; later, the eve of a festival; a candidate for knighthood would keep a night's vigil of prayer and dedication in a church before being initiated.

Mansell Collection

Villa of the Mysteries
Cult centre of Dionysus at Pompeii, the town which was overwhelmed by eruptions of Vesuvius in 63 and 79 AD; murals depict the rituals of the cult.
See DIONYSUS.

Vine

Through its connection with intoxicating wine, often linked with life-energy and a state of closeness to the divine: plant of Dionysus as god of wine; in the Old Testament God's people are the vine which he brought out of Egypt and tended (Psalm 80, Isaiah, chapter 5); Jesus said, 'I am the true vine, and my Father is the vinedresser ... I am the vine, you are the branches' (John, chapter 15).
See DIONYSUS; SYMBOLISM.

Virgil

Publius Vergilius Maro (70–19 BC), author of the *Aeneid*, the *Eclogues* and the *Georgics*; in the Middle Ages his fourth eclogue, predicting the birth of a child who would usher in a new Golden Age, was taken to refer to Christ, and in legend he became a master magician; he guides Dante through the afterworld in the *Divine Comedy*.

'There are not many pre-Christian stories of virgin births, and there are perhaps none in which virginity is the main point'

VIRGIN BIRTHS

WHEREVER CHRISTIANITY is the official religion, the phrase 'virgin birth' carries a special meaning. It does not refer to a theme of myth or folklore, or to a biological hypothesis, but to a single, unique event: the birth of Jesus Christ to the Virgin Mary. Jesus's miraculous origin, setting him apart from the rest of mankind, has seldom been publicly questioned by professed Christians until fairly recent years.

Of the four canonical gospels, only Matthew and Luke contain a birth narrative; no clear allusions to any such narrative occur elsewhere in the New Testament. The scriptural basis of the Virgin Birth doctrine is confined to Matthew 1. 18–25 and Luke 1. 26–38. Other accounts are given in apocryphal writings, but the Church rejected these as devoid of authority.

Matthew relates that Mary, when engaged to her future husband Joseph, was found to be pregnant. Joseph planned to proceed with the marriage and divorce her quietly afterwards. But an angel appeared to him in a dream and told him to keep her as his wife. Her child was not due to any sexual union, but to divine action, immaterial and mysterious: 'that which is conceived in her is of the Holy Spirit'. Luke gives Mary's side of the story. Before the events recorded in Matthew, the angel Gabriel came to her at Nazareth and prophesied that she would bear the promised Messiah. She protested that she was a virgin. Gabriel replied that God alone was responsible for what would happen and Mary consented to her destiny.

Virgin birth is often alleged to be a recurrent theme in mythology, so that material for comparison should be plentiful. Objective study, however, has been rare. Most

'Divine parentage was claimed for famous men, well into historical times': Alexander the Great was said to have been born to Olympias, Philip of Macedon's wife, after Zeus embraced her in the form of a serpent; 14th century miniature of Alexander with his horse Bucephalus

British Museum

C. M. Dixon

writers who accept the Christian dogma discuss it in isolation. Conversely, writers on comparative religion tend to hunt out 'parallels' that are not parallel, and distort the facts in the process.

Actually there are not many pre-Christian stories of virgin births, and there are perhaps none in which virginity is the main point. Goddesses occasionally conceive without male assistance. The Great Mother of the ancient Mediterranean world may have initiated life in this way. Certainly Neith, an Egyptian form of the Great Mother, gives birth to the sun god Re by her own power. In a much later age the divine Sophia (Wisdom) of Gnosticism was regarded, by some, as a virgin-mother. One gnostic sect even gave her a child named Jesus. But here Christian influence is apparent, and in any case this 'Jesus' is another spiritual entity, not a human one; the birth does not take place in the world we know.

Impregnation by a Flower

When we descend to that world, we do not find a distinct 'virgin birth' motif before Christianity. What we do find is an 'abnormal impregnation' motif. A woman is said to have achieved motherhood in some extraordinary way. She may or may not have been a virgin, usually not, but it is seldom of any consequence to the story.

Such legends fall into two classes. The first is the more important — the 'divine begetting' type of legend, which confers honour on a hero by making out that his father was a god. Sometimes the deity

Other religious leaders besides Christ have been credited with miraculous births. The conception of the Buddha was immaculate, although his mother was not a virgin but a married woman: Queen Maya dreams that the Buddha enters her womb as a little white elephant

appears to the future mother in his own person, taking a shape, generally but not always human, which permits sexual intercourse. This is a popular Hindu theme. Several heroes in the epic *Mahabharata* are the sons of gods who came to their mothers undisguised. Or the god may impersonate a mortal — the woman's husband, for instance, as when Zeus fathers Hercules by assuming the likeness of Amphitryon (see HERCULES). Or the god may cause pregnancy by a means which is not frankly sexual but remains material, as when Zeus enters Danae in a shower of gold.

Divine parentage was claimed for famous men well into historical times. Pythagoras and Plato were allegedly sons of Apollo. Alexander the Great was born to Olympias, Philip of Macedon's wife, after Zeus embraced her in the form of a serpent. An Indian legend tells more cryptically how Buddha projected himself into the womb of Maya, his chosen earthly mother, and she dreamed that she conceived a white elephant (see GAUTAMA). The story exists in several versions, some of which add fantastic details, but there is no claim that Maya was a virgin. Like the mothers of most of the other famous men, she lived as a married woman in normal relations with a husband.

The second, more primitive type of legend concerns pregnancies induced by magic. Here the father is apt to be secondary, or wholly absent, and the stress is on the magic. The remote inspiration of all such tales is to be sought in an early phase of society when conception was imperfectly understood, and the sexual act was not recognized as the cause, or as the sole cause. Generation might be ascribed to the wind, to certain foods, to unseen spirits. Even when the process was better grasped, magical objects or substances might still be used to make women bear children.

Stories reflecting this naive state of mind are numerous. Sometimes the heroine conceives when a man looks at her. More often she does it alone, through swallowing a pebble, a blade of grass or some other potent object. Fo-hi, the legendary founder of the Chinese Empire, was conceived by a girl who ate a flower which clung to her garment as she bathed. In such tales there is no working of divine power, no miracle in the religious sense. Impregnation occurs by material means; only the means are nonsexual, and probably suggested by ancient misinformation. Virginity, even when it is part of the story (as it is with Fo-hi), is incidental.

The orthodox Christian statement is that Jesus, an historical person, was conceived through a divinely-ordained exception to the laws of Nature. God's Holy Spirit caused an embryo to exist in Mary's womb. The gospels — though, unavoidably, they use sexual metaphors — do not describe a physical act or a material means; and the virginity is crucial. To equate what happens with the various 'divine begettings' is to obscure a profound difference of idea.

Christ's Family Tree

Nor are the origins of the story at all obvious. Theories of a gradual growth of legend, long after everyone who knew the truth was dead, are hard to sustain. The gospels of Matthew and Luke were composed within the lifetime of many of Christ's younger contemporaries. The two narratives are different, but not contradictory. Both seem to reflect an early and widespread belief.

Biblical scholars have claimed to detect a contrast in style between the opening passages of Luke and the rest. This could

suggest interpolation, but it could also suggest that the author incorporated a memoir by someone close to Mary herself.

The strongest counter-argument is that the two genealogies, Matthew 1. 1–16, and Luke 3. 23–38, tracing Jesus's descent from David through Joseph, his nominal father, would be pointless if Joseph were not his true father; so that their Christian compilers must have thought he was. But this does not follow. The relations with Joseph would have established the legal Davidic lineage which was a mark of the Messiah, even if it were only adoptive. Here for once a pre-Christian case is helpful: Alexander's being the son of Zeus did not prevent his being counted also as a descendant of Hercules through Philip. Joseph's status

as an adoptive parent is likewise enough to account for the references to him in the gospels as the father of Jesus.

The Virgin Birth seems, then, to have been a Christian tenet well before the close of the 1st century AD. There is no reliable trace of its being challenged as an innovation, except by one sect, the Ebionites (see EBIONITES). Nor is there any trace of

Divine parentage was claimed for many heroes of legend. Perseus was the son of the supreme god Zeus, who visited his mother Danae in the form of a shower of gold: painting by Charles Natoire (*right*). It was prophesied that the child would kill his grandfather, so Danae and the young Perseus were put into a chest and cast adrift: drawing by Arthur Rackham (*below*)

Chris Barker

Giraudon

Ikon illustrating the story of Christ's nativity, from the Church of the Virgin at Potamies, Crete. The belief that Jesus was born of a virgin as a result of divine action was accepted by the Church well before the end of the 1st century AD; earlier, non-Christian accounts of divine births generally do not claim that the mother was a virgin

a rival tradition outside the Church. Jews said that Jesus was conceived through Mary's misconduct; but since they gave her seducer's name as Pantheros — which is variously spelt and corrupted, but originally merely an anagram of *parthenos*, 'virgin' — the rumour is a scandal without historical substance (see JESUS).

Catholic tradition adds that Mary stayed a virgin always, with Joseph living in voluntary celibacy, accepting that she belonged to no man. If she did, several references to Jesus's 'brothers' in the Bible and in the historian Josephus have to be explained away. The vagueness of relation-words among Jews at that time would allow the 'brothers' to be cousins. But an established Christian belief in Mary's perpetual virginity is hard to trace in the early centuries, though several Fathers of the Church endorse it. Misunderstanding of the further dogma of the Immaculate Conception (which states that Mary was conceived sinless, as the chosen and predestined vessel) has fostered a mistaken notion that she too, in Catholic belief, was born of a virgin. This is an error.

Queries have been raised as to whether the Virgin Birth might have happened without a miracle. Parthenogenesis in mammals is not impossible. It has been induced in rabbits, though all the offspring were female. Cases are cited of women conceiving after bathing in the same water as a man; and of a twin being 'born' as an embryo inside the other twin and eventually expelled. If a rationalization of the Christian story is wanted, it could be argued that Jesus was the child of an abnormal pregnancy sincerely regarded as miraculous, and that this helped to invest him with a supernatural aura. But such a theory cannot be more than speculative.

(See also MARY.)

GEOFFREY ASHE

FURTHER READING: Thomas Boslooper, *The Virgin Birth* (S.C.M. Press, 1962).

Virginity

State valued in various religious and magical traditions, because it implies innocence, or concentration on spiritual things, or because it implies a reservoir of untapped force; the taking of a woman's virginity is frequently hedged about with taboos; in legend, only a virgin can tame a unicorn; objects used in ritual magic are required to be 'virgin'.

See RITUAL MAGIC; SELF-DENIAL; SEX; UNICORN; WOMAN.

Virgin Mary

The mother of Jesus; numerous legends grew up about her, and in popular Christian belief she was elevated to the level of a goddess; her cult demonstrates 'the importance of the female in the thought and feelings of ordinary people when expressed in religious faith and practice'.

See MARY; VIRGIN BIRTHS.

VIRGO

THIS is one of the 'mutable' signs in traditional astrology (the others being Gemini, Sagittarius and Pisces), so termed because the Sun is 'in' them at times of the year when one season is changing into another. In Virgo's case the dates are 23 August to 22 September, when summer gives way to autumn, and the effect on you, if Virgo is important in your birth chart, is to give you a strong impulse to be of service to others, as a parallel to the way in which the old season is making way for the new to further the progress of the year. Astrologers also say that you will be changeable and adaptable, but this is modified by the fact that Virgo is associated with the element of earth, which in terms of personality analysis is translated into 'keeping one's feet on the ground'.

Those born under the sign of the Virgin do not, of course, necessarily have defective love-lives as a result, but they are expected to be quiet and undemonstrative in affairs of the heart. They may be genuinely affectionate but not fully involved with their partners, and in general they tend to keep themselves to themselves and to shrink away from very close relationships with other people. Unassuming and retiring, they are modest, prudent, and possessed of considerable cool charm. Strong Virgo influence is said to produce a personality that is spinsterish in the bad sense.

The influence of Mercury, the sign's ruling planet, brings intelligence, excellent communicative abilities, possibly a knack for languages. The Virgo person is likely to be logical and tidy-minded, suspicious of abstract ideas and emotional attitudes, fond of exactitude, perhaps pedantic.

Sensible, reliable, busy, cautious, careful with money, the Virgo person's preference for practical concerns is not a mark of materialism but is harnessed to his genuine and idealistic bent for service. Natives of Virgo are said to make good doctors, teachers, accountants and secretaries.

'The Virgo person's preference for practical concerns is not a mark of materialism but is harnessed to his genuine and idealistic bent for service': 15th century astrological treatise

British Museum

In early Hindu mythology Vishnu was relatively unimportant, but through coalescing with other gods he achieved – with Shiva – a supreme place in the Hindu pantheon

VISHNU

THE HINDUS are not monotheists, strictly speaking, but they all agree that there is one supreme and eternal Principle, one abiding reality behind the whole phenomenal universe which is in a state of perpetual flux. This belief is central to Hinduism and because neither the Buddhists nor the Jains (see JAINS) believe in such a Principle, the Hindus call them *nastikas*, 'heretics', or more literally, 'people who do not believe in Being', that is to say in immutable Being beyond all becoming. This 'Being' is the Absolute, and in theology it is called Brahman or simply the 'Self' (see BRAHMAN). Brahman is beyond all attributes and all characterization: but if you conceive of it as possessing attributes such as omnipotence, omniscience, and sovereignty, then it is God.

Hinduism, however, started as a polytheistic religion and only gradually came to an awareness of Brahman as the eternal ground of all existence. Later still it arrived at the idea that the ground of existence is also the Lord of existence – is God. In an early hymn the question is asked: '*What* god shall we revere with the oblation?' The answer is 'Prajapati, the Lord of Creatures.' But this solution was really no solution at

all, for it implies the further question, 'Which of the many gods mentioned in the early scriptures is the Lord of Creation? Which of the many gods is the one true God?' For a time Prajapati enjoyed this honour, but Prajapati came to be identified with the sacrifice, both sacrifice as it is performed in ritual and with the cosmic sacrifice of Prajapati himself which was said to have resulted in the manifestation of this multiple world out of an original unity. At about the same period we find Vishnu too being identified with the sacrifice and therefore with Prajapati, 'the Lord of Creatures'.

In the earliest Hindu scripture, the *Rig-Veda*, Vishnu turns up from time to time but he is quite unimportant. He is the faithful companion of Indra who, during the period of the *Rig-Veda*, was the greatest of the gods, the patron of the Aryans as they swept into India and the chastizer of the aboriginal inhabitants, the god of the storm and of war (see INDIA). The only action attributed separately to Vishnu is his striding out three paces:

> I will proclaim the manly powers of Vishnu
> Who measured out earth's broad expanses,
> Propped up the highest place of meeting:
> Three steps he paced, the widely striding!
>
> Though one, in threefold wise he has propped up Heaven and earth, all beings and all worlds . . .
>
> There indeed the widely striding Bull's Highest footstep, copious, downward shines.

From this hymn it is clear that Vishnu's

three paces represent the 'measuring out', that is, the creation of the universe; and his highest step seems to be the sky. Later it was to be identified with Being itself, that is, Brahman or the Absolute.

Creator, Sustainer, Destroyer

The seed from which Vishnu developed to his full stature as the supreme deity is already here; but it is a very small seed from which so immense a tree should have grown. It was, however, not the only seed, for the full-fledged Vishnu is clearly the result of the coalescence of many gods, none of which belong to the oldest mythology of the *Veda*. In the course of time he coalesced with Narayana, who appears in a rather later Vedic text as a divine sage who offers sacrifice and 'becomes this whole universe'. In the Great Epic, the *Mahabharata*, Narayana dwells, though invisible himself, in a mythical 'White Island' where he is surrounded by his devotees – strange beings by any standards, since their heads are like umbrellas and they each have four testicles – who revere him alone as the one God and thereby partake of his eternal essence. The cult of Narayana in conjunction with

Vishnu is made real to his worshippers through his ten incarnations *Right* Vishnu in his aspect as man-lion *Below left* Vishnu as Rama, hero of the Rama Yana who was cheated of his throne *Below right* Vishnu as Krishna, the youth whose affairs with the cowherd's daughters are held to be an analogy of the love affair between God and the soul

G. L. Carlisle

G. L. Carlisle

'For the protection of the good, for the destruction of evil-doers . . . I come into being age after age': Vishnu, in carvings from the magnificent rock temple of Mahabalipuram, south India, 7th century AD

Vasudeva is attested by an inscription from the 2nd century BC.

But who was Vasudeva? In the Epic and the *Puranas* (300 BC – 1000 AD) Vasudeva is the patronymic of Krishna (see KRISHNA) whose father was Vasudeva; and this adds a new complication, for the origins of the Krishna cult are even more obscure than the cult of Vishnu himself. By the time of the Epic in which the man Krishna plays a leading part, he is already identified with Vishnu and is his incarnation on earth. As such he delivers the most celebrated of all the Hindu scriptures, the *Bhagavad Gita* (see BHAGAVAD GITA), in which he explains his own nature as God, reveals himself in a quite terrifying vision as all-consuming Time, shows how he is not only identical with Brahman, the Absolute, but actually transcends it, explains the supreme merit and efficacy of loving devotion to the one God, and also explains the purpose of God's incarnation as man. 'Whenever the law of righteousness withers away,' he says, 'and lawlessness arises, then do I generate myself on earth. For the protection of the good, for the destruction of evil-doers, for the setting up of the law of righteousness I come into being age after age.'

In the Great Epic, Krishna is Vishnu incarnate, but Vishnu himself, though he appears in most of this enormous poem as the supreme deity, is not undisputedly so. He is Bhagavan, 'the Lord', but in the background there lurks disconcertingly Mahadeva, the 'Great God' Shiva (see SHIVA), whose supremacy Krishna himself acclaims on occasion. The two gods are still clearly rivals, but a compromise is reached whereby the one true God is invoked as Hari-Hara, *hari*, the 'tawny' or 'he who takes away (sin)', being one of the stock epithets of Vishnu, and *hara* the 'seizer' being one of Shiva's. For from the time of the Great Epic until today God has been worshipped by the Hindus either in the form of Vishnu or of Shiva: for the worshippers of Vishnu, Vishnu (and his incarnations) alone is God, for the worshippers of Shiva the same is true of Shiva. In the so-called Hindu Trinity (the Trimurti or 'three-form' of God, consisting of Brahma, Vishnu and Shiva) Brahma is associated with creation, Vishnu with sustaining, and Shiva with destruction, just as in Christianity, the Father came to be associated with creation, the Son with redemption, and the Holy Spirit with sanctification. This, however, is a purely theological device and in no way influenced the actual practice of the two dominant trends of Hinduism for which either Vishnu or Shiva is the one God who creates, sustains, and destroys the universe in unending cycles of ever-revolving time.

The Creation myth associated with Vishnu is rather naive. At the end of each cosmic cycle Vishnu falls asleep on the cosmic serpent Shesha. When he wakes up, a lotus grows out of his navel and in the middle of the flower Brahma is seated, and Brahma then proceeds with the creation of the universe. Meanwhile the wrathful Shiva emerges from his forehead ready to destroy all that Brahma has created.

Among the followers of Shiva, Shiva is worshipped directly or in the form of his erect phallus; but for the devotees of Vishnu, Vishnu is made real to them through his incarnations or avatars, as they are called in most Indian languages (from the Sanskrit *avatara* meaning a 'descent'). These avatars are either a full incarnation of the supreme God or a partial one. The number of incarnations varies but the generally accepted number is ten. These are incarnations as fish, as tortoise, as boar, as man-lion, as dwarf, as Parashurama ('Rama with the axe'), as Rama-candra, as Krishna, as the Buddha, and as Kalkin who is yet to come.

Heroic Incarnations

The first four incarnations need not detain us although some of them have a respectable antiquity. Vishnu became incarnate as Rama 'with the axe' in order to extirpate the warrior class who had come to challenge the supremacy of the Brahmins, but this Rama is a purely literary character with no cultic significance. Vishnu's incarnation as the Buddha, however, is very surprising and the orthodox explanation that the Buddha's function was to lead astray many from the true faith as formulated in the Vedas is even more surprising. In actual practice Vishnu is worshipped either in his incarnation as Krishna or as Rama(candra), the heroes of the *Mahabharata* and the *Rama Yana* respectively. Of the two cults, that of Krishna is the more emotional, for the object of worship is not so much the Krishna of the *Mahabharata* or the *Bhagavad Gita* as of the youthful and wayward Krishna of the *Puranas* whose love affairs with the cowherds' daughters in Vrindavan are held to be an analogy of the love affair between God and the soul.

The history of the elevation of Rama-(candra) to the rank of an incarnation of Vishnu is no less obscure. In the *Rama Yana* (except in the first and last books which are generally regarded as being a later addition) Rama is simply the virtuous hero, the heir-apparent cheated of his throne by a vindictive queen, the faithful husband, and the just destroyer of the demon king who had carried off his wife. But by the time that the *Rama Yana* was refashioned in Hindi by the 17th century poet Tulsi Das, Rama had for long been accepted as an incarnation of Vishnu, and his earthly life (almost entirely mythical) was held up as a model for the ordinary man to follow. Rama had become quite as much an incarnation of Vishnu as had Krishna, and the Hindi form of his name, Ram, had come to mean God. And so it was that Mahatma Gandhi, assassinated by an 'orthodox' Hindu fanatic, died with the name 'Ram' on his lips.
(See also HINDUISM.)

R. C. ZAEHNER

FURTHER READING: Alain Daniélou, *Hindu Polytheism* (Routledge, 1964).

At Limpias in Spain, in 1919, a girl said that she had seen the figure of Christ in the parish church perspire visibly and move its eyes, and between 1930 and 1950 the Roman Catholic Church investigated 300 cases of apparitions to children and 30 sets of appearances of the Virgin Mary: but 'the wisdom of the Church and the teaching of its greatest intellects and holiest saints has made it circumspect'

VISIONS

THE WORD vision is used in the religious sphere to mean what elsewhere is called an apparition. The percipient of an apparition has the experience of 'seeing' (in some sense or other) something which is not present in the same way as ordinary physical objects are. Sir Francis Galton (1822–1911), in his researches into human faculties, encountered a perfect example of an apparition. A lady novelist assured him that she once saw the principal character of one of her novels come through the door and glide towards her. As the character was fictional there was no possibility that the apparition corresponded to any external cause. The experience thus originated within the lady's mind and can be described as *endogenic* (caused from within).

Apparitions are sometimes loosely called hallucinations (from Latin *hallucinatio* – I dream) bearing the implication that they are endogenic. This is because apparitions commonly result from drugs, fever, exhaustion or mental illness. The present writer prefers to reserve the term hallucination for endogenic hallucinations, and to use the word apparition or vision for an appearance whose cause may be internal or external.

Are there in fact any apparitions which are *exogenic* (with an external cause)? Religious visions are difficult to interpret but psychical research provides good evidence of exogenic apparitions (see GHOSTS; HAUNTED HOUSES; SPONTANEOUS PSI EXPERIENCES). Occasionally, at a time of death or crisis the likeness of the person concerned appears in recognizable form to a friend or relative, perhaps on the other side of the world. The apparitions are sometimes clearly unreal, being transparent or appearing in a 'pool of light' or in a 'picture frame', but quite often they are natural enough to be mistaken for the actual person. Theories differ as to how these crisis apparitions come about. Some writers claim that the person whose apparition is seen has an 'astral body' which is a duplicate of his physical body (including clothes) and is 'projected' to the vicinity of the percipient (see ASTRAL BODY). I prefer an explanation by telepathy or 'thought-transference'; a violent 'thought wave' impinges on some level of the percipient's mind and is translated into a picture of the person in crisis.

The Vision of Father Simon by Francesca Ribalta: Simon was a 16th century Italian aesthete who walked the streets at night meditating on the Road to Calvary; one night he heard trumpets and saw Christ, carrying the cross, turn to look at him

About 1899 the Society for Psychical Research carried out a census of apparitions and obtained 17,000 replies to their questionnaire. It appeared that about one person in 16 sees an apparition about once in the course of a lifetime. About a third of all apparitions are of animals, lights, indefinite or inanimate objects, but the remaining two-thirds are of realistically human figures. More than half of these human apparitions are of persons living or dead and known to the percipient. It was found also that about one in 30 of all apparitions are of a religious, exalted or highly poetic nature. In mentally normal persons only a very small proportion of apparitions are grotesque or horrible. Even if an apparition is not frightening in itself it may puzzle the percipient who often fears that his reason is failing, but this alarm is unnecessary, because the statistics quoted refer mainly to people in normal physical and mental health.

A large proportion of apparitions are *hypnagogic* hallucinations (from Greek *hypnos* – sleep) and occur on the borderline between sleeping and waking, being very akin to dreams. Like dreams, these apparitions are mainly endogenic but some may, like crisis apparitions, have an external cause, because there is evidence of telepathic or clairvoyant effects both in dreams and in the hypnagogic state.

All the same, many interesting visionary experiences cannot be reliably distinguished from dreams. In a classic case, a Dr Wittse seemed (in his own recollection) to leave his body, observe his own corpse and the physicians standing by, and travel through a mysterious landscape; but we cannot confidently accept that this adventure was not illusory. All endogenic hallucinations are likely to have features in common with dreams. They contain revived memories, but in new combinations. If the Jungian and Freudian psychologies are true, hallucinations may also contain symbolic representations of unconscious urges, aspirations or anxieties. This is true of normal people and especially true of the hallucinations of the insane.

Modern brain surgery has given some insight into the causes of some hallucinations (though less than is sometimes claimed). If the normal functioning of a part of the brain concerned in ocular perception is prevented, the person may have *compensatory hallucinations*. Thus a patient with a tumour in the right temporal lobe had consequently no normal vision of things on the left. But while in darkness he 'saw' a non-existent man to his left sitting at a non-existent fireside. Visions of this sort consist of re-activated memories; men blind from birth have no visual hallucinations, although they can have auditory ones. Occasionally, sane and intelligent persons have spontaneous electrical discharges in the brain which, besides producing involuntary movements of the limbs, engender remarkably vivid hallucinations often identifiable as revived memories. When in the course of remedial brain surgery certain areas of the cerebral cortex are stimulated mildly with an electrode, *sensory hallucinations* result – effects of dispersed light or shade, coloured lights, stars, wheels. Stimulation of the temporal lobe and the posterior parietal cortex produce more elaborate hallucinations. Some neurologists tend therefore to refer all apparitions to random electrical flickers in the brain, but on the evidence of crisis apparitions I would deny this.

Emotion certainly is productive of visions. Carl Jung (see JUNG) speaks of a spontaneous vision experienced as a child while in a choking fit. He saw above him a glowing blue circle about the size of the full moon. Within it there moved golden figures which he took to be angels. Once, when my own father, a sea-captain, was trying to extricate his vessel from a whirlpool and debating whether to change course, my mother's apparition appeared before him on the ship's bridge and told him, with emphasis, 'You *will* get out if you change course!'; as in fact he did.

A Wavering Rose

Many hallucinations are extremely vivid and lifelike so that, as with some crisis apparitions, the percipient may think he is actually seeing in the ordinary way. But with many visions, particularly in the religious sphere, it is hard to decide from the visionary's words exactly in what sense the vision was 'seen'. Roman Catholic theorists such as St Thomas Aquinas (1226–74) recognized three types of vision; the intellectual vision, the imaginative vision and the corporeal vision. The theory of the corporeal vision was akin to the modern astral body explanation of crisis apparitions. If one had a vision of Jesus, it *might* be a corporeal vision; one was actually seeing either the resurrection body of the Christ or alternatively a kind of wraith fashioned by the angels, the handymen of heaven. On the other hand, it might be that the percipient received only an imaginative vision – a purely mental image, though a vivid one and induced by the action of God. St Thomas, of course, like all reputable theologians, reserved the possibility of a vision being an endogenic hallucination not divinely caused.

The 'intellectual vision' of the theologians corresponds to ordinary mental imagery. If the average person thinks of an object, say, a duck, he will form a mental image; he 'sees' it in the mind's eye. His mental picture will be somewhat generalized and lacking in detail (unless he is a zoologist or a farmer), as he discovers if he tries to draw it. An artist will do better because, both by nature and training, he has a capacity for more vivid mental imagery. The lack of sharp detail in the average mental image is shown by the effort which a hypnotist has to make when establishing a hallucination in a person under hypnosis. The hypnotist has to suggest in a persuasive manner the characteristics of the figure that he wishes the hypnotized person to 'see', and to catalogue the hat, the hairstyle, the blue eyes, the jewellery and so on.

Some people, however, have a remarkable power of mental visualization, so that what they 'see' in the mind's eye can be as vivid as things actually seen. Such exceptionally clear imagery is described as *eidetic* (from Greek *eidos* – form), and is sometimes aided by looking at a plain or dark background. When Goethe shut his eyes and thought of a rose he would clearly see a rosette for as long as he wished, though it wavered a little and moved its petals. The Rev George Henslow, a friend of Francis Galton, had a similar faculty and attempted with partial success to control the form of the objects he 'saw'. When he thought of a gun he saw only the stock; the vision then drifted into the form of a tuning fork. By mental effort he recovered the gun in the form of a flint-lock: a type of fire-arm he had not consciously intended.

Galton came across a few visionaries who said that they received their visions in two entirely distinct ways. Thus one informant could experience eidetic images at conscious command but these were vague and shadowy in comparison with his spontaneous visions, which occurred unexpectedly and quite outside his mental control. These visions were of landscapes more strange and beautiful than any he had ever seen in the ordinary way. Such visions which arise, as it were, of their own motion can be called autonomous, but they are not necessarily exogenic. Not all autonomous visions are idyllic or romantic. A visionary who bought a Dutch cheese at a shop in Tottenham Court Road, London, saw the shopkeeper roll it on the counter. He told Galton that chancing to close his eyes the next day, he saw a bodiless head rolling on a white surface. Its face was that of the cheesemonger. Such visions resemble the more trivial type of dream which is a patchwork of recent experiences and jumbled recollections, but the visions of people with a poetic or literary bent, like their dreams, have an intellectual and idyllic content. In 1944 Jung, who was recovering after a heart attack, would awake at midnight and would spend an hour or so in 'an utterly transformed state' as if 'in ecstasy'. He saw unfolding before him various mythical occurrences such as the wedding of the cabalistic beings Malkhuth and Tifereth in the 'garden of pomegranates' or the sacred marriage of Zeus and Hera in a classical amphitheatre.

Ecstasy is a peculiar state which is sometimes entered spontaneously or in the course of prayer or meditation on sublime themes (see ECSTASY). During it the ecstatic person consciously experiences any or all of a variety of thoughts and feelings. Visions are common but there can be also a sense of bliss or of union with the deity or a benign cosmic power. Contact with the surroundings is not always completely lost. Jung could eat his supper and comment to the night nurse on his visions.

One of the most remarkable visionaries of all time, Emanuel Swedenborg (see SWEDENBORG), spoke of three distinct kinds of 'spiritual sight' (apart from dreams). There was vision 'with the eyes closed, which is as vivid as with the eyes open'. At other times, when wide awake and walking in the city streets, Swedenborg would be 'in vision, seeing groves, rivers, palaces and men'. He described his third type of experience as differing entirely from 'the common imagination of men' and as a state 'when those things which are in heaven, such as spirits and other objects, are represented'. Swedenborg believed that he had some kind of direct sight of actual spirits and divine beings in these latter visions which, he said, came to him only when in ecstasy or 'trance'.

The English poet and painter William Blake (see BLAKE), was erroneously regarded by some as mad because of his visions which he described in poems and epics. Chastized by his mother for seeing the prophet Ezekiel in the garden, at the age of eight he saw 'a tree filled with angels; bright angelic wings bespangled every bough like stars'. It is likely that children experience eidetic imagery and autonomous visions more commonly than adults realize. In Blake's case his visionary faculty expanded to cosmic proportions in adulthood. Once by the seashore, everything in the world appeared as 'men seen afar'. Eventually all objects fused and combined into 'One Man, the Christ' on whose bosom Blake reposed. When asked about the reality of his visions he replied that he saw them 'in imagination' and pointing to his forehead said that he saw them 'in here'. The visions reported by prophets and saints were, he believed, merely poetic.

Numerous visions of divinity have been described by their recipients as ineffable and incapable of expression in words. The German mystic John Tauler (1300–61) said that, 'sometimes the grace is so manifest that it is impossible to doubt that God has actually shown Himself', but '. . . no (distinct) idea of what has been seen is

retained. We cannot understand what it was. Only we know with certainty that we cannot analyse it.' Tauler's comment suggests not only ineffability but, with visions as with dreams, a tendency to forget them. We may suppose also that some visions, like dreams, are subject to the process of 'secondary elaboration' by which they are modified in the recollection. This is to be suspected in the case of such rhapsodical visionaries as Venerable Marina of Escobar (1554–1633) who found herself before the heavenly Jerusalem, which was encircled by an exceedingly vast river. When interrogated by her confessor Marina declared that her clearness of perception was not much inferior to St Paul's.

Moving Statues

Other mystics have described their experiences in rather different terms. Blessed Angela of Foligno (1248–1309) said that, 'when the most high God comes into the rational soul . . . and she (the soul) seeth Him within her, without any bodily form . . . , the eyes of the soul behold a fulness, spiritual not bodily'. Such visions seem to be essentially cases of seeing with 'the mind's eye'. However, St Ignatius of Loyola (1491–1556), founder of the Jesuits, whose

The Angels of Mons were the creation of an English journalist, but many British soldiers came to believe that they had actually seen the heavenly warriors hold back the might of the German army at Mons in 1914: French painting of the event, 1920

description of his visions can be relied on, perceived 'the Divine Being, not obscurely but in a vivid and highly luminous brightness'.

Loyola distinguished between visions of this compelling sort and 'intellectual perceptions' (that is, mental imagery) which he also had, particularly when gazing into running water. This recalls the German mystic Jacob Boehme (see BOEHME), who once saw a vision in a shining pewter dish, and also the phenomenon of crystal-gazing or 'scrying' (see SCRYING). It is estimated that about one person in 20, if gazing at a crystal ball or similar surface, will see some picture in it. Scrying is often spoken of as a kind of auto-hypnosis. Be this as it may, an element of auto-suggestion doubtless comes into play. If the scryer has been told that he is likely to see a certain picture in the crystal, then often he will see it with striking vividness. This accords with research on eidetic imagery in children which indicates that the more suggestible personalities tend to be the best 'eidetikers'.

The factors that seem to be operative in scrying − suggestibility, expectancy and narrowing of attention onto a single object − are perhaps adequate to explain some of the famous cases in which numerous observers have seen statues move or weep. In 1919 at Limpias near Santander in Spain, a girl of 12 said that during the sermon she had seen the figure of Christ on the altar of the parish church perspire visibly and move its eyes. Before long the number of daily pilgrims rose to 4,000. The majority saw nothing, but some visitors saw tears in the Saviour's

Photolensens

eyes, others saw blood on the brow, and yet others saw the head turning. Significantly most of these prodigies occurred only after the percipients had stared for long hours at the altar.

The Accuracy of Visions

Literary problems arise with the very extensive writings in which a long series of mystical ladies have reported their revelations received during ecstasies. St Bridget (1302–73), patron saint of Sweden, said that our Lord remarked to her that she retouched her visions through not having properly understood them; but he approved her secretaries for adding 'colour and ornamentation'. St Bridget often saw heaven, earth and hell simultaneously, as did St Lidwine of Schiedam (1330–1433) every night for 28 years. The vision of hell had been, of course, a common literary theme ever since Plato wrote the *Phaedo*. Visionaries, one suspects, are somewhat at the mercy of what they have read.

St Hildegard, Abbess of Rupertsberg in the Rhineland (see HILDEGARD), received her scientific knowledge from a 'divine light' experienced in ecstasies from the age of four. Her numerous treatises are, unfortunately, replete with just those factual errors prevalent in the 12th century. Confidence in her treatment of the sapphire or the lodestone evaporates on encountering her scientific explanation of the griffin and the unicorn. St Frances of Rome (1384–1440) failed in astronomy. When she visited the celestial regions in her visions she distinctly saw the sky as a hollow sphere of blue crystal; an admissible idea in the 15th century, but tending to be outmoded even in Spain when Blessed Maria of Agreda repeated the same error in her *Mystical City of God*. Maria, a woman of intellect and good sense, actually doubted the accuracy of her visions, until her faith became absolute after a visit to the throne of God. The Eternal Father produced a richly decorated book which the Blessed Virgin certified to be her own true history. Maria was gratified to find the text in perfect agreement with her own *Life of the Virgin*. However, the biographical details appear to have been revealed in two earlier books, a *Nativity of the Blessed Virgin* and the *Raptures of Blessed Amadeus*.

To conflict with edicts of the Church is less serious than to contradict scripture, because the Church can revise its own judgements, as in the case of Joan of Arc. But some embarrassment was felt at the beatification process of St Catharine of Ricci (1522–90), in whose visions Savonarola (burnt as a heretic at Florence in 1498) appeared in the role of saint and martyr. However, Pope Benedict XIII cut the Gordian knot by decreeing that the saint's virtues had to be considered separately from her visions. Much controversy attached to the recommendation of the Carmelite scapular

The Vision, by Chagall: a census in 1899 suggested that approximately one person in 16 sees an apparition once in the course of a lifetime, and that about one in 30 of these is of a religious, exalted or highly poetic nature

which the Blessed Virgin was supposed to have made to St Simon Stock at Cambridge, England, in the 13th century. It was decided that the assurance that anyone who died wearing the scapular would certainly be saved ought not to be taken literally. This decision was probably a wise one because no contemporary memoir of Simon was written. (It was said of this saint, a strict vegetarian, that when offered a fried fish, he ordered it to be put back in the river whereupon it swam cheerfully away.)

The greatest of the mystical doctors of the Church, St Francis of Sales (see FRANCIS) and St John of the Cross (see JOHN) were profoundly suspicious of the accuracy of visions. St John used to quote with some relish the posthumous appearance of St Teresa of Avila (see TERESA) to a Carmelite nun. The great foundress and mystic warned the visionary that the vast majority of visions were untrustworthy. Whether the saint actually returned from paradise is uncertain, but her advice was in character. In his old age Loyola doubted the validity of his own youthful visions.

The wisdom of the Church and the teaching of its greatest intellects and holiest saints has made it circumspect. In the 17th century it denounced more than a score of false visionaries. When it specifically approves an apparition or revelation, it does so in terms of a formula laid down by the learned Pope Benedict XIV (1675–1758). Even approved revelations are accorded only the probability of being true, and have at most the credibility 'of human faith according to the rules of prudence', and any Catholic is at liberty to reject or criticize. Discretion is certainly justified because in Western Europe between 1930 and 1950 the Church investigated 30 series of apparitions of the Virgin Mary alone, and 300 cases of individual apparitions to children. Only three apparitions have been recognized in the present century: Fátima, Beauraing and Banneux, though the Church sometimes authorizes shrines without officially endorsing the visions which have led to their foundation.

It is clear that visionaries often make gross errors in matters of ascertainable fact. And in questions where the truth is not verifiable they are apt to conflict with the Church, or with scripture or with one another. Are they ever right? It is easy to satirize the poor visionaries. But occasionally, it must be admitted, they gather information by other than normal means. While in prayer on 26 July 1570, St Teresa found herself, as it were, present in spirit on the high seas and witnessed the massacre by pirates of 40 priests and novices on the way to Brazil, among them her cousin Francis Godoi. She immediately told her confessor. News of the tragedy reached Spain a month later. Among the reams of unverifiable material that Catherine Emmerich (1774–1824) dictated concerning the life of Jesus are many accurate topographical details concerning the Holy Land, including place names. In view of the limited knowledge of Palestine available in Europe in her day, it is hard to see how she could have acquired this information by normal means. St Teresa's experience,

apart from its religious setting, could be interpreted as a simple case of a crisis apparition. Catherine's archeological knowledge presents a more elaborate problem. It might be the case that divine agency was operative in both instances. On the other hand, such phenomena occurring in a secular context are not nowadays judged supernatural but 'paranormal' or 'parapsychological'. The modern view tends to ascribe such experiences to rare natural occurrences – telepathy, clairvoyance, and the rest. Thus verifiable revelations of secular facts do not constitute rigorous evidence for divine intervention.

But what of the apparitions of Jesus, or the Eternal Father or the Holy Virgin? Do they represent communications from God or from Mary? From theology we know that the visionary cannot be receiving a direct view of God in the same sense that he sees Mr Jones who lives down the road, because God is unlimited and immaterial. The visionary is therefore either seeing a wraith fashioned by the angels or is experiencing a mental image. In the first case the agency would be supernatural, but there is no real evidence that any visions are 'corporeal ones' in the sense of Aquinas. In the second case the image *may* be purely endogenic. But this cannot be logically proved to be so.

We would be helped in this enquiry if we really knew what value to put on mystic experience in general. The mystic feels a sense of certainty as to the 'truth' of his experiences and a feeling of union with the ultimate power in the universe. These are certainly weights to be thrown into the scales of judgement, but it is difficult to know just what weight to give them. St Teresa, describing some of her feelings of spiritual comfort and assurance while in ecstasy, compared the soul to the silkworm in the cocoon it has spun for itself. And many scholars have wondered if mystical experience is not just this, a comforting illusion which the mind in spiritual or other travail spins for itself.

It cannot be denied that there are 'fashions' in visions. In the Middle Ages visionaries saw saints and martyrs and, in certain limited circles, apparitions of the child Jesus were extemely frequent. Later, visions of the suffering and wounded Jesus or of his Sacred Heart were favoured. In recent times the Virgin Mary has almost monopolized the field. Since Lourdes (see LOURDES) there have been definite series of apparitions occurring at dates announced in advance by the Virgin to her visionaries. On a sceptical view, this conformity of visions to fashion points rather to their being the products of auto-suggestion in harmony with the prevailing climate of religious devotion. But it needs to be said that this argument is something of a two-edged sword if we accept the possibility that a mental impulse, actuated from on high, may be elaborated into a vision from such materials as are available in the mental storehouse of the recipient. Religious psychology is no less replete with subtleties than ordinary psychology, and the present writer would consider it foolish to hasten to a final conclusion concerning the presence or absence of the supernatural in religious visions.

John Webb

National Gallery

Despite the evidence of numerous saints and holy persons who have experienced visions, the Roman Catholic Church has remained circumspect, and even approved revelations are accorded only the probability of being true: *The Vision of the Blessed Gabriele*, by Crivelli

It is sometimes argued that the divine origin of apparitions can be inferred from other strange phenomena attendant on the visionary such as the presence of the stigmata (see STIGMATA) or levitation. But this is unsound because a strong case can be made for regarding stigmata as having a natural cause. Levitation, though an obscure happening, may well prove eventually to be a natural (though paranormal) one. Be this as it may, it is already an axiom of the Church that such additional phenomena do not constitute an adequate proof.

A. R. G. OWEN

FURTHER READING: John Beevers, *The Sun Her Mantle* (Browne & Nolan, Dublin, 1953); C. C. Martindale, *The Message of Fatima* (Burns & Oates, 1950); Herbert Thurston, *Beauraing and Other Apparitions* (Burns & Oates, 1934).

VON DANIKEN, ERICH

BORN IN SWITZERLAND, in 1935, Erich Von Däniken is one of the best known writers on the theory that space voyagers visited earth thousands of years ago, and his books have sold in millions. He claims that the voyagers from space 'created' man by careful selection and genetic breeding. Von Däniken culls evidence from all over the world in support of his ideas – he wrote that epics in the Indian Mahabarata texts actually tell of wars between the gods, and contain descriptions of weapons similar to ray-guns and advanced atomic devices. Another claim he puts forward is that the massive Easter Island statues could not have been carved by the islanders, and must have been made by the spacemen, who used them to signal to each other. He also said that a 16th century map called the Piri Reis map shows the Atlantic coastlines as they would appear from an orbiting satellite. One of his other famous interpretations is his claim that a relief carving in a Mexican Mayan temple shows an astronaut wearing a space helmet, seated at the controls of his space rocket. Archaeologists say that the hieroglyphics on the relief clearly identify the grave of an important Mayan priest. In fact, all of Von Däniken's theories turn out to have perfectly reasonable explanations supplied by respected archaeologists. It is evident that Von Däniken has discovered a great *need* to believe in his ideas, as the sales of his books prove. However, the fact that he so completely disregards the cautious work of archaeologists and scholars undermines his fascinating premise: that the gods of ancient civilizations were astronauts who came to Earth in sophisticated space craft.

FURTHER READING: Von Däniken's books are: *Chariots of the Gods?* (pap) (Berkley Pub., 1980); *Miracles of the Gods* (pap) (Dell, 1976); *Signs of the Gods* (Berkley Pub.).

Foto Hetzel/C. Waterson

Herbert List

VOODOO

Dissociation, possession by and marriage to the gods are the central facts around which the ceremonies and superstitions of Voodoo are organized; Voodoo treats the 'Invisibles' as enemies to be won over and powers to be used, and the supernatural as a disease to be turned to good account

THE WORD VOODOO comes from *vodun*, meaning god, spirit or sacred object in the Fon language of West Africa. It is applied especially to the beliefs and practices found in Haiti, whose inhabitants are, for the most part, descendants of slaves imported from many parts of Africa, and by extension to similar practices in other Caribbean islands, in the Southern states of America, and in Brazil, where plantation slavery was also customary.

To Westerners, the word usually denotes black magic and uncouth superstition, such as sticking pins into dolls, casting spells, lighting black candles in cemeteries to Baron Samedi, the lord of the underworld and patron of all black magic, calling up the dead and being familiar with monsters, spirits and zombies. In Jamaica such activities are known as *obeah*, and certainly Haitians are quite familiar with them. However, Voodoo also refers to a systematic religion in which the gods descend and possess their worshippers, and in which the ancestral spirits are invoked to give oracles and be a power in the household.

These two aspects of Voodoo make a

Pocomania ceremonies in Jamaica parallel Haitian Voodoo, involving drumming, chanting and dancing which may continue for days on end. The initiates collapse in trances in which they have experiences in the world of spirits. Voodoo and similar West Indian and South American cults are based on African religions

whole, and it is not always easy to distinguish them because the superstitions of Voodoo provide a forcing ground for the religion, which in turn supports and develops their meaning. From the start, children are brought up to be good by being made afraid of the supernatural, and this leaves an indelible imprint on the minds even of highly educated people. They are taught not to get their heads wet, especially with dew, because

2967

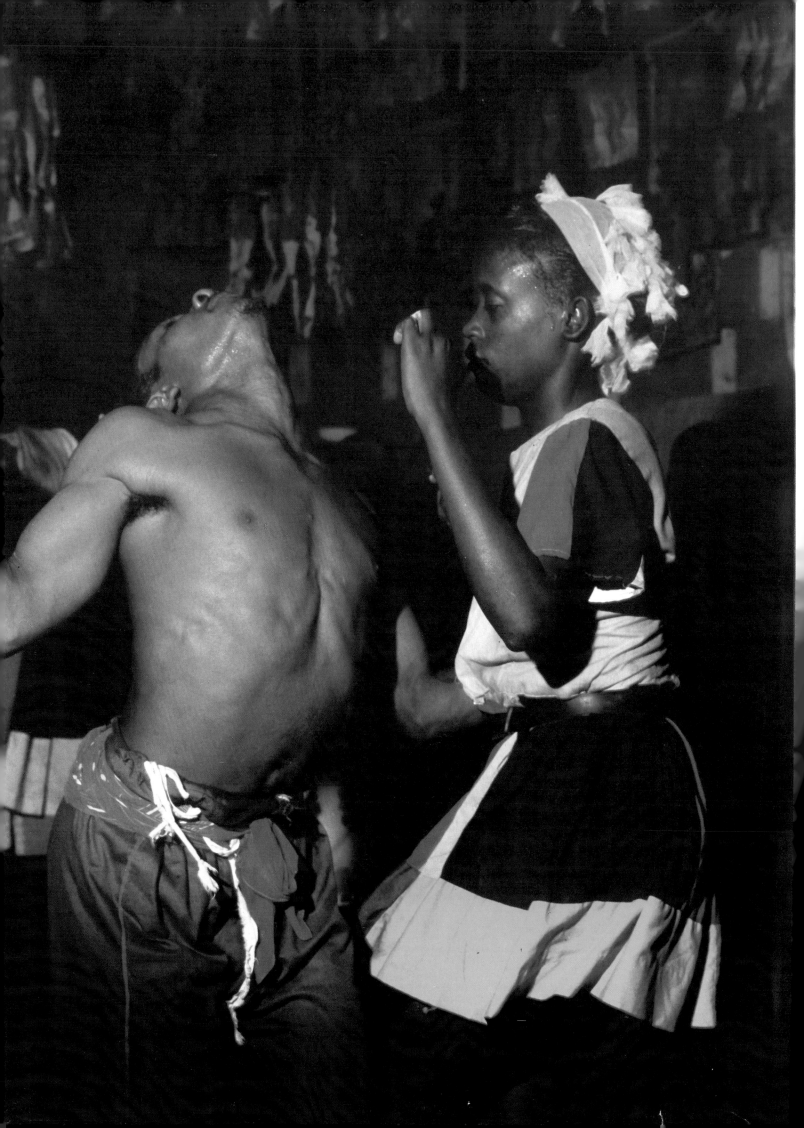

There are bogies who can get through the thatch: the loupgarous or witches who like sucking children's blood, and who are sometimes seen whizzing through the night like fireworks

water is both a solvent and a magnet for spirits, and a man's spirit lives in his head. At night, besides, there are bogies about, and doors and windows are carefully closed to keep them at bay. There are some who can get through the thatch: these are the loupgarous or witches who like sucking children's blood, and who are sometimes seen whizzing through the night like fireworks. Midday is another dangerous time, for then no man casts a shadow; which is as much as to say that his soul has temporarily disappeared, soul and shadow being equated, and that the air is full of invisible spirits looking for an abode. Children are forbidden to play with their shadows by candlelight lest they tie them in knots or mislay them. And there is always the *tonton macoute*, the travelling magician with a satchel over his shoulder in which he has magical and medicinal plants, dried bits of wild cat, black candles, and other paraphernalia. Mothers threaten children that if they are not good, the tonton will make off with them: it is fitting that the name was given to the bully-boys of the Duvalier regime, who carried out this threat upon their political rivals.

In such an atmosphere, 'obeah' is used either to counter such hobgoblins of the mind or to make use of them, and its practitioners are medicine-men. A medicine in this sense is something with either magical or pharmacological properties, sometimes both. Consider, for example, the treatment given to a child suffering from the attacks of a loupgarou. It is pale, fretful, wasted, and sometimes goes into convulsions; its mother is anxious, suspecting foul play, and her anxiety makes the child worse. The medicine-man – he may be a *tonton macoute*, a *bokor*, sorcerer, or *houngan*, Voodoo priest – has thus to kill one bird, and he does it with two stones. He discovers who the witch is – usually a relative or a neighbour who is jealous and resentful of the mother – and works a magic to protect the child and send the magic back to its creator. But he also

Left and **right** Scenes from Voodoo ceremonies, photographed at Port au Prince in Haiti: in Voodoo belief, magic and superstition are inextricably enmeshed with 'a systematic religion in which the gods descend and possess their worshippers, and in which the ancestral spirits are invoked to give oracles and be a power in the household'

Picturepoint London

doses the child with castor oil, because intestinal worms can produce convulsions in young children. The child gets better, the mother is relieved, the witch confesses, and the poisonous atmosphere is dissipated.

The Large Good Angel

The object of magic is to affect the soul either of the victim or of the persecutor. The soul is called the *gros bon ange*, the large good angel, and is manifested in the shadow and the breath. It coexists with the *'ti bon ange*, the little good angel, which is equated with the penumbra, the spirit, the conscience – it is sometimes also called the zombie. Both inhabit the *corps cadavre* or corpse body. The weak element in this ensemble is the gros bon ange, without which the other two elements lose contact. It is easily infected by emotions, especially those of suspicion, resentment, envy, anger and lust, by sudden shocks such as a death in the family, a failure in business or being jilted. It can also be stimulated magically by the casting of spells, the use of magical powders or of complicated pieces of apparatus called *wanga*. For instance, a girl being courted will try to 'hook' her man by serving him dishes in which she has put a piece of bacon she has worn in her shoe for three days running, or her nail and hair clippings, even her menstrual blood. If she is cold towards him, he may discreetly blow on her a powder composed of dried humming-bird flesh and a large number of potent herbs. If she is living with another man, however, he will

Right African fertility doll: the pervasive fear of the supernatural in Haiti means that nearly everyone expects to be the victim of magical attack and seeks to protect himself and promote his own well-being through magic *Far right* Baron Samedi, the greedy and lascivious king of the Voodoo cemetery spirits, who is dominant on All Souls' Day when he possesses women who flock to the graveyards

first use a powder called 'break the household', which causes quarrels. To defeat an enemy he can have recourse to another kind of leaf powder, often containing dead men's bones and cemetery earth, and held to cause paralysis, blindness, impotence or death. Smearing the door of an enemy's house with human dung causes much anxiety; to dig up the bones of his father's corpse (as happened to the late President Duvalier) is even worse, for highly sophisticated kinds of black magic and necromancy can be performed with them.

Magic is nothing less than an underhand intention given symbolic form and used to create an expectation in its victim. Given the atmosphere in Haiti, nearly everyone expects the worst from some of his neighbours and hopes for the best for himself. There are two dangers in using magic, however. If improperly used, or sent back by a strong magician onto its perpetrator, it can cause what is called a 'shock in return', which is difficult to cope with. On the other hand, it may be so powerful that it needs constant attention. The entity embodying this kind of magic is called a *baka*, and the owner of this supernatural monster must be prepared to offer it the life of one of his relatives every year unless he is to be devoured by it himself. Bakas are greedy, and are used by greedy men to gain power and money: the service they require shows that paranoia is not far in the offing.

The Invisibles

Paranoia is defined as a form of insanity marked by fixed delusions, especially those of grandeur, pride and persecution. On one level it can be said that its most innocuous form is the common sulk, or what Haitians call *mauvais sang*, bad blood, caused by a failure of expectation and authority, and with a plentiful admixture of suspicious resentment. Mauvais sang sometimes becomes so involuted that a *saisissement* or seizure results, whereupon a magician or Voodoo priest is called in to diagnose and treat the disorder. The diagnosis is usually straightforward, and the main treatment is to wash the patient's head with water in which seven or 21 leaves of different plants have been shredded. This cools the head and brings the gros bon ange back to its proper place; a counter-magic is employed to influence the person the sulker is involved with.

Popperfoto

William MacQuitty

But sometimes the diagnosis and treatment are both at fault, and the victim is left to his mania until, if he is lucky — which he frequently is — he has a vision in which his malady is personified as a spirit. The spirit prescribes a remedy for the illness, such as a diet of charred maize and water, but remains with the patient even when the cure is completed. For it also gives a formula by which it can be invoked in the future, such as looking at a candle flame, or reciting the *Pater Noster* backwards seven times: and this allows the patient to set up as a small-time oracular priest or priestess, diagnosing and treating illness, giving advice, and doing black and white magic for a fee.

The case histories of these Voodooists show that disordered emotions of long standing can be precipitated by an apparently trivial incident. A man may smoke a cigarette or drink a cup of coffee given him by a neighbour he has long mistrusted and who has given him a meaningful glance: he goes off in agitation, becomes hysterically dissociated and vomits up such unlikely emblems of his discomfort as lizards, pieces of bark, or a large and poisonous centipede. This is equivalent to a possession, and the vomiting brings him back to himself. He then puts what he has vomited in a bottle and tops it up with rum. It becomes his guardian spirit and oracle, while the liquor can be used as a universal medicine for those in need of treatment. Other sufferers vomit up needles, which they later use in their magical practice, swallowing them when the

Voodoo has its origins in the spirit possession cults of the old Slave Coast of West Africa *Left* Figures of spirits on sale in a Dahomey market *Below left* Pupils emerge from a school of instruction in tribal customs and religions, again in Dahomey

spirit leaves them in readiness for the next occasion. Still others go sleepwalking and pick up interestingly shaped stones to which the spirit leads them. These stones are placed in saucers, hot rum is poured over them and set aflame, and the liquor again used as a medicine – usually an embrocation. What happens in these and similar cases is that the gros bon ange has externalized its infection, which is then used homoeopathically to treat the infections of other sufferers.

Possession by the Loa

Initiation into Voodoo follows a parallel course under the guidance of a priest and in the context of a traditional rite. There are several reasons for being initiated. The novice may be suffering from a saisissement, or from a series of calamities in his daily life, which the priest diagnoses as coming from the *loa* (gods), if he has failed to observe his religious duties. Equally, the illness or calamity may be sent on him by his dead parents, whose souls have been 'living in the waters of penitence' and have finished their term there: the duty of their descendant is to bring them up out of the waters and install them upon the family altar. His persecutors are now not the living, who can be countered by black magic, but the dead and the loa: the Invisibles, in fact, who are the principles of grandeur, pride and power, and who are only propitiated by a man changing his own attitude to life. Freud noted a similar course of events in Europeans who make a pact with the Devil: typically after their fathers had died. He saw it as a consequence of guilt and despair which transforms the object of mourning into a source of comfort and power. (Interestingly enough, he made these observations soon after his own father had died.) If the Invisibles plague men, therefore, they do so because they also represent the unused faculties and energies which exist in everyone behind the bars of repression, and which make themselves felt when the agent of this repression has died. Initiation into Voodoo not only placates the Invisibles, but transforms them from repressors of desire into helpers for action.

The process of initiation the world over is the undergoing of a mock death followed by the experience of a rebirth (see INITIATION). It is the same in Haiti, where a not uncommon rider is added, that the death is preceded by

Initiation by Fire

The novices were brought in. There was a turmoil at the door of the seclusion hut, as the hounsis struggled to get through the crowd — for each novice is hidden under a white sheet and has to be carried on the back of a hounsi, as limp as a corpse . . .

Idem attended to them in turn. She smeared her hands with cold oil, took the novice's left hand from beneath the sheet and smeared that too. Scooping a handful of the now seething mixture from the zin she pressed it into the novice's hand and closed the fingers over it, for four or five seconds. The père savanne peered anxiously over Idem's shoulder, his candle still alight.

This is the central moment of initiation, when the novice is made to grasp heat without flinching — a heat which will sear the flesh only if the loa are displeased through some lapse on the novice's part. For the nature of the loa themselves is fire, and it requires much courage and preparation to support them.

From one to another of these crouching figures Idem moved, lit by the small fires till all was finished and the novices were humped back through the crowd like unwilling dragons. The pots were now emptied and a mixture of rum and oil brushed onto them, inside and out. Oil was poured into the fires below till ribbons of flame towered into the air, each pot a crucible for some gros-bon-

ange. Back the novices were called, still carried by the hounsis, their arms and legs seized and passed through the blaze . . .

A hounsi called Zett became possessed. Sobgwe, a thunder loa, took her, and she whirled, radiantly good-natured, about the centre post. Idem became possessed: now peering round with staring eyes and nostrils, as Ogoun; now with eyes shut and eyebrows raised, one hand touched the thatch above, as Louis André, the spirit of her grandfather; now as Brave Tonerre Crasé, with hunched shoulders and a lengthened jaw working lugubriously under a hollowed face; or as the Baron, an intimate, self-satisfied death.

Francis Huxley *The Invisibles*

an illness, and the rebirth is seen as a cure.

The state and future of the novice is diagnosed in terms of the entity which is plaguing him. If his ancestors are calling upon him to serve them, he can only do so if he serves the loa also. The problem then is which loa he is to serve. There are for a start several nations of loa, so called because they originated as gods of the various African tribes whose members came to Haiti. Slavery mixed these tribes so well that their descendants all came to be Haitian, and only the gods retained their nationalities. These nations are called Rada from Dahomey, Wangol from Angola, Siniga from Senegal, Congo, Ibo and Naga: there is also an indigenous nation, the revengeful Petro loa, who appear to stem both from the aboriginal Indian population of the island and from the slave population. Families tend to serve the same nation of gods, each of which is a pantheon. The novice may already know which loa destiny has devoted him to, or the priest may have to diagnose it by examining the novice's disorder and matching it to the known character of a suitable loa. The loa are in fact character patterns which can be seen working both in man and in Nature: Ogoun the blacksmith god, for instance, is a martial demiurge whose hammer is a thunderbolt, and who controls the head of those who are strong-minded. But he may also patronize those who strongly resent strong-mindedness in others, according to the adage: 'The character of the loa is that of his mount.' In either case the loa is invoked to settle a disorder and to lay the foundation for future development, for an initiate may become possessed by many loa during the course of his life.

Once accepted for initiation, the novice has to buy the magical and ritual apparatus for the ceremony, and during one week he goes nightly to the preparatory rites. During these, songs and prayers are intoned which speak of the time of misery which is passing, of the spirit unsheathing itself from the body, of the novices as patients whose cure will benefit the dead, and of the mapou tree, haunt of evil spirits, being felled by the blows of the rite; and interspersed with these songs and prayers is the frequent exclamation: 'There is malice, oh!' On the last evening their heads are washed, and on the Saturday morning they are formally inducted into a room where they will be secluded for another week. The

songs at this time speak of the novices being saddled ready for the loa, like a horse for its rider, the usual phrase describing a possession. Strips of palm leaves are shredded to protect and master the novices: these strips are called *aizan* after a female loa said to be a traitor and a cannibal. A song and a rite to *Grand Bois*, Great Tree, is performed, the novices are turned brusquely till they are giddy and then thrust into their chamber.

Inside, they lie upon their left sides eating white foods such as are offered to the dead; they learn more passwords and secret gestures, songs and prayers, their heads are again washed with leaves, and everything is done to prepare them for a possession by the loa on whose 'point' they are lying. The next Saturday, fowls are sacrificed and parts of them placed in a *govi* or ritual pot together with the novice's hair and nail clippings, and his gros bon ange is transferred into the govi. In the temple, cauldrons are set up over small fires and a mixture of flour and oil boiled inside them. The novices are carried out swathed in white sheets, a lump of the boiling mixture is pressed into their hands, and their arms and legs are passed through the flames. They return to their seclusion until the Sunday morning when they come out barefoot, dressed in white, collars of beads about their necks representing the loa, and hats on their heads to protect them from erring spirits; they are seated at a table under a white sheet, are baptized with a leaf dipped into water and given their new names in Voodoo. The drums strike up, they dance, and the loa possess their new servants.

After 40 days, during which they are forbidden to wash or change their clothes in order to absorb the force of the ritual, they and the priest go into a dark room where he calls up the spirits of those ancestors they wish to serve. Curious flapping sounds are heard as he draws these souls out of the waters of death, and they are made to speak through the ventriloquial medium of the priest; then they are placed in the govis reserved for them, which are also passed through the flames of a fire to heat them and give them life. These govis, together with the one containing the gros bon ange, can either be kept by the initiate or given into the safe keeping of the priest. The novice is now called a *hounsi canzo*, literally, the initiated spouse of the god.

These rites accomplish a number of different things. They emphasize the misery and malice of the world and the sickness of the novice. Seclusion allows this sickness to be incubated, and to hatch out as a loa which becomes the master of the novice's head. His gros bon ange is separated from him and placed in a govi, and so are the spirits of the dead, much as a centipede is put into a bottle of rum: this means that he is protected from further infection and can make use of the spiritual principles involved through ritual forms. He becomes familiar with the complicated rites of Voodoo and becomes one of a congregation. Finally he learns how to endure the fear of dissociation and the pain of possession.

The rites in fact spell out a number of images which carry him through this process. Dissociation at first is not a pleasant experience, being heralded by giddiness, the unstringing of the limbs and the mounting to the head of a nauseating darkness. It can be brought on in an uninitiated person by the atmosphere of a ceremony, and he will stagger about as though in the throes of a saisissement without being fully possessed by a loa. This state is often personified by the loa Grand Bois, a violent and speechless entity who can only grunt and gibber, and is referred to in the song about the felling of the mapou tree with its cargo of evil spirits. In the initiation of priests, the novice is made to stand with his back against the central post of the temple, down which the loa are held to come when they are invoked. This post is sacred to Legba, guardian of the passage between this world and the other, and he is sometimes called Legba Grand Bois Chemin, Legba the Path of the Great Tree. This tree is also equated with the backbone. But for the loa to come down this tree, its guardian, the gros bon ange, must be displaced. In ritual terms it occupies the nape of the neck, and physiologically it is represented by a large number of postural reflexes which affect the eyes, the neck, the spinal column and the heartbeat. Subvert these reflexes by suggestion, theatricality, rhythm, dancing, drumming and strong emotions, and dissociation sets in: the body falling like a felled tree. But after training, the dormant energies represented by the loa can inhabit the place the gros bon ange has vacated, and the body is held upright around the central post sacred to

It is not unknown for a man to be overwhelmed by the sexual advances of the woman dancing with him so that he falls to the floor in orgasmic dissociation

Legba. This is to be possessed by a loa, who though they live in water are fiery by nature: and to test the novice's ability to contain this influx of energy without going mad, he is made to grasp a boiling paste and to have his limbs washed by flame.

Spouse of the God

The term *hounsi*, spouse of the god, is also significant. In Haiti, lack of social organization starts in the family; women long to be married properly but all they usually achieve is the status of a common law wife, or *plaçée*. At regular marriages the bride is received at her husband's home by a group of young girls singing Catholic verses against Voodoo and plaçage whose refrain goes: 'pas plaçée, pas plaçée!' – meaning properly married.

Some women do not even become plaçée but turn *jeunesses*, good-time girls who have a financial understanding with their lovers, or even *bousins*, prostitutes, and they will often turn to Voodoo to keep their suitors' ardours aflame, to procure abortions, or just to maintain a clientele. They, and womanizing men, excuse their behaviour by saying it is the loa who make them do it, who prevent them from marrying or from keeping a partner more than a week or so. Many of them are overtaken during sleep by erotic dreams in which the loa possess them sexually, with such sweetness that they will have nothing to do with love-making for days afterwards. Curiously enough, women are often made love to by Erzulie, the goddess of love, who comes to them in masculine form; thus it is not surprising to find that many of them indulge in homosexual play as well.

The sexuality of the loa produce saisissements of a particular kind. At ordinary dances, for instance, it is not unknown for a man to be overwhelmed by the sexual advances of the woman dancing with him so that he falls to the floor in an orgasmic dissociation. The proper treatment for this, as for nocturnal visits by the loa, is to set one or two nights apart for them every week, when the sufferer sleeps alone. If he or she is married and the spouse objects to such an interruption of his pleasures, a full-blown saisissement may well erupt with disastrous results. But even if this does not happen the loa may be so pressing in its attentions that it demands to be married in proper style. This occurs at a Voodoo temple where the loa is invoked to possess an attendant, the marriage ceremony is performed with the human spouse, rings are exchanged, a document drawn up and attested.

These marriages do not always stop the lecherous behaviour of the human spouses – sometimes, indeed, it seems they encourage it, by giving it a religious justification. Priests are certainly not above using sexual magic for their own advantage, for instance by always lying on their backs when they make love in order to be possessed in the act of possession. It is also said that they sleep with their novices during the initiation rites, though this is probably pure slander. What does often occur is that the priest uses his position to sleep with the women of his congregation, who are by no means averse to his attentions, and that priestesses, who often started in life as jeunesses, use their old arts to enlarge the circle of their faithful. In addition, the hounsis, who have made the temple the centre of their life and attend all the rites as singers and dancers, frequently act as temple prostitutes and indulge in small perversions amongst themselves. This is logical enough if the hounsi is a spouse of the god, and if the temple is the god's house. A consequence very much to the advantage of the priest is that he can bring various pressures to bear on those with

Like Voodoo, Brazil's Umbanda cult involves possession by spirits, drum beats, candles and healing: Umbanda worshippers (*left* and *right*) at Copacabana Beach, Rio de Janeiro on New Year's Eve

Foto Hetzel/C. Waterson

Foto Hetzel/C. Waterson

whom his hounsis sleep, who also provide him with a great deal of interesting gossip which he can turn to good advantage when he has to diagnose an illness.

The loa most often concerned in these marriages are perhaps Ogoun and Erzulie. But underlying all these matters is Guédé, a collective title for the cemetery spirits whose king is Baron Samedi. The Baron is the first person to be buried in a churchyard – his female counterpart is called Maman Brigit – and Guédé was the first soul to be drawn up out of the waters of death by Legba. Though he can and does appear at any ceremony, being a greedy and tricky spirit whose prerogative is to devour the offerings made to any loa before they get at it, he is dominant on All Souls' Day, when he possesses a large number of women who go flocking to the cemeteries in his honour. They dress in black and purple, sing coldly lascivious songs and, using a stick as a mock penis, dance the *banda*. This dance is highly suggestive and combines sexual fascination with a scorn for pleasure and wilful contempt of love.

That women are the especial mounts for the Guédés at this moment suggests that they are getting their own back against the men who usually dominate them. It also shows the close and universal connection between death, magic and sexuality. It is one

Voodoo has had a profound influence on the surrealist, otherworldly quality of Haitian art: *The Inauguration of La Citadelle,* by J. R. Cléry, from the Morland Lee Collection

of the priest's duties to control this power, and he does it by means of the asson, a gourd rattle filled with pebbles, snake bones, earth from a cemetery and magical powders, and circled by a network of coloured beads and snake vertebrae. With this instrument he can command the dead and bring them out of the waters, he can inflame and control the Guédés, and he can master the living by beating out the rhythms which the drums then pick up and to which the attendants dance.

In theory, the use of the asson should go together with the gift of a spiritual power known as *la prise des yeux*, the taking hold of the eyes. This allows the priest to remain conscious while the loa possess themselves of his being, unlike minor initiates who black out when they are ridden and who have no memory of what they did when possessed. The state is marked by a sensation of weight on the neck or shoulders, and a feeling of enormous power: the priest can hear the loa whispering in his ear, and he is endowed with second sight and other paranormal powers. So, at least, say those who have

undergone la prise des yeux and those who have witnessed its effects, and it may well be that their claims are sometimes justified.

Dissociation, possession, marriage to the gods and la prise des yeux: these are the central facts around which the many and diverse ceremonies of Voodoo are organized, and the superstitions also.

Voodoo treats the Invisibles as enemies to be made friends of and powers to be used, and the supernatural as a disease to be turned to good account. To do so the priest must use his left hand as well as his right, that is, he must know as much about black as about white magic, and keep both in the context of the religion. What he does is sometimes cruel and often alarming, besides being mystifying in the good and bad senses of the word. But then the gods that the magician serves are jealous as well as powerful, and those who enter their mysteries must expect to pay the price.
(See also DAHOMEY; POSSESSION; SOUTH AMERICA; TRANCE; ZOMBIES.)

FRANCIS HUXLEY

FURTHER READING: Maya Deren, *Divine Horsemen* (Dell Publishing, 1972); F. Huxley, *The Invisibles* (Humanities, 1966); A. Métraux, *Voodoo in Haiti* (Schocken, 1972).

Wagner's operas have exerted a powerful influence on occultists, who have regarded him as a 'natural magician' and a 'Gnostic saint': he has been credited with an intuitive grasp of the principles of sexual magic, and one enthusiast translated the names of Wagner's characters into Hebrew to find important numerological formulas

WAGNER

'LORD OF LIFE and Joy . . . . . . though adored of us upon heaths and in woods, on mountains and in caves, openly in the market-places and secretly in the chambers of our houses . . . we worthily commemorate them worthy that did of old adore thee and manifest thy glory unto men, Lao-tze and Siddartha and Krishna and Tahuti . . . and these also . . . Thomas Vaughan, Elias Ashmole, Molinos, Adam Weishaupt, Wolfgang von Goethe, Ludovicus Rex Bavariae, Richard Wagner . . .'

So reads the Collect for the Saints in the Gnostic Catholic Mass written by Aleister Crowley (see CROWLEY) for his followers. At first sight it may seem surprising that Crowley included Richard Wagner in his rag-bag collection of Gnostic 'saints' — others were the Borgia pope, Alexander VI, and a syphilitic and eccentric 15th century Lutheran named Ulrich von Hutten — but Wagner's indebtedness to Nordic myth, legend and mystical interpretations of Christianity has convinced many occultists that the great composer was one of their own number. Sar Péladan, the French magician, novelist and poet, who broke away from the Kabalistic Rose-Croix of Stanislas de Guaita to found his own Catholic Rose-Croix of the Temple and the Grail (see BATTLE OF BEWITCHMENT; ROSICRUCIANS), made a pilgrimage to the Wagner festival at Bayreuth and was so deeply affected by his attendance at a performance of *Parsifal* that thereafter he not only claimed that Wagner had possessed 'the soul of a natural magician' but insisted that from now on his own novels must be referred to, not as novels, but as *wagneriennes*. Other occultists have made even more extravagant claims. Aleister Crowley's disciple Frater Achad (Charles Stansfeld Jones) wrote that: '. . . Wagner

himself had received Instruction in the great Principles of the Holy Order from certain of the Secret Chiefs and this accounts for the great harmony between his Work and that of other members of the Great Brotherhood.'

Wagner was born at Leipzig in 1813; officially, he was the son of Karl Wagner, a petty bureaucrat who had risen to the command of the Leipzig police. There is some reason to suppose, however, that he was in reality the offspring of an illicit liaison between his mother and Ludwig Geyer, a portrait painter, actor and dramatist who had for some time been a guest in the Wagner household. Karl Wagner died of typhoid six months after the child's birth, and in the following year his widow married Geyer — significantly enough, she gave birth to a daughter only six months later. The young Richard was brought up in Dresden as Geyer's son and did not adopt the surname of Wagner until his confirmation at the age of 14.

As a boy, Wagner seemed more interested in the theatre than he did in music and it was not until 1828 that he began the serious study of composition; just two years later his work achieved its first public performance — a fiasco — when an overture composed by him was played in the Leipzig Hoftheater. This work has not survived, but its most notable characteristic, apart from the unusual physical appearance of the score — brass appeared in black, strings in red and woodwind in green — seems to have been a ludicrously *fortissimo* drumbeat every

Harshness and Compassion
If so many contrary emotions can be brought so intimately into relationship by the music, the implication is that the grievousness and the resignation, the harshness and the compassion, belong to one another. Evil is not a foreign body which some clever surgeon of morals can neatly excise; it is a part of ourselves which we have to learn to live with. Grief is not a poison we can vomit out of the system; it is an ingredient in human experience which we have to assimilate. We can accept all this, and still be in love with life, which we cannot really be if we merely repudiate the darker side of it.

Robert Donington *Wagner's 'Ring' and Its Symbols*

fourth bar, productive of intense and, at every repetition, increasingly hysterical laughter from the audience.

Politics and Exile
Throughout his life Wagner enjoyed melodramatic fiction and as a young man fell under the spell of English Gothic novels in German translation; even in his last years he re-read with enjoyment the occult thrillers of the English novelist and occultist Bulwer Lytton (see LYTTON). According to Houston Stewart Chamberlain, Wagner was particularly fond of *Zanoni* and *A Strange Story*. It was with *Rienzi*, an opera derived from Lytton's novel of the same name, that Wagner achieved, in 1842, the public acclaim that had eluded him 12 years before. *Rienzi* was followed by *The Flying Dutchman*, first produced in 1843 and found perplexing by its audience, and in the same year its composer achieved a temporary financial security as Director of the Dresden Opera.

Wagner, who is sometimes seen, probably incorrectly, as an arch-reactionary and an important formative influence on the ideology of Nazism, was deeply involved in the German revolutionary-democratic movement of 1848–49 in spite of the fact that he was, as Director of the Opera, an official of the Royal Court of Saxony. Wagner's relationship with the Court had become strained in 1847 when he had submitted to the Intendant of the Opera — an amiable aristocratic bureaucrat who had previously been in charge of the Department of Woods and Forests — a memorandum calling for a radical reform of all aspects of Saxon musical life. The memorandum was pigeon-holed for a year and then rejected; simultaneously Wagner was informed that as a mark of royal displeasure the first performance of his new opera *Lohengrin* was to be indefinitely postponed. Wagner, annoyed that his suggestions should be disregarded, rewrote his memorandum in stronger form, demanded the abolition of the office of Intendant and, in May 1848, joined the *Vaterlandsverein*, a society whose objects included universal suffrage, a united Germany and the abolition of the Saxon monarchy. Wagner was an enthusiastic advocate of this programme and read a paper to the society, later published in its official journal, calling for a republican Saxony.

In May 1849 civil war broke out; Wagner fought (briefly) on the barricades and a provisional government was declared, but enjoyed only a brief existence before it was snuffed out by the combined efforts of Saxon and Prussian troops. Evidence of Wagner's involvement in (as distinct from his sympathy with) treasonable activities was scanty and it was not until May 1850 that he fled Saxony after a warrant had been issued for his arrest.

For the next 11 years Wagner was an exile, living at various times in Paris, London and Zurich, usually in poverty – for while he earned considerable sums his expenditure always exceeded his income – suffering from violent headaches and the eczema that had plagued him since childhood, and always longing for a return to his beloved Germany. But these unhappy years of exile were also years of great artistic achievement. *Das Rheingold*, the first part of *The Ring*, was completed in 1854; *Die Walküre* in 1856; and *Tristan und Isolde* in 1859.

Wagner's exile ended in 1861 but, dogged by creditors and unpaid debts, his life was still far from happy. He was actually in hiding from debt collectors when, in 1864, he was summoned to Munich by Ludwig II, then aged 19, the spendthrift, homosexual and half-mad king of Bavaria – another 'saint' of the Gnostic Catholic Church. Within six weeks of his arrival at Munich Wagner was one of the young monarch's principal advisers: '. . . the young King', wrote Wagner, '. . . resolves to give me all that I require in this life; I in return do nothing but compose and advise him. He calls me two and even three times in one day; talks to me for hours, and is . . . devoted heart and soul to me.'

From 1864 until 1876 Wagner received considerable, although often erratic, material support from Ludwig II. The first two parts of *The Ring* were performed at Munich in 1869 and 1870, and the score of the third part *(Siegfried)* was completed by the beginning of 1871. By the end of that year Wagner had decided that no existing German theatre was really suitable for the staging of *The Ring* and that he would himself build one at Bayreuth.

By almost superhuman exertions, supplemented by a loan from Ludwig II, Wagner managed to build his theatre and to stage, in August 1876, all four parts of *The Ring*: the last part, *Götterdämmerung*, had been completed in the previous year. In spite of the fact that this performance, the first Bayreuth festival, resulted in a loss, a second festival took place in 1882, and in July and August of that year there were 16 performances of *Parsifal*, Wagner's last opera, at Bayreuth. Wagner died, of heart failure, in 1883.

Blind Forces
It has been said of Wagner that 'he invented little but adapted much'. Certainly this was true of his plots, and it is his reliance on traditional 'supernatural' material that, coupled with the emotional appeal of his music, largely accounts for the esteem in which he has been held by occultists. Significantly enough, it has been those works in

Richard Wagner at Triebschen, in 1868: the operas in which he drew most heavily on myth and legend are those which have particularly fascinated occultists

Radio Times Hulton Picture Library

which Wagner drew most heavily from myth and legend – the cycle of *The Ring, Tannhäuser* and *Parsifal* – that have held the most fascination for occultists and even a brief examination of them gives some indication of the way in which Wagner managed to transmute unpromising material into great art, and to select those incidents in a story that should be left out in its re-telling.

Jessie Weston has summed up this selective aspect of Wagner's genius: 'the original stories . . . were too full, too complicated, for dramatic representation . . . Wagner selected those incidents which would tell most effectively on the stage, re-combined them so as to preserve (in some cases restore) the original simplicity of the story, developed the characters, and grasped with unerring instinct hints of his predecessors which, superfluous for the epic, were big with possibilities for the dramatic form . . .'

Wagner took the story of *The Ring* from a Scandinavian source, the older and so-called 'poetic' Edda. The German version, the *Nibelungenlied*, is a 13th century compilation derived from material of much earlier date and bearing much the same relationship to subsequent German poetry as the *Iliad* bore to the literature of classical Greece (see NIBELUNGENLIED). It is odd that Wagner, that most German of musicians, relied principally upon the Icelandic source, making very little use of the *Nibelungenlied* except in *The Twilight of the Gods*, the last part of *The Ring*.

The world of *The Ring* is the world of the Nordic gods, not the world of Christianity; we are in a doom-laden universe, completely lacking in free will, moving inevitably towards the predestined collapse of order and the triumph of chaos – the veritable Doom of the Gods (see SCANDINAVIA). The primitive feeling that all living things are subject to the mindless play of blind forces is terrifyingly re-created.

The Budding Staff
While *Tannhäuser* is a much earlier work than *The Ring*, historically and theologically it comes between *The Ring* and *Parsifal*; in the former we are in the world of the old Teutonic gods, in the latter we are in the world of mystical Christianity, and in *Tannhäuser* we see the conflict between the old faith and the new. There are many surviving medieval ballads of Tannhäuser, and their basic plot is simple enough. Tannhäuser spends a year with Venus in her pleasure-gardens beneath the mountain known as the Venusberg; repents, leaves, goes to confession and is told that only the Pope can absolve him. He travels to Rome on pilgrimage and is told by the Pope that God will not forgive him until his dry pilgrim's staff bursts into leaf; immediately it puts forth buds, leaves and flowers – moral, the forgiveness of God is infinite.

Wagner transformed this simple and trite story into a conflict between earthly love and paganism on the one hand (represented by Venus) and heavenly love and Christianity on the other (represented by Tannhäuser's sweetheart Elizabeth). Only when Tannhäuser, rejected by heaven and earth alike, chooses the dead body of Elizabeth in preference to the delights of Venus does the staff burst into flower – forgiveness is achieved through love and death.

There are many versions of the story of Parsifal, but Wagner relied exclusively on that of Wolfram von Eschenbach (see PARSIFAL) and retold the latter's version of the knight's quest for the Spear and the Grail with great fidelity. *Parsifal* bears more resemblance to a mystery play, a religious rite, than it does to a conventional opera, and Wagner regarded it as such, refusing to let it be performed except at Bayreuth.

The Swan of Ecstasy
Throughout the present century, Wagner's operas and writings have exerted a considerable, although sometimes hidden, influence on many of the more intellectual occultists. While a few of them have been attracted by the more repellent aspects of Wagner's personal philosophy – the followers of the German mystagogue Lanz von Liebenfels (see NEW TEMPLARS) elevated Wagner to the status of a Teutonic guru and folk-hero, not because of his music but because of his antisemitism – most have found Wagner's use of myth and legend attractive in itself and also surprisingly compatible with their own interpretations of occidental esotericism. Theodor Reuss, a practitioner of sex-magic (he was Crowley's predecessor as chief of the *Ordo Templi Orientis*) and an ardent Wagnerian, looked upon Wagner as a sort of intuitive sex-magician and attached a sexual symbolism to the Spear and the Grail of *Parsifal*.

Crowley himself also found much of occult significance in *Parsifal* and, to give only one example, regarded the swan shot by Parsifal as symbolizing that ecstasy which is the ultimate goal of the magician. He wrote: 'There is a Swan whose name is Ecstasy . . . In all the Universe it alone is motionless . . . Motion is relative: there is Nothing that is still. Against this Swan I shot an arrow; the white breast poured forth blood. Men smote me; then perceiving that I was Pure Fool, they let me pass. Thus and not otherwise I came to the Temple of the Grail.'

Link With the Cabala

The fascination of *Parsifal* for occultists has been a perennial one: at least one follower of Rudolf Steiner (see STEINER) looks upon it as a brilliant exposition of the doctrines of anthroposophy. But the most ingenious and perhaps the maddest occult exegisis of it was made by C. S. Jones, in his book *Chalice of Ecstasy*, published in Chicago in 1923. His basic thesis was that Wagner had been either a great cabalist or, quite literally, inspired. In any case the

important thing was that *Parsifal* was a vehicle conveying important cabalistic secrets. When the names of the principal characters were turned into Hebrew (each Hebrew letter has its own numerical value), they added up into important numerical formulas. Thus the name of the evil magician Klingsor added up to 333, the number of 'that mighty devil' Choronzon, whom Aleister Crowley had evoked to visible appearance in the Sahara Desert. Even more important, Monsalvat, the mountain of Salvation, added up to 666 – clear proof of Wagner's inspiration and Aleister Crowley's divine mission. These were only two of Jones's cabalistic discoveries; there were many more, and those who care to read *The Chalice of Ecstasy* will find out for

themselves the answers to such recondite problems as the occult significance of the destruction of Klingsor's garden, and the reason why the flask from which oil is poured on Parsifal's feet should be shaped like a female breast and stoppered with a ruby. (See also TRISTAN.)

FRANCIS KING

FURTHER READING: Derek Watson, *Richard Wagner* (Schirmer Books, 1981); W. H. Hadow, *Richard Wagner* (AMS Press reprint). Jessie L. Weston, *The Legends of the Wagner Drama* (Nutt, London, 1896); for an interpretation of *The Ring* in Jungian terms, see Robert Donington, *Wagner's 'Ring' and Its Symbols* (St Martin, rev. edn., 1969).

A. E. WAITE

Mansell Collection

A SELF-PROCLAIMED MYSTIC whose theories have become accepted occult doctrine, Arthur Edward Waite was born in 1857 in the unromantic Brooklyn area of New York. Soon after his birth his mother returned with him to England, where she became a Roman Catholic; and Waite was to remain under the influence of Church ceremony all his life. He considered himself to be a late developer, not having reached 'intellectual puberty' at 21; and he passed through a succession of enthusiasms before

arriving at the occult by way of Spiritualism and Mme Blavatsky's book *Isis Unveiled* (see BLAVATSKY).

In 1881 Waite discovered the writings of the French magus Eliphas Levi (see LEVI), and his first 'occult' work (1885) was a digest and codification of Levi's teaching. The year before had seen the publication of A. P. Sinnett's *Occult World*, with its account of the miraculous phenomena produced by Mme Blavatsky. Waite joined her Theosophical Society at a time of great fluttering in the occult dovecots and when the newly-converted Annie Besant was in the first flush of her theosophical enthusiasm (see BESANT; THEOSOPHY). In theosophical circles Waite met other prominent occultists, including Edward Maitland of the Hermetic Society, W. B. Yeats, and the writer Arthur Machen who remained a lifelong friend. With the theosophists, Waite's connections became increasingly tenuous until he finally refused the post of Librarian at the Society, because of his inability to accept the existence of Mahatmas (see MAHATMAS; MASTERS).

It is not with Theosophy that Waite's name is chiefly linked, but with ritual magic as practised in the Hermetic Order of the Golden Dawn under the direction of S. L. Macgregor Mathers and Wynn Westcott (see GOLDEN DAWN). Waite made two ventures into ritual magic, but it was not his true vocation. The first time he entered the Golden Dawn he passed through the grades of the First Order, but resigned on the suspicion of questionable legal practice on the

part of his superiors. Some years later he rejoined the Order in a period of dissension among its members, and contrived to gain control of the Golden Dawn's Isis-Urania temple (mother-lodge in London), whose ceremonies he entirely rewrote from the point of view of Christian mysticism.

From his encounter with cabalistic magic, Waite derived one lasting source of inspiration: the idea of the soul ascending the Tree of Life towards the Godhead (see CABALA). But he came more and more to distrust 'occult' practices, and there was little love lost between him and the posturing Mathers, who claimed to admire Waite's poetry, but proved most suspicious of any attempt to encroach on his personal province of the mystical. Waite's chief concerns became Freemasonry and the charting of a 'Secret Tradition' underlying alchemy, masonry and the Cabala, expressed in the 'Hidden Church of the Holy Grail', a mystical body of the elect contained in and concealed by the Christian Church. Whereas his early belief – recorded in 1891 – was that magic could provide the solution to the problems of 'the origin and destiny of Man', his mature conviction of some 20 years later was that the place of the Seeker was within the Church, 'that body in which the work of regeneration takes place'. His poetry is forgotten, his vaunted scholarship seems both tedious and defective, and his chief legacy is his conception of an all-pervasive secret tradition.

JAMES WEBB

For centuries ferociously persecuted by Church and state for their unorthodox interpretation of the Bible, the Waldenses have survived into the 20th century by sheer faith and courage

WALDENSES

A CHRISTIAN COMMUNITY which has had its focus in the Cottian Alps on the borders of France and Italy for nearly 800 years, the Waldenses (also Valdenses, Valdesi, Vaudois) have been given various labels. They have been thought of as the forerunners of St Francis because they were originally mendicant preachers; as the

forerunners of the Baptists because of their views on infant baptism; as the forerunners of the Bible-Reading Movement because their founder had the New Testament translated into the vernacular; and as the forerunners of the Reformation because they emphasized the authority of the Bible and vigorously opposed the worldliness of the Roman Church and many of its practices. That they have survived the centuries can be largely attributed to the nature of the territory in which they settled: the mountain valleys which debouch into the plain of Piedmont about 30 miles west of Turin are inhospitable and isolated; thus the region afforded seclusion, assisted flight and hindered attack.

Claiming a geographical derivation *(valles densae)* for the name of the sect, some historians asserted that the community was founded by St Paul during a pause in a journey from Rome to Spain (see Romans 15.28). This theory was discredited in the middle of the 19th century after critical examination of the available manuscript evidence.

Renouncing a Worldly Life

It is now generally thought that the community was founded towards the end of the 12th century by Peter Waldo, a wealthy Lyonnaise merchant, businessman and money-lender, who was abruptly converted to religion. By one account, he was startled

Federico Patellani

into appreciating the uncertainty of life by the sudden death of a friend; by another, the spiritual richness of evangelical poverty was thrust upon his notice by the chance hearing of the legend of St Alexis sung by a wandering minstrel. The son of wealthy Roman parents, St Alexis parted from his wife during the post-nuptial festivities, forwent his inheritance and thereafter lived a life of great piety and extreme asceticism.

Whatever the truth, Peter Waldo asked a pious scholar the surest way to God. He received the answer given by Jesus to the rich young man: 'If you would be perfect, go, sell what you possess and give to the poor . . .' Waldo, too, had great possessions; but he was neither sad nor went away grieved. Only setting aside sufficient money to pay for a translation of the New Testament and other theological writings into the Provençal dialect, he paid his creditors, provided for his wife, portioned his daughters and placed them in the care of the Abbess of Fontrevrault, and spent the last of his money buying food for the starving poor of Lyons. Thereafter, dressed in the manner of the Apostles, he tramped the countryside, preaching wherever he went and begging his daily bread. He studied the New Testament intensively, interpreting it in the light of his private judgement.

Waldo soon attracted followers, who copied his example of penury and evangelism. The literate read the gospels regularly; the illiterate learnt them by heart, sentence by sentence, chapter by chapter, book by book. As their numbers increased Waldo

The Waldensian pastor of Prali walks to church before dawn; Prali is a village high in the Italian Alps and the spiritual capital of the Italian Waldenses, who after suffering some 500 years of persecution are now able to practise their faith in peace

sent them out as wandering preachers, two by two, men and women alike. From their profession of poverty and city of origin they became known as the 'Poor Men of Lyons', and from their custom of wearing sandals, 'Sandaliati', 'Insabbatati', 'Sabbatati' or 'Sabotiers'.

At that time the Church forbade all private translations of the Bible as well as preaching without licence. Inevitably, the Archbishop of Lyons prohibited the activities of the Poor Men of Lyons; whereupon Waldo decided to carry the matter to Rome. The Pope, Alexander III, wavered. At first he received Waldo as a favourite son and gave him a solemn embrace; then he refused to licence him; and finally, in 1179, approving the Waldensian vows of poverty, gave permission to preach, subject to the approval of the archbishop. That approval was withheld, whereupon the Poor Men, declaring proudly that they ought to obey God rather than man, ignored the papal injunction and continued as if nothing had happened. The Church replied with excommunication and in 1184 the Waldenses were anathematized by Pope Lucius III in a decree issued from Verona.

The Waldenses dispersed. Colonies and small cells were established throughout Europe, but the main body of the heretics, as they now were, took refuge in an isolated corner of the Alps. There they found other sects, reported to number 17, who were also opposed to Rome. In 1212 the Waldenses made a second approach to the papacy. It was ineffectual. In 1218 a conference of all the demonimations lurking in the valleys was held at Bergamo, and from it emerged the Valdesian Society or Associates of Valdes. The Waldenses now became known in French as the Vaudois and in Italian as the Valdesi.

Barbarous Cruelty

In 1215 the Fourth Lateran Council decreed the extermination of the Waldenses, together with the Cathars (see CATHARS). In 1230, although thousands of heretics had by then been butchered, Pope Gregory IX initiated a decade of fierce armed attack against the settlements. In 1233, he instituted the Inquisition to destroy the remnants of heresy and appointed the Dominicans as the official Inquisitors for the south of France. Relentless and ruthless, the 'Hounds of God' besmirched their early history by their cruelties.

In the following centuries the persecution of the Waldenses, alternately by the Church, the king of France and the duke of Savoy (the last two urged on by the pope) was in no way abated. Thousands of martyrs were burnt at the stake; French and Irish mercenaries marched into the valleys and slaughtered many hundreds of men, women, and children.

In the 17th century the barbarities reached such a height that international concern was roused and voiced. Cromwell sent letters, written in Latin by Milton who also composed a sonnet *On the late Massacre in the Piedmont*, to the Duke of Savoy, and sent a special commissioner, Sir Samuel Morland, to investigate the 'Bloudy Massacre, 1655' and 'the barbarous and horrid cruelties'. Despite this, the valleys were depopulated when in 1686 Louis XIV, following the Revocation of the Edict of Nantes, ordered the Duke of Savoy to compel the Waldenses to adopt Roman Catholicism. Thousands were carried away and imprisoned in Turin, all their property being confiscated and handed over to Roman Catholics. Four years later a mere handful, under the command of the heroic Henri Arnaud, pastor and historian, struggled back to their homeland.

In the 18th century life in the valleys became easier as physical persecution waned, though spiritual liberty was still all but denied. The kings of England joined with other European monarchs in granting annuities for the support of the pastors and the maintenance of schools. From 1816 onwards gradual concessions were made until 1848, when Charles Albert, King of Piedmont, gave them political and religious rights equal to those of their Roman Catholic fellow subjects.

Rejecting the House of Lies

From the beginning the Waldenses were a missionary society, though with increasing numbers it became impossible for all to preach. They became divided into two classes, on the same pattern as the Cathars, the laity known as the *amici* or *credentes*, and the pastorate known as the *perfecti*. The pastors were all expected to undertake missionary work and, still travelling two by two, they made long journeys, undeterred by the likelihood of martyrdom. Italy was their main, though far from only, field. Congregations were established in all the principal towns and elsewhere in the peninsula, and those in Florence, Rome, Naples and Venice numbered several thousand each. There are thought to have been approximately 40,000 Waldenses in the valleys and Piedmont alone in the middle of the 16th century.

The Waldenses held that the authority of the Bible is supreme, and that anything not authorized by it is fabulous. They further said that the Bible should be understood according to its exact wording and not according to any doctrine or tradition of the Church of Rome or to the glosses of popish scholars.

They maintained the vital doctrine of justification through grace, holding that God bestowed grace because of his nature irrespective of the worthiness of the recipient. Infant baptism they declared

The Waldenses held that the authority of the Bible is supreme, and that it should be 'understood according to its exact wording and not according to any doctrine or tradition of the Church of Rome or to the glosses of popish scholars': Waldensian service at Prali

to be of no avail. They held that matrimony is freely open to all: for nowhere in the New Testament is it forbidden – some of the Apostles were married – and God has left it to each man's discretion. Some of the pastors married in order to show approval of matrimony; but the greater number remained single because of the hazardous nature of their calling.

They threw off the authority of the Pope and the bishops generally, though good bishops (that is, bishops who modelled their lives on the Apostles) were to be obeyed. They argued that the Church, admittedly originally the true Church, had been seduced by the Donation of Constantine (a document transferring temporal power from the Emperor Constantine to the papacy, which was in the 15th century proved a forgery) and was now corrupt and a house of lies, with the Pope as the 'Head of Error'.

They denied the power of unworthy priests either to consecrate or absolve, holding that in each case the ability to do so lay in the merits, not in the ordination, of the ministrant. They held that a pious layman or laywoman could in the case of necessity administer the sacraments or hear confessions, and that the sacraments could be consecrated in the vulgar tongue since sanctification has the same effect in the vernacular as in Latin.

The Mass, beyond the words of consecration, they thought to be worth nothing because neither Christ nor the Apostles ever

Federico Patellani

sang any liturgy in celebration of the Lord's Supper. They declared that the plainsong of the Church was no more than the barking of dogs and that any merit lay in the words rather than the melody. One Lord's Prayer, they said was of greater efficacy than many Masses.

They abominated all those matters that venal priests turned to personal profit, such as the granting of indulgences, the invocation of the saints, alms, Masses and prayers for the dead. They thought the doctrine of purgatory (see PURGATORY) to be without warrant, saying that after death there were but two roads for the disembodied soul — either heaven or hell. They reprobated all practices not expressly approved by the New Testament, believing the use of crosses and ornaments in churches and the adoration of images to be idolatrous; benedictions, dedications and pilgrimages to be vain and superfluous; and holy water ridiculous. They denied the lawfulness of capital punishment, oaths and the bearing of arms; though on the latter points their views had to be modified later in order to prevent the total destruction of the sect. Some of the Waldenses refused to worship in churches, deriding them as mere heaps of stones, and quoting Acts 18.24: 'God . . . does not live in shrines made by men.'

At the Reformation the Waldenses gravitated towards Calvinism. Their great synod held in 1532 at Chanforans, above the Angrogne valley, at which they decided to join the Reformation and the family of Reformed Churches, was attended by

Guillaume Farel, preacher in Geneva and subsequently friend of, and assistant to, Calvin. Also present was the scholar Olivetan, who three years later produced for the Waldenses a second translation of the Bible, this time in French. At a council held in 1559 the Waldenses adopted a new Confession of Faith, of a Calvinistic type.

Today the Waldensian Church is a member of the Reformed and Presbyterian Alliance and the Federal Council of Protestants. It is flourishing, and there are Waldenses in the valleys, throughout Italy (where in 1965 there were about 35,000 members with 115 churches), Switzerland and the south of France, whilst emigrants have carried the faith throughout the world. There are ten overseas congregations, five in Uruguay and two in Argentina with about 20,000 communicants between them, and one each in the states of Texas, Carolina and Missouri. The Church is governed by a synod, and the moderator, who presides over the executive committee, is elected for one year only (though he may be re-elected annually for a maximum term of seven years).

The miracle of the Waldensian survival was undoubtedly grounded in glowing faith and immense physical courage.

Below left **Pope Gregory IX (1227–41), the father of the Inquisition, initiated a decade of fierce attack against Waldensian settlements** *Below right* **Pope Alexander III, who at first welcomed the Waldensian movement and approved their vows of poverty**

Ingenuity may have helped. It was argued by Harold Bayley (in *A New Light on the Renaissance*) that they, with one or two other pre-Reformation Protestant sects, derived great encouragement and strength from their ability to keep in touch with one another without the knowledge of the Inquisition. He maintained that the watermarks in paper were often emblems of religious faith and were used to 'flash signals of hope and encouragement to exiles in far distant countries . . .'

If watermarks were so used, why not other symbols? One tradition suggests that the Waldenses were the originators of the Tarot (see TAROT), the pack of cards with 22 trumps of mysterious design used for fortune telling by many and the game of *tarocchi* by a few. Whilst its origins are not certainly known, it is worth noticing that the earliest documentary evidence of the Tarot is dated c 1450, that is to say at the very same time when pressure on the Waldenses was at its height. Speculation suggests that these trumps were used by the pastors as visual teaching aids, that they were carried as part of the full pack and in consequence were easily explainable to the Inquisition, and at safe times were brought out as texts for sermons and reminders of points of faith.

ROGER TILLEY

FURTHER READING: Ellen Scott Davidson, *Forerunners of St. Francis* (Houghton, Miflin, 1927); Henry Charles Lea, *A History of the Inquisition* (AMS Press reprint).

WALSINGHAM

THE QUIET VILLAGE of Walsingham in the Vale of Stiffkey, in Norfolk, England, was a notable place of pilgrimage in honour of the Virgin Mary in the Middle Ages. From the 11th century until the Reformation, its fame throughout England and even throughout Christendom rivalled that of Canterbury and some of the ancient European shrines; and it is now, once more, among both Anglicans and Roman Catholics, one of Britain's principal centres of the cult of Mary.

Some years before the Norman conquest, a Norman family named de Faverches had settled in this remote Saxon hamlet and become lords of its manor. In 1061 Lady Richeldis, the young and intensely pious wife of the lord of the manor, had a vision which has much in common with those recorded as the inspiration of other celebrated shrines, such as the much later ones at Lourdes (see LOURDES) and Fátima. The Virgin Mary, she said, had appeared to her, taken her in spirit to the house at Nazareth in which the Holy Family had lived, and commanded her to build an exact replica of it at Walsingham.

Richeldis obeyed, and set her ample estate staff to prepare the work. As at other such places, water had welled copiously from the ground at the scene of the apparition; and one morning, after a heavy dew, Richeldis noted two dry patches, and chose one of these for the site of the Holy House, as it was to be called. Everything went wrong with the work; and Richeldis spent a night in prayer asking for the Virgin's guidance. In the morning she found the house correctly completed – and moved, apparently by supernatural means, to a site 200 feet away.

Such was the legend of the founding of the Walsingham shrine, which soon became famous. Many kings – Richard Coeur de Lion, Edward the Confessor, and even Henry VIII among them – made this pilgrimage; so, with equal devotion, did Erasmus. Healing miracles were claimed. The Franciscans opened a friary in the village. Augustinian canons built a great priory church, now in ruins. Medieval pilgrims carried away water from the holy well in small leaden flasks, marked with a crowned 'W'.

With the Reformation, almost all that had made Walsingham famous was destroyed. The image of the Virgin, on which the pilgrims' devotion had concentrated, was burned at Chelsea. Of the ballads that survive, one is especially poignant:

> Bitter, bitter oh! to behould,
>   The grasse to growe
> Where the walles of Walsingam
>   So statly did shewe . .
> Level, level with the ground
>   The towers do lye . . .

So Walsingham slept until – after only a few modest signs of homage to its past – in 1921 a new vicar, Alfred Hope Patten, was appointed to the living of Walsingham. He was 36 years old and had a very small

Spectrum Colour Library

Interior of the Anglican shrine of Our Lady of Walsingham: the original shrine was said to have been built as a replica of the house at Nazareth in which Joseph, Mary and Jesus had lived; it was a major centre of pilgrimage, its fame rivalling that of Canterbury, until its destruction during the Reformation. The new shrine church was built in 1931

stipend, three churches to serve and a large vicarage to keep up. But he was a man of extraordinary determination and powerful personality: within a few years he had revived the medieval devotion to Mary and the pilgrimage – at first in the parish church of Little Walsingham, then in a separate shrine church, which he had built and adorned in the most flamboyant Italianate style. The replica of the Holy House was built within this church; the seated image of the Virgin was copied from a medieval seal.

The difficulties Fr Hope Patten had to contend with were many. One may have been paranormal. He always said that, when he first came there, the parish church was 'full of evil spirits'. He had 'some very unpleasant experiences' when alone in it. The moment he began the *Asperges*, the sprinkling of the congregation with holy water which precedes the Western Mass, the spirits 'almost visibly retreated'. Then, too, he had to convert the villagers, from whom conservative opposition might have been expected. He faced, and gradually overcame, the strong disapproval of his diocesan bishop, Bertram Pollock of Norwich.

When the new shrine church was built in 1931, Patten put on the foundation-stone an inscription in Latin recording that it had been built in the pontificate of Pope Pius XI and the episcopate of Bertram of Norwich. The Bishop insisted on the removal of his name and, when he visited Walsingham, exclaimed: 'It is far worse than I expected . . . All these things which you have put in must be cleared away.'

They were not. Walsingham remains the most extreme latter-day expression of the doctrine and forms of worship rediscovered by the Oxford pioneers of the 19th century Catholic revival in the Church of England. A century ago such Anglican priests as Fr Tooth of Hatcham were sent to prison for introducing such practices.

While Fr Patten was alive, there was a certain sense of rivalry between his flock and the Roman Catholics – as he called them, 'our fellow-Catholics who are not in communion with Canterbury'. The Roman Catholics have a far smaller shrine a mile away, in the Slipper Chapel, so called because medieval pilgrims took off their shoes here and walked barefoot for the last stage of the journey. Now all such differences are melting in ecumenical charity: many Roman Catholics were among the 7000 who attended the Anglican national pilgrimage on Whit Monday, 1971.

On such an occasion as this, and on most major festivals, the churches and streets of the village are crowded with visitors. In the afternoon Mass is sung in the shrine church (usually, now, with a number of priests concelebrating). Then the priests, carrying the image of the Virgin, lead a long procession of pilgrims round the village. As they walk, they sing the 37-verse pilgrimage hymn, which retells in simple form the history of the shrine and is sung to the same tune as the Lourdes hymn. As they return, the service of Benediction is already beginning. Afterwards they queue at the holy well, also within the shrine church, to drink of its water and be sprinkled with it. It is a phenomenon the speed of whose triumphant revival can hardly be equalled elsewhere in the Anglican communion – and the founder, Fr Hope Patten, saw its climax before his death in 1958.

TOM DRIBERG.

Told by Christ to be his divine messenger, Mary Anne Girling preached the communal sharing of goods and celibacy to her disciples

WALWORTH JUMPERS

THE SECT of Walworth Jumpers, also known as the Girlingites, Bible Christians, Children of God, or English Shakers, first met in Suffolk and later in London. Around 1870 they held religious services of an unorthodox order under a converted railway arch in Sutherland Street, Walworth Road, South London. Here large crowds of poor people assembled to listen to the preaching of the founder and leader of the sect, a tall, thin, Suffolk woman with high cheek-bones and dark piercing eyes whose name was Mary Anne Girling.

Mrs Girling, whose maiden name was Claughton, was illiterate. She married a sailor who died young, and for some months after her husband's death she was overcome by grief; it was then that she proclaimed that she had seen visions. While praying in her room, she said, she saw Christ standing before her, telling her she was to be his divine messenger. She claimed to have had two further visions, and in 1868 she gave her first sermon outside the Wesleyan chapel in Suffolk where she worshipped.

The main belief of the sect was that if its members stayed celibate they would never die. From the date of their full conversion, they considered themselves immortal. A characteristic feature of the Girlingite services was the dancing and jumping of the believers, who often fell down on the floor in fits, made trance utterings, and screamed in religious fervour.

From the noisy railway arch Mrs Girling moved with her loyal followers to a small chapel in College Place, Chelsea, where a charge of threepence was demanded from all non-Jumpers attending. Among the new disciples was a wealthy woman named Mrs Julia Wood, who was persuaded to buy a large house in Battersea in South London as a home for the sect. Here Mrs Girling had another vision, that 'God had given her New Forest Lodge at Hordle in Hampshire', as a country headquarters. She said she had no idea where it was, but God would direct her to it. Sure enough, the house and estate were soon revealed, and the faithful Mrs Wood went to her bank and bought the property for Mrs Girling.

All the Children of God, with their spiritual Mother leading them, now moved to the New Forest, where they were joined by several farmers and labourers; and by 1874 there were 164 members living in the house surrounded by grounds which could not adequately support them. Everyone led a communal life, handing over all they possessed when they entered the colony, but as Mrs Girling forbade all working for profit, or trading with the outside world, her followers were soon in debt; they were dispossessed of the house and forced to live in tents in a field near the hamlet of Tiptoe, also in Hampshire.

A correspondent of *The Times*, visiting Mrs Girling in February 1875, reported how after a few sentences of prayer she began leaping rhythmically from foot to foot, waving her arms with a beckoning motion, while repeating short sentences of religious exhortation. A young woman on a front seat

Mary Anne Girling, who styled herself the 'Bride of Christ', was the leader of an ecstatic sect known as the Walworth Jumpers because they jumped and danced up and down at their meetings held under a Walworth arch

MARY ANN GIRLING.

John Montgomery

joined in, starting a strange dance with springy, elastic movements and considerable waving of her arms. Three-quarters of the disciples at this time were women, some had been servants, one had been a Wesleyan school-teacher, and there was also a blacksmith, a shoemaker and a tailor. But most were farm labourers, and all were at that time unemployed.

The Bride of Christ

Mrs Girling rejected the title given to her followers of English Shakers, preferring to call them Bible Christians. She pointed out that the American Shakers believed in Christ only as a prophet, whereas her followers believed in Christ as God-Man. But celibacy and the communal sharing of goods were common to both sects (see SHAKERS).

Men and women leaving the colony had spread rumours in the district that the dancers took off their clothes, but Mrs Girling denied this was ever done under direction, although it sometimes happened when the worshippers became over-excited.

Cold weather, the hostility and curiosity of neighbours, and lack of money, contributed to the collapse of the colony. Several members died of consumption, due to undernourishment. In about 1878, Mrs Girling announced that she was greater than the Holy Ghost, and henceforth was to be known as the God-Mother, the Bride of Christ. To prove her claim, she displayed the nail marks of the Crucifixion on her feet and hands. A few months later she announced that she was the reincarnation of Jesus, saying, 'It was prophesied that false Christs should come and all others are false, for besides me there is none other.'

In 1885 Mrs Girling was taken ill with a sore throat, which confined her to bed. Malignant cancer was diagnosed and, after suffering excruciating pain, she arose from her sick bed to declare that she would never die. Her followers believed her, and she lingered on, the colony being sadly reduced to a few ardent disciples. Finally on 18 September 1886, she died, and was buried next to those of her sect who had preceded her, in Hordle churchyard, near Lymington, Hampshire, where the curious may still see the graves of the Mother and some of her disciples.

JOHN MONTGOMERY

The royal sceptre, the Lord Chancellor's staff, the sergeant major's swagger stick and the conductor's baton are all derived from the magic wands of kings and priests

WAND

AS SYMBOLS of authority, the wand and the rod can be traced back to the staffs of the priest kings and magician healers of antiquity. The sceptre is an old symbol of kingship. A herald, the inviolable emissary of a king, carried a staff of office and the caduceus of the Greek god Hermes (see HERMES) was his herald's wand. The shepherd's crook was an emblem of royal authority in Egypt. Medieval physicians inherited the custom of carrying wands from their priestly predecessors. Red Indian chieftains bore carved wands as their badges of office.

In its simplest form, as a stick or staff, the wand must have been one of man's earliest weapons, enabling him to subjugate wild animals and human enemies alike. It has also long been recognized as a phallic symbol. It is a sign of power and virility, supernatural and physical (and consequently, clerical or secular) in a wide variety of forms.

In its supernatural context, the wand is an agent of transformation, a well-known example being the fairy wand, which is supposed to draw its power from the sun, represented by the star at its tip. The wand is also a means of aiming power at a given object; like the pointing finger or the pointing bone, it was once regarded as the agency of intense psychic power.

The construction of a wand was carried out in great secrecy and accompanied by mystical ceremonies. The wand of the wizard was usually of hazel-wood (see HAZEL) cut from the tree at sunrise, in order to draw upon the untouched solar energy; the knife used in the operation would be baptized in blood. At the same time special prayers were addressed to the high gods imploring

The rods of Moses and Aaron are the most famous examples of magic wands: Moses striking water from a rock as the Israelites cross the wilderness: 14th century French Bible

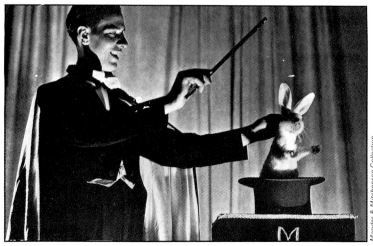

their help in endowing the wand with power and authority. The wands of the English and Welsh Druids were usually constructed of yew, and those of the Irish Druids of yew, hawthorn or rowan, all of these being sacred trees. The medieval magician would often fix a magnetized steel cap to the end and tip of his wand with the object of projecting an extremely powerful magnetic force. He would use it sparingly, reserving it for important acts of magic and concealing it from view within his voluminous sleeve.

In ancient grimoires and annals of sorcery there are many curious references to the employment of special types of wands for the various magical rites. Those who sought to communicate with Satan used wands of cypress wood – the cypress being well-known as a tree of death – and with this inscribed a magical circle at a crossroads at midnight. When attempting to communicate with the spirit of a suicide, the magician would touch the corpse nine times and then order it to answer his questions, under threat of torment. The use of a sword, in place of a wand, occurs in the records of English witchcraft past and present.

References to a special type of wand used by witches can be found in an anonymous 15th century work, *Errores Gazariorum*, which states that the witch received a special stick at the time of her initiation. In the early 17th century, the demonologist Henri Boguet declared that witches travelled through the air on white staffs, and this statement confirms that of Lambert Daneau, who had said in his work *Les Sorciers* (1564) that the witch received from the Devil a staff or rod which she used for flying (see also BROOMSTICK; FLYING OINTMENT). Modern witches use wands and staffs for purposes of divination; their riding staff is in fact a phallic emblem.

Wands were used by sorcerers for the detection of hidden treasures and other valuables. This is referred to in one of Sheppard's epigrams, dated 1651:

Some sorcerers do boast they have a rod
Gathered with Vowes and Sacrifice
And (borne about) will strangely nod
To hidden treasure where it lies.

The wand of divination has close affinities with the forked hazel twig of the ancient miners and water diviners (see DOWSING)

Above The conjuror's wand is a descendant of the wand of power of the magician *Below* Leader of a British witch coven dressed to represent the jackal-headed Egyptian god Anubis: in one hand he holds a wand topped by an ankh, the symbol of life, and in the other a sistrum or ceremonial rattle: the magic wand probably goes back to the early use of sticks and staffs as natural weapons against human and animal enemies

which, like the wand, had to be cut at either sunrise or sunset, with the sun's rays shining through the forks of the twig at the time.

There are references in some old works to the use of the wand in tests of chastity. In a tale in the *Mabinogion* (see MABINOGION), the wand of the wizard Math is used to determine whether or not the Lady Arianrhod has remained a virgin. Probably the old belief that walking over a magic wand served as a test of virginity was the origin of a Welsh wedding custom, in which the couple solemnized their union by stepping over a broomstick. Wands were also employed for the detection of thieves and murderers.

Rural wise men were often credited with

the power to capture hares and other small game by waving or pointing their walking sticks in their direction; a practice which continued until the middle of the 19th century. On some farms men known as 'goose-charmers' were called in to bless the flocks, and would reinforce their incantations by waving a short stick.

As the instrument of transformation, the wand occurs in the Celtic legend of Diarmaid and Grainne, in which the sorcerer transforms his own son into 'a cropped pig having neither ears nor tail'. In another Celtic legend a fairy woman strikes her rival with a wand and she becomes a beautiful wolfhound. In the *Odyssey,* the enchantress Circe strikes Odysseus's men with her wand, turning them into swine (see CIRCE).

To the physician priests of antiquity, the wand conferred not only the divine authority of the healer, but also the power to detect diseases. Medieval physicians were immediately recognizable by the wands which they bore. It was the custom for physicians to carry a walking stick down into the 18th century; the last of the line of 'wand carriers' being apparently the famous London physician, Dr John Radcliffe, whose goldheaded cane is preserved by the Royal College of Physicians. Charm-wands were still in use by rustic healers for the treatment of ague in the East Anglia marshlands up to about 150 years ago.

Aaron's Rod
Perhaps the most famous examples of wands used for supernatural purposes were the rods of Moses and Aaron, which were employed to divide the waters of the Red Sea, to cause water to gush forth from a rock in the desert, and to confound the enchantment of Pharaoh's magicians. According to an old Mohammedan legend, after the wand had been transformed into a serpent before Pharoah (Exodus, chapter 7) it suddenly grasped his throne and, suspending it in the air for a moment, announced: 'If it please Allah, I could swallow up not only the throne with thee and all that are here present but even thy palace and all that it contains without anyone seeing the slightest change in me.'

In a curious Jewish legend, Aaron's rod is described as having been created on the sixth day of Creation, and then taken by Adam out of Eden, and subsequently handed down through a succession of patriarchs. An early

Christian tradition relates how this miraculous rod had originally been cut from the Tree of Knowledge in Eden. It finally came into the hands of Judas, and provided the beam of the cross upon which Christ was crucified. In one of the earliest portraits of Christ, incidentally, discovered in a catacomb in the 3rd century, the Saviour is depicted with a wand in his hands.

In the form of the sceptre, the wand is the emblem of temporal power. In Britain, the royal sceptre which is placed in the monarch's right hand at his coronation endows him with his kingly authority, while his other sceptres symbolize mercy and justice. The Ivory Rod, which is over three feet long, is another royal wand of office which expresses the supernatural authority vested in an anointed king. It has been suggested that the monarch's sceptre is derived from the sacred spear upon which the war chief leaned when delivering judgement; yet another example of the magic wand.

The great officers of state are presented with special wands at the time of their appointment, to endow them with part of the royal authority. The white staff carried by the Lord Chancellor signifies not only that he acts on the monarch's behalf but that his duties will be carried out with uprightness and purity. At one time the Earl Marshal would be presented with a wooden staff, but from the reign of Richard II onwards the holder of this office has been entitled to a gold staff bearing both the king's arms and his own as the symbol of his authority. The swagger stick carried by army officers provides yet a further example of the wand of power, and similarly, the baton of the conductor of an orchestra.

The modern conjuror's wand is traceable to the magician's wand of medieval days, if not to the staffs carried by court jesters. In the past, the conjuror was regarded as identical with the sorcerer, the two terms being interchangeable. As members of the Magic Circle are well aware, a magician without his wand is as ineffective as a soldier without his gun. Any appearance on stage without this ancient symbol of psychic powers dissipates both the magician's authority as a worker of wonders and his power of command over his audience.

ERIC MAPLE

Thorns in the flesh of the major Christian Churches, these eccentric and sometimes disreputable ecclesiastics can nevertheless claim apostolic succession and a valid, if irregular, consecration

WANDERING BISHOPS

IN THE LATE 1950s, the staider inhabitants of Brittany began to be both scandalized and alarmed by the unusual ecclesiastical activities of His Whiteness the Humble (Sa Blancheur L'Humble) Tugdual I, Archbishop of Dol, Primate of the Holy Celtic Church in Brittany, Abbot of St Dolay, Kayermo, and Keroussek. It was not so much the Archbishop's custom of administering the sacrament of baptism on the seashore at midnight that gave offence — although in such a traditionally Catholic area as rural Brittany it was naturally the cause of some surprise — but the fact that, save for his headgear (an imposing mitre of vaguely Gothic Revival pattern), it was alleged that he wore nothing at all while conducting this simple, but no doubt reverent, ceremony. Even the Archbishop's worst enemies, however, were forced to agree that, whatever his dress, he never failed to carry his crozier while performing his archiepiscopal duties.

Like most of the smaller Churches of Christendom, the Holy Celtic Church founded by Archbishop Tugdual suffers from 'too many Chiefs and not enough Indians'. Indeed, in the year 1970 it had no less than 14 bishops to administer to the spiritual needs of its nine lay members and to achieve its aim of reviving the Celtic invocation of 'Hum-Hum-Hum' (mysteriously spelt Oiv-Oiv-Oiv). Odd as this Church undoubtedly is, the oddest thing about it is that its bishops have the authentic apostolic succession (see PRIESTS) and that they have been validly, although highly irregularly, consecrated. For these unusual ecclesiastics are some of the *episcopi vagantes*, wandering bishops, whose existence and increasing numbers have been a cause of annoyance to the Orthodox, Anglican and Roman Catholic Churches since the beginning of this century.

One authority has estimated that there are something like 800 of these wandering bishops, most of them still active, though some have retired into private life. Some of them teach a syncretistic neo-gnosticism and practise faith healing, occultism and magic; others preach the historic creeds of Christianity, although these are divided on certain points of doctrine. Some are unquestionably rogues, and one or two of them have suffered long terms of imprisonment. Others live lives of great holiness — the present writer has met at least one who could be described as a saintly eccentric. Most of them are in schism from one another, but divided as they are, almost all of them have three things in common: a disregard of, and contempt for, the ecclesiastical disciplines of Rome, Constantinople and Canterbury; an almost magical belief in the importance of a valid apostolic succession; and an episcopal status ultimately derived from the Dutch Old Catholic (Jansenist) Church through either the Polish Mariavite Church or one or other of the successors of Archbishop Mathew, an eccentric Englishman who died in 1919.

Live Tiger in the Pulpit

Archbishop Mathew was a most erratic and unstable character. Born in 1852, of a Roman Catholic father and an Anglican mother, he underwent baptism in both Churches. Perhaps this early influence was the cause of the religious indecision that made him first an Anglican theological student, then a Roman priest — at this period his lifelong love of animals was responsible for his terrorizing the faithful of St Mary's, Bath, by introducing a live tiger into his pulpit — then a Unitarian, then a curate of the Church of England, then a Catholic layman, and finally an Old Catholic Archbishop. Even this last period was marked by one submission to Rome, one recantation of this submission, and a brief spiritual flirtation with Annie Besant and the Theosophical Society.

Mathew was consecrated a Bishop on 28 April 1908 by Archbishop Gul of Utrecht. On historical grounds the validity of his consecration seems unquestionable, for although the Dutch Old Catholic Church had been in schism from Rome since 1739 its episcopal line of succession could be traced back in an unbroken line to Cardinal Antonio Barberini, nephew of Pope Urban VIII. Nevertheless, the consecration was clearly obtained by fraud, for while both the Old Catholic bishops, and Mathew himself, were sincerely convinced that the latter represented a large and growing body of English Catholics who desired independence from Rome, the reality was very different. For Mathew was no more than the innocent tool of a tiny body of disgruntled, excommunicated, and possibly financially dishonest Catholic priests.

These were led by two Monsignori, Herbert Beale and Arthur Howarth, who had at one time been in charge of parishes in the diocese of Nottingham. Both had been on good terms with Bishop Bagshawe, who had been Bishop of Nottingham until his forcible retirement in 1901. Bagshawe has been described as saintly, in spite of occasional flashes of bad temper — on one occasion he excommunicated the entire membership of that High Tory body, the Primrose League — and he was usually prepared to turn a blind eye on the behaviour of his clergy, however outrageous, and to appoint to responsible positions priests who had been sacked from other dioceses. So great was Bagshawe's tolerance that his diocese became known as *refugium peccatorum*, the refuge of sinners. Bishop Brindle, Bagshawe's successor, was a man of quite a different type and engaged in a general clean-up — he sacked Beale and Howarth for various alleged financial irregularities. These two seem to have had no other motive for getting Mathew to establish an English branch of the Old Catholic Church than a desire to annoy their lawful ecclesiastical superiors, Bishop Brindle and Cardinal Bourne.

On his return from Holland, poor Mathew soon realized that he had been the victim of fraud, that the 'seventeen priests' and 'eight parishes' who had supposedly chosen him to be consecrated as their bishop existed solely in the imaginations of Beale and Howarth. For the rest of his life he devoted his efforts to holding together his tiny personal following, usually numbering no more than three or four, consoling himself for his lonely life by writing lengthy essays designed to prove the Baconian authorship of Shakespeare, and dreaming of a National Catholic Church under his own leadership. Unfortunately Mathew attempted to put

his dreams into practice and consecrated a number of bishops; he was a poor judge of character and many of those he consecrated were clearly quite unsuitable candidates for any ecclesiastical position.

Mathew performed comparatively few consecrations but there were some bishops who were prepared to confer the episcopate on anyone who could pay a sufficiently large fee. It is through such fee-snatching activities that the lines of succession of many of the wandering bishops of the present day are derived.

The Archbishop of Utrecht, 18 months after his consecration of Mathew, obligingly supplied the Polish Mariavites with their first bishop, a certain Michael Kowalski. The Mariavite Church had approximately 20,000 members and had come into existence as a result of the mystical experiences of a woman named Maria Kozlowska. Maria, who had started her adult life as a poverty-stricken sewing-woman, had founded, in 1887, a community of Franciscan Tertiaries (lay members of a monastic order), all female. The Virgin, said Maria, had instructed her to found a mixed religious community dedicated to the life of Mary. This organization, the Mariavite (Life of Mary) Union, was duly established and met with considerable success, for it appealed strongly to the messianic elements in Polish Catholicism. Maria began to be known as 'Little Mother', was venerated as a living saint, and continued to have further revelations.

By 1904 the Polish hierarchy had become

The wandering bishops have 'an almost magical belief in the importance of a valid apostolic succession' *Left* **His Whiteness the Humble Tugdual I, Archbishop of Dol, Primate of the Holy Celtic Church in Brittany, Abbot of St Dolay, Kayermo, and Keroussek: a fondness for resounding titles is characteristic of the wandering bishops, who have been a cause of annoyance to the more orthodox Churches all this century** *Right* **Joseph Rene Villate derived his episcopal status ultimately from the Jacobite Patriarch of Antioch, and bishops of the African Orthodox Churches in turn derive their succession from him**

alarmed by the growing strength of the Mariavite Union and by rumours of immoral activities in its mixed monasteries. An investigation was undertaken and a report sent to Rome. The Holy See, always suspicious of saints, declared that Maria's revelations were spurious, that her visions were hallucinations, and ordered the dissolution of the Mariavite Union and its communities. The Mariavites disregarded the Pope's ruling and were excommunicated.

Marriage in a Monastery
With Kowalski as its presiding Archbishop the Mariavite Church became ever more eccentric. Monks and nuns entered into 'spiritual marriages' — and sometimes carnal relations — with one another, women were ordained, and idolization of the Virgin Mary was encouraged. By 1930 Kowalski had actually consecrated his spiritual directress, a nun named Sister Isabella, as a female

bishop and concluded that both he and she were infallible and impeccable.

Kowalski seems to have enjoyed nothing more than manufacturing bishops and carried out many consecrations; Sister Isabella was just as keen to make female bishops, and in just two months she consecrated 11 of them. In their turn Kowalski's bishops made more bishops, and today most of the episcopi vagantes who are not in the Mathew succession derive their status from the Mariavite line — although, of course, many have both lines of succession, for the conditional reconsecration of one another is a favourite recreation of the wandering bishops.

Two other lines of episcopal succession were created as a result of the activities of Joseph Rene Villate (d. 1929) and Julius Ferrete (d. 1904). Both these prelates ultimately derived their episcopal status from Peter the Humble, the Jacobite Patriarch of Antioch. There is some doubt as to the validity of the consecrations of both Villate and Ferrete, but because of cross-consecrations almost all the wandering bishops can claim an undoubted line of descent from Mathew or the Mariavites.

Aleister Crowley – Bishop
Many of the wandering bishops have chosen to involve themselves in faith healing, magic and occultism. On the other hand, quite a few magicians have sought the episcopate for their own purposes. Thus Julius Hussay, who became a bishop of the Villate line in 1904, seems to have acquired his episcopal status only because he believed that it would greatly enhance his magical powers. Hussay, who wrote several extremely boring books on magic, conditionally consecrated a number of bishops of the Gnostic Catholic Church, a mysterious body which still survives in several offshoots, each claiming the only orthodoxy. The consecrations were conditional because these French Gnostic bishops had already had the episcopate conferred upon them by A. Doinel, who himself claimed to have been 'twice spiritually consecrated a Bishop'; on the first occasion by Jesus Christ who had, so Doinel said, made one of his rare personal appearances, and on the second by the ghosts of two medieval Cathar bishops who had chosen to manifest themselves at a Spiritualist seance. Hussay also consecrated an ex-Trappist monk named Giraud, and he in turn, consecrated as a Gnostic bishop Joanny Bricaud, a prolific writer on magic.

At about the same time Dr Encausse, who wrote on occultism under the name of Papus (see PAPUS) and was a Gnostic bishop, had various masonic dignities conferred upon him by Theodor Reuss, as head of the *Ordo Templi Orientis,* an organization specializing in sexual magic (see CROWLEY). Dr Encausse returned the compliment by consecrating Reuss, an action which seems to have led to Aleister Crowley becoming a bishop! For when Crowley visited Reuss in Berlin and had conferred upon himself the chieftainship of the British section of the O.T.O., he was also consecrated as a Gnostic Catholic bishop — or so Reuss claimed. Crowley, however, does not appear to have been aware of his new status; certainly he never made any attempt to exercise his ecclesiastical functions, although, it is true, he did write a special Mass for the Gnostic Church.

Of all the hundreds of independent Churches spanned by the wandering Bishops, only two groups have shown any real capacity for survival and growth. The first of these groups is that of the African Orthodox Churches which, in spite of numerous schisms, have made considerable inroads amongst the membership of those African Churches which are still, to some extent, under the control of the ecclesiastical hierarchies of the former colonial powers. The second group consists of those Churches deriving from the Theosophical followers of Archbishop Mathew.

The African Orthodox Churches derive their episcopal succession from Villate who, in 1921, consecrated George Alexander McGuire, a former Episcopalian missionary in the West Indies, as 'Patriarch Alexander of the African Orthodox Church of the World'. Within a short time this new Church achieved a sizeable membership among the Negro population of the United States, almost certainly because of its appeal to black nationalism; it is significant that *The Negro Churchman*, the newspaper of the new Church, described McGuire's consecration as being 'the germ of a Racial Church'.

Throughout the years of the Depression the Church continued to grow, but after McGuire's death in 1935 various schisms occurred and there was a consequent decline in membership. At the present time, however, there are at least four Churches active in the United States and the West Indies deriving from the McGuire organization.

Saviour of African Christianity
It is in Africa itself that the African Orthodox Church has met with its greatest successes and has in certain areas become a powerful rival to the missionary-led Churches in general and to the Anglican Church in particular.

McGuire extended his influence to Africa in 1928, when Daniel William Alexander, the son of an American father and a coloured South African mother, returned to South Africa after his consecration by McGuire in the previous year. Alexander established his cathedral in Kimberley and, significantly, dedicated it to an African saint, Augustine of Hippo. He soon made converts and within a few years had a considerable following in Kenya, in Uganda and in South Africa. Bishop Alexander was a man of intellectual ability, charm, and even holiness, being held in high regard by Anglicans.

In Buganda — now part of the Republic of Uganda — a schismatic section of the African Orthodox Church has actually been brought into full communion with one of the ancient Patriarchates of Eastern Christendom. This, the African Greek Orthodox Church, came into existence as a result of the activities of a certain Reuben Spartas, a young African Christian who had rebelled against the theology of Anglican evangelicism.

The internal theological disputes of the world-wide Anglican communion have been reflected in the missionary activities of the Church of England and the Protestant Episcopal Church of the United States. Thus, in Africa, the Universities' Mission to Central Africa has occupied the extreme Anglo-Catholic position, the Society for the Propagation of the Gospel has been in the middle of the road, and the Church Missionary Society has represented the evangelical viewpoint.

Reuben Spartas had been brought up by

Certificate of the consecration of Ernest Odell Cope by Ralph Whitman, Regionary Old Catholic Bishop of Wales, who himself had been consecrated by Archbishop Mathew, an eccentric Englishman from whom many wandering bishops are 'apostolically' descended

the Christian Missionary Society as an evangelical and had become the cook of a missionary archdeacon. He soon rebelled against both Low Church theology and the white colonialism which he believed it represented, writing to Cosmo Gordon Lang, then Archbishop of Canterbury, to tell him that the Church of England had 'no Catholic faith, Doctrine and Real Principles' and to McGuire that he had resolved 'to go to hell, gaol, or die for the redemption of Africa'.

Spartas was consecrated by Alexander in 1932 and rapidly gained converts, establishing schools and churches throughout Buganda. In 1934 he broke away from Alexander, and his African Greek Orthodox Church was finally admitted into full communion with the Patriarchate of Alexandria

CERTIFICATE OF CONSECRATION
+
In the Name of God. Amen.

WE, Ralph Whitman, Regionary Old Catholic Bishop For Wales, consecrated by the late Archbishop Mathew on the 8th day of June 1910 as Bishop for Llanthony Abbey, Do Hereby Certify that for the purpose of re-establishing the monastic vocation at Llanthony (which has been lying in abeyance since the death of the late Father Ignatius) and providing spiritual ministrations for the Order of Llanthony Abbey Brothers, We did on the 19th day of July 1940 at Repton, by the laying-on of Hands with Prayer and Anointing, Apostolically Consecrate to the Office of a Bishop in the One Holy Catholic and Apostolic Church of Jesus Christ Ernest Odell Cope, whom We had previously ordained Priest on the 11th day of July 1939 at Gloucester.

As Witness Our Signature and Seal this 19th day of July 1940.

Ralph Whitman +
Regionary Bishop

Witnesses:

Harold Sugden
Thomas Hall
Thomas Frederick Appleby
Robert Edmund Langton
James Walter Slater

Society for Promoting Christian Knowledge

in 1946; today there is not only a Metropolitan for East Africa, appointed by the Patriarch of Alexandria, but the African Greek Orthodox Church uses the full liturgy of St John Chrysostom, translated into Luganda by Spartas himself.

It seems at least possible that such independent African Churches as that of Spartas offer the best hope for the survival of Christianity in Black Africa. More and more those Churches which, rightly or wrongly, are associated with the former colonial powers are falling into disfavour with newly-independent governments. It is an odd thought that the activities of such an ecclesiastical clown as Villate may ultimately prove to have been the salvation of African Christianity.

Liberal Catholicism

The theosophically-inclined Liberal Catholic Church came into existence when most of Archbishop Mathew's clerical and lay followers went into schism as a result of Mathew declaring that membership of the Theosophical Society was incompatible with membership of his own organization. The schismatics chose James Wedgwood, a member of the famous pottery family, as their leader and he was duly consecrated. The leadership of the Liberal Catholic Church, in practice if not in theory, passed to C. W. Leadbeater, a former Anglican curate and theosophist, who held this position until his death in the 1930s. He developed a strange neo-gnostic interpretation of Catholic Christianity and wrote *The Science of the Sacraments*, putting forward his ideas. The growth of Liberal Catholicism has not been spectacular but has nevertheless continued at a steady rate: today there are around 50,000 members of the Church.

The Churches founded by the wandering bishops are peculiar in every sense of the word. It is unlikely that we shall hear the last of them for many years to come.

FRANCIS KING

FURTHER READING: Peter Anson, *Bishops at Large* (Faber, 1964); H. R. T. Brandreth, *Episcopi Vagantes and the Anglican Communion* (S.P.C.K., 1947); C. W. Leadbeater, *The Science of the Sacraments* (Theosophical Publishing House, 1929).

WANDERING JEW

The Wandering Jew, from a 17th century engraving: the name by which he was known, Ahasuerus, probably comes from King Ahasuerus, the villain and laughing-stock of the Old Testament book of Esther

AHASUERUS, the unwilling immortal, has been a well-known figure of European legend since 1602, when he was introduced to the public in a German pamphlet. It declared that Paulus von Eizen, the late Lutheran Bishop of Schleswig, had once met a Jew in Hamburg and learnt that he was more than 15 centuries old. This man had been a cobbler in Jerusalem in the time of Christ, one of the crowd that shouted 'Crucify him'. When Jesus, carrying the cross, tried to rest on his doorstep, the Jew pushed him away saying, 'Go where you belong.' Jesus looked at him sternly and replied, 'I will stand here and rest, but you shall go on till I return.' Ever since – Bishop von Eizen gathered – Ahasuerus had been wandering from country to country awaiting the Second Coming.

The pamphlet of 1602 appeared anonymously. Even its alleged place of printing, Leiden, is very doubtful. A later edition gives the author as Chrysostomus Dudulaeus of Westphalia, otherwise unknown. Whatever its origin the legend became popular at once, partly, perhaps, because of anti-semitic prophecies about the advent of Antichrist with Jewish support; partly also because this discovery of an eyewitness confirmed the Christian narrative. Besides many German editions of the pamphlet, there were soon eight in Dutch and Flemish, and others in French, Danish and Swedish, besides an English parody. The story grew as it spread.

The Immortal

Ahasuerus's title varies. In German-speaking countries, he is the 'immortal' or 'eternal' Jew. The epithet 'wandering' has its source in the French version, which made him 'le juif errant', from which the English title was derived. With other nationalities he has acquired different names: in Spain he is Juan Espera-en-Dios ('trust in God') and in Belgium, Isaac Laquedem. Some versions stress the mystery of his immortality, some stress the curse of wandering, some make him symbolic of his race. The French account portrays him as a rebel against his doom, constantly seeking death in vain.

About 20 recognitions of the Wandering Jew are on record. Besides his Hamburg appearance in 1542 or 1547, he is said to have been seen and known in Spain in 1575, Vienna in 1599, Ypres in 1623, Brussels in 1640 and Paris in 1644; and at various other places, mostly in Central Europe, at various other dates in the 17th century.

Some of the reports may be due to impostors having played the part. Later appearances are rarer, although they include one in Newcastle in 1790, and one in Salt Lake City in 1868, when the wanderer met a Mormon named O'Grady – an event duly reported in the *Deseret News*.

While Ahasuerus cannot be documented before 1602, he has older antecedents. The notion does go back to a saying of Jesus, though a canonical one: 'Truly, I say to you, there are some standing here who will not taste death before they see the Son of Man coming in his kingdom' (Matthew 16.28). The obvious meaning is that the Second Coming will occur soon, in the lifetime of contemporaries. Its failure to do so has made this prophecy a problem for Christians – among them the famous missionary and doctor, Albert Schweitzer, who inferred from it that Christ could be wrong, a conclusion with immense implications.

For the early Christians, Schweitzer's view was ruled out. Instead, as the years passed, they began to speculate that somebody would be kept alive by divine favour till Christ did return. Such hopes centred for a while on John, the beloved disciple, to whom Jesus had made a rather similar cryptic remark about 'remaining until I come' (John 21. 20–23). But John died, and the rumour died with him.

Then, at an unknown period, the same story was revived in the Middle East with new characters. The historian Roger of Wendover says that in 1228 an Armenian archbishop visited England, and told the monks of St Albans that he had seen a man called Cartaphilus who was a witness of the Crucifixion. When Jesus had passed him bearing the cross, he shouted, 'Go on faster', and Jesus answered, 'I go; but you shall wait till I come.'

Cartaphilus (a door-keeper in Pilate's house, therefore a Roman, not a Jew) was afterwards baptized by Ananias and given the Christian name Joseph; 12 centuries later he was living a quiet, penitential life, cheifly as a guest of religious communities. He would age till he appeared to be 100 years old and would then be miraculously restored to 30. Travelling Armenian priests seem to have made much of this tale, not only at St Albans – more than once – but at Tournai in Flanders in 1243. It is repeated in the chronicle of Matthew Paris, as a proof of Christianity.

Medieval accounts of the Holy Land hint

at a second figure of the same type. In 1250 a French author, returned from residence in Jerusalem, speaks of 'Jehan Boute Dieu' as proverbially long-lived. In Italian legend the same person becomes John Bottadio, 'God-smiter'. He is stated to have been the officer who struck Christ before the high priest, sometimes further identified with Malchus (John 18. 10, 22). Bottadio is mentioned by Guido Bonnati, an astrologer known to Dante. There are reports of his being seen in Italy early in the 15th century.

The names given to these two immortals, Cartaphilus ('most beloved') and John, imply that the ultimate source of inspiration is the far earlier belief about the apostle. But at some stage, divine favour has been turned into punishment. The motif occurs in

Buddhist legend: Pindola, an unworthy follower of Buddha, was condemned to be unable to die.

Villain and Laughing-Stock

No direct links of influence have been traced, either between Pindola and the two medieval immortals, or between them and Ahasuerus. But the inventor of the Jew must have known something of the older stories. He repeats the tale of the insult to Christ. He takes up and strengthens the idea of a curse. The name Ahasuerus suggests an acquaintance with Jewish plays that were acted at the feast of Purim. These were based on the book of Esther, and brought in King Ahasuerus as a villain and laughing-stock.

The Wandering Jew has inspired many works of literature and art. There is a ballad in Percy's *Reliques of Ancient English Poetry* (1765). Goethe and Shelley were attracted to the theme, Shelley more than once.

William Godwin introduced it into his novel *St Leon* (1799). Eugène Sue's romance *Le Juif Errant* (1844) is the most famous of several French treatments, which include a pictorial series by Gustav Doré. A Jewish dramatist, David Pinski, has given the legend a Jewish form, portraying the wanderer as searching for the Messiah. The most recent literary addition is an episode in Evelyn Waugh's novel *Helena* (1950).

GEOFFREY ASHE

Some of the bloodiest wars in history have been waged in the name of God; even those religions which exalt mercy and peace have put the need to stamp out unorthodoxy before humanitarian considerations

WAR

HISTORY RECORDS few instances of aggressive wars in which the antagonists have not professed some high or altruistic motive. There seems to be an innate reluctance on the part of rulers and governments to admit, even to themselves, to waging war for material gain or self-aggrandizement. Generally it has been left to individuals such as the Italian *condottieri* and other mercenaries, to use their swords unabashedly for gain. This moral or psychological need to justify resort to war, which has been shown even by cynical statesmen, probably operated in earlier ages to produce the idea of a holy war, waged in obedience to divine command. Such professedly holy wars were doubtless motivated often by secular aims or inspired by personal ambition. However, the idea of war as a sacred task has been a powerful factor in earlier societies, and there are some notable examples that repay study for the insight they give into human nature.

The two earliest civilizations, of which we have written records, provide evidence of the waging of holy wars as far back as the third millennium BC. The most remarkable document, both for its antiquity and vivid depiction, is a ceremonial slate palette which commemorates the victorious wars of the Egyptian Pharaoh Narmer (c 3000 BC). On one side of the palette the commanding figure of the pharaoh is portrayed striking down an enemy with his mace. The sacred character of the conflict is symbolized by a curious group of figures close to the pharaoh's right. A hawk is shown holding, by a human hand, a short cable which is hooked into the nose of a man's head, which has features similar to those of the man struck down by Narmer. This head protrudes from a rectangular object, from

The hawk god Horus assists the Egyptian Pharaoh Narmer in his victorious wars: the palette of Narmer

C. M. Dixon

Left Christ as a warrior, holding a book which reads, 'I am the way, the truth and the life': mosaic from Ravenna *Right* 15th century view of Jerusalem, the heart of centuries of holy war between Islam and Christianity

which six papyrus plants are growing. The significance of the imagery seems clear, although there is no explanatory inscription. The hawk doubtless represents the hawk god Horus (see HORUS), the divine patron of the early kings of Egypt. It is shown as assisting the king in subduing his enemies, who probably dwelt in the marshlands of the Delta, signified by the papyrus plants. On the other side of the palette, the victorious pharaoh, preceded by the standards of his gods, goes to view the decapitated bodies of his enemies. Over both scenes the twin heads of the cow goddess Hathor preside. Thus, by this quaint but graphic imagery the victory of Narmer is recorded as the triumphant outcome of a war sanctified and assisted by the gods.

Of similar significance is the memorial set up by Eannatum, ruler of the Sumerian city of Lagash, to record his victory over the neighbouring city of Umma. The memorial, of which only fragments exist today, depicted the war as seen in its practical and its religious aspects. Thus, on one side, Eannatum is depicted advancing on foot at the head of his troops over the prostrate bodies of the foe, and also in his war chariot. Fragments of other scenes show the corpses of the slain being devoured by lions and vultures or ceremonially buried. These realistic scenes of war are paired by a representation, on a gigantic scale, of the god Ningirsu holding within a net the bodies of the men of Umma. This scene is surely intended to signify that it was the god who had really secured the victory for his faithful

deputy, Eannatum. The memorial thus attests that in ancient Sumer, about 2500 BC, men also invested war with a sacred character, as they did in Egypt, believing that they served their god and that he helped them to victory.

When Egypt became an imperial power during the New Kingdom period (1567–1085 BC), its pharaohs claimed that their wars of conquest were ordained by their gods, pre-eminently by Amun. The army which Rameses II (c 1300–1234 BC) led against the Hittites mustered in four divisions, significantly named after four Egyptian gods: Amun, Re, Ptah and Seth. In the critical battle of Kadesh, Rameses tells how Amun succoured and inspired him: 'Amun hearkeneth unto me and cometh, when I cry to him. He stretcheth out his hand to me, and I rejoice; he calleth out behind me: "Forward, forward! I am with thee, I thy father"'. In like manner the kings of Babylon and Assyria claimed that they had fought at the command and with the aid of their respective gods.

Fighting for Yahweh

Examples such as these of royal claims to divine authority for wars of conquest could be multiplied; but more notable, and of far greater consequence, has been the Jewish idea of the holy war. The idea was basic to the peculiar covenant relationship that existed between Israel and its god Yahweh (see YAHWEH). It first finds expression in the belief that Yahweh had promised the land of Canaan (that is, Palestine) to

Abraham, the progenitor of Israel: 'on that day the Lord made a covenant with Abram, saying, To your descendants I give this land, from the river of Egypt to the great river, the river Euphrates' (Genesis, 15,18). The translation of this promise into reality required a war of conquest, to wrest the land from its inhabitants and exterminate them in the process. In the Hebrew Bible this war is described in the book of Joshua. That it was essentially a holy war is dramatically portrayed in the instructions given by Joshua to the Israelite tribes as they emerged from the desert and prepared to cross the river Jordan into Canaan. The priests are told to bear the Ark of the Covenant, the mysterious portable shrine of Yahweh, to the brink of the Jordan and halt there. Then Joshua exhorted the people: 'Hereby you shall know that the living God is among you, and that he will without fail drive out from before you the Canaanites, the Hittites, the Hivites, and the Perizzites, the Girgashites, the Amorites, and the Jebusites. Behold, the ark of the covenant of the Lord of all the earth is to pass over before you into the Jordan' (Joshua 3. 10–11). According to the account, Yahweh then signified his presence by stopping the flow of the Jordan so that the Israelites passed over the river dry-shod.

The Israelite warriors then prepared for the holy war by circumcising themselves (Joshua 5. 2–9). After recovering from the operation, the army's first objective was Jericho. The city was taken by a combination of military tactics and ritual magic (see SEVEN); its inhabitants were slaughtered, with the exception of the harlot Rahab and her household, who had sheltered Israelite spies. All the booty was devoted to Yahweh. But the breaking of this 'war ban' by one Israelite soldier named Achan resulted in an Israelite defeat when the Canaanite city of Ai was next attacked. Joshua was then told by the affronted Yahweh that Israel would suffer further defeat unless expiation was made. This took the form of stoning Achan and all his family and animals, and the burning of their bodies and all their goods, together with the tabooed articles retained by Achan (Joshua 8. 24–6). With Yahweh thus appeased, the holy war could continue with his blessing and cooperation.

After their initial establishment in Canaan, the Israelites continued to be involved in wars with neighbouring peoples. These struggles usually were regarded as holy wars. A notable example of their fanatical character is recorded in 1. Samuel (chapter 15). The prophet Samuel informs Saul, Israel's first king: 'Thus says the Lord of hosts . . . "go and smite Amalek, and utterly destroy all that they have, do not spare them, but kill both man and woman, infant and suckling, ox and sheep, camel and ass."' Saul carried out his orders, but spared the Amalekite king, Agag, and the best of the cattle in order to sacrifice them to Yahweh. But because he had not exactly done as he was commanded, Yahweh withdrew his favour from Saul as king. After informing Saul of Yahweh's anger, Samuel himself 'hewed Agag in pieces before Yahweh in Gilgal'.

Owing to the passionate attachment of the Jews to their land, which was for them the Holy Land of Yahweh's ancient promise, all their struggles against foreign invaders assumed the character of holy wars. Thus the Maccabaean War (166–157 BC) was not only a patriotic struggle for freedom from the oppressive foreign government of the Seleucid kings of Syria; it was a fierce reaction against the Seleucid attempt to impose pagan Greek customs on the people of Yahweh. Mattathias, the father of Judas Maccabaeus, clearly proclaimed the nature of the war at its start: 'Whosoever is zealous for the Law, and maintaineth the Covenant, let him come forth after me' (I Maccabees 2.27). The same motive inspired Jewish resistance to the domination of heathen Rome in the 1st century AD. It found apocalyptic expression in the Dead Sea Scroll known as *The War of the Sons of Light against the Sons of Darkness*. And it moved the Zealots (see ZEALOTS) to precipitate the fatal war against Rome that destroyed Jerusalem in 70 AD, and ended Israel's national life for nearly 19 centuries.

Islam has also been characterized by its attachment to the idea of the holy war. The *jihad* ('striving') has been reckoned by many Moslems among the 'five pillars' of practical religion. Authority for this belief is found in various parts of the Koran. Thus in sura 9.29: 'Fight against those who believe not Allah nor in the Last Day, who do not prohibit what Allah and His Messenger have prohibited, and do not practise the True Faith of those who have received the Book, until they submit and pay the *jizya* (tribute).' Those Moslems who died fighting in the jihad are accounted martyrs and assured of eternal bliss with Allah. Mohammed resorted to arms to suppress his idolatrous opponents in Mecca and Jewish tribes in Arabia (see MOHAMMED). After his death, the armies of Islam launched successful campaigns, with a sense of divine mission, against the Eastern Roman and the Persian Empires. Within a century of Mohammed's death, the religion of Islam had been established throughout the Middle East, Egypt, North Africa and Spain, and its spread into Europe was only halted by the Franks under Charles Martel at the battle of Tours in 732. Later Moslem rulers often proclaimed jihads, and there have been attempts to present the current struggle of the Arab states against the state of Israel as a jihad.

Against the Infidel

The classic example of the holy war in Western Christianity has been the Crusades. Several factors combined to launch the first of the crusading armies against the Moslems in the latter years of the 11th century. Medieval society was organized mainly in the interests of a military aristocracy and the Church. The institution of knighthood represented the Church's attempt to Christianize the warlike instincts and ideas of this aristocracy. In the 11th century the struggle against the Moslem powers in Spain had assumed the character of a holy war, and in 1073 Pope Gregory VII had urged Christian princes and knights to help there in subduing the infidel. But events in Palestine were soon to present militant Christendom with a new cause. The Moslem conquest of Palestine in the 7th century had resulted in the holy places of Christianity passing under Moslem control, though Christian pilgrims still continued to have access to them. But the situation changed in 1071 when the Seljuk Turks, who were Moslems, captured Jerusalem. Moved by reports of the sufferings of pilgrims at their hands, Pope Urban II at the Council of

Clermont in 1095 called on the faithful, rich and poor, to free the holy places of their faith. The response was instant and fervent. The Pope's passionate exhortation evoked cries of 'Deus le volt' ('God wills it'). Remission from temporal penalties for sins was promised to all who went. Their dedication to the holy war was symbolized by the wearing of a red cross on their surcoats. Urban's exhortations were assisted and exceeded by those of Peter the Hermit, an itinerant monk. Without waiting for the expedition organized by the princes, Peter led a People's Crusade as far as Anatolia, where its unruly host perished at the hands of the Turks.

The First Crusade, led by Godfrey de Bouillon and other lords, was surprisingly

Siege of Jerusalem, from a Flemish manuscript, late 15th century: the capture of the city by the Seljuk Turks in 1071 precipitated the Crusades

successful. Jerusalem was captured in 1099; the Christian victory being sullied by the massacre of the city's Moslem and Jewish inhabitants. A Latin kingdom of Jerusalem was set up; but the city was recaptured by Moslem forces under Saladin in 1187. Further crusades were organized to succour the Christian forces in Palestine and win back Jerusalem. But all these efforts failed, and the last significant Christian stronghold at Acre was lost in 1291. The Fourth Crusade, in 1202, was a shameful affair; instead of attacking the Moslems, it stormed and pillaged the city of Constantinople, the great Christian bulwark in eastern Europe against the Turks. Constantinople never recovered from this blow, and when it was besieged by the Ottoman Turks in 1453, Pope Pius failed in his effort to organize a crusade to save it.

The Crusades produced two remarkable orders of military monks who epitomized the medieval Christian conception of the holy war: they were the Knights Templar and the Knights Hospitaller – the former were destined ultimately to sordid destruction at the hands of fellow Christians (see KNIGHTS TEMPLAR); the latter to stop the Turkish advance into the Mediterranean by their heroic defence of Malta in 1565.

Against the Heretic

The history of the Christian Church records many other wars regarded as 'holy' by the participants. These were waged not against the infidel, but against heretics. Thus Pope Innocent III ordered a crusade, under Simon de Montfort, against the Albigenses, a heretical sect of Languedoc, in southern France (see CATHARS). The war, which was conducted with great cruelty, included a massacre at Béziers in 1209. The Reformation caused a series of wars between Catholic and Protestants, which were often fought with great ferocity, and marked by such atrocities as the Massacre of St Bartholomew's Day (1572), when between 5000 and 10,000 French Protestants were killed.

In these wars political motives were usually compounded with religious aims; but the religious issue was the original cause of the conflict and it remained basic. That Christianity, which exalts the virtues of love, mercy and peace, should have generated such wars is not surprising on analysis. The belief that Christianity embodies God's plan for mankind's salvation has caused its adherents to lay absolute emphasis upon holding the correct form of the faith, and to be intolerant towards any deviation from what they regard as orthodoxy. Hence the extirpation of heresy or false doctrine has been deemed a sacred duty that transcended humanitarian considerations. It is significant that with the secularization of European society from the 18th century, religious wars ceased.

The idea of the holy war has found its most notable instances in the prophetically inspired religions of Judaism, Christianity and

Islam. But the idea has occurred elsewhere, as we have seen. Ancient Greece knew of three sacred wars, which were so declared by the Delphic Amphictyony, a league of states under the patronage of Apollo of Delphi. A sacred war was declared by the league on any member state deemed to have committed sacrilege against Apollo by such acts as levying tolls on pilgrims or seizing control of the Delphic sanctuary and its famous oracle. However, the real causes of these wars, and indeed the underlying purpose of the Amphictyony itself, were political. War was a sacred necessity for the Aztecs of ancient Mexico, in order to maintain a supply of human victims for sacrifice to their gods. Headhunting, which has been practised by various primitive peoples,

may also be regarded as a form of holy war, since the heads were required for fertility rites to promote good harvests (see HEAD).

The sacred character that war has had for many peoples is evident in their customs. For example in Rome, at the start of a war, the general commanding shook the sacred spears of Mars. The standards carried by troops have often borne sacred emblems — the Roman legionaries offered sacrifices to theirs. The triumph decreed by the Roman Senate to a successful general was essentially a religious ceremony which ended with

Pope Urban II preaching the First Crusade at the Council of Clermont: the response was passionate cries of 'God wills it': 15th century manuscript

sacrifice offered to Jupiter Capitolinus by the victor, while the enemy leader was executed in the adjacent Mamertine prison. Prisoners have often been sacrificed to war gods — the *Orkneyinga Saga* records a particularly grim example. Torf-Einar, Jarl of Orkney, cut the ribs from the back of a rebel chief, symbolizing the 'blood-eagle', and 'gave' him to Odin.

S. G. F. BRANDON

FURTHER READING: S. G. F. Brandon ed., *Dictionary of Comparative Religion* (Scribner, 1970); see article on Jihad, *Jesus and the Zealots* (Scribner, 1968); S. Runciman, *A History of the Crusades* (Cambridge Univ. Press, 3 vols).

Bibliotheque Nationale

WATER

Water of life, water of chaos, water of destruction — these three principal elements flow and mingle in shifting patterns in the symbolism of water

THE SPANISH conquistador Ponce de Leon, governor of Puerto Rico in the early 16th century, set out with three ships in search of the land of Bimini, where he hoped to find the fountain of youth. What he actually discovered was Florida and, by a curious irony, near the site where he landed in 1513 there now stands the city of St Augustine, a famous last retreat for the old, who wait there in the sunshine for death.

The theme of the fountain of youth, the spring of living water, the well at the world's end, the water of life, is old and widespread. In numerous folktales and fairy tales there is a magic liquid which cures all diseases, brings the dead to life and makes anyone who drinks it immortal. Alexander the Great, it was said, went to the world's end to find the water of immortality. Cranach's painting of *The Fountain of Youth* shows old women entering the water which transforms them into young girls, and in Bosch's *Garden of Terrestrial Delights* a fountain of curious and alarming design is the source of the river of life which waters Eden (see ALEXANDER THE GREAT; ELIXIR OF LIFE; FOUNTAIN). Correspondingly, lack of water is associated with death, not only in this world but in the next. In Near Eastern and Christian traditions the dead thirst for cool water, because they exist in dry, dusty places or in burning hot ones, where the water of refreshment and life is missing (see REFRIGERIUM).

Water is naturally linked with life because living things cannot survive without it, and liquids in general are regarded as life-giving. Rain makes the plants grow, babies are generated by sperm and nourished on milk, the chick forms in the liquid of the egg, the child in the womb is lapped in waters which break at its coming, the sap is the life of the tree, and blood is the life of men and animals for when they lose it they weaken and die. Intoxicating liquids are connected with life because they make people 'lively', and this

Father and Mother Nile, from an Egyptian tomb of the 19th Dynasty: one of the principal strands in the symbolism of water is its connection with life — the rain which fertilizes the soil, the river which irrigates it

We wash away physical dirt with water, and so we wash away spiritual dirt with it too and this may be an essential pre-requisite for approaching the divine

is reflected in the words for alcohol in various languages – *aqua vitae, eau de vie, lebenswasser,* all meaning 'water of life' – and in the term 'spirit', referring to the principle which vivifies matter. Liquids are also life-giving because they flow, they move about while lifeless things stay still. Mercury was called quicksilver, 'living silver', because it is mobile, which was the basis of its importance as the 'spirit' in alchemy, and one of the processes in the alchemical work was the 'bath of rebirth' (see ALCHEMY; MERCURY).

The Spring of Eternal Life

The life-giving divine spirit and the life-giving rain are linked in Isaiah (chapter 44), when God says to Israel: 'For I will pour water on the thirsty land, and streams on the dry ground; I will pour my Spirit upon your descendants, and my blessing on your offspring', and that God 'pours' his material and spiritual blessings on man, as rain pours from the sky, has become a common figure of speech. In Jeremiah (2.13) God is called 'the fountain of living waters'. In Ezekiel (chapter 47), the river of life flows out from Jerusalem to irrigate the desert, to freshen the waters of the Dead Sea and make it swarm with fish. The book of Zechariah (chapter 14), describing the coming 'day of the Lord' when God will become king over the whole earth, says that he will stand on the Mount of Olives and 'living waters shall flow out from Jerusalem . . . it shall continue in summer as in winter'. And the people will go up to Jerusalem every year to worship God and to keep the Feast of Booths. If any fail to go up, 'there will be no rain upon them' (except for the Egyptians, who did not depend directly on rainfall and so are threatened with plague).

This prophecy links the river of life and the rain with the Feast of Booths, or Tabernacles, a harvest festival during which the people lived outdoors in arbours covered with foliage, in memory of the passage of their ancestors through the wilderness, when God had miraculously supplied them with water and had 'rained' manna from heaven for them to eat (Exodus 16.4). The green arbours recall the garden of Eden, which was watered by a river that divided into four rivers (Genesis, chapter 2). The new Jerusalem, the heavenly paradise of the book of Revelation (chapter 22) contains 'the river of the water of life, bright as crystal', which is the river of Eden, and the tree of life which stood in Eden.

It was during the Feast of Booths, apparently as the libation of water was being poured out, that Jesus said, 'If any one thirst, let him come to me and drink' (John, chapter 7), and earlier he had told the woman by the well in Samaria: 'Everyone who drinks of the water that I shall give him will never thirst; the water that I shall give him will become in him a spring of water welling up to eternal life' (John, chapter 4). In Christian symbolism the four rivers of Eden were identified with the four gospels which brought the life-giving message of Christ, and the living water with the water which flowed from Christ's side on the cross.

Clean Hands and Pure Heart

'Cleanliness is next to godliness', the proverb says, and in many societies washing in water or being sprinkled with it cleans away pollution, the contamination which may arise from many sources, including blood, childbirth, sex, the dead, a sin or a breach of custom (though water is by no means the only purifying agent – fire, blood, sand and other substances have also been used). We wash away physical dirt with water, and so we wash away spiritual dirt with it too, and this may be an essential pre-requisite for approaching the divine. In Islam the faithful must wash before each of the five daily sayings of prayer, and tanks or wells are provided at mosques for the worshippers' ablutions. The priests of ancient Egypt shaved their entire bodies every three days and washed themselves in cold water twice each day and twice each night. In Hinduism a ritual bath, which achieves both physical and spiritual cleanliness, is most effectively taken in a river or a sacred pool or a tank provided at a temple. The 'ghats' or sites of ritual bathing are regarded as spiritual 'centres' at which the bather is linked with both earth and heaven. The European magical textbooks put a high value on cleanliness, to rid the magician of impurities on which a spirit might fasten and as a sign of dedication to the work in hand (see RITUAL MAGIC).

There are numerous references in the Old Testament to ritual purification with water. In Exodus (chapter 30), priests are instructed on pain of death to wash their hands and feet before approaching the altar. Anyone who touched the bed of a menstruating woman was required to wash himself and his clothes in water (Leviticus, chapter 15), and people and things which had been in contact with the dead had to be sprinkled with water or washed in it (Numbers, chapter 19). In Psalms 18 and 24 clean hands are equated with 'righteousness' and 'a pure heart'. In strict Jewish households the hands must be washed before saying prayers and before any meal which includes bread. Jewish families which do not keep a separate set of dishes and glasses for the Passover meal may purify their ordinary tableware by dipping it in boiling water.

Roman Catholic priests wash their hands in a basin called a lavabo before saying Mass. 'Holy water', specially blessed by a priest, is provided at the doors of churches so that worshippers can sprinkle themselves with it before going in. It is also sprinkled on the congregation at Mass on Sundays, and it has long been regarded as a powerful defence against evil forces.

In Christian baptism, as in ancient Egyptian mortuary ritual, the two ideas of the

Below **Physical dirt is washed away with water, and so symbolically is spiritual dirt and guilt: Pilate 'washing his hands' of Jesus, a stained glass window in Lincoln Cathedral**
Right **Detail from Veronese's *Marriage at Cana*, where Jesus turned water into wine: liquids, especially intoxicating liquids which make people 'lively', are generally connected with life in symbolism**

Sonia Halliday

God of Waters

By dread deeds thou dost answer us with
  deliverance,
    O God of our salvation,
who art the hope of all the ends of the earth,
    and of the farthest seas;
who by thy strength hast established the
  mountains,
    being girded with might;
who dost still the roaring of the seas,
    the roaring of their waves,
    the tumult of the peoples;

so that those who dwell at earth's farthest
  bounds
    are afraid at thy signs;
thou makest the outgoings of the morning
    and the evening
    to shout for joy.

Thou visitest the earth and waterest it,
    thou greatly enrichest it;
the river of God is full of water;
    thou providest their grain,
    for so thou hast prepared it.

Thou waterest its furrows abundantly,
    settling its ridges,
softening it with showers,
    and blessing its growth.
Thou crownest the year with thy bounty;
    the tracks of thy chariot drip with
    fatness.
The pastures of the wilderness drip,
    the hills gird themselves with joy,
the meadows clothe themselves with flocks,
    the valleys deck themselves with grain,
    they shout and sing together for joy.

Psalm 65. 5-13

water of life and the water of cleanliness were brought together. The water which washes away dirt and corruption became also the water of life, effecting a spiritual rebirth. In Romans (chapter 6) St Paul presented baptism as 'a ritual death and rebirth, which simulates the death and resurrection of Christ' (see BAPTISM).

In the background of this view of baptism is the notion of water as *fons et origo*, the fount and origin of all forms of life. In some

Left In Christian baptism the two ideas of the water of life and the water of purification are brought together: *Jesus baptized in Jordan,* by Verrocchio and Leonardo *Below* Satirical view of baptisms at the Brooklyn Tabernacle, New York, from *Puck*

creation myths, there existed in the beginning a chaos of water, from which the world or the god who made the world emerged (see CREATION MYTHS). But though water is sometimes regarded as the vital principle – the rain which fertilizes the soil, the river which irrigates it – the vital principle may alternatively be air, breath or spirit (see BREATH), which injects vitality into the formless waters of chaos and creates forms – the structures and bodies of the phenomena of our world. Mircea Eliade comments on the symbolism of baptism and initiation by water in this light: 'Immersion in water symbolizes a return to the pre-formal, a total regeneration, a new birth, for immersion means a dissolution of forms, a reintegration into the formlessness of pre-existence; and

emerging from the water is a repetition of the act of creation in which form was first expressed.' This brings to mind the parallel, which the alchemists drew, between the Holy Spirit descending on Jesus at his baptism in the waters of Jordan and the Spirit of God moving over the primeval waters in Genesis.

The writer of 2 Peter (chapter 3) observed that God made the world out of the water of chaos and through this same water destroyed the world again in the Flood. Later writers saw a parallel between the waters of the Flood and the water of baptism, and saw Noah's ark, riding out the Flood, as a foreshadowing of salvation through Christ. 'Christ the firstborn of every creature,' said Justin Martyr (2nd century AD), 'has become

Illustration by W. Heath Robinson to Charles Kingsley's children's book *The Water Babies* (1863): small beings in human form were believed by many American Indian peoples to live in lakes, springs and streams, and were usually feared as uncanny

waters of potential life. Many alchemists regarded their processes as a repetition, in miniature, of the process of creation described in Genesis. 'Perform no operation till all be made water,' they said, meaning that the material in the vessel, or spiritually the alchemist himself, must be reduced to the state of watery primeval chaos before 'philosophical mercury', the divine spirit of life, could move over the waters to create a new material or a new condition.

The Mind's Depths

As the fount and origin of life water may naturally be connected with woman. Aphrodite, the Greek love goddess, was born of the sea, the fountain is one of the emblems of the Virgin Mary, and in the Cabala the Sefirah Binah (see CABALA) is called the Mother, the Throne, the Great Sea. In modern magical systems it is linked with the waters of chaos in Genesis and with female symbols, the cup, circle, oval and diamond. Water is also linked with the moon, which 'flows' in the sense that it constantly changes shape, and which is connected with the flow of the tides and the ebbing and flowing of all the rhythms of life (see MOON).

Both water and the moon are connected by many modern interpreters of symbolism and mythology with the 'depths' of the mind, the unconscious, the swirling currents of the inner self. According to C. G. Jung, the sea or any large expanse of water appearing in dreams and fantasies is an image of the unconscious. Here again, the depths of the self are chaotic, formless, and pregnant with violence and destruction, but are also the wellsprings of the life of the conscious mind. 'If attention is directed to the unconscious,' Jung said, 'the unconscious will yield up its contents, and these in turn will fructify the conscious like a fountain of living water.'

(See also BRIDGES; DRAGON; ELEMENTS; FISH; GANGES; LANDSCAPE SYMBOLISM; MERMAIDS; MIRROR; NYMPHS; SEA; SPRINGS AND WELLS.)

RICHARD CAVENDISH

FURTHER READING: S. G. F. Brandon, *Creation Legends of the Ancient Near East* (Verry, Lawrence, 1963); M. Eliade, *Patterns in Comparative Religion* (New American Library).

in a new sense the head of another race, of those whom he has brought to birth by water, faith and the wood that holds the mystery of the Cross, just as Noah was saved in the wood of the Ark.' Noah's ark is related to the symbolism of the Church as a ship, in which the faithful ride out the storms and perils of this world (see SHIP), and baptism was also taken to have been prefigured in the crossing of the Red Sea, the triumphant and miraculous passage through water in which the Israelites escaped from bondage in Egypt, as the Christian in baptism escaped from slavery to the Devil.

The story of the Flood, with its parallels in other traditions (see END OF THE WORLD; FLOOD), is an example of yet another aspect of water symbolism, which stems from the

fact that too much water is as harmful to life as too little: you can drown in it. There is in water, especially in the sea, a power of violence, turbulence and destruction which threatens life and good order. In Babylonian mythology the monstrous sea, Tiamat, whose 'eyes' were the rivers Tigris and Euphrates, threatened to overthrow the gods. In Canaan, Baal conquered Yam, the god of seas and rivers and waters underground, and there are passages in the Old Testament referring to Yahweh's conquest of a sea monster, the ancestor of the Great Beast of Revelation (see GREAT BEAST) and more distantly of the threatening monsters which in science fiction come up out of the depths to destroy the world as incarnations of primeval chaos.

But the waters of chaos are also the

Many apparently magical methods of forecasting the weather have proved to have a scientific basis; but whether medicine-men and witches have been able to influence the elements, and if so how, has not been properly explored

WEATHER MAGIC

THERE HAS BEEN no time in human history when people have not needed to know something about the weather. Probably under modern conditions we have less knowledge of the weather than ever before. In the great civilized countries of the world, the red sky at night is no longer a warning that the cloud will disappear and fine weather will come on the morrow, but it tells us of the glare of neon signs in peace and of the burning of cities in time of war. We fill our world with artificial light so that it is only in the more remote areas that one can take a walk at night to admire the moon and the stars. Within the great city the moon is less brilliant than the street lights.

To our unsophisticated ancestors the world was a place full of magic, and most important of all the phenomena of Nature were the coming and going of rain and snow, which determined the growth of the food crops for the primitive farmer; and for the hunters the rainfall determined the amount of fresh grass available for the migrating herds of deer and bison. Sometimes quite alarming falls of coloured dust of unknown origin caused red rains, white rains and black rains which were carefully noted in the historical annals of past times. Hail storms occurred with sudden changes of temperature, sometimes blighting new crops by a layer of thin frozen ice, but more often actively destroying crops through the massive battering of larger hailstones crashing to the ground and beating everything flat beneath them.

Demons of the Desert

Then there were the winds; to most of us the winds have simply come from the four directions of north, south, east and west. We, who live in the great cities of the world just notice whether a day is windy or not, but to the seaman and the farmer each wind still has its own character, bringing its specific blessing or danger to the crops and animals. In addition to the normal winds there are the sudden and more violent winds, the waterspouts and the hurricanes; terrible things which cause tremendous damage as they sweep across the country. Sometimes, after a waterspout has passed, the ground is seen to be covered with small frogs or even fishes. Sometimes leaves of trees from far distant places are cast down as the storm passes. To primitive man all these phenomena are not only beyond his control, as indeed they are today, but also totally

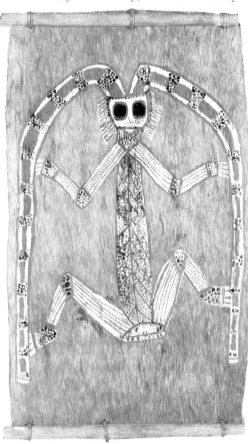

'To our unsophisticated ancestors the world was a place full of magic', and weather phenomena were linked with gods and spirits *Left* Head of a basalt figure of the Aztec goddess Chalchihuitlicue, consort of the rain god: she was the spring rains, the whirlwinds, the whirlpools in the water and all young growing plants *Above* Australian aboriginal lightning spirit

British Museum/Michael Holford

Axel Poignant

beyond his rational understanding. The frogs from the waterspout are sent by the gods, to convey a warning to the local population. The dust storms running along the edge of the deserts are inhabited by terrifying jinn, dangerous whirling spirits who, if they come your way, must not be looked upon. You take cover and wrap your face in a cloth so as to avoid breathing in the hot burning sand which comes with them.

All around the skies of the world lightning plays from time to time. To the North American Indians this is the flashing beak of the great thunder-bird as she flies through the storm. To the classical Europeans these were the thunderbolts cast, by the king of the gods. Even in far Tibet the philosophy of Mahayana Buddhism involves the use of

the metal *Dorje*, which represents a thunderbolt, in the temple services. It is a symbol of destruction, even to the point of annihilation. In some circumstances it is the symbol of terror, but in others those who possess the secret inner knowledge see it as a symbol of an ultimate blessing when a soul is set entirely free from the wishes and dislikes of normal existence; the past chains of earthly existence are broken and the soul moves through to a state of unbeing. However, few people have the philosophic detachment of a highly trained lama in his mountain monastery. Nevertheless, what happens with the weather has always been of great importance, not only for the practice of hunting and agriculture, but also as a means of divination of the quality of great events.

Winds in a Bag

Among the world's greatest weather watchers in ancient times were the Etruscans of northern Italy (see ETRUSCANS). Their diviners, who cast prophecies from the state of the sky, achieved great fame and it was customary in the early days of Rome for the Senate to send deputations to Etruscan cities to ask for advice when their own oracles seemed doubtful. The Etruscan soothsayers preferred to work from a high clear mountain with an even view of the sky in all directions; if it was situated above oak woods, so much the better. The oak (see OAK) was a sacred magical tree with tremendous strength and so it had a relationship with the strength of the thunderbolt-throwing god Tinia, who was the Etruscan

equivalent of Jupiter. They divided the sky not only into four directions, but each of these were again divided into four, so that there were 16 wind directions to be regarded. Particularly in thundery weather, the observers would wait on the hilltops, marking the direction of lightning flashes exactly, taking note of their brilliance and of the places where they appeared to 'strike. From this study they calculated the incidence of danger, and of blessings coming from the different directions. The augurs then assessed their particular meanings for the person or city on whose behalf they were consulting the elements.

By no means all people had the skill of the Etruscans in observing the weather. But there is no known group who do not take notice of the quality of the sky and of what it forebodes to them in the way of success or failure in hunting and agriculture.

For most people, knowledge of the sky sufficient to give a clue to tomorrow's weather is quite enough. But quite often a much fuller knowledge is demanded, even in primitive society, and this is expected from the weather specialists, the shamans (see SHAMAN) who have watched the skies sufficiently long and thoroughly to form judgements. They make their estimates from wind, cloud, the flight of birds and the colour of the sky, particularly at sunrise and sunset.

Such specialists included the magicians of Northern Europe, who were said to have the power to tie the winds in a length of rope. This power might be used for evil magic, by pulling the knots tight, when it was believed that the winds would be stopped and ships becalmed, with consequent loss of business and even health, if the calm lasted for a long time. The way in which the knots were used to tie up the bag in which the wind was symbolically trapped is reminiscent of Greek mythology. The magician would have his wind bag, which he would use like the bellows of a bagpipe for sympathetic magic, thus inducing the real winds to follow the example of the air

'Red sky at night, shepherd's delight': chimney-pots silhouetted against the sunset in London. Many simple methods of weather forecasting have survived into modern times and have proved to have some scientific basis

being expelled. Such men were powerful far back into history.

The Viking navigators were naturally deeply interested in this form of magic. And among their crews there were people who knew the weather sufficiently well in summer, which was the period when the great voyages were undertaken, to navigate the North Atlantic from Oslo fjord right across to Iceland and on to Greenland. In the Vinland Sagas we hear of the noble Thorfinn Karlsefni, who was so sure of the navigation of the ocean that long before the discovery of the mariner's compass he left Norway with the intention of missing Iceland and making his landfall at Brattahlid in Greenland. He succeeded in the adventure, and as he landed, saw a beautiful lady sitting spinning wool beside her father's house. And that led to a romance which in turn led to the first white settlement in North America. But weather magic on the scale necessary to the great northern voyages was by no means common in the world.

Continual Rain in Paradise

Perhaps the most difficult of all forecasting performed by people living the simple life was that of predicting the coming of rain in semi-desert areas. Some successful meteorological observers probably possessed clairvoyant powers; in Africa, Masai shamans would sit on the hilltops near Mt Kenya and look at the sky, knowing from the position of the stars what season of the year it was. By the colour of the sky, by the appearance of little drifts of clouds forming near the snowcap of the mountain, they would estimate whether the rains would be early or late, in order to give the farmers a few days' warning of the coming rain, so that the planting could be achieved in time. When the forecasts proved wrong the rain-maker would be considered to have been abandoned by his spiritual helpers and therefore of no further importance. He might be lucky if he escaped simply with insults and a beating. Usually each of the older forecasters would have an apprentice who was learning the mysteries of the sky, and so other rain-makers would be able to assume their duties when necessary.

Among the Pueblo Indians of Arizona (see PUEBLO INDIANS) there were also many wise shamans who observed the weather. In this semi-desert country, where the water supply was dependent largely on seasonal thunderstorms, it was important to know whether the storms were likely to be light or heavy, early or late. All good observers in the hilltop villages could detect at a glance which way a storm-cloud was moving, and by looking at the shadows of rain or hail falling from its base, they would be able to estimate any possible danger to their crops either by flooding or battering of hail.

In central Mexico (see AZTECS; MEXICO) the weather gods were very important. Tlaloc, the lord of the rain and master of thunder, was a great spirit who controlled the four kinds of rain and brought life and fertility to the earth. His importance was so great that the high priest of the Aztecs was called the Tlaloc Tlamacazqui. He was a sacrificing priest who brought life and

Witches working magic to create a hailstorm, a 15th century woodcut: witches were widely believed to be able to affect the weather, and methods of applying electrical and heat energy to weather magic are still being used by modern witches

fertility to the land, although most of his sacrifices were made to the more brutal sun god. The consort of the rain god was the beautiful princess Chalchihuitlicue, who was the spring rains, the whirlwinds, the whirlpools in the water and all young growing plants. Between them they looked after the fertility of the material earth. People who had been struck by lightning or drowned were believed to have been claimed by these deities, and their souls would live in the wonderful paradise where flowers bloomed continually, there were myriads of butterflies, and thin rain fell constantly amid the rainbows. To the Mexicans of the semi-desert highland, this indeed was the most beautiful place which could exist.

Scientific Magic

The importance of thunder gods seems to have been greatest in countries with similarly arid types of climate. The Palestinian god Hadad, lord of the storms and thunder, was worshipped under slight variants of his name far into Babylonia and up into the Persian highlands (see BAAL; SYRIA). Even in the early days of the Jewish faith, Yahweh is often described as the wielder of thunderbolts and storms. There was a natural relationship between the tremendous power which gave life to all plants, and its other destructive manifestation in the lightning and thunder which were so intimately connected with the rain. This, of course, is part of a universal tradition, wherever man lives in civilized town states which depend to a great extent on agriculture.

There are many simple ways of forecasting weather which have survived into modern times; the old saying 'Red sky at morning, shepherd's warning; red sky at night, shepherd's delight', belongs to the weather of the Northern Hemisphere, and has some scientific basis.

One can tell a great deal from the flight of birds because many birds sweep through the air almost like gliders and naturally the height of their flight depends upon the pressure of the air; the higher the pressure, the higher the birds can float into the sky. In the advent of stormy conditions, ripples and whirlpools in the atmosphere in advance of the depression cause the birds to fly in little clusters, where normally they would fly in large groups. So there is some justification for observing the birds flying home at sunset in order to predict the next day's weather.

One of the most solidly based methods of forecasting, traditionally used by farmers and shepherds and surviving into modern times, was demonstrated to me recently by a farmer in south Wiltshire. Every morning he would consult his well about the weather outlook for that day. He would look down the well at the surface of the water, and decide whether it was curved slightly upwards at the edges or slightly downwards; this was an indication of air pressure, the water acting as an Aneroid barometer. He would also observe the height of the dampness on the sides of the well. If the damp was at the top of the well and running downwards, he would expect rain, if there was moisture from the surface of the water rising upwards a little, he would expect the weather to remain cold. There were many observations possible in this way, dependent on the state of humidity in the air. His own practical knowledge of the run of seasonal weather, linked with the detailed observations, were sufficient to give him a very good estimate of the weather for the next 24 hours. In this case we were able to check his observations with our own meteorological studies and both sides found a great deal of interest in observing the skill involved in the other's way of forecasting.

A good deal of information about forthcoming weather can also be gleaned from the behaviour of flowers, the way animals turn their backs to the wind, how cows in a field will take shelter from expected rain before its arrival, and so on. Much of the sensitivity of animals with regard to rain is now known to be due to increasing atmospheric humidity causing the hair of their coats to expand and irritate them.

In the busy life of a farming community, day-to-day weather observation was everybody's concern because it was so important. However, in doubtful situations the specialist, with his greater knowledge and experience, would be consulted. He would be asked to predict a date for the end of a spell of dreary wet weather which had made it impossible to plough the ground or plant the seeds, or when a drought would end. The weather-wise seer was looked upon with special respect. He may have observed that spells of fine weather usually go in units of four days, but that in wintertime this would apply to spells of quiet, grey weather. In other words, in the middle latitudes of the Northern Hemisphere, areas of high pressure usually circulate for four days and then either move away or reform. Such knowledge for the primitive observer without written records depends upon personal observation.

The Celtic Druids were skilled in weather magic. Their very name means 'men of the oak-tree' and associates them with ideas of the knowledge of trees and of the inner life of trees. This was magically expressed for them by the appearance of mistletoe on oak trees (see DRUIDS; MISTLETOE), showing that the god had fertilized the earth and was giving new strength and power. Their traditional knowledge has been preserved for us in many little nursery rhymes and riddles which refer to the wind and the sky. Like all people concerned with the natural growth of crops, the Druids realized that the power behind the weather had spiritual connotations, that the life of man was closely linked with the movements of wind and rain.

Splitting a Cloud

At all times magicians, witches and ecstatics of various kinds have been credited with influencing the weather; not only the shaman tying knots in his rope, but also the witches in their magical rituals, flying through the air on their broomsticks. They swept along among the clouds, they brought mists, they threw the hail, they were able to charm the winds on the ocean so that they could float to sea in a sieve.

Even under modern civilized conditions, there are various curious phenomena to be found in the experience of witchcraft. In periods when the atmosphere is highly charged with electricity and the skin is dry, a group of naked dancers in a circle may find themselves producing sudden little flashes of fire all over their bodies. This is due entirely to the electrical static discharge between the atmosphere and their skins. These discharges may often be very beautiful in the dark, like veils of flashing pale blue diamonds appearing all over the dancer. Such things in the past must indeed have seemed magical and mysterious, although to a modern mind they are simply curious and rather beautiful. There is also the possibility of a group dancing in a circle producing electrical or even heat energy of a mild form. When the atmosphere is unstable, this may be sufficient to cause some change in the structure of cloud.

Although nothing has been reported in recent years to compare with the storm-raising powers credited to medieval witches, or with the bringing of thunder and lightning from the heavens which was attributed to priests and magicians in classical times, in practice it has been found possible to split a small cloud in unstable weather conditions. A few years ago, three friends walking along a path in thundery weather observed a small cloud blowing up directly towards them. By looking towards it and assuming that the cloud would divide, they witnessed the actual splitting of the cloud into two portions as it approached and then passed in its separate halves overhead.

This one experiment is by no means proof of the power of projected energy, but it was suggestive in that the projection of thought in this emotional state is accompanied by a slight increase in heat energy; and it may just have been possible that this was directed at, and helped to disperse, some of the water droplets at the front of the approaching cloud and so set up conditions under which it would divide. In this case the people concerned were totally naked, and therefore energy was reflected from the surface of their bodies.

Unimpressive as this little experiment may seem, it did give a clue to the possibility that people much more devoted to such activity, and with a deeper occult knowledge than is available in these days, were able to cause clouds to disperse.

However, the whole of this field of weather control by magic is insufficiently explored in modern times, and a good deal more research is necessary in order to lay down any sound principles. The main importance of weather magic today is that without the scientific work of a professional meteorologist, it is possible for ordinary people to look at the sky and say what tomorrow's weather will be. That in itself is a phenomenon worth noting and an achievement of the human personality.
(See also SKY.)

C. A. BURLAND

Wedding Customs

The giving of gifts is usually an important part of a marriage ceremony, and so is the eating of food, certain items being essentially symbolic; new clothes are often required, and the couple may be showered with rice, sweets or other symbols of fertility; the wedding ring stands for marital union and constancy; many wedding customs reflect the fact that marriage means the transfer of one of the couple to a different kin group. See MARRIAGE AND BETROTHAL; RING; THRESHOLD.

Weighing of the Soul

Motif in the judgement of the dead; in ancient Egyptian accounts the dead person's heart is weighed in the balance against a feather, the symbol of truth; in medieval Christian representations of the Last Judgement the Archangel Michael weighs the souls of the dead.
See JUDGEMENT OF THE DEAD.

THOMAS WEIR

IT WAS the curious fate of Thomas Weir to enjoy during his lifetime a reputation for extreme religious zeal and piety, and to be remembered after his death as one of Scotland's most notorious witches. He was born in Lanark about 1600, the son of a family of some standing in Clydesdale, and was executed in Edinburgh in 1670 for crimes of which he had never been suspected until he suddenly and quite spontaneously confessed to them. In between these two dates, he had been well known as an ardent Covenanter, one of the promoters of the Western Remonstrance in 1650, a violent anti-royalist during the Civil Wars, and a fanatical opponent at all times of the Established Church.

In 1641 Weir served as a lieutenant in the army sent by the Covenanting Estates into Ireland, and in 1649 and 1650 he was a commander in the City Guard of Edinburgh. He was then a major, and he was known by that title for the rest of his life. He is said to have shown great severity and cruelty to any Royalists who fell into his hands, and to have gone out of his way to insult and humiliate his wretched prisoners. In his later years, when he was a member of an extreme Presbyterian sect, sometimes called the Bowhead Saints, he was renowned throughout Edinburgh for his remarkable gifts of extemporary prayer and exhortation. Many flocked to his house to hear him pray, and he was constantly called upon to take part in private meetings, to bless the families of the faithful, and to offer up prayers by the bedsides of the sick. He always carried a black staff with a thorn-wood head, and leant upon it while he prayed; and it was noticed that if he became separated from it for any reason, his power and fluency seemed to desert him.

In 1670, this respected man suddenly confessed to a number of abominable crimes, secretly committed over many years. He told the appalled and incredulous members of his own sect that he had been guilty of adultery with 'several and diverse persons', and of long-continued fornication with his maid-servant; of incest with his stepdaughter, and also with his sister, Jean, from the time she was 16 till she was 50 years old; and of bestiality with animals, particularly one of his own riding-mares. His horrified co-religionists at first refused to believe these wild statements and then, for fear of being involved in the inevitable scandal, tried to conceal them. Eventually, however, the Provost of Edinburgh was informed. He not unnaturally concluded that the Major was demented, and sent doctors to examine him. They reported that he was quite sane, and suffering only from an outraged conscience. Some ministers subsequently sent by the Provost also declared that he was not mad, but driven by 'the terrors of God that were upon his soul'. He was therefore arrested, and with him, the sister he had implicated in part of his confession.

Notwithstanding his posthumous reputation, Weir was never indicted for witchcraft, nor does he seem to have acknowledged that offence in so many words, though it formed part of the evidence at the trial. His sister, however, was accused of sorcery as well as incest, and confessed to both. One of the charges brought against her was that she had a familiar spirit which kept her constantly supplied with quantities of good yarn. In fact, there is no evidence that she ever kept a familiar spirit in the usual sense of that phrase; but she admitted that, many years before, when she lived in Dalkeith, she had trafficked with messengers from the 'Queen of Farie', and with one of these she had gone through a ritual equivalent to the renunciation of her baptism. From then on, she was never without yarn 'ready for her upon the spindle, whatever business she had been about'.

She also said that, in 1648, she and her brother had been transported in a coach 'which seemed all of fire' to Musselburgh, and there the Major heard from the Devil news of the battle of Preston which did not reach Scotland by normal means for several days afterwards. As soon as they were both arrested, she drew the guards' attention to his staff, saying that it had magical powers, and that he had received it from the Devil himself. It was perhaps after this that so many people remembered that he could not pray without it.

'Nothing But Darkness'

While he was in prison, Weir was visited by several well-intentioned ministers, who urged him to repent and ask God's pardon for his sins. He would not listen to any of them. He said he knew he was already damned beyond hope, and that no prayers or exhortations could save him. 'I find nothing within me,' he declared on one occasion, 'but blackness and darkness, brimstone, and burning to the bottom of Hell.' In that despairing state he continued until the end.

The evidence against both the Weirs depended almost entirely upon their own confessions. Several witnesses at the trial testified to statements made earlier in their presence, including one man who said he had asked Thomas if he had seen the Devil, and had been told only that 'any feeling he ever had of him was in the dark'. His sister-in-law stated that once she had surprised him in the act of incest with his sister and heard scandalous talk between them. Another woman said she had seen him committing bestiality with a mare, and had complained to the minister of the parish; but because she could not prove the charge, she had been publicly whipped for slandering 'such an eminent holy man'.

Except for the evidence of these witnesses, there were only the confessions, reiterated and steadily persisted in with a fervour that suggests the Provost's original suspicions may have been right. Both prisoners were convicted. The Major was strangled and then burnt on 11 April 1670, his staff being burnt with him, and on the following day his sister was hanged.

Weir's house in the West Bow survived him for about 150 years. It was said to be haunted by his ghost, who was sometimes seen issuing from it on foot, or on horseback, or driving away from it in a spectral coach in the small hours of the morning. Neighbours and passers-by often heard sounds as of howling, and dancing, and the hum of a spinning-wheel. No one had the hardihood to live in it, or pass a night there; it was finally pulled down in the 1830s, and no trace now remains of this dwelling of evil memory.

CHRISTINA HOLE

Stories of men having the power to change themselves into ravening beasts have gained currency in almost every part of the world; a universality which suggests that the underlying idea emanates from deep within man's own mind

WEREWOLF

IN LEGEND, the werewolf is a living person who has the magical power to change his or her shape. In its bestial form it is a terrorizer, a killer, an eater of human flesh. These two elements – metamorphosis and murder – form the basis, and much of the substance, of the legend. But the werewolf's family tree is ancient, vast and has many spreading branches. Some branches lead to the realm of revenants (those who have returned from the dead), where ghosts and vampires walk; others lead to evil sorcery, witchcraft and diabolism.

The idea of the werewolf is based on the acknowledgement of 'the beast in man' – our dual nature, which was no doubt as much of a commonplace in the Stone Age as in our Age of Psychoanalysis. Primitive mythology, naturally, makes much of the concept. Sometimes we are said to be descended from original, semi-divine animals, and sometimes the primitive feels a mystical and total identity with an animal, in the religious belief called 'totemism' (see TOTEM). In folktale, the culture heroes appear in indeterminate, human or animal form, like Coyote and the other tricksters of American Indian myth (see TRICKSTER). And there are numerous tales of intermarriage, when a humanized animal takes a human mate, perhaps producing offspring with the power of shape-shifting. These and other elements of primitive myth establish the widespread belief in metamorphosis (see SHAPE-SHIFTING). When the assumed shape was that of a dangerous animal, a carnivorous enemy of man, the element of murder enters the picture as well, and the werewolf idea begins to emerge.

But not only the werewolf emerges. The world's folklore is full of other were-animals. ('Were' may come from the Old English word for 'man', and the corresponding terms in other languages are mostly similar compounds meaning 'man-wolf'.) Even those lands where the wolf is or was native have tales of other were-creatures: were-bears in Russia and Scandinavia, for instance. Lands without wolves have tales of were-hyenas, were-lions, were-crocodiles, were-jackals. In 1933 a respectable British doctor reported that he had seen two Africans turn themselves into jackals during a ceremony (see ATAVISM). But the were-leopard dominates the African tradition, assisted by sensationalized tales of the secret cult of the Leopard Men (see AFRICA), which gained much attention earlier in this century.

Similarly, were-tigers have been noted in the supernatural lore of India and other Asian lands; were-jaguars and sometimes were-snakes terrorize South American tribesmen. And though occasionally the were-animal is not of the most ferocious species (the Chinese have tales of were-foxes, for instance, rather like the cats or hares that witches are said to become, in European tales), in general the metamorphosis and murder theme predominates.

The Beast in Man

Ancient civilizations provide a number of antecedents for the werewolf. The maenads of ancient Greece (see DIONYSUS) flaunted the 'beast in man' in their ecstasies, and apparently sometimes wore wolf masks during their hunts through the forests. Also from Greece comes the legend of Lycaon, a man who became over-zealous in his worship of Zeus and sacrificed a child to the god, making an offering of the child's flesh. Zeus changed him into a wolf, as punishment. But later there grew up an ecstatic cult of the worship of Zeus Lycaeus, in which the participants wore wolf masks.

Several notable Greek writers, including Herodotus and Plato, gave credence, or at least currency, to the werewolf idea, and so helped its spread into Europe in later centuries. In ancient Rome, Pliny discussed the idea seriously, Petronius mocked it in the *Satyricon*, and Ovid drew the Lycaeon story into the *Metamorphoses*.

Perhaps all the beast-men and wild men, found in folklore all over the world, are also distant kindred of the werewolf: the satyrs and centaurs of Greece, the Abominable Snowman, human children fostered by animals, as in Kipling's story of Mowgli.

But the metamorphosis and murder is absent, or of minor importance, in such tales. Mowgli is not a werewolf, nor Tarzan a were-ape. More explicitly and directly behind our idea of the werewolf are two strands of folklore from the chillier regions of Europe. Northern peoples generally seem to have viewed the wolf with a fear and hate bordering on hysteria – the kind usually reserved for the worst supernatural monsters (see WOLF). Of course, the wolf was always a dangerous predator that cared little whether its dinner was a prize sheep or the shepherd. But there is more to the fear of the wolf than a mere antipathy to a beast of prey. The wolf seems to be regarded by Europeans as somehow in itself demonic. Wolves are semi-nocturnal, usually greyish in colour, and move in an almost ghostly silence. They have slanting eyes that glow yellow-green in moonlight, red in reflected firelight. And their chilling, banshee-like howl completes the eerie picture.

So the wolf unsettles us, on some deep atavistic level. Which may explain why even today men seek to exterminate this beast, while intending only to control other predators. The wolf has vanished from America (except Alaska), Britain, Germany, Switzerland and France. The French suffered terribly from wolves in the past, which explains the abundance of werewolf (*loup-garou*) tales from that country. In 1963 it was thought that a small pack of wolves had been sighted in France; and though some people believed it was just a pack of half-wild dogs, the mere thought of wolves returning to France made international headlines.

Wolves are still said to roam in eastern Europe, in Russia, and in Spain and Portugal. They exist also in Canada (a man was attacked by wolves in Ontario in 1963), but probably not for long. The hysterical urge to exterminate wolves is well described by the Canadian writer Farley Mowat, in *Cry Wolf*, a book that offers facts about the animal which counter its traditional typecasting as an evil, voracious monster.

No doubt that view will persist, and will pursue the wolf into extinction. Our responses have been conditioned by centuries of horror stories about wolves. Invariably these stories concern the wolf's cruel ferocity and murderousness, and his insatiable hunger. The Bible compares false prophets to 'ravening wolves' in sheep's clothing. A comparable disguise was used by the wolf in the tale of Little Red Riding Hood, which is part of the furniture of the mind of nearly every Western European and North American child. There are a number of old wives' tales of hunters caught out in the northern woods as darkness falls, hearing that echoing howl in the distance, approaching; or of that famous Russian sled, from which members of a family are thrown one at a time in vain sacrifices to a pursuing pack. In common catchphrases, villains

grin wolfishly, and gluttons wolf down their food. Above all, there is the Fenris wolf, the most terrible monster of Northern mythology, and the eventual killer of Odin himself (END OF THE WORLD; SCANDINAVIA).

The Fenris wolf points to the second strand of folklore that has contributed directly to the werewolf legend. Scandinavian and Teutonic myth and folklore are full of the combination of metamorphosis and murder. The Norse gods took animal form even more often, it seems, than those of the Greeks. Scandinavian heroes are also often shape-shifters: one Bodvar Bjarhi took the shape of a bear to fight in a great battle in Denmark, recounted in the Norse sagas, and a bear motif appears in the tales of many other heroes (see BEAR; BEOWULF). Clearly

there is a link here with the 'berserkers' of Scandinavian legend – the warriors who fell into a battle madness that made them preternaturally powerful, causing them to roar like beasts and foam at the mouth. We use 'berserk' to mean that kind of maniacal fury, but it is said to derive from the Old Norse for 'bear-shirt', referring to the fur garments of these warriors. It was not much of an imaginative step (for their victims especially) to believe that the berserkers not only released the 'beast within' but actually transformed themselves into wild beasts.

The werewolf's impressive European ancestry became focused in the Christian era's dark centuries of superstition and witch hunting. The old horror tales of those

Man into ravening beast, a film still from *Dr Jekyll and Mr Hyde*: Robert Louis Stevenson's book used the theme of 'the beast within' which lies behind the stories of werewolves and other were-animals

'Northern peoples generally seem to have viewed the wolf with a fear and hate bordering on hysteria', and the human being who turns into a wolf and prowls in search of human victims is a persistent figure of folklore and fantasy
Top and *centre* The werewolf of Eschenbach, Germany, 1685, said to have preyed on children *Below* Werewolf attacking a man, from a 15th century German work *Facing page* The Wild Beast of Gévaudan, France, 1765, said to have devoured more than 100 people and to have a particular liking for the flesh of girls

centuries showed the witches in possession of the shape-shifting power, conferred on them by Satan. The witches were believed to change into cats, hares, toads, and the like. But the ancient wolf fear rose up too, became projected onto Satan's minions, and led to the idea that werewolves were witches who chose to take wolf form, ravaging the countryside as part of their diabolic duties. So the Renaissance witch trials recorded many gory accounts of werewolfism, especially in France and Germany. Often the 'confessions' of witches asserted that whole sabbaths changed into wolf packs; one old Latvian tale described a 12 day march at Christmastide of thousands of demonic werewolves, led by Satan himself in wolf form.

Sometimes the demonologists argued that werewolves were actual demons or imps, rather than metamorphosed human witches. But a few clearer minds, like that of Reginald Scot, author of *Discovery of Witchcraft* (1584), suggested that shape-shifting was unlikely, that certain kinds of insanity might lead people to imagine that they became wolves. Usually such insanity was ascribed to demonic possession and so although the mental illness known as lycanthropy was recognized quite early, the recognition had little effect on the superstition.

A Belt of Wolfskin

Out of the 16th century obsession with witches and like horrors come some of the world's most famous documented accounts of 'werewolves'. In 1573 a French village was terrorized by a monster that had killed and partially eaten several children. Then a group of villagers rescued another child from an attack by a huge wolf which, they swore, had the face of a local recluse named Gilles Garnier. Garnier was duly induced, by the usual means, to 'confess' to being a werewolf. The authorities, who seemed especially incensed that he had engaged in some of his gruesome feasts on meatless Fridays, ordered him to be burned alive.

Even more fearful was the punishment meted out to Peter Stubb, or Stump, in Germany in 1589. Stubb's 'confession' revealed him explicitly as a diabolist werewolf: he shifted his shape by means of a magical 'girdle' or belt of wolfskin, given to him by the Devil. And as a wolf, Stubb went forth on the Devil's work, to wreak 'his malice on men, women and children'. Apparently he had been doing so for some 25 years before he was caught. He sometimes killed livestock, and occasionally men whom he disliked; but he principally preyed on women and girl children, whom (he claimed) he raped, killed and ate. As a sideline he committed a good deal of ordinary if sinful fornication, as well as incest with his sister and his daughter, and capped his crimes, as the story goes, by killing and eating his own son. Finally he was captured, but the wolfskin belt was not found, which seems to have proved its diabolic origin to the witch-hunters' satisfaction: clearly the Devil had taken it back. Stubb died fearfully, under the most terrible tortures and mutilations.

Somewhat less ugly was the story of Jean

Grenier (see GRENIER), a clearly mentally defective youth accused of being a werewolf in southwest France in 1603. He brought it on himself, boasting of having killed and eaten many girls; and since several children had been killed in the area, he was believed and brought to trial. He claimed that he shifted his shape by means of a magic ointment and a wolfskin cloak given to him by a 'black man', whom he called 'Maître de la Forêt'. The judges sensibly decided that Grenier was suffering from the mental illness of lycanthropy, though they added that it was caused by demonic possession. Grenier was merely imprisoned for life, in a monastery.

Tell-Tale Signs

Since the days of medieval superstition and demonology, the werewolf legend – like so many others – has become a tangled web of older semi-pagan folklore and Christian strands of belief. But out of the tangle can be extracted a fairly clear picture of the werewolf's nature and habits, as he is known in modern European and American lore, and in those Hollywood films in which Lon Chaney Jr created the Wolfman.

The creature's appearance is fairly standardized, in the legends. When there are any visual clues that a man is a werewolf, they include extreme hairiness, straight eyebrows meeting over the nose, strong and claw-like fingernails, small flat ears, or sometimes pointed ears, and the third finger on each hand at least as long as the second.

In wolf form, the werewolf tends generally to be merely an extra large and ferocious wolf. But in some traditions (including the French) the shape-shifting is not complete, which adds to the werewolf's detectability. Gilles Garnier was said to have retained his human features while in wolf form; other tales speak of werewolves with human hands or feet. In the early 20th century, according to the French folklorist Claude Seignolle, a French farmer told of seeing two great wolves who conversed in human voices and who took snuff from a box produced from under the tail of one of them.

But it is rare for a werewolf, after the transformation, to be mainly humanoid – as is the Hollywood Wolfman, who after shape-shifting is simply a man with extra hair, teeth and agility. Even in the Middle Ages, when a hairy man began howling and saying he was a wolf, the experts generally agreed that he was mentally ill, suffering from lycanthropy. If he was a werewolf, those experts knew, he would be able to change into a wolf. Still, controversy often arose over occasional lycanthropes who claimed that they did change into wolves, but wore their hair on the inside. In northern Italy in 1541, one such claimant died under the knives of officials probing for proof of his statement.

These were the same kind of officials who generally agreed that werewolves had made a pact with Satan, who then bestowed upon them the power of metamorphosis. But it is clear that the Christian authorities were trying to patch much older werewolf beliefs onto their systematized accounts of devils. They did not succeed entirely: the seams show. For it is obviously odd and inconsistent that a would-be servant of Satan, who signed that pact, should ask only for the power of shape-shifting. One would have to be a Satanist of very limited ambition to want to be merely a werewolf; after all, any rank-and-file witch could change her shape – as the accounts of 16th century witch trials tell us – and a witch could also raise storms, wither crops, fly on a broomstick or other conveyance and cast a multitude of useful spells.

Of course, much laborious medieval argument arose over whether an actual metamorphosis took place, whether Satan placed the minion's soul in the 'effigy' of a wolf, or whatever. More rewarding, however, are the older, non-Christian ideas about how a werewolf becomes one in the first place. Several of these seem to involve the summoning of a demon to confer the power, but the being who is summoned is quite often obviously an elemental, a pagan spirit (like Jean Grenier's Maître de la Forêt).

How to Become a Werewolf

This conjuring up of an evil spirit is done by a complex ceremony, involving a magic circle, a fire, an incantation or two, application of magical ointment (like the witches' flying ointment) to the nude body, and final donning of a wolfskin cloak or belt. But the shape-shifting power can, in other traditions, come more easily. Sometimes it can come whether you want it or not – if you infringe some taboo. Italian folklore says that if you were conceived at the time of the new moon or if you sleep outdoors on a Friday under a full moon – you will become a werewolf. An obscure flower will, if eaten, confer the power of metamorphosis, according to Balkan legend; so will drinking from a stream where a wolf pack has drunk. Drinking water from a wolf's paw-print, eating a wolf's brains, or eating the flesh of a rabid wolf are the simple do-it-yourself magic for the would-be shape-shifter.

A few ancient writers thought that the power might be hereditary, while others thought that it might grow within a person who lived an especially evil life. An old French tradition tells of priests putting curses on criminals that forced them to be werewolves for seven years. And Paracelsus wrote that particularly evil, bestial men might return after death as werewolves.

The ghost werewolf occurs in a few other places. England's cruel King John was said to have risen after death as a werewolf. And several ghost wolves seen in Britain during the 19th century had human features, which identified them as belonging to this species. It seems that this minor aspect of the legend affected Hollywood: the Wolfman was a resurrected corpse, turned into a werewolf by an accidental combining of magical elements like the plant wolf's-bane and a full moon. But the living men with shape-shifting powers vastly outnumber the revenants, in werewolf traditions.

The technique by which the metamorphosis is accomplished is often the same as that by which the power has been acquired: so many legends say that the change requires, each time, the full ritual and summoning of the evil spirit mentioned before. But as always, folklore likes its simple magics too. Often the mere act of putting on the wolfskin belt will cause the change. In a few gruesome variants, the belt is supposed to be of human skin, preferably from a criminal executed on the gibbet. Some French tales say the werewolf must immerse himself in water, besides putting on the belt, in order to change – though elsewhere in Europe, the werewolf is supposed to exhibit a fear of water, a clear transference from the 'hydrophobia' idea of rabies.

Quite often the werewolf changes by stripping himself under a full moon and urinating in a circle on the earth, a technique used by Guy Endore for the hero of his excellent novel *Werewolf of Paris*, as definitive a work for this body of legend as Bram Stoker's *Dracula* is for the vampire. In a few tales, and in Hollywood's films, the full moon alone may effect the change; in a few others, though not as yet in films, stripping nude and rolling about on the ground may do the trick.

Changing back to human form may require the repetition of certain of these actions, like the rolling about or the immersion in water. Some legends say that the werewolf changes back automatically, at daybreak. Most tales agree that the creature instantly changes back to human form if it is injured or killed. From this idea come all those stories in which a hunter shoots and wounds a marauding wolf, later to learn that some local person has suffered an injury to the same part of the anatomy.

Chris Barker

The legends disagree widely on how a werewolf may be injured or killed. In many European tales, it can be caught or destroyed by the same means that would be used against an ordinary wolf. Peter Stubb, for instance, was pursued by men and dogs, and captured when he changed to human form in an attempt to outwit the pursuers. No one seemed surprised that he was as easily killed as any man; many other werewolves in European tales have been simply shot, clubbed or stabbed to death.

In other traditions, however, it seems that the power of the creature must be opposed by some kind of magic. In those traditions where werewolves are believed to be possessed by demons, the holy magic of the Church goes into action, to exorcize them. So a Catholic priest in French Canada is said, in an old tale, to have rescued a man from a loup-garou by magically changing it into its human form. And an old legend from colonial New England mentions a simpler exorcism, when a colonist drove off a pack of werewolves simply by speaking the name of Jesus.

Otherwise, rather more pagan magic is mingled with Christian elements in the werewolf antidotes. In England, Scotland and parts of France the creature is said to be immune to ordinary bullets; although, like vampires and witches, he can be killed by a silver bullet, especially if it is first consecrated in a church. In some instances a cure will be effected if the werewolf is called by his human name, or if he is called three times by his Christian name. French lore says that you may cure the loup-garou by taking three drops of blood from him, or merely pricking him to bleeding point, when he is in wolf form; it is not clear how you get close enough to him, in safety. And those who become werewolves involuntarily can cure themselves, it is said, if they have the strength of character to abstain from human flesh for nine years.

Monster From the Mind's Deeps

A fragment of fact, is to be found at the roots of the werewolf tradition. It has long been recognized that the mental illness known as lycanthropy is associated with a pathological condition in which the sufferer believes himself to be a wild beast and, as the old case histories show, develops a taste for raw or putrid meat, a desire to howl and run naked

Les Lupins by Maurice Sand: these werewolves of Normandy were believed to steal into cemeteries and dig up corpses to violate and devour

through the woods, and sometimes a wish to kill, rape and eat young girls. Although it is a rare malady, it may not have been so rare in past centuries; or perhaps other, more common types of sex murderers and child rapists of the past were assumed to be lycanthropes, the more so because such killings often involve an element of mutilation which might make Europeans think of wolves. Assuredly the werewolf is just as sexual a figure as the vampire (see VAMPIRE). But he lacks the sado-erotic subtlety of the vampire: werewolves are crude rapists and murderers, with a few ghoulish or cannibalistic overtones.

Despite this basis of fact, the werewolf belongs rather in the realm of sado-masochistic fantasies. Robert Eisler has thrown

The Lupins

In many parts of France, but more especially perhaps in Britanny, *Le Meneur des Loups* is a well-known figure. He is generally considered to be a wizard, who when the werewolves of the district have met and sit in a hideous circle round a fire kindled in the heart of some forest, leads forth the howling pack and looses them on to their horrid chase. Sometimes he himself assumes the form of a wolf, but speaks with human voice. Gathering his flock around him he gives them directions, telling them what farm-towns are ill-guarded that night, what flocks, what herds, are negligently kept, which path the lonely wayfarer setting out from the inn is taking . . .

In Normandy tradition tells of certain fantastic beings known as *lupins* or *lubins*. They pass the night chattering together and twattling in an unknown tongue. They take their stand by the walls of country cemeteries, and howl dismally at the moon. Timorous and fearful of man they will flee away scared at a footstep or distant voice. In some districts, however, they are fierce and of the werewolf race, since they are said to scratch up the graves with their hands, and gnaw the poor dead bones.

Montague Summers *The Werewolf*

some interesting light on these connections, in a theory based firmly on Jungian ideas. Eisler tries to trace the idea of the werewolf back to prehistory, seeing its origin in a primeval clash of cultures between peaceable, vegetarian early man and the brutal, fur-wearing, carnivorous creature that he was forced (by, say, an Ice Age) to become. The clash left scars on the collective unconscious that have still not healed.

Even in this over-simplified form of Eisler's theory, the argument cannot be easily dismissed. The werewolf *is* a monster of the unconscious, one to which folklore and superstition formerly gave fleshly reality and occasionally still do, in modern times: a French farmer in 1930 was accused of changing into a wolf at night; and in 1946 in America a Navaho Indian reservation was terrorized by a murderous beast which was widely reported as a werewolf. (Both Navaho and French traditions are rich in werewolf tales.)

But today the legend has generally retreated to a more subjective reality, without losing any of its horror. Nandor Fodor, the American psychologist and psychical researcher, has collected a number of dreams reported by people under psychoanalysis in which the werewolf theme — metamorphosis and murder — was brutally explicit. 'The old, savage lycanthropic beliefs have been relegated to our dream life where they are still active . . .' Fodor comments, 'the transformation is used symbolically as self-denunciation for secret deeds, fantasies or desires.'

Coming full circle, these psychological insights merely confirm that age-old and universal truth about the inner duality of man, the ravening beast within each of us. As Lord Byron put it:

Lycanthropy
I comprehend, for without transformation
Men become wolves on any slight occasion.

History as well as folklore shows that many of us are more than likely to let the beast take over, in an inner 'shape-shifting'. (See also BERTRAND.)

DOUGLAS HILL

FURTHER READING: Robert Eisler, *Man Into Wolf* (Ross-Erikson, 1978); Montague Summers, *The Werewolf* (Citadel Press, 1973).

WHALE

THE ANCESTORS of the whale were probably land mammals, whose structure became adapted to living in the sea. Because of its immense size and energy, the whale has attracted a wealth of superstition and folk-lore. In medieval times, for instance, it was regarded as an aggressive creature armed with huge tusks, a misconception that probably arose from a confusion between the whale and the walrus.

The whale is called 'Fastitocalon' in an Anglo-Saxon bestiary and is described as a deceptive floater on ocean streams, upon which men build a fire and sink to the hall of death; in other words, when the immense bulk of a whale was at rest on the ocean's surface it would occasionally be mistaken for an island by naïve sailors who, in attempting to land upon it, would be suddenly plunged to a watery grave. A similar story is told about the kraken (see KRAKEN). Perhaps because ambergris was an ingredient in perfume the whale was said to have so sweet a breath that fish were lured into its wide-open jaws. As a result of this mistaken belief the creature became the symbol of deceitfulness. It also stood for unintelligent immensity, violent passion and lust.

The whale was worshipped as Mama-cocha, or 'Mother Sea', among the Indians on the east coast of Central America. The Arabians believed that a fabulous whale, Bahamut, provided the base upon which the whole world rested, and that earthquakes were the result of its movements. (The beast referred to in Job 40.15, by the similar name of Behemoth, is now considered to have been the hippopotamus.) The whale that swallowed Jonah (see JONAH), and in whose belly the prophet spent three days and three nights, is one of the ten animals that have been allowed to enter paradise, according to Mohammedan legend.

In Christian thought the whale became

According to Mohammedan legend, the whale that swallowed Jonah, and in whose belly the prophet spent three days and three nights, is one of the ten animals allowed to enter paradise: *Jonah and the Whale* by David Jones

an allegory of evil, the emblem of the Devil, the archetypal snare, baited with sweet aromas, which lured the unwary to eternal damnation. The whale's mouth has often been depicted as the gateway to the otherworld, while its belly has been said to symbolize the infernal regions.

Among some Indian tribes on the western coast of America, the whale was regarded as a totem animal, and was thought to have the power to sink enemy canoes. Whales' teeth and whalebone are both supposed to be extremely effective as amulets; in fact, the teeth have been used for that purpose since Neolithic times. Chieftains of Tonga, Soma and Fiji wore necklaces of whales' teeth, shaped like curved claws, as signs

An allegory of evil in Christian thought, the whale was the emblem of the Devil; its mouth has been regarded as the gateway to the otherworld, while its belly symbolized the infernal regions: a demonic whale threatens a fisherman, illustration from Collin de Plancy's *Dictionnaire Infernal* (1863)

of high rank. Pieces of whalebone were highly valued as charms since they were supposed to confer some of the physical powers of the whale upon the owners.

Ambergris, a grey waxy substance found in the intestines of the sperm-whale, is supposed to be a powerful aphrodisiac. According to Boswell, the biographer of Dr Johnson, it produces 'a greater activity in

the intellectual faculties, a disposition to cheerfulness, and venereal desires'.

Primitive whale hunts were associated with a number of specially devised magic rituals which were thought to be necessary because of the dangers involved in hunting. Among the Eskimo, the hereditary role of whaler verged on shamanism, and the whaler was skilled in the art of psychic mimicry and the imposition of taboos. Ritual purity was essential among Greenland hunters if the chase was to be successful, and anyone who wore soiled garments, or who had been in physical contact with a corpse, was excluded from the party. Chastity on the part of the tribal chief was obligatory in many communities. Siberian whale-hunters sought to pacify the mother whale, whose offspring they proposed to kill, with prayers for forgiveness.

Among the Indians of the Bering Straits all work was suspended for four days after a whale had been slaughtered, in the belief that its ghost lingered in the vicinity of its body for this length of time. The Annamese, of what is now Vietnam, regarded even a dead whale washed up on the beach with considerable awe, and always buried the body with elaborate ceremonies which included burning incense and firing crackers.

Shape-shifting between the whale and other creatures of land and sea was not unknown. An Icelandic myth tells of a godless youth who was condemned to assume the shape of a whale as a punishment, and who was killed when he attempted to swim up a waterfall. North American Indians have legends of a terrible killer whale which approaches the shore and assumes the shape of a ravening wolf. In 887 AD a snow-white mermaid, 190 feet long, was reported and was said to be the metamorphosis of a white whale.

The whale represents one of the great cosmic forces of the universe. This symbolism is found in Herman Melville's *Moby Dick*, which tells how Captain Ahab pursues, and finally destroys, the great white whale. This has been interpreted as the eternal conflict between good (Ahab) and evil (the whale), as the war in heaven which led to the downfall of Lucifer. On the other hand, some have maintained that the white whale is the spirit of absolute goodness, while the proud Ahab is evil.

WHEEL

THE WHEEL ranks with money and writing as one of the greatest single contributions to human progress and, like them, it evolved (and is still evolving) rather than coming into existence as the result of a unique act of invention. No one will ever know for certain where, when and how the decisive stages in this evolution were achieved, but present archeological evidence suggests that the first object we should recognize as a wheel was used under a kind of sledge in Mesopotamia, c 3500 BC. This early wheel was solid, and the axle was an integral part of it. It may have been another five centuries before a wheel which revolved about its axle was

invented. The connection between this primitive cartwheel and the potter's wheel is not known, but some archeologists believe that the two kinds of wheel came into existence at about the same period.

At an early stage in its evolution, the wheel became a cult object, with religious, mythological and magic attributes. Here again, the actual process by which these attributes were acquired is lost in the mists of prehistory, but the wheel became associated with the sun, which Stone Age man had already represented as a disc in rock carvings, before the wheel as such was known. The association, being very ancient, is widespread. In Scandinavian myths, elves call the sun 'fair wheel', and in the far away Java Sea, the Balinese fire god is always represented as dancing on

a fiery wheel, the symbol of the sun. The ancient Egyptians used to place a winged solar disc over the gateway of every temple forecourt. The stages by which this disc evolved into a spoked wheel can be traced in places as far apart as Greece and Japan.

Wheel of Time

Connected with the sun wheel is the wheel as a symbol of the year, and also of time, which is found in various Indian myths. In the belief of one Indian sect, the Jains (see JAINS), time is endless, and is pictured as a wheel of 12 spokes. The spokes are divided into two sets of six, one representing a 'descending' phase, in which good things gradually give place to bad, and the other an 'ascending' phase, which shows the opposite tendency. According to the Jains, we are living now in the fifth 'spoke' of the descending phase.

A similar notion of descending and ascending phases is symbolized in the Wheel of Fortune of the Tarot cards, and there may be a link with ancient ideas about good and evil, or constructive and destructive forces in the universe. Thus, in the characteristically dualist system of Manichean beliefs, the Creator builds a cosmic wheel, also representing the two opposed forces. The 12 spokes of the Jain wheel of time are obviously linked with the 12 equal parts of the zodiac. The Manichean cosmic wheel also contains 12 buckets for the raising of souls, another reference to zodiacal ideas.

In magic and religion, however, the symbolic wheel has four spokes more often than 12. In Greek mythology, Ixion is bound to an eternally revolving four-spoked wheel as a punishment for trying to seduce Hera, the queen of heaven. In his great work on Zeus, A. B. Cook argued that Ixion represents a long line of human beings who were sacrificed in bygone ages 'as effete embodiments of the sun-god'. Cook also believed that a sun wheel like Ixion's was represented in the love charm which Aphrodite devised to enable Jason to win the love of Medea. A bird, the wryneck, itself the nymph Iynx transformed by Hera as a punishment for seducing Zeus, was fastened to a magic wheel, which also had four spokes. In later Greek love magic, the bird was largely forgotten, and the charm was merely a simple wheel, pierced with two holes and threaded with string, which was made to rotate by pulling the string. This magic wheel, sometimes with jagged edges representing the rays of the sun, and often with four spokes, occurs frequently as a motif on certain types of ancient Greek pottery. The same wheel was hung on the gables of a temple at Delphi, and an ancient Babylonian tablet, depicting an event which took place c 870 BC, shows a sun disc with two sets of four spokes suspended on ropes held in the hands of two divine beings poised on the roof of a shrine. The prayer wheel of Tibetan monks comes to mind in this connection, and here also there is an essential link with sun worship.

Temple wheels and prayer wheels, found in India, Tibet, ancient Egypt and Gaul, Greece and Japan, have a long ancestry, going back, as with many widespread ideas and objects, to the Babylonians. Worshippers were supposed to turn them in paying adoration to the gods, either imitating the rotatory movement of the heavens, or turning from one god to another. Some bronze wheels suspended on the doorposts of Egyptian sanctuaries emitted water, so that worshippers could sprinkle themselves. In medieval churches in Europe, the Wheel of Fortune hung up to the roof was a common sight. It was worked with a rope, and regarded as an oracle. The ancient Roman goddess Fortuna was depicted in statuettes and on coins seated on a wheel, and Roman writers from Cicero onwards frequently mention Fortuna's wheel. Fortuna is not the only ancient goddess to be represented with a

wheel: so are Nemesis and Isis. Perhaps the inevitability and randomness, which can both easily be associated with the turn of a wheel, are present here, but the original connection may well have been with the worship of the sun. Scholars have drawn attention to the fact that one of Fortuna's temples (associated with her interest in

Below **Prayer wheels in the Golden Temple, Tibet; they convey a blessing when turned to the right, the side of good, but a curse when the movement is to the left, the side of evil** *Bottom* **The belief that all men are shackled to the 'wheel of life', and that they must be reborn on earth until all karma is expended, is a basic concept in Hinduism and Buddhism: Tibetan 'wheel of life'**

farms and gardens) was dedicated on the summer solstice.

The summer solstice, or Midsummer Day (see MIDSUMMER EVE), was certainly associated with magic wheels (relics of sun worship) in medieval Europe. There is a possible link with Druidic worship in the custom at Douai, in northern France, of carrying a large Wheel of Fortune in procession before a wickerwork giant. But more commonly, a blazing wheel was rolled down hill, burning discs or wheels were flung into the air, or fresh fire was kindled by rotating a wheel on a wooden axle. Another custom was to set fire to a tar barrel and swing it round a pole. There is a possible reference to such customs in connection with the celebration of St John the Baptist's

William MacQuitty

C. Nelson Stewart

day as early as the 7th century. An 11th century writer describes quite clearly a wheel set alight and brandished in the air. An edict issued in a German principality in 1566 expressly forbids the use of fire wheels on St John the Baptist's day, which it lumps with 'other heathen and superstitious practices'. The wheel in question certainly was a relic of pagan sun worship and of imitative magic intended to ensure good weather for the harvest, but the connection with St John the Baptist was rationalized by referring to him as a 'burning and shining light' who was the forerunner of the true light.

The rolling of the wheel was taken to signify the rising of the sun to the highest part of its orbit before it must descend, which was

again analogous to the role of the Baptist, who says of Christ (John 3.30), 'He must increase, but I must decrease.' The wheel, by a not entirely coincidental analogy, is also a symbol of contraction and expansion as well as of ascent and descent. But here, one cannot tell which idea came first, for the celebration of St John's day at the summer solstice, as the turning point of the year, must surely be connected with his prophecy about increase and decrease.

Ezekiel's Vision
More trivial magic was also associated with wheels in the Middle Ages, all of it no doubt deriving ultimately from the sun magic. For example, before the spring sowing, peas were allowed to trickle through the spokes

of a cartwheel in some parts of central Europe. In the Tyrol it was believed that some kinds of swelling could be cured by rubbing against a cartwheel, and magic powers of marksmanship were believed to be conferred by mixing part of a molten spoke from a wheel on which a miscreant had been broken in the manufacture of shot. In folktales in many parts of the world, magic wheels or wheel tracks guide the hero or heroine on the right way.

The wheel also has other more mysterious magical and religious connotations, going beyond its association with the sun. The famous wheels seen by the prophet Ezekiel in his vision (Ezekiel, chapter 1) are susceptible of many interpretations: the 17th century mystic Jacob Boehme, for example,

British Museum

The association between the sun and the wheel is widespread; in Scandinavian mythology elves call the sun 'fair wheel', while the Balinese fire god is represented dancing on a fiery wheel symbolizing the sun *Facing page* Although the Wheel of Fortune is generally accepted as being a symbol of the inevitability of fate, it may originally have been connected with sun worship; one of the temples of the Roman goddess Fortuna, who was depicted with a wheel in statuettes and on coins, was dedicated on the summer solstice: Fortune with her wheel, from a 15th century French manuscript *Right* Detail from the Gundestrup cauldron; a Celtic deity who is thought to be Taranis, 'the thunderer', is shown holding a spoked wheel which may possibly be a symbol of the sun

C. M. Dixon

took them to be symbols of the spiritual and the natural life. Because a wheel is most simply represented by four spokes making a cross, and because four is a natural number of wheels for a vehicle, there is a link between the wheel and the four elements of alchemy. But the symbolism can become so diffuse as to cease to be specific. So Jung reads a 'symbol of the self' into Ezekiel's wheels, and through the four faces of the creatures associated with the wheels he traces a link with the four elements, thus connecting alchemy with his own version of psychoanalysis. As Ezekiel remarked, there are wheels within wheels, and the subject is a much larger one than most people in this wheel-crazed era of history would guess.

DAVID PHILLIPS

WHITE

WHITE has both positive and negative qualities. It symbolizes good, light, purity, peace, modesty and innocence, gaiety and happiness; but it is also traditionally the colour of weakness, delicacy, infirmity and cowardice. The more dominant associations of white are derived from its link with the light-giving sun and the other heavenly bodies, including the silver moon. Romans wore white robes when they sacrificed white cattle in honour of Jupiter, and the priests of the Egyptian god Osiris were also robed in white.

In northern Europe the Druids sacrificed white cattle in their sacred groves, and in general white sacrificial animals are regarded as unblemished and so suitable as offerings to the gods. Zeus was said to take the shape of a white bull, representing the twin forces of solar light and creative energy, and the sacred steed of the sun in antiquity was a white horse. In Teutonic mythology the god Odin is sometimes depicted riding on a white horse, and even today to dream of a white horse promises success.

The Vestal Virgins, who tended the sacred fire brought to Rome from Troy by Aeneas, were clothed in white, to represent virginity and innocence. The same qualities belong to white in Christian symbolism, and a bride wears white as a mark of virginity.

In Christian art, Jesus is generally shown robed in white after the Resurrection, and angels and the righteous dead are shown in white robes in heaven. Churches are hung in white at the festivals of all saints except martyrs. The white lily is an emblem of Easter Sunday, and processions of newly-baptized worshippers, garbed in white, gave Whit Sunday its present name. Curiously enough, in early 19th century England, the hallmark of a Radical was a white top hat, which was no doubt worn as a token of impeccable political principles.

White draws its negative symbolism from the fact that paleness has always been equated with bloodlessness and lack of vigour. The white feather is the badge of the coward and the white flag the banner of defeat. White could also be imposed as a badge of shame and repentance, as girls in the 17th century, who had loved not wisely but too well, found to their cost; they were made to stand in front of the congregation in church, dressed in white sheets.

In magic white was associated with the good magician and black with his opposite, the Devil's agent. Although the former were generally immune from charges of heresy, and the latter were the main targets of

White is connected with death, innocence, purity and the radiant light of the heavenly bodies, and in Christian art the angels and the righteous dead are shown in white robes in heaven: *Jesus Ministered to by the Angels*, a painting by James Tissot

Sonia Halliday

witch-hunters, white magicians were frequently sent to the stake during outbursts of witch mania, particularly in Scotland and on the mainland of Europe, under suspicion of working for the Devil.

The White Lady
There is a close association between white and death. Small white pebbles have been found in prehistoric graves, and until the late medieval period white was the colour of mourning in England, as it is today in China. The departing soul was commonly thought to take the shape of a white bird, usually a dove and occasionally a sea bird. Moslems believe that the souls of the just assume the forms of white birds, and wait beneath the throne of God for the resurrection. The belief that

all ghosts materialize in white winding-sheets is widespread, and spectres have been described as emitting a curious white light.

Fairy lore contains many curious allusions to a mysterious being, called 'the white lady', who is sometimes seen in the vicinity of bridges and is an omen of death. In Wales and on the Welsh borders she carries a torch with a vivid white flame. More recently she has begun to haunt motorways in Britain.

White animals and birds are often regarded with awe because of their rarity. American Indians classed albino animals as sacred and, in the past, sacrificed the white buffalo and the white dog. The Chinese consider the white tiger to be the

king of beasts, while a white fox with nine tails is regarded as an omen of good luck in many Eastern countries. In Scotland it was customary to give young children necklaces of white nuts in the belief that they would turn black at the first sign of threatening evil.

The racial problems of the 20th century have been exacerbated by the Caucasian superstition that white is inherently superior to black, which is in some mysterious manner devilish and debased (see RACE MYTHS). This is in spite of the fact that a pallid skin is symptomatic of weakness and ill-health and that the sign of physical vitality and virility in a 'white' man is usually a ruddy glow or a deep suntan.
(See also COLOURS; CORRESPONDENCES.)

The white magician of the past, like the psychiatrist of today, was basically a healer, and the complaints treated and the methods used were similar: whether we attribute our ills to devils or neuroses, the result is anxiety – and 'where anxiety exists, measures will always be taken to allay it'

WHITE MAGIC

DESCRIBED as an 'ancestral science' and also as 'the art of compulsion of the supernatural', magic is in practice a human technique designed to control the environment. It is based on the belief that the forces of Nature can be recruited to serve man's interests. In many primitive societies the control of these forces was one of the most important functions of priesthood, and it is only comparatively recently that magic has become divorced from religion.

The battle between good and evil or light and darkness, between white magic and black, may have existed only in the imagination, but it has always been conducted by dedicated individuals who were assumed to have access to psychic powers. The practitioner of white magic may have been a priest, magician or psychically endowed layman, but he always insisted that his supernatural operations were dedicated to the service of man, a claim that led to a great deal of contention. Both priests and magicians tend to insist that they and they alone have the qualifications to perform their vital role. This is why the clergy so often attacked magicians as agents of the Devil.

Magic has its positive and negative aspects, its active and passive principles. Similarly, magical practitioners may be divided into two basic personality types. One is the seeker after power, who strives to overcome his personal deficiencies by dominating others. The other is the seeker after wisdom who, driven by the same unconscious impulses, attempts to find the key to the hidden treasures of truth. The white magician, traditionally, calls upon God, angels and elemental spirits to supply the power he needs for his operations. The black magician is supposed to derive his particular powers from devils, and to have ghouls and other night monsters as his agents. Black

magic should not be written off for it can implant a degree of terror in a victim that may seriously harm him (see CURSE).

The history of the conflict between black magic and white suggests that in the main it is not the highly specialized magician who is held responsible for psychic attacks, but ordinary individuals, usually neighbours, who are thought to have the Evil Eye (see EYE) or 'evil mouth', and to be involuntary agents of evil. Among people who believe in bewitchment, the fear of being caught by it, unprotected, is ever present; drowsiness, for example, is supposed to be a vulnerable state which must be avoided at all costs unless one has taken steps to protect oneself by white magic, such as by wearing an amulet. The gospel of St John hung on a cord around the neck was thought to be effective for this purpose, as was the Lord's Prayer inscribed on a piece of paper and kept in one's shoe. The charm bracelet, which has become universally popular as a luck-bringer since its introduction about 100 years ago, is probably the last of the traditional protective devices, but many

people observe eccentric rites to which they resort when agitated. An unexpected example which I came across recently was the wearing of a violin 'D' string around the waist in order to benefit from its favourable vibrations. In the past, whenever personal systems of protection failed to put the mind at ease, a white magician was called in, in much the same way that a psychiatrist is consulted today.

In the country the white magician used to be a kind of general practitioner, the village Cunning Man or conjuror, while his urban counterpart, particularly in the upper ranks of society, tended to specialize in one particular art, such as astrology. In fact, the role of white magician will always remain important in a community that fears magic, or in one that has been convinced by its clergy of the presence of devils.

Doctor, Vet and Detective
It is not generally realized that in its heyday white magic involved a wide variety of socially useful activities which are not readily associated with sorcery. The country magician was likely also to be the local veterinary surgeon, treating sick animals with a combination of muttered spells and a sound knowledge of animal diseases. The name of God was frequently on his lips when he supplied his human patients with simples or ointments, or exorcized their ghosts and devils. When cross-examining someone who had asked him to divine the whereabouts of a lost object, he would combine incantations with painstaking interrogation. The white magician's status was sustained by the awe with which he was regarded in his community and, unless he was driven underground by persecution, he survived for just as long as people had need of his services, and while they accepted his peculiar version of reality.

An inveterate enemy of the clergy, whom

Corn dolly in Wales; made from the last sheaf of the harvest, which was thought to contain the spirit of the corn, dollies were kept until the beginning of the next season's ploughing to ensure continuity; this old custom, which was widespread throughout Europe, reflects the belief, a basic concept of magic, that the forces of Nature can be controlled and used for the benefit of man

Spectrum Colour Library

he tended to regard as presumptuous inter-lopers, the white wizard in Europe assumed a semi-divine authority, comparable with that of the African witch-doctor. This might be conferred upon him during his initiation, or it might be based upon some unusual circumstance of birth – in England, for instance, he might be the seventh son of a seventh son – or on an inherited power.

In medieval Germany and 19th century North America the charmer whispered or sang his patient back to health. At Castel-mellano in southern Italy, a small village which is regarded as a centre of witchcraft by people for many miles around, the *maciara* or sorceress treats her emotionally disturbed clients by tying knots in a length of string which is buried in a cemetery at the conclusion of the ceremony. The spirit of evil is destroyed by this ritual 'killing'. In 19th century England a wizard of Amer-sham in Buckinghamshire was reputed to have cured a sick child by instructing its parents to 'take the length of the child with a stick, measure so much ground in the church-yard, and there dig and bury the stick'.

The Spanish village of Mojacar, famous for its witches, was the home of a celebrated Almerian wise woman Tia Carrica, until about 20 years ago. She achieved some remarkable cures by tracing a cross with a finger on the foreheads of sick clients. She would then enter into a trance state during the course of which the sickness passed from her client's body into her own. She often recited the following spell over individuals suffering from the Evil Eye:

Three have done evil to you.
Three have to be taken away.
Who are the three persons of the Holy
    Trinity?
Father, Son and Holy Ghost.
Shepherd who came to the fountain
And came from the fountain,
Take away the Evil Eye
From whom you put it on.

The white magician in medieval England confronted with the same type of case used a very similar technique and recited:

Three biters hast thou bitten
The hart, ill eye, ill tongue.
Three biters shall be thy Boote,
Father, Sonne and Holy Ghost or God's
    name.
In worship of the five wounds of our
    Lorde.

Magic as a force can probably best be defined as the interaction of one mind upon another, with suggestion as its primary mechanism; psychic power is nothing more nor less than a peculiarly effective type of thinking. In Africa the witch-doctor is believed to possess an indwelling power which enables him not only to heal the sick but also to identify witches in the com-munity (see FINDING OF WITCHES). This consciousness of an inner force is common to most psychic healers and white magi-cians, and they usually believe that it can be preserved only if they observe an extremely strict code of conduct. If the witch-doctor submits to the temptation to practise magic

Colorific

Charms, amulets and talismans of various kinds play their part in white magic: in Mauritius fishermen attached images of fish to a tree; a form of imitative magic, this is thought to ensure a plentiful supply of fish

for illicit ends his power will leave him, or he will become a witch himself.

English folklorists report a similar moral code among the Cunning Men of the past (see EAST ANGLIAN AND ESSEX WITCHES). It seems that they always refused to work for reward since they believed that this would result in a subconscious pandering to the client's wishes, and that they would tell him what he wanted to hear rather than what he needed to know. Such insight, though rare, is not uncommon among white magicians.

The practitioner of white magic is com-pelled to be rigidly disciplined in his atti-tudes to day-to-day affairs, as he may other-wise fall from grace and his spells may fail to work. This leads to a permanent state of tension, which is in itself a sign of instability, a measure of the emotional disturbance common to 'possessed' people (see POSSES-SION). It is a widely-held view today that the witches of the past were often people who would nowadays be classed as suffering from some form of mental illness (see HYSTERI-CAL POSSESSION; OLD AGE; WITCHCRAFT), and the same could be said of witch-doctors. The Siberian shaman became frenzied as he entered the trance state (see SHAMAN), and it is well known that many white magicians have been emotionally disturbed.

Sonia Halliday

The social value of the white magician was to some extent counterbalanced by the dangers inherent in his methods of treatment. In his extremely informative book *Scared to Death*, Dr J. C. Barker devotes considerable attention to this problem. There are cases in which fortune tellers have implanted troublesome thoughts and eroding fears in the minds of clients, with disastrous results. It is a curious situation when the sick are treated by the sick, and when the rustic psychiatrist who sets up shop to abreact the community's traumas could be said to be in need of treatment himself.

Another aspect of witch-doctor practice, and one which led to many tragedies, was the hunting down and execution of so-called black witches at the instigation of white ones. Isolated examples have occurred in the 20th century. Some 40 years ago, for instance, the Pow Wow men of Pennsylvania were indirectly responsible for the murders of a number of innocent victims of popular prejudice. More recently similar cases have been reported from West Germany, where the belief in magic is today, if anything, even stronger than in pre-war years.

Aura of Responsibility

Although the definitive history of white magic in the British Isles has yet to be written, it is clear that much of it is of Germanic origin. The white magicians and healers of Anglo-Saxon times treated their patients with a combination of prayer, magical incantations and herbal medicines, based on the Doctrine of Signatures, the

Whether the practitioner of white magic was a priest, magician or psychically endowed layman, he always insisted that his supernatural powers were dedicated to the service of man; the most important of his roles was that of healer, in emulation of Jesus whose aid he often called upon when carrying out his healing operations: *Jesus Raising Lazarus from the Dead,* **wall painting in Cyprus**

principle that 'like cures like' (see DISEASE). They healed by touch, breath, and suggestion, and this in their day was probably the best type of medicine available. Medieval healing charms were often supplemented by a type of amulet that goes back to prehistoric times, and which is still used today to bring luck. This is the flint arrowhead or the holed stone, sometimes called a fairy stone, which protected both the byre and the bedroom from demonic attacks. The consecration of a fairy stone was an elaborate affair, and included the following incantation:

> I conjure thee, by all Hosts of Heaven,
> By the Living God, the True God,
> By the Blessed and Omnipotent God . . .

At the conclusion of the ceremony the magician cried out: 'May it protect you against all evil forces and curses, Amen.'

Such a blasphemous combination of paganism and Christianity was a constant affront to many Christians and gave offence to the ecclesiastical authorities, but there seems to have been very little they could do about it. Basically there appears to have been little difference between the magicians'

claims that sickness was the work of evil spirits, and the Church's belief that Satan was responsible.

White magic was apparently sanctioned, if not sanctified, because it was socially necessary. Given the choice between the faith healing of the Church and that of the more skilful wizard, the outcome was generally predictable. Love magic (see LOVE MAGIC), a primitive type of marriage guidance, was in constant demand by all classes in spite of the fulminations of the bishops. Geomancy and many other divinatory arts had the same meaning for medieval man as the newspaper astrologer has for his 20th century counterpart. Where anxiety exists, measures will always be taken to allay it. The law of supply and demand applies to every type of human need.

The white magician of medieval days competed successfully with the clergy for the exorcism of ghosts and devils, transferred the evils of sickness from the living sufferer to inanimate objects which were then ritually buried, and at the same time maintained his aura of respectability by insisting that God, Christ and the 12 Apostles were on his side. This is probably the reason why English white magicians were allowed to operate relatively unimpeded.

From a study of modern white magic it is possible to reconstruct some of the techniques used by healers until well into the 19th century. Magic circles with cabalistic symbols were drawn in order to conjure up what would now be described as psychic energy. Modern witches call this process creating the 'cone of power', and insist that it be directed to social ends. A variety of spells were used to combat black witchcraft, the most remarkable being the witch bottle (see BLOOD; IRON; MURRELL), which was used when the identity of a witch was unknown to her victim. A bottle which was often made of glass but sometimes of welded iron, and which contained blood, hair, nail parings, urine and excreta from the bewitched person, was heated on the hearth fire at midnight; at the same time the assembled company intoned the Lord's Prayer backwards. The witch was presumed to be undergoing excruciating agonies while the contents of the bottle boiled, with all the blood in her body afire, and this pain continued until she had removed her spell. If the bottle exploded she was expected to die. Witch bottles are not unknown, even today. It is possible that a few hysterics may have been cured by this bizarre rite, but it is doubtful that it could have had much effect upon organic diseases.

From White Magic to Black Box

The state's attitude towards semi-heretical magicians began to harden after the Reformation, despite the sympathy directed towards white magicians by the community generally. A few eminent European jurists, such as Paulus Grillandus, a 16th century writer on witchcraft who was a papal judge in the witch trials in Rome, were even prepared to tolerate white magic, at a time when witches generally were being persecuted, provided it was socially useful. However, strict adherence to the law of God, particularly to the command in Exodus 22.18, which is translated in the Authorised Version of the Bible as 'Thou shalt not suffer a witch to live', made it imperative that every kind of witch should be eliminated. The Bible also decreed that 'There shall not be found among you anyone who . . . practises divination, or a soothsayer, or an augur, or a sorcerer, or a charmer, or a medium, or a wizard, or a necromancer. For whoever does these things is an abomination to the Lord' (Deuteronomy 18.10-12).

Religious purists instituted witch-hunts to eliminate both black and white sorcerers. The Scots tortured and burned both classes indiscriminately, but elsewhere in the British Isles white magicians were awarded minor punishments unless it could be proved that they were heretics. These prosecutions were at their fiercest during the reign of Queen Elizabeth I, and gradually died down during the following century. As late as 1651 John Lock of Colchester was placed in the pillory for setting up as a diviner of lost and stolen property, and many other white magicians were sent to prison. Jane Wenham, the last woman in England to be found guilty of witchcraft, who was tried and pardoned in 1712, was a former white magician whose clientele had turned against her.

Although the Witchcraft Act of 1735 abolished the death penalty for witchcraft, practitioners of white magic were theoretically liable to be put in the pillory and sent to prison. However, there is no evidence that legal proceedings were ever taken against white magicians.

The traditional type of white magic is

Tibetan exorcizing dagger: the belief that sickness is the work of evil spirits is found in many cultures; in England the white magician competed successfully with the clergy for the exorcism of ghosts and devils, and maintained his aura of respectability, at the same time, by insisting that God, Christ and the 12 Apostles were on his side

still dispensed in the Channel Islands by bone-setters and healers, who often claim to be seventh sons of seventh sons. On the mainland the older type of magician had almost disappeared by the beginning of the 20th century, although a report published by the British Medical Association just before the First World War revealed that a few healing witches still survived in remote places.

Today the successors of the white magician may be found in the sphere of unorthodox or 'fringe' medicine. The 'Black Box', for instance (see RADIESTHESIA), which it is claimed can diagnose disease in the absence of the patient, so that it can be treated on homoeopathic principles going back to Paracelsus, has become a vogue in the present century; and there are even radionic instruments which are said to be able to 'broadcast' treatment from a distance. Healing by the laying on of hands – by ordinary men and women rather than priests – is as popular today as it was in the Middle Ages. Astrologers and diviners of every kind dispense their psychic powers in cities and towns, while in the countryside wart charmers and rustic healers have their following. Yet another manifestation of white magic in Britain is in the form of witch covens which flourish in some cities (see MODERN WITCHCRAFT). Modern witches insist that they are the only true heirs of the old magical healers. Needless to say, the Church looks on their activities with a jaundiced eye.

There is a certain similarity between the methods used by modern psychiatrists and those of the old magicians, and in recent years psychiatry has begun to examine sympathetically the functions of witchdoctors, medicine-men and shamans. If white magic may be defined as the power of the imagination to effect changes in mental states by helping the sufferer to relive his past experiences, and by this means externalize his problems and reduce them to manageable proportions, the comparison becomes obvious.

The Evil Eye may have ceased to trouble civilized man, but the 'evil mouth' in the shape of adverse news continues to assault his peace of mind and to require the ministrations of the healer. Although white magic can have no effect on the objective world, it profoundly influences the way in which it is seen. In an age of anxiety the white magician in one form or another can still perform a useful role; for this reason, white magic is likely to be with us for the foreseeable future.

ERIC MAPLE

FURTHER READING: David G. Phillips, *White Magic* (Scholarly, 1981); E. Maple, *Magic, Medicine and Quackery* (A. S. Barnes, 1968).

Whitsun

The season of Pentecost, commemorating the descent of the Holy Spirit to the apostles of Jesus (Acts, chapter 2): Whit Sunday is literally 'white Sunday', probably because newly baptized Christians wore white robes on that day; still a holiday season in Britain, it used to be celebrated with feasting, games and processions.
See PENTECOSTALIST MOVEMENT; SPEAKING IN TONGUES.

Widdershins

Or withershins, the direction contrary to the sun's apparent course, to the left, or anticlockwise; deliberate movement in this direction is sinister, associated with witches and worshippers of the Devil, because it reverses the normal and proper order of things.

Mansell Collection

Men fled to their homes when they heard the Wild Hunt approaching and took care not to look out of their windows; the leader was sometimes said to be the Devil, and his hounds were demon dogs, or the spirits of unbaptized children

WILD HUNT

A TERRIFYING BAND of spectral riders and hounds led by some divine, or demonic, or ghostly leader, the Wild Hunt could be heard on dark and stormy nights of midwinter (and sometimes at other seasons also), rushing through the air with a great clamour of shouts and horn-blowing and the baying of hounds.

Belief in its existence was at one time widespread all over northern Europe, Germany, France, and Great Britain, and traces of that belief are still to be found in the folk traditions of all these lands. It has been known by various names in various regions: the Yule Host in Iceland, the Raging or Furious Host in Germany, the *Chasse Maccabei,* or *Chasse Artu,* or *Mesnie Hellequin* in different parts of France, and numerous others elsewhere. In the West of England, it was the Yeth Hounds or Wish Hounds, in Durham and north Yorkshire the Gabriel Hounds or Gabble Ratchets. This last name literally means 'corpse hounds', from the medieval *gabares,* a corpse, and *rache,* a hound that hunts by scent and gives tongue. In some north-country dialects, it is also a term used for night-flying wild geese, whose cries, heard in darkness, so strikingly suggest the noise of an invisible pack of hounds passing far overhead.

It was commonly believed that to see the Wild Hunt as it swept by was dangerous. Men fled to their homes when they heard it approaching and took care not to look out of their windows. One version of the legend says that any person who could not find shelter in time was liable to be seized, carried away over long distances, and finally abandoned in some unknown region far from his home. He could save himself only by falling face downwards on the ground so that he could see nothing, and holding fast to any available plant or tuft of grass until the dark company had passed. To look deliberately at the riders, or to speak to their leader, was to court instant death or madness, or at best, some dreadful personal misfortune.

Odin, god of the dead, or Woden, his Germanic counterpart (see GERMANIC MYTHOLOGY; ODIN), is generally thought to have been the original leader of the Wild Hunt. Later on, when Christianity had dimmed the memory of the ancient deities in the minds of men, his place was often filled by the Devil. He too rode with a great company who were sometimes fiends like himself and sometimes the souls of the lost dead. His hounds were demon dogs, or the spirits of unbaptized children. The unnamed spectral huntsman who is sometimes encountered on Dartmoor and in other lonely places, riding without followers but with a pack of jet-black hounds, is almost certainly a direct descendant of the Devil as leader of the Wild Hunt. So also is the anonymous being who, in later legends, drives a sinister black coach in which the souls of dying sinners are fetched from the death chamber and driven away to hell.

The Night Hounds

In the Middle Ages, the leader was frequently neither god nor devil, but some human individual of heroic stature, renowned, locally or nationally, for the splendour of his former deeds or, quite as often, for the magnitude of his sins or his misfortunes. Dietrich von Bern (the legendary name of Theodoric the Great) was one of these; so was Charlemagne, and King Wenzel (or Wenceslas) of Bohemia, and Duke Abel, the fratricide. In one district of France, it was Hugh Capet, King of France in the 10th century, who led the host, in another, King Herod, the murderer of the Innocents. Gervase of Tilbury, writing in the 13th century, refers to a belief that Arthur hunted in the forests of England and Brittany, and that companies of his knights, with their hounds, had been seen there by foresters, at midday, or on nights of the full moon. At Cadbury Fort in Somerset (see CAMELOT), which is one of the places where Arthur is said to abide until the day when he will come again, local tradition asserts that he and his men rode round the hill when the moon was full, and watered their horses at a nearby spring. So too, on wild winter nights, he went hunting down an ancient trackway running from Cadbury towards Glastonbury, which is still known as King Arthur's Causeway. No one saw him then, but those who lived near the old track sometimes heard his hounds and his horses rushing by in the windy darkness.

In Shropshire, Wild Edric, the resistance hero who held out against William the Conqueror for nearly three years and was never defeated or captured, appeared before a war, riding furiously with his followers in the direction of the enemy country. Whoever encountered them had to cover his eyes immediately and keep silent until the cavalcade had passed. If he failed to do so, he would be smitten with madness. A rather uncertain tradition says that Sir Francis Drake used to drive over Dartmoor in a black coach, drawn by headless horses and followed by a pack of hounds whose baying killed every earthly dog that heard it. In this late tale we see a transitional stage between the ancient Wild Hunt and the spectral coach which eventually took its place in folk tradition. Here is the human leader who was once a god, and here are the hounds; but the hero does not ride, and the perils of his passage fall, not upon men, but upon dogs.

A faint memory of the legend lingered until fairly recently in the Meon Hills of south Warwickshire. On Christmas Eve and New Year's Eve, a solitary huntsman was often seen with a pack of hounds whose cries could be heard a long way off, and who were locally known as Hell Hounds, or Night Hounds, or Hooter. No one knew who he was; some said he was a master of foxhounds who hunted on the Sabbath and was consequently condemned to hunt until the Day of Judgement. Others said he was a man who had been torn to pieces by his own hounds. In one version of the tale he hunted a phantom fox through the countryside; but in another, he rode quietly with his hounds round him, as though returning from a day's sport. If he encountered any night wayfarer, he often asked the man to open a gate for him, or do some other little thing that a horseman might reasonably ask of a man on foot. But to grant these requests was dangerous. Whoever did so ran the risk, like his pagan ancestor long ago, of being suddenly swept away, not to be seen again in his home for a very long time, and perhaps never.

CHRISTINA HOLE

WILDWOOD

The forest of legend and folklore is often strange and eerie, an otherworld, the realm of Nature untamed by man, of unearthly and potentially dangerous beings

THE MOLE, in Kenneth Grahame's children's classic *The Wind in the Willows*, set off by himself one winter's day to explore the Wild Wood. It stretched before him 'low and threatening, like a black reef in some still southern sea', and once inside it he became increasingly uneasy. Growths of fungus on tree stumps looked like faces, and he thought he saw faces watching him from the holes in the banks. Nervously plunging away into the trackless depths of the wood, he heard a faint shrill whistling sound that came first from one direction, then another. There was the rustling patter of feet. 'The whole wood seemed running now, running hard, hunting, chasing, closing in round something or – somebody?'

Suddenly the Mole was in a panic, running aimlessly to and fro, bumping into things, falling over things, dodging round things, until he took refuge in the dark hollow of an old beech tree, where he covered himself with leaves and hoped he was safe. The Rat, who came to his rescue, told him that no one should walk in the Wild Wood without protection: 'I mean passwords, and signs, and sayings which have power and effect, and plants you carry in your pocket, and verses you repeat and tricks you practise.'

The uncanny quality of woods is part of the lore of childhood. In the forest you are far from home, from fireside warmth and kindliness and the settled accustomed order of things. In the forest you are lost. In the forest the trees put out roots to trip you, and reach out for you with crooked, skinny fingers. In the forest, very often, lives the witch. In the story of Hansel and Gretel, for instance, the two children are abandoned in the woods, where they become hopelessly lost. They find a little house made of gingerbread and sugar, and break off pieces of it to eat, but it is a treacherous sanctuary, for it belongs to a cannibal witch, who puts Hansel in a cage to fatten him up for cooking.

In another, peculiarly nasty, German fairy tale a little girl goes to the house of Frau Trude in the forest. She looks in through the window and sees no sign of Frau Trude, but she does see the Devil with a fiery head. When she tells Frau Trude this, the latter says, 'Oho, then you have seen the witch in her true colours: I have been waiting for you for years, longing for you to shine for me.' She turns the little girl into a block of wood and throws her on the fire. 'And when she was in full flame, Frau Trude sat down beside the blaze, warmed herself and said, "Now at last it shines bright."'

There is another highly disagreeable forest witch in Russian folklore, Baba Yaga, an ogress who cooks and eats small children. She lives in a hut, surrounded by a fence topped with skulls, in a clearing in the woods, and the hut spins round and round on chickens' legs. She is evidently an incarnation of wild Nature, for she guards the

Previous page The forest of legend and folklore is a strange and eerie place, an otherworld of unearthly and potentially dangerous beings; in modern interpretations it is frequently taken as a symbol of the dark, tangled depths of the mind *Above* 'The uncanny quality of woods is part of the lore of childhood', and in the forest trees put out roots to trip you and reach out for you with crooked, skinny fingers: *Jo's Wild Wood*, a drawing by Anne Said

fountain of the water of life, her teeth are of stone, she rides through the air in an iron kettle to stir up storms, and she is served by three horsemen, a bright one, a red one and a dark one, who are her day, her sun and her night.

Forest Primeval

Groves and woods have many symbolic connotations and are by no means always places of evil (see TREES). They may be a place of retreat from the bustle of the noisy human world to the peace of Nature, or the scene of amorous dalliance away from the neighbours' eyes, or the arena of the hunting of boar or stag. The forest of legend and folklore is not always what Edgar Allan Poe characteristically called 'ghoul-haunted woodland', but it does tend to be strange and eerie. It is an otherworld, the realm of Nature untamed by man, of unearthly and potentially dangerous beings. In modern interpretations it is frequently taken as a symbol of the dark depths of the mind, the wild and tangled growths of the unconscious.

In the forest you are lost. In the forest the trees put out roots to trip you up, and reach out for you with crooked, skinny fingers. In the forest, very often, lives the witch

In the *Odyssey*, the house of Circe, the enchantress (see CIRCE), is in a forest clearing. Dante's *Inferno* begins in a gloomy wood and in Shakespeare's *Midsummer Night's Dream* a wood is the setting for Oberon, Titania, Puck and the fairies. There is an old uneasy saying that 'woods have ears', and when we are still caught in some entangling thicket of difficulties we say we are not yet out of the wood.

One strand in the theme of the wildwood is the feeling of its immense antiquity, 'the forest primeval' of Longfellow's famous lines in *Evangeline*, where the murmuring pines and the hemlocks 'stand like Druids of old'. The Druids worshipped in woodland sanctuaries (see DRUIDS), and the Celtic and Germanic reverence for sacred trees and groves contributes to the haunted, numinous quality attributed to woods in northern Europe.

Another strand is the terror that the trees might move. In a frightening passage early in J. R. R. Tolkien's *Lord of the Rings* the heroes traverse the Old Forest, where the trees do not like strangers. At night they seem to be whispering to each other, passing news and plots along in an unintelligible language, and the branches sway and grope even when there is no wind. 'They do say the trees do actually move, and can surround strangers and hem them in.' One of the hobbits is trapped by a great grey willow tree, and Old Man Willow has an old and peculiarly sinister reputation among trees, as does the elder (see ELDER; WILLOW). Oak coppices, where the trees have been felled, are also dangerous places in which to walk at night, for the stumps hunger for revenge and swiftly grow new shoots which reach out for passers-by.

The Questing Beast
In Arthurian legend, the wild forest is frequently the scene of enchantments and encounters with supernatural beings and wonders, or the way to these beings and wonders lies through the forest. The Forest Perilous, located in North Wales in Malory's *Morte D'Arthur*, was the home of an enchantress who lured King Arthur there to seduce him, and he would have died there if he had not been rescued by Sir Tristram. It was deep in a forest that Arthur saw the Questing Beast, a most extraordinary creature (with which T. H. White had great

fun in *The Once and Future King*). It had the head of a serpent, the body of a leopard, a lion's hindquarters and the feet of a stag, and from its belly came the noise of 30 couple of hounds baying.

In *Perlesvaus*, a French romance of the 13th century, the Questing Beast is a white animal which has 12 barking hounds in her womb. When she gives birth to these hounds, they tear her to pieces but cannot eat her flesh. The author explains that the beast is a figure of Christ and the hounds are the Jews, who sacrificed Christ but cannot consume his body in the sacrament of the Mass.

In the *Didot Perceval*, of the same period, a young knight enters the land of Avalon and in an enchanted forest meets a beautiful maiden sitting by a fountain. They wander lovingly through the woodland till they come to a green meadow where the knight becomes unaccountably drowsy. He falls asleep, and when he wakes up finds himself the maiden's prisoner in an invisible castle. A similar story was told of Merlin, who was tricked and made prisoner by an enchantress (see MERLIN), a scene sometimes set in the Forest Perilous.

Sir Gawain and the Green Knight (see GAWAIN) describes how the hero, riding north to seek out the Green Knight, travels through the Wilderness of Wirral, on the borders of Cheshire and Lancashire, which in the 14th century was so infested with dangerous outlaws and outcasts that in 1376, at the request of the citizens of Chester, Edward III ordered it to be deforested. Pressing on through unknown country, he fights dragons to the death and battles with wolves, woodwouses (wild men of the woods), bulls, bears, boars, and ogres on the high fells. Cleaving his way through all these perils, he reaches 'a wondrously wild wood', a forest of oak, hazel and hawthorn (all of them magical trees), and when he comes to the Green Knight's castle he sees it shimmering through the oaks which hem it in.

Among his other adventures, Gawain reached the hall of the Grail after riding through a forest, and the causeway which led to the hall was roofed by trees which grew on either side, making it dark and eerie. Another Grail hero, Perceval (see GRAIL; PARSIFAL), was brought up in the forested wilds of Wales. Emma Jung and Marie-Louise von Franz (in *The Grail Legend*) see in this an image of both the

mother and the unconscious. The forest in which Perceval grows up is Nature in her maternal role as nourisher and protector, and: 'with its plant and animal life, its twilight and its restricted horizon, the forest aptly illustrates the as yet barely conscious condition of the child . . .' They also suggest that in general when the forest is the starting point of a hero's adventures, it 'represents the emergence from a relatively unconscious situation into a far more conscious one'.

The Wild Man
One of the alarming creatures to be found in the forest of legend, and in the old days in the forest of reality, is a woodwouse (spelt in various ways, including woodwose and woodhouse), a wild man of the woods. Perceval is something of a wild man himself, in the sense of a 'natural man' or 'noble savage', brought up close to Nature and far from civilization, so ignorant of the ways of the world that when he first sees mailed knights of Arthur's court he takes them for angels.

A more orthodox woodwouse, is the hero of *Sir Orfeo*, a medieval English poem based on the Greek legend of Orpheus, the great singer (see ORPHEUS). Sir Orfeo takes to the forest when his beloved wife is snatched away by the fairies. In his desperate grief he decides never to look at a woman again but to go to the wilderness, to live with wild beasts in the ancient woods. There he sleeps on the ground, gathering fruit and berries in the summer and in the winter reduced to grubbing up roots and gnawing on grass and bark. He grows cruelly thin, his beard long and shaggy, but on bright clear days he plays his harp. All the beasts of the forest gather round and the birds cluster on the branches to hear the sweetness of his harping.

In the woods Sir Orfeo sees the King of Fairyland at his hunting, with the sounding of horns and baying of hounds. He sees armed fairy knights riding with swords drawn and banners unfurled, and knights and ladies dancing in the glades. One day he recognizes one of the ladies as his lost love and unlike his Greek original, is able to win her back.

It was said that Merlin had been driven mad and sent wandering through the woods as a punishment for causing war. There was a Scottish legend of a forest wild man, said to have been encountered by St Kentigern.

C. Barker

He was naked and hairy, his name was Lailoken, and he had been punished for his sins by being made to live apart from humanity with only wild beasts for company: some said he was Merlin. In Irish legend, Suibne Gelt, King of Dal nAraide, was said to have gone mad after the battle of Moira in 673. He fled to the woods where, since he could fly like a bird, he spent much of his time roosting in the tops of trees.

The fact that the coat of arms of the Earls of Atholl in Scotland had a wild man in fetters as a supporter was explained by the story that a wild man had lived among the rocks at Craigiebarns, ravaging the countryside and terrifying everyone. After several attempts to catch him had failed, a man named Murray trapped him by

filling the pool from which the wild man drank with Atholl brose — whisky and honey — and so putting him into a sound sleep. As a reward the Earl of Atholl gave Murray the hand of his daughter in marriage, and Murray eventually succeeded to the earldom. (In fact, the Murrays did succeed to the title through a marriage with the heiress of Atholl in the 17th century.)

A celebrated wild man of modern fiction is Ben Gunn, in *Treasure Island*. He has been marooned on the island and has survived there alone for three years, living on goats, berries and oysters, and wistfully longing for toasted cheese. Shaggy, black with sunburn, dressed in rags and tatters, he is almost as timid as an animal, desperately anxious for human company and

Previous page In Arthurian legend, the wild forest is frequently the scene of enchantments, wonders and supernatural beings, or the way to them is through the forest: Sir Lancelot in the enchanted forest, from a French 14th century MS
Above In its beneficent aspects the forest has been described as representing Nature in her maternal role, nourishing and protecting, a concept reflected in the story of the 'Babes in the Wood' in which two lost children are fed and cared for by the animals of the forest: *Babes in the Wood* by Ralph Caldecott
Far right Robin Hood, the most famous of all forest outlaws, feasting in the Greenwood: in the outlaw legends the forest is a place of refuge and freedom from the demands of conventional society

yet scared of it. Robinson Crusoe, the Swiss Family Robinson, Tarzan of the apes, and Kipling's Mowgli are other fictional explorations of the same basic theme.

Outlaws of the Greenwood

The wild man of legend has his prototypes in real madmen who took to the woods to escape from the hostility of the sane, but his closeness to Nature connects him with two other figures, the Green Man who personifies the life of vegetation (see GREEN; VEGETATION SPIRITS), and the unearthly woodman who is the keeper of the forest and its creatures (Tom Bombadil in *The Lord of the Rings*). In 'The Lady of the Fountain', one of the stories in the *Mabinogion* (see MABINOGION), Cynon rides through the forest and comes to a clearing with a mound in the middle of it. On the mound sits a huge black man who has one foot, one eye in the centre of his forehead, and a massive iron club. He is the woodman, ugly to look at but not ugly in disposition, and he has power over animals. He demonstrates this to Cynon, who describes the scene. 'He took the club in his hand and with it struck a stag a mighty blow till it gave a mighty belling, and in answer to its belling wild animals came till they were as numerous as stars in the firmament . . . And he looked on them and bade them go graze. And then they bowed down their heads and did him obeisance, even as humble subjects would do to their lord.'

A giant guards the cedar forest in the Babylonian *Epic of Gilgamesh* (see GILGAMESH) and in some of his aspects seems to personify a forest fire. His roaring is like the storm, his mouth is fire, his breath is death. Gilgamesh and his friend Enkidu, another 'natural man', penetrate the forest through an enchanted gate, which paralyses Enkidu's hand when he touches it. They come to the mountain which is the home of the gods, and the sacred cedar which Gilgamesh fells with an axe. When the giant, Humbaba or Huwawa, appears, the sight terrifies even the valorous Gilgamesh, but the sun god sends eight great winds which hold Humbaba fast, and Gilgamesh cuts off his head.

Another variety of forest wild man is the outlaw, wild because he has been placed outside the pale of society and outside the protection of the law, and wild in the sense that, as Maurice Keen says, he is 'a desperate man and he has recourse to desperate

Mansell Collection

and violent remedies' and 'a cold and callous brutality'. The forests of medieval England sheltered thieves, vagabonds, fugitives from justice, men who had been turned off their land, rebels and misfits of all sorts. The poor, themselves suffering in a hard, rigidly stratified society, romanticized them and credited them with superhuman abilities. There grew up the picture of the merry outlaw in the greenwood, free as a bird, roistering on good ale and forbidden venison, robbing the rich and giving to the poor, the enemy of pomp, privilege and tyranny. Far the most famous of them is Robin Hood who, dressed in Lincoln green, has a connection with the Green Man and the May Day ceremonies (see ROBIN HOOD).

The forest is now a sanctuary and the wild man or natural man a proud, heroic figure, admired because he is free of the chains and shackles of society. The same aura surrounds highwaymen, and romantic wanderers and free spirits, nomadic motor cyclists, tramps and hippies, but here the lure of the wildwood has turned into the longing for the open road.

RICHARD CAVENDISH

FURTHER READING: *The Mabinogion,* trans. G. and T. Jones (Biblio Dist., 1976); *Sir Orfeo* is translated by Brian Stone in *Medieval English Verse* (Penguin, 1964). See also E. Jung and M. L. von Franz, *The Grail Legend* (Sigo Press); M. Keen, *The Outlaws of Medieval Legend* (Univ. of Toronto Press, 1961).

In many respects a typical member of Victorian society, 'Mrs Willett' was also a non-professional medium who played an essential part in the 'cross-correspondences', communications which purported to come from the spirit world

MRS WILLETT

UNTIL AFTER her death on 31 August 1956, Mrs Charles Coombe Tennant was known in the literature of psychical research as 'Mrs Willett'. She was a most remarkable non-professional medium.

Born on 1 November 1874, and christened Winifred Margaret, she was the only child of George Edward Pearce-Serocold (1828–1912) by his second wife, Mary Richardson of Derwen Fawr, near Swansea. Her paternal ancestors had been closely connected since the middle of the 18th century with the University of Cambridge and with the vicarage of the neighbouring village of Cherryhinton.

On 12 December 1895, in her 22nd year, she married Charles Coombe Tennant (1852–1928) of Cadoxton Lodge, Glamorganshire. He was the head of a wealthy and able family, originally of industrialists, who had sprung from northern England and had in the 18th century settled in Glamorganshire and acquired and developed property there. One of his sisters, Eveleen, had married F. W. H. Myers (see MYERS), one of the pioneers of psychical research in England. Mrs Coombe Tennant, thus related by marriage to him, came to like and admire him greatly; but she actively disliked his wife Eveleen, and she had no very friendly feelings for the latter's sister Dorothy, who married the explorer H. M. Stanley and eventually wrote his biography.

The Coombe Tennants had four children. The eldest son, George Christopher, and the only daughter, Daphne, died in youth. Daphne, who was born in 1907, lived only one year and seven months, but exhibited during that short period a most remarkable personality. Christopher, a young man of brilliant promise who became an officer in the Welsh Guards, was killed in Flanders in 1917 in his 20th year. Naturally, these early deaths of two very remarkable children had a profound effect on their mother. In August 1908 she wrote, and had privately printed, a memoir of Daphne. And she contributed a memoir of her eldest son to the book, entitled *Christopher*, containing many of his letters, which was compiled by Sir Oliver Lodge and published in 1918.

Mrs Coombe Tennant combined marked practical interests and abilities with outstanding gifts of mediumship. She was in many aspects a typical Victorian society lady, but she combined this with strong, and rather unusually radical, social and political interests. She was an early and enthusiastic supporter of women's suffrage. In politics she was a strong Liberal, and for a time a great admirer of Lloyd George. She took an active part in local administration in Glamorganshire, and was one of the first women JPs on the bench there. After the end of the First World War the British Government appointed her a delegate to the Assembly of the newly founded League of Nations. Of Welsh descent on her mother's side, she became a keen Welsh nationalist; played an active part and held high office in the National Eisteddfod; and was a discriminating patron of Welsh painting. Beside this, she made for herself a fine collection of modern French pictures.

It was probably through her brother-in-law, F. W. H. Myers, that she first became aware of the Society for Psychical Research and met some of its prominent Cambridge members, such as Mrs Sidgwick, Mrs Verrall, and the latter's daughter Helen (afterwards Mrs W. H. Salter). But it was not until after the death of her daughter Daphne that her interest in psychical research became strong and her own very distinctive type of mediumship developed. Its nature, and the course of its development, are thoroughly described in Gerald Balfour's 'Study of the Psychological Aspects of Mrs. Willett's Mediumship', which he contributed to the S.P.R. *Proceedings* in 1935.

The 'Palm Sunday' Case

The salient points are as follows. She had attempted automatic writing in the summer of 1908, after Daphne's death, and had obtained messages purporting to come from Myers, who had died in 1901. She had not been much impressed with these, but had nevertheless continued. Then, early in January 1909, came a sudden development. In a script, ostensibly coming from Myers, she received an order to stop writing, and to try to apprehend the ideas which would be put into her head, and to record them in ordinary writing as soon afterwards as possible. It was stated in the scripts that Edmund Gurney (see GURNEY), who had died in 1888, was involved with Myers in a special experiment which they were to make 'from the other side' with her help.

The next stage was that the 'Myers-persona' and the 'Gurney-persona', as we may call them, expressed and reiterated in the scripts the wish that she should give sittings in the presence of Sir Oliver Lodge, who had been a friend and collaborator of theirs in their lifetimes, and should dictate to him the impressions which she would receive from them. After considerable resistance she consented to approach Lodge, who was then a complete stranger to her. They first met on 17 May 1909 and she afterwards had many sittings in his presence, with him as note-taker.

Next, the Gurney-persona insisted that Gerald Balfour (later the second Earl of Balfour) should be introduced as a sitter and note-taker. He had been a close friend of Gurney's, had co-operated with him in psychical research, and was deeply read in philosophy. Mrs Coombe Tennant, who had never met him, resisted the suggestion, but eventually consented to approach him. The first sitting was on 4 June 1911. Thereafter he became almost the only sitter with her, and during the next 20 years hundreds of sittings were held, sometimes at Cadoxton and sometimes at the Balfours' home at Fisher's Hill, Woking, in Surrey.

These sittings largely took the form of elaborate conversations, with questions and answers, between the sitter and the ostensible communicators. The latter, purporting to be the surviving spirits of Myers and Gurney, explained the use which they claimed to be making deliberately of Mrs Coombe Tennant, the methods which they employed and the difficulties which they met in attempting various kinds of communication through her. Whatever their origin, these communications are on a high intellectual level. They are some of the most impressive recorded products of trance-mediumship.

Long before Balfour's study was published, two papers, one by Sir Oliver Lodge and the other by Mrs Verrall, appeared in 1911 in the S.P.R. *Proceedings* concerning the 'cross correspondences' in which 'Mrs Willett' played an essential part (see CROSS-CORRESPONDENCES). Balfour himself published two papers on the same subject, in 1914 and 1917. These four papers have become classics in the literature of psychical research. Between them they make it plain in detail that in her scripts 'Mrs Willett' showed a knowledge of particular facts and incidents and of highly recondite classical lore, which cannot plausibly be assigned to any source normally available to Mrs Coombe Tennant. These are, moreover, highly characteristic of the interests, the learning, and the idiosyncrasies of the deceased scholars, in particular Myers, Verrall, and Butcher, who were ostensibly communicating through her.

In 1960 Joan Balfour, daughter-in-law of Gerald, published in the S.P.R. *Proceedings* a long paper on the 'Palm Sunday' case. This describes how 'Mrs Willett', in a long series of automatic scripts and trance-utterances, between 1912 and 1929, seems to be referring cryptically, but unmistakably, to a certain very private and personal matter in the early life of Gerald's elder brother, the Conservative statesman Arthur Balfour (1848–1930). This was his love for Catherine Mary Lyttelton and her tragic death from typhus on Palm Sunday 1875, before he had declared himself. A sitting between Balfour and 'Mrs Willett' in 1916 is referred to and certain incidents in his last illness are described, when he was a very old man in 1929, in which 'Mrs Willett', who was staying in the house, seemed to be aware of the presence and intervention of Catherine Lyttelton's surviving spirit.

Mrs Coombe Tennant died in 1956 in her 82nd year, but on the face of it this was by no means the end of her psychic activities. For from 7 August 1957 to 6 March 1960, Miss Geraldine Cummins, who had been unknown to her personally, obtained a series of 40 automatic scripts purporting to come from her surviving spirit. They were published in 1965 under the title *Swan on a Black Sea*, and they have been the subject of much discussion since. Whatever may be their ultimate origin, they seem to be redolent of Mrs Coombe Tennant's personality, and to contain bits of highly individual information about her doings and feelings throughout her earthly life. (See also AUTOMATIC ART.)

C. D. BROAD

WILL-O-THE-WISP

MYSTERIOUS LIGHTS seen hovering or moving about in an eerie manner, especially over fens and marshes or in churchyards, have acquired a grim reputation in Europe under a great variety of names: including will-o-the-wisp, jack-o-lantern, fox fire, fairy fire, *ignis fatuus* ('foolish fire', because only a fool follows it), elf light, friar's lantern, corpse light, corpse candle, William with the little flame, Jack of the bright light, fetch candle or fetch light, a 'fetch' being a person's shadowy counterpart or double (see DOUBLE). The lights may be caused by atmospheric conditions or possibly by ignition of gases emanating from decaying plant or animal matter. They look like small, glowing balls of fire or like candle flames and are generally associated with the souls of the dead (see CANDLE). In northern Europe spectral fires were seen on burial mounds and were believed to be the souls of dead warriors, guarding the treasure which had been buried with them.

A will-o-the-wisp, jack-o-lantern or ignis fatuus, sometimes believed to be a wandering soul which cannot find refuge in heaven or hell, or sometimes a malignant imp, wanders about in an erratic way and, if you follow it, it is likely at best to get you hopelessly lost and at worst to lead you to your death in a bog or pool, though there are a few reports of the light being helpful and leading people out of danger. There are also stories of the will-o-the-wisp chasing a terrified victim through mud and brambles until he is confused and then leaving him with the sound of mocking laughter.

In German folklore, the light is thought to be the soul of someone who in life moved or disregarded a boundary marker, a way of stealing part of a neighbour's land which has been a particularly detested crime in many societies. The Finnish *liekkio*, 'flaming one', is the soul of a child who has been buried in the forest.

A corpse candle or fetch light, like a small flame moving through the air in the dark, may be a warning of your own imminent death if it hovers before you, or of the death of someone you love. Or it may hover at a place which will soon be the scene of a death. It may cross your line of vision between your home and the grave which waits for you in the churchyard. More often, it is seen going from the churchyard to the house of a person who is near death, in which case it is tracing in reverse the route which the funeral will take, or lingering on the roof of a house in which a death will follow.

The sea-going equivalent of the corpse candle is a glowing light called St Elmo's Fire, which is caused by electrical discharges during thunderstorms and is accompanied by a crackling sound, like the noise of twigs burning. It is seen on the masts and yards of ships and is generally interpreted, correctly, as a sign that the worst of the storm is over. However, if it comes down onto the deck, this is an ominous sign, and if it is seen glowing round a sailor's head, his death is very close to him.

An alternative name, corposant, is derived from Portuguese *corpo santo*, 'holy body', the body being that of St Elmo himself, the patron saint of Mediterranean seamen. His name is probably a corruption of Erasmus, the name of a martyr of the early 4th century who was said to have died at sea during a storm, after promising the crew that if they were not fated to die in the storm, he would come back and show himself to them. They waited anxiously and presently a glowing light appeared at the masthead.

A glowing ball of fire, the will-o-the-wisp, jack-o-lantern or *ignis fatuus*, has been known to lead men to their deaths: *Ignis Fatuus*, an imaginative 19th century relief by Henry Alfred Pegram

Tate Gallery London

WILLOW

A TRADITIONAL EMBLEM of grief and melancholy, the willow is also a symbol of forsaken love, and it was once customary for the jilted to wear a willow garland. In *The Merchant of Venice* Shakespeare describes the forsaken Queen of Carthage:

> In such a night
> Stood Dido, with a willow in her hand,
> Upon the wild sea-banks. . . .

Ophelia hangs her symbolic bunch of wild flowers upon a willow that 'grows aslant a brook', and Desdemona sings 'a song of "willow"' about a jilted girl, which ends 'Sing all a green willow must be my garland'. Unkind people would even send a willow garland to someone who had been jilted, often on the occasion of the unfaithful lover's marriage to another. In Wales the willow wreath was replaced by a peeled hazel wand.

It was not only the jilted but the bereaved who should wear the willow. In *Henry IV* (Part 3) when Bona, sister of the Queen of France, hears of Edward IV's marriage with Elizabeth Grey, she says: 'Tell him, in hope he'll prove a widower shortly, I'll wear the willow-garland for his sake.'

The association with grief dates only from the late Middle Ages; there is little doubt that the biblical 'willows' upon which the exiled Jews hung their harps as they wept by the rivers of Babylon were the Euphrates aspen, a kind of poplar. Even the 18th century Swedish botanist Linnaeus was misled by the Bible into christening the weeping willow, which actually comes from China, *Salix babylonica*.

There is, however, an ancient association between the willow and death. In the 2nd century AD Pausanias, the Greek historian, wrote of a grove sacred to Persephone, queen of the underworld, where willow and poplars grew, and also describes Orpheus holding a willow branch in the underworld. On the island of the enchantress Circe there was said to be a grove of willows, from which corpses hung. In China coffins were covered

Tate Gallery London

with willow boughs, and the trees were planted in cemeteries to suggest immortality. The Chinese also considered the tree to be magical and capable of averting harm and illness, a belief that is also found in Ireland, where the pussy willow, one of the 'seven noble trees of the land', was a charm against enchantment.

Because of its ancient sacredness the willow is one of the trees that should be invoked when a person 'touches wood'. The pussy willow provided the English substitute for palm branches on Palm Sunday (see PALM). It is sometimes thought to be unlucky to take the catkins or 'pussies' indoors, but more often this is said to bring good luck, especially if they are brought into the house on May Day.

In certain places the willow was associated with festivals held on St John's Eve, 23 June. In the Ile de France a figure made from pliable willow wands was ceremoniously burnt and at Luchon, in southern France, a representation of an actual willow tree was made from the wands. Snakes were thrown upon it and it was then set

Associated with death by the ancient Greeks, the. willow is traditionally an emblem of forsaken love; in *Hamlet* Ophelia hangs her wild flowers on a 'willow aslant a brook' before drowning herself: painting by Millais

alight. The background to these two extraordinary rites is obscure.

As with hazel, wands of willow were important in various magical operations, especially divination. In northern England, a girl who wanted to know whom she would marry could perform an alarming ritual. With her willow wand in her left hand, she had to leave the house secretly and run three times around it, saying, 'He that's to be my gude man come and grip the end of it'. On the third time round a likeness of her future husband would grasp the other end.

Because willow trees are often hollow, and decay easily, it was believed that a child beaten with a willow rod would be stunted, while an animal so beaten would suffer internal pains. However, willow trees were sometimes used in an ancient cure for children's ailments, notably rupture.

The child was passed through a natural hole or artificial cleft in the tree, which was then bound or closed up with willow twigs.

Willow is one of the few cases where the Doctrine of Signatures, the theory that 'like cures like' (see DISEASE), has proved to have a scientific basis. Because the tree grows in wet places it was believed to be a remedy for rheumatism, which can be caused by damp. A magical method recorded in the Netherlands was for the afflicted person to make three knots in a branch on an old tree, saying 'Good morning, Old One, I give thee the cold.' Later, according to Gerard, the 16th century herbalist, branches of osier, a kind of willow, would be brought into the sick-room; but the country remedy was to take an infusion of the bark. During the 19th century this remedy was investigated and willow (*salix*) was found to contain salicylic acid, which is now used in the treatment of rheumatism.

In the language of flowers, the weeping willow is not surprisingly the code for mourning, but the water willow represents freedom.

A. J. HUXLEY

'O for the wings of a dove': the human longing for wings and flight has been accomplished in one sense, for man can and does fly in his dreams

WINGS

PERHAPS BECAUSE man's body, wingless and earth-bound, has never normally been able to levitate, let alone fly, the ability to take off and soar freely away from terra firma, as demonstrated by birds, has aroused man's awe and longing. Ancient man peopled the mysterious upper and lower regions of his world with imagined creatures of unhampered mobility, often with winged

appendages, whether for flight or not, as a symbol of extra-terrestrial power.

In some ancient myths, the sky itself was depicted as a winged vulture, and the Egyptian sun god Re, when he was disenchanted with human beings, was advised to mount the Heavenly Cow, rise up and become the sky itself. The Mesopotamian god Anum created a winged bull, called the Bull of Heaven, and sent it to earth to redress a slight to his daughter Ishtar (the wings, however, did not prevent the bull from being slain).

In Greek myths Hermes (see HERMES), messenger of the god Zeus, wore winged sandals and a winged hat to make him invincibly swift and mobile. Eros, a beautiful

winged youth, sped where he willed to shoot his victims with arrows of love (see EROS). The Sphinx, a woman-fronted lion with an impressive wing-spread, killed people who could not answer her riddles, epitomizing the evil use of supernatural flight.

The Fall of Icarus

Of several winged horses in ancient myth, Pegasus, steadfast and courageous, travelled the air faster than the wind, attained the heights of Olympus and drew the thunder-chariots of Zeus across the heavens. Al Borak ('Lightning'), milk-white and with the wings of an eagle, carried Mohammed to the seventh heaven.

Less appealing, the winged Harpies,

which were partly women but had eagle's claws and beaks, swooped down viciously to seize man's food and depart, leaving a terrible stench (see HARPY). The griffin (or gryphon) had the head, wings and feet of an eagle and the hind-part of a lion. Only the female was winged; the male counterpart had protruding spikes instead. Aeschylus called griffins 'the hounds of Zeus, who never bark, with beaks like birds', and they were considered fierce guardians against theft. Nemesis, avenger of wrongdoing, was a winged woman carrying a sword or whip, who travelled the air in a griffin-drawn chariot. The hippogriff was a variant of the griffin, with the body of a horse, the forefront of a griffin and an eagle's wings and claws.

The terrifying dragons that appear in many legends are a compound of many creatures, including serpent, lion, antelope, fish and eagle. Although some alternately ran and flew, many seem to have been able to fly a considerable distance, and most were depicted with wings, signifying the ultimate in supernatural endowment (see DRAGON). The wings of the Roc (or Rukh), according to Marco Polo, who had heard of it from many sources, had a span of '30 paces', and the wing feathers were '12 paces long'. It could rise to great heights, swoop down on an elephant, bear it far up, then drop it and smash it, and, of course, descend to eat it (see ROC).

A moral lay in the experience of Daedalus, architect of the labyrinth for the Minotaur in Crete. Daedalus did not have wings at all, but when King Minos imprisoned him and his son Icarus in the labyrinth, Daedalus fashioned some with wax and glue, and he and Icarus took to the one available escape route, the air. Icarus, however, intoxicated by his new-found freedom and power, did not heed his father's warning to fly a middle course between the sun and the sea. He flew too near the sun and his beautiful wings melted. He fell into the sea and drowned. His sorrowful father flew safely on to Sicily.

Peter Pan

In later folklore (and theology), both angels and devils had the power of flight, and angels were generally illustrated with feathered wings, which they apparently did not need to flap to encompass distance; angels' thoughts and desires sped them without this effort.

By the 17th century, it was generally believed that angels ruled all spheres above the moon, and devils all below. The seraphim, highest order of angels, had no less than six wings. The main business of angels was the salvation of men's souls, and of devils the damnation of them. By purity of character, men might themselves become angels when they died, thus finally acquiring the supremacy of wings.

Although angels were generally depicted as having feathered wings in medieval art, they apparently did not need to flap them to encompass distance; it was believed that their thoughts and desires alone were able to move them: winged cherubs surrounding a statue, in Sicily

Fairies were considered nearer to devils than angels. Supposedly composed of condensed or congealed air, they took countless shapes, and were more often earth-oriented than celestial, though some were said to have been descended from gods. How, when and why they first acquired wings, is uncertain, though probably the form of angels was an influence.

Though fairies are frequently without them, their ability to become invisible in one place and visible in another, to steal in and out of shapes and sizes, has the same supernatural freedom of movement. In Shakespeare's *Midsummer Night's Dream*, Oberon has just arrived from India, and Puck takes but a few minutes to travel from England to Athens and back. Oberon

summarizes the fairies' eerie form of flight when he says to Titania:

Then my queen in silence sad,
Trip we after the night's shade;
We the globe can compass soon,
Swifter than the wandering moon.

The human child's longing for wings, or their equivalent for flight, is never more vividly portrayed or more happily fulfilled than in J. M. Barrie's *Peter Pan*. Peter, the boy who refused to grow up, knew how to fly. He taught the Darling children how to do it by simply believing they could, and then taking a huge jump from their beds into the air. Suddenly, as if wing-borne, they lifted up and followed him out of the window, gliding with speed and exhilarating ease to

Jeffrey Craig

Michael Holford

'Never-Never Land'. That their escape from adulthood had sad repercussions did not linger in children's minds as much as the identification with Peter's magic ability.

The art of flying, with or without wings, has been accomplished in one sense – man can and does fly in his dreams. In dreams man may have the pleasure of being conscious that he has risen out of his body's limited sphere. He may ascend only a short way, looking down at his still reclining and inert body, or rise high into the sky and fly across an ocean. Techniques range from a rapid flapping with the elbows, a forward thrust and outspread of arms that now act as wings, to a controlled tilting and angling of the body to balance it in relation to the air. Flying dreams of any kind are primarily

Above Symbols of extra-terrestrial power, wings were the attributes of many deities of the ancient world: winged sun disc, detail from painting on the coffin of a priestess of the Egyptian god Amen-Re *Below* Although fairies are more often earth-orientated than celestial beings, they are frequently depicted with wings

satisfying and delightful; whether man merely rises above his normal confinement, or right out of it, the added dimension of levitation and flight removes frustrating barriers to the supernatural.

Scientists are not sure how real wings were evolved, and it is now believed that they may not be appendages at all, but the extension of the *chitin*, the outer integument

or body wall. In any case, the outstretched human arm is just similar enough to the wing structure of birds to tantalize man with the possibility of developing flight power. Man has spent untold amounts of time strengthening appropriate muscles and appending strange devices to his person, to no avail. In vicarious achievement of his desire, he has flown kites and balloons, invented metal wings and even rocket propulsion. He has become airborne, but still cannot elevate himself more than a few feet off the earth, and this for but a fleet moment. Until he can do so, man will continue to be fascinated with the supernatural connotations of wings and flight.
(See also ANGELS; BAT; BIRDS; FAIRIES; SKY.)

NONA COXHEAD

Mansell Collection

WINTER

'There is food everywhere, heavy, rich food. And laughter. A positive urge to spend seizes on everyone . . .' What sounds like our modern Christmas is in fact an account of a pagan winter festival in the 4th century AD

IN NORTHERN LANDS the season of cold, wet and darkness has also traditionally been the time when the freest rein is given to fantasy. It was in winter that whole families in bygone ages huddled together in smoky huts listening, as the storms raged outside, to sagas and folktales. In winter, more than any other season, ghosts stalk abroad, and in the countryside a solitary light, glimpsed in the distance by a lone wayfarer, can flood the soul with emotion. Winter has always been, too, a time for feasting and celebrating. When harsh weather made warfare and even trivial disputes between neighbours impossible, and the concerted hostility of the elements made men mindful of their own essential brotherhood, it was natural to think of winter as the season of goodwill. There was also the gloom and tedium of long nights crying out for relief, and when the days began at last to lengthen, however imperceptibly, men looked upon it as the rebirth of the sun, and celebrated the nativity of a god.

The earliest of these winter festivals about which we know anything was the Sacaea in Babylon, a celebration of the New Year, lasting several days. From the third millennium down to the very end of Mesopotamian civilization, a few centuries before the Christian era, mock battles were held every year, in which the king impersonated the god Marduk, who had won a mighty victory over Tiamat, the watery goddess of chaos, on the very first New Year's day, when the world had been created (see CREATION MYTHS; MARDUK). In Babylonia new temples were inaugurated only on New Year's day, and from this day a king officially dated the beginning of his reign. According to later Greek writers, the Babylonian Sacaea was a time of sexual licence, feasting and disguising. Slaves gave orders to their masters during the days of the festival, and a criminal was chosen to have royal rights conferred upon him, only to be executed at the end of the celebrations. Whether these Greeks are reading contemporary practices in the Roman world into the Babylonian setting it is impossible to say, but if their reports are accurate, then the Babylonian festival must have been the ancestor of a number of similar celebrations in the ancient world.

The Roman Saturnalia, celebrated at the end of December, was a festival of merry-making and exchanging gifts which left its mark on our own Christmas celebrations. All work and business was suspended, originally for three days, but eventually for seven, and slaves were free to say and do what they liked. Gambling, usually punishable with a fine fixed at four times the value of the stakes, was officially permitted on these 'best of days', as the Roman poet Catullus calls the Saturnalia. Rich men gave their 'clients' presents of silverware, and children received little wax dolls.

A Greek writer of the 4th century AD, the sophist Libanius, has left a description of the winter festival as it was celebrated in his own city of Antioch: 'There is food everywhere, heavy, rich food. And laughter. A positive urge to spend seizes on everyone, so that people who have taken pleasure in saving up the whole year, now think it's a good idea to squander. The streets are full of people and coaches, staggering under the load of gifts. Children are free of the dread of their teachers, and for slaves the festival is as good as a holiday. Another good thing about it – it teaches people not to be too fond of money, but to let it circulate from hand to hand.'

Libanius was an early opponent of Christianity who nevertheless had Christians among his pupils, one of them St John Chrysostom. He is here describing pagan festivities in general, though he seems to have had the Saturnalia particularly in mind. The corresponding Greek festival, the Kronia, was celebrated at harvest time, but the Greeks had winter festivals, including the rustic Dionysia, held in December, and celebrated in villages with a burlesque procession; the Lenaea, or feast of the wine vats, celebrated in January with a procession, sacrifice and competing plays; and the Anthesteria, held during three days about the time that we call February, when the casks were opened and the new wine was tasted.

All the winter festivals were connected in some way with Dionysus, the god of wine (see DIONYSUS), and the Greeks in fact divided the cult-year into two halves, the Dionysiac and the Apollonian, corresponding to winter and summer. A similar division was made by the ancient Hindus, for whom winter was the time for ancestor worship and summer for the gods of Nature. In other parts of the world, too, winter is the time for appeasing the spirits of the dead. On the third day of the Anthesteria, the celebrations were held within the family circle, with rites in appeasement of ancestors. This festival came at the end of winter in Greece – indeed, it was to celebrate the end of winter marked by the appearance of the year's first flowers – but in northern Europe the cult of the dead was celebrated either in autumn, as among the Saxons, or in early or midwinter, as among the Scandinavians and Celts. In these pre-Christian festivals, bonfires were lighted to represent the waning and waxing sun. The rites were absorbed into Christianity in the guise of All Saints' day on 1 November and All Souls' on 2 November. Winter festivals in commemoration of the dead were also celebrated in China until comparatively recent times.

The Last Winter
Connected perhaps with the cult of dead souls, but also with the general harshness of winter, is the widespread notion that the world will come to an end in the middle of a terrible winter. This is the *fimbul-vetr* of the Icelandic sagas. In one of these poems, Odin, the god of the dead (see ODIN), asks the wise giant Vafthrudnir which of mankind will survive the mighty winter, and is told Lif and Lifthrasir, hidden in Hoddmimir's wood. In a prose saga of the 13th century, it is prophesied that winter will precede the great Doom (see SCANDINAVIA). Snow will drive from all quarters, with sharp frost and cruel wind. The sun will have no power. Three such winters will follow in succession, without an intervening summer. There will be fighting all over the earth, with brother slaying brother.

In Iranian mythology, the rain of Malkosh devastates the earth, and snow and ice cause most of mankind to die of cold and famine. The only men and animals saved from this destructive winter are those who are herded together by one of the gods in a great enclosure. There is a related idea in St Mark's gospel (13.18), when Christ, in prophesying the misery and destruction

There is a widespread notion that the world will come to an end in the middle of a terrible winter

which will precede the Second Coming, urges his disciples to 'pray that it may not happen in winter'. Other verses in the same chapter may have inspired the passage in the Eddic saga about brother slaying brother, but whether the Iranian myth shows Christian influence, or whether even older notions connecting the end of the world with winter underlie both the myth and the gospel prophecy, is impossible to determine.

The Sleep of God

In astronomical terms, winter begins at the solstice on 21 or 22 December, and ends at the vernal equinox, on 20 March, but in northern latitudes winter begins, in popular estimation, much earlier. In many villages in the Upper Styria region of Austria, it was the custom to 'ring in' the winter as early as 24 August, the purpose of the ceremony being to frighten away the malevolent spirits of winter by making a loud noise. According to a saying current at one time in Aachen, Charlemagne goes to his winter quarters on St Giles's day (1 September) and leaves them on Ascension Day, a reference to the army of ghosts stationed in a magic mountain that Charlemagne still commands. In other parts of northern Europe, winter begins on 28 October, 1 November, or 11 November – St Martin's day, the saint riding on a white horse as the harbinger of snow. Colder weather is supposed to set in on St Catherine's day (25 November), but in a warm year when winter is late, St Andrew's day (30 November) finally marks the real onset of winter.

The day most commonly taken as midwinter is that of the conversion of St Paul (25 January). In more southerly climates, January and February are regarded as the true winter months. But it is curious that

Left Illustration depicting the month of February, from the *Très Riches Heures*; probably as a result of the general harshness of the season, there is a widespread belief that the world will come to an end in the middle of a terrible winter *Above right* Christmas mummers and (*right*) the 'Wassail Bowl'; winter has always been a time for feasting and celebration, when the hostility of the elements made men conscious of their essential brotherhood; these traditional Christmas scenes reflect the pagan elements that are still an essential part of the Christian festival

Mansell Collection

Mansell Collection

Victoria & Albert Museum

In myth and folklore winter may be personified as a storm god or in the form of frost, ice or snow spirits *Left* Probably because of its beautiful, sparkling quality, frost seems to have stimulated man's myth-making faculty more than either snow or ice: *Jack Frost*, illustration by Arthur Rackham *Far right* Ice is the original stuff out of which the world is made in the myths of some Northern peoples: *Ice Fairy*, statuette by J. Causse

summed up in an oracle quoted by a Latin author about the time of the birth of Christ: 'The highest God is called Hades in winter.' Here again, there is a link with the winter cults of the dead already mentioned, and with ghosts, which are especially active in winter. In Nordic myths, winter is the time of the wanderings of Odin, or Wotan, the god of the dead.

The belief that dead ancestors are present in winter explains the practice of the Kwakiutl Indians of British Columbia who change their names at the beginning of winter, when the ghosts arrive, and adopt the names of their ancestors. They also form secret societies in winter, in place of their ordinary summer family life. The practice of exorcizing evil and evil spirits at either the beginning or end of winter is widespread among primitive peoples.

Probably owing to its beautiful, sparkling quality, frost seems to have stimulated the myth-making faculty of man more than either snow or ice. Jack Frost is our own personification of frost, and he seems quite a friendly figure compared with the evil frost giants of the Eddic sagas. These giants, the Hrimthursar, represent snow and ice as well as frost, and were descended from the giant Ymir, who was himself created out of ice. They had been driven out of their ancestral home by Odin and his band of Aesir, and dwelt in Utgard, the outlying world.

Porridge for the Frost Man

Frost is personified in Finnish magic songs, and Frost man appears as the brother of Mist man in a charming Japanese legend. But the frost spirits were taken most seriously by the Finnish tribes of Russia and Siberia, the Votiaks, the Cheremiss, the Mordvins and the Ostiaks. There was a 'Frost woman' as well as a 'Frost man' to whom sacrifices were made. It was the custom among the Mordvins (who live in the district lying between Nizhni Novgorod and Saratov, and who in Byzantine times scored many victories over the Russians) to place porridge for the 'Frost man' in the smoke outlet of their huts on the Thursday before Easter, in order to protect the spring sowings, for although the Mordvins had accepted baptism, they still clung to their ancient mythology and to many pagan beliefs and practices. The Lapps also paid

the Greek and Latin words for 'winter' (*kheimon, hiems*) are related to words in prehistoric languages meaning 'snow': the name Himalaya is cognate. In northern European languages, on the other hand, the words denoting winter are cognate with words meaning 'water' and 'wet'. The Greeks probably brought their word with them when they migrated in prehistoric times into their present country. In literature, at any rate, one can find as many references to rain as to snow and ice: 'The winter is past, the rain is over', says the Song of Solomon (2.11), words which Chaucer echoes: 'The winter is goon, with alle his reynes wete.'

In myth and folktale, winter is personified, either in himself, as a storm god (Kari

in Nordic legend), or through frost, ice and snow spirits of one kind or another. There are traces in prehistoric myths of a single god or goddess wielding power over both winter and summer. The Asiatic Nature goddess known to the Greeks as Kubele (see CYBELE) held the keys of the earth, which she opened in summer and shut in winter. The Teutonic lunar goddess Holda (the Frau Holle or White Woman of German folklore) holds summer captive in her underworld kingdom during winter. When she shakes her bedclothes, it snows.

The idea that Nature is asleep in winter is an ancient one, and the Phrygians believed that the Deity himself was asleep in winter. In primitive belief, winter and death are often equated, a notion strikingly

In central Europe, ice in winter was connected with good crops the following year

great respect to the 'Frost man', who was more like a god than a man, as he was believed to govern the weather, the snow and the ice, and sacrifices were offered to him so that 'the ice should not harm the reindeer and that the blizzard should cease'.

But frost is not the monopoly of the northern hemisphere. A tribe of Australian aborigines have the following myth about the origin of frost. The seven Pleiades (called by them the Meamei) once lived on earth as seven sisters, whose bodies sparkled with beautiful icicles. Several brothers followed the girls about and tried to seduce them with gifts, but without success. A man stole two of the girls, but could not manage to thaw off the icicles. These two girls flew up to the sky, where they found their five sisters already waiting. Once every year, the sisters break off ice from themselves and throw it down to earth. Then members of this Australian tribe say, 'The Meamei have not forgotten us.'

Snow Maiden

In the mythology of sub-arctic peoples, ice is the original stuff out of which the world is made. Ymir the ice giant has been mentioned already. He is one of many such giants, the personification, perhaps, of icebergs. In the Eddas, the god Buri, grandfather of Odin, was licked into life from a block of ice by the magic cow Audhumla. A legend of the ice sea was recounted even in the western mountains of Czechoslovakia, which told of twelve ice giants, enemies of the sun. It is these giants, says the legend, that cause eclipses of the sun. The ice wolf, who threatens both sun and moon with his baying, lives with these giants on an island in the ice sea.

In central Europe, ice in winter was connected with good crops the following year, if it came in the period between Christmas and Twelfth Night. Smooth ice in March was taken as a sign that fruit would be plentiful in some places, while elsewhere it was taken to mean the opposite. Long icicles indicated that the flax would grow long in the following year, and again, their appearance in the days following Christmas was especially important. Sometimes the appearance and the time of formation of icicles was taken as a guide as to the best time to sow. If icicles were forked, the flax would also be forked.

Snow is personified in the myths and folktales of many peoples. In Japanese lore, Yuki-onne, the snow woman, is a young woman with a ghastly white complexion, with a slim figure, and a gentle and alluring manner. She appears to any wayfarer caught in a snowstorm and exhausted in the struggle. She soothes him and lulls him to sleep, until he loses consciousness and dies. Sometimes, it is said, she incarnates herself as a beautiful woman and marries a mortal, but she kills her unlucky husband.

Other people picture snow, in personified form, as a man. In Nordic mythology, Snow is an aged king of cold Finland, with the name Snaer, 'the old man'. His father is Iceberg or Frost, and his three daughters are Thick Snow, Snowstorm and Fine Snow. Snaer is 300 years old, and when people wish one another a long life, they say, 'May you live as long as Snaer.'

Snow is not always personified as a powerful or fearful figure. A Russian folk song tells of an elderly childless couple who made a snow doll in their garden, which a passing stranger blessed, whereupon it became a living child. The blue-eyed, golden-haired little girl was very precocious – she was like a child of 14 by the time winter had passed. As the snow melted from the fields in spring, little Snow child avoided the sun, in which she wilted, and sought out the shade of the willow trees. Most of all, she liked heavy showers, and if there was a hailstorm she was as gay as if she had found a treasure trove. But on St John the Baptist's day (24 June) her friends took her on an outing. They were careful to keep her in the shade of the forest, but when night came, they lit a bonfire and leapt back and forth across it. Suddenly they heard a dreadful noise behind them. They could see nothing when they turned to look, but Snow child had disappeared, and though they looked for her for several days, combing the forest tree by tree, they could find no trace of their little pale companion. The old couple were inconsolable, and imagined that a cruel beast had carried Snow child off. But, says the song, it was not a beast. When Snow child followed her friends over the glowing embers, she turned into fine vapour, and rose as a cloudlet to heaven.

It would be possible to read a symbolic meaning into this apparently very simple story. The Snow child, sweet and innocent

Erich Lessing/Magnum

A feature of Greek and Roman winter festivals, the custom of giving gifts has been perpetuated in the Christian counterpart of these celebrations; according to legend, the Three Magi brought gifts of gold, frankincense and myrrh to the infant Jesus. Village schoolchildren dressed as the Magi walk through a snow laden forest in Austria to announce the birth of Christ to people living on nearby farms

as she is, represents the cruel winter, but for all the care she takes to avoid the sun, she is vanquished in the end. It is interesting that it is not the sun itself which melts her, but the bonfire which in pagan times was lit to celebrate the sun god at the height of his power, about the time of the summer solstice. With the triumph of Christianity, these pagan rites were transferred to the celebration of St John the Baptist (see also WHEEL), and in this Russian tale there may also be a barely conscious reference to the triumph of the Son over the powers of darkness, symbolized by the wintry phenomenon of snow.

(See also ALL HALLOWS' EVE; CHRISTMAS; NEW YEAR.)

DAVID PHILLIPS

Wisdom Literature

General term for writings of the ancient East concerned with practical rules of conduct or with philosophical wisdom; including the books of Job, Proverbs and Ecclesiastes in the Old Testament, and the Wisdom of Solomon and Ecclesiasticus in the Apocrypha; in Proverbs, chapters 1 to 9, Wisdom is a personified female aspect of God.

Wish

Among numerous traditional occasions for making a wish which will come true are on seeing a chimney-sweep, a white horse, a loaded hay-wain coming towards you, or a horseshoe in the road, provided you spit; when putting on new clothes for the first time; on seeing a hare or the first star of evening; or on seeing the new moon, provided you turn your apron back to front.

Wish-Bone

Or merrythought, the forked bone between a fowl's neck and breast; two people grip the bone and pull, while wishing, and the wish of the one who breaks off the larger piece will come true, provided he does not speak or laugh while the contest is going on, or reveal his wish.

Wishing-Well

A well at which you formulate an unspoken wish, dropping a coin, a pin or perhaps a pebble into the well as an offering; the belief that the wish will come true is part of the old lore of wells as the dwelling-places of powerful spirits.
See SPRINGS AND WELLS.

John Moss

'Although the epidemic character and the religious entanglement of European witch-beliefs make them different from the beliefs anthropologists have discovered among existing non-literate tribes, there are still many points of parallel'

WITCHCRAFT

IN MOST ENGLISH dictionaries 'witchcraft' and 'sorcery' are roughly synonymous. In anthropological usage they have acquired distinct meanings because an African tribe, the Azande (see AZANDE), are more precise in their categories of the supernatural than we are; and E. E. Evans-Pritchard, the

anthropologist who studied them and wrote what has become a classic on the ethnography of witchcraft and similar belief systems, found the existence in English of these two words a useful means of translating the Zande distinction. Witchcraft and sorcery are words referring to systems of belief centred on the idea that certain human beings in a community may harm their fellow men by supernatural means. According to the Zande usage now adopted by most of the anthropological profession, both witches and sorcerers are believed illegitimately to kill others or make them ill, to cause them to fall victim to accident or other misfortune, or to destroy their property. 'Both alike are enemies of men,' as Evans-Pritchard puts it.

Although people who practise witchcraft are generally regarded as being agents of misfortune, an exception is made for 'white' witches, who use their powers for the benefit of man; modern witches usually emphasize that they are concerned only with white magic: witches' wedding

They differ, however, in method and motivation. The techniques of the witch are 'more supernatural' than those of the sorcerer in that they are beyond the comprehension of ordinary folk, whereas those of the sorcerer are acts of destructive magic that are well known and reasonably accessible to most adult members of the community. As to motive, witches are believed to be slaves of aberration and addiction;

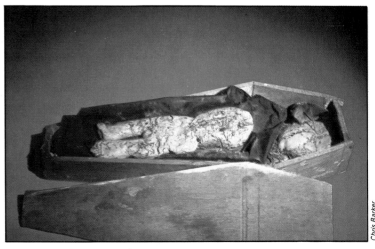

thus considered, they are weird, sometimes tragic characters. Sorcerers, on the other hand, are considered to be ordinary people driven by understandable, if disapproved, urges such as malice, envy or revenge, which are part of everyone's experience.

The propensity to be a witch is usually attributed to heredity or at least is considered constitutional, in the sense of having been implanted at an early age through mother's milk or, as among the Cewa of Central Africa, through a child's having been magically inoculated by a senior relative against the dermatitis believed to result from eating human flesh, an activity attributed to Cewa witches. Sorcery, on the other hand, usually demands no special personal attributes and is believed to be practised by anyone who can acquire the necessary magical substances (in Africa) or spells (in Oceania).

Most anthropologists see the advantage of agreement on the meanings of these terms as outlined; but there are some, particularly those writing on Oceania, who treat the term 'sorcery' as socially or morally neutral, using it for all forms of destructive magic regardless of whether it is socially approved — as it may be in property protection for instance — or considered illicit. Similarly, and this applies to historical studies of European witchcraft, the term 'witch' does not invariably have a sinister or evil connotation, especially if it is qualified by the adjective 'white', in which case it may be used in reference to those who cure people rather than kill them, or who help to find lost possessions rather than destroy them (see WHITE MAGIC). However, in most societies, more often than not, witches, like sorcerers, are believed to be agents of evil and misfortune.

The self-styled witches of modern society usually emphasize that they are not involved in antisocial practices such as black magic. This makes doubtful their inclusion in the anthropologist's definition of either sorcerer or witch. Their continued existence is as much a tribute to the inventive genius of Margaret Murray or of Gerald Gardner as it is to the strength of any continuing tradition (see MODERN WITCHCRAFT).

The Universal Witch

Beliefs in witchcraft (which from this point will be used in a generic sense to include sorcery) have been so widely observed that it has been suggested that the more important elements were probably common to Paleolithic man and spread with him to most of the presently inhabited parts of the world. There are certainly close resemblances between the beliefs in witchcraft revealed by the studies of modern anthropologists and those shown by historical and literary sources to have been characteristic of classical and medieval Europe. As Philip Mayer remarks, 'Shakespeare writing in 17th century England about mediaeval Scottish witches makes them recite a list of creatures that would be just as appropriate to witches in primitive Africa. Or again: the Pueblo Indians in Mexico say that witches go round at night carrying lights that alternately flare up and die down; exactly the same thing was said to me in Western Kenya by the Bantu tribe among whom I worked.' One might add that these widely dispersed elements would also have been familiar to Lucius Apuleius, author of *The Golden Ass*, a useful source for witch-beliefs in classical times.

Many of the works on European witchcraft, dealing with the early modern period, are concerned with a phenomenon very different from the witch-beliefs of surviving primitive societies or those of classical or medieval Europe. In the Dark Age, as Trevor-Roper puts it, 'there were witch-beliefs, of course — a scattered folklore of peasant superstitions, the casting of spells, the making of storms, converse with spirits, sympathetic magic . . . but on the whole

the mediaeval Church succeeded in containing them.' But the 16th and 17th centuries saw so great an upsurge in Europeans' preoccupation with witch-beliefs, with the craze encouraged 'by the cultivated Popes of the Renaissance, by the great Protestant Reformers, by the saints of the Counter-Reformation, by the scholars, lawyers and churchmen of an enlightened age', that Trevor-Roper is led to summarize: 'If these two centuries were the age of light, we have to admit that, in one respect at least, the Dark Age was more civilized.'

Servants of Satan

This means that the witch-beliefs of primitive peoples and those of early modern Europeans are in many ways not comparable. The first represent a chronic state, active but kept unremarkable by a society's normal mechanisms of tension management. The second reflect times of profound change when witch-beliefs, as sensitive symptoms of social strain, became intertwined with the religious, political and economic conflicts that punctuated the relatively sudden emergence of modern European society from feudalism. For this reason the events relating to witchcraft in early modern Europe might more appropriately be compared with the cult movements which, since the second half of the 19th century, have been reported from virtually every part of the world where native peoples have had to adjust themselves suddenly to the advent of Western ways of life. Just as the cargo cults of Melanesia, the ghost dance and peyote movements of North America and the anti-witchcraft crazes of Central Africa represent, as Worsley has put it, 'desperate searchings for more and more effective ways of understanding and modifying' a confused environment, so may the witch-scares of Europe and of Old and New England have played a similar role in blasting away the creaking and groaning remnants of an outdated social structure (see CARGO CULTS; GHOST DANCE; NEW RELIGIOUS MOVEMENTS; PEYOTE CULTS).

The most important respect in which the epidemic character of European witch-beliefs made them differ from those of non-literate societies was the fact that they were taken up in the conflicts of the late medieval Church, the Reformation and the Counter-Reformation. An early mistaken

Some of the witchcraft beliefs found in classical and medieval Europe still exist today *Facing page* The custom of using a doll to kill or injure the person it represents was known in Greece and Rome, and is still widespread *Above right* A doll in a coffin, found recently by firemen in a house in London to which they were called *Above left* The figure of a naked woman, and a sheep's heart, both pierced by slivers of hawthorn, found at a castle in Norfolk in 1964
Left In primitive rituals curses are directed at an effigy of the intended victim *Right* A witch with her familiars; animals and insects associated with witches include hyenas, owls and red ants in Africa, as well as the creatures which are generally associated with European witchcraft

identification of witches and heretics had the effect of marshalling a pre-Christian moral indignation against those who failed to conform with official Christianity. This fact probably prompted Margaret Murray's now discredited theory that European witches were the lingering adherents of a pagan religion. However, it also accounts for the fact that, whereas in all societies witches personify evil, in the society of early modern Europe they did this in a very specific way, being regarded as the earthly representatives of the Prince of Evil. In the course of time the chief criterion for identifying a witch in Europe or New England came to be whether he or she had made a compact with the Devil. Evidence of such a compact included the presence of a 'Devil's mark'

on his or her body (see PACT; PRICKING).

Witches were often accused of appearing in spectral form to tempt and torment their believed victims. In the Salem trials in New England in 1692, the screaming teen-age girls, who were the main witnesses for the prosecution, regularly claimed to see — in the very courtroom — the spectres of the accused (see SALEM WITCHES). The idea that the Devil could not use the spectral counterparts of people without their connivance was an important principle in establishing the guilt of the accused. It was sufficient for an accuser to state that he had seen the accused witch's spectre; and it was only when theological opinion questioned this principle that the rate of conviction by the courts declined.

British Museum

C. Barker

The Hoot of an Owl

Although the epidemic character and the religious entanglement of European witch-beliefs make them different from the beliefs anthropologists have discovered among existing non-literate tribes, there are still many points of parallel. The ethnography of witchcraft, the systematic description of this complex of beliefs in relation to the total way of life of the people or the period, has shown many similarities between societies separated in space and time.

Wherever beliefs in them are found, witches are conceived as having supernatural powers, antisocial tendencies and disgusting practices. They are believed to travel around at night by flying through the air on broomsticks (in Europe) or in saucer-shaped winnowing baskets (in Central Africa), or to move over the ground by riding on the backs of animal familiars such as baboons (in southern Africa). The range of animals and insects they are believed to induce to run their evil errands for them is wide, and includes dogs and cats in Europe and hyenas, owls, night-jars and red ants in Africa. In the Cewa language an owl's hoot is heard, not as a meaningless inanity such as 'To wit-to woo!', but as a clear and sinister *Muphe! Muphe! Nimkukute!* (Kill him! Kill him! That I may munch him!), and this inevitably links this weird bird with the necrophagous sorcerers who, the Cewa believe, bring them a large share of their misfortunes, such as illness, death and accident. Witches are usually credited with extra-sensory powers approaching omniscience, knowing by a sixth sense where a death has occurred and consequently where the next ghoulish feast will be held.

European beliefs reflect the medieval concern over sins of the flesh; for witches appeared to men as voluptuous succubi and to women as seducing incubi (see INCUBUS). A somewhat similar treatment of illicit sexual relationships occurs in the beliefs of the Pondo of south-eastern Africa: their beliefs seem to be related to the fact that custom excludes large categories of individuals living in the same neighbourhood from marrying or flirting with one another, and that the modern South African colour-caste system forbids sexual relationships between persons of different race. The less sex-ridden but more food-conscious Nyakyusa of south-western Tanzania, on the other hand, consider them as motivated by greed rather than lust.

From one society to another, ideas vary regarding the relationships between witches and their familiars, whether these be spirits, mythical creatures or animals. Among the south-eastern Bantu-speaking tribes of Africa, including the Pondo, witches are believed to have sexual relationships with their familiars, particularly with a dwarf-like creature called *tokoloshe* or *tikoloshe.* Although familiars are usually regarded as the servants or the messengers of witches, they are sometimes believed to urge their masters and mistresses on, giving their aberrant addiction a more feasible, comprehensible and somewhat tragic character. Even where no sexual relationship is postulated between witch and familiar, some kind of mystical link may be claimed. It was said of a reputed sorcerer among the Cewa that, when he had imbibed heavily, drunken hyenas were to be found in his house and that, when he died, his hyena-familiars died with him.

Attributed with special powers, witches are believed to be particularly difficult to bring to terms. Eternal vigilance and protective medicines have to be employed while they are at large and, once they have been caught, special methods of killing them have to be followed, such as burning them alive or driving stakes, pegs or nails into various parts of their bodies. Such practices, of widespread occurrence, are probably related to the belief that witches have special spirit-helpers or that they possess elusive souls, though not all those who follow these procedures are explicit about their reasons for carrying them out.

Supernatural Terrorists

Owing to their supposed deviant and often revolting practices, witches are everywhere looked upon as beyond the pale of decent living. They provide moralists with shorthand concrete descriptions of evil and parents with effective bogymen. To accuse anyone of witchcraft is a condensed way of charging him with a long list of the foulest crimes, and this action throws into sharper relief the moral precepts of the society to which he belongs. The fact that the witch is

used for making children more circumspect about their conduct is no doubt related to the tendency in many societies for beliefs in witchcraft to provide plausible points of backward reference in the explanation of misfortune. If someone falls ill or has an accident, both he and his fellow men can usually find some incident in his prior social interaction which will explain why someone had reason to have a grudge against him and why he should now be the victim of witchcraft. He may have quarrelled with someone of dubious reputation, or he may have failed to discharge an obligation towards someone who, though in a superior moral position, is now believed to have resorted to an immoral form of retribution.

This leads to the paradox that, though witches provide mainly negative instances of conduct, they may also play positive moral roles in being the points of retrospective projection for the 'victim's' feelings of guilt resulting from acts of foolishness and meanness. This moral import of beliefs in witchcraft can be illustrated from all those societies, contemporary and historical, on which data on such beliefs exist, and this represents an important convergence of the findings of historians and anthropologists. Witches are unmitigated supernatural terrorists in all societies in which beliefs in them occur; and sufferers of misfortune find in the witches' supposed actions the means of expressing their feelings of guilt.

Another anthropological finding has been more difficult to substantiate from historical materials. It has been found that, in contemporary non-literate societies, accusations of witchcraft and believed instances of attack by witches occur typically between persons whom the social structure throws into uncontrolled competition and tension, for instance, rivals in love or in politics. Accusations, which represent crises in the relationship between the alleged witch and the accuser, may thus be regarded as 'social strain-gauges', indicating where the tensions and role conflicts in the social structure lie. Believed instances of attack, involving the relationship between alleged witch and believed victim, have a similar significance but, since all witchcraft and most sorcery exist in the uneasy minds of their believed victims, they are on a different plane of reality and illuminate the society's own model of strained social relationships rather than the anthropologist's.

Closed Circle

These two models often differ from each other and either may differ from the accepted picture. For instance, people in most societies where beliefs in witchcraft exist usually claim that witches are almost invariably women; yet, if the anthropologist keeps a tally of actual instances of accusation or of believed attack, he is likely to discover that men, who are generally more socially involved and more in competition for positions of leadership, form a much higher proportion of those accused or suspected than informants' general statements would suggest. In our society, statements about women drivers are a parallel case.

Until recently the nature of the historical

Facing page While witches are believed to be slaves to aberration and addiction, other practitioners of magic may be ordinary people driven by urges such as malice or envy: illustration of a wizard by Arthur Rackham *Right* South African witch-doctor; like his European counterparts he uses his powers mainly to cure disease

COMPENDII
MALEFICARVM
LIBER SECVNDVS.

In quo agitur de diuerfis generibus Maleficiorum,
& de quibufdam alijs fcitu dignis.

De Maleficio Somnifico. **Cap. I.**

Doctrina !

 Onfueuere Sagæ,& Malefici, alios potione,malo car
mine,& certis ritibus foporare, vt interea illis ve-
nenum infundant, vel infantulos rapiant, aut ne-
cent,vel furto quid fubtrahant, vel ftupro, adulte-
rioue contaminent, & hoc fieri poteft naturalibus
venenis foporiferis,vt erit videre per exempla. Et
he non funt fabulæ,quia fi multa funt, quæ naturaliter,vel infufa,
vel admota, non fomnium aut foporem tantùm,fed etiam ftupo-
rem

Symptoms of social strain, the witch-beliefs of 16th and 17th century Europe reflected a period of profound change, and became intertwined with the religious, economic and political conflicts that arose during the emergence of modern European society from feudalism; an early mistaken identification of witches and heretics resulted in the belief that witches are the earthly representatives of the Devil: title page of *Compendium Maleficarum*, a late 15th century treatise on witchcraft

to specialization, not only in economic processes, but also in human relationships, with some of the latter personal and others impersonal. Instead of having everyone in the community breathing intimately down our necks, we manage in our modern way of life to escape, even if momentarily, the prison of personal relationships with their high potential for influence and control of our conduct, for love and hate, and, in general, for the ingredients of those delusions which in the right social setting become standardized and infuse the world with fellow humans wielding supernatural power. It is significant that, in most reports of accusations and believed instances of witchcraft, the main characters, like most of those involved in crimes of violence in even our impersonal society, have been intimately acquainted with one another.

An Open Society
Though modern man may have given up the more specific beliefs in witchcraft, he has retained many of its associated tendencies. He has not yet completely escaped from the charmed circle of taboos and magical beings that confines primitive man, and moved into an open society in which he has no qualms about adjusting his social institutions in the light of rational analysis. Some 20th century movements have many of the characteristics of a 16th century European or a contemporary primitive witch-scare. An accusation of political deviance may, like an accusation of witchcraft, prove an infallible means of destroying a reputation or a career. Arthur Miller's play *The Crucible*, which attacked Joseph McCarthy's anti-Communist cult in the idiom of 17th century Salem, brought out this parallel with brilliant insight.
(See also FAMILIARS; OLD AGE; SORCERY; and articles on European Witchcraft.)

M. G. MARWICK

FURTHER READING: Apuleius, *The Golden Ass* (Indiana Univ. Press, 1962); J. C. Baroja, *The World of Witches* (Univ. of Chicago Press, 1965); E. E. Evans-Pritchard, *Witchcraft, Oracles and Magic among the Azande* (Oxford Univ. Press, 1976); A. D. J. Macfarlane, *Witchcraft in Tudor and Stuart England* (Harper and Row, 1970); M. G. Marwick, *Sorcery in its Social Setting: a Study of the Northern Rhodesian Cewa* (Humanities, 1965); R. H. Robbins, *Witchcraft* (Kraus Intl., 1978); John Middleton and E. H. Winter ed., *Witchcraft and Sorcery in East Africa* (Praeger, 1963); H. R. Trevor-Roper, *Crisis of the Seventeenth Century: Religion, the Reformation and Social Change* (Harper and Row, 1967).

materials made it difficult to apply the 'social strain-gauge' hypothesis to European data. The historical sources that have been analysed have often not revealed enough specific information about the relationships between the important triad of accuser, accused witch and believed victim; nor have they always thrown light on the nature of the issues between them. However, with Macfarlane's recent meticulous combination of the latest techniques of English local history and the theoretical orientations of social anthropology in his study of witchcraft in Essex between 1560 and 1680, an ever closer convergence in this field is promised.

In any society that uses witchcraft as a regular explanatory principle, two features may be expected to be prominent. Firstly, there will be practices such as consulting diviners and oracles, and submitting suspects to ordeals (see FINDING OF WITCHES). Secondly, prevailing thought processes will be closed, in the sense that misfortunes, witch-beliefs and the techniques of witch-finding form a circular sequence in which each case of misfortune that is attributed to witchcraft reinforces the belief in witchcraft and renders a sceptical escape from the sequence unlikely.

As yet we have no satisfactory explanation of how some societies, including our own, have broken from this closed circle and abandoned beliefs in witchcraft. Part of the answer seems to lie in the larger scale of modern societies with their related tendency

WOLF

FEW EUROPEAN MAMMALS equal or surpass the wolf in the richness of its folklore, though in the British Isles wolf lore is much scantier than on the Continent, where in some mountainous forested regions the animals are still to be found. By the mid-13th century there can have been few wolves left in England but not until the 18th were the last wolves killed in Ireland and Scotland.

Much European wolf lore is pervaded by a fearsome awe, less apparent in North American wolf traditions. But although fear of wolves is a natural human reaction, the friendly wolf appears fairly frequently in myths and legends, indicating that the animal awakens ambivalent responses. The *Rig-Veda* tells of Rijrasva, whom his father blinded because with misplaced generosity he gave 101 sheep to a bitch wolf: the wolf prayed for her benefactor, to the Asvins, benevolent deities, and they restored his sight. On the other hand, according to ancient Iranian doctrines the wolf was created by the evil spirit Ahriman (see AHRIMAN). A similar belief is still current among the Voguls of Siberia.

The associations of Greek gods and goddesses with wolves hint at older traditions beneath the mythology of the anthropomorphic divinities. It was said that the priest of Zeus could take the form of a wolf. Hecate could also take wolf shape (see HECATE). Leto, the mother of Apollo and Artemis, appeared as a she-wolf and a wolf was emblazoned on the shield of Artemis, the huntress. Apollo (see APOLLO) was said to have expelled wolves from Athens and any citizen who killed one had to bury it by public subscription. Sophocles called Apollo 'the wolf-slayer', yet a number of myths describe how his children by mortal girls were fostered by wolves. This motif of children tended by a she-wolf reappears in the story of Romulus and Remus (see FOUNDING OF ROME) and in later legends. Despite this myth of the kindly wolf the Romans associated the animal with Mars, the god of war.

In Scandinavian mythology the Fenris wolf is one of the three children of Loki, the others being the Midgard serpent and Hel (Death). Fenris, whose jaws stretched from heaven to earth, created much trouble among the gods until they managed to bind him with a magic cord. However, as the representative of Fate he bides his time, until at the end of the world he swallows up the sun (see SCANDINAVIA).

'The friendly wolf appears fairly frequently in myths and legends, indicating that the animal awakens ambivalent responses' *Above right* Kipling draws on legends of human children reared by wolves, in his stories about an Indian boy who becomes a member of a wolf pack: illustration to the *Jungle Book* by Rudyard Kipling *Right* A famous legend tells how St Francis of Assisi tamed the ferocious wolf of Gubbio: a painting by Sassetta shows the saint arbitrating between the citizens of Gubbio and the wolf

The wolf was feared as an uncanny and evil creature, and credited with preternatural cunning *Left* in Scandinavian legend the Fenris wolf is a force of terror and destruction, brother to death and the World Serpent: the god Tyr sacrifices his hand in order to bind the Fenris Wolf, in an illustration from an *Edda* MS
Right The wolf seizes Little Red Riding Hood, after tricking her into climbing into bed with him: illustration from a 19th century children's book

The wolf has innumerable associations with the Devil, especially in Germany. According to one saying the Devil squats between the beast's eyes, according to another he appears as a black wolf. A legend relates that the Devil made the wolf out of mixed constituents – his head from a stump of wood, his heart from stone, his breast from roots, and so forth. The Devil of the witches sometimes took wolf shape. The cross drives away all such diabolical lupine apparitions, and although great ferocity is attributed to the animal it is said to have been cowardly ever since Christ struck it with his staff.

Because wolves were seen on battlefields feeding on corpses, the animals were transformed by imagination into sinister supernatural creatures. They were thought of as corpse demons, connected with Odin (see ODIN) and the fierce Norns or Fates. In Normandy horrible spirits disguised as wolves were said to haunt cemeteries in order to devour corpses. In Finland it was said that unbaptized children wandered around in the shape of wolves.

In Sheep's Clothing

Wolves have ancient associations with witchcraft. The Latin term of opprobrium *lupula* (little wolf) signifies 'witch'. Thessalian witches were said to howl like wolves and to use portions of the animals in their charms, as Shakespeare recalled when he included a wolf's tooth in the witches' brew in *Macbeth*. On the Continent gypsies would say on hearing a wolf howling, 'Take care, it may be a witch.' In Germany witches were said to ride wolves and in Lorraine the 'witch-master' turned into a wolf to go to the witches' sabbath. It was also thought that witches could transform themselves and other people into wolves. A priest who was turned into a wolf remained identifiable by his white collar. In the 17th century men and women were hanged for ravages believed to have been committed by them as wolves, although a century earlier Reginald Scot in his *Discoverie of Witchcraft* had ridiculed such ideas. The Navaho and other American Indians believe that a man disguised as a wolf goes around practising witchcraft.

The New Testament reference to false prophets as wolves dressed up in sheep's clothing (Matthew 7.15) embodies the belief that wolves are crafty as well as malicious, and the allusion served to perpetuate these ideas. In a beast fable the crafty wolf sings Psalm 23, the Shepherd Psalm.

On the principle that evil combats evil and what frightens a man also terrifies evil spirits, parts of wolves were used to scare

Victoria & Albert Museum/Mark Gerson

such beings. A pierced wolf's tooth was sometimes worn as a protective charm, and a tooth placed under a pillow was thought to enable the dreamer to identify a robber. In Spain and Sicily a scrap of the animal's skin was believed to avert the Evil Eye, and in some localities was even thought to be effective in keeping flies out of the house. A wolf's hair placed in the rafters was a protection against fire and a wolf-bite made a person immune to witchcraft. According to an ancient tradition if a man came on a wolf and the wolf saw him first he would be struck dumb.

So prominent a place in the imagination of the people was occupied by the wolf that it entered into expressions describing the time of day and the weather. In France dusk is commonly described poetically as 'between the dog and the wolf' – the one being thought of as a creature of the day, the other as nocturnal. Elsewhere, when the wind whistles, 'the wolf sharpens his teeth', and a strong, destructive wind is 'the wolf'. If the sun shines when it is raining, it is 'the wolves' wedding'. Around Düsseldorf, when the sky is filled with woolly clouds they say, 'today little sheep, tomorrow wolves'.

The Wolf of Gubbio

The tradition of the kindly wolf appears in a number of Christian legends. Sculptures in some churches illustrate the benevolent beast which kept guard over the head of the martyred St Edmund. Probably the best known of such legends is the story of St Francis of Assisi and the wolf of Gubbio. The animal was so fierce that the citizens were afraid to venture forth from the little town. The saint reproved him and, bowing his head, he indicated that he would abandon his evil ways. He accompanied St Francis into Gubbio and henceforth lived amicably among the citizens. This legend is a version of a much older story. Friendships developed between Irish saints and wolves. St Maedoc provided a feast for a pack, while the blind St Hervé was led around by a wolf. In other tales we hear of a wolf killing an animal drawing a plough or waggon and being compelled by a saint to take the place of the dead beast. Thus the wolf legends in which saints are involved embody the ambivalence characteristic of much wolf folklore. The fierceness and the friendliness of the animal both tend to be exaggerated.

From the Babylonian *Epic of Gilgamesh* to medieval tales of wolves invading monasteries and devouring heretical monks, the wolf has been represented as much more dangerous to man than it is. It was, and still is, a menace to domestic animals, but there are hardly any authenticated accounts of a wolf attacking an able-bodied man. It is possible that during times of famine in the Middle Ages wolves broke into flimsy dwellings and seized children or invalids, but stories of packs pursuing travellers on sledges in Russian forests do not deserve credence. They are the inventions of myth-makers in comparatively recent times.
(See also WEREWOLF.)

E. A. ARMSTRONG

WOMAN

'Through women doth the Enemy lay siege to mortal men': the myth of the evilness and inferiority of woman has grown out of social conditions, which in turn it has powerfully influenced

GODDESS, VICTIM, idol, plaything, mother, virgin, harlot, ministering angel, slut, enchantress, hag, 'better half' or 'weaker vessel' — woman plays all these roles in supernatural contexts, partly in reflection of man's frequently professed inability to understand her. Women, in male eyes, are supposed to be contrary and mysterious creatures, bewilderingly combining all sorts of opposite characteristics, as change-able as chameleons, and yet somehow vexingly in touch with reality through

intuition, through a secret sympathy with the heart of things.

Among the most powerful strands in the web of the mythical female are that she is man's inferior and that she is essentially evil. In the Jewish, Christian and classical traditions, evil came into the world through woman. In many societies, including our own, women's bodies are hung about with a miasma of impurity and pollution which does not cling to men. In many parts of the world women do not eat with men, they walk a few paces behind their husbands as a sign of their inferiority, and they are often excluded altogether from important mascu-line activities, including religion.

Orthodox Hindus believe that women cannot attain salvation as women, but only

through being reborn as men. Women are evil and unclean, and the virtuous Hindu woman, who must treat her husband as if he was a god, is considered inferior to the worst of men. In the West the more import-ant religious roles are still reserved for men and denied to women, and it is only in the face of stubborn resistance that women have begun to invade male preserves. In religious and magical traditions which classify phenomena in terms of opposites, male is generally classed with good, positive, active, and female with evil, negative, passive. It is characteristic that one of the dictionary meanings of the word 'female' is 'epithet of various material and immaterial things, denoting simplicity, inferiority, weakness, or the like'.

In male eyes, women are supposed to be contrary and mysterious creatures, as changeable as chameleons, and yet somehow in touch with reality through a secret sympathy with the heart of things

The Terrible Mother

All this has the weight of hundreds of years of tradition and custom behind it: some women welcome it, many accept it, and almost all are brought up to behave in accordance with it and so perpetuate it. But how it began, how hatred, fear and contempt came to be injected into the image of woman – remembering that a child's first love is his mother, that men and women do fall in love and live happily together, and that what may be the oldest known representation of a deity is a figure of a woman – is a question to which there is no certain answer. Psychoanalysts in search of an answer have created new myths of their own, including those of penis envy and the castration complex. Stated in a very brief and over-simplified way, the theory is that the little girl, lacking a penis, feels a sense of inferiority to males which lasts her the rest of her life: and that the little boy fears losing his penis when he sees that little girls have none, and fears that his father will castrate him because he is a rival for the affections of the mother, these fears mingling with desire in his attitude to women, who become both love-objects and hate-objects.

It is true that the theme of castration occurs in mythology and religious practice (in the worship of Cybele, for instance – see CYBELE; MUTILATION), and the motif of woman as castrator has enjoyed some literary popularity in the wake of Freud, but it seems unlikely that fear of castration is really a crucial element in the myth of

Woman's inferiority to man is one of the most powerful strands in the web of the mythical female; the legend of Eve's subordination to Adam, and the numerous representations of her in art as the acme of physical desirability, have contributed to a stereotype described by Germaine Greer in *The Female Eunuch* as being 'more body than soul, more soul than mind . . . the Sexual Object sought by all men, and by all women'
Facing page, left to right **Raquel Welch, Marilyn Monroe and Mae West, three 20th century examples of 'the perfect woman'** *Right* **The concept of woman as a passive sexual object or plaything classed on a level with wine and song as a masculine diversion, is ancient and widespread: wall painting in an Egyptian tomb showing women at their toilet**

woman's evilness. A simpler approach sees the source of this myth in the difference between the sexes itself. Women are different from men, and tolerance of what is different is not a marked feature of human societies. When what is different and 'other' is also desired, it may be resented, hated and feared, as well as loved and idealized.

The fact that it is woman who bears and rears children means that it is first and foremost a child's mother who not only loves and protects him but also thwarts and punishes him. The twin experiences of mother's love and mother's rage seem to implant an ambivalent attitude to women in general, which is reflected in beliefs about the supernatural. For example, Spartan boys were flogged, or ritually 'punished',

on the altar of Artemis Orthia, which had a fondness for human blood. In the Cabala the sefirah Din or Geburah, which represents the punishing judgement of God, is on the female pillar of the Tree of Life (see CABALA). In the Near East mother goddesses and love goddesses were also wrathful war goddesses. Kali, the goddess of terror in Hinduism, significantly presides over undeserved retribution as 'the Mother who nourishes but also punishes'. She typifies 'the deep-seated dread aroused by the unpredictable hazards of man's existence', which in terms of childish experience starts with the bewildering terror of the mother's anger. The age-old assertion that woman is fickle and changeable may have the same root.

William MacQuitty

The All-Devouring Curse

The supposed inferiority of woman follows from the fact that human societies have been dominated by men, presumably because men's greater physical strength has enabled them to dominate. The theory that early societies passed through a stage of matriarchy, followed by patriarchy when men seized power from women and enslaved them, is now generally doubted (though there are myths of the reign of women – see BRAZIL) and even matrilineal societies, where descent is reckoned from the mother, are not usually woman-dominated.

Because women are physically weaker, it is concluded that they must also be inferior mentally and spiritually. A German neurologist named Paul Möbius published in 1907 a book on *The Physiological Intellectual Feebleness of Women* in which he pronounced that the regions of the brain 'necessary for spiritual life' are 'less well developed in women', and concluded that since women are mentally inferior to men lying is 'the natural and indispensable womanly weapon'. He thought it was for the best, since if woman could compete with man in masculine fields her function as a mother would suffer.

Many attempts have been made, unsuccessfully, to show that woman is biologically inferior to man, and the argument that the emancipation of women would wreck home and family life, and the female character, is old and tenacious. But the pronouncements of Möbius pale into insignificance as a condemnation of woman beside the tirade in the Indian epic, the *Mahabharata*: 'Woman is an all-devouring curse. In her body the evil cycle of life begins afresh, born out of lust engendered by blood and semen. Man emerges mixed with excrement and water, fouled with the impurities of woman. A wise man will avoid the contaminating society of women

Although woman has been regarded as subordinate to man in cultures throughout the world, sometimes excluded entirely from masculine activities such as religion, modern women are rebelling against this traditional concept of their role; these two contrasting aspects of woman are reflected in *The Favourite of the Harem*, a 19th century engraving by Thomas Hallom, coloured by Laura Lushington *(left)* and members of the Women's Liberation movement at a rally in New York *(above right)*

as he would the touch of bodies infested with vermin.'

This diatribe contains two themes found elsewhere. The first is that when our earthly lives and our earthly bodies are condemned as evil and dangerous, distracting the mind from spiritual things and imprisoning us in ignorance and wrong, then sexual intercourse is considered evil, and so is woman, who tempts man to sex and from whose body yet more imprisoned spirits emerge to earthly life: though in other contexts, of course, woman as mother and fount of life is deified and revered (see EARTH; FERTILITY; ICONOGRAPHY; MOTHER GODDESS).

The second theme is that women are unclean. The fact that they bleed at regular intervals has aroused fear and disgust, especially when menstrual blood is regarded as the substance which should have formed the body of a child and as charged with potent and dangerous energy. Contact with this blood and with a menstruating woman has been widely feared as contaminating, and so has contact with a pregnant woman or with childbirth. If women are unclean, then they must be kept at a distance from men's fighting and hunting activities and equipment, and from religious ceremonies, because they might pollute them.

The Great Whore

Another physically-based reason for masculine fear of woman is that the male organ 'dies' in orgasm, and the emission of sperm has frequently been regarded as a loss to

the male of some of his life-energy. H. R. Hays quotes an Australian aborigine as saying, 'The vagina is very hot, it is fire and each time the penis goes in, it dies.' The Roman poet Ovid used the same image in hoping to die making love: 'Let me go in the act of coming to Venus; in more senses than one let my last dying be done.' In *Paradise Lost*, when Adam and Eve make love after the Fall, Adam rises afterwards as Samson rose from Delilah's harlot lap, 'shorn of his strength'.

This motif combines with the fact that women are unlike men in being capable of sex at any time and able to go on longer, to create the myth of woman's insatiable lustfulness and to paint a picture of her as a voracious monster who ensnares a man to devour him, subjecting him to orgasmic 'deaths' until she destroys him.

Greek men were horrified by the worship of Dionysus (see DIONYSUS), partly because it took women away from their 'proper place' in the home, but also because the frenzied rites unleashed all the murderous carnality felt to be inherent in the female nature. In later centuries people were similarly horrified by the cannibalism and orgiastic excesses of witches. It was once customary to refer to women as 'the sex', as though sensuality was a peculiarly female trait.

Jean de Meung, 13th century continuator of the *Roman de la Rose*, put it succinctly: 'Every woman is a whore.' In the book of Revelation (chapter 17) the personification of lust and murder is the great harlot who sits on a scarlet beast, arrayed in purple

Victoria & Albert Museum/Mark Gerson

Previous page Although there are myths that tell of the reign of women, the theory that societies went through a stage of matriarchy before men seized power from women and enslaved them is generally doubted; in fact, woman's influence over man has generally been based on her sexual role. In *Lysistrata*, a comedy by the Greek writer Aristophanes, the women of Athens force the men to make peace with Sparta by going on a 'sex strike': scene from a modern Greek production of the play *Right* Woman's traditional reliance on man's goodwill is reflected in the story of Cinderella, who is finally rescued from a life of drudgery by a prince: *Cinderella*, illustrated by Arthur Rackham

and scarlet and jewels, holding a golden cup full of abominations and the impurities of her fornication, drunk with the blood of saints and martyrs. The German writer Otto Weininger, who detested both women and Jews, published in 1903 a book called *Sex and Character*, which went through numerous editions, in which he maintained that women are monsters of devouring sexuality: 'Woman wants man sexually because she only succeeds in existing through her sensuality.'

The same stereotype, of woman as a being whose existence depends on draining the life from men, appears in the legends of Lilith, the lamias, the sirens, vampires and demonesses who prey on men sexually (see INCUBUS; LILITH; SIRENS; VAMPIRE). She appears again in modern novels, for instance as the Great Bitch in Norman Mailer's *An American Dream*, who 'delivers extermination to any bucko brave enough to take carnal knowledge of her', and in the fantasy characters, described by Germaine Greer in *The Female Eunuch* as 'those extraordinary springing women with slanting eyes and swirling clouds of hair who prowl through thriller comics on the balls of their feet, wheeling suddenly upon the hero, talons unsheathed for the kill. Their mouths are large, curved and shining like scimitars: the musculature of their shoulders and thighs is incredible, their breasts like grenades, their waists encircled with steel belts as narrow as Cretan bull-dancers'.'

The great bitch or cat-woman, the seducer and slayer, is also related to the *femme fatale* or *la belle dame sans merci*, the enchantress for whom men feel an irresistible longing and who pitilessly enslaves and degrades them. She appears in Arthurian legends, she is Delilah, who robbed Samson of his strength and his freedom, or Cleopatra, 'who lost Mark Antony the world'. She is Wilde's Salome and the Dolores, 'Our Lady of Pain', of Swinburne's masochistic fancy.

The Jar of Evils

The *femme fatale* may herself be essentially passive: her loveliness by itself entraps men and destroys them, as in the case of Helen, whose beauty launched the thousand ships of the avenging Greeks and caused the fall of Troy. Another example is Pandora, whose story was told by Hesiod in his *Works*

and Days and *Theogony*. Zeus determined to make men pay for the gift of fire, which Prometheus had stolen (see PROMETHEUS), and instructed the divine craftsman Hephaestus to manufacture a 'beautiful evil', a woman, made of soil mixed with water. The goddess Athene taught her to sew, golden Aphrodite 'shed grace upon her head and cruel longing and cares that weary the limbs', and Hermes bestowed on her 'a shameless mind and a deceitful nature'.

Pandora was, in fact, a typical woman as seen by Hesiod, and Zeus presented her to Epimetheus, Prometheus's brother, who foolishly accepted the gift. She then raised the lid of a jar, which contained all evils, and the evils escaped and have been loose

in the world ever since. Before this, Hesiod says, 'men lived on earth remote and free from ills and hard toil and heavy sicknesses . . . but the woman took off the great lid of the jar with her hands and scattered all these and her thought caused sorrow and mischief to men.' All women are descended from her, 'the deadly race and tribe of women who live amongst mortal men to their great trouble', for Zeus 'made women to be an evil to mortal men, with a nature to do evil'.

Pandora's name may mean 'all-giving' and was perhaps originally a title of the Earth Goddess. Her jar (*pithos*) was turned into a box (*pyxis*) by Erasmus, the 16th century humanist, and 'Pandora's box' became a phrase for any source of multiple

Reflections on Woman

What man has assurance enough to pretend to know thoroughly the riddle of a woman's mind, and who could ever hope to fix her mutable nature?

Cervantes

From a woman sin had its beginning, and because of her we all die

Ecclesiasticus

Women are only children of a larger growth

Lord Chesterfield

The goal of female education has invariably to be the future mother

Hitler

There's nothing sooner dry than women's tears

Webster

Nature has given women so much power that the law has very wisely given them little

Dr Johnson

Dissimulation is innate in woman

Schopenhauer

What female heart can gold despise?
What cat's averse to fish?

Gray

The female of the species is more deadly than the male

Kipling

A woman is necessarily an evil, but he that gets the most tolerable one is lucky

Menander

Thou goest to women? Don't forget thy whip!

Nietzsche

Here lies my wife: here let her lie!
Now she's at rest, and so am I

Dryden

Here's to Woman! Would we could fall into her arms without falling into her hands

Ambrose Bierce

The modern individual family is founded on the open or concealed slavery of the wife

Engels

Women have very little idea of how much men hate them

Germaine Greer

---

disasters. Early Christian writers likened her to Eve and the Renaissance rediscovered her, though usually not as the source of evil but as the 'all-gifted' one, on whom the gods had bestowed their treasures. However, Jean Olivier, author of *Pandora* (1541), said: 'Eve in Scripture opened the forbidden fruit by her bite, by which death invaded the world. So did Pandora open the box in defiance of a divine injunction, whereby all the evils and infinite calamities broke loose and overwhelmed the hapless mortals with countless miseries . . .'

In the late 18th century, the painter James Barry, who executed an enormous *Creation of Pandora,* called her story 'one of the most splendid of the many specimens of the Heathen manner of adumbrating and allegorizing that introduction of Evil or fall of mankind which is celebrated in Genesis'. Pandora's box was occasionally identified with her genitals, and Paul Klee's drawing of *Pandora's Box* (1920) brings in the menstruation motif, for it shows a goblet shaped like the female genitals, containing some flowers and emitting evil vapours.

The Devil's Gateway

The Jewish legend of the Watchers traces the introduction of evil into the world to the angels who descended from heaven, significantly drawn to earth by the sexual attractions of human women (see DEVIL), but the story of Adam and Eve has had a greater influence in the West in reinforcing the belief in woman's inherent wickedness. In the account in Genesis it is the woman who succumbs to the serpent's temptation and persuades Adam to eat the forbidden fruit, the action which caused the Fall and implanted the taint of original sin in all human beings (see EVIL; FIRST MAN). In some paintings of the scene, including Michelangelo's in the Sistine Chapel, the serpent itself is female.

Genesis also stresses the inferiority of woman. She is created after Adam, and fashioned from one of his ribs, and the pangs of childbirth and the subjection of woman to man are among the penalties for the crime, so providing divine authority for the actual situation in patriarchal Hebrew society. The story in Genesis may have been influenced by the Babylonian Epic of Gilgamesh (see GILGAMESH), in which Enkidu, the 'noble savage' who is man in

his natural primitive state, is seduced by a temple prostitute. She teaches him the delights of sex, instructs him in civilized behaviour, and finally lures him away from his peaceful life with the animals and takes him to the city, and so ultimately to his doom. When he is dying, Enkidu curses her for coaxing him away from his simple life in the wild.

Eve, who coaxed Adam into eating the forbidden fruit of sexual and civilizing knowledge, entered the Christian tradition as the supreme example of woman as both intensely desirable and intensely dangerous. Tertullian (2nd century AD), who castigated women as Eves, Devil's gateways, destroyers of man and ultimately responsible for the death of Christ, said that they ought all to wear permanent mourning as a sign of penitence for the wickedness they derived from Eve. And Eve's creation from Adam's rib was for hundreds of years one of the stock arguments against the emancipation of women. There is a story about one of the desert hermits, the holy Arsenius, who was visited by a devout woman, a virgin, who went all the way from Rome to see him. Arsenius was furious and said, 'Dost thou not know that thou art a woman, and ought not to go anywhere? And wilt thou now go to Rome and say to the other women, "I have seen Arsenius", and turn the sea into a high road of women coming to see me?' She asked him to pray for her but he said that on the contrary he would pray to God to wipe the memory of her from his mind. When she told the archbishop what had happened, he said, 'Knowest thou not that thou art a woman, and through women doth the Enemy lay siege to mortal men?'

It is not as easy to generalize about Christian attitudes to sex and woman as authors embattled in these particular lists have sometimes suggested. Few Christians went as far as a Church Council in 585 which ruled that a male corpse must not be buried beside a female corpse until the latter had decomposed. But though generally by no means as hostile to women as orthodox Hinduism or as appalled by sex as some of the European heretical sects, Christianity did contain a powerful strain of mistrust of sex and the body, as obstacles to spiritual advancement, which engendered disapproval of women as evil temptresses, and which lies behind the lauding of the

virgin state as a condition closer to God than the married, the establishment of monasteries and nunneries, and the insistence on clerical celibacy.

The God of Jews and Christians is emphatically male and, unlike pagan gods, has no female consort (except in mystical imagery about the Shekhinah or Wisdom or the Sophia of the Gnostics, or the mystic himself, as God's bride). Jesus did not marry, and any suggestion that he had ever been involved in a love affair would probably strike most Christians to this day as blasphemous and deeply offensive. The nearest thing to a goddess in Christianity is a virgin, though she has clearly brought into patriarchal Christianity a feminine element which multitudes of worshippers have refused to do without (see MARY).

The fact that St Paul, in the much discussed passages of 1 Corinthians (chapters 6 and 7), keeps insisting that it is not a sin to marry suggests that the Corinthian Christians thought it was. 'It is well for a man not to touch a woman,' he says, though conceding that many men, unlike himself, cannot refrain from touching one; and so, 'it is better to marry than to be aflame with passion'. St Paul was writing at a time when Christians expected the world to come to an end at any moment, and he advised people to stay as they were if they could, single or married, slave or free, 'for the appointed time has grown very short'. Later Christian writers continued to recommend virginity, not necessarily condemning marriage but regarding it as a second best, because involvement in things of the flesh distracts attention from the things of God. Sex was necessary for the procreation of children, and the Almighty for his own inscrutable reasons had instituted it for that purpose, but it was still something of a barrier between humanity and God.

Many Christian authors have disapproved of cosmetics and other feminine adornments because they excite men's passions, and much of the element of distrust of woman in Christianity stems from the observation that sex causes man to lose his self-control. This is part of the widespread human feeling that desire is supernatural, awesome and dangerous, sweeping over human beings from outside and carrying them away in an uncontrollable tide. Both St Albertus Magnus and St Thomas Aquinas

Giraudon

Roger Wood

maintained that what is sinful in sexual intercourse is not the pleasure of the act but the fact that fallen man in his weakness cannot enjoy so intense a pleasure without losing sight of God. Earlier, St Augustine had also been horrified by the irrationality of erotic passion, the whirling away of reason and self-control in the hurricane of desire. He thought that what Adam and Eve really discovered, when their eyes were opened and they knew that they were naked, was 'concupiscence' – desire which was beyond their control.

Wine, Women and Song

If at one end of the scale woman is whore, temptress, murderess, at the other she is a toy or doll, a passive sexual object and plaything, the occupant of a real or psychological harem, classed on a level with wine and song as masculine diversions. The legendary Eve's subordination to Adam, and the numerous representations of her in art as the acme of physical desirability, in styles varying with male tastes of different periods and places, have contributed to this stereotype, which is blisteringly described by Germaine Greer. 'She is more body than soul, more soul than mind . . . She is the Sexual Object sought by all men, and by all women. Her value is solely attested by the demand she excites in others. All she must contribute is her existence. She need achieve nothing, for she is the reward of achievement . . . Because she is the emblem of spending ability and the chief spender, she is also the most effective seller of this

In legends of sirens and vampires woman is depicted as a being whose existence depends on draining the life from men; this stereotype is related to the enchantress for whom men feel an irresistible longing, a *femme fatale* who may in fact be essentially passive, and whose loveliness by itself entraps and destroys men *Above left* Helen's beauty caused the fall of Troy: *Helen on the Ramparts of Troy* by Moreau *Above right* Head of Nefertiti, wife of the heretic Pharaoh Ikhnaten *Below* Pandora, who raised the lid of a jar containing all evils and allowed them to escape to plague the world, has been described as a typical woman: *Pandora* by François Quesnel

Facing page Relief depicting an Egyptian queen, said to be Cleopatra who 'lost Mark Antony the world'

Corvina, Budapest

world's goods. Every survey ever held has shown that the image of an attractive woman is the most effective advertising gimmick.'

There is far more to Eve in Genesis, and to woman in supernatural contexts generally, than evil and passive inferiority, but the note of wickedness, darkness, danger and death does sound constantly. *Cherchez la femme,* men say, if there's trouble there's a woman at the bottom of it. In *Paradise Lost* Milton, whose relations with women were not of the happiest, depicts Sin sitting at the gate of hell. She is female, a beautiful woman to the waist and a foul scaly serpent below, and her womb is the kennel for demonic dogs. Many of the mother goddesses of the distant past were deities who gave life but who also gave death, and their worshippers seem to have regarded them with the same mingled emotions of love and terror, trust and fear, admiration and resentment, desire and disgust, which men have blended in their image of woman all through recorded history. (See also AMAZONS; BIRTH; HYSTERICAL POSSESSION; MENSTRUATION; OLD AGE; SELF-DENIAL; SEX; TANTRISM.)

RICHARD CAVENDISH

FURTHER READING: D. S. Bailey, *The Sexual Relation in Christian Thought* (Harper and Row, 1959); H. R. Hays, *The Dangerous Sex* (Putnam, 1964); D. and E. Panofsky, *Pandora's Box* (Princeton Univ. Press, 2nd edn., 1962); B. Walker, *Hindu World* (Praeger, 1968, 2 vols). See also G. Greer, *The Female Eunuch* (McGraw-Hill, 1980).

WOODPECKER

MOST WOODPECKERS assert their possession of a nesting territory not by song, but by a rattling noise or 'drumming' made by striking the bill rapidly on a branch – a distinctive drum-roll quite different from the sound made by a woodpecker when pecking at a branch to extract an insect or make a hole for its nest. This drumming was of great significance to our ancestors who, living mainly out of doors and dependent for their well-being on propitious weather, paid much attention to birds which seemed to them to be not only weather-wise but actually able to influence the weather, especially the amount of rainfall.

Listening to the woodpecker drumming in a tree high up towards the sky, they assumed that he was making miniature thunder, calling for and bringing down rain. Such a bird, in league with the higher powers, deserved respect and could teach men how to act when they needed rain for their crops. It is a widespread practice for people anxiously desiring rain to make imitation thunder by drumming, the underlying idea being that like would attract like. In Estonia, during times of drought, a man used to climb a tree in a sacred grove, carrying a small cask or kettle, and rattle a stick in it: he acted the part of a woodpecker making thunder.

It is still believed in the English countryside that the loud and frequent calling of the green woodpecker foretells rain, although observation shows that this has no foundation in fact. In Scandinavia, also, the woodpecker is considered a weather prophet. Frenchmen call the bird 'the miller's advocate', because in times of drought it is thought to plead insistently for water to turn the mill wheel.

The red crowns of European woodpeckers have also played a part in gaining them their status as thunderbirds and rainbirds. Species with conspicuous red markings tend to be associated with fire, and so the woodpecker came to be connected not only with thunder but also with the lightning which accompanies it.

Perhaps the first hint in literature that the woodpecker was considered a rainmaker and thunderbird is its name in Babylonian, meaning 'the axe of Ishtar', for Ishtar was a fertility goddess. The earliest written evidence of the bird's exalted status is a reference by Aristophanes: 'Zeus won't in a hurry the sceptre restore to the woodpecker tapping the oak.' There appears to have been a belief that the bird once occupied the throne of the High God and received reverence such as Zeus received in Aristophanes's time.

There is definite evidence that the woodpecker was consulted as an oracle, if not actually worshipped. An account survives of an oracle connected with Mars in the Apennine Mountains, where an image of a woodpecker was placed on a wooden pillar; engraved gems show a warrior consulting such an oracle. Mars was originally associated with fertility as much as with war (see MARS), which perhaps explains his association with the fertility-bringing woodpecker.

The First Ploughman

There is further evidence that the woodpecker is a bird of fertility. Greek myth relates that Celeus, whose name means 'green woodpecker', attempted to steal the honey which nourished Zeus while he was an infant. As a punishment the angry god turned Celeus into a green woodpecker. Celeus was the father of Triptolemus, the inventor of the plough – a king or chieftain instructed by Demeter, the Earth Mother, in the ritual which procured the fertility of the soil.

The significance of all this is obscure until we realize that the green woodpecker often feeds on the ground, picking up ants, and that its beak could be regarded as serving the same purpose as the primitive plough, which was not much more than a single prong drawn through the soil. The story says in effect that the green woodpecker was the first ploughman.

More recent legends confirm the woodpecker's connection with ploughing. According to a tale of the Letts, a people of the eastern Baltic, God and the Devil engaged in a ploughing match. God had a woodpecker to draw his plough, but the Devil had horses and quickly ploughed a whole field, while the woodpecker was making little progress. During the night God borrowed the horses and ploughed a field. The Devil was so impressed next day that he stupidly exchanged his horses for the woodpecker. When the bird lagged behind he angrily struck it on the head and this is why the woodpecker has a blood-coloured crown. In a veiled way this story tells of the suppression of ancient beliefs.

There are plenty of other indications of the association between the woodpecker, rain and fertility. In France, Germany, Austria and Denmark it is given names equivalent to the English local name 'rain bird'. In Italy there is a saying, 'When the woodpecker pecks, expect rain or storm.' In France the story goes that at the Creation, when God had made the earth, he called on the birds to help by hollowing out places which could be filled with water and so become seas, lakes and ponds. Only the woodpecker refused to join in. A German version says that it was because she would not dirty her fine plumage. So the bird was condemned to peck wood and to drink nothing but rain. That is why she clings to the tree trunk with beak upwards calling, 'Rain, Rain'.

It was at one time believed, or half-believed, that the mysterious herb springwort, with which doors and locks could be opened, could be obtained by blocking the woodpecker's nesting hole. The bird would fetch the herb and apply it to the blocked entrance. If a strip of red cloth was placed below the nest, the bird, mistaking it for fire, would drop the sprig on it. Another plan was to watch where the woodpecker went to fetch the plant.

The legend seems to be an Eastern tale in Western dress. A version was current in Greece but the bird concerned was the hoopoe. It had its nest in a wall, but three times the owner plastered it up and three times the bird removed the plaster by applying the springwort. The tale as told in Germany is similar to a version quoted by Pliny.

Probably it passed from Greek literature into Latin and is not, as might at first appear, the concoction of simple country-folk. What may be an embellished and distorted version was current in a region of Germany. It was said that a princess incarcerated in the Markgrabenstein could be released by the man who went to the place at midnight on a Friday carrying a white woodpecker.

E. A. ARMSTRONG

FURTHER READING: E. A. Armstrong, *The Folklore of Birds* (Dover, N.Y., 1970).

Wraith

The double or apparition of someone who is alive; its appearance is generally taken as an omen of the person's imminent death, or as a sign that he is in serious danger or trouble.
See ASTRAL BODY; DOUBLE; SPONTANEOUS PSI EXPERIENCES.

Wreath

A circle or garland of flowers or leaves, bestowed as a mark of distinction, or placed in a grave or on a coffin to honour the dead; evergreen wreaths are used as Christmas decorations; in Greece and Rome poets, athletes and other persons of note were honoured with laurel wreaths or crowns.
See BURIAL; LAUREL.

The custom of killing a wren at midwinter and parading it with elaborate ceremony through the neighbourhood, observed in parts of France and Ireland, was probably connected with ancient sun rituals

WREN

Bodleian Library Colour Filmstrip

ALTHOUGH IT IS nearly our smallest bird, inconspicuously coloured and unlikely to call attention to itself, except when it utters its relatively loud song, the wren is a familiar bird to most people because it is common, and besides inhabiting woods is to be seen in hedgerows and gardens. The folklore of the wren is of exceptional interest as it is the only bird associated with a fairly elaborate ritual in the British Isles, besides being represented in legends and oral traditions.

Wren ritual is performed throughout most of Ireland and to a limited extent in the Isle of Man. It seems to have disappeared in Wales, as it has in England, but scraps of evidence and local traditions indicate that it persisted until not very long ago, in one form or another, in many of the southern countries. It was never established in Ulster or Scotland.

The Wren Hunt and Procession as performed in Ireland may be briefly described. In those localities where an actual wren figures in the ceremonial it may be caught by beating the hedgerows or captured in its roost. On St Stephen's Day (26 December) a number of lads and young men form a party and visit the houses in neighbouring villages, carrying the corpse of the bird with them, or more often now a toy bird or some other object representing a wren. Girls occasionally take part, another indication that the custom has deteriorated. The 'Wren Boys' dress up for the occasion in odds and ends such as pyjama jackets and fantastic headgear. When they call at a cottage they sing a Wren Song in English or Irish, seeking a contribution from the householder. When the Wren Boys have finished their calls they hold a celebration, paid for by the collections made during the day.

French wren ceremonies were enacted in an area stretching from Marseilles northwestwards up to Brittany. They were more elaborate than in Ireland, probably indicating that the cult was carried to the British Isles from France and lost some of its characteristics on the way. At Carcassonne, the Wren Boys of the Rue St Jean assembled towards the end of the year and went into the countryside to beat the bushes and obtain a wren. The first lad to kill one was proclaimed King and to him fell the duty of carrying the bird back to town on a pole. The King proceeded through the streets on the last day of the year with all who had participated in the Hunt, accompanied by a drum and fife band and carrying torches. Here and there they would halt and a lad would chalk on a house 'Vive le Roi' and the number of the New Year. On Twelfth Day, the King arrayed himself in a blue robe and, wearing a crown and carrying a sceptre, went to High Mass at the parish church; he was preceded by a man carrying the wren fastened to the top of a pole, which was decorated with a wreath of olive leaves, oak or mistletoe cut from an oak. After the service the King, together with his retinue, paid visits to the bishop, the mayor, the magistrates and other notable citizens. Money was given to the participants, a banquet was held in the evening, and the celebrations concluded with a dance. Unfortunately this picturesque ceremony was suppressed in 1830. In some places in France and the Isle of Man the wren was solemnly buried in a churchyard.

The ceremonies are certainly very ancient and probably date from the Bronze Age. Unfortunately, documentary evidence earlier than the 19th century is practically nonexistent, so we have to piece together an interpretation from a variety of scattered clues. The geographical distribution of the ritual is significant. It would seem that the people amongst whom wren ceremonies were important reached southern France from elsewhere in the Mediterranean and carried elements of their culture northwestwards, eventually reaching the British Isles. There are grounds for believing that these same folk may have been the builders of some of the megalithic monuments which are found in areas where wren ritual was practised.

Through the Keyhole of Hell

The date of the custom provides a valuable clue to its meaning. Midwinter was for our ancestors a crucial turning-point of the year and many ceremonies performed at this time were intended to combat or chase away the powers of darkness and co-operate with the sun in restoring light, warmth and growth to the world. The wren frequents thickets and penetrates holes, crevices and other dark places, as its scientific name *Troglodytes troglodytes*, 'dweller in caves', indicates. It was therefore a suitable representative of the powers opposed to or complementary to the sun.

This view is borne out by the well-known fable of the competition between the eagle and the wren to decide which could fly highest. The wren defeated the eagle – the bird of the sun – by trickery. In many languages the wren is called 'king', suggesting that long ago it was regarded as allied with mysterious powers; these may have been the dark potencies believed to reside in the earth. An ancient Irish document refers to the wren as a bird with oracular powers.

As heat proceeds from the sun, it was natural that birds, being creatures of the sky, should be regarded as fire-bringers. Such birds were commonly identified by the red badge of fire on their plumage. The robin (see ROBIN) was one of these and in France the wren was also a fire-bringer, perhaps because when it is in its full spring plumage some of its feathers have a ruddy tinge. It was said that when the wren fetched fire from heaven most of its plumage was scorched away. The other birds compassionately donated some of their feathers, but the robin came too close and its breast feathers were burnt. Another French version relates that as the wren was flying to earth with the fire its wings burst into flame; it passed the brand to the robin, whose breast feathers also became alight. The high-flying lark then came to the rescue and brought the precious burden to mankind. The Bretons explain that the wren fetched fire, not from heaven but from hell. Her plumage became scorched as she escaped the infernal regions through the keyhole.

So closely were the robin and wren associated in folklore that they were regarded as male and female of the same species – a notion which has lingered to the present time in some localities.

> The robin redbreast and the wren
> Are God Almighty's cock and hen.

A Scots ballad refers to their marriage tiff over who ate the porridge:

> The robin redbreast and the wran
> Coost out about the parritch pan;
> And ere the robin got a spune
> The wran she had the parritch dune.

Although in many localities the wren was hunted and killed at the winter solstice, this does not imply that it was generally regarded as in any sense an evil creature. On the contrary, it was usual for birds and beasts held in high respect to be sacrificed on some special occasion during the year. In France it was said that the crime of robbing a wren's nest would entail the destruction by fire of the culprit's house, or that his fingers would shrivel and drop off.

An indication of the affection in which the wren was held in France is provided by its appearance in legends connected with various saints. A delightful story records that St Malo, finding that a wren had built a nest in his habit, which he had laid on a bush while working in the monastery vineyard, went without the garment until the bird had reared its young. St Dol, noticing that the monks at his monastery were distracted during their devotions by the calls of the birds in the neighbouring woods, ordered the birds to depart. He made an exception of the wren, because its sparkling song cheered the brethren without interfering with their concentration on prayer and praise.

E. A. ARMSTRONG

FURTHER READING: E. A. Armstrong, *The Wren* (Collins, 1955).

Ironically, the lasting influence of this Polish Messianist was not in his hoped-for 'Absolute Reform of Human Knowledge' but in passing on to the famous magician Eliphas Levi, the secrets of occultism which he had so long attempted to hide

J.M.H.-WRONSKI

Polish Institute

JOSEPH MARIA HOËNE-WRONSKI was born at Wolsztyn in Poland in 1776. His career led him from misfortune to misfortune, until he died in Paris in 1853 in a condition which the intrigued observers of a man believed variously to be a fraud, a genius, a madman and a divinity, unite in calling miserable. But he left disciples, and after the First World War a 'Hoëne-Wronski Institute of Messianism' was set up in Warsaw. More recently, a lengthy bibliography of Wronskiite works was issued by the Polish Academy. To Wronski's credit must be placed the crucial influence in the life of Eliphas Levi (see LEVI), various mechanical inventions, including what seems to have been a tank, and the discovery in 1803 of 'the Absolute'.

This misplaced Renaissance figure was the son of Antoine Hoëne, the court architect (the 'Wronski' was added later). When the Poles rebelled in 1794 against the partition of their country between Russia and Prussia, Wronski distinguished himself in the fighting but was eventually captured by the Russians, with whom he took the opportunity to enlist. Eventually he left the Russian service with the rank of major, and spent the next three years studying philosophy in Germany, chiefly the system of Immanuel Kant. In 1800 his dormant sense of patriotism revived, and he set off to join the legions gathering in Italy under Dombrowski to free Poland. But the patriot succumbed to the man of science and Wronski returned to scientific researches at the Observatory of Marseilles. In 1810 he

married the daughter of a well-known French astronomer: by that date he had discovered the Absolute.

The Absolute is the knowledge of truth attained through human reason. At least, Wronski always claimed he had reached this state through rational thought, but as his philosophical works are couched in mathematical terms, it is almost impossible for the layman to understand him. From the sum of his sense impressions, a man could 'create reality' in accordance with Wronski's 'Law of Creation', a mathematical expression of no meaning to those who are not mathematicians, and little enough significance to some who are. Wronski's supporters derive his theory from pure mathematics and the influence of Kant; but it is just as likely that it comes from mystical experiences and a knowledge of the Cabala (see CABALA).

Christ among Nations

The rebellion in which Wronski changed sides was one in a series of ill-starred attempts by the Poles to reassert their nationhood. Perpetually fought over and partitioned, Poland became for Romantic Europe, and for France in particular, the epitome of heroic resistance. Another rebellion, hopelessly ill-timed, took place in 1830–31 and the Tsarist regime allowed the wholesale emigration of the Polish officer corps.

About 12,000 Polish refugees were allowed to enter France, where they became national heroes. Until that time Wronski had enjoyed a monopoly of 'Messianism', the Polish national philosophy; he became most disgruntled when one of the late arrivals, the great Polish poet Adam Mickiewicz, started lecturing at the Collège de France. Mickiewicz, when told that Wronski was accusing him of stealing his ideas, asked whether Jesus Christ had taken out a patent.

Polish Messianism compared the Polish and Jewish nations. The perpetual suffering of the Poles was seen as a counterpart to the sufferings of the dispersed tribes of Israel, forever denied the right to exist as a free nation. Nevertheless they were the chosen people: to justify the national run of bad luck it was argued that Poland was the Christ among nations. Just as Christ, by his suffering, had redeemed each individual human being, Poland, by hers, would redeem all nations.

Sage in Tatters

The apocalyptic mood of these doctrines was emphasized by two factors. The first was the existence in 18th century Poland of the very influential Jewish revivalist movement known as Hasidism (see HASIDISM). Founded by Israel Baal Shem, who died in 1760, this represented an attempt to make of the Jewish Cabala a really popular tradition. Some of this cabalistic enthusiasm was imported by the Polish immigrants into France where, transformed by the romantic imagination of Eliphas Levi, it became the basis of the later revival of ritual magic. The second current of thought was that represented by Martinism (see

MARTINISTS) and other forms of occult Freemasonry, which had thoroughly penetrated the Masonic orders in Poland and Russia and were prominent in liberal and anti-Tsarist circles. Such doctrines, with their symbolic interpretation of Masonic ritual and ideas of 'Hidden Chiefs' behind the apparent superiors of the Order, were also markedly to influence the development of modern occultism (see MASTERS).

But Wronski, although he had read the German mystic Boehme, and was expert in the Cabala and familiar with the teachings of the early Gnostics, was most anxious to conceal his occult studies, according to Eliphas Levi. His teachings were supposedly strictly rationalist: he had, after all, to earn his living. He was soon forced into penury by the withdrawal of a subsidy which the French Academy had paid him when he studied at Marseilles. The publication of his first work was enough, embodying as it did the 'Supreme Law of Algorithmy'.

Wronski's devotion to his own genius was admirable. He survived by schoolmastering in Montmartre; he went about in wooden clogs; his little child died. In this state, he is hardly to be blamed for fastening onto a gullible businessman called Arson, who had made a fortune and wanted to improve himself. In 1812 Arson met Wronski through a mutual friend and was overwhelmed by the wisdom of the sage in tatters. He agreed to take a course of instruction from Wronski, and eventually financed the publication of his Messianic works, which were soon rolling off the presses in indigestible volumes. Then Arson was initiated into the secret of the Absolute. Perhaps this was less illuminating than he had expected, for the businessman decided that he wanted to go back on the bargain and published a pamphlet entitled *Materials towards a History of the World's Great Frauds*. Wronski replied, and a polemical battle began, which was continued in the courts to the total discomfiture of Arson, who had foolishly signed a binding contract. Wronski ever afterwards declared Arson to be a real incarnation of Satan.

Sum of Human Knowledge

To do Wronski justice, if he was out to exploit Arson it was solely to publish his books. This seems all he was ever interested in; but it rapidly became necessary to seek new sources of income. In the hope of claiming a reward offered by the British Board of Longitude for improvements in their system of navigation, Wronski pounced on an error in the *Nautical Almanac,* sent the Board a complex correction to their theory of refractions and followed it to London. Here he was soon reduced again to extreme poverty. The *Nautical Almanac* incorporated his correction without payment or acknowledgement; Wronski petitioned Parliament, showered Sir Humphry Davy with letters, and persuaded a clergyman to swear before the Lord Mayor as to the justice of his case. The learned bodies maintained a stony silence.

In this period of total catastrophe Wronski began yet another project, which for some time seemed to promise not merely relief from poverty but positive riches. It was a system for steam engines which he called the 'dynamogenic system': the engine could dispense with rails, travelling on specially reinforced roads. By 1833 he had actually signed a contract with a French company which would have kept him comfortably for at least 15 years. But Wronski's soaring mind had deduced from his invention further principles of mechanics, which he conceived it his duty to publish. The company objected to Wronski's making public property of their experiments, using, moreover, the money given to him to build working models. They broke the contract and Wronski was again without support.

He was not to find a new patron till 1850; but somehow his works were still printed. Appeals to the Tsar failed to produce the expected summons to implement his political programme immediately. But at this time he met Eliphas Levi, whom he is said to have initiated into the secrets of the Cabala.

It is indeed ironic to think that the lasting influence of the Polish Messianist was not in his hoped-for 'Absolute Reform of Human Knowledge', but in passing on the secrets of occultism which he had so long attempted to hide. For this encounter gave a completely new direction to the life of the former Abbé Constant, turning Levi from the lunatic fringe of politics

towards magic. Shortly afterwards he adopted his pseudonym.

One day in 1873 Eliphas Levi discovered in a junk shop Wronski's pride and joy. This was the Prognometer. Whilst the Pole had been alive, the disciple had never been allowed to touch it; now he bought the machine. Inside the central globe of this curious construction was another, inscribed with equations. By adjusting the machine, the operator could bring together on any given point the sum of human knowledge. The Prognometer contained the solution to every problem. Wronski's widow survived him, poverty-stricken, but believing herself to have been married to a god.

J. C. N. WEBB

WRYNECK

THE WRYNECK is a rather inconspicuous, slim, greyish-brown bird with mottled and streaked plumage, which lives in woodland and is related to the woodpeckers. Both its common name and its specific scientific name, *torquilla*, refer to the way in which the bird twists and turns its neck when disturbed at the nest or handled.

Today the wryneck is commoner on the Continent and attracted the attention of the Greeks in classical times. Aristotle gives an excellent description of it in his *Natural History*. Among the Greeks it had importance in ritual as well as mythology. It seems that the bird was spread out on a wheel with

four spokes, which was then rotated as part of a magical procedure, probably as a love charm. In all probability this custom, in which the wryneck was associated with a revolving wheel, arose from observation of the peculiar manner in which it rotates its neck. Until recently the wheel had many magical associations (see WHEEL), arising in large part from its movement seeming to resemble the curved path of the sun and moon across the sky.

As the rotating wheel had magical power, it was assumed that the bird which rotated its head and arrived from abroad when the sun was rising higher in the sky also had magical significance. Thus it became involved with a complex of ideas — fire and fertility, sun and moon, witchcraft and

love, gods and goddesses. On a Greek vase Adonis is depicted holding out a wryneck to the goddess of love, Aphrodite. On another, Cupid, winged and nude, revolves a wheel in front of Adonis while a female figure holds out a wryneck.

When the bird was commoner in England countryfolk noticed that it returned in spring about the same time as the cuckoo or a little before it; hence it was called in Norfolk 'cuckoo's leader', in Gloucestershire 'cuckoo's footman' and in East Anglia 'cuckoo's mate'. Other names are derived from peculiarities in its behaviour — 'turkey bird' because of the way it ruffles its neck feathers when disturbed, 'writhe neck' and 'snake bird' from its neck-twisting and 'tongue bird' because of its long tongue.

The god of Israel revealed himself to Moses in the burning bush with the words 'I am who I am': modern scholarship suggests an origin and development of the cult of Yahweh far different from that presented in the Bible

YAHWEH

ACCORDING TO modern academic opinion, 'Yahweh' represents the personal name of the god of Israel. In the ancient religions, gods had personal names as well as titles: thus in the Hebrew Bible the god of Israel is called Yahweh as well as 'God' (in Hebrew, *Elohim*), or 'God Almighty' (*El Shaddai*). Yahweh is actually a vocalized form of what

is known as the divine Tetragrammaton, the four consonantal letters YHWH by which the personal name of Israel's god is written in the Hebrew scriptures (see NAMES).

Hebrew was originally written in a consonantal script, the vowels being supplied by the reader. But the name signified by YHWH gradually became too sacred to be pronounced, with the result that the original vowels were forgotten. Instead of pronouncing the name where it occurred in the scriptures, the Jews substituted *Adonai* (My Lord). For this reason, in English translations of the Bible YHWH has generally been rendered as 'the Lord'. Another English rendering of the name, often used in hymns, is 'Jehovah', but the form derives from a medieval usage for which there is no

authority. Some scholars think that another early form of the name was 'Yahu', which could have been a primitive cultic invocation: *ya-hu*, 'oh He!'

There has been much speculation about the meaning of the name Yahweh. This speculation can even be traced far back into the Bible itself, for the Hebrew author of Exodus 3. 14, who may have written about 800 BC, tried to explain the name. The passage is very important and merits quotation. It occurs in the dramatic account of Moses and the burning bush, which was intended to explain how Yahweh first revealed his concern for the Israelites, who were then in bondage to the Egyptians.

The episode begins by telling how the attention of Moses was attracted, one day in the desert of Horeb, by a burning bush. On going near to investigate, Moses heard a voice announcing: 'I am the God of your fathers, the God of Abraham, the God of Isaac, and the God of Jacob.' The mysterious presence then revealed his intention to deliver the people of Israel from Egypt and settle them in the land of Canaan, and that Moses should be his agent in effecting this. In reply, the astounded Moses asked: 'If I come to the people of Israel and say to them, "The God of your fathers has sent me to you," and they ask me, "What is his name?" what shall I say to them?' The answer then given is in fact an attempt to explain the meaning of 'Yahweh'. Moses is told by the strange divinity: 'I AM WHO I AM . . . Say this to the people of Israel, "I AM has sent me to you."'

In this curious statement the ancient Hebrew writer was trying to connect the name Yahweh with the verb 'to be' (hayah). Today scholars still debate its meaning; it has recently been suggested by a specialist of great authority that the name signifies 'he causes to be, or brings into being'.

Another passage in the book of Exodus (6.2–3) reveals that the ancient Jews were aware that Yahweh had not always been worshipped under that name by their ancestors: 'And God said to Moses, "I am Yahweh. I appeared to Abraham, to Isaac, and to Jacob as God Almighty (El Shaddai), but by my name Yahweh I was not known to them."' This consciousness that Yahweh had become the god of Israel at some definite point in the past finds graphic expression in the account of the covenant made between Yahweh and Israel at Mt Sinai, as recorded in Exodus. This momentous event is described as having taken place shortly after Israel's marvellous deliverance from the bondage of Egypt. Moses had led the Israelite tribes into the Sinai desert, to the sacred mountain of Yahweh. The mysterious god, into whose presence Moses then ascends, is represented as promising the terms of the covenant to Israel: 'Now therefore, if you will obey my voice and keep my covenant, you shall be my own possession among all peoples; for all the earth is mine, and you shall be to me a kingdom of priests and a holy nation' (Exodus 19.5–6).

The Sacred History

Belief in this ancient covenant has conferred on the Jewish people their distinctive character and destiny in the history of mankind. Their unique achievements and awful sufferings stem from their conviction that Yahweh, whom they identify with the divine Creator of the universe, made them his Elect People (see ELECTION). The records of his dealings with their race constitute their holy scriptures, on which both their cultural and religious life have been continuously nourished. It is from these scriptures, however, that modern scholars have reconstructed a very different account of the origin and development of the cult of Yahweh.

Nearly a century of critical study of the Hexateuch (the first six books of the Bible) has shown that a single writer or a succession of writers were responsible for presenting Yahweh as the unique god of Israel. It appears that the ancient Hebrew writers who created the tradition about Yahweh were the literary representatives of a powerful group of Yahwist devotees concerned to promote the cult of Yahweh. They were obliged to do this because Yahweh was not originally the god of many of the tribes which came to form the people of Israel.

In the Hexateuch three distinct cycles of tradition about Yahweh can be discerned. The first can best be designated the 'Primeval History'. It starts at Genesis 2.4 with Yahweh's creation of Adam and ends by telling how the original unity of mankind was broken by the confusion of languages, as divine punishment for the building of the Tower of Babel (Genesis 11.1–9). In this Primeval History, Yahweh is presented in a universalist setting as the Creator of the human race. The Jews do not figure specifically in the narrative; but a hint is given about their future settlement in the land of Canaan in the curious episode concerning Ham's offence against his father Noah, recorded in Genesis 9. 20–27. Instead of cursing Ham, Noah curses Ham's son, Canaan, and decrees that he shall be the slave of Noah's other sons, Shem and Japheth. From Shem, we are told, the Hebrews descended, and the Philistines from Japheth. Thus the Yahwist writer prepared the way for his later narrative: for the Hebrews and the Philistines were to dispossess the Canaanites of Canaan, their land.

The next cycle of Yahwist tradition can be aptly termed the 'Patriarchal Saga'; for it describes the careers of four generations of Hebrew patriarchs who are presented as the ancestors of the Israelites. They are Abraham, Isaac, Jacob and the sons of Jacob, the most notable being Joseph. It concludes with a series of vividly described episodes concerning the fortunes of Joseph, used by the Yahwist writer to explain how the descendants of the patriarchs came to settle in Egypt instead of Canaan.

The third cycle of Yahwist tradition begins in the first chapter of the book of Exodus. A long period has elapsed since the sons of Jacob first settled in Egypt, and their offspring have now grown into a populous nation. Their increasing numbers so alarm the Egyptians that they enslave them. It is to deliver Israel from this oppression that Yahweh appears to Moses in the burning bush, and commissions him to tell Pharaoh to release the people. The colourful account of the ten plagues that precede the exodus from Egypt, and the marvellous crossing of the Red Sea, reveal the power of Yahweh and his care for his chosen people. This cycle of tradition concludes with Israel's conquest of Canaan, fulfilling Yahweh's ancient promise to Abraham.

The Yahwist narrative is thus a most impressive demonstration of how Yahweh had guided world events from the Fall of Adam to the settlement of Israel in the land of Canaan. But, impressive though it is and influential as it has been, this sacred history is essentially a propagandist work.

It was designed to show two things: that the various Israelite tribes in Canaan had a common ancestry, and that Yahweh was their ancestral god. Modern research has revealed that this version of Israel's past was composed because the real situation had been very different.

War God of the Desert

Of the three cycles of Yahwist tradition which have been outlined here, that concerning the exodus from Egypt and the conquest of Canaan is historically the most important. For it is clearly based on a firmly established memory among the Hebrews that their ancestors had escaped from servitude in Egypt and had succeeded in conquering Canaan, and that Yahweh had been essentially connected with these momentous events. There was also a memory that the cult of Yahweh had started with a covenant made at Mount Sinai, in which Moses was the mediator between Yahweh and the Israelite tribes.

After much study of the traditions concerning the exodus and the conquest of Canaan, modern scholars have reached something like the following interpretation of the historical events which lie behind them. It would appear that certain Semite tribes, possibly those known as the Joseph tribes, escaped from Egypt under a leader called Moses. These tribes believed that they owed their deliverance to a war god of the desert, whom they came to know as Yahweh. This deity, who seems to have been associated with fire and storm, may possibly have been worshipped by the Kenites, a nomadic people dwelling in the desert land of Midian. The tribes, led by Moses, united with other Semite tribes for the purpose of invading and settling in Canaan. This union was placed under the patronage of Yahweh, whose prestige as a potent war god was high. Yahweh's presence among the marching tribes was located in a portable wooden ark; this ark was sheltered in a tabernacle or tent, which formed the focus of worship when the tribes encamped.

After the tribes had established themselves in Canaan the ark of Yahweh was deposited at Shiloh, which became his cult centre. However, despite the success gained under his patronage, Yahweh's hold on the allegiance of many of the tribes was insecure. Although these tribes had accepted Yahweh as the divine patron of their federation, they still remained loyal to their ancestral gods or tended to adopt the Canaanite gods. The attraction of these latter gods was great, since they were fertility deities and their help was needed by the nomadic invaders as they settled down to an agricultural economy (see VEGETATION SPIRITS). Doubtless many reasoned that Yahweh was indeed a powerful god in the desert and in war, but how could he make the corn grow in fertile Canaan?

This desertion of Yahweh was vehemently opposed by his devotees, and they were soon able to back their exhortations to loyalty by military facts. The Israelite conquest of Canaan had not been complete, and the Canaanites began to fight back; moreover, the Philistines who had settled in

the coastal area became aggressive. The Israelites' original success had lain in their unity; when their tribal federation broke up, they became an easy prey to their enemies. Thus the Yahwist prophets had a strong case. They could argue that when the tribes had been loyal to Yahweh, he had fulfilled his covenant and given them victory; but when they deserted him for other gods, he had punished them by defeat. The book of Judges records the pattern of Hebrew history at this time. Israel is subjugated by its enemies; a Yahwist leader then recalls them to their allegiance to Yahweh and victory follows; but later the tribes again revert to other gods and the process is repeated.

Shrine at Jerusalem

However, the persistent endeavour of the Yahwists gradually bore fruit, and under Saul and David, the first Israelite kings, the cult of Yahweh was established as the national religion. After David's capture of Jerusalem from the Jebusites (c 1000 BC), the Ark of Yahweh was brought there and placed in the Temple which David's son, Solomon, built for Yahweh on Mt Moriah. The place was reputed to be the site where Abraham had attempted to offer up Isaac, his son, as a sacrifice to Yahweh. Thus began Yahweh's association with that historic site, which is still commemorated in the celebrated Wailing Wall of the Jews.

The construction of a national shrine to Yahweh at Jerusalem was indeed a momentous event, and its consequences have been immense not only for the Jews

The god of Israel, Yahweh is depicted in the first part of the book of Genesis as the divine creator of the world: *Creation of the World,* **17th century painting by Fiamminga**

but for a large part of mankind (see JERU-SALEM). But it did not mean that the supremacy of Yahweh was yet assured, or that the Israelites had been consolidated into a single nation under the protection of Yahweh. Indeed, after Solomon's death the people split into two separate kingdoms: that of Israel with its capital at Samaria, and that of Judah with Jerusalem as its centre (see LOST TRIBES). Moreover, as the books of Kings show, there was still a deep-rooted tendency to worship the Canaanite gods, or to serve Yahweh with ritual practices appropriate to Baal, the Canaanite god (see BAAL; SYRIA AND PALESTINE).

It was to counteract these dangers that the Yahwist version of Israel's past, which is contained in the Hexateuch, was constructed. The intentions behind its three distinctive parts varied, but they all supported the major theme of the composition as a whole: to reveal the purpose and power of Yahweh. Thus the account of the exodus and the conquest of Canaan commemorated the two momentous events that marked the beginning of Israel's life as a nation, together with its covenant with Yahweh at Mt Sinai. The preceding Patriarchal Saga was designed to show that the various tribes which had settled in Canaan were really a homogeneous people, descended from common ancestors. It also taught these tribes

that their possession of Canaan was the fulfilment of the promise that Yahweh had made to their ancestors. To this national history the Primeval History served as a most impressive introduction, revealing that Yahweh, the god of Israel, was the divine Creator of the world and had guided its affairs from the beginning for the good of his chosen people, Israel.

This Yahwist philosophy of history succeeded in its purpose. It established the idea of the 12 tribes of Israel forming a single nation, united in a common past and a common faith. It has subsequently been a major factor in preserving the national consciousness of the Jews during all the painful vicissitudes of their long history; and its influence on Christianity has been incalculable (see HISTORY).

The conception of Yahweh underwent much change during the course of centuries. In origin and nature Yahwism was an ethnic religion. It was essentially concerned with the relationship between Yahweh and his chosen people, Israel. Individual persons were significant only in so far as they affected, by their conduct, this relationship for good or ill. They could look forward to no life after death, for Yahweh had decreed man's fate when he sentenced Adam for his original sin: 'You are dust, and to dust you shall return' (Genesis 3.19). The most that was promised to the individual was that Yahweh would reward his pious service with a long life in this world, economic prosperity, and sons to inherit him. But at death the same grim fate awaited all persons, good

Corvina, Budapest

It was essential for the early Christians to preserve the Hebraic message of the creator god, who was active in history and who loved his world, and Yahweh was eventually transmuted into the Christian god who 'so loved the world that he gave his only Son, that whoever believes in him may have eternal life (John 3.16): *God the Father* by Tiepolo

or bad. What survived the physical disintegration of death descended to Sheol, which was conceived as an immense pit, far below the foundations of the world, shrouded in dust and gloom (see HELL).

This view of human destiny became increasingly intolerable, as prophets emphasized that Yahweh was not only omnipotent, but also a just god, who required just dealing from his people. For experience showed that only too often it was the just who suffered in this world, while the unjust prospered. Consequently, because there was no hope of recompense after death, the justice of Yahweh was questioned. The book of Job illustrates the tension that built up for the faithful Israelite (see JOB).

When the book of Job was written, the problems of innocent suffering could not be solved since there could be no redress after death. But by the middle of the 2nd century BC belief in a resurrection and judgement of the dead had become established in Israel (see JUDGEMENT OF THE DEAD). However, although this development made Yahwism a more satisfactory personal faith, the old ethnic character of the religion remained. Indeed, it became more vehemently presented owing to the worsening of Israel's political fortunes.

The basic tenet of Yahwism was that Yahweh had settled Israel in Canaan, and had consented to dwell in the Temple built for him at Jerusalem. But Israel was a small

nation, and it became a victim of the power politics of the ancient Near East. Solomon's Temple was destroyed in 586 BC by the Babylonian forces of Nebuchadnezzar, and the better part of the people sent in captivity into Babylonia. On the return from this exile in 538, the Temple was rebuilt on a modest scale. But the Holy Land of Yahweh continued to be controlled, except for a brief period, by foreign powers or uncongenial native rulers until its incorporation into the Roman Empire in 6 AD. One of these rulers, Herod the Great (37–4 BC), an Idumean by race and Jewish by profession, whom the Jews hated exceedingly, rebuilt the Temple on a most magnificent scale, but it failed to placate the Jews. The subjugation of Israel contradicted their ideal of it as a theocracy. This contradiction led to a fervently held belief that Yahweh would ultimately intervene, or send his Messiah, to overthrow Israel's enemies and restore its sovereignty in its Holy Land.

The belief eventually proved fatal to Israel. The yoke of heathen Rome was increasingly felt to be intolerable, and in 66 AD the people revolted (see ZEALOTS). They trusted that Yahweh would interpose with some miracle to save them. But after a bitter struggle, in 70 AD the Romans captured Jerusalem and burnt the Temple. Israel's national life in the land of Yahweh's promise ended then in awful disaster, until its restoration in 1948.
(See also HIGH GODS; JUDAISM; SKY.)

S. G. F. BRANDON

FURTHER READING: W. F. Albright, *Yahweh and the Gods of Canaan* (Eisenbrauns, 1978); S. G. F. Brandon, *Jesus and the Zealots* (Scribner, 1968); M. North, *History of Israel* (Harper and Row, 2nd edn., 1960); H. H. Rowley, *From Joseph to Joshua* (Oxford Univ. Press, 1950) and *Worship in Ancient Israel* (Fortress, 1967).

W.B.YEATS

'I HAD NOT taken up these subjects wilfully, nor through love of strangeness, nor love of excitement, nor because I found myself in some experimental circle, but because unaccountable things happened in my childhood, and because of an ungovernable craving. When supernatural events begin, a man first doubts his own testimony, but when they repeat themselves again and again, he doubts all human testimony. At least he knows his own bias, and may perhaps allow for it, but how trust historian and psychologist that have for some three hundred years ignored in writing the history of the world, or of the human mind, so

momentous a part of human experience? What else had they ignored and distorted?'

The view current among Yeats's younger contemporaries during his lifetime was that, considering the nonsense Yeats took seriously, his verse was surprisingly good; T. S. Eliot, by contrast, was regarded as learned in all that it befitted a poet to know. Time has worked a reversal of that judgement: there is a tradition of spiritual knowledge which comprises a body of learning not taught in the schools, with its own great literature, besides its unwritten gnosis, accessible only to those who submit themselves, as Yeats did, to a spiritual discipline. Yeats was in his own field a learned, even a scholarly poet, though not in an academic sense.

The son of Anglo-Irish parents of

Protestant stock, William Butler Yeats (1865–1939) did not inherit the Catholic faith of the nation for whose cause he worked as a member of the Young Ireland movement, and in whose parliament he afterwards became a Senator. His father, the portrait painter J. B. Yeats, a member of a Pre-Raphaelite community at Bedford Park, in London, felt no need for any religion beyond his own courteous humanism. Yeats's mother, a Pollexfen from Sligo, was imaginative rather than religious; and Yeats's sense of the supernatural was first aroused by the country people of Sligo, the paradise of his childhood.

As an art student in Dublin Yeats formed a friendship with a class-mate, George Russell (A. E.) a natural mystic and visionary (see RUSSELL). Under the influence of A. P. Sinnett's *Esoteric Buddhism* the Dublin Hermetic Society was founded. On the invitation of this society the theosophist Mohini Chatterjee (named in a poem written many years later) came to Dublin, and from him Yeats learned the rudiments of Hindu philosophy, which remained a lifelong study. (Sri Purohit Swami dedicated to Yeats on his 70th birthday his translation of the *Gita*; and the poet collaborated with the Swami in translating the *Ten Principal Upanishads*, published in 1937.) Yeats and A.E. both became members of the Theosophical Society; in *The Trembling of the Veil* Yeats has described with amusement and sympathy his impressions on meeting Mme Blavatsky (see BLAVATSKY; THEOSOPHY).

Among his father's friends was Edwin J. Ellis, a minor poet and painter interested in esoteric matters. Blake was, during the 1880s, much in vogue in Pre-Raphaelite circles and Yeats, in collaboration with Ellis, set to work on the Blake manuscripts in the possession of the Linnell family to produce the first edition of his longer poems, the three-volume Quaritch edition (1893). The commentary is based upon the authors' esoteric knowledge; they rightly surmised that Blake had access to an esoteric tradition, though they had at that time no exact knowledge of Blake's sources. Yeats may have come to Swedenborg (see SWEDENBORG) through his Blake studies.

Education in Magic

While working on Blake in the British Museum Reading Room Yeats noticed a figure who captured his imagination: S. Liddell Mathers, afterwards known as MacGregor Mathers, was copying magical manuscripts and rituals. Yeats afterwards described him as 'a learned, but not a scholarly man'. In 1887 Mathers became, with two distinguished English Rosicrucians a co-founder of the Hermetic Society of the Golden Dawn (see GOLDEN DAWN). Yeats was initiated in May or June 1887 under the motto *Diabolus est Deus Inversus* (Frater D.E.D.I.). Yeats helped Mathers to write the rituals, drawing upon the Chaldean Oracles, the Egyptian Book of the Dead, and (evidently Yeats's contribution) William Blake.

Yeats's fictitious figure Michael Robartes (who first appears in the early romance *Rosa Alchemica*) is no doubt based upon Mathers, 'who seemed, before I heard his name, or knew the nature of his studies, a figure of romance'. *Rosa Alchemica* describes a magical initiation, in which superhuman beings descend to dance with mortals on a marbled floor in 'an agony of trance', long afterwards recalled in the poem *Byzantium*. Michael Robartes appears again as the Initiator of *A Vision*; this work, an 'arbitrary, harsh and difficult' diagrammatic system relating historical cycles and human character to the 28 phases of the moon, resembles related systems by Eliphas Levi (see LEVI) and others, which Yeats had studied as an initiate of the Golden Dawn.

Through Yeats a number of his friends, including Florence Farr and Maud Gonne, became members of the Order. Nearly all the early members were high-minded people, including Anglo-Catholic clergymen and even for a time Evelyn Underhill, the writer on mysticism. The volumes of the ritual, since published by Israel Regardie, do not include the many essays on prayer, the Catholic sacraments, the doctrines of the Virgin Birth, Apostolic Succession and the like, circulated among adepts. The original object of the Society was, beyond the study of magical techniques of various kinds, the alchemical 'great work' of self perfection (see ALCHEMY). Subsequent quarrels arose from Mathers's dictatorial attitude and increasing interest in black magic. Yeats was the leader of the movement to throw out Mathers's pupil Aleister Crowley, who under the name and number of 'the Great Beast' of the Apocalypse openly identified himself with the Antichrist, and practised a form of sexual magic (see CROWLEY). Yeats was at no time anti-Christian, nor was sexual magic practised by the Golden Dawn.

In the troubles which followed the expulsion of Crowley, and afterwards of Mathers, other fragmentations disrupted the Order. A. E. Waite (see WAITE), author of scholarly works on the Cabala and Rosicrucianism, resigned, with a group of adherents who wished to devote themselves exclusively to spiritual development; Yeats was among those who wished to study magic. In 1901 he published a pamphlet circulated among members of the Lodge, *Is the Order of R.R. and A.C. to Remain a Magical Order?* (R.R. and A.C. stand for Rosea Rubiae and Aurea

Yeats's interest since boyhood in the fairy lore of Ireland, still a living tradition at the end of the 19th century, was an important element in his widespread knowledge of occult matters: *Mr W. B. Yeats presenting Mr George Moore to the Queen of the Fairies*, a caricature by Max Beerbohm

Crucis, the higher grades of the Golden Dawn). In it he urged the continuation of the strict examination system by which initiates worked their way through the degrees of adeptship. This document, written to be read by friends who shared his deepest beliefs, is perhaps Yeats's most open declaration of faith. In 1905 Yeats, Wynn Westcott and Arthur Machen resigned; the poet had been a member of the Order for nearly eight years.

The Golden Dawn taught the Western esoteric tradition; the Cabala was central, and adeptship was based upon the Tree of Life and the sefiroth, to which were added the Tarot symbols, the Egyptian pantheon and other mythological equivalents (see CABALA; TAROT). Such was the real ground of all Yeats's subsequent thought: he received no formal education after leaving school; and his true education was a most thorough, serious and practical knowledge of magic and its literature, including alchemy, through the Golden Dawn, together with an introduction to the Platonic and Eastern traditions, through the Theosophical Society. In the pamphlet already mentioned he defines magic as he understood it: 'The central principle of all the Magic of power is that everything we formulate in the imagination, if we formulate it strongly enough, realizes itself in the circumstances of life, acting either through our own souls, or through the spirit of nature.'

The course of Yeats's wide and deep reading was to a great extent determined by these studies. The publications of the Theosophical Society, and publishers and authors under theosophical influence, give a good idea of the scope of his interests. The level of scholarship in this circle was high: learning remained in the hands of such scholars as G. R. S. Mead, A. E. Waite, Harold Bayley and Stephen McKenna, whose qualifications were more than academic.

Yeats also studied history, comparative mythology (the *Golden Bough* set its stamp upon a generation), works on symbolism by Harold S. Bayley and others. Among English poets he preferred the Platonists – Spenser, Shakespeare, Shelley, Blake. He was widely read in philosophy, from the Cambridge Platonists and Berkeley to Kant, Hegel, Spengler and Wittgenstein.

He was also interested in Spiritualism: he maintained a critical attitude, not from scepticism but because he understood that many explanations of the undoubted phenomena were possible. His play *The Words upon the Window Pane* is drawn from his knowledge of mediumship and seances.

A no less important tributary of Yeats's knowledge of occult matters was his interest (continuous from boyhood) in the fairy lore of Ireland, still a living tradition at the end of the 19th century. The collection of folklore by Douglas Hyde and others inspired Yeats to follow their example. *The Celtic Twilight* contains material gathered round Sligo; and he presently inspired Lady Gregory to collect similar material in Galway. In his introduction and notes to her *Visions and Beliefs* he relates folklore to the learned tradition of the Platonists and to Swedenborg. W. Y. Evens-Wentz, since famous as the translator of the Tibetan Buddhist scriptures, dedicated to Yeats his first book, *The Fairy Faith in Celtic Countries*, in which he argues that the Irish folk-beliefs are a remote memory of learned Druidism.

Yeats dreamed of establishing, with the help of Maud Gonne, a Hermetic order in Ireland, whose temple was to be in a castle on an island in Lough Key. The rituals were to be Irish in character, substituting perhaps for the Egyptian gods of the Golden Dawn, Irish gods; as he hoped to do in an epic. 'Patrick or Columcille, Oisin or Finn in Prometheus' stead; and, instead of the Caucasus, Cro-Patrick or Ben Bulben. Have not all races had their first unity from a mythology that marries them to rock or hill?'

In Byzantium, a city at once Christian and Hellenic, Yeats found a symbol which seemed to epitomize the imaginative integration of 'unity of being' within that 'unity of culture' without which no true unity of being is possible to the individual. 'I think that in early Byzantium, maybe never before or since in recorded history, religious, aesthetic and practical life were one, that architect and artificers – though not, it may be, poets, for language had been the instrument of controversy and must have grown abstract – spoke to the multitude and the few alike. The painter, the mosaic worker, the worker in gold and silver, the illuminator of sacred books, were almost impersonal, almost perhaps without the consciousness of individual design, absorbed in their subject-matter and that the vision of a whole people.'

To restore to the Irish nation a unity of culture founded upon a mythology expressed in works of art was the ambition of the poet; who could not endure 'an international art, picking stories and symbols where it pleased'. It was his purpose as a poet so to 'deepen the political passion of the nation that all, artist and poet, craftsman and day-labourer would accept a common design. Perhaps even these images, once created and associated with river and mountain, might move of themselves and with some powerful, even turbulent life, like those painted horses that trampled the ricefields of Japan.'

'Age-long Memoried Self'

His biographer, Joseph Hone, played down Yeats's concern with occultism, which most of his academic readers and admirers also dismiss as being either discreditable or irrelevant. Others defend their poet on the grounds that he studied magic only for the sake of his poetry; quoting in support of this too facile judgement a phrase from *A Vision* in which Instructors say, 'we have come to give you metaphors for poetry'.

The evidence is rather that Yeats regarded poetry as a special kind of magic, than magic as a special kind of poetry. In a postscript to the pamphlet already quoted he makes it clear that for him symbols are agents of power whose operation upon the unconscious mind is independent of conscious intention. 'It is a first principle of our

A learned, even a scholarly, poet in his own field, Yeats's true education was a thorough and serious practical knowledge of magic and its literature; in *A Vision* he expounds a diagrammatic system which relates historical cycles and human character to the 28 phases of the moon, and which resembles related systems by Eliphas Levi and others: 'The Great Wheel' from the *Speculum Angelorum et Hominum*, one of the illustrations in *A Vision*

illumination that symbols and formulae are powers, which act in their own right, and with little consideration for our intentions.' This is because such formulae act upon 'the agelong memoried self' whose Daimons 'may move through the Great Year like individual men and women and are said to use men and women as their bodies, to gather and disperse those bodies at will'; for such reasons as this Yeats told Florence Farr that 'individuality is not as important as our age has imagined'. In his *Autobiographies* he gives instances of subjects made to see visions by symbols exhibited to them in a state of trance.

As a member of a Hermetic order Yeats was under vows of secrecy; his work was grounded in a body of knowledge which he never disclosed. The rituals of the Golden Dawn have since been published, in part by Crowley and fully by Israel Regardie; but these cannot be understood by merely reading the text.

Before Jung and long before Surrealism, and with greater learning and surer metaphysical foundations than either of these or than any psychical research since undertaken, Yeats had divined the existence of a collective mind, a source of imaginative knowledge and poetic images beyond normal consciousness. It is Henry More's *anima mundi*, the oversoul, or collective unconscious. 'I know now that revelation is not from the self but from that age-long memoried self, that shapes the elaborate shell of the mollusc and the child in the womb, that teaches the birds to make their nest; and that genius is a crisis that joins that buried self for certain moments to our trivial daily mind.'

From this collective and shared mind great poetry derives, and to that imaginative ground in each reader it addresses itself. Certain myths, images and incantations speak to the imagination with an immediacy

that overlaps reason, in whoever will allow this to happen. Yeats's symbols, his incantatory speech, all his themes, are addressed to that mind; his design is to awaken recollection, in the Platonic sense of the word, by the use of symbolic images. His poetry is at once oracular and evocative. He held strong views on the declamation of verse which should be (so he held) incantatory, because rhythmic incantation also addresses itself immediately to the imagination.

Yeats believed that the evocatory power of symbols had little to do with the conscious mind. He describes how a certain diagrammatic symbol had the power of evoking visions of 'Eden', with tree, walled garden on the top of a high mountain, birds among the boughs, and from the trunk the sound of 'continual clashing of swords'. Whence came that fine thought of music-making swords, that image of the garden, and many like images and thoughts? I had as yet no clear answer, but knew myself face to face with the Anima Mundi described by Platonic philosophers, and more especially in modern times by Henry More, which has a memory independent of embodied individual memories, though they constantly enrich it with their images and thoughts.'

To those who regard such symbolist art as 'inhuman' it may be replied that such is the abiding ground of our collective humanity. Symbolist art is a form of religious art; one might even say that when religious art ceases to be symbolist it is no longer religious, for it no longer joins the 'age-long memoried self' at certain moments to 'our trivial daily mind'. A demythologized religion is no longer a religion at all, since it no longer possesses the means of binding the individual self to the universal life.

Yeats is never more a symbolist than when in such occasional poems as *Parnell's Funeral* or *All Souls' Night* he relates events of national history or of personal life to that cosmic whole which alone confers upon each part its dignity and significance.

Yeats must be seen in the context of that 'revolt of soul against intellect now beginning in the world' (Yeats here uses the word 'intellect' in the sense of 'reason') of which the Theosophical Movement, Freud and Jung, the Surrealist Movement and the revival of magical studies are various aspects. Of those named it is possible that Yeats himself reached the most profound understanding, as he gave the most enduring expression, to a great reversal of the cycles of history.

KATHLEEN RAINE

FURTHER READING: The principal works of W. B. Yeats are *The Collected Poems* (Macmillan, 2nd edn., 1956), *The Collected Plays* (Macmillan, 2nd edn., 1953), *Mythologies* (Macmillan, 1969), *Autobiography* (Collier Macmillan, 1966), *A Vision* (Collier Macmillan, rev. edn., 1961) and *The Letters of W. B. Yeats* (Macmillan, 1954); see also the official biography by Joseph Hone, *W. B. Yeats 1865–1939* (St Martin, 2nd edn., 1962); Mary C. Flannery, *Yeats & Magic: The Earlier Works* (Barnes & Noble, 1977) and *Yeats' Iconography* (Macmillan, 1960).

YEW

THE EVERGREEN YEW lives to an immense age for it can continue to grow with a completely hollow centre. It has been claimed that the tree can survive for over 3000 years, but this seems unlikely. However, like other conifers, it had an ancient reputation for immortality and became a symbol of life after death. Mourners carried yew branches at funerals, which were placed in the grave; and shoots of yew were sometimes put in a dead person's shroud.

As a symbol of the Resurrection, yew was often incorporated in Eastertide church decorations and used on Palm Sunday. However, it was considered unlucky to bring it into a house, and for this reason it is not used for Christmas decorations. Because of its sacred associations, in Ireland yew wood was made into croziers and shrines. While a common yew was valued at 15 pence in the Middle Ages, a consecrated yew was worth a pound.

It was most unlucky to cut down or damage a growing yew tree; this is not surprising for the yew was among the most potent of trees for protection against evil, and was therefore often planted alongside a house, or where it might form a windbreak against the invisible wind as well as against the unknown powers of evil. Doubtless its planting in churchyards was largely to prevent witchcraft and to restrain the spirits of the buried dead.

However, Robert Turner, writing in 1664, suggested that its main function in churchyards was that it 'attracts and imbibes putrefaction and gross oleaginous vapours exhaled out of the Graves by the setting Sun, and sometimes drawn into those Meteors called *Ignes Fatui*'. Its protectiveness presumably arose from its longevity, its very tough tim-

Said to be among the most potent of trees for protection against evil, the yew was probably planted in churchyards to prevent witchcraft and to restrain the spirits of the buried dead; a symbol of life after death, it had an ancient reputation for immortality, and mourners at funerals carried yew branches which were placed in the grave: yew tree in Stoke Poges churchyard

John Moss

ber, and its red 'berries'. It was, of course, also prized for making bows, although most English bows were made from imported yew, for the native variety was often too brittle and too full of knots. The most antique wooden weapons known are early Paleolithic spears made from yew.

Unrejoicing Berries

The yew cannot be called a cheerful tree, although its autumn display of what Wordsworth called 'unrejoicing berries' is spectacular. Its churchyard affinities have given it funereal associations, and it was also considered a malign tree, perhaps because its foliage is poisonous. Because of this, and because weapons were made from it, Shakespeare referred to it as 'double

fatal' *(Richard II)*. It seems likely that the 'cursed ebenon' referred to by the ghost in *Hamlet* is of yew; Marlowe also mentions 'juice of hebon' in *The Jew of Malta*. Yew forms part of the witches' brew in *Macbeth*:

> Gall of goat, and slips of yew
> Sliver'd in the moon's eclipse.

'Slivered' refers to the wind breaking branches of the trees; any branch broken in this way was unlucky and dangerous to use, for the evil spirit of the storm remained within it.

There are various other intriguing pieces of folklore about the yew. In the north of England it was used in a variant of dowsing to find lost property: the seeker held a yew branch in front of him, which led

him to the goods and turned in his hand when he was by them. A very odd Scottish tradition was that a chieftain could, if holding a piece of churchyard yew in his left hand, threaten or denounce his enemy without the latter hearing. Others present did hear, however, so that it could not be said that he attacked his enemy without warning.

A Herefordshire belief was that if a girl placed a sprig of yew under her pillow, which she had picked in a churchyard she had not previously visited, she would dream of her future husband.

To dream of yew presages the death of some old person which will be of benefit to the dreamer. In the Victorian language of flowers yew meant sorrow.

Yggdrasil

In Scandinavian mythology, the world ash tree; standing at the centre of the universe, it connects together the heavens, the earth and the underworld; after the doom of the gods at the end of the world the man and woman who will repopulate the earth emerge from the world tree.
See ASH; SCANDINAVIA; TREES.

Yin and Yang

In Chinese philosophy, two great opposite principles or forces, on whose interplay everything in the universe depends; Yang is male, light and positive, Yin is female, dark and negative, and all phenomena can be classified in terms of them; in Taoism, the Tao is the principle which unites and transcends the opposites.
See ACUPUNCTURE; CHINA; DUALISM; I CHING; OPPOSITES; TAOISM.

Both a form of meditation and a practical discipline, yoga is a path to liberation from the bondage of rebirth. The best known form is hatha *yoga, which charts the course towards mystical union with the Universal Soul, through the physical body, in a long series of arduous exercises*

YOGA

ESSENTIALLY yoga is a voyage of self-discovery, for it means the linking of the lesser self with the Greater Self. Paradoxically, the Greater Self is contained within the lesser, personal self, just as the farthest horizon of an undiscovered continent is contained within the ship that rides at anchor waiting the captain's word of command. Yoga charts the course, tells how to get there, and describes what will be encountered on the way.

Yoga has sometimes been defined as a religion, and there are as many kinds of yoga as there are sects and cults in any great denomination. In this general sense yoga can mean all things to all men. It has been recommended as a method of beauty culture and a means of getting rich. Its advocates have prescribed it for migraine and falling hair, for insomnia and flatulence. The great adventure has been bypassed altogether, and yoga made into a plaything.

Nonetheless, yoga has a more conservative meaning. It is a system of philosophy;

one of the six recognized systems of orthodox Hinduism (see HINDUISM). The other five are concerned with logic (this is called *Nyaya*), with physical concepts like space, time, causality and matter (*Vaisheshika*), with the objects of abstract philosophical inquiry (*Samkhya*), with ritual (*Mimamsa*), and with the metaphysics of the Ultimate Principle (*Vedanta;* see VEDANTA). But yoga is not a philosophy in the ordinary sense, and a yogi is not a mere 'knower of words'. It is essentially practical, and its discipline down to earth.

The chief textbook on yoga and the first systematic presentation of its philosophy is found in the work of Patanjali, who lived in the 3rd century BC. He is not regarded as the founder, only as the codifier of a doctrine that had already been in existence in India for about 1000 years before his time. He set forth its philosophy in a series of *sutras*, aphorisms or brief sentences, which in the course of centuries, have been subject to considerable interpretation.

As yoga evolved a number of subsidiary systems were added to it, many of them taking as their starting point a verse or even a phrase or word from Patanjali's sutras, and these developed along their own specialist lines, just as modern exponents speak of the 'yoga of business efficiency' or the 'yoga of marital happiness'. But the aim of all the orthodox systems of yoga was permanent liberation from the bondage of rebirth in another incarnation, and ultimate union with the Infinite. Each of these yogas was a 'path' to that goal. The powers that

one might pick up along the way, such as an enhanced mental and physical power, are regarded as of no great consequence in themselves, and a preoccupation with them is a hindrance. Anyone who takes up yoga solely for the powers it might confer is disqualified from the higher teachings.

There are about ten traditionally recognized yogas, acceptable as a path to Realization. *Bhakti* yoga is the way of devotion love and faith, usually directed to God. Yoga, like most of the orthodox Hindu systems of philosophy, was originally atheistic, and even later, when a concept of of a divine soul was introduced, did not refer to God in the ordinary sense as Creator and ruler of the universe. He was only one, albeit the chief, of a whole class of souls (according to Nyaya philosophy), or the fashioner of the world out of material elements which were already in existence (according to Vaisheshika), or an impersonal spirit, the animating principle which united with inert matter to form the universe (Samkhya). Mimamsa held that God was not necessary for salvation, which could be achieved by ritual acts. But bhakti yoga presupposes a personal creator who desires men's devotion and responds to their faith.

Dhyana yoga is the method of contemplation. It is a purely mental discipline, much of which is also embodied in the yoga of physical culture, *hatha* yoga, the yoga familiar to most people today. Dhyana yoga teaches mental discipline, concentration, and the forms of meditation leading to trance states, of which *samadhi* is the culmination.

There is a yoga of works and deeds called *karma* yoga, expressed in charitable acts, forgiveness, penance, asceticism. It is to be distinguished from *kriya* yoga, which is primarily concerned with religious action and ritualism, particularly as expounded in the Mimamsa philosophy. The yoga of knowledge, called *jnana* yoga, relates to the understanding of the sacred books, the *Vedas*, especially the *Upanishads*, where many esoteric doctrines are expounded. *Mantra* yoga deals with magical spells and mystic syllables and the verses of sacred lore, whose correct recitation is believed to confer supernatural gifts (see MANTRA).

In addition to these there are certain yogas concerned with the subtle plexuses of the etheric body, called *chakras*, of which one, called *laya* yoga, teaches their activation, with special emphasis on the *kundalini* (see KUNDALINI) lying at the base of the spine, hence also known as kundalini yoga. It is connected with the recitation of sacred mantras which stimulate the chakras.

Often regarded as the highest form of yoga is *raja* yoga, the royal path to spiritual perfection, which deals almost entirely with mental and psychic development leading to spiritual enlightenment. It is sometimes given the honorific title of *rajadhiraja* yoga, the king of kings yoga.

The Yoga of Physical Power

The best known of all the yogas, and the one whose practice is linked with all the procedures usually associated in the popular mind with Indian religious and occult practice is hatha yoga, the yoga of physical power, or the development of the physical body. It is yoga as commonly understood, the yoga of the cross-legged posture, of standing on the head, the yoga of the wonder-worker. Like the other yogas it follows a series of 'stages', working progressively from the easy to the more difficult. Like the others its aim is release from the bondage of rebirth, and attaining union with the Absolute. It has adopted several features of the other yogas and embodied them within its own discipline.

There are eight stages in hatha yoga, and so comprehensively are they formulated that they are usually taken as the prototype of all forms of yogic discipline. Starting with simple restraints it proceeds through a system of physical and mental culture until it reaches the final stage which cannot be taught but will be experienced by the yogi when he is ready for it. The whole course is long and arduous, and most practitioners are content to confine themselves to the earlier stages and opt for health and efficiency, leaving the Ultimate to the more aspiring.

Whatever spiritual goals may ultimately

The yoga of physical power, hatha yoga consists of eight stages which are usually taken as the prototype of all forms of yogic discipline; the third stage teaches the asanas or bodily positions which are assumed as an exercise and during meditation: statuette of a deity sitting in the lotus position. The most common of the asanas, and the simplest for people accustomed to sitting on the ground, it obviates any danger of the student falling over during trance

underlie yogic training, it is the physical body that is the instrument through which they are achieved, and the physical body must be trained for it. We can go through life ignoring our 'soul', indeed even denying its existence, without doing ourselves apparent harm; we may neglect the intellectual side of our personalities and still savour a great deal of life without detriment to ourselves. But the physical, or gross body of flesh and blood, makes insistent demands on us. Breath is needed every few seconds; food every few hours; sleep once a day. And unless the body receives this recurrent sustenance and replenishment it will demand attention in such a manner that all other considerations will have to be subordinated until it is satisfied.

Therefore, even though the aim of yoga might reach beyond and above the range of the physical, we have to begin at the beginning, that is, on the physical plane. Our attitude to worldly and unworldly matters has to be settled and our priorities fixed and it is in the arrangement of these that hatha yoga has laid down its eight stages.

The first two preliminary stages are called *yama* and *niyama*, and are to do with external and internal control. They cover the ethical rules governing personal and social conduct, and various methods of self-discipline connected with non-injury, continence, equanimity and right thinking.

Non-injury, or *ahimsa*, implies a restraint on all aggressive emotions, such as hatred, anger, jealousy, revenge. It totally forbids

physical injury to any living thing and this idea lies behind the dietary prohibition against the eating of meat. The true yogi is a vegetarian, and a pacifist. One should not 'flail one's arms about', in case one injures someone standing near by. One should not even think in violent and aggressive terms.

Ahimsa is closely connected with the idea of equanimity, which is one of the basic tenets of the Hindu ethical code. It means that a person should be tranquil in the face

Executed in combination with breathing techniques, the recitation of mantras, and mandalas or mystic diagrams, asanas are believed to draw down etheric forces from the invisible world which imbue the body of the student with power: mandala, 17th or 18th century

of every provocation, defeat, personal and financial loss, indignity, insult. It is the mark of self-conquest, to be acquired long before the regular yogic disciplines are undertaken. It is to be learned in the school of life, as a householder or man of affairs. Anger, desire to avenge an insult or redress a personal injury, retaliation, are all marks of pride. According to the great Indian epic, the *Mahabharata*, only the fool imagines that anger or indignation are signs of energy or of the superior man. A man given to anger is a man in chains, not a free person. Self-restraint or self-control are aimed at in the early stages, but as one advances even these fall short of the true ideal, for they imply the existence of emotions that need restraining. True equanimity is the absence even of the seeds of anger.

Another item usually included in the yama and niyama exercises is *brahmacharya* or abstinence from sex, and this is generally insisted on for those who desire to devote themselves totally to the spiritual life. But for all persons, irrespective of their occupation, moderation in sexual activity is of the highest importance. Married people are enjoined to guard against self-indulgence. Aspirants to the higher reaches must abstain altogether, for while sex has its proper place in the life of the householder, it is considered a definite hindrance to the higher life. The lawgiver Manu said, 'Irresistible power comes from chastity.'

For the man of the world yama and niyama present an eminently rational way of life. Certain things are essential, but our attitude to them must be reasonable. Food is necessary but not greed; sex but not sensuality; self-respect but not arrogance.

The Beneficial Headstand
The third stage in hatha yoga teaches the *asanas* or bodily positions, the postures assumed both as an exercise and during meditation. Patanjali said that the best posture was one that was 'firm and pleasant', that is, fit for its purpose and not uncomfortable. Yogic meditation involves long periods of motionless sitting and it is partly to accustom the student to a fixed and easy position in which he can remain longest without discomfort that the basic yogic asanas have been devised.

Many of the positions involve great bodily contortion, and though the practice of such devious attitudes is frowned upon by the adept, it is with these asanas that most people associate yoga. The exponent with his legs twisted about his neck or in some other peculiar stance is the traditional Western image of the yogi in action.

Asanas are called after their supposed resemblance to some object, plant or animal. There are asanas named after the lion, the bull, tortoise, frog, fish, scorpion, lotus, plough, wheel and sun, and many other such things. The names are bestowed on them partly to describe their appearance and also to suggest the quality they impart. The asana named after the swan gives one discrimination, for this is the chief attribute of that bird; the asana named after the frog gives one the main quality of this animal, which is strength of purpose.

In the *simhasana*, or lion pose, the yogi bends his legs till the knees touch the floor and places his hands on his knees. He protrudes his tongue as far out as it will go, stares at its tip, and then tenses the shoulders, arms and neck, making the whole frame taut so as to give the body the appearance of a fierce lion. This asana gives one leonine attributes.

The most common of yogic asanas is the well-known cross-legged pose called the *siddha* (power) asana and, in a slight variation, the *padma* (lotus) asana. This is the squatting position, with legs crossed. To people who are accustomed to sitting on the ground this is the simplest of all the asanas, although it presents some difficulty to those who have never tried it. It is a very stable posture, which enables one to keep the spine straight and obviates any danger of falling over and injuring oneself.

Another popular posture is the *shirsha* asana or 'head position', the ordinary headstand, which is done in several ways. The simplest method is to stand facing the wall, a convenient distance away from it, to bend forward till the head touches the ground, and finally to throw the legs up till they touch the wall for support. The legs are then shifted off the wall and the body straightened out. There are numerous variations on this.

The headstand pose is one of great antiquity. As an occult exercise it was known to the early Taoists of China (see TAOISM) who recommended it as a means of making certain subtle fluids descend to the head in order to 'repair the brain'. The mysterious sect of the Cabiri of Greece practised the headstand as a sacred rite, and the statue of a woman standing on her head in a Cabiri shrine aroused the uncontrollable laughter of the Persian king Cambyses II (d. 522 BC) who could not understand what the inverse attitude had to do with religion. In Europe standing on the head was long recommended as a cure for colic.

In yoga the purpose of this asana is to reverse the direction of the flow of certain fluids running in the internal channels of the body and direct them to the hidden reservoirs of the brain. The perfect execution of the headstand is said to be a profound mystery for it unites 'upper with lower', 'running with still', and 'male with female' in the 'nuptial chambers' situated in the cranium. The fluids become etherialized and then ignite, so that a state of illumination may be reached through this asana alone, if one knows the hidden art.

Many blessings attend its proper performance. In addition to the physical benefits of longevity, youthfulness and sexual vigour, and the intellectual benefits of an improved memory, great concentration and increased will-power, the spiritual blessings include the ability to perform miracles and fly through the air. This latter has been interpreted to mean that the adept can travel at will in the astral body (see ASTRAL BODY).

Associated with the asanas are certain accompanying gestures of the hand called *mudras*, which are believed to direct the latent potencies of each bodily posture by channelling them along particular paths.

The hand is the focus of immense power, and certain gestures made by the hands are universally recognized as having an almost magical quality (see GESTURE). The human hand has been called the second brain and the visible part of the mind. Benedictions are bestowed by the hand. Diseases are healed and strength communicated by the laying on of hands. Gestures of anger, appeal, supplication, and command are familiar throughout the world. A hand gesture not only articulates and concentrates the internal forces and directs them outwards, it also receives power from the invisible world. It is the channel of communication between the two worlds.

Pranic Winds
In their highest form yogic asanas are executed in combination with breathing techniques, with the recitation of mantras, with mudras, and with *mandalas*, or mystic diagrams (see MANDALA). In such an asana the whole body becomes a plastic mould, as it were, a fixed symbolic pose, into which etheric forces are drawn down and poured forth from the invisible world, filling the mould represented by the asana and imbuing it with the desired power.

The fourth stage of hatha yoga is concerned with *pranayama* or breath control, which takes into account a number of factors. First, comes the simple technique of inhalation, retention and exhalation, for which a ratio has to be established. For instance, if we breathe in for the duration of six seconds, hold our breath for nine seconds and breathe out for three seconds, the ratio would be shown as 6.9.3., a ratio that is regarded as good for a specific purpose. In order to increase the efficacy of the ratio the yogi might double it to 12.18.6., and breathe with this frequency, or treble it to 18.27.9., and use this timing in his breathing. The commonest ratios are 1.4.2., or 2.5.3., or 5.4.3. Sometimes another item is added to the rhythm of inhalation, retention and exhalation, namely, retention of breath after exhalation, and we then have to add a fourth element to our ratio, thus getting 1.4.2.3., or whatever the ratio may be.

When further refinements are added to these factors, such as breathing with the mouth open or closed throughout, or with the mouth closed during inhalation and open during exhalation, or with one nostril closed with the finger, breathing shallowly or deeply, hot or cold, or inhaling and exhaling while blowing, panting, sniffing, snoring, or while making the noises of animals like barking, cooing, mooing, or roaring, the permutations are increased almost to infinity.

The full range of possibilities in pranayama has therefore never been worked out and its systems of breathing are of unending variety. The chief kinds of breathing are taught by various schools, their benefits explained in brief, and their continuance strongly advocated. As a rule the subtleties are ignored. For the important thing about breathing is not so much the manner in which it is done, as the way the breath is used, for it is believed to be a very subtle essence full of energy.

The air breathed in is not in itself the essential element utilized by the yogi, but another far more refined ingredient which is diffused in the atmosphere all round, and impregnated with a vivifying power. The air we breathe only serves as the conductor for this subtle force. This energy is called *prana*, generally translated as 'wind', and pranayama teaches the method of absorbing it.

Several kinds of these pranic winds or airs are distinguished, each with its own function. Prana, when taken in, moves from the lungs and lodges in the heart, and from here directs the movement of the vital airs to the other parts of the bodily frame. Pranas in their various forms are responsible for the beating of the heart, for respiration, the circulation of the blood, for digestion, speech, sleep, hunger and thirst, and all the physiological processes of the body, which are continuously activated through the subtle body. Essentially, pranayama is the controlled means by which the invisible energy of the cosmos is channelled to act directly on the physical system.

The next stage, *pratyahara*, involves a deliberate procedure of abstraction and withdrawal of the senses from the turmoil of the outside world. The obvious way to do this is to retire to a quiet secluded chamber free from all disturbances; or to shut the eyes and ears and so prevent the sights and sounds from impinging on them. There is a specific way of performing this act, which involves the actual closing of the organs of sense.

Again, the instrument used is the body itself. One must 'block' the passages of the body by using the body, without recourse to external apparatus. A special mudra has been devised which shuts the gates of the body. The yogi sits in a cross-legged position, performs the prescribed breathing rituals, utters a few mantras, then raising his hands to his face he shuts his ears with his thumbs, his eyes with his index fingers, his nostrils with the middle fingers; the ring fingers press on the upper lip and the little fingers on the lower. With his heel he applies a firm pressure to the perineum, and thus effectively seals the chief orifices of his body.

But this gesture is only a symbolical rite, and is always accompanied by special mental exercises, which eventually lead to mastery of the secret of sealing the gates without the mudra. The ordinary person may take anything up to 21 years before he can perfect the technique to such an extent that his senses are totally impervious to every sensation of sound, sight, hearing, touch, taste and smell. Since his sensory reactions are also effectively blocked, he remains unperturbed by anything that happens around him.

Next comes the stage of *dharana* or concentration, fixing the mind on a single object to the exclusion of all else. In a small way everyone has moments of dharana — the child playing with his toys, the student cramming for his examinations, the mathematician engrossed in his problem. It is also spoken of as 'one-pointedness', and a number of yogic exercises are designed to heighten one's capacity to concentrate. The purpose of dharana is to fill the mind, already emptied by pratyahara, with the thought one wishes to hold, and then to hold that thought without any flickering of consciousness. The mind must burn steadily and purely, 'like a flame in a windless place'.

Among the many different methods used to increase the powers of concentration is one called *trataka*, or 'fixing', in which the gaze is directed without blinking and with full concentration on an external object. One might start with an object far off, such as a hilltop, or a window in a distant house, or the branch of a tree. The mind must be collected and focused on the object without wavering. In time, nearer objects may be used for the purpose, and then in the quiet of the room one can mark the wall with a small dot at eye level and, sitting about six feet away from the wall, stare at it. In the case of such exercises one must think of nothing else but the dot. But concentration being an 'inward' matter, is best achieved by exercising the mind to dwell on the body itself. Thus we have exercises concentrating on the tip of the nose, the centre of the forehead, or the navel.

The seventh stage is called dhyana, or contemplation and in it one must lose oneself. The operation is still 'mental', and mental forces are required to attain it. There is a total direction of thought on the goal sought. The range of subjects for dhyana is limitless for the higher adept, but is confined to certain specific items for the beginner.

Not all subjects are suitable for meditation. It is easy to concentrate on material

Although the ultimate aim of yoga is permanent liberation from the bondage of rebirth, the body is the physical instrument through which these goals are achieved, and its demands must therefore be disciplined and controlled before samadhi, 'final bliss', can be attained
Above, left to right Some of the bodily positions assumed in hatha yoga are called after the objects or animals they supposedly resemble: triangle pose; the 'head position' which unites 'upper with lower', 'running with still', and 'male with female' in the cranium; lotus position in the headstand; shoulder stand; the 'plough'; the 'tortoise'
Facing page, below left A twisting position and *(below right)* a sitting position assumed for pranayama or breath control, the fourth stage of hatha yoga

things, and think of money, sex or pleasure, but the moral dangers of such objectives are very great. Similarly, symbols casually selected without taking into account one's religious, racial, family and personal background can also lead to spiritual disharmony. In India the matter is very simply decided. One can meditate on one's guru or mentor, or on a deity, but for the Western mind the unfamiliar character of such meditation will present difficulties, apart from the psychological barriers in the way of his acceptance of such objects to meditate upon.

Symbols too have a strong psychic dynamism and every religion charges its own symbols with its own current of power, which can be picked up by anyone who meditates on such a symbol with sufficient faith. The mandalas and mystic diagrams are all capable of putting one in rapport with the powers inherent in them. Great care has to be exercised before adopting a symbol for dhyana.

Attainment of Ecstasy

The eighth and final stage of hatha yoga is samadhi, which has been variously translated as trance, super-consciousness, or final bliss. This is no longer an intellectual state, for it transcends the merely mental condition of intellectual contemplation, and goes on to the state of ecstasy. The attainment of such a condition for the ordinary man is difficult in the extreme and needs long practice, for he is constantly hindered by physical and mental distractions. An

uncomfortable posture will result in the mind being diverted to the aching limbs; lack of sufficient self-discipline and training will make one aware of the pangs of hunger or the need for sleep. If one has mastered the early stages of yoga sufficiently to withstand these distractions, one is faced with the distractions of the mind and spirit as one moves along the path. It is precisely in order to remove all possible sources of distraction that the stages of yoga have to be systematically followed through.

Samadhi is the mystic union of the individual soul with the Universal Soul. The earlier stages of dharana and dhyana may be defined as concrete meditation. Samadhi may be regarded as abstract meditation on the Void. The earlier stage is active; the latter is passive. The earlier is achieving, this is receiving. One is seeking, the other absorbing and being absorbed. There is no trace of mental activity, no trace of self or the ego. The fevers of the flesh are far behind, the petty emotions that perturb the soul and shatter the peace of mind. The ego is lost, the mind transcended.

True samadhi must be clearly distinguished from certain kinds of extraordinary trance states that have on occasion been achieved by practitioners of the magical arts, and that have been attested by more than one dependable witness. Some exponents have allowed themselves to be buried alive. A well-authenticated case took place in Lahore (now in Pakistan) in 1838 in the presence of the distinguished Sikh leader, Maharajah Ranjit Singh, a British general, Sir Claude Wade, and other British officers. The man was a professional magician who made a living by feats of this kind. He took a few days to get himself in readiness by fasting and meditation, and then presented himself to the distinguished gathering. He sat cross-legged on a sheet of white cloth and went into a trance, after which the corners of the cloth were drawn up and tied over his head. He was then buried still seated, in a padlocked box, in an underground pit within a garden pavilion. The doors were locked and sealed. British soldiers stood on 24-hour guard outside. He remained in the grave for 30 days, after which the pit was dug up in the presence of the Maharajah, Sir Claude Wade, Dr

McGregor and several others, and the box lifted out intact. After the man's apparently lifeless body had been gently massaged by his assistant he recovered consciousness, and two hours later was able to speak.

This kind of performance is emphatically discouraged by the true adept. But so close is the inherited association of yoga with the magical arts of the wonder-worker that the term *jogi* (colloquial adaptation of yogi) has become synonymous with the magician, and jogis have been credited with some very bizarre feats. They are the fakirs and naked *sadhus* of the tourist. Some of them sleep on beds of nails, or remain standing in one place, often on one leg, for several months. Some remain in the same spot throughout their lives, never moving outside the confines of the area they have assigned for themselves, which may be a tiny hut, with only a short walk for the calls of nature. Others remain submerged up to the waist in a stream for weeks on end; or sit in the open in the full blaze of the midsummer sun surrounded by five fierce fires kept alive by their disciples. Some hold the face up until the neck muscles harden and they are unable to look down upon the earth again; some reverse the position and look downwards so that the sky is no more within their normal vision. Others keep the fist closed permanently until the nails grow into the flesh (see FAKIR).

But some remarkable claims have been made on behalf of the orthodox yogi too, especially concerning the control of the physiological processes of the body. Yogis are able to suspend their breathing to an abnormal extent; show different pulse rates at will on the right and left wrists; lower the respiratory rate till it is barely perceptible; become totally immunized to the effects of heat and cold; remain in trance for days at a time; go without food and water for several weeks; exert an almost supernatural control over wild animals.

Although the exercise of the powers that come to the practitioner of yoga is regarded as an obstacle in the path towards the aspirant's spiritual progress, many people practise yoga for precisely these powers, or *siddhis* as they are called, and are not greatly concerned about the non-material benefits accruing from its practice.

There are said to be eight traditional siddhis, as follows: making oneself infinitely small; infinitely large; infinitely heavy; weightless; transporting oneself anywhere instantaneously; gaining all one's desires; controlling people; achieving overlordship over all things. Patanjali's enigmatic statement that 'Perfection may arise from birth (inherited faculty), drugs, spells, austerities or concentration', has been the subject of considerable commentary and interpretation. The inclusion of drugs has divided opinion on the matter, some suggesting that the philosopher mentioned drugs as one means of emancipation from the bondage of rebirth, others contending that he merely included them to complete the catalogue of items that could be used for the purpose of reaching samadhi, but did not give drug-taking his approval.

A matter of considerable interest to researchers in the field today is the close similarity between the powers developed by yoga and the experiences of the drug-state, particularly those induced by LSD. Drugs produce the tranquillity, provide the vision, and create the illusions of power. Subjects of LSD experiments report experiences that parallel every one of the traditional siddhis, produced as a result of visual, auditory and other sensory distortion. Session records indicate that subjects have the feeling that they have shrunk to near vanishing point, while the consciousness of others expands to such an extent that they imagine themselves 'as big as a galaxy'. Some feel that they have a vastly greater or lesser density, and become extremely heavy and virtually immovable, or in some cases, almost weightless. The feeling of being transported to other places is quite common in LSD experiments. This kind of drug-induced 'travelling clairvoyance', where the subject visits distant places, is perhaps also comparable to the flying of medieval witches, who rubbed the sensitive mucous membranes of the nasal and sexual orifices with drug-impregnated ointments which induced a trance, and returned to bring back accounts of wonderful adventures at the sabbath (see FLYING OINTMENT). The power of attaining one's desires is again met within the hallucinogenic state where the subject, depending on his personal predispositions, projects himself into his vision and thus attains what he seeks. Likewise the power to control people and the illusion of overlordship over all things is another commonplace of psychedelic experience, and on a smaller scale is exhibited by the subject who jumps off a tall building under the delusion that he has suddenly acquired the ability to fly; or who stands in a busy thoroughfare, steps off the pavement and wills a speeding bus to come to a halt.

But many regard these resemblances as superficial. The differences between the genuine and controlled powers acquired after many years of self-culture and the erratic hallucinations produced instantaneously by drugs are so considerable that the analogy need not be pursued any further. On the other hand it is easy to exaggerate the benefits of yoga, for it is well known that many other disciplines of physical culture and mental training can bring about the same results, and are not the monopoly of any one system of spiritual development.

Yoga is said to give one a higher IQ, exceptional sexual vigour, ESP, and even a kind of earthly immortality. Yet yogis in their prime die every year like other mortals. They are not notable for their IQs. Attempts by exponents to walk on water have always come to a watery end. And extraordinary breathing feats have been recorded all over the world from China to Peru. The ascetic disciplines of the sadhus find a parallel in the Christian desert hermits of the 4th and 5th centuries. Yogis have been buried alive, but so have Moslem sufis, and Western magicians. Yogis have walked on fire, but so have natives from the South Seas, who perform the much more difficult feat of walking on red-hot stones.

Putting the whole of the miraculous element aside, it may be said that yoga is a discipline which in moderation and by the use of common sense, may be practised with benefit.

(see BREATH; MEDITATION; SELF-DENIAL.)

BENJAMIN WALKER

FURTHER READING: Theos Bernard, *Hatha Yoga* (Wehman); Paul Dukes, *The Yoga of Health, Youth and Joy* (Harper and Row, 1960); Mircea Eliade, *Yoga, Immortality and Freedom* (Princeton Univ. Press, 1970); S. K. Majumdar, *Introduction to Yoga: Principles and Practice* (University Books, 1967); R. E. L. Masters and Jean Houston, *The Varieties of Psychedelic Experience* (Holt, Rinehart and Winston, 1966); Lar Caughlan, *Yoga: The Spirit of Union* (Kendall-Hunt, 1981).

Yoni

The female sex organ, as an emblem of both sexual pleasure and generation; connected with fertility, the earth, the mother goddess; worshipped in India alone or in conjunction with the male symbol, the lingam, expressing the fruitful union of opposites; sometimes symbolized by a shell, a perforated stone, a woman, lotus, cow or triangle.

See PHALLIC SYMBOLISM.

Yule

Old-fashioned term for the Christmas season, from the Norse winter fire festival over which the god Odin presided; the Yule-log should be brought into the house with ceremony on Christmas Eve and should be lighted from a piece of the previous year's log, which has been kept all year to preserve the luck of the household.

See CHRISTMAS.

Mansell Collection

When the Roman army entered the smoking ruins of the Zealot stronghold of Masada, mounds of corpses testified to the resolution of this Jewish sect to die rather than to recognize any other lord than Yahweh

ZEALOTS

THE EMPEROR AUGUSTUS ordered the incorporation of Judaea into the Roman Empire in the year 6 AD. The change was to prove disastrous to the Jews because, for the first time, it brought them up against the realities of subjugation to Roman rule. Other peoples had naturally resented the imposition of Roman rule as the Empire expanded: but for the Jews such subjection was not only an affront to their national pride, it profoundly affected their religion. It touched them at their most sensitive point; for they cherished the idea of Israel as a theocracy, with Yahweh (see YAHWEH) as their supreme Lord and a godly high priest as his earthly representative.

One of the first measures taken by the Romans to implement the new decree was to order a census of the population of Judaea for the purpose of taxation. The Jews had been accustomed to pay taxes to their own kings; but to pay them to Rome challenged a fundamental tenet of their religion. For it meant giving of the resources of the Holy Land of Yahweh to the heathen emperor of Rome. As soon as the new measure was known, a rabbi called Judas of Galilee incited the people to revolt − to pay the taxes, he proclaimed was an act of apostasy toward Yahweh, and tantamount to recognizing Caesar as lord (*despotes*) instead of the god of Israel.

The revolt was suppressed, and Judas was slain. But those of his followers who survived took to the deserts of Judaea, to maintain a guerilla resistance against the Romans. They became known as the Zealots, which was a Greek translation of their Hebrew name *Kanna'im*. The name probably derived from the ancient example of Phinehas, as recorded in the book of Numbers 25.6–13. Angered by the liaison of a fellow Jew with a non-Jewish woman, Phinehas had slain both. For his action he had been praised by Yahweh, 'in that he was zealous with my zeal', and a perpetual priesthood was conferred on him and his descendants, 'because he was zealous for his God, and made atonement for the people of Israel'.

Phinehas was thus the divinely commended prototype of the Zealots, who served Yahweh their god with a fanatical devotion, ready to resort to violent action or suffer martyrdom in his cause. Their enemies were not only the heathen Romans, who had imposed their rule on Israel, but also those Jews who collaborated with them. Such Jewish 'quislings' were mainly members of the Sadducean aristocracy, who monopolized the chief ecclesiastical offices connected with the great Temple of Yahweh at Jerusalem. From this aristocracy the high priest was chosen by the Romans, who recognized him as the head of the Jewish state for internal affairs. These sacerdotal aristocrats were not popular with the mass of their fellow-countrymen. Consequently, since their positions depended on Roman support, they co-operated with the Roman government of their land.

Suppression of the Truth

It has only been since the Second World War that the real character of the Zealot movement has been understood. There have been three main reasons for this. The excavation of the rock fortress of Masada beside the Dead Sea, and the discovery of the Dead Sea Scrolls have provided new information about the Zealots and the background of Jewish religio-political thinking at this time (see DEAD SEA SCROLLS). Then, the 'resistance' movements in Nazi-occupied countries during the Second World War have promoted a more sympathetic insight into the Zealot 'resistance' against ancient Rome. These factors, in turn, have led to a more critical evaluation of what Josephus, the Jewish historian of the 1st century, wrote about the Zealots. Josephus is our chief informant concerning the Zealots; but it is now realized that he denigrated them for personal reasons. In the war against Rome which started in 66 AD, Josephus deserted to the Romans, and later wrote an account of the war for his Roman patron, the Emperor Vespasian: In this account, Josephus blames the Zealots for the war, representing them as evilly-disposed desperadoes who would stop at no atrocity to force their peaceably-minded countrymen to revolt against Rome. His favourite term for them was *lestai* ('brigands'), which was undoubtedly also how the Romans described them. He conceals the fact that the Zealots were patriots, and that their actions were inspired by their intense devotion to Yahweh, the god of Israel.

Owing to the apologetical character of Josephus' account of Jewish affairs during this period, it is impossible to trace out the development of the Zealot movement. However, the Christian gospels afford some significant evidence, although this is also of an enigmatical kind. Thus it is recorded that one of the apostles chosen by Jesus was 'Simon the Zealot' (Luke 6.15); but Mark tries to disguise the fact by giving only the unexplained Aramaic equivalent 'the Cananaean' for 'the Zealot' (Mark 3.18). Jesus was also implicated in some way with Barabbas, a Zealot leader of a rising against the Romans (see JESUS); and Pontius Pilate ordered Jesus to be crucified between two *lestai*, who were doubtless Zealots captured in the recent rising in which Barabbas was involved.

Like other resistance forces, the ancient Zealots adopted guerilla tactics in operating against the Romans and their Jewish collaborators from hide-outs in the desert areas of Judaea and Galilee. They probably had the sympathy and clandestine support of the mass of their own countrymen, whose social interests and antipathies they shared. It is significant that one of their first acts, on gaining control of Jerusalem in 66 AD, was to burn the public archives which contained the money-lenders' bonds − in order, so Josephus complains, to encourage the poor to rise against the rich; a sympathy showed also by Jesus.

Death Before Surrender

The Zealot movement seems to have had a dynastic leadership. After the death of Judas of Galilee, the founder, in 6 AD, his sons apparently organized the movement; for Josephus records that the Roman governor Tiberius Alexander, during his term of office in 46–8 AD, crucified Jacob and Simon, sons of Judas. At the beginning of the revolt in 66 another son, Menahem, assumed the leadership, and the last surviving Zealots at Masada were commanded by a descendant of Judas, named Eleazar.

Capture by the Romans usually meant crucifixion for a Zealot. It is probable that the warning given by Jesus of the likely consequences of joining his movement already had a Zealot currency: 'If any man would come after me, let him deny himself, and take up his cross, and follow me' (Mark 8.34). In Judaea at that time crucifixion was the Roman penalty for sedition. It is significant that Josephus also records that the Romans tortured Zealots to make them 'acknowledge Caesar as lord'.

According to Josephus, a new group of

St Simon, 12th century wall painting in Cappadocia; one of the apostles chosen by Jesus, he is described in St Luke's gospel as 'Simon the Zealot'

Zealots appeared when Felix was the Roman governor (52–60 AD). They were called 'Sicarii', or daggermen, from the *sica* or dagger with which they were armed. They were evidently formed as a terrorist group to carry out clandestine assassinations, particularly of notable Jewish collaborators with the Romans. Concealing their daggers in their loose garments, they struck at their victims in crowded places – thus they killed the high priest Jonathan in the Temple.

During the 60 years from 6 to 66 AD, Jewish history has the appearance of a Greek tragedy moving relentlessly to its fatal climax. Even if the Roman procurators of Judaea had been consistently wise and just in their rule, it is unlikely that the Jews would ever have settled down quietly as subjects of heathen Rome. For the fundamental tenets of their religion forbade their recognition of any other sovereign lord of Israel than Yahweh. These tenets the Zealots fanatically maintained, and their exhortations to their fellow Jews were powerfully reinforced by the evidence of Roman injustice and such outrages as the attempt of the Emperor Caligula in 39–40 to place his image, in the form of Zeus, in the very sanctuary of Yahweh at Jerusalem.

The final explosion came in 66 AD, when the lower order of the priests, who were infected by Zealotism and persecuted by the sacerdotal aristocracy, refused to offer the daily sacrifice in the Temple for the well-being of the Roman emperor and people. These sacrifices were regarded as signifying Jewish loyalty to Rome, so that their cessation was tantamount to rebellion. The aristocracy endeavoured to restore the situation by force, and fighting broke out. The rebel priests were soon reinforced by the Zealots. Opposition was wiped out, and the Roman garrisons in Jerusalem and elsewhere were massacred. Once in possession of the Temple, the Zealots elected a new high priest according to the directions of the Torah.

The first Roman attempt to suppress the revolt in 66 failed disastrously, and encouraged the Jews to believe that Yahweh would save them. It took four years of bitter fighting before the Romans could capture Jerusalem. In the final assault on the city, the Temple, which was fiercely defended by the Zealots, was burnt. The fall of Jerusalem in 70 AD was fated to mark the end of the Jewish national state in Palestine until its re-establishment in 1948. The Jewish overthrow is commemorated in the sculptured panels of the Arch of Titus in Rome, where the exultant legionaries are shown bearing the spoils of the Temple in triumph through the streets of the capital.

The final drama of Zealot resistance was, however, played out at Masada, on the shores of the Dead Sea. There a Zealot garrison, with their families, held out until 73 AD. When the Romans, by a prodigious feat of military engineering, at last succeeded in breaking the walls, the Zealots preferred suicide to surrender. The men killed their wives and children; then they drew lots for the order in which they themselves should be killed by their comrades. Finally, on that fatal night, the last remaining Zealot, having seen that all were dead, set fire to the fortress and killed himself. The next morning, when the Romans entered the smoking ruins, 960 corpses testified to Zealot resolution to recognize no other lord than Yahweh, the god of their fathers.

S. G. F. BRANDON

FURTHER READING: The best edition of the works of Josephus, including Greek text and English translation, is published in the Loeb Classical Library; vols 1–3 concern the Zealots. See also: S. G. F. Brandon, *Jesus and the Zealots* (Manchester Univ. Press, 1967); Y. Yadin, *Masada: Herod's Fortress and the Zealots' Last Stand* (Weidenfeld & Nicolson, 1966).

Sonia Halliday

ZEN

An emphasis on direct intuitive experience characterizes Zen, a conviction that penetration to the heart of life's meaning cannot be brought about by the mind alone; unexpectedly to the Western mind, its deeply serious truths are often conveyed in humour and also in seeming irreverence

ZEN is a Chinese-Japanese branch of Mahayana Buddhism. Although nowhere within the boundaries of its special teachings is there demanded faith in a God external to the universe who has created the cosmos and man, nor is there any single sacrosanct collection of revealed scriptures to be venerated like the Christian Bible or Hinduism's *Vedas*, Zen followers and teachers nevertheless consider Zen a religion. In their view, Zen's form of Buddhism is a natural, indeed inevitable development from such challenging and iconoclastic statements by the founder of this major world faith as 'Look within, *thou* art the Buddha'. Zen is concerned with teaching that all men, with disciplined individual effort, are capable of attaining the Buddha's Enlightenment, known as *satori* in the Zen vocabulary.

Zen's emphasis, in the present as well as the past, falls on specific meditative practices designed to 'see into one's nature', a descriptive phrase attributed to one of the most important figures in the annals of early Zen, the Chinese master of the 7th century, Hui-Neng (638-713; in Japanese, Eno). The late author and scholarly authority on Zen Buddhism, D. T. Suzuki, called Hui-Neng's statement 'the most significant phrase ever coined in the development of Zen'. Some 13 centuries have passed since Hui-Neng uttered these words but they remain as basic to Zen teaching as they were when he spoke them, and it is this phrase, and others similar to it, that have turned a number of Western psychoanalysts and psychiatrists — including

Although one of the characteristics of Zen is a zany sense of humour this springs from the wish to avoid self-conscious religiosity or smugness about spiritual attainment, and it has not stopped Buddhists from prostrating themselves in front of Buddha images as an act that 'horizontalizes the ego-mast': statue of Buddha in Kamakura, Japan

Alan Irvine

Carl Jung, Erich Fromm and Karen Horney — to a serious study of Zen methods in relation to their own interests in the attainment of self-knowledge. Existentialists, also, of the stature of Martin Heidegger, have claimed to find in ancient Zen writings some of the very ideas they have been developing in modern times.

The recent phenomenon of a steadily growing interest in Zen teachings in Europe and the United States arises, it has been suggested, in part because Zen's emphasis on 'finding out for oneself' appeals to modern people who have difficulty accepting fixed dogma or traditional religious authority in a world now in scientific and philosophic flux. It is not only Japanese *roshis* (venerable spiritual teachers) but Westerners as well who, after training in Japanese monasteries, are today carrying to the West Zen's interpretation and extension of original Buddhist teachings. Through body-mind techniques of 'quiet sitting' as well as through the challenge of the dynamic conundrum known as the *koan*, Zen aims to establish unshaken personal faith in life's 'Is-ness', the universe seen as an indissoluble unity, a single totality of which man is but a part.

In Buddhism's slow but irresistible spread over all Asia the Mahayana branch of teaching reached China around 525 AD. From China in time it moved on to Korea and to Japan acquiring, in the usual flexible Mahayana style, certain colourations from the cultures encountered in its passage (see BUDDHISM; JAPAN). The ancient

Indian mystic root, along with strong pragmatic and humanistic influences from China, the land of Confucius and Lao-Tze, are so clearly traceable in Zen's development that Zen as known today might be fairly described as a unique blend of Indian mysticism and Chinese naturalism sieved through the special mesh of the Japanese character. The very origins of its name indicate its historical genesis. Zen is the Japanese way of writing and speaking the Chinese word *ch'an*, which is a transliteration of the Sanskrit word *dhyana*, meaning meditation or, more fully, 'contemplation leading to a higher state of Consciousness' or 'union with Reality'.

It was in the 12th century that the special development of Buddhist philosophy known in China as ch'an was definitely established in Japan under the name of Zen. Prior to this date, however, there had been a significant exchange of Buddhist monks and teachers between the two countries; a traffic of inestimable importance not only to Japanese culture but to the history of Zen philosophy and the world's art. These religious emissaries acted, in effect, as disseminators and preservers of Chinese civilization at its brilliant height in the great Sung Dynasty. When the Sung idyll was brought to its end by an invasion of Mongols, Japan escaped the invaders and thus became the sanctuary not only for the scriptures and teachings of a new-old, India-born, Chinese-influenced philosophy but for its intimately related arts as well.

So allied with Zen philosophy is its

The Zen belief that the Buddha nature is immanent not only in man, but in everything that exists, animate or inanimate, is reflected in the traditional culture of Japan; qualities such as tranquillity and emptiness are expressed in the design of gardens and house interiors, in plays and poetry *Above* **Sand garden in Kyoto, symbolizing the sea** *Above right* **A temple garden, also in Kyoto**

unique aesthetic that one cannot separate the two and still have a profound comprehension of Zen's underlying precepts. This is true in particular of those swiftly-executed 'spontaneous' ink paintings which manage to express with consummate subtlety both a passionate love of Nature and a singular harmony with it. Waterfalls, mountain peaks, birds, stones, flowers, bamboo, pines in mist all speak of a hidden Unity, of the belief that the Buddha nature is immanent not alone in man but in everything that exists, animate or inanimate. The traditional culture of Japan is grounded in Zen perceptions which have been preserved, encouraged and practised in an amazingly pure stream of transmission right up to modern times. Qualities such as naturalness, simplicity, tranquillity, asymmetry, emptiness are expressed in Japanese plays and poetry, in flower arrangement (a highly regarded art in Japan), in *sumi* ink painting and calligraphy, in the subject matter and performances of the traditional theatre, in the design of gardens and house interiors. The room in which the tea ceremony is held, for example, is known as

'the abode of vacancy' and taking tea might be fairly described as a Zen practice in unfaltering awareness and joy in simple objects. The precise disciplines of judo, archery and ceremonial swordsmanship are also rooted deep in Zen. Most importantly the stripped, evocative 17-syllable Japanese verse form known as *haiku* affords special clues to the Zen state of mind:

> The water-fowl
> Lays its beak in its breast
> And sleeps as it floats.

> An old pine tree preaches wisdom
> And a wild bird is crying truth.

> How marvellous, how miraculous
> I draw water,
> I gather fuel.

What is being said in lines like these is that one should come to rest in the great Emptiness, that in every moment of life there is chance for enlightenment and that in the very seeming commonplaceness of existence one may discover the deepest mystery and wonder.

Buddha's Truth Beyond Words

Zen claims to be the direct inheritor of principles of thought and behaviour first promulgated by the historic Buddha (see GAUTAMA BUDDHA). In the 6th century BC the Buddha preached a new doctrine of a Middle Way of Understanding. He taught that certain methods of thought and behaviour could lead a follower to freedom from attachment to objects and to the eventual

release from that cramping and illusory sense of a special self or ego which, cutting off man from his fellows and from all other forms of life, gave human existence its tragic tone.

The Buddha's illuminating perception that he was, in a strictly personal sense, 'no-thing' and 'no-body', his profound realization of the indescribable, existential indivisibility or One-ness of all life, freed him forever from the fetters of *maya* (illusion) and from the necessity for rebirth or participation in the ceaseless round of 'becoming'. At this point in the spiritual history of Buddhism it is assumed that the Enlightened One might of his own volition have left the physical plane. Instead, after a period of doubt and uncertainty he accepted the sacrifice and responsibility of going forth to try to teach the unteachable; a truth that could not be described in words, that must instead be individually experienced as he had experienced it in his own moment of supreme clarity while seated under the Tree of Wisdom.

It is this act of profound selflessness on the part of the historic Buddha which has led to the development in Mahayana Buddhism of the theory of Bodhisattvas, enlightened beings who have taken the vow to postpone their own release in order to assist all other creatures in the attainment of Nirvana, a state of total inner Peace and Freedom, in other words, Buddhahood itself (see NIRVANA). Although this profoundly mystical and, in a sense,

paradoxical concept of Bodhisattvas as personifications of the highest wisdom and compassion did not originate in Zen, they preside in spirit over Zen halls of instruction and meditation, and the chanting of a Bodhisattva's four vows of dedication to the Buddha's Way are a part of each day's routine in teaching centres and monasteries. Sculptured or painted forms of such great Bodhisattvas as Kuan-Yin (Japanese Kwannon), Manjusri, Maitreya (Miroku) and others, are found in the priceless art collections of Zen monasteries, and are numbered among Japan's greatest national treasures. In old Chinese and Japanese art one can even find the Buddha himself depicted as a Bodhisattva, notably in such a moving masterpiece as the 12th century Chinese painter Liang K'ai's picture of the Great Teacher leaving the mountain top of his Enlightenment preparing to descend again into the world. Shown as a worn, weary, shabby ascetic, he stares down with an expression of profound questioning into the valley below, where he must now go on his self-determined mission to carry a light into the 'darkness of the world'.

From the annals of early Indian Buddhism, Zennists pluck certain stories which to them represent the very crux and significance of Buddhist teaching. One is the Buddha's rebuke to a disciple who kept demanding intellectual answers to such questions as the nature of the First Cause, life after death and similar insoluble mysteries. To this typical sophist the Buddha

Intuitive understanding of that which 'goes beyond the Word' is basic to Zen; one of the criteria by which Noh drama, rooted in Zen, is judged is whether a performance expresses that which is 'ineffable, indescribable yet communicable and capable of being intuitively experienced': child actor in Noh drama

remarked that his demands were comparable to those of a man who refuses to leave his burning house until he has found out who set the house on fire; or like a man who, shot with a poisoned arrow, will not remove it until he has ascertained all the facts about the arrow's source. In other words, speculation can only lead to further speculation with no possibility of any final solution; individual penetration to the heart of life's meaning cannot be brought about by the mind alone.

Silent Sermon
The second story in this general style describes the Buddha's so-called Silent Sermon, to a Zennist perhaps the most eloquent of all the Buddha's discourses. On one occasion before a great gathering of followers and disciples, the Buddha sat without speaking, turning a flower quietly in his hand. Some of the versions relate that he regarded the flower with joy, that he even broke into laughter. As he, without words, turned the flower in his hand he also looked into the faces of his followers waiting for a flash of understanding. At last it came. One disciple, Kasyapa, smiled, a serene inward-turning smile of awareness which told the Buddha that he had really *seen* the flower, had grasped that 'which goes beyond the Word'. It is significant that this perceptive disciple was subsequently chosen by the Buddha as his successor in the role of teacher. It is also worth mention in passing that to this day a canon of judgment brought to bear on Japan's ancient Zen-rooted Noh drama, is whether a performance does or does not possess 'the true flower', in other words express that which is ineffable, indescribable yet communicable and capable of being intuitively experienced. This basic Zen emphasis on an understanding that lies outside verbalism has been put succinctly in a famous four-line statement:

A special transmission outside the
  Scriptures;
No dependence upon words and letters;
Direct pointing to the soul of man;
Seeing into one's own nature and thereby
  attaining Buddhahood.

These four lines, expressive of the very essence of Zen, might be said to find their original embodiment in a semi-legendary

Morris Newcombe

missionary monk from India known as Bodhidharma (in Japanese, Daruma). The date of his first appearance in Zen annals is uncertain but we are told that Buddhism was already established in China when he arrived. It is related that he came all the way from India, a journey of incredible hardship, with the purpose of restoring to Buddhism its original directness and meaningful simplicity; to teach Buddhist followers that 'the finger pointing at the moon was not the moon (Enlightenment) itself'.

Although the precise date of Bodhidharma's arrival in China is lost in the mists of time, we do know the dates (502-550) of the devout Buddhist Emperor Wu Ti who received him in private audience. It can be assumed therefore that sometime around the middle of the 6th century a most important dialogue took place between the devout emperor and his noted visitor from the sacred land of the Original Teacher. The significance of this perhaps apocryphal conversation lies in the fact that it has set the tone for many hundreds of Zen dialogues, commentaries, *mondo* ('question and answer'), and *koans*, those apparently senseless Zen conundrums which do not lend themselves to solution by ordinary thought processes, which are in fact deliberately designed by their nonsensical formulation to break down habitual mental patterns.

Vast Emptiness

The emperor began the interview with Bodhidharma by describing his personal efforts on behalf of the newly transplanted religion, Buddhism. He told of the many temples he had built, the scriptures he had ordered copied, the special privileges he was granting Buddhist monks in his kingdom. What special merit, he wished to know, had accrued to him from these activities. Without hesitation Bodhidharma bluntly replied, 'No merit whatsoever.' The astonished but not yet daunted emperor went on to inquire which among the holy teachings his learned visitor considered a first principle of Buddhism. 'Vast Emptiness,' replied the sage. Taken aback, in fact a little nettled by this second statement, the emperor then demanded, 'Who are you who thus reply to me?': to which he received the jolting answer, 'I do not

Picturepoint London

Enlightenment may be found in every moment of life, according to Zen belief, and it is possible to discover the deepest mystery and wonder in what appears to be the commonplaceness of existence *Left* Flower arranging, a highly regarded art in Japan, reflects the Zen philosophy of joy in simplicity, and unfaltering awareness *Below right* 16th century scroll painting of a floral arrangement

conundrum on which Zen students have been testing their powers of comprehension for centuries. It suggests the impossibility of replying in words to the immense question, 'Who are you?' Yet the question is considered answerable in non-verbal terms, for as the Buddha nature is inherent in every sentient being there can be achieved, with the right effort, a lasting realization that one's own consciousness is the very Buddha Mind itself or Absolute Reality.

The Shortcomings of Reason

Zen's unswerving centuries-old emphasis on direct intuitive experience, rather than reliance on words *about* experience, has been described in modern psychological terms as a way of connecting with the deep unconscious to the end that one becomes what one truly is, as the tree grows, the bird flies, the cloud forms. Zen holds that the so-called rational mind is incapable of solving an individual's deepest problem: his meaning to himself and life. In Zen, reason is not allowed to assume the place of mastery that it has occupied for centuries in Western philosophy, the inheritor of the Greek viewpoint. Reason, in the Zen view, is incapable of bringing lasting spiritual or psychological equilibrium for it is the very nature of the reasoning process to produce contradictory yet equally valid theories that lead on and on endlessly, arriving nowhere. Talking about water will not quench a thirst any more than speaking of food will satisfy hunger. Again and again Zen teachings stress that it is not possible to take hold of the true merely by abandoning the false, nor can one reach peace of mind or any final answer by argument or the use of logic. Final awareness and lasting freedom come only when the deepest intuitional faculties of the human being are tapped and put to use.

In reaching these perceptions and releasing these invisible energies Zen employs its own singular techniques. In the Soto school, founded by a brilliant religious genius, the Japanese Zen master Dogen (1200-1253), one finds rather more emphasis on 'quiet sitting' than in the Rinzai school with its dynamic use of the koan. Since each school, however, employs not only specific periods of meditation (walking and running, as well as sitting) along

know'. Then, without further words, Bodhidharma took himself off (some legends and many paintings have him journeying upright on a reed, a leaf, or a straw across the wide Yangtze river – calmly fearless because one-with-all) to take up a nine year term of deep meditation (*zazen* in the Zen vocabulary), facing a cave wall. One of Japan's most valued national treasures, a monumental painting by Sesshu, the famous 15th century artist-monk, depicts Bodhidharma in this cave with the disciple Hui-Ko (in Japanese, Eko) who has cut off a hand to indicate his invincible will to work for enlightenment.

In his part of the dialogue with the conventionally pious emperor Bodhidharma was not being merely cheeky or captious.

By denying any 'merit', that is, reward or value, to formal temple worship or the copying and slavish study of approved scriptures, he was placing emphasis on the more profound and subtle, indeed the ultimate Buddhist goal of self-knowledge, the one true road to final liberation from life's anxieties and enigmas. His answer 'Vast Emptiness' to the question of the nature of Buddhism's first principle was a positive not a negative retort. His words did not imply mere emptiness in the usual sense of the term. In Zen the non-dualistic eternal Void, when truly comprehended, is seen as the rich source of all life and all wonders. Bodhidharma's third reply, 'I do not know', to the Emperor's question concerning his personal identity is a

Zen teachings stress that it is not possible to take hold of the true merely by abandoning the false, nor can one reach peace of mind or any final answer by argument or the use of logic

with the mind-boggling koan it seems safe to say that their similarities are more numerous than their differences.

The Rinzai School was founded somewhat earlier than the Soto by another brilliant spiritual genius, Eisai (1141-1215), generally accepted as the actual founder of Japanese Zen. It was Eisai who, after several visits to Chinese Zen centres, became convinced that this religious philosophy or way of life, then at its height, could be transplanted to Japan and bring about there a Buddhist awakening. Although Eisai was forced by circumstances to make concessions to types of Buddhism considered less pure, he belongs in the true Zen lineage and stands out among many names of missionary

monks who brought the teaching across the sea from China to Japan. Eisai is also honoured as the father of Japanese tea culture, although tea itself had already been introduced from China some time before.

Since the Soto school teaches what is called 'sitting with a single mind', 'observing one's mind in tranquillity' or even 'sitting just to sit', it has been designated as the 'Gradual School', in contrast to the Rinzai which is popularly known as the 'Sudden School', due to its greater emphasis on the abrupt breakthrough into a new state of consciousness, of heightened awareness, by means of the dynamic thrust of the koan. The word koan comes from the Chinese term *kung-an* and originally meant a precedent-establishing formulation in the legal

sense. In its origin the koan was a spontaneous expression of the exuberant enlightenment which came to the spiritual heirs of Bodhidharma during the Tang era in China; part of a general desire to get rid of religious rules, to throw away form and ritual in order to be carried 'by the storm of the spirit', as Heinrich Dumoulin has expressed it. In due course this highly original and vigorous expression of a rejuvenated Buddhism faded away and it was then deemed expedient, by certain wise teachers, to maintain some records of this first flowering to serve as guide lines in less inspired or vital periods. Thus it came about, in spite of Zen's strong emphasis on 'that which goes beyond the word', that a surprising number of koan, mondo, chronicles, dialogues

and sayings from the past are to be found in the literature of the Zen branch of the many-branched Buddhist tree.

The irrational Lewis Carroll nonsensicality of the koan has, in recent years, caught the imagination of many Westerners who find in them what Alan Watts has described as 'an itchy fascination'. The koan is deliberately designed to throw the mind off its accustomed track, to detach it from familiar habits of classification, division, comparison of this with that.

There can be no mentally worked-out answer to 'What is the sound of one hand clapping?' or 'What was your original face before you were born?' Answers, when they come, come in the form of illuminating perceptions and they are found not by

thinking about the koan but rather by trying to gaze at it quietly. The student is advised to become concentrated, but not in thought. To achieve this kind of perception requires total absorption day and night in the koan itself. Even when attending to the duties of everyday life it should remain firmly fixed in the unconscious mind. Zen does not believe it necessary to occupy Bodhidharma's cave in order to practise zazen; there is needed only an unshaken determination to find the Buddha's answer. Yet paradoxically, the seeker should never strive for the goal itself. He should just sit, breathe properly (very important in Soto) or concentrate single-pointedly on the koan until he perceives 'What Is'. Then he has at last grasped the truth that one's

self and the everyday world in all its manifold manifestations, forever in flux and transformation, are together only an eternally changing and transforming, appearing and disappearing, expression of 'This', of 'Is-ness' or 'Such-ness'. Once this state has been reached the Zennist does not give up all action, but rather his actions rise spontaneously out of the flow of Being itself. Understanding and use of 'This-ness' or 'Is-ness' is well described in Euben Herrigel's small classic, *Zen in the Art of Archery*, which tells how, after long and arduous effort, the author at last learns to let 'it' shoot for him so that the arrow reaches its target as effortlessly, as naturally, as a fruit which is ripe falls from a tree.

Two favourite characters in Zen art are the so-called 'idiots', Han-shan (Kanzan) and Shih-te (Jittoku), invariably depicted in rustic garb, often leaning on garden brooms, watching leaves fall or birds quarrel, or just standing, laughing. They are not only expressing their simple joy in life's 'Is-ness' but also sharing their amusement at the folly of man's usual way of living. The haiku that might well accompany these carefree lunatics is one which reads:

Sitting quietly, doing nothing
Spring comes and the grass grows by
    itself.

Any interpretation of these lines, however, as an argument for non-participation,

idleness or lack of concern could hardly be farther off the mark. In Zen no labour is beneath one's dignity; in fact all work is considered a basic and necessary part of existence. An ancient Zen monastery rule states baldly, 'No work, no food!'

Humour: Antidote to Smugness

One of Zen's outstanding characteristics is a zany sense of humour which has found expression not only in its literature but in a coexisting art of sharp and subtle commentary. The famous roshi Hakuin (1685-1768), known in his time as 'the greatest sage in 500 years' was not only a master teacher but also a great artist in the spontaneous free style favoured by Zen painters and calligraphers. Among his astringent

Zen teachings stress that final awareness and lasting freedom come only when man's deepest intuitional faculties are tapped, a concept that is reflected in Japanese art; in this the world was perceived intuitively from within, and the artist attempted to represent not physical space but an internally apprehended space: print by Yashima Gatutei

masterpieces there is a cartoon-like drawing of a one-eyed monster in company with a simple blind man. The grotesque creature, depicted with a single fierce headlight-eye in the centre of his forehead, is glaring at the unconcerned blind man as he exclaims, 'Hey! I am a one-eyed monster. Aren't you afraid of me?' 'I have no eyes,' replied the blind man, 'Why should I be

Described as 'a unique blend of Indian mysticism and Chinese naturalism sieved through the special mesh of the Japanese character', Zen claims to be the direct inheritor of the principles of thought and behaviour promulgated by the historic Buddha in the 6th century BC: worshippers entering the Kamigamo shrine in Kyoto

murky irresolution was instantly resolved. Afterwards he told everyone he met, 'Since I received that kick from Ma Tsu, I haven't been able to stop laughing.'

A number of modern students of Zen feel that the koan exercise has been over-stressed in Western literature about Zen, and that too much has been made of practices followed in certain Zen training centres: the swift thwack on the drowsy or irresolute student's shoulders by an attendant with a special stick (invariably accompanied, however, by low bows on the part of both the dealer of the blow and its recipient) or the loud rude shouts of disapproval and dismissal from an impatient roshi to whom a student has brought an obviously thought-out answer. There are also critics who are disturbed by the West's over-emphasis on the idea of the suddenness of the breakthrough into satori which tends to give the impression of 'instant Zen' when in truth illumination, though it may be sudden in its impact, is experienced only after prolonged effort and a number of satori-like experiences (*kensho*) prior to the Great Enlightenment in all its stunning finality.

Something of the nature of Zen may be discovered from the words of an old poem:

> When one looks at it, one cannot see it;
> When one listens for it, one cannot hear it;
> However, when one uses it, it is
> inexhaustible.

Zen claims to point a paradoxical Way, at once abstract and personal, that is markedly different from the practices of more conventional religions.

NANCY WILSON ROSS

FURTHER READING: Heinrich Dumoulin, *A History of Zen Buddhism* (Pantheon Books, 1963); Erich Fromm, D. T. Suzuki and Richard de Martino, *Zen Buddhism and Psychoanalysis* (Harper and Row, 1960); Eugene Herrigel, *Zen in the Art of Archery* (Random, 1971); Nancy Wilson Ross ed., *The World of Zen* (Random House, 1960); Nancy Wilson Ross, *Three Ways of Asian Wisdom: Hinduism, Buddhism and Zen* (Simon and Schuster, 1966); Philip Kapleau, *Zen East & West* (Doubleday, 1980).

afraid of you? You should be scared of me'. A comical sketch, by another painter-monk, shows a neophyte warming his backside at a burning statue of a Bodhisattva. The accompanying anecdote tells that when caught in this irreverent act the culprit innocently replied that since there had appeared in the ashes no sign of *sarira* (a special substance found only in the remains of cremated saints) he concluded it was only a wooden statue — and it was a very cold day.

This kind of rough humour and seeming irreverence has in no way prevented Zen temples and monasteries from remaining repositories of great religious art, nor has it stopped Buddhists from prostrating themselves before Buddha images as an act which 'horizontalizes the ego-mast' as one interpreter has put it. Zen's countless humorous anecdotes spring from the wish to avoid self-conscious religiosity or pompous smugness about spiritual attainment. Satori, in Zen annals, is often accompanied by a kind of transcendental laughter, as in the story of the monk who came to his roshi for help with one of the classic questions assigned to neophytes: 'What is the meaning of Bodhidharma's coming from India?' The master, to whom the question was put, suggested that before proceeding with the problem the inquiring monk should make him a low salaam. As he was dutifully prostrating himself the teacher administered a good swift kick. At this unexpected impact the disciple's

Olympian Zeus, lord of storms and rain, supreme in his mountain stronghold, had an earthly prototype in the Mycenean Great King: but Cretan and other influences also contributed to his nature

ZEUS

THERE IS good reason to suppose that the hierarchical organization of the Olympian deities of the Homeric poems reflects the social and political conditions of the Mycenean period, when the gods and goddesses were gathered together in a single heavenly stronghold under the monarchical hegemony of Zeus (see GREECE). Their dwellings, built by Hephaestus, surrounded the central palace of Zeus. The authority of the supreme male deity was now fairly stable but was still by no means unchallenged. The Mycenean pantheon spread its influence as the Mycenean social and economic system became dominant elsewhere. The ensuing conflict and fusion is paralleled by an increasing complexity in cult and mythology and in the composition and organization of the pantheon.

In its most dramatic form this process had assumed the character of a struggle between the older conception of an Aegean goddess and a newer conception of a dominant male god, Zeus, whose name is certainly Indo-European. Crete had been the centre of Minoan civilization and had now become part of the fringe of the Mycenean. The study of the all-pervasive cult of Zeus in Greek religion helps us to understand the means whereby, and in what diverse forms, the Minoan religion, with its prime allegiance to a Great Goddess (though already familiar with the growing power of its own Cretan male god), became reconciled with the Mycenean pantheon (see also CRETE).

Significantly, it has been claimed that the earliest representation of Zeus occurs on the Geometric lid from a tomb at Fortetsa near Cnossus. That this representation is traditionally Cretan is indicated by the presence of birds, one of them carried on the left hand of the figure traditionally supposed to be Zeus, who strides towards a tripod. There is another bird on top of the tripod. Between the figure and the tripod is yet another, larger bird with its head lifted towards the handle of the tripod. The principal figure carries in his right hand an object which consists of three wavy verticals – the thunderbolt, or at least fire, perhaps resembling the bolts depicted on Syro-Hittite reliefs. Underneath the tripod is a human bust – perhaps the Minoan goddess herself, associated with, but not yet displaced by Zeus. We could then have here represented a double epiphany or manifestation of Cretan Zeus and the older Cretan goddess, heralded by the birds of Minoan tradition.

The thunderbolt of Zeus was itself traditionally regarded as a means of bringing death so that immortality might be conferred. The tripod, a three-legged cauldron to be put over a fire, goes back in its origins to the 14th century BC. Real or simulated boiling in a cauldron is a familiar prelude to rejuvenation, immortality and apotheosis. The infant Dionysus-Zagreus, for instance, was slain, his limbs cooked in a cauldron, and restored to life again. In the boiling cauldron mortality and old age are shed, perennial youth is gained, rebirth follows upon death, the initiate is born again. Thunderbolt and tripod can be accompaniments of initiation; and Cretan Zeus, pre-Olympian in origin, was an initiation god. It is tempting to imagine that the mystery of Cretan Zeus himself is celebrated in this scene on the Fortetsa lid in the form of a double epiphany, reflecting the combination of the new Dorian with the traditional Cretan background, as it were newly Hellenic yet abidingly Minoan.

Background of the Gods
However that may be, other evidence illustrates the growth of the cult of Mycenean Zeus against the old Minoan background in Crete itself. Homer and Hesiod were the first to compose theogonies, to give the gods their epithets, allot them their offices

God of the sky and of storms, Zeus is traditionally depicted carrying a thunderbolt, which was itself regarded as a means of bringing death so that immortality might be conferred *Below left* Bronze statue of Zeus, c 5th century BC *Below* Bronze cast for a statue of Jupiter, the Roman god who was identified with the Greek Zeus, 2nd century AD

C. M. Dixon

C. M. Dixon

and occupations, and describe their forms, in the tradition reported by the historian Herodotus. This means that these customary Greek theogonies derived from the epic tradition, rooted in the Mycenean period. In the Homeric Catalogue of Ships (in the *Iliad*, book 2) Crete is described as having 100 towns. Seven of these are mentioned by name, including Cnossus, Gortyna and Phaistus, all of them from central Crete, which was apparently the chief area of Achaean occupation.

Though they are by no means principal characters in the *Iliad*, it is quite clear that the Cretan captains were of some importance, consistent with the island's contribution to the Trojan expedition. For Idomeneus and Meriones had a considerable contingent of 80 ships. This number can be compared with 100 ships under the command of Agamemnon himself, 90 under Nestor, 60 under Menelaus, brother of Agamemnon, and a mere 12 under Odysseus.

Idomeneus boasts of his descent from Zeus. Like other similar leaders of the Heroic Age of Greece he had quite a short pedigree, which goes up to a god in the third generation before the Trojan War. Aerope, his first cousin, was connected by marriage with the Atreidai, the family of his allies. She married Atreus and was herself a grand-daughter of Minos. In the *Iliad*, Idomeneus kills Phaistus, son of the Maionian Boras from Tarne and the eponymous hero of this great Cretan city. There was another Phaistus in the Peloponnese, and again another in Thessalian Achaia. The opponents of Idomeneus, Oinomaos and Alkathoos, have associations with Pelops and the Peloponnese; and his father Deucalion has associations with Thessaly. The implication is that he was an intrusive northerner by extraction, a bringer of strife to Crete before he went to Troy.

Europa and the Bull

Zeus, the god ancestor of Idomeneus, the one member of the Olympian pantheon with an Indo-European name, rose to his eminence with the growing power of the Achaeans. The result was that, in Crete, the name of their sky god was attached to a Minoan deity whose original ritual and character can be discerned from the evidence of later times. It was not until after the Minoan period that this originally secondary deity, this youthful god, pushed his way to the forefront in a variety of forms and under a variety of names. The myth of the Minotaur (see BULL; MAZE; THESEUS) implies that he was identified at Cnossus with the bull; and the story of the love of Queen Pasiphae for the Minotaur may derive from a form of the sacred marriage, the male partner in the ritual being played by the king masked in the head of a bull. The sacred marriage was closely involved with the fertility of the crops. This association is clearly to be observed – as is also the association with central Crete – in the famous legend of Zeus and Europa.

An archaic kind of Europa, riding on a bull, features in the earliest (5th century BC) coins of the city of Gortyna and also of

Phaistus. The type persists on the coins of Gortyna throughout the 5th century. Their pictorial character has plausibly suggested a derivation from local frescoes. This relation is even more conspicuous in the 4th century coins both of Gortyna and of Phaistus. On one type of coin from Phaistus Europa is sitting on a rock and is welcoming with her raised hand the bull who is approaching her. A coin series from contemporary Gortyna tells vividly the story of the marriage of Zeus and Europa, with Zeus changing from a bull into an eagle. Coins of Cnossus, probably struck in 220 BC, when that city was closely allied with Gortyna, are similar to the Gortynian type which features Europa; and Europa on the bull remained as one of the chief coin types of the Roman province of Crete – probably struck at Gortyna between 66 and 31 BC.

It appears to be likely that the final evolution of the male deity from a bull into an anthropomorphic Zeus, the Zeus who later became involved with Europa, must have occured in the Mycenean period. Zeus is featured as the partner of Europa not only in Hesiod, but already in the *Iliad*. Animal sacrifices continued to be conspicuous in the rituals of Zeus, the victims normally being either rams or, more frequently, oxen. Both of these animals are associated with sky gods in general and with Zeus in particular. They were the most precious victims that pastoral peoples could offer, considered to be most possessed of fertilizing power and most essential to their economic survival. Various traditions combine to associate mainland settlers at Gortyna, or its neighbourhood, with the Arcadian area where the Achaean dialect survived. It is therefore perhaps significant that Gortynian Zeus shared the title of *Hekatombaios* ('to whom hecatombs are offered') with the Arcadian Zeus.

A celestial Zeus of Gortyna called Zeus *Asterios* ('Starry Zeus') was known to Byzantine writers and he was associated with Europa by earlier writers including Hesiod and Bacchylides. After his affair with Europa, Zeus reputedly gave her in marriage to a Cretan king Asterion (or Asterios, or Asteros) who, childless himself, reared the children of Zeus and Europa; and, according to the Byzantine writer Tzetzes, Sarpedon, Minos and Rhadamanthys were sons of Zeus Asterios. The Minotaur of Cnossus was also called Asterios or Asterion. There were sacred herds of cattle of the sun god at Gortyna, a cult of a solar deity called Atymnos, brother of Europa, whose early death was mourned; and an inscription of the 5th century BC confirms the worship of the sun.

The art and the literary and numismatic evidence of historical times all indicate how the sacred marriage of Zeus and Europa combined Mycenean with Minoan and even more primitive traditions of cult. Europa often features in art on the bull, holding in one hand his fertilizing horn and in the other hand a flower, symbol of her fertility and also of earlier magical associations before the bull had been deified.

The marriage of Zeus and Europa traditionally occurred in or under a plane

tree near a stream at Gortyna. Coins of Gortyna of the 5th century BC show a goddess in a tree, generally considered to be Europa, possessed by Zeus in the form of an eagle and thus identified with Hera (see HERA). A bull's head, however, is apparently often fixed to the trunk of the tree. The tree on the coins seems to be a pollard willow and not a plane tree. Yet we need not go so far as to accept the suggestion that Europa was actually a willow goddess and that Zeus, as a nursling of the willow, might naturally be mated with a willow bride. Magical plant and tree associations of this kind must have existed long before either Zeus or Europa. Such earlier connections, prior to the time when Zeus became involved with the willow at Gortyna, were indicated in the mention of the tree where the sacred marriage took place and the stream nearby, where the goddess bathed.

Putting Away Childish Things

The cult of the goddess Leto at Phaistus, not far away from Gortyna in southern Crete, is of particular interest. We have evidence to prove that Cretan youths, when they reached the last stage of initiation into manhood and citizenship, cast aside their boys' garments before assuming their warriors' costumes. The formality of this particular ritual was embedded in the festival which was known at Phaistus as the *Ekdysia* ('Casting off'), during which the youth cast off his boys' clothes. This festival was associated with the local cult of Leto and was connected with the myth of Leucippus, who was changed from a girl into a boy. According to the myth, Galatea, daughter of Eurytus and wife of Lamprus, bore a daughter; and she persuaded Leto to let the girl change sex when she grew up.

The change was commemorated in the Phaistian festival of the Ekdysia. When the Phaistians married they lay down beside the statue of Leucippus, which was presumably in the sanctuary of Leto. The festival and the mythology suggest a combination of fertility, initiation and marriage ritual. The youths of Phaistus were apparently initiated into manhood, citizenship and marriage at the same period of life. The local Leto, as her epithet *Phytia* ('Causing Growth') indicates, promoted growth and fertility in the young. When growth had been promoted, the boy died and was reborn as a man, casting away his boy's clothes and dressing like a man.

Leto Phytia and her Phaistian festival were rooted in the earliest stratum of Cretan religion. It has been suggested that, because the cock was dear to Leto (as to all women in childbirth) since he stood by to lighten her labour, Leto Phytia was somehow related to Zeus *Welkhanos* of Phaistus, whose sacred bird was the cock.

Both Zeus and Jupiter, his Roman counterpart, were renowned in mythology for their many love affairs; Semele, the mother of Dionysus, was loved by Zeus but was consumed by the fire of his thunderbolt when the god appeared to her in his divine form: *Jupiter and Semele*, painting by Gustave Moreau

Coins of Phaistus in the period from about 430 to 300 BC show Welkhanos as a youthful, beardless god, his right hand caressing a cock; on the reverse side there is a bull. The Cretan identification of Zeus with Welkhanos is also confirmed by lexicography.

The discovery of numerous tiles with the name of the god *Weukhanos* (Welkhanos) was made years ago at neighbouring Hagia Triada. Significantly, the temple of Zeus Welkhanos was here built upon the ruins of the old palace of Hagia Triada. An associated month name and spring festival is attested in three other towns of Crete.

A. B. Cook (author of *Zeus*) thought the meaning of Welkhanos could have been 'god of the willow-tree', confirming his idea that Zeus at Phaistus, as at Gortyna, was consort of a willow goddess. For he had a cock (instead of his usual eagle), since the cock, as the crest of the Phaistian Idomeneus, had a long-standing mythical association with the town. There was also a tradition that Idomeneus was descended from the sun, sire of Pasiphae, and that the cock was sacred to the sun. Though these associations may be true, there is no reason but to suppose that Cook's identification strained the evidence.

It is nevertheless possible to conclude, from the nature and provenance of the cult, that Zeus Welkhanos was a product of the Minoan god of fertility. There is clear similarity between the coins of Phaistus showing Welkhanos with a cock in the branches of a tree and the coins of Gortyna showing Zeus, Europa and the eagle. The cock, like the eagle, seems to signify a bird epiphany. Welkhanos must surely have been yet another male partner in a sacred marriage with the old Minoan mother goddess.

Thunderbolt and Aegis

The evidence about Zeus Welkhanos and the representation (if it be of Zeus) on the lid from Fortetsa serve alike to emphasize the difficulty of clearly distinguishing Olympian Zeus from the specifically Cretan Zeus. The weather god, lord of storms, rain, lightning and thunder, who acquired supremacy in his mountain stronghold, had an earthly prototype in the Mycenean Great King. Nevertheless, the Cretan Zeus who survived with such dominant traits of his original nature long after the Olympian pantheon became supreme in officially sponsored religion, is but one symbol – though one of outstanding importance – through which old prehistoric cult exercised its influence. The later Zeus, Olympian though he might be, exhibited himself in many forms, as is evident in those various distinguishing epithets attached to his name, which not only reveal his many-sided nature but often a pre-Olympian basis.

In eastern Crete, 'the Cretan-born Zeus' was specifically associated with Dicte by the epithet *Diktaios* (Dictean). The geographer Strabo expressly connected the temple of Dictean Zeus with the old Bronze Age population of the area. Although the Hellenic temple which stood on the site of the Minoan town of Palaicastro had been destroyed, sufficient numbers of votive

offerings were found there in the course of archeological investigation to define its position; and the site of the alter was fixed by a bed of ashes. It was the discovery of the inscription of the famous Hymn of the Curetes (see CORYBANTES), addressed to Zeus of Dicte, which confirmed with certainty that the temple was that of Dictean Zeus. Or again, there is Zeus *Idaios* ('of Ida'), similar to Dictean Zeus, mentioned in a much-discussed fragment of *The Cretans* of Euripides, delivered by a chorus of inspired devotees of Zeus.

The ancient Greeks themselves believed that the Pelasgians were the aboriginal inhabitants of Greece and they tended also to associate Pelasgians with Carians (people from south-west Asia Minor) and the Leleges of the Greek islands. The name survived in the ancient shrine of Zeus *Pelasgios* at Dodona in Epirus, in north-west Greece. Here was the most ancient oracle in Greece, the divine responses obtained from the rustling of sacred trees and from brazen vessels suspended from them (see ORACLES). The cult of Zeus *Karios* ('Carian Zeus'), centred at Mylasa, the Carian capital, was also found in Boeotia and Attica, in mainland Greece.

The eagle was associated with Zeus in mythology, and the god is said to have assumed the form of this bird when he carried Ganymede off to heaven to be his cup-bearer *Facing page* Zeus abducting Ganymede, a painting by Rembrandt *Below* Statue of Ganymede astride an eagle, by Cellini

Scala

'The portion of Zeus is the broad heaven among the clouds in the upper air,' says Homer in the *Iliad*. Hence a repeatedly recurrent Homeric epithet of Zeus is the Cloud-gatherer, sending rain, lightning, thunder. Small wonder that altars have been found in Greek houses dedicated to Zeus *Kataibates* – Zeus who descends (in thunder and lightning) – and sacrifices were made on these altars to appease him and ward off destruction from the house.

Beside the thunderbolt, the aegis (skin shield) is a peculiar attribute of Zeus. In keeping with his rise to eminence in the Heroic Age of Mycenean Greece, Zeus, as god of manly strength and prowess, was especially honoured at two of the four great athletic festivals of Greece, the Olympian and the Nemean, besides many others. From the 4th century BC onwards, Greek historians reckoned time in Olympiads, the periods corresponding to the Olympic Games, which were quadrennial and claimed uninterrupted celebration from 776 BC (see GAMES).

The sacred precinct of Zeus at Olympia, the Altis, was surrounded by a wall with several entrances. In the southern part stood the great temple of Zeus, with the famous gold and ivory statue of Zeus by Pheidias, which was classed as one of the seven wonders of the world until it perished in 462 AD, and which was more praised in antiquity than any other work of art.

Lord of the City State

Zeus was of supreme importance in the daily life of the Greek city state. As Nilsson explained, in *A History of Greek Religion*: 'Just as the father of the household is Zeus's priest, so Zeus himself in the patriarchal monarchy of earlier times is the special protector of the king and hence the supreme custodian of the social order. Thus in Homer Agamemnon is under the special protection of Zeus. The god was not dethroned with the fall of the monarchy. As Zeus *Polieus* he is the divine overlord of the city state.'

As protector and guardian of the house he was Zeus *Herkeios* ('Of the front court'). As Zeus *Ktesios* ('the Acquirer') he was similarly protector of house and property. Hence Nilsson's conclusion that where Zeus appears in the shape of a snake under such names as *Ktesios*, *Meilikhios* ('the Kindly One') and *Philios* ('the Friendly One'), the name of Zeus had been added to the house deity which appeared as a snake, because Zeus was also protector and guardian of the house. A deity, male in later Greece, female in the Minoan Age, developed out of a domestic snake cult.

Zeus was also protector of the fugitive suppliant, as Zeus *Hikesios*. He had a part to play in the sanctity attaching to the duties of friendly hospitality (*Ksenios*). From the beginning of the 5th century BC, there grew up, in the city of Athens and its neighbourhood, a special class of resident aliens called *metoikoi*. They were attracted by the opportunities of trade in a flourishing commercial centre, and the government encouraged them, despite the fact that, as foreigners, they were really excluded from civic rights and from public ceremonies associated with the official religion of the state. Nevertheless, once a year, at the national festival of the Panathenaea, these resident aliens were not merely permitted to take part but were allowed special marks of honour. They also had a separate Zeus *Metoikios* as their special patron.

As the governments of the city states, like that of Athens, tended to become more

democratic in form, they still continued to have allegiance in council and assembly to Zeus as, for example, to Zeus *Agoraios* ('Of the market place'). That epithet was not peculiar to Zeus, but no doubt derived from the location in the market place of a shrine or altar of the deity to whom it applied. Functional shades of meaning must have been derived from the various functions of the *agora*, the market place, chiefly as a place of assembly and also as a market place in the strict sense. Zeus Agoraios would therefore have been a special patron of those mustered in assembly at the agora. From this special association with the assembly of citizens, Zeus Agoraios could be described in literature as patron of eloquence or of public supplication.

In later antiquity, among the more sophisticated, as religious belief tended to become more monotheistic, there was a tendency for Zeus to become conceptualized as the one, single god, the beginning and the end of all things.
(See also HIGH GODS; SKY.)

R. F. WILLETTS

FURTHER READING: A. B. Cook, *Zeus* (Biblo & Tannen reprint, 3 vols); M. P. Nilsson, *Minoan-Mycenaean Religion* (Lund, Sweden, 1950); M. P. Nilsson, *A History of Greek Religion* (Greenwood, 1980); W. K. C. Guthrie, *The Greeks and their Gods* (Beacon Press, 1968); R. F. Willetts, *Cretan Cults and Festivals* (Greenwood, 1980).

Zeus rose to pre-eminence with the growing power of the Achaean Greeks, but traces of the Cretan Zeus survived in Greek mythology: according to legend, the god was born in Crete and hidden in a cave from his father Cronus, who would otherwise have devoured him: the cave of Zeus, Crete

Ronald Sheridan

Zion

Or Sion, one of the hills of the city of Jerusalem, often used in the Old Testament as an alternative name for the city itself as the spiritual centre and capital of the world; in Christian literature frequently used to mean the heavenly city of God, or the Church; Zionism is the modern movement to create a Jewish national home in Palestine, which culminated in the establishment of the state of Israel.
See JERUSALEM.

Mansell Collection

Zodiac

In astrology, a circle in the sky through which the sun, moon and planets appear to move; divided into 12 'signs', each allotted 30 degrees; a planet's position in the zodiac is believed to affect the way in which it influences people and events on earth; the signs of the traditional 'tropical' zodiac are not identical with the actual constellations in the sky, the 'sidereal' zodiac.
See AQUARIUS; ASTROLOGY; and articles on each of the signs.

Mansell Collection

The risk of being turned into a zombie, a soul-less, automaton-like body or a disembodied soul, by poison or enchantment, is still feared and guarded against in Haiti

ZOMBIES

ONE CANNOT live long in Haiti without hearing talk of zombies, dead bodies brought back to a half-life by magic, and many stories about them have appeared in print. In 1939, for instance, Zora Hurston published a now classic account of a young girl from a well-to-do family who was discovered four years after her death working as a slavey in a shop; she was rescued by French nuns and placed in a nunnery.

The tale was still current in Haiti 20 years later, with several additions: four or five quite different towns were named as the place where she had been found, and some said that her rescuers had been Baptists. They also declared that she had been recognized on account of her bent neck, the result of her having been buried in a coffin too small for her, and by a scar on her foot made by a candle which had overturned and burnt her during the wake. But these distinguishing marks are first known in a story told to the writer Alfred Métraux in about 1950. It concerned a young woman who over-brusquely turned down the amorous advances of a *houngan*, or Voodoo priest (see VOODOO), who bewitched her in revenge, dug her up after her presumed death and used her as a zombie until the Catholic anti-superstition campaign caused him to set her loose.

Whatever the original truth of these stories, their combination has produced something approaching a myth which will probably be gaining credence 100 years from now, because of its apparently factual detail and its compact sense of the superstitions involved. It is certain anyhow that few stories told about zombies are to be taken literally.

Many of the people thought to be zombies are in fact morons or idiots, of which Haiti has its fair share. Métraux tells of one such who escaped from the house where her parents had locked her up, and whose behaviour alarmed the neighbouring peasants sufficiently to make them believe she was a zombie. Zora Hurston took a photograph of a woman zombie in a hospital who almost certainly was a mental defective. The mistake is easy enough to make, for both zombies and morons have certain things in common. The zombie, for instance, walks with a shambling gait and downcast eyes, speaks gibberish in a nasal voice if it speaks at all, does not answer when spoken to, and is bereft of the usual marks of sanity.

Equally important, Haitians delight in telling tall stories about things supernatural, which serve to amaze their audience and even to convince themselves, if only for a moment. A magistrate, for instance, told a convincing story about a Catholic priest who went blind after seeing a troupe of zombies in the hills, remarking that one shouldn't laugh at such matters. But he immediately followed up his cautionary tale with an eye-witness account of a corpse being dug out of its grave and then re-animated, which was a mere hoax: he examined the grave the following day and found a pipe leading from it to the air so that the supposed corpse — the houngan's accomplice — could breathe before his exhumation.

Few people have actually seen zombies. The following incident was said to have occurred in 1959, and was vouched for by a Catholic priest. (It must be remembered, however, that Voodoo and its superstitions are the great enemy of the Church in Haiti, and that even the most upright of men will slander his enemy in a good cause.) A zombie had come wandering into the village where he lived, entered the courtyard of a house and promptly had his hands tied together by the owner, who took him to the police station. The police wished to have nothing to do with such an ominous creature, and so he was left outside the station for some hours, chewing at his bonds, until he was given salt water to drink — the instant cure for zombification. He then found his voice again and told his name. His aunt, who was living in the

Tales of zombies, dead bodies magically brought back to half-life, proliferate in Haiti where the superstitions of Voodoo are an integral part of life; President Duvalier's private army was named after the *tontons macoute*, or magicians of Haiti, and some were believed to be zombies

village, was sent for: she not only recognized him but declared she had seen him dead and buried four years previously.

The Catholic priest also arrived on the scene and learnt from the man that he had been one of a large number of zombies set to work by the houngan who had enchanted them. This announcement frightened the police even more, and they sent word to the houngan that he could have his zombie back for a consideration. Two days later, however, the man died, and it was generally presumed that the houngan had murdered him for having spilt the beans. He was arrested, but his wife fled into the hills with the remaining zombies.

The educated classes also tell of zombies, as in Métraux's account of a *monsieur* whose car broke down outside the house of a houngan. The houngan, assuring him that the matter was no mere accident, invited him inside and showed him a zombie, in whom the monsieur recognized a great friend, dead some six months previously. Full of pity the monsieur offered the zombie a drink, but was stopped by the houngan who warned him of terrible dangers if he did so.

Return to the Grave

Perhaps the most sensational zombie tale is the one recounted by W. B. Seabrook, about a number of zombies owned by a houngan called Joseph and looked after by his wife. One day, not realizing what she was doing, she gave them salted biscuits to eat. Awoken from their deathly trance and knowing themselves for the walking corpses they were, they made straight for the cemetery, brushing aside all who would stop them. There they hurled themselves upon their graves and tried to dig themselves back into the earth, but turned into carrion as they did so.

The most feared consequence of releasing a zombie from his bondage is that he will revenge himself physically and magically upon his owner. Those who own zombies thus make a point of treating them with great harshness – another point which they have in common with the mentally deranged, for it is normal practice in Haiti to beat lunatics and keep them frightened. The parallel is in fact recognized obliquely by all who claim knowledge of how to make a man into a zombie: there are two major ways, by poison and by enchantment. The plants usually cited as poison are manchineel, whose apple-like fruit was often used by resentful slaves in plantation days to kill their owners and their livestock, and datura, the thorn apple, which contains atropine, and belladonna or deadly nightshade. A further poison can be made from the legendary three drops which escape from the nose of a corpse hung upside down.

Besides these, houngans also prepare a number of leaf powders of different kinds with various magical and, it is said, pharmacological properties. One of these powders, containing pepper wood, is very effective in bringing on possessions by the gods. The powder seems to have no effect other than to stimulate the mucous membranes of the nose, but this is enough to trigger off a dissociation when people are highly suggestible, as they are during a ceremony. It is quite possible, therefore, that such a powder used in the right context can magically zombify a man, by entrapping his soul and leaving him with nothing but his body (called the corpse body in Haitian parlance) and his spirit, also termed the zombie.

Spider into Zombie

Initiates into Voodoo pass through a similar state but with proper safeguards. To become possessed by a god their souls must first be displaced or, as we should say, they must be dissociated. During their initiation, their souls are incubated and finally transferred into a sacred vessel called the *pot de tête*, or head-pot, where they are safe from the attacks of evil-doers and under the protection of the gods. At their death, a rite called *dessounin* is practised which sends their spirits into the waters of death and again captures their souls in a head-pot to await their spiritual resurrection. An initiate is thus a purified zombie whose activity when possessed is controlled by a god, not a magician.

Significantly enough, the dessounin rite is copied by those who want a dying man's zombie. This is done by placing a pot, containing 21 seeds of *pois congo* and a length of string knotted 21 times, under the pillow of the moribund. After his death the string turns into a spider, and the pot containing it is placed in a dark room. To turn the spider into the dead man's zombie

---

Banquet with Corpses

In the centre of the room was an elegantly set table with damask cloth, flowers, glittering silver. Four men, also in evening clothes, but badly fitting, were already seated at this table. There were two vacant chairs at its head and foot. The seated men did not arise when the girl in her bride-clothes entered on her husband's arm. They sat slumped down in their chairs and did not even turn their heads to greet her . . .

As she sat down mechanically in the chair to which Toussel led her, seating himself facing her, with the four guests ranged between them, two on either side, he said, in an unnatural strained way, the stress increasing as he spoke:

"I beg of you . . . to forgive my guests their . . . seeming rudeness. It has been a long time . . . since . . . they have . . . tasted wine . . . sat like this at table . . . with so fair a hostess . . . But, ah, presently . . . they will drink with you, yes . . . lift . . . their arms, as I lift mine . . . clink glasses with you . . . more . . . they will arise and . . . dance with you . . . more . . . they will . . ."

Near her, the black fingers of one silent guest were clutched rigidly around the fragile stem of a wine-glass, tilted, spilling. The horror pent up in her overflowed. She seized a candle, thrust it close to the slumped, bowed face, and saw the man was dead. She was sitting at a banquet table with four propped-up corpses.

W. B. Seabrook *The Magic Island*

---

all you need do is to knock three times at the door, taking care to stand with your back to it, and to threaten it with a whip when you give it its orders.

In southern Haiti this kind of zombie is known as a *vivi*: it is the equivalent of a jinn trapped in a bottle. Another way of making a vivi is to exchange a man's soul while he is still alive for that of a lizard, chicken, butterfly or other small animal. The man is no wiser for the substitution, but the animal which embodies his soul cannot die, and merely vanishes if an attempt is made to kill it. The word 'soul' is probably a misnomer here: a better word is 'talent', for it is men talented in law, accountancy, business or some such skill who are sought for as zombies, and for whom the dessounin rite is practised even if they are not initiates into Voodoo proper.

In any case, it is difficult to tell a vivi from a *baka*, that monster of the supernatural created by black magic to bring luck, power or wealth. Both have to be served in the proper manner or their owner is destroyed by their ungoverned force; both are best invoked in cemeteries. One kind of zombie can be made of a man long dead (by whipping his grave with sticks of pois congo) and is used in several branches of magic: for instance a tired prostitute can have her private parts inhabited by such a 'mort' or dead man, paradoxically to liven them up and make her clients come back for more.

It is to stop this kind of zombification that people enter into Voodoo, have their souls placed in head-pots and undergo the dessounin rite. But even this is not enough to stop the corpse answering the magician's voice as it lies in its grave, and being turned into a zombie. In certain parts of Haiti, therefore, the corpse is buried face down with its mouth full of earth, or its lips are sewn together; sometimes a knife is placed in its hand with which it can defend itself. In other places sesame seed is scattered in the grave so that the ghost will be eternally occupied in counting how many there are. As a last resort the corpse is strangled or shot through the head.

Zombies thus come in two major forms: as a body without a soul, and as a soul without a body. These last are not easily distinguishable from magical spells, and both from confidence tricks. The word zombie itself, however, comes from the Arawak Indian term *zemi*, a god or a spirit, which also lies at the origin of the name Baron Samedi, god of the dead: by which we may infer that a zombie is properly to be understood in religious terms, as a body resurrected by spiritual means. It is not impossible for such means to be used for profane ends, nor that a man can truly exist as a body without a soul. So far, however, this is still a moot point.

FRANCIS HUXLEY

FURTHER READING: Zora Hurston, *Tell My Horse* (Lippincott, 1938); Francis Huxley *The Invisibles* (Humanities, 1966); Alfred Métraux, *Voodoo in Haiti* (Schocken, 1972); W. B. Seabrook, *The Magic Island* (Folcroft, 1977).

From a monotheistic faith with Ahura Mazdah as its supreme deity, Zoroastrianism progressed towards a dualistic concept of Ohrmazd, principle of goodness and light, and Ahriman, principle of evil and darkness; in all its phases, however, Zoroastrianism remained primarily a religion of free will

ZOROASTRIANISM

ZOROASTRIANISM is the name given to the religion founded by the Iranian prophet Zoroaster, probably in the 6th–7th centuries BC. Modern scholarship tends to accept the traditional date of the prophet, '258 years before Alexander'. For the Iranians, 'before Alexander' could only mean the final extinction of the First Persian Empire at the sack of Persepolis by Alexander the Great in 330 BC. Hence Zoroaster's 'date' would be 588 BC. But what period in his life would this refer to? It might refer to his birth, to his first revelation at the age of 30, to his conversion of the local king Vishtaspa at the age of 40, or to his death at the age of 77. Whichever date we accept, Zoroaster's life will have spanned the 7th and 6th centuries BC. This, however, like so much in Zoroastrian studies, cannot be regarded as at all certain. So too with the place in which he operated. The later tradition placed him in western Iran, in what is today Azerbaijan; but this is almost certainly not true, for the internal evidence – the dialect and the place names mentioned in the early Zoroastrian texts – points to the east, the country near the Oxus River, now in Soviet Central Asia. Modern scholarship would have it that Zoroaster's field of activity was in ancient Chorasmia, corresponding roughly to what is today the Turkmen Republic of the Soviet Union. This again is highly probable but not certain.

Gods and Demons

It must be emphasized at the outset that in practically every aspect of Zoroastrian studies uncertainty prevails, and this for a variety of reasons. The principal reason is that our main sources do not agree. The sacred text, the *Avesta*, itself only a fraction of the original scripture and handed down orally for at least 1000 years, is (as is the way of sacred scriptures) not consistent with itself, nor is it consistent with the contemporary sources – the inscriptions of the Achaemenian kings and the Greek accounts of Iranian religion from Herodotus onwards. The same is true of the second period of Zoroastrian supremacy during the Second Persian Empire, the so-called Sassanian Empire, which lasted from 226–651 AD. It cannot be claimed, then, that all that will be said in this brief article is authoritative; for Zoroastrian scholars have disagreed with a vehemence of acerbity rare even among academics.

Zoroaster, or Zarathushtra, as he is called in the *Avesta,* was born some time in the 7th century BC, fled from his native land because he preached a doctrine which his fellow-countrymen refused to accept, and found asylum with a certain King Vishtaspa in eastern Iran who finally accepted his teaching. That his teaching was at variance with the traditional religion is clear. Just what that earlier religion was is less clear. One thing is certain, however: that the Aryans, the common ancestors of the 'Aryan' invaders of India (who were responsible for the earliest sacred book of the Hindus, the *Veda*) and the Iranians who inhabited the Iranian plateau, had a common religion which was polytheistic (see INDIA). The original Aryan pantheon

Roger Wood Studio

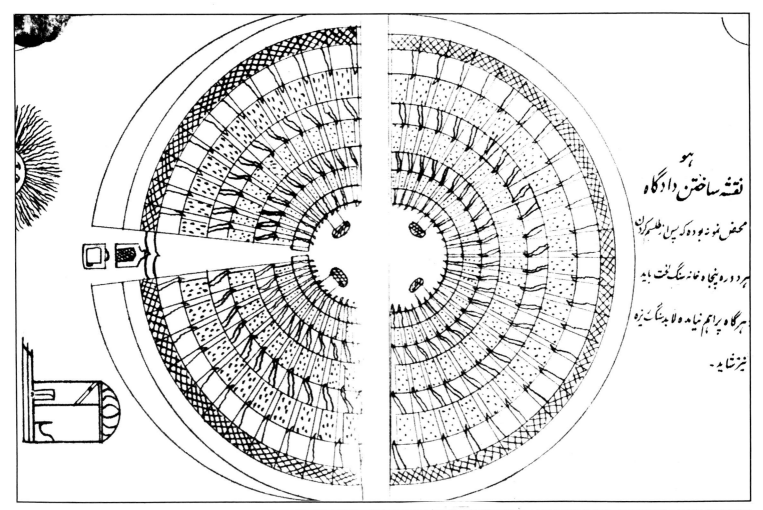

was, it seems, divided into two distinct groups of deities, the *asuras* (or *ahuras*) on the one hand and the *daivas* on the other. The asuras seem to have been remote gods who dwelt in the sky, while the daivas were nearer to men and more intimately associated with them. From the beginning there seems to have been tension between the two groups. In India the asuras, because they were held to possess magic powers which they were prone to use against men, finished up by becoming demons. In Iran precisely the opposite happened. The ahuras (the Iranian form of the Indian asuras) retained their divine status whereas the daivas were reduced to the status of demons. This probably happened before the appearance of Zoroaster, as the terms *ahuro-tkaesha* ('the religion of the ahuras') and *daevo-data* ('the law of the daivas') would seem to show. Already, it would appear, the ahuras were considered to be beneficent powers, the daivas maleficent.

New Message from God

Zoroastrianism has been described both as an ethical monotheism and as a classical form of dualism (see DUALISM; EVIL). How can one religion be described in two such contradictory ways? The answer is that Zoroastrianism, like any other religion, developed and changed, now emphasizing one aspect of the prophet's message, now another. In any case the Zoroastrianism of the prophet himself was very different from the Zoroastrianism which became prevalent in the later stages of the First (Achaemenian) Persian Empire (550–330 BC), and this again differed considerably from the official Zoroastrianism of the Second (Sassanian) Empire (226–651 AD). The first could be called monotheism, the second modified monotheism, and the third dualism.

Zoroaster was born into a priestly family but he saw himself as a prophet, the bringer of a new message from a god called Ahura Mazdah, the 'Wise Lord', who revealed himself as the true God. This message is preserved in the oldest part of the *Avesta,* the *Gathas* or 'Songs' of Zoroaster himself. Zoroaster was a prophet every bit as much as were the Hebrew prophets who prophesied at much the same time. He was convinced that he was inspired by God and that he was charged with a message from him to man. He claimed to 'see' him and to hear his voice. Indeed, his relationship is so close that he can speak of it as one of 'friend to friend'.

The essence of Zoroaster's message is that God is One, holy, righteous, the Creator of all things, both material and spiritual, through his Holy Spirit, the living and the giver of life. He is good because he is productive and gives increase. His 'oneness', however, is a unity in diversity, for he manifests himself under various aspects: the Holy Spirit, as and through whom God creates; the Good Mind, as and through which he inspires the prophet and sanctifies man; Truth, Righteousness, or Cosmic Order (*Asha*), as and through which he shows man how to conform himself to the cosmos in accordance with righteousness; Sovereignty, as and through which he rules creation; Wholeness, which is the plenitude of his being; and Immortality, as and through which he will annihilate death.

The Bounteous Immortals
These aspects of the Wise Lord were later to be called the 'Bounteous Immortals', and in the later periods of Zoroastrianism were to be associated with various material elements: they appear as God's creatures and are thus assimilated to the archangels

of other traditions. Two of them demand special notice: Truth and the Holy Spirit. Like the other Bounteous Immortals these have acknowledged opposites or 'adversaries' which thwart and restrict them. Ahura Mazdah, as Supreme Deity, has no opposite but, in so far as he is associated with Truth and the Holy Spirit, he is indirectly at variance with the 'Lie' and the 'Destructive Spirit', the later Ahriman, just as the Hebrew God is opposed to Satan in the later Judaeo-Christian scriptures. Hence it is not wholly illogical to describe the Zoroastrianism of the prophet himself as both a 'monotheism' and a 'dualism'; and in so far as Ahura Mazdah reveals himself under different aspects, it is not wholly absurd to describe it as a modified 'polytheism'.

Truth and the Lie
In the *Gathas* the basic dualism is between Truth and the Lie – Asha and Druj – which can also mean the established cosmic order and what disrupts it. This dualism remains throughout all phases of Zoroastrianism. The Lie also means the disruption of the established political order (Darius described the rebels against his authority as 'liars'), and the disruption of the truthfully spoken word, or what we normally understand by a lie. As God, Ahura Mazdah is beyond both Truth and the Lie, but as and through Truth he is inexorably opposed to its opposite, which is also the spirit of disruption.

Similarly in the case of the Holy Spirit. The Holy Spirit is irreconcilably opposed to the Destructive Spirit (see AHRIMAN) and this opposition was later to be regarded as characteristic of Zoroastrian dualism. Of these two Spirits it is written:

In the beginning those two Spirits who are the well-endowed(?) twins were known as the one good and the other evil in thought, word and deed. . . And when these Spirits met they established in the beginning life and death that in the end the followers of the Lie should meet with the worst existence, but the followers of Truth with the Best Mind. Of these two Spirits he who was of the Lie chose

to do the worst things; but the most Holy Spirit, clothed in rugged heaven, (chose) Truth as did (all) who sought with zeal to do the pleasure of the Wise Lord by (doing) good works.

Although the two Spirits choose to do good and evil, the Holy Spirit can nevertheless say to 'him who is Evil: "Neither our thoughts, nor our teachings, nor our wills, nor our choices, nor our words, nor our deeds, nor our consciences, nor yet our souls agree."'

Ahura Mazdah, the Wise Lord, is himself described as being the 'father' of the Holy Spirit (as he is of several other Bounteous Immortals), but he is also in a sense identical with him. As and through the Holy Spirit, then, he is as irreconcilably opposed to the Evil or Destructive Spirit, the author of death, as he is to the Lie, for he is both Life and Truth. But if he is the father of the Holy Spirit, and the Holy Spirit is the Destructive Spirit's twin, does it not follow that he is the father of the Destructive Spirit too? In the later literature, the Wise Lord is roundly identified with the Holy Spirit, and once this has happened Zoroastrianism becomes a classically dualist religion (see OHRMAZD). A minority, however, remembering that the two Spirits had been spoken of as twins, insisted that they must have a common father. This could no longer be Ahura Mazdah (the later Ohrmazd), so some other entity had to be found. They finally settled on 'Infinite Time' (see ZURVAN), who thus became the supreme principle beyond good and evil.

The Two Houses
In all its phases Zoroastrianism is the religion of free will. Man is judged in accordance with the nature of the thoughts, words and deeds he has thought, spoken and done in his lifetime. The reward of the good is heaven, the 'Best Existence'; that of the wicked is hell, an 'evil existence'. At death the soul must cross the 'Bridge of the Requiter' which, in the later literature, is broad and free from danger for the righteous but becomes as narrow as a razor's edge for the wicked, who thereby fall helplessly into hell (see BRIDGES; JUDGEMENT OF THE DEAD). In the *Gathas* it is Zoroaster himself who guides the righteous across the awesome bridge, but when the wicked reach it 'their souls and consciences trouble them when they come to the Bridge of the Requiter, guests for all eternity in the House of the Lie'.

Heaven and hell are states rather than places – the best existence and the worst existence or, more graphically, the House of the Good Mind and the House of the Worst Mind, the House of Song and the

On New Year's Day, at the beginning of spring, a great festival was held at Persepolis under the auspices of Ahura Mazdah, supreme deity of Zoroastrianism, during which representatives of all the nations of the Persian Empire brought tributes to the king *Left* Relief at Persepolis showing a procession of Median nobles *Right* Symbol of Ahura Mazdah

William MacQuitty

House of the Lie. In the one there is 'ease and benefit', in the other discomfort and torment, 'a long age of darkness, foul food, and cries of woe'.

In addition there is a final reckoning 'at the last turning-point of existence', when there will be a Last Judgement in the form of an ordeal by fire and molten metal which will allot to the righteous and the unrighteous their final destiny of weal or woe. The Last Judgement then, merely confirms the individual judgement at death: salvation and damnation are fixed for all eternity. This 'black and white' doctrine was to enter Judaism and, through Judaism, Christianity and Islam. The Zoroastrians, however, were later to modify it themselves, for in the later texts the

Last Judgement (which seems unnecessary anyhow) becomes not a judgement at all but a purgation by molten metal in which the wicked are finally purged of their sins and the just suffer nothing since the molten metal has no terrors for them: they experience it as if it were warm milk.

These, then, are the basic doctrines preached by the prophet Zoroaster himself: there is one supreme God, Creator of all things, spiritual and material; aside from him there are two irreconcilable principles — Truth and the Lie, the Holy Spirit and the Destructive Spirit. Alongside these there are 'aspects' of God and also, though less markedly, 'aspects' of the Lie and the Destructive Spirit. Man must choose between the two, and in

accordance with his choice he will either be blessed with eternal bliss or chastized with everlasting torment. By 'good' is meant Truth, the proper ordering of things, life, and prosperity: by evil, the Lie, disorder, death, and misery. The dualism is not one of spirit and matter but one of spirit and spirit, matter being in itself good because created by God, though later corrupted by the Devil.

The Later Avesta

Only the *Gathas* purport to be the work of the prophet Zoroaster himself. The rest of the *Avesta* (or rather what survives of it) is later and contains much material that seems to be totally at variance with the prophet's teaching. According to the

later tradition the 'original' *Avesta* consisted of 21 *Nasks* or 'books', a summary of which survives in the *Denkart*, a work, like all the works written in Pahlavi (Zoroastrian 'middle' Persian), that dates from after the Mohammedan conquest but which draws on much earlier material. Of these 21 *Nasks* only one remains in its entirety – the *Videvdat* or 'Law against the Demons', a tiresome book largely concerned with the punishments of sins, ritual purification and mythology. Apart from this there is the *Yasna*, the 'sacrifice', or ritual texts accompanying the main Zoroastrian liturgy together with minor liturgical texts, and the *Yashts* or 'hymns of praise' celebrating a whole gamut of pre-Zoroastrian deities which the prophet had certainly ignored and may even have proscribed.

The *Yasna*, or sacrificial liturgy, centres round the immolation of the sacred plant haoma (the Iranian equivalent of the Indian soma), the juice of which is considered to be the elixir of immortality. The *Yasna* is both sacrifice and sacrament: the plant god is slain by being pounded in a mortar and its juice is consumed in order to win eternal life. There seem to be references to this cult in the *Gathas* themselves, and it seems certain from these references that the prophet disapproved of it strongly, at least as practised by the 'worshippers of the daivas'. Be that as it may, the haoma cult appears very soon to have become central to Zoroastrian worship and it has remained so to this day, both among the

Born during the 7th century BC, Zoroaster saw himself as a prophet, the bringer of a new message from a god called Ahura Mazdah, the 'Wise Lord', who was the true God: *Zoroaster in his study,* **a 15th century Flemish miniature**

10,000 Zoroastrians who still survive in Iran and among the 100,000 Parsees ('Persians'), as the Zoroastrians who emigrated from Iran to India some centuries after the Mohammedan conquest are called (see PARSEES). The haoma sacrifice is the central act of the liturgy, but from beginning to end the material object around which the rite is celebrated is the sacred fire which, like haoma itself, is called the 'son' of Ahura Mazdah.

The Sacrificial Haoma

The sacrifice opens with a confession of faith in the following terms: 'I confess myself a worshipper of Mazdah, a Zoroastrian, a renouncer of the daivas, an upholder of the ahuras.' The formula helps us to see how the Zoroastrians of a later date regarded their religion. They are worshippers of (Ahùra) Mazdah, the only God, proclaimed by Zoroaster as supreme Creator and Lord: hence they are 'Zoroastrians'. But when they add that they are 'renouncers of the daivas' and 'upholders of the ahuras', they seem to be upholding a religion that probably preceded the coming of the prophet and in which there were many ahuras or gods just as there were many daivas or demons who, like Satan and his angels in the Judaeo-

Christian tradition, had once themselves been gods. In any case the ahuras, now called *yazatas* or 'worshipful ones', are constantly invoked throughout the *Yasna*. They may either be material manifestations of divinity, pre-eminently fire and water, but also the winds, mountains, and so on, or they may be spiritual, invisible beings who are in fact the ancient Aryan gods, once common to Iran and India; slightly refurbished, it is true, in that they are subjected to the ultimate authority of Ahura Mazdah, the Wise Lord.

But these divinities though they are constantly invoked throughout the *Yasna*, are not essential to it. The central figure, as we have seen, is the sacrificial haoma, but next to him and the sacred fire is a 'god' who figures quite prominently in the *Gathas*, Sraosha. In the *Gathas* he is, like the Bounteous Immortals, an abstract idea. He is the faculty of 'hearing' God's word and therefore of obeying it. In the *Yasna* he is fully personified and is, in a sense, the mediator between man and God. As the spirit of obedience, he also enforces obedience among men and chastizes the wicked, as he chastizes the demons. His continued importance, his relevance, and his popularity are attested by the fact that he alone among all the Zoroastrian pantheon was later identified with a Mohammedan angel (with the angel Gabriel, so familiar to Christians too).

The second main division of the later *Avesta* is the *Yashts* and it is in some ways remarkable that they have survived;

for they are hymns of praise to deities, some of whom are quite certainly pre-Zoroastrian and others almost certainly so. In the *Yasna* these deities are always clearly subordinate to Ahura Mazdah but this is not always so in the *Yashts*, for in two cases at least Ahura Mazdah himself is represented as doing obeisance to them – to Vayu, the wind god, and to Anahita, the goddess of the waters.

The Faith of the Achaemenids

From the Achaemenian inscriptions, from proper names like Mithradates, from rock reliefs of much later date, and from the extraordinary diffusion of the cult of Mithras (see MITHRAS) throughout the Roman Empire shortly after the rise of Christianity, it is clear that the most important of these ancient deities was Mithra – like Ahura Mazdah himself originally a god of the sky and later identified with the sun.

As with everything connected with Zoroastrianism, there has been furious debate as to whether or not the Achaemenid kings were Zoroastrians. About the religion of the earliest of them, Cyrus and Cambyses, there is no evidence, but about that of Darius the Great (521–485 BC) there is plenty, for there are many inscriptions dictated by him. Ahura Mazdah is the only god the Great King invokes. He is the great god 'who created this earth, who created yonder sky, who created man, who created happiness for man, who made Darius king.' This is recognizably the same god as that of Zoroaster. Similarly, when speaking of the rebels against his authority, Darius says they 'lied' in that they claimed to be kings, 'lying' thus being equivalent to the disruption of the established order – again a Zoroastrian conception. Thus, in his conception of the nature and supremacy of Ahura Mazdah and in his identification of evil with the 'Lie', Darius is at one with Zoroaster. Though it can be argued that he was not formally a 'Zoroastrian', he was certainly a 'worshipper of Mazdah'.

The case of Darius's successor Xerxes (485–466) is even clearer, for he claims to have suppressed the cult of the daivas and to have established some sort of 'Mazdean' orthodoxy: 'Where the daivas had previously been worshipped, there did I worship Ahura Mazdah in accordance with Truth and using the proper rite.' Further he refers to an afterlife in which the good will be 'blessed': 'The man who has respect for the law which Ahura Mazdah has established and who worships Ahura Mazdah in accordance with Truth and using the proper rite, may he be both happy when alive and blessed when dead.' Xerxes, then, was both a 'worshipper of Mazdah' and a 'renouncer of the daivas', and since he refers to 'the law which Ahura Mazdah established', presumably through his prophet Zoroaster, he was almost certainly a 'Zoroastrian'.

During the reign of Artaxerxes I (465–425) the Zoroastrian calendar was introduced, but in this calendar the days and months are named not only after Ahura Mazdah and the Bounteous Immortals but also after the ancient gods who now appear beside them. The Zoroastrianism of the later Achaemenian kings was that of the *Yasna* rather than that of the *Gathas*. And so we find in the rare inscriptions of Artaxerxes II and III the god Mithra and the goddess Anahita invoked together with the supreme god, Ahura Mazdah.

The Last Contest

With the collapse of the Achaemenian Empire, Zoroastrianism disappears as an organized religion until it becomes once more the state religion of the Second (Sassanian) Empire from 226 to 651 AD. To judge from rock reliefs during this period, it would appear that Mithra and Anahita still enjoyed considerable favour both with the royal house and among the people. It was, however, the policy of the new dynasty to seek to establish religious conformity throughout the empire. Now for the first time one can speak of religious orthodoxy; and this, to judge from the Pahlavi books which draw their material from this period, was a rigid dualism in which the Bounteous Immortals and the ancient gods resuscitated in the late Achaemenian period were reduced to the status of angels. The scene was now dominated by two eternal principles, Ohrmazd (Ahura Mazdah) and Ahriman, Ohrmazd being identified with all goodness and light and dwelling in the Endless Light above, Ahriman being equated with all evil and darkness and dwelling in the Endless Darkness below. The two kingdoms are totally separate and independent, but the time comes when Ahriman becomes conscious of the light of Ohrmazd, envies it, attacks it, and invades the material world which Ohrmazd had created as a bulwark against him. For 3000 years the issue of the battle is in doubt, but in the last 3000 years of the existence of this world the power of evil is slowly but relentlessly ground down until the Saviour, the Saoshyans, appears to make all things new. The souls of men, whether they be in heaven or in hell, are reunited with their bodies and are purged in a sea of molten metal. When this is done, Ahriman is expelled back into his native darkness and rendered unconscious for ever. Then the whole creation enjoys eternal bliss in the presence of Ohrmazd, the Lord.

This dualist orthodoxy, however, was questioned by a theological deviation called 'Zurvanism' which subordinated both Ohrmazd and Ahriman to a higher principle, Infinite Time or Zurvan. However, no matter what the main theological trend may have been at the time, Sassanian Zoroastrianism was so wedded to the Sassanian state that, when the latter was overthrown by the forces of the new religion, Islam, which had arisen in the Arabian desert in the 7th century AD, the Zoroastrian Church, no longer being the 'established' Church, rapidly and irreversibly declined. Iran, once the centre of two great empires of which Zoroastrianism had been the official religion, now became a Moslem country; and the Zoroastrian community, having steadily lost ground throughout the centuries, has now been reduced to a mere 10,000 souls living mainly in Yazd and Kerman in the southeast, while another 100,000 or so, descendants of refugees from persecution, survive as the rich and enlightened community of the Parsees in Bombay and other Indian cities. Such has been the fate of a religion that once ruled proudly throughout the Iranian lands.

R. C. ZAEHNER

FURTHER READING: tr. by M. Henning, *The Hymns of Zarathustra* (Hyperion, 1980); R. C. Zaehner, *The Dawn and Twilight of Zoroastrianism* (Putnam, 1961), *The Teachings of the Magi* (Oxford University Press, 1976).

Men become sorcerers by their own choice, but women become witches because they are inherently evil; yet it is the female whom the ancestor spirits possess, who has the power to heal and make the crops grow. Deep-seated conflicts of this sort are reflected in Zulu social customs

ZULU

TO UNDERSTAND the religion and the magic of the Zulu, it is necessary to know something of their historical background. The Zulu kingdom existed as an independent unit in south-eastern Africa (the present province of Natal in the Republic of South Africa) in the 19th century. It was established when Shaka (or Chaka), the chief of a small tribe, conquered many of the tribes of the region between 1818 and 1824, while others either fled from him or fled under attacks from tribes driven away by his onslaught. The repercussions of these events were far-reaching, and various nations were created as a direct or indirect result of Shaka's wars.

The Boers inflicted a first major defeat on the Zulu, then under one of Shaka's brothers, in 1838, and took over part of the Zulu territory. The Zulu were finally beaten as a major military power in the region by the British in 1880: they were then ruled by Cetshwayo (or Cetewayo), son of another of Shaka's brothers. Part of the kingdom was ruled by the British, who by then had taken over Natal from the Boers, and the remainder was divided under independent chiefs, including Cetshwayo, who was left with a remnant of his kingdom. Internecine war between these chiefs led to the British establishing rule over the remainder of the kingdom. The former united nation was now organized within British (and from 1910, South African) administration; but in the 1930s there was a revival of Zulu nationalism in adherence to the head of the Royal House, then established as chief of one of the many small chiefdoms into which

Zululand was divided. In the 1960s, Zululand was established as one of the Bantustans under present South African apartheid policy, with the agreement of the legitimate successor of the Zulu kings, now Paramount Chief.

Early Zulu history has been worked out from tribal traditions, from the records of shipwrecked mariners, and from the records of white travellers, traders, missionaries and administrators, of whom some English settled among the Zulu in 1825.

Zululand is one of the pleasantest regions of Africa, the main part consisting of rolling, well-pastured hills, lying between the Indian Ocean and the Drakensberg Mountains. The soils were fertile, but are now much eroded. It has a monsoon climate, and records show that there are bad droughts only once in five years. Rain often comes in severe thunderstorms accompanied by lightning, of which the forked form is most destructive. Then the rivers come down from the hills in walls of flood. Cattle thrived, though since the early 1900s they have been plagued by various diseases. The main crops of the Zulu were sorghum and millet, and in later years maize, with gourds, pulses and pumpkins. Their houses were originally made of grass on a framework of branches, beehive-shaped, but later these were replaced by mudded cylinders with a thatched conical roof. The houses were spread in small clusters over the hillsides, each inhabited by an extended family, the core of which was an agnatic lineage, men related to one another by descent through males. The capitals of the kings, and the military barracks in which they housed their warriors and their royal women were once inhabited by thousands, and were three to four miles in circumference. They were abolished after the Anglo-Zulu War.

Regicide and Civil War

Records show that until late in the 18th century the region was inhabited by many small tribes, ranging in total population from 500 to perhaps 5000. The relationships between the tribes oscillated between friendly peaceable intermarriage, and short sharp skirmishes. The tribes were also split up periodically by civil wars, or sections of a tribe would move off amicably to newfound independence. This system came to an end about the end of the 18th century, when a number of stronger tribes began to extend their sway over their neighbours. The most plausible explanation for this change is that the population of both human beings and cattle (which breed quickly) increased in the well-favoured region until it exceeded the carrying capacity of the land under the prevailing methods of husbandry. A series of battles between dominant tribes ensued: Shaka, head of a very small tribe, took over the disintegrating kingdom of his overlord when the latter was killed, and in a few years built a great nation of 250,000 people. His wars solved the crisis of population; he was successful because he invented more lethal weapons and methods of fighting, as well as new tactics for battle.

Shaka administered his nation in a system almost, but not absolutely, dictated by the system of husbandry which entailed a widespread dispersal of population. It was divided into counties ruled by chiefs. Some of the counties comprised defeated tribes: they were ruled sometimes by their legitimate chiefs or their heirs, sometimes by a scion of the chiefly family who was favoured by Shaka, while occasionally he placed favoured 'strangers' over them. Other counties he constituted out of broken tribes, or by settling people in areas whose inhabitants had been killed or had fled: the chiefs appointed there were those who had helped him in his struggles.

Shaka himself had experienced an unhappy childhood, for his mother and he had been driven from their home: therefore he killed all his paternal half-brothers (the Zulu were polygamous), except for three. He did not give these surviving half-brothers counties to rule, but he gave a distant cadet of the Zulu royal family such a county. Shaka's major innovation was to organize the men of his kingdom into

Camera Press London

A proud and warlike people, the Zulus were welded into a formidable fighting force by Shaka, the warrior chief, who organized all men within a certain age group into regiments, and housed them in royal barracks; this martial history is reflected in the ritual dances still performed by Zulus on ceremonial occasions *Left* Tribal dance *Facing page* Young men prepare to take part in a war dance

regiments, consisting of all the men of a narrow age range, housing them for most of the year in royal barracks. The men were forbidden to marry until they were in their mid-30s, when they were allowed to marry a much younger regiment of women (similarly organized), who at that point would be around 23 years old.

Shaka ruled tyrannously, and 12 years after he acceded to the Zulu chieftainship, he was killed by two of his brothers, one of whom succeeded him. The successor was also a tyrant, and 12 years later another brother fled with 17,000 people to the Boers, and with their help defeated and drove out the king. The new king was the last of that generation: he was also the first Zulu king to marry, and he had many wives and sons. Seventeen years later the sons of two of the queens fought over the succession to the throne, and Cetshwayo was successful. He ruled till his defeat by the British 23 years later. Thus assassination of kings and civil war were endemic in the Zulu nation, as they had been in the earlier polity of small tribes: and this fact was reflected in certain ceremonies.

The Maiden Goddess

The Zulu have a conception of a High God, who broke off the nations from a reed-bed, but he plays little part in their daily life and is not worshipped. Distinct from him is Heaven, a concept of a great power in the sky, barely anthropomorphized, present in storms and particularly in lightning, and manifested in the thunderbolts which are numerous because of the violence of the storms. These thunderbolts are thought to be the excreta of a thunderbird. Heaven is believed to influence certain persons who begin to get drowsy, become ill, and wander far from the habitations of men. They are then initiated as Heaven doctors, and can plant magical substances around villages to protect them from lightning, while during storms they go out on the hilltops and fight the storms with weapons and magic. Several people are killed each year by lightning, and these magicians are much respected.

These beliefs about lightning are not reconciled with the idea that dangerous forked lightning is female, while harmless sheet lightning is male, or with a belief in a goddess who is supposed to make the rain and who is associated with the rainbow, which is believed to be the rafter of her hut in the sky. This goddess is graphically described: '. . . presenting the appearance of a beautiful landscape with verdant forests on some parts of her body, grass-covered slopes on others, and cultivated slopes on others . . . robed with light as a garment . . .' The Zulu had few myths of origin or of creation, but they speak of the goddess, who is a maiden, as having come from heaven to teach people to make beer, to plant, to harvest, and all the useful arts.

The most important spiritual beings in Zulu belief are the spirits of their ancestors. These are believed to live below

Keystone

the earth or in the sky, or to appear in the villages in the form of particular kinds of snakes, sometimes dangerous species, but believed to behave peaceably and to be recognizable as their deceased 'inhabitants' by marks on the body. The ancestors are one of the two principal agencies in Zulu belief influencing good and ill fortune: they expect their descendants, those related to them by descent through males, to place all milk and beer in the 'great hut' of the village for them to taste and to pour it into the ground of the cattle corral round which houses are built, in periodic offerings. They also require that sacrifices of cattle be offered to them. Should their descendants neglect to make these offerings, the ancestors will send disease; and they will also do so if their descendants default in their obligations to other kinsmen. They are prayed to at ceremonies for birth, initiation and marriage, and at funerals, and also at sowing first fruits, and harvest, as well as on other occasions. The ancestors of kings and chiefs look after their political dependents.

During illness, diviners of various kinds are consulted to find which ancestor is sending the misfortune so that it can be besought to remove the disease. It is believed that male ancestors are reasonable and will remove the misfortune if it has been sent for neglect of offerings, or when the breach of obligation which provoked the affliction has been redressed. On the other hand, female ancestral spirits are

capricious, and may allow the misfortune to continue even after amends have been made.

Inherently Evil Female

This belief, like the belief in the femaleness of forked lightning, reflects a deep-seated conception in Zulu belief that femininity is inherently full of threatening evil occult power. This fear appears in the many taboos that attach to menstruating women and their effluxes, which threaten all things male and all virile enterprises. The belief is marked in a distinction made between sorcerers and witches who, like the ancestral spirits, are occult agencies of good and evil. The Zulu have a very rich assortment of magical substances to treat disease in humans and livestock (50% of which achieve their intended purposes, according to pharmacological tests), to obtain fertility of women, cattle and crops, to protect themselves against thieves and lightning, to influence those in power, to reintroduce murderers into social life, and so forth. Some of these substances are also believed to be used for sorcery, for making others fall ill or even to kill them. It is believed that men, and not women, make the conscious moral decision to learn these evil arts: men are evil deliberately. But women become witches by an inherent evil in their voracious sexuality, which attracts to them sexual familiars, who then demand the lives of the close kinsmen of the husband, or of his children by his other wives. Again,

Camera Press London

there is an inherent evil in femininity, since a woman does not deliberately seek a familiar.

On the other hand, women also contain much occult power for good: the great majority of those who become possessed by ancestral spirits, which speak through them and divine the cause of illness and dictate cures, are women. Nevertheless, for a woman to become socially valuable in this way she has to pass through a very painful illness. In addition, women provide rituals of fruitfulness: pregnant women perform rites to bless the crops, and women and girls enact ceremonies to the maiden goddess at seedtime and when blight affects the grain.

Songs of Hate

These ceremonies exhibit the ritualization of social roles and relationships which is characteristic of tribal societies (see RITES OF PASSAGE; RITUAL). In supplicating at seedtime for a good harvest, the young unmarried girls would don men's garments and carry shields and spears. They drove out the cattle (normally taboo to them) to pasture and milked them. Meanwhile their mothers planted a garden far out in the veld, and poured a libation of beer to the goddess. Thereafter this garden was neglected. At various stages of the ceremonies women and girls went naked, and sang lewd songs. Men and boys hid inside their huts, and might not go near the females; if they did, they were attacked by the women.

Zulu warriors and the maidens who have been given to them in marriage perform a marriage dance in the royal kraal; although women are regarded as being inherently evil, they also contain much occult power for good, and enact ceremonies to the maiden goddess when blight affects the grain, and at seedtime

In order to understand how this ceremony, so expressive of conflict in society, operated, it is necessary to probe deeply into the position of women. The present writer has maintained that women's position in Zulu society was highly ambivalent. A woman was expected to bear many sons to strengthen the agnatic lineage of her husband, and it was feared that if she was barren she might turn to witchcraft, and she was generally treated very harshly by others.

On the other hand, when a woman produced sons she in fact produced competitors for the limited property and social positions in the lineage, thus introducing strife into the lineage that was supposed to be strengthened. It is arguable that the occult beliefs about women concealed this deep contradiction in their social position and that in the rites previously mentioned the ambivalent emotions generated were transposed to social ends.

Similar analysis can be applied to the national ceremonies performed at festivals of the first fruits. During these ceremonies, warriors sang songs of hate and hurled insults against the king, in order to strengthen the nation through the king.

Comparative research shows that such ceremonies occur where civil war and royal assassination are endemic, but where king and subjects are not cut off from one another by class barriers. The symbolic representation of deep existing conflicts seems to release emotions which become fixed positively on socially approved groups and values.

Of the many Zulu who have been converted to Christianity since 1880, the majority are women. As in European Christianity, many sects have developed and, as throughout South Africa, they are markedly influenced by the colour bar under apartheid. Some Zulu independent sects are organized as are mission churches; others are syncretistic of Zulu and Christian belief, and combine possession by the Holy Spirit, speaking with tongues, laying on of hands for healing, cults against witchcraft and sorcery (demons), with sometimes the ancestral spirits reappearing as angels.

MAX GLUCKMAN

FURTHER READING: M. Gluckman, *Custom and Conflict in Africa* (Barnes and Noble, 1969); *Analysis of a Social Situation in Modern Zululand* (Manchester Univ. Press, Manchester, 1958), *Order and Rebellion in Tribal Africa* (Free Press, 1963), *Politics, Law and Ritual in Tribal Society* (Biblio Dist., 1977); E. J. Krige, *The Social System of the Zulus* (Tri-Ocean); D. Burness, *Shaka, King of the Zulus* (Three Continents, 1976).

ZURVAN

ZOROASTRIANISM and Manicheanism are commonly regarded as being the two classical dualist religions: and this is true. But there is all the difference in the world between them, for Manicheanism is a dualism of spirit and matter, spirit being identified with good, matter with evil. Zoroastrianism, on the other hand, is a spiritual dualism of two spirits, the one good and the other evil, and they are irreconcilably opposed. Matter, however, is created by Ohrmazd, the good God, though it comes to be corrupted by Ahriman, the 'pure' spirit of evil (see AHRIMAN; DUALISM; MANICHEANS; OHRMAZD; ZOROASTRIANISM). The basic text for this dualism is to be found in the *Gathas* or 'Songs' of Zoroaster himself where the prophet is represented as saying: 'I will speak out concerning the two Spirits of whom, at the beginning of existence, the Holier thus spoke to him who is Evil: "Neither our thoughts, nor our teachings, nor our wills, nor our choices, nor our words, nor our deeds, nor our consciences, nor yet our souls agree." '

The irreducible antagonism between the two Spirits seems clear enough here. But there is another text (quoted in the article on Zoroastrianism) in which it is unambiguously stated that the two Spirits were twins; and that would imply that they had a common father.

God of Infinite Time

Now in the later *Avesta,* as the sacred book of the Zoroastrians is called, an entity with the name of *Zrvan akarena* ('Infinite Time') is sometimes mentioned. Nothing much is said about him, but at least he is infinite, whereas Ohrmazd and Ahriman, God and the Devil, had by now become independent principles, each limiting the other. A different view is quoted by Eudemus of Rhodes, a pupil of Aristotle, who lived in the 4th century BC. He is reported as having said that 'the Magi and the whole Aryan race call the whole intelligible and unitary universe either Space or Time from which a good god and an evil demon were separated out, or, according to others, light and darkness before these . . . One of these (higher principles) is ruled by Ohrmazd, the other by Ahriman.'

This is the philosophical account of the 'Zurvanite' position. Light and darkness are ruled respectively by Ohrmazd and Ahriman, God and the Devil; but the highest principle is beyond all these, and this principle is Space-Time, Zrvan akarena, who in the later language becomes *Zurvan i akanarak,* 'Infinite Zurvan-Time.'

By the time of the Sassanian Empire (226-651 AD), however, Zurvan had become a proper name and a personal god, the word for 'time' in Persian now being *zaman,* as it is to this day. During the Sassanian period, to judge from the Zoroastrian books which, though actually written as late as the 9th century AD, are generally held to represent the views of Zoroastrian orthodoxy during the last century or so of the Sassanian Empire, one would not realize that the god Zurvan was of any importance at all, let alone that he was regarded by some as being the father of both Ohrmazd and Ahriman. Indeed, in these so-called 'Pahlavi' books, Zoroastrianism (or the 'Good Religion' as the Zoroastrians themselves now called it) was defined as the religion of the two principles as distinct from the monotheism of the Jews and Christians. 'I must have no doubt,' a Zoroastrian catechism reads, 'but that there are two first principles, one the Creator, and the other the Destroyer. The Creator is Ohrmazd who is all goodness and all light; and the Destroyer is the accursed Ahriman who is all wickedness and full of death, a liar and a deceiver.' Nothing could be clearer than that.

There is no question that there is a principle beyond these two. In the whole corpus of the Pahlavi books there is only one mention of the theory (explicitly stated in the *Gathas* though it is) that Ohrmazd and Ahriman are twins, and in this one passage it is denounced as a doctrine thought up by a demon.

The Pahlavi books, as they now stand, reflect a doctrine that was current at the end of the Sassanian period, and we can be fairly certain that this complete dualism was official doctrine then. So too was it after the death of Shapur (Sapor) I in 271 AD as we now know from a long inscription of the high priest of that time, one Kartir. Unfortunately this agreement between the 9th century books and the 3rd century inscription is not conclusive; for if neither had survived and we had to rely exclusively on Christian, Manichean and Moslem sources, we would be inclined to think that Zurvanism was the predominant trend in the Zoroastrianism of the Sassanian period, not the neat dualism of the Pahlavi texts, and this for two principal reasons. First, when the Christians attack Zoroastrianism, they attack not the dualism we know from the Pahlavi books but the theory that Ohrmazd and Ahriman are twins. Secondly, when the Manichees started to translate their own scriptures into Persian they called their own supreme Spirit, the 'Father of Greatness' and king of the kingdom of light – not Ohrmazd but Zurvan. And this is very odd indeed since the Zoroastrian Ohrmazd who is 'all goodness and all light' corresponds as exactly as you could wish to the Manichean 'Father of Greatness'. The Zoroastrian Zurvan, on the other hand, as we know him from the Christian sources, is rather 'the whole intelligible and unitary universe, either Space or Time', of Eudemus, but now transferred onto a purely mythological plane.

The Zurvanite myth is preserved in several sources which substantially agree and must go back to a common original. In this myth (quoted in the article on Ahriman) Zurvan is the father of Ohrmazd and Ahriman.

The message of the myth is clear. In the beginning, all is One in Zurvan who, philosophically, is Time-Space. Basically he is good and light, but there is a fundamental flaw in his nature represented by his 'doubt', and this is materialized in the shape of Ahriman who is 'dark and stinking', 'a liar and a deceiver'. Unless Zurvan is to be false to his vow, he must make Ahriman king of this world for 9000 years, though Ohrmazd may be high priest in heaven above. In any case, Ahriman's power will be broken in the end, and then Ohrmazd will be 'all in all' in 'infinite time' of which Zurvan is the mythological representation.

Form of Fire

In the *Selections of Zadspram,* the only one of the Pahlavi books where Zurvan plays a prominent part, we learn a little more about his 'testament' to Ohrmazd and Ahriman and about Ahriman's 9000-year rule:

> When first creation began to move and Zurvan, for the sake of movement, brought that form, the black and ashen garment to Ahriman, he made a treaty in this wise: 'This is that implement like unto fire, blazing, harassing all creatures, that hath the very substance of Az (Greed, Lust, Concupiscence). When the period of nine thousand years comes to an end, if thou hast not perfectly fulfilled that which thou didst threaten at the beginning, that thou wouldst bring all material existence to hate Ohrmazd and to love thee, . . . then, by means of this weapon, Az will devour . . . thy creation; and she herself will starve.'

From other texts we can deduce that Zurvan gave a corresponding 'implement' or 'form' to Ohrmazd – 'a form of fire – bright, white, round, and manifest afar', which is associated with priesthood and wisdom as it is in the 'classic' Zurvanite myth.

How are we to interpret all this? The birth of Ahriman from Zurvan's doubt is a 'Fall' in the divine nature itself, the manifestation of an essential imperfection in the godhead. To compensate for this Fall Zurvan endows Ohrmazd with wisdom, the priestly virtue par excellence, but to Ahriman he gives Az who is Greed, Lust, Concupiscence, Acquisitiveness, and who is insatiable. Ultimately, then, Az is self-destructive and so in the end Ahriman's kingdom is destroyed by the very 'implement' he had accepted from Zurvan and made into his own 'selfhood'. Having supplied Ohrmazd and Ahriman with the 'implements' appropriate to each, Zurvan plays no further part in the cosmic struggle. Only at the very end does he appear to help Ohrmazd administer the *coup de grâce* to Ahriman, Az, and their evil creation. Even so, Zurvan must be seen as a God that failed.

(See also TIME.)

R. C. ZAEHNER

FURTHER READING: R. C. Zaehner, *The Dawn and Twilight of Zoroastrianism* (Putnam, 1961); *Zurvan, a Zoroastrian Dilemma* (Biblo and Tanner, 1973).